THE
OFFICIAL
ENCYCLOPEDIA OF

SCOTLAND
YARD

First published in 1999 by
Virgin Books
An imprint of
Virgin Publishing Ltd
Thames Wharf Studios
Rainville Road
London
W6 9HT

ISBN 1-85227-712-2

Printed and bound by Graphicom, Italy.

All photographs are reproduced courtesy of the Metropolitan Police Museum,
with the exception of the following:
Alpha/Sport and General: 174, 293
by courtesy of Stewart Evans: 123, 135
by courtesy of Peter Kennison: 142
Royal Archives, Windsor Castle: 37
by courtesy of Harry Spain: 109
Topham Picturepoint: 36, 141, 167

Every attempt has been made to credit the source of photographs used in this
book. Any omissions brought to the attention of Virgin Publishing will be
corrected in a future edition.

THE OFFICIAL ENCYCLOPEDIA OF

SCOTLAND YARD

MARTIN FIDO AND KEITH SKINNER

Virgin

AUTHORS' FOREWORD

Neither of us is or ever has been a member or employee of any police force. We are accordingly extremely honoured that the Commissioner and Policy Board should have entrusted us with producing this book after the concept had been initiated by Assistant Commissioner Paul Manning.

Our brief was to produce a book that a tired constable might happily browse through at his own fireside. We are both accustomed to holding a tired audience by the expression of quirky opinions. But such things are not appropriate to an Official Encyclopedia of Scotland Yard. Where they have slipped through, we apologise, and stress that they are ours and the Met should not be blamed.

While writing, we have most often been asked, "Is it a whitewash?" The belief that Scotland Yard hides dark secrets was not one we personally held when we started writing. The only files withheld from us have been those statutorily sealed under the Lord Chancellor's rules, and only constraints of time have prevented us from untying their knotted red tape. It has been accepted without question that we will not put our names to anything we do not believe to be true. The Branches and Departments who have checked our work for accuracy have not asked us to remove adverse comments.

But are we 100 per cent accurate and up to date? We do not believe anyone could be. Just as we were about to go to press, the news broke that Libya accepted responsibility for Yvonne Fletcher's death. The Metropolitan Police Service is a huge organisation undergoing constant and bewildering change. The sheer volume of primary and secondary source material is almost overwhelming. Authorised work published as little as five years ago is often out of date. We spent several weeks laboriously sorting out the Divisions and SubDivisions, only to scrap our work because of the forthcoming introduction of Borough Policing. New Branches come into being all the time as the need arises. We hope we have it right at the time of writing. We believe it will serve as a reliable reference book for others to build on. But mindful of the need for accuracy, we will happily accept precise and documented corrections of names, dates or numbers.

Finally we hope the tired constable, and every other reader, enjoys picking up new facts about the history and practice of the world's premier apolitical civilian peacekeeping service, and feels as proud as we do to be associated with it.

Martin Fido and Keith Skinner
Kent and London, June 1999

COMMISSIONER'S FOREWORD

When I was reflecting about the advent of the new millennium and wondering what the Metropolitan Police might do to mark the occasion, a colleague suggested a historically based, easy-to-read book which could be used for reference for many years to come. I did not fully realise at the time how much work would be involved!

Martin Fido and Keith Skinner have produced a magnificent book, far beyond my expectations, in a very short period. The bibliography reflects the enormous amount of research carried out into previously published material about the Metropolitan Police, and the authors have added many points and entries which have brought the book up to date.

Reading this book gives some valuable insight into how our policing style has developed, how relationships with the community and the media have changed and how my predecessors faced and dealt with problems. As we approach the new millennium we must look to learn the lessons from history while exploiting the opportunities afforded by the advance of technology and other disciplines.

Colonel Rowan, one of the first joint Commissioners, played an invaluable part in setting the tone of police and public relations within a framework of enlightened discipline which was remarkable for his day. It was Rowan's adaptation of military tactics in the Peninsular War which bequeathed to us the beat system. It is hard now to imagine policing without the phrase "bobbies on the beat".

The attitude of inquest juries to the deaths of Joseph Grantham and Robert Culley, two of the first officers killed on duty, seems remarkably callous by today's standards, but it was a reflection of the public hostility towards the first police officers on the streets of London and it shows how difficult policing was in their day. By contrast, the 1948 death of Nathanael Edgar, to whom we recently dedicated a plaque at Muswell Hill, was the inspiration for the plot of the film *The Blue Lamp* which in turn led to the *Dixon of Dock Green* TV series.

The book will enrich discussions about ending the tradition of an unarmed Police Service by its reference to the fact that Constables on outer Divisions were permitted to carry revolvers on night duty between 1884 and 1936, while the first recorded case of a Metropolitan officer firing his revolver was in 1887.

Any historical book on the Met needs to deal fairly with the facts of scandals which have occurred, and the authors have not shirked that challenge. The 1877 Trial of the Detectives shows that corruption existed in the early days of the Force, but the Royal Commission 1908 and the case of Irene Savidge showed that not all complaints were well founded.

If one had to choose one single thing which built the reputation of New Scotland Yard it would probably be the development of the fingerprint system by one of my predecessors Sir Edward Henry, who also laid many foundations for the way the Met was run for much of the twentieth century. He was shot and badly wounded. Another of my predecessors, Brigadier Horwood, was nearly killed by poisoned chocolates. Life as a Commissioner has never been free of risk!

One of the initiatives which we have undertaken in recent years has been the Officer Safety Programme, aimed at reducing injuries to officers from assault. When you look at the Appendices containing the Roll of Honour of those who have died in the course of their duty, and the officers who have been awarded medals for gallantry, you will no doubt be sobered by the sheer number of officers who have risked their lives on behalf of London's public, and share some of the sense of pride and duty which the Metropolitan Police Service carries in its heart.

It should be pointed out that the views and opinions expressed about my predecessors and former Home Secretaries reflect historical judgements rather than any official Metropolitan Police position.

I have always felt privileged to lead what I believe to be the finest capital city Police Service in the world; after reading this book you will understand why.

Paul Condon

P. L. Condon
Commissioner of Police of the Metropolis
New Scotland Yard, June 1999

A DIVISION Originally known as Whitehall, subsequently Westminster, and unofficially known as 'Royal A.' Since the Division included the original Scotland Yard, and the royal parks and palaces, it was from the outset one of the most important of all Divisions. Its first Superintendent (John May) was used by Commissioners Rowan and Mayne as a sort of informal Chief Constable, liaising between them and the rest of the force.

ABBISS, SIR GEORGE (1884–1966) Second officer to rise from the ranks to Assistant Commissioner. Born Hitchin, Herts. Gardener at Sir Saville Crossley's estate, Somerleyton Hall, Lowestoft, prior to joining the Met in 1905. Warrant No. 91801. Served as PC on T (Richmond) and B (Chelsea) Divisions, Sergeant and Station Sergeant on Hammersmith and Paddington Divisions, and promoted Inspector at A2 Branch, Scotland Yard in 1919. Sub-Divisional Inspector, C Division (Westminster), 1922. Chief Inspector Y Division (Haringey), 1924. Transferred E Division (Holborn), January 1926. Returned to Commissioner's Office, A2, April 1926. MBE, 1929. Chief Constable, 1930. OBE, 1932. Deputy Assistant Commissioner, 1933. Assistant Commissioner D (Personnel), 1936, following the retirement of Sir Percy Laurie. Knight Bachelor, 1941. Retd, 1946.

For many years Abbiss was closely associated

ASSISTANT COMMISSIONER SIR GEORGE ABBISS.

with Peel House and the training of recruits. He became Commissioner Sir Philip Game's right-hand man when Game, a former Air Marshal recommended by Lord Trenchard, wisely recognized the need to have advice from an experienced professional police officer. This was especially important because the rank and file were unhappy about the possibility that Hendon Police College would close the traditional avenues of promotion by letting in upper class supervisory officers over the heads of rankers. Abbiss, who had risen further than any ranker since Sir James Olive, was ideally placed to explain this discontent, and may have played no small part in Game's decision to slow down the growth of Hendon and discontinue the rank of Junior Station Inspector for its graduates. He was characterized by Sgt Harry Daley as approachable, straight as a die, and possessed of a sense of humour rare among senior officers of the time. His promotions, in Daley's view, contributed signally to the diminution of malpractices in the 1930s.

Abbiss was noted for his interest in police history and his excellent power of recall. He assembled a collection of police paraphernalia which included an outstanding set of truncheons from all periods. This was passed to the Bow Street museum and is now held in the Historical Museum.

ACIS Article Classification Identification System. An inexpensive computer database of stolen objects giving the necessary data on their nature and provenance, present or last known whereabouts, etc., with small coloured pictures of each object, which can be laser-printed and enlarged to full size. It is maintained by the Art and Antiques Unit – Organised Crime Group.

ACRONYMS See Appendix 5 for a list of acronyms and abbreviations.

ACSO Acronym for Assistant Commissioner, Specialist Operations. With command of the Organised Crime Group since the reorganization of 1996, and command of SO1 International and Organised Crime ever since the formation of Specialist Operations, ACSO effectively takes over much of the role of the former Assistant Commissioner C as head of specialist detective policing at Scotland Yard. His portfolio includes the Directorate of Intelligence, the Organised Crime Group, the Fraud Squad, the National Identification Service, Special Branch, the Anti-Terrorist Branch, the Royalty and Diplomatic Protection Department, the Palace of Westminster Division and the Firearms Unit.

ACSO'S SUPPORT BRANCH See Crime Support Branch.

ACTO Assistant Commissioner, Territorial Operations; a post extant between 1986 and 1996. Effectively superseded Assistant Commissioners A and B following the Newman Restructuring. Responsible for the eight Area DACs and with a Deputy (DACTO) responsible for much of the Headquarters department of Territorial Operations.

ADELE, HELENE (B.1907) Victim of attempt to pervert the course of justice by two Metropolitan constables, one of whose advances she refused.

In July 1928, Miss Adele, whose lifestyle was described by Mr Justice Humphreys as immoral, though not actually one of prostitution, had come to a private arrangement with a taxicab washer that she might sleep overnight in a cab garaged near Caledonian Road. PCs John William Clayton (Divisional No. 541Y) and Charles Victor Stevens (383Y) inspected the garage on their patrol, and Clayton entered the cab and tried to make Miss Adele have sexual intercourse. She refused volubly, and threatened to report him to his Sergeant. Clayton and Stevens thereupon arrested her and charged her with insulting words and behaviour, claiming that they had found her in the street shouting at a man who was running away.

Confused and contradictory testimony was given at Clerkenwell Magistrates' court. The cab washer admitted that a man had got into the cab and annoyed Miss Adele, but pretended not to know that he was a policeman. A 16-year-old boy working in the garage, however, testified to finding a piece of leather inside the cab which matched an obviously missing piece from Clayton's belt. The Magistrate dismissed the case against Helene Adele, and remarked that this was a serious abuse of police powers among a class of people who were effectively at their mercy.

The two constables were charged with perjury and attempting to pervert the course of justice, and at their trial, Acting-Sergeant Smith swore that Clayton had been in Caledonian Road station at the time of the offence. This evidence was contradicted by other officers, and although Mr Justice Humphreys made it clear that he was not happy about the quality of evidence for the prosecution, it took the jury only half an hour to find both officers guilty, whereupon the judge said that he agreed with their verdict, and severely sentenced the two men to 18 months hard labour. Acting-Sergeant Smith was dismissed from the Force.

In the wake of the Irene Savidge affair and the context of criticism of the police which led to the Macmillan Committee and Lee Commission enquiries, the case was used by opponents of the Met to claim that all the police were corrupt, and by the Met's defenders to show that 'rotten apples' were quickly and decisively dealt with. In point of fact, it was the only one of many complaints that could be upheld in the run-up to the Sergeant Goddard scandal.

AFO Acronym for Authorised Firearms Officer. Approximately 2000 officers are given regular firearms training and permitted to carry arms when special duties require. Such duties may include protection of principals whose lives are known to be under threat, the arrest of criminals known to be armed and dangerous, or preventive patrolling in crowded areas or in road blocks where terrorist activities are feared. In addition to Special Branch and the specialized units of the Royalty and Diplomatic Protection Department, Divisions have a small number of AFOs who may be called upon to draw weapons for appropriate incidents.

AFOs are volunteers, and their training is in the hands of the Force Firearms Unit. Women are much less inclined than men to volunteer for firearms training, and the 50 Women Police AFOs disproportionately under-represent their gender.

METROPOLITAN POLICE BELL 222 HELICOPTER ABOVE TOWER BRIDGE, 1989.

AIR SUPPORT UNIT (CO53) Includes the Surrey Police, and is officially titled the South East Region Police Air Support Unit. Currently, three Eurocopter AS 355N 'Twin Squirrel' helicopters, operating from two bases – Lippitts Hill in north-east London and Fairoaks Airport in Surrey – provide air support in the policing of the Metropolitan District and Surrey Constabulary. The bases, codenamed 'I. L.' and 'I. F.', are staffed jointly by Metropolitan Police and Surrey Sergeants and constables. An aircraft is on standby at each base for 16 hours each day.

Able to react rapidly to an appropriate call, it can be overhead anywhere in its radius of cover within a maximum of 12 minutes.

The helicopters are platforms for observation, search and communications. In addition to the radio system that enables the crew to talk to any police officer on the ground or in the air anywhere in the UK, an array of sophisticated equipment is carried to support the search role. A nose-mounted spherical turret, able to rotate through 360 degrees, contains a TV camera with x64 zoom and thermal imager. The imager, using heat emission to create an image on a CCD screen, allows the controller, sitting next to the pilot, to see the ground below even in total darkness. An incident seen on screen can be transmitted to Scotland Yard's Central Communications Complex and recorded on videotape in the aircraft. This is a valuable asset for decision-making by senior officers. Night searches can be further supported by the 30 million candlepower searchlight (NITESUN). The 400 watt public address system can be used to send instructions to crowds at festivals or sporting occasions in the event of a serious incident.

The primary role of the region's helicopters is to support the policing of major events where public order or security could be an issue. The historical origins stem from the use of a captive balloon at the 1924 Epsom Derby, the use of autogyros from 1934 and the hiring of helicopters before the Unit's foundation in 1980.

ALIENS REGISTRATION OFFICE
Formed 1915. Branch of the Directorate of Identification, located in Borough High Street from March 1999, and run by Civil Staff. Recently renamed as Overseas Visitors Records Office. Required under the Immigration Act 1971 to keep records with photographs of adult aliens in the Metropolitan Police District seeking or holding employment for more than three months, or remaining for any purpose for more than six months. European Union citizens and certain other categories are exempt.

The Office processes about 60,000 registrations each year, and holds approximately 140,000 'live' records and an archive of about 300,000 'dead' records. The staff are well aware that their involuntary customers may not especially enjoy having to visit them, and every effort is therefore made to make the environment as comfortable and friendly as possible.

Registration of aliens visiting England started in 1792 as a response to the French Revolution. Its conditions were varied by the Aliens Acts of 1826 and 1905, and the duty of registering aliens in London was passed to the Metropolitan Police when regulations were tightened again at the outbreak of WWI. The office has been housed in various places, including Bow Street, Vine Street and Lamb's Conduit Street before reaching its present home.

AMBULANCES Prior to WWI the word 'ambulance' almost invariably referred to the police hand ambulance (manufactured by Bischoffsheim), a 2.7m (9ft) long stretcher mounted on the axle of a pair of large wheels halfway down its length, with a third small support wheel at the front. It was equipped with an oilcloth hood and cover, a locker under the hood end, and three straps to fasten down violent or incapable passengers, for its primary purpose was not rescue of the sick or injured but the transport of drunks or obstreperous prisoners to the station. Introduced into occasional service in 1860, the hand ambulance soon became an essential piece of police station equipment, kept in special sheds in police station yards. A few more were kept under cover at usefully accessible points for beat patrols. In his short story 'Brugglesmith,' Kipling makes entertaining use of his knowledge that one was kept in the Strand, near his Villiers Street digs. They passed out of use in 1938. An old hand ambulance is held in the Historical Museum.

From about 1884, the Metropolitan Police ran a small horse ambulance service for the sick. Ambulance wagons were maintained at Stoke Newington and Carter Street stations, and could be hired. The cheapest rate was five shillings (25p) for a journey up to 3.2km (2 miles), the

THE BISCHOFFSHEIM POLICE HAND AMBULANCE IN USE AROUND 1920.

most expensive 10 shillings for a journey of 9.6–16km (6–10 miles). The police were authorized to use their telegraph to summon the horse ambulance if asked to do so by a doctor, and the charges might be dropped for needy cases. Other small ambulance services were operated by the Fire Service and the London Asylums Board. In 1915 the Fire Service was authorized to open a number of specific motor ambulance stations. The way was paved for the London Ambulance Service, and the Metropolitan Police ambulance service was discontinued.

ANDERSON, SIR ROBERT (1841–1918)
Assistant Commissioner (Crime), 1888–1901.
B. Dublin, son of Crown Solicitor and younger brother of Vice-Regal Attorney-General. Educ. Trinity College, Dublin. Called to the bar, King's Inn, Dublin, 1863. Reviewed Fenian activities for Vice-Regal Government, and, 1876, transferred to London Home Office as adviser on Fenian matters. Controlled spies infiltrating or reporting on Fenian activities, 1876–86. Secretary to the Prison Commissioners, 1887–8, then Assistant Commissioner, retiring with knighthood. Wrote 23 books on theology and two on police and criminal affairs, *On Criminals and Crime* (1907) and *The Lighter Side of My Official Life* (1910). Also numerous articles in journals, including anonymous contributions to the 1887 series 'Parnellism

and Crime' in *The Times*, for which he made improper (but fascinating) use of secret official information.

Anderson's appointment to Scotland Yard was made the justification for abolishing the post of legal adviser to the Commissioner, since Anderson was a trained lawyer. This was, perhaps, unfortunate for Sir Charles Warren, since Anderson was away on sick leave and then taken up with the Jack the Ripper case during the climactic months when the Commissioner most needed advice on his powers and responsibilities with respect to the Home Office.

Anderson's term of office in Scotland Yard included the most substantial reduction in recorded crime in the history of the Met, the crime figures for 1899 being the lowest ever. This achievement was noted by early historians of the police but has been overshadowed since by the introduction of fingerprinting by his successor, Sir Edward Henry.

ANGRY BRIGADE Anarchist group which carried out anti-establishment bomb attacks in London, Birmingham and Manchester in 1970 and 1971. Their London targets included the homes of Attorney-General Sir Peter Rawlinson, Home Secretary Robert Carr, Trade and Industry Minister John Davies and Metropolitan Police Commissioner Sir John Waldron.

Following the attack on Robert Carr's home in January 1971, Sir John Waldron set up a special squad commanded by Detective Chief Superintendent Roy Habershon to track down the bombers. In July he beefed it up with the addition of Flying Squad and Special Branch officers headed by Commander Ernie Bond. In August the squad arrested the three men and two women responsible, and when it was shown that the Angry Brigade had inherited members and weapons from the First of May Group the squad was made permanent as the Bomb Squad.

ANGUILLA Tiny Caribbean island which was effectively under the executive government of a Metropolitan Police Unit from 1969–1972.

Anguilla, with a population of about 6000 in 1969, resented being administered jointly with and from neighbouring St Kitts (pop. about 40,000) since the practice began back in colonial days in 1871. After the dissolution of the British West Indies Federation in 1962, when St Kitts-Nevis-Anguilla was offered self-administration as an 'Associated Territory' under the Foreign and Commonwealth Office, many Anguillans objected profoundly, and in a number of incidents starting in 1967 finally precipitated British intervention. Government House in Anguilla was burned down, several private businesses and the police station were attacked with firearms and the Anguillan police force (12 strong) was disarmed and expelled from the island. For over a year the islanders tried to assert their independence and set up unconstitutional governing councils, while the Kittitian government, headed by Robert Bradshaw, refused to recognize their demands. In March 1969, after an unofficial referendum in Anguilla had favoured a Unilateral Declaration of Independence by 1739 votes to 4, Mr William Whitlock, Parliamentary Under Secretary of State for Foreign and Commonwealth Affairs, was threatened with guns and hustled off the island when he came to mediate.

Eight days later a Royal Naval frigate, 140 British soldiers and a volunteer contingent from the Metropolitan Police called the Anguilla Police Unit all descended on Anguilla. The 40 constables, 3 Sergeants and 2 Inspectors from Special Patrol Group, supported by a DCI and a Detective Sergeant from Special Branch, an Inspector and a Sergeant from Branch A8 (Public Order) and one civilian wireless operator, were all under the command of Assistant Commissioner A, Andrew Way. The operation, codenamed 'Sheepskin', was anticipated to last about a month. In the event, more than 700 Metropolitan officers served tours of duty on Anguilla over the next three years, the last five finally leaving on 29 March 1972. Seven other senior officers succeeded Mr Way in commanding Operation Sheepskin. This was the longest containment of a civil disturbance in the Service's history.

Rumours that American mafiosi were attempting to profit by the anarchic situation proved untrue, though an American citizen named Jack Holcombe, variously described as an ex-policeman or private detective, had collaborated with local secessionist politician Ronald

Webster to draw up a new constitution and set in place various business enterprises and arrangements. Mr Holcombe was speedily deported, and Mr A. C. W. Lee, the senior British FCO official, was installed as Commissioner.

Though the islanders were suspicious of British intervention at first, the police quickly made themselves accepted. In fact, it was the devout wish of many islanders that they should be restored to direct colonial government outside the jurisdiction of Bradshaw's St Kitts-Nevis administration which, Anguillans felt, always treated them as an inferior third partner. The police, however, had to maintain neutrality and distance. The coterie of pro-Bradshaw Anguillans had to be protected from the threats of the majority secessionists, and security had to be maintained for visiting dignitaries who continued to take soundings and organize negotiations. On 11 April 1969, in the most serious incident, when Commissioner Lee and UN ambassador Lord Caradon were felt to have been too placatory to Bradshaw, a crowd of 300 tried to attack the Commissioner's residence. Despite being injured, PC Jack T. W. Gooday held them back at pistol point, until the military arrived to break up the riot.

Criminal law enforcement was less demanding than the maintenance of public order. The

Anguillans are a deeply Christian and intensely moral community and crime prevention was largely directed against Virgin Islanders poaching fish from the minuscule off-islands. Three Puerto Rican prostitutes who tried to start a brothel were quickly arrested and deported, to the satisfaction of the Anguillans.

However, the operation was not, as the press liked to imagine, a tropical holiday. For most of the time, housing was primitive and extremely uncomfortable. There was no electricity and no running water on the island. The unexpected length of the operation caused stress to officers separated from their families. Travel to and from the UK by RAF Hercules aircraft was so appallingly uncomfortable that Commissioner Sir John Waldron made immediate arrangements to expedite commercial flights for all officers after he had made a tour of inspection. PC James Dady contracted double pneumonia while on night duty at Anguilla HQ, and died in hospital in nearby Antigua on 10 November 1971. His death lowered the spirits of the Anguilla Police Unit for the remainder of the tour of duty.

Before leaving Anguilla, Operation Sheepskin

POLICE AND NAVAL PERSONNEL, JOINED BY LOCAL CHILDREN, ENJOY THE CARIBBEAN SUN.

was strengthened by the addition of two Training Sergeants from Hendon Training Centre, who implemented a special syllabus drawn up by Martin Murray (later Chief Inspector), and trained a new Anguillan Police Force to the point of a passing out parade on 28 February 1972 and a handover of responsibility for policing the island to Chief of Police Mr Claudius Matthias Roberts, MBE. When the last Metropolitan officers left the island the following month, the Foreign and Commonwealth Office had met the Anguillans' essential demands, and the island reverted effectively to provisional crown colony status, separate from St Kitts and Nevis, with Mr Robert Webster as its first minister.

The Anguillan experience is recalled by the Metropolitan Police Anguilla Society, which holds social events and reunions and issues the regular magazine *Arrow*. The Society is about 200 strong, and welcomes members of the armed forces who served on Anguilla and whose overseas postings make the maintenance of a regular Army or Navy Anguilla Society impossible.

ANNUAL CONCERT The Annual Metropolitan Police Concert was first given in Central Hall, Westminster in December 1946. It was performed by the recently formed Choral Society (see choir) and the Police Band, two groups which remained the mainstay of the programmes until the Band's dissolution in 1997. In 1952 the concerts moved from Central Hall to the Festival Hall, and an organ recital was added in the interval. The concerts by now regularly featured professional entertainers alongside the police amateurs, including Semprini, Max Jaffa, Vera Lynn and Sir Harry Secombe and comedians Tommy Trinder, Harry Worth, Roy Hudd and Roy Castle. The East London male voice choir and various military and other bands have performed at the concerts. The police groups included the Women's Choir, the Commissioner's Office male voice choir and assembled Divisional choirs.

When the Festival Hall ceased to accept the regular 'one-night stand' booking in 1986, experiments were made with a return to Central Hall and then with the Queen Elizabeth Conference Centre, neither of which proved satisfactory.

Since 1990 the annual concert has taken place in the Barbican Centre and the use of professional platform entertainers has been abandoned, though bands from places which have hosted the Police Choir and professional jazz soloists continue to appear from time to time. The Blue Vein Dance Band, composed of officers from the Metropolitan and City Police, has made popular appearances, as have police jazz trumpeters. Comperes, however, continue to be drawn from the world of radio and television. Alvar Liddell, Frank Phillips and Richard Dimbleby were among great BBC names who compered the concert in the early years, and Shaw Taylor, presenter of *Police Five*, MC'd almost without a break from 1968 to 1990. Since 1992 the programme has been introduced by Richard Baker.

'ANTECEDENTS' Police jargon for a person's criminal record and any other information held on file about their past life.

ANTHROPOMETRY DEPARTMENT Section of Scotland Yard responsible for maintaining criminal records for identification purposes between 1895 and 1901. 'Anthropometry' ('the measurement of man') was the term used by Francis Galton in the laboratory he ran for experiments in Bertillonage. The Anthropometry Department, which was set up on the recommendation of the Troup Committee, used five of Bertillon's proposed measurements of bones, and added eye colours and fingerprints. As the Committee had always feared, Bertillon's system proved flawed because tired or lax officers were not always precise in recording accurate measurements, but until Edward Henry's classification system made fingerprinting viable it was the best system available. Its first real success came in 1898, when a waiter called James Coots, awaiting sentence for stealing a clock from Lord Raglan and claiming to have no previous convictions, was shown to have been previously sentenced to three years' penal servitude and anthropometrically registered under the name Frank Foley. When the Anthropometry Department abandoned feet and inches for the more scientific metric system, it was quickly nicknamed the 'Metric Department'.

The failure of the Department to achieve its prime purpose – correctly identifying habitual offenders – was made notorious shortly after its demise by the Adolf Beck case.

ANTI-TERRORIST BRANCH (SO13) Enlarged and enhanced expansion of the Bomb Squad to approximately 130 staff dedicated to providing the Metropolitan and City of London police with a secure service capable of investigating acts of terrorism and kindred offences and bringing specific types of kidnappings to a successful prosecution. The staff gather, store and utilize intelligence and evidence in relation to those offences. In addition, they liaise and train with other branches, forces and outside organizations to maintain high professional standards of investigation and evidential presentation. Their explosives officers are also responsible for rendering safe explosives that are endangering the public as well as for specialist counter-terrorist and search advice and techniques.

The Anti-Terrorist branch was founded in 1976, when preventing IRA terrorist activities had become a major responsibility for the Metropolitan Police. Other concerns which dominated SO13 work were Middle Eastern terrorism during the 1980s and extreme animal rights activism. In 1985, after the Libyan People's Bureau Siege (see Yvonne Fletcher), a counter-terrorist contingency planning unit was established. Until the Northern Irish Peace Accords of 1998, the Anti-Terrorist Branch was constantly engaged with members of the IRA on the mainland both in London and elswhere under the leadership of the Head of SO13, the National Co-ordinator of Terrorist Investigations.

'APPOINTMENTS' Police jargon for the whistle, truncheon (or baton), handcuffs, personal radio, notebook and (according to some officers) headgear which have to be carried by police officers on beat duty and which were once routinely and are now occasionally inspected by supervising officers before constables leave the station. The list of appointments changes from time to time, for instance with the introduction of CS sprays.

TRADITIONAL BASIC 'APPOINTMENTS': TRUNCHEON, NOTEBOOK AND WHISTLE c. 1985.

ARCHIVES Archives is the colloquial term for Departmental Records (Archives), a section of Records Management Branch (QPP3). Civil Staff are responsible for the appraisal and review of non-current records. A First Review Team decides, in consultation with relevant branches where necessary, which files are of no further administrative or historical value and may be destroyed to avoid the expense of retaining useless records. It sets a date for further review of files which are retained.

A second Review Team continually reviews files over 25 years old to decide whether they should be sent to the Public Record Office, destroyed, or retained for administrative purposes. Files which are sent to the PRO are normally made available to researchers 30 years after the last action on them. Before transfer to the PRO, however, files are subject to a sensitivity review to decide whether the privacy of surviving individuals, or the security of ongoing police opera-

tions, requires that they be closed to the public for a specified number of years. Sensitivity reviews are also carried out on previously closed records in the PRO in accordance with the Open Government Initiative. The transfer of records to the PRO or other agencies is not limited to paper files; also included are books and forms, photographs, plans, sound recordings, films and computer records. All aspects of the appraisal and review of records are overseen by the PRO and any variations to the 30-year rule for access requires the approval of the Lord Chancellor.

The Archives Section monitors record-keeping (creation, maintenance, retrieval, storage, disposal and so forth) throughout the MPS through an ongoing process of inspection. It also answers questions from members of the public about the history of the Metropolitan Police, and assists police officers and civil staff with historical research.

ARCOS RAID Highly public three-day search of the All Russian Co-operative Society's premises in Moorgate by 200 officers in 1927. Climax of Assistant Commissioner C Sir Wyndham

Childs' attempts to outlaw the Communist Party of Great Britain.

Childs described his period in Scotland Yard as seven years of fruitlessly trying to make the government see the need to ban the CPGB. After his success in having 12 members of the party's executive jailed for subversion in 1925, he turned his attention to their Russian paymasters. Most were protected by diplomatic privilege, but their Trade Mission, the All Russian Co-operative Society (ARCOS) in Moorgate, incorporated a British registered bank and an import company which could be legitimately searched on a magistrate's warrant. Believing (correctly) that ARCOS was a hotbed of espionage, Childs set up a sting with marked papers which were 'allowed' to go missing from the War Office.

The Arcos raid, carried out by 40 Special Branch men while 160 City of London Police officers emptied and guarded the premises, completely failed to discover the expropriated papers, but it did find an unnecessarily large number of unusually concealed safes as well as papers which put the overseas addresses of a number of Soviet espionage agents into Special Branch's hands.

AREA MAJOR INVESTIGATION POOLS Teams of CID officers based at Area headquarters to investigate murders and other major crimes or events which appear to cross Divisional boundaries or represent too demanding an investigation for Divisional CIDs. Non-domestic murders have always been investigated by non-Divisional senior detectives, but the AMIPs were important for the principle of having a dedicated team of junior detectives always in place, thus avoiding the need to negotiate for the abstraction of officers from Divisions to staff major investigations.

As was the case with CI Branch officers at Scotland Yard, the concept of officers at leisure on standby is more notional than real. In fact all CID officers are always busy. AMIPs simply undertake the most serious investigations on their Areas.

AREA POLICING The normal term for the work of the localized territorially based Divisions and Sub-Divisions in the Areas.

AREAS From 1999, three major territorial districts into which the total Metropolitan Police District is divided. Prior to 1999, five major territories, thus No. 1 Area Central, No. 2 Area North West, No. 3 Area North East, No. 4 Area South East, No. 5 Area South West.

The original division of the MPD into four large sectors embracing several Divisions created the Districts (1) in 1869. The name 'Area' was not used until the institution of the 'Big Four' District Detective Superintendents in 1919, and then only unofficially. F. P. Wensley's memoirs rather tended to suggest that he had invented the idea of Area detective policing to override possible Divisional jealousies, and this may have led the press to give the term currency. The status of the old District commands varied considerably from time to time, some District command positions occasionally remaining unfilled when Commissioners deemed them of secondary importance. The Sports Centres established by Lord Trenchard were originally located so that each served one of the four Districts, subsequently becoming Area Sports Clubs.

Under the Waldron Reforms, 1970, the previous four Districts were renamed Areas. Divisions became Districts, and Sub-Divisions became Divisions. There was also a large-scale regrading of police ranks above Chief Inspector. Deputy Assistant Commissioners thereby commanded Areas; Commanders, Districts; and Chief Superintendents, Divisions.

The Newman Restructuring (1985) created eight Areas and removed Commanders from having any direct responsibility for a geographic territory, and Sir Kenneth Newman made it clear that the Division was to be seen as the basic unit of policing.

The Service Restructuring Exercise in 1995 reduced the Areas to five, but upgraded the officer in charge to Assistant Commissioner rank. The reduction to three Areas was first planned in 1998 to coincide with the foreseeable realignment linked with the Borough policing model.

ARMED RESPONSE VEHICLES Up to 11 vehicles for rapid transport of Authorised Firearms Officers from the Firearms Unit. Equipped with Glock 9mm self-loading pistols

and Heckler & Koch carbines (see firearms).

Each ARV is crewed by three officers, undertaking normal police car patrols unless directed to incidents requiring an armed presence. Some care is taken that their normal patrol duties should never involve incidents likely to detain them for long periods.

Six ARVs are constantly on patrol. They are marked with a yellow spot on the top to enable their instant identification by police helicopters. ARV officers are given elementary training in negotiation because of the likelihood of their being summoned to siege and hostage situations.

ARMLET A broad band of navy blue and white vertically striped cloth to be worn on the left forearm uniform sleeve by constables and Sergeants when on duty between 1830 and 1968. Initially the stripes were horizontal. Necessitated originally because officers were required to wear uniform at all times, whether on or off duty. Between 1835 and 1864 Sergeants were given armlets with narrower blue and broader white stripes and required to wear them on the right arm as a badge of rank. With the introduction of tunics and chevrons they reverted to the bands of equal width worn on the left arm. From 1895, loops to hold the armlets were tailored into tunic sleeves. Traffic patrols were exempted from wearing armlets

DUTY ARMLET IN USE c.1950, AS AN OFFICER DIRECTS A MOTORIST ON WESTMINSTER BRIDGE.

because they could accidentally catch the indicator arms of motor cars.

The withdrawal of armlets in 1968 prompted an exceptionally large correspondence in *The Job*. According to PC Harry Cole, author of several entertaining books of memoirs, no issue except capital punishment ever stirred up such intense feeling (pro and con) while he served with the Force!

ARREST Constables' power of arrest without warrant is specified by PACE, which regularized the numerous different powers contained in previous Acts of Parliament by creating 'arrestable offences' (including theft, assaults, and other crimes which may be punished by certain lengths of imprisonment). Any person may arrest anyone found in the act of committing an arrestable offence, or reasonably suspected of having done so after the event.

Constables have the additional power to arrest someone reasonably suspected of being about to commit an arrestable offence, and to arrest persons for other offences (such as motoring offences) if it is not possible to obtain their proper names and addresses.

See also 'Sus laws', warrant.

ART AND ANTIQUES UNIT – ORGANISED CRIME GROUP Small Specialist Operations Unit originally set up by Sir Joseph Simpson in 1967 as two small squads: Art Squad and Antiques and Philately Squad in C1 Branch, Serious Crimes. 'I don't know a Botticelli from my backside,' was the view of one detective drafted into this new duty. He went on to become an international authority on fine art forgery.

The unit was at one point disbanded as part of a cost-efficiency initiative but was re-formed when the art world complained that there were no longer expert and informed officers in Scotland Yard. The current purpose of this unit is the selective investigation of allegations of crime concerning works of art which have been stolen, dishonestly handled, faked or used by major criminals for illegal purposes in the London markets. It manages the ACIS database of stolen objects.

ASSESSMENTS Obligatory compensation payments for the loss or damage of appointments or other equipment. These became a real grievance when, for example, an officer might be injured in attempting to prevent a bomb explosion, and then be personally charged for equipment destroyed in the blast. An appeals system usually upheld the assessment. In 1968 Sir Robert Mark abolished assessments for sums under £50.

ASSISTANT COMMISSIONERS Senior officers, outranked only by the Commissioner and Deputy Commissioner. One is Assistant Commissioner, Specialist Operations, while between 1995 and 1999 another five were numbered by the Areas they commanded, ACs 1–5.

The Police Act, 1856 authorized the appointment of two Assistant Commissioners. Although Commissioner Sir Richard Mayne kept very tight personal control of all business and declined to delegate efficiently, by the time of his death they had fairly clearly determined duties, Captain Labalmondière having responsibility for internal discipline and administration of the uniformed force, and Captain W. C. Harris managing executive business, supplies and buildings. These would ultimately develop into Departments A and B. Like the Commissioners, ACs were sworn in as executive justices of the peace (magistrates who would swear in and command constables, but could not try criminal cases), a practice which was not discontinued until 1973.

In 1884 the third Assistant Commissioner's post was created to take over Howard Vincent's role as Director of Criminal Intelligence. In 1887 it was decided that one of the Assistant Commissioners might usefully be a qualified lawyer (as Mayne had been), saving the necessity of Commissioners drawn from the military having to engage a special legal adviser. Accordingly Dr Robert Anderson (Ll.D., London, member of the Dublin and London bars) was appointed AC (Crime).

By 1906 the Administrative and Executive ACs embraced unwieldy portfolios of responsibilities, and Commissioner Sir Edward Henry told the Royal Commission, 1908 that the overall managerial command responsibilities were too great for himself and his three Assistants. Accordingly he appointed a fourth AC in 1909, and reorganized their responsibilities in the four lettered departments, A, B, C and D, with D taking many of the former executive ACs' duties. From then until the Newman Restructuring in 1986, the ACs were identified by the letters of their departments. AC A was informally accepted as the Deputy Commissioner until the rank was formally established as separate from the four ACs in the 1930s.

After WWI, traffic in London became such a huge problem that AC B was given Traffic and Lost Property as his entire remit, the

RECRUITS AT PEEL HOUSE IN REGENCY STREET LEARN HOW TO MAKE AN ARREST c. 1930.

remaining duties being divided between AC A and AC D (who, until 1931, was also head of L or Legal Department). In 1931, when L Department's duties were redistributed, AC D headed the Organisation Department with responsibility for policy and planning.

By the post-WWII period, the duties of the ACs were reasonably rational. AC A headed all uniformed police (including the Mounted Branch, River Police and Women Police) except for those specifically allocated to Traffic Duties, who came under AC B. AC C continued to head the CID and its ancillary units. AC D took on what remained a curious lumping of recruitment, training, welfare, communications and dogs. The Waldron Reforms (1970) followed PA management consultants' recommendations which included the suggestion that the AC responsible for personnel and welfare (at that time AC D) should always be seen as the senior AC.

By the 1980s the need for closer integration of territorial policing made reform necessary. Sir Kenneth Newman cut the Gordian knot by scrapping the system that had held sway for 80 years and creating ACTO, ACSO, ACPT (Personnel and Training) and ACMS (Management Support) to head, respectively, what had now become Area policing (with its ancillary Territorial Operations Units), Specialist Operations (which largely took over the work of specialist CID and its ancillaries), Personnel and Training, and the branches and departments concerned with strategic planning, management services, public relations and other functions.

The system was adjusted again by Sir Peter Imbert as part of the PLUS programme. ACMS became known as ACIR (Inspection and Review) and a stronger Central Staff was created to deal with Area performance information. In 1995, rather than going on with eight Areas commanded by Deputy Assistant Commissioners, Sir Paul Condon's restructuring reduced the Areas to five, each commanded by an Assistant Commissioner, each of whom also managed a portfolio of Headquarters Operations and Branches from the former Territorial Operations. These were given CO numbers starting with a digit from 1 to 5 according to which Area Assistant Commissioner managed them, a system which was quite logical until changes in personnel meant that ACs might change Areas, taking their HQ Portfolio

PC FREDERICK ATKINS.

Branches with them. ACSO still survived in charge of Specialist Operations, without responsibility for a territorial Area.

Assistant Commissioners are Crown appointments. They have had the power to hear appeals against the decisions of Disciplinary Boards and since the mid-1990s have regularly done so in place of the Commissioner.

ATKINS, PC FREDERICK (1858–1881)
Murdered police officer, whose death started the agitation to arm constables on lonely beats in the outer divisions. Joined the Met, 1877, serving in T Division (Richmond) and, from 1881, V Division (Kingston).

On 22 September 1881, PC Atkins (Warrant No. 61462, Divisional No. 356V) routinely visited a large house in Kingston on his beat. In the drive he was shot in the abdomen, chest and groin by a gunman whom he did not see and whose presence he had not suspected. Subsequent investigation discovered a burglar's cold chisel and lantern beside a ground floor window, from which one bar had been removed. Atkins died in hospital 24 hours later.

Despite the offer of a reward of £100 for information, the killer was never traced. PC Atkins was the only murdered Metropolitan Police Officer whose case remained unsolved between 1846 (PC Clark) and 1991 (DC Morrison). In 1996, a plaque to his memory was placed in New Malden Police Station, following detailed historical research on the case by PC Nick Mann.

ATKINSON, PC WILLIAM (FL.1829)
First police constable attested, almost immediately dismissed for drunkenness. Warrant No. 1.

Atkinson and PC William Alcock, the holder of Warrant No. 2, were both dismissed for drunkenness on the streets on 29 September 1829, the first day that patrols began. Police historian John Price expressed doubt about their dismissal and the accuracy of the Nominal Roll listing them as Warrant Nos. 1 and 2, but further research by Ken Stone of the Historical Museum has established that the delightful story of the first two policemen enrolled being sacked almost before the force hit the ground is absolutely true.

ATTESTATION
Being sworn-in (attested) in 'the office of constable' by a Commissioner or Assistant Commissioner (formerly a magistrate), gives the new constable greater powers of arrest than other citizens, and (depending on the precise state of the law at the time) certain powers to stop and search persons arousing justifiable suspicion of their criminal activities or intent (see Arrest). The attested officer's legal status is confirmed by his warrant card.

BACK HALL The front entrance to New Scotland Yard. The foyer contains a permanently staffed reception desk, seats for waiting visitors, an eternal flame commemorating members of the Service who have died on duty or in war, and illuminated Rolls of Honour whose pages are turned daily. Small ceremonies may occasionally be held there, such as the annual Remembrance Day service conducted by the Chaplain.

The curious traditional name derives from the period 1829–90, when the back hall of No. 4 Whitehall Place, opening on to Great Scotland Yard, was the direct means of entrance for anyone wishing to see 'the police' or 'a policeman' as opposed to formally visiting the Commissioners.

BADGES OF RANK These are mainly derived from military uniform. They were not featured on the original uniform issue of 1829, but were introduced later.

BALCOMBE STREET SIEGE Successful operation culminating in the arrest of four IRA terrorist murderers.

The IRA bombing and terror campaign of 1974–5 caused loss of life in London and Birmingham, journalist Ross McWhirter, informant Kenneth Lennon, PC Stephen Tibble QPM and Explosives Officer Captain Roger Goad GC BEM being among the fatalities. An intelligence-led response by the Met exhaustively surveyed the sites and times of IRA actions in London and calculated the likely times and places of future targets. In consequence, when four terrorists drove past Scott's Restaurant in Mount Street, Mayfair on 6 December 1975, a body of police was standing by awaiting their possible assault on a target they had attacked previously. The gang was pursued by car to Balcombe Street, Marylebone, where they entered the flat of a middle-aged couple, Mr and Mrs Matthews, and took them hostage, hoping to bargain their way out.

Commissioner Sir Robert Mark used experience gained in the Spaghetti House Siege to conduct a similar operation, monitoring the flat interior with hi-tech surveillance equipment, consulting psychiatrist Dr Peter Scott of the Maudsley Hospital and using the negotiating skills of Peter (later Lord) Imbert and others to prevent

the terrorists from taking panicky action against the hostages and to persuade them to leave peaceably. In addition, in view of the dangerous record of these men, the SAS was called in, and the site was screened from television and news cameras so that an element of surprise could be sustained.

In the event this proved unnecessary. Once they learned the SAS was standing by, the terrorists gave themselves up after nearly six days under siege.

BAND Metropolitan Police Band, 1932–1997.

Several Divisions formed their own local amateur bands from 1840 onwards, employing civilian bandmasters. In 1927 a central Metropolitan Police Band was organized, and in 1932 Commissioner Lord Trenchard gave it official recognition. Thereafter it played at events such as the Annual Concert and the Metropolitan Police Horse Show and at some ceremonial occasions, including certain funerals. Demands for its services became such that serving officers could not be spared from duty to attend all the rehearsals and public performances. The band thereupon became a full-time institution of civil staff musicians attached to the Directorate of Public Affairs and kitted out with a uniform similar to police for public appearances. As such it was vulnerable to economy measures, and was regretfully dissolved in 1997.

THE DIVISIONAL BAND OF K DIVISION, PICTURED AT SOME TIME BETWEEN 1906 AND 1909.

BASIC TRAINING From 1829 to 1907, the basic training of Metropolitan Police officers consisted of two weeks' foot drill, followed by a period accompanying experienced constables or Sergeants on beat patrol. Knowledge of the Instruction Book was required, but was not formally taught or examined. Candidates were sworn in and attested at the end of their training.

In 1907 Commissioner Sir Edward Henry established Peel House in Regency Street, Westminster, to give recruits a four-week programme of drill and elementary instruction in law and law enforcement (including deportment, writing reports and giving evidence in court). In 1908 self-defence was added. Over the years the course increased, until by 1927 it lasted 10 weeks.

After 1946, the former Hendon Police College became the Metropolitan Police Training School, and basic training was undertaken there as well as at Peel House. In 1968 Peel House was closed down and Hendon took over all responsibility for basic training, being renamed Peel Centre in 1974. Today all recruits report to Hendon for their basic training.

The residential training programme now lasts 18 weeks. Intakes of 50–200 recruits are admitted at five-week intervals. At the end of their training, passing-out parades in the presence of a very senior officer or distinguished visitor mark the recruits' formal induction into active policing. (But see O Division). They are still given some basic drill, with emphasis on speedy and competent bussing and de-bussing for quick transportation to crowd control. There is also training in tactical crowd control and the use of shields. Self-defence has now been absorbed in a larger programme of Officer Safety Training, including First Aid to standards set by the St John Ambulance Brigade exams. Swimming and life-saving used to be compulsory, though the Service now takes the view that people in difficulties are often better helped by officers giving assistance with lifesaving equipment from the bank than by an officer in the water struggling against the current. Physical education is compulsory to ensure the necessary standard of fitness.

Instruction in basic law and law enforcement remains essential, but as far as possible the material is introduced through role-playing exercises or video simulations of reality. The mock courtroom introduces students to presentation of evidence, and police duties such as tactful intervention in domestic disputes and sensitively informing relatives of bereavement are practised. The goal is good Community Policing. The best student in each intake receives a presentation and has his or her name recorded on a trophy.

The remainder of the recruit's first two years in the service is still probationary, and includes further training on Division. His or her continuance in the police force is dependent on continuous evidence of suitability.

BATHER, ELIZABETH CONSTANCE, OBE (1904–1988) Superintendent and Chief Superintendent i/c women police, 1946–60.

Daughter of a housemaster at Winchester College. Educ. St Swithun's School, Winchester. As a young woman served on Hampshire County Council, and became the youngest JP in the country. Joined WAAF on outbreak of WWII, rising to Senior Staff Officer i/c WAAF attachment to Bomber Command. Seconded to Canada to help establish Canadian WRAF. Left WAAF with rank of Group Officer and OBE for services. Joined Met Police, 1945, answering advertisement for (first) woman Chief Inspector. Barely reached 162.5cm (5ft 4in) height requirement. Superintendent, succeeding Miss Dorothy Peto as head of Women's Branch, 1946. Regraded Chief Superintendent, 1949. Retired 1960 and returned to local government interests, serving on parish councils in Hartley Wintney and Hart.

As Head of Women's Branch A4, Miss Bather consolidated and extended the positions gained by Sofia Stanley, Bertha Clayden and Dorothy Peto. With the support of Commissioner Sir Harold Scott and Home Secretary Chuter Ede, she made recruiting easier by promoting uniforms with a more feminine image and saw to it that women played their part in all areas of crime prevention, including the CID and Special Branch. She achieved her target of bringing the women's strength up to 300 and the prohibition on recruiting married women was dropped. Miss Bather represented sensible modernity and one of her last public services before her retirement was to give evidence to the Wolfenden Commission

SUPERINTENDENT ELIZABETH BATHER (LEFT) AND SUPERINTENDENT DOROTHY PETO.

which paved the way to the decriminalization of homosexual acts between consenting adult men.

BATON CHARGES Method of crowd dispersal to prevent an angry demonstration from turning into a riot. Proposed to Commissioner Rowan in November 1830 by the Radical reformer Francis Place (1771–1854), when it was apparent that the successful police use of passive resistance to wrong-foot potential rioters in Hyde Park the previous month was a tactic that could not survive determined violent demonstrators.

The method is self-explanatory. A small, disciplined body of men advancing swiftly with drawn truncheons on a large crowd has every chance of evoking a panicky retreat before large-scale resistance can begin.

BATTLE OF BOW STREET, 1919 Riot in which 50 policemen held back a crowd of US, Canadian and Australian servicemen estimated at 2000 strong.

In March 1919, police officers patrolling the Strand came across American soldiers and sailors playing dice on the pavement outside the Eagle Hut. When advised that this was illegal, the servicemen protested that they had won the war for the British and would do what they liked. When the policemen arrested three of them, they were set upon by the crowd and a pitched battle started. Police whistles brought reinforcements, and several servicemen were struck with truncheons, until a tall corporal named Zimmerman addressed the crowd, saying they would settle this in their own way. At that point, several officers believed he pulled his pistol. He was immediately felled with a truncheon blow across the head, whereafter the police fought their way back to Bow Street station, taking Zimmerman and several others who were under arrest.

An hour later the rumour went round that Zimmerman had died in the cells, and despite the efforts of YMCA employees and American officers to assure the mob that this was untrue, the crowd started throwing stones and bricks at Bow Street station. About 20 officers forced them back with a baton charge, and then, joined by about 30 more, formed a 'thin blue line' to hold

DEMONSTRATORS FLEEING FROM A BARRICADE ERECTED TO STOP A BRITISH UNION OF FASCISTS MARCH IN 1936.

the street. They repeated the successful baton charge when the mob tried to overwhelm them. Finally mounted police cleared the street, and a large body of police remained on duty well into the night to prevent any renewed disturbance.

About 30 servicemen were arrested, and seven American sailors and four soldiers were handed over to the US Military Police to be disciplined. Four Canadian soldiers appeared at Bow Street magistrates' court charged with rioting, and six servicemen who were severely injured and hospitalized were also held under guard for punishment.

The press estimate that a crowd of 2000 was successfully kept at bay by the determination of 50 policemen is probably an exaggeration, but there can be no doubt that the Metropolitan officers acquitted themselves well against heavy odds. It was noted that several of the policemen wore Mons and other WWI campaign ribbons (see Epsom Police Station Siege).

BATTLE OF CABLE STREET Anti-Fascist disturbance in 1936.

Sir Oswald Mosley's British Union of Fas-

cists, formed in 1932, habitually challenged Jewish East-Enders with strident anti-Semitic speeches and the chanting of anti-Semitic slogans. Their meetings were frequently attended by violence, and Mosley was deliberately provocative when he called a march for 4 October 1936 which was intended to go to the London Docks and rally support among dock workers. He had misread the temper of Gentile dockers, however, many of whom had been helped by Jewish sympathizers when they were children during the 1912 Dock Strike. As a result, Mosley's march was stopped at the junction of Cable Street and Dock Street by overturned vehicles and a vast united crowd of dockers, Jews and Popular Front leftists, armed with simple weapons such as chair legs or pick handles. Mosley demanded that the police help his men force a way through, but despite a violent struggle in which 70 people, many of them police officers, were seriously injured, and 88 arrests were made, the anti-Fascist forces were successful and Mosley's march had to turn tail.

It became a matter of pride for the East End that they had stopped Mosley, and he never again attempted such a mass rally in the docklands. The neighbourhood remembered it as a triumph, not a riot, and the site is marked by a plaque and a nearby mural which, happily, minimizes the police involvement in its idealized representation of the scene. Many policemen involved were disgusted by having to apply the law in favour of anti-Semitic Fascists.

BATTLE OF HEATHROW Triumphant Flying Squad operation which exemplified cases where 'minimum force' involves considerable violence.

In July 1948, squadmen received information from a warehouseman at BOAC (British Overseas Air Corporation, forerunner of BA) that he had been suborned by a gang of thieves to drug the tea and coffee of guards protecting a £250,000 consignment of bullion. The Squad promptly mounted an ambush. The guards were given the night off, and three squadmen donned their uniform and slumped in their chairs, pretending to be drugged. Two more hid in the van which transported the bullion and another nine lurked in the vicinity dressed as mechanics. The warehouseman, acting on police instructions, then telephoned the gang to say that the guards were doped. Eight men wearing stocking masks and armed with iron bars came into the warehouse and started searching for keys. The 'drugged guards' arose from their chairs to arrest them, supported by the squadmen from the van and by those who had waited outside. There was a furious and violent fight, in which several officers and several thieves were concussed. But the Flying Squad prevailed, and the robbers were arrested and convicted, receiving average sentences of 10 years.

BEALE, PC THOMAS, KPM (B.1893) The last policeman awarded the KPM (KPFSM) for Gallantry after having tackled a runaway horse.

Joined the Metropolitan Police on 27 October 1919. Warrant Number 107247 (363 G).

At about 2.30 p.m. on 2 February 1948, PC Beale was standing at the corner of Grahame Street and Noel Street, Islington, when a horse and van came flying towards him. A pneumatic

drill starting up in Noel Street had panicked the horse just as its driver was about to get back up on his seat. The horse collided with a lamp post before reaching PC Beale, who made an unsuccessful grab at its bridle. He then leaped on to a passing lorry and, as it overtook the horse, jumped off on to the horse's neck and succeeded in bringing it quickly to a halt.

The incident was the last of its kind. There had been no other recorded runaway horses stopped by policemen in the UK since WWII, and during the war years there had been more such incidents in Glasgow than in London. The action took its toll on a man then aged 54, and PC Beale suffered from shock and nervous debility.

BEAT CRIMES Minor offences which, it was decided in 1967, should be dealt with and investigated by the uniformed branch without reference to CID.

BEAT PATROL The basis of the original police system of 1829. Adapted from the military 'Shorncliffe system' of small communicating scout patrols. (See under Sir Charles Rowan.)

Under the original arrangements, eight constables would be paraded and inspected by their Section Sergeant at the station, and then marched formally out to independent positions in the Section from which each would start to patrol a small area of streets following a regular pattern. Details of the beats were kept on numbered cards. In the crowded inner London districts the beat would be about 1.6–2.4km (1–1 ½ miles) in total distance. Rowan's instruction book said 'he should be able to see every part of his beat at least once in ten minutes or a quarter of an hour; and this he will be expected to do.'

The inner city beats were so spaced and timed that it might be assumed there was always an officer within 15 minutes' walking distance from any point in London. As the newer Divisions in the outer suburbs were established, the beats there became longer, since much of the territory was open fields between residential areas. These parts had long been the territory of highwaymen and footpads (although the Bow Street Mounted Patrol had done much to diminish their numbers by 1829) and lone constables were at sufficient risk to

warrant their being armed with cutlasses for the first 20 years of the Force's existence. For a few decades after 1870, beat constables in the outer sections were allowed to carry pistols if they wished. (See under firearms.)

The beat patrol officer was forbidden to talk to colleagues whose beats abutted on his, unless about a necessary matter of duty. He was not allowed to enter pubs while on patrol, nor to smoke, and during the 19th century there were no arrangements for him to take a refreshment break, so officers tended to carry snacks in their pockets. Well into the 20th century, while gas lighting survived on the streets, officers equipped themselves with metal flasks which could be left discreetly next to the burner in a street lamp to provide a refreshing cup of hot tea as the night wore on.

The beats were planned and drawn up as new Divisions were created, and changed from time to time as the street plans and housing densities changed. The beat wheel was used to ensure that lengths of beats were approximately equal. But by the 1880s, Commissioner Sir Charles Warren noted that his men were walking up to 32km (20 miles) a night in all weathers with extremely ill-made boots whose clumsiness won them a popular reputation for having huge feet, and the nickname of 'flatfoot'. The frequent entry 'worn out,' explaining a constable's retirement on his record and pension papers, points to the very heavy physical demands the beat patrol made on middle-aged men.

The 'bobby on the beat' has long been the public ideal of policing. The highly visible presence of a uniformed officer guarding the streets offered constant reassurance and the regular patrols were perceived as preventing vandalism and public disorder by juveniles, street prostitutes or drunks. However, beat policing is extremely manpower-intensive and supplying 'full geographical coverage', especially in the scattered outlying Sections, soon proved impossible. Commissioner Sir Harold Scott introduced patrol cars, which enabled officers to cover greater areas more rapidly, and Unit Beat policing tried to combine the 'rapid response' of motorized patrols with the reassurance of home beat officers. By the 1970s it seemed that the bobby on the beat was becoming rare and, since increased mechanical traffic control by traffic lights had also virtually eliminated point duty, the public complained that a police officer could never be found when one was wanted. American urban experience was showing the desirability of a return to the original ideal of serving local communities with regular and familiar foot patrols, and so the Home Beat Officer was introduced, especially for housing estates and areas where juvenile disorder, vandalism and street drug dealing were prevalent.

Today the beat is patrolled with a good deal of discretion at all levels. Senior Divisional officers will make their own assessment of the best balance between Permanent Beat and Relief officers on their own patch. Personal radios have obviated the need for regular personal reports of untoward occurrences and the modern widespread ownership of telephones has made this method the first resort of the member of public who wants police assistance. Beat policing has become a focal aspect of Community policing.

See also Police boxes.

BEAT WHEEL Wooden spoked wheel of approximately 60cm (2ft) diameter mounted on an axle at the end of a handle roughly 75cm (2 ½ft) long, and fitted with a distance-measuring dial. Introduced in the 19th century for measuring

A BEAT WHEEL IN USE.

constables' beats, and discontinued c.1930. Examples are held in the Historical Museum and on display at the Peel Centre.

BECK, ADOLF (D.1909) Twice-imprisoned victim of misidentification. Beck, a middle-aged man of Norwegian extraction, was imprisoned in 1896 on the evidence of several women who testified to his having defrauded them, using the alias 'Lord Willoughby'. The prosecution believed that he was a previous offender, convicted under the name 'John Smith' for identical offences two years earlier, but dropped certain charges made against 'Smith' when Beck's defence could establish a good alibi for him. While Beck was in prison, however, his defence team realized that 'Smith' was circumcized and Beck was not. Their appeal to Assistant Commissioner Robert Anderson for access to the papers to reopen the case was curtly refused. Home Office officials who were told of the proof that the two men were different dismissed the issue as unimportant since Beck had been convicted of several offences that did not stand in 'Smith's' name.

In 1904, two years after his release from prison, Beck was rearrested and reconvicted for offences following the pattern of 'Smith's' crimes. This time the Home Office knew very well he was not 'Smith', but kept silent. Ten days after his conviction, Inspector John Kane recognized a man brought in to Tottenham Court Road Police Station as the real 'John Smith' (who, indeed, looked very like Adolf Beck), and started the procedures which secured Beck's release.

A Home Office Inquiry established that no police officers were ever made aware of the proof that 'Smith' and Adolf Beck were different men. Kane's observation had been been properly followed up, and Scotland Yard itself had effectively secured Beck's release. The only blame attaching to the Met was Anderson's peremptory refusal to let the defence lawyers see the papers.

The proven possibility of genuine misidentification by honest witnesses went far to win respect for fingerprinting, and the case also highlighted the need for a Court of Criminal Appeal.

BECKE, COMMANDER SHIRLEY CAMERON, OBE, OSTJ, QPM (B.1917) Last head of A4 Branch and for many years the most senior woman police officer in the country. B. Shirley Jennings in Chiswick, daughter of a gas engineer. Educ. Westminster Technical Institute, becoming the first woman to qualify as Higher Grade Gas Engineer. Employed by Gas, Light and Coke Co. (subsequently North Thames Gas Board) until 1941, when joined the Met anticipating service for the duration of the war only. WPC C Division, (478C). CID, West End Central, 1945. Det Sgt, 1952. Married chartered accountant Justice Becke (later the Rev. Justice Becke, MBE), 1954. Detective Chief Inspector, 1959, and most senior woman CID officer. Superintendent i/c women police of No.1 District. Chief Superintendent and head of A4 Branch, 1966, from which time until her retirement she was the most senior woman police officer in the UK. Commander, 1969. On dissolution of A4 Branch in 1973 served in force Inspectorate and energetically ensured the employment of women on an equal basis throughout the force. Retired 1974.

Shirley Becke gave high priority to the recruitment of women police, frequently noting the inevitable 'wastage' through marriage and (especially) maternity, for which reason she always hoped to increase the intake of women in their late twenties or early thirties. In 1970 she was included in a volume of distinguished women (including Barbara Castle and Barbara Hepworth) with pen portraits by William Wordsworth (great-great-grandson of the poet) and charcoal sketches by Pietro Annigoni's former pupil ZsuZsi Roboz.

BELPER COMMITTEE Five-man Home Office committee chaired by Lord Belper which sat in 1900 to consider the relative merits of anthropometry and fingerprinting. Both Dr John Garson, president of the Anthropometry Society, and Edward Henry appeared before it and argued for their respective systems. Henry's practical demonstration from a collection of 7000 prints easily convinced the committee. Their report recommended that fingerprints should routinely be taken and added to anthropometric cards.

BERTILLONAGE System of recording body measurements for the purpose of confirming the identities of convicted criminals. Invented by Alphonse Bertillon in 1880 and introduced to Scotland Yard (where it was known as Anthropometry) in 1894 on the recommendation of the Troup Committee. Its advocates in France strenuously resisted its replacement by fingerprinting for many years as, with less success, did Dr John Garson, president of the Anthropometry Society, who set up the Anthropometry Register for Scotland Yard. See also Anthropometry Department.

BICYCLES Experiments with tricycles as a means of transport, especially for Sergeants inspecting beat patrols, were the subject of memoranda in 1888, but they do not appear to have been authorized on a regular basis. In 1904, by which time bicycling had become a common form of transportation, *Police Orders* approved allowances over an experimental period of two years for Inspectors, Sergeants and constables using their own bicycles for service duties, provided the officers cleaned and maintained the bicycles at their own expense and in their own time. By 1906 bicycles had proved their worth and were accepted as one of the useful means of transportation, especially across the greater distances in the outer Divisions.

'BIG FIVE, THE' Journalists' nickname for the four Area (or District) Detective Chief Superintendents from 1919 (see 'The Big Four') together with their colleague commanding HQ CID (Branch C1) in Scotland Yard, when he was raised to their rank in 1921.

'BIG FOUR, THE' Journalists' sobriquet for Superintendents F. P. Wensley and Arthur Hawkins, and acting Superintendents Arthur Neil and Francis Carlin, in 1919 when they were each given command over a quarter of the CID operations in the MPD. Subsequently applied to their successors as Area (or District) Detective

Superintendents (or higher ranks, up to Commander, as nomenclature and grades changed over the years). The name 'Big Four' was copied from the popular description of President Woodrow Wilson and premiers Lloyd George, Clemenceau and Orlando, who dominated the

OPTIMISTIC ADVERTISING AT A TIME WHEN THE FORCE WAS EXPERIMENTING WITH VARIOUS FORMS OF CYCLE.

Versailles peace conference. The officers' promotions realized proposals Wensley had put to Sir Basil Thomson in 1916 for amalgamating groups of Divisions under an external command so that territorial CIDs could work together without being compelled to respect strict Divisional boundaries.

With offices in New Scotland Yard (1), Wensley and his confreres were partly liaison officers between Divisional CIDs and HQ and partly general officers commanding strategy and receiving reports from the field. The titles 'Big Four' and 'Big Five' were never formally recognized in

Scotland Yard, although Wensley rejoiced in them and used them in his memoirs (*Detective Days*, 1931), as did several of his successors. While certain other operational posts, like Commander of the Flying Squad or senior officer in the 'Murder Squad' came to seem more glamorous to newspapermen, Chief Superintendent Ted Greeno's publishers thought his membership of the 'Big Five' worth recording on the jacket of his memoirs. The sobriquets fell out of favour completely when Sir Robert Mark moved the Area Detective Commanders out of Scotland Yard and deployed them under the Area Deputy Assistant Commissioners.

BILL, THE Television drama series noted for serious attempt to present an authentic Metropolitan Police setting. Made by Thames Television since 1983, developed from a naturalistic play called *Woodentop* about a police recruit's experiences.

BILLY, THE WHITE HORSE OF WEMBLEY (FL.1923) Mounted Police grey gelding, acquired from Yorkshire, and allocated to PC George Scorey in 1920. Acquired fame at the first FA Cup Final to be played at Wembley, 1923, when Scorey led him to clear the pitch of invasive crowds. Thereafter both were famous, and their presence was requested at many events.

Billy died in 1930, and Sir Percy Laurie, head of the Mounted Branch, presented Scorey with one of his hooves, polished and mounted. Although the real achievement was Scorey's, Billy's name is the one that is always remembered in connection with the Cup Final.

BLACK MARIA Nickname for secure police vans with separate locked cubicles, used for the transportation of prisoners. Borrowed from America, where a large and powerful black lodging-house keeper named Maria Lee is supposed to have helped the constables of Boston, Massachusetts in the 1830s whenever they needed to escort recalcitrant drunks to the cells, hence the

BLACK MARIA OUTSIDE SOUTH WESTERN COURT, LAVENDER HILL, IN 1902.

phrase 'We're sending for Black Maria'.

The Met's first vehicle of any kind was a Black Maria drawn by two dray horses, acquired in 1858. Within 30 years the number had increased to eight, and a special area in the yard of Bow Street Police Court was reserved for them to load and unload their charges. In 1914 the horse-drawn vans started to be replaced by black motorized vans. These in turn gave way to white buses in the 1970s, and the whole fleet passed out of service when the Courts Escort Service was contracted out in 1995.

BLACK MONDAY See Trafalgar Square Demonstration and Riot, 1886.

'BLACK MUSEUM' Popular name for the Metropolitan Police Crime Museum, an L-shaped room on the first floor of New Scotland Yard. The first section, a space about 8 x 5m (26 x 16ft), has been decorated to replicate the original crime museum in Great Scotland Yard, with an iron-grated fireplace and tables in the centre and on two walls displays of weapons which have been involved in crimes. A high shelf car-

ries death masks of executed 19th-century convicts, collected from 1824 at the request of the Phrenological Society. A collection of more recent hangman's nooses with labels identifying their victims hangs beside the door. The first plate camera used at a crime scene is on display, and freestanding cabinets exhibit Himmler's death mask and assorted criminalia.

The second section, measuring about 13 x 5m (43 x 16ft), holds 13 cabinets, two of them devoted to famous murder cases and the remainder with displays on such subjects as terrorism, murdered police officers, sieges, the Great Train Robbery, attacks on royalty, espionage, counterfeiting, burglary and safebreaking. An illicit still, the bath and cooker with which serial murderer Denis Nilsen disposed of his victims, a cross on which an eccentric visionary tried to have himself crucified on Hampstead Heath and fetishistic equipment from a Victorian brothel are among the more striking freestanding exhibits. The notorious 'electric box' with which the Richardson brothers interrogated gangland enemies in the 1960s is displayed on a shelf, as is a selection of ingeniously rigged gaming equipment. The arms of murderer Ronald Chesney (aka Donald Merrett), pickled in formaldehyde, are the most obviously gruesome exhibit. The entire museum, though fascinating to all students of true crime, is

much smaller than its worldwide reputation might suggest.

The museum was started some time after the Prisoners' Property Act of 1869, which clarified responsibilities for the safe keeping of belongings taken from prisoners when they were charged or convicted. In 1874 Commissioner Sir Edmund Henderson allocated No. 1 Palace Place, Great Scotland Yard, behind Whitehall Place, to be used as a store for this property until it could be returned to its owners on release. Burglary tools and weapons were kept separately as they were not going to be returned.

Inspector Percy Neame (Warrant No. 48294) and PC Randall, who were appointed to duty in the property store in April 1875, were probably the first to see the value of showing young constables the kind of 'innocuous' items that marked their possessors as housebreakers, and they were probably exhibiting examples by 1874. In 1875 an official collection was approved, and from the time of a visit from the Commissioner and Assistant Commissioners in 1877 a Visitors' Book was kept, detailing the interested dignitaries and celebrities who came to see the collection. The drawing of 1884 from which the current layout of the opening section was taken shows a party of ladies and gentlemen peering at the weapons on display. When Scotland Yard moved to the Norman Shaw Building on the Embankment, the museum was consigned to a basement initially under the care of Randall (by then an Inspector) assisted by two Sergeants and two constables. Its fortunes fluctuated according to the interests of various AC Cs, and it was closed during both wars. A note in *Police Review* in 1896 complained that Assistant Commissioner Robert Anderson had taken charge of it, and was admitting very few visitors. The Visitors Book for the period shows that Anderson indeed conducted people around personally, as did the later AC C Melville Macnaghten, between 1903 and 1914. In 1897, however, Percy Neame, by then a Superintendent, took charge of it again as part of his duties in charge of the Convict Supervision Office. What exactly he did wrong is not clear, but six months after his retirement in 1902, the newly appointed Assistant Commissioner Edward Henry asked him to explain 'certain irregularities', and he shot himself.

THE PRESENT DAY ENTRANCE ROOM OF THE BLACK
MUSEUM, LAID OUT TO REPLICATE THE EARLIEST KNOWN
PICTURE OF THE ORIGINAL CRIME MUSEUM.

The museum's primary purpose was and is
instructional. The weapons displayed in quasi-
Victorian surroundings today are largely selected
to show how knives and guns may be disguised
as anything from combs and pens to briefcases.
The burglary and drugs exhibits expose inge-
nious camouflages and places of concealment.
The name 'Black Museum' was coined in 1877
by a journalist on the *Observer*, disgruntled at
being refused admission. Yet, had the museum
ever been maintained simply to gratify the curious, it would have fallen victim to the first economy drive imposed on the Met. Had it been

transferred to other premises and opened purely
as a commercial undertaking, its dangerous
weapons and drugs would have required
extremely expensive secure exhibition, and it
would have had to be purged of so many gruesome and arguably distasteful items that it would
have lost much of its historical interest. A certain
amount of early pilfering by (it is suspected)
rather eminent people led to some exhibits (for
example the original 'Jack the Ripper' letter) going
missing for a number of years, but their descen-
dants (such as those of the judge who retained a
pistol from the Siege of Sidney Street as a souvenir) have often seen that the criminalia return
to their rightful place.

In 1954 Alexander Hannay, a Principal Executive Officer on the Civil Staff, retired, and then
accepted junior rank to become the first full-time

and only civilian curator of the museum. Since
his death the following year, the museum has
always been in the care of a full-time curator
drawn from the ranks of ex-police officers. They
have had to train themselves in Forensic Science,
Law, Pathology and Investigative Techniques for
the lectures they are required to give to various
visiting bodies of police and their files contain
fascinating records of English crime history and
the exhibits under their care. Curator Bill Wad-
dell, who oversaw the 1981 refit which created
the imitation Victorian section, raised the museum's profile with television appearances and
writing during the 1980s. The present curator,
John Ross, is noted for his sympathetic approach
to scholarly inquirers.

The museum Visitors' Book has been carefully maintained, retaining records of visits by many

members of the royal family, such notables as Sir Arthur Conan Doyle and Harry Houdini, and many stars of stage and screen such as Stan Laurel and Oliver Hardy. But despite the famous radio series opening with the formula 'I am in the Black Museum at Scotland Yard,' there is no evidence that Orson Welles ever set foot in it.

BLACK POLICE ASSOCIATION Founded

in August 1994, with the aim of improving the working environment of Metropolitan Police officers and Civil Staff of African, African-Caribbean and Asian origin; working for equality of opportunity and cultivating better relationships between the minority communities and the police; and assisting with the recruiting and retention of black personnel. The launch at New Scotland Yard was publicly supported by Commissioner Sir Paul Condon and Sir Herman Ouseley, Chairman of the Commission for Racial Equality (CRE). The Association was actively involved in the Macpherson Inquiry into the Stephen Lawrence murder investigation, providing written and oral submissions to Part II of the Inquiry. The Black Police Association provides a mechanism for officially airing the concerns of minority ethnic employees, and is active in debates surrounding issues of race and diversity management.

BLAKELOCK, PC KEITH (1945–1985)

Policeman murdered by rioters on 6th October 1985.

Joined the Metropolitan Police on 14 November 1980 (Warrant Number 176050). A Home Beat Officer working a peaceful district in Muswell Hill, PC Blakelock was one of the officers called to the Broadwater Farm riot, where he was issued with riot gear, and put in the *ad hoc* serial of only 11 men headed by Sergeant David Pengelly. At 9.30 p.m., Sgt Pengelly led his serial to the assistance of firemen who had been driven off the first-floor deck of Tangmere Building,

where a fire had been started in a newsagent's. The serial, too, were beaten back by rioters. As they retreated, PC Blakelock slipped and fell. Immediately he was surrounded by masked and balaclava'd rioters armed with sticks, knives and a machete who proceeded to hack him to death. PC Richard Coombes tried to run to his help, but was felled by a tremendous blow to the face which broke his jaw and left him unconscious. Sgt Pengelly, followed by PC Ricky Pandya, raced back to the killers who were slashing at PC

BLOODY SUNDAY, 1887. DEMONSTRATORS OVERWHELM POLICE IN ST MARTIN'S LANE.

Blakelock, and despite being hit by rocks thrown at them and risking severe injury, frightened the murderers away. Chief Superintendent Colin Couch, who was in charge of the incident, then ran to Blakelock's assistance with PC Maxwell Roberts, helped Blakelock to his feet, and urged him to run. PC Blakelock, his face covered with blood and a wooden-handled knife stuck in his neck, managed three strides before collapsing. He was dead on arrival at North Middlesex Hospital with 40 separate wounds, several of them blows to the head and face with a machete. A very severe cut which had smashed the right side of his jawbone led to the canard that the rioters intended to decapitate him and put his head on a pole.

Blakelock left a wife and three children, and the distress his death caused the Metropolitan Police was intense. In 1989 Broadwater Farm

residents converted the site of PC Blakelock's death into a memorial garden for him and for Mrs Cynthia Jarrett, whose death in the course of a police search of her home was the proximate cause of the riot.

It is a tragic irony that PC Blakelock should have been attached to Muswell Hill and was pronounced dead in the North Middlesex Hospital, in both cases exactly like PC Nat Edgar.

BLOODY SUNDAY, 1866 See Hyde Park Riot, 1866.

BLOODY SUNDAY, 1887

13 November 1887. Battle in Trafalgar Square between police and would-be demonstrators against unemployment which caused many injuries and some alleged loss of life, and led to a sustained and ultimately successful press campaign against the Commissioner.

In the summer of 1887, large numbers of the destitute unemployed took to camping in Trafalgar Square. Their presence made the square a centre for political agitation, and by September Commissioner Sir Charles Warren, fearing that London would once again be at the mercy of a mob, asked the Home Secretary to ban all meetings in the square. The City had already banned political processions for the time being, and tradesmen, the Mayor of Westminster and the Metropolitan Board of Works were all anxious to see demonstrations stopped. Home Secretary Henry Matthews procrastinated throughout October, during which time Warren had to post up to 2000 policemen around the square and at its approaches on weekends to ensure public order. The great extent of the area policed, and the approval of the middle classes, is shown by a personal note from Florence Nightingale to the Commissioner, asking his permission to give cups of tea to the officers regularly stationed outside her house in Park Street, Mayfair.

In November, Matthews suddenly gave way and allowed Warren to declare meetings in or around the square prohibited. This appeared to have been done on Warren's sole authority and was seen as unlawful and provocative by the left-wing press, which had previously looked with favour on Warren as a desirable intellectual progressive. A meeting to challenge his order was called for 2.30 p.m., Sunday 13 November, and Warren responded by expressly prohibiting any procession from entering the square on that day. Predictably, radicals took this as a 'dare', and took a lofty moral tone in snatching up the gauntlet.

Warren stationed his 2000 men and took up a position to oversee events at the square himself, from which he sent reports at intervals to the Home Secretary, so that the progress of this riot can be described unusually precisely:

1.00pm: although all was quiet and the police had held the square undisturbed for an hour, Warren took the precaution of requesting four squadrons of Life Guards to take up position at Horse Guards Parade, behind the Admiralty, with two magistrates to read the Riot Act if necessary.

2.45 p.m.: Bands of men were reported to be assembling at Clerkenwell Green and other spots near the centre of London.

3.45 p.m.: Large disorderly crowds armed with sticks were approaching the square and declared their intention of taking it. Warren was concerned that there were a large number of Irishmen among those coming from the east and north. He thought the police could hold the square until the onset of darkness.

4.05 p.m.: There was serious fighting at Waterloo Place and near Bow Street. Warren ordered two squadrons of Life Guards into the Square to relieve the police who were unable to keep the mobs back.

4.30 p.m.: The two squadrons of Life Guards in the Square were holding it with difficulty, surrounded by disorderly mobs in all directions. A third had joined the fray in Waterloo Place. Warren sent for more mounted troops to be placed in reserve at Horse Guards Parade and 400 foot soldiers to 'liberate' the police lining the north side of the Square. John Burns, the dockers' union leader, was arrested, and so was the radical MP R. B. Cunninghame Graham, who had been injured in the fighting.

5.00 p.m.: The square was quietening down. The worst rioting had been in Waterloo Place, but the police had controlled it before the Life Guards arrived. The mobs were starting to drift away, though reports came in that new ones were approaching from Parliament Street and Southwark. Warren sent troops to disperse the Parliament Street crowd, and hoped that before the estimated 10,000 mob from Southwark appeared he would have complete control of the Square.

5.15 p.m.: The troops restored order at Parliament Street, where a mob with sticks had fought the police, stabbing one officer in the back and cutting the reins of a mounted policeman. The squadron that had gone to Waterloo Place was sent to patrol Pall Mall and Lower Regent Street, to prevent the retreating mobs from stoning club windows as they had done on Black Monday the previous year.

6.00 p.m.: The mob still held Northumberland Avenue and some other approaches to the square, and had broken windows in Northumberland Avenue and Charing Cross. 'A very low class of roughs' had been prowling around and throwing stones at the police, but Warren hoped that in half an hour he might be able to reduce the number of men on duty.

6.20 p.m.: The Life Guards had returned to Horse Guards Parade. The Foot Guards were holding the square, but Warren expected to dismiss them in a few minutes. The streets were returning to normal, and over 50 arrests had been made for riotous conduct or assaulting the police.

Trafalgar Square was a mess, and Charing Cross Hospital was filled with casualties. The left-wing press reported that one or more people had subsequently died of their injuries. The demonstrators felt cheated that the military had been called in when they could have fought the police to a standstill. John Burns was sentenced to six weeks' imprisonment for resisting the police. Sulky skirmishes continued on and off until December, including one huge brawl in Westminster Abbey. The radicals held regular weekly demonstrations in Trafalgar Square for the next two years, and Warren's unfortunate policemen were marshalled for extra weekend duties to exercise crowd control.

Warren was henceforth excoriated in papers which had previously admired him. When he resigned over a policy dispute with the Home Office on the day of the last Jack the Ripper murder, the Star crowed 'Whitechapel has avenged us for Trafalgar Square' and set the seal on his unjustified unhappy reputation.

BLUE LAMP Identifying sign for a police station. The origins are obscure. Westminster City Council ordered police stations to identify themselves by posting lights outside the buildings early in the 19th century. The practice of surrounding them with blue glass began as gas lighting reached London stations piecemeal until, in 1861, Police Orders directed Superintendents to requisition blue glasses to surround the external lamps at all their stations on at least three sides. The blue lamp at Bow Street, however, was removed at the request of Queen Victoria, who disliked seeing it when she went to the opera.

BLUE LAMP, THE An Ealing Studios feature film made in 1949 which revolved around police duties at Paddington Green Station. The style was influenced by contemporary Crown Documentary pictures, using realistic and location settings, with rather self-consciously warm and human characterization to illustrate such routine events as beat duty, contact with the public, supervision of the cells and so forth before moving to the narrative climax of the murder of a policeman on duty and the hunt for the young tearaway who killed him. Made with the approval of Commissioner Sir Harold Scott and consultative assistance from the Met, the film gave a convincing if slightly rose-tinted picture of normal police life. Unusual care was taken with getting details of uniforms, Divisional numbers and equipment correct. Jack Warner's portrayal of the murder victim, fatherly constable George Dixon, made a lasting contribution to the image of the Metropolitan bobby, especially when the role was revived and transferred to a fictional station for the long-running television series, Dixon of Dock Green (see also PC Nathanael Edgar.)

'BOBBY ON THE BEAT' Although the familiar nickname 'bobby' (derived from Sir

BOROUGH POLICING Proposed reorganization of the MPS structure to be introduced in 1999 as part of the Greater London Local Government reforms associated with the Greater London Authority and elected Mayor of London. The planning was led by Assistant Commissioner Paul Manning.

Ever since the 1965–66 reorganization of the Met boundaries, Divisional boundary lines have, as far as possible, clung to Borough boundaries. Where the busier Boroughs (for example Lambeth or Hackney) comprised two, three or four Divisions, there were obviously additional Divisional boundaries inside the Borough perimeters. Districts (2) as established under the Waldron reforms included one or more London Boroughs.

Under Sir Peter Imbert's PLUS programme, a gradual move began to reduce the number of Divisions and to align them more closely with the Boroughs. Thus the Borough of Chelsea and Kensington (B District under the Waldron Reforms), for instance, was pulled back from three Divisions to two.

At the end of the century the Blair government declared its intention of making the MPD co-terminous with the electoral area of the new Greater London Authority by the year 2000. Those small sections of the MPD encroaching on the administrative counties of Surrey, Hertfordshire and Essex would be handed over to the County Constabularies. At the same time, the Crime and Disorder Act of 1998 gave local authorities increased responsibilities for crime prevention. It was thereupon felt that regardless of the varying sizes of territory to be policed, it would be necessary to make command units coincide completely with the London Boroughs. This would have the advantage of giving each Borough a single officer of Chief Superintendent rank in charge of policing, apart from the City of Westminster which, due to its Central London size and nature, would have a Commander.

BOW STREET Site of the first Police Office and subsequently the premier London magistrates' court; also housed the exhibition founding the Historical Museum.

In 1739, Colonel Thomas de Veil (1664–1746) occupied No. 4 Bow Street on the

'A SERIOUS CASE OF POACHING': THE 1891 BOBBY ON THE BEAT SHARES A WORD WITH CHILDREN IN TRAFALGAR SQUARE.

Robert Peel's forename) is today more commonly used in the north of England than the south, the expanded term 'bobby on the beat' remains a warm and positive way of summarizing the regular uniformed foot patrol, comparable with the rural idyll of the 'village policeman'.

BOMB SQUAD Familiar name for Anti-Terrorist Branch C13 (now SO13) between its initial informal establishment by Sir John Waldron in 1970 and its permanent establishment in 1976.

Originally an *ad hoc* team of 20 Special Branch and 10 CID officers headed by Detective Chief Superintendent Roy Habershon, who was investigating the Angry Brigade bombing of Home Secretary Robert Carr's house. Expanded with the addition of Explosives Officers formerly attached to C7 (laboratory liaison staff), familiarly known as 'Expos' to the remainder of the Service. At one time organized under Commander Ernie Bond to meet the ongoing, if fluctuating, threat from terrorism in London.

west side, a site subsequently covered by the Floral Hall's adjacent flower market and a warehouse. De Veil made a name as the first notably honest magistrate in the era of London's 'trading justices' (who took bribes as a matter of course and brokered deals between thieves and their victims). His 'office' was regarded as the best source of street-level justice in the capital.

After his death, a magistrate named Poulson continued to use De Veil's office for his public business for two years. The newly appointed Henry Fielding then moved into the Bow Street Office and remained there until his death in 1754, whereupon his blind half-brother John Fielding took over, remaining the chief Bow Street magistrate until his own death in 1780. In 1762 John (by then Sir John) published A Plan for Preventing Robberies within Twenty Miles of London. This proposed that stipendiary magistrates in 'Rotation Offices' should work under the direction of Bow Street (the 'Police Centre'). The magistrates should keep registers of all criminals brought to their notice by their constables and the registers should be held centrally at Bow Street, incremented with lists of deserters from the

BOW STREET MAGISTRATES COURT AND POLICE
STATION, c.1882.

army, and published in a regular *Police Gazette*. The funds for running the Offices, derived from the pooled fees accruing to justices' clerks, should pay for the registers and paperwork, and for the retention of a solicitor to advise the police. A short-lived experiment with the scheme collapsed for lack of proper funding, but Fielding had anticipated a remarkable amount of the future structure of crime prevention, and his and Henry Fielding's basic formula of magistrates controlling permanent constables from fixed offices would lie at the heart of the Middlesex Justices Act (1792). Prior to the Act, Sir John had clearly felt that his jurisdiction extended over London and the home counties although, oddly, there was no statutory basis at all for Bow Street's authority.

Shortly after Sir John Fielding's retirement, the Bow Street office was attacked and damaged, and its contents burned in the Gordon Riots (1780). It was rebuilt by his successor, Sampson Wright, who, like De Veil and the Fieldings before him, privately leased the building from the Duke of Bedford's Covent Garden Estate, as the Bow Street office would continue to be leased by his successors until 1842. This independence, and the Bow Street magistrates' payment from Home Department funds (whereas the other Middlesex magis-

trates were paid out of the Consolidated Fund), gave Bow Street a distinctly superior standing, and its Chief Magistrate was semi-officially regarded as the Chief Magistrate of London.

A tavern called the Brown Bear on the opposite side of the street was, ironically, known as a 'flash ken', or haunt of thieves and malefactors. In 1797 the landlord agreed to make a room available for holding manacled and fettered arrestees awaiting their appearance before the magistrate, and the Bow Street establishment recorded the employment of an 'assistant jailer' in addition to three clerks and a messenger. Thus Bow Street pragmatically pioneered the idea of cells and Civil Staff at Police Offices.

In 1811 a new courtroom was added to the building, and in 1812 the Treasury granted James Read £1295 to extend the Office by converting the adjacent No. 3 Bow Street, whose lease he had acquired. The new property included a building designated 'Felons Rooms' behind the back yard, the ancestral custody suite.

When the Metropolitan Police was founded in 1829, the Commissioners placed the station house on the other side of the road on the site of Nos 25 and 27. Bow Street Station became the Divisional Station of the original F Division (Covent Garden), and remained the Divisional Station for Holborn and Covent Garden when E and F Divisions were merged in 1869 and F Division ceased to exist for several years.

The 1839 Metropolitan Police Act quietly put an end to the Bow Street magistrates' anomalous legal independence, defining them as Stipendiary Magistrates like any others within the meaning of the Act, and in 1842 the Home Office took over the lease of Nos 3 and 4 Bow Street from the magistrates. Nevertheless, Bow Street would continue to be seen as the premier London Magistrates Court, and committal proceedings for great criminal

cases such as that of Dr Crippen continued to take place at Bow Street.

When Blue Lamps were introduced to demarcate police stations in 1861, Queen Victoria objected to having this distressing reminder of the blue room in which Prince Albert died confronting her whenever she visited the Opera House. So Bow Street, rather proudly, became the major London police station which famously did not have a blue lamp but a white one. In the public mind Bow Street Station remained the prototypical Police Office and it was a cause of grave concern that Bow Street officers were prominent in the abortive Police Strikes of 1872 and 1890.

By 1860, the historic magistrate's offices at Nos 3 and 4 were in need of repair, rebuilding or extension, and discussions as to their replacement continued until, in 1876, a 99-year lease on a site across the road and adjacent to the police station was acquired. Construction of the new purpose-built Bow Street Police Court and Station, with a Section House for 106 PCs, was started in 1878 and completed in 1881, whereupon the entire business of the magistrates transferred across the road. After use for a few years as a theatrical wigmakers' premises, Nos 3 and 4 Bow Street were demolished, never to be replaced.

In 1920 temporary buildings were erected in the yard for the Aliens Registration Office. These were demolished in 1925, when the Section House was closed, and the ARO moved to the basement. In 1949 a collection of police artefacts was put on display at Bow Street, and remained there until, as the Metropolitan Police Historical Museum (a name it received in 1967), it was transferred to temporary storage accommodation in Brixton in 1983, and subsequently Charlton.

The revision of Divisional boundaries to correspond better with the new London Boroughs created in 1963 led to Bow Street's being incorporated in C Division in 1965. When the new purpose-built Charing Cross station was opened in 1985, most of the police functions were transferred there. Bow Street retained its famous magistrates' courts, but the Metropolitan Police presence was reduced to a temporary use of the station to accommodate parts of West End Central while it was being refurbished. The Courts Division offi-

cers attached to the court itself were removed when the contracted-out Court Escort Service was introduced to relieve police officers from the task of transporting and guarding prisoners. The only continuous police presence there now is that of the local Division's Prosecution Liaison Officer. It is the passionate hope of the Friends of the Metropolitan Police Museum and others that plans to establish a Police Museum at Bow Street will be fulfilled. See also Battle of Bow Street.

BOW STREET POLICE FUND Also known as the Bow Street Magistrates Court Reward Fund, and branched into the additional Police Relief Fund.

Endowed by Mr Henry Whiting in 1868 following the bravery of Detective Inspector James Jacob Thomson (Warrant No. 43692) in arresting Richard Burke, the Fenian terrorist (see Clerkenwell Bombing). Mr Whiting placed £1000 in the form of shares at the disposal of the Bow Street magistrates, to reward in perpetuity members of the Metropolitan Police who distinguished themselves by 'gallant conduct'. In 1872 he added another £1000. Three years later, learning that many brave officers suffered hardship and incapacitation after injury, he offered to donate another £1000 which, with £500 of the £2000 Reward Fund money, could go to setting up a new Relief Fund, to be disbursed at the discretion of the Commissioner. Another £1000 was donated to the Reward Fund in 1952 by an elderly lady who wished to remain anonymous. About 20 awards a year are given.

The awards have always been small. Sums between 7/6d (37p) and £2 were common in the 19th century; and at times as the invested capital fluctuated there has been concern about the continuance of the scheme. Since 1930 'smart police work' without reference to gallantry has been brought within the scope of the fund, and by that time it was normal for a Commissioner's High Commendation to be given to recipients. Since 1972 the reward has been restricted to officers of the rank of Inspector and under. Today the awards are unlikely to exceed £200, but they are highly valued by the recipients for the certificate of meritorious service which accompanies them.

BOW STREET RUNNERS Also other Bow Street Patrols and Officers. Prototype police force. To be strictly accurate, the term 'Bow Street Runners' was only properly applied to the small plainclothes detective force (never more than eight men) which was the original creation, but the name of Bow Street was also attached to the uniformed Horse and Foot Patrols whose success in putting down highway robbery on the outskirts of London and footpads on dark streets played a large part in encouraging the experiment of a permanent metropolis-wide peacekeeping force. The Bow Street Horse Patrols ultimately became the nucleus of the Metropolitan Mounted Police, and detective Runners continued to function alongside the Met for 12 years.

Henry Fielding (1707–54) devised the idea of permanent paid magistrates commanding small forces of permanent constables in district Police Offices and in 1753 he put it into operation. With the help of his brother John and Saunders Welch, the High Constable of Holborn, he recruited seven respectable householders, all but one of whom had served their year as parish constable. As 'Mr Fielding's men', they agreed to continue their peace-keeping activities in concert and under Fielding's direction. By going out and looking for information they swiftly broke up a large gang of thieves, something that had hardly been seen in London since the corrupt receiver and informer Jonathan Wild destroyed his rivals in the 1720s. Unfortunately for Fielding's plan, Wild was still vividly remembered, and Mr Fielding's men, like Wild, were described as 'thief-takers' – a word of ill-omen since Wild's exposure and hanging in 1724. Fielding was unable to obtain proper funding for his men and the Recorder of London would not give them the rewards (or 'blood money') to which they were entitled. In consequence, suspicion and unpopularity attached to the Bow Street men from the outset, and the little force was soon disbanded. But it is noteworthy as the first attempt at policing a district with a permanent force of dedicated peace officers.

Brother John carried the good work much further. He published *A History and Effects of the late Henry Fielding's Police* in 1758, and revived the band of thief-takers. The first printed reference to them under the name 'Bow Street Runners' came in the *Morning Herald* in 1785, but the name did not become really familiar until the 19th century.

The Bow Street Runners were more than watchmen or constables: they actively sought to detect the perpetrators of crimes, not merely to impede those who might be contemplating some villainy or arrest those against whom the magistrates had received information. They were paid a 'retainer' of 11/6d (57p) a week and allowed up to 14/- (70p) expenses. On the recommendation of the bench, they received a share of more substantial rewards for successful prosecutions of burglars and highwaymen, though the lion's share of such rewards went to the private prosecutors (the victims of the crime) who were put to the expense of bringing the case. When the Middlesex Justices Act copied the Fielding system in seven other offices, constables' pay was set at a guinea a week (£1.05p) and the Bow Street men's retainer rose accordingly, rising once more to 25s (£1.25p) shortly before their disbandment.

They wore no uniforms, but carried short tipstaves with gilt crowns as warrant of their constabulary standing. Their method of detection was essentially the rapid pursuit and arrest of suspects indicated by the earliest information of any crime, and the use of information from petty criminals. To this day the use of informants remains central to detective work.

Sir John Fielding had a further short-lived success with his proposals for the suppression of highwaymen when he was given funds to raise a horse patrol of eight (later 10) men to police the turnpikes around London in 1763. They rapidly proved their worth, but Treasury parsimony led to their dissolution after 18 months. Nevertheless, Fielding had set the example, and private patrols were set up at Bayswater, Islington and Highbury. At the same time Fielding organized occasional *ad hoc* foot patrols under the direction of a Bow Street Runner to search areas where footpads were suspected of hiding.

Fielding's successor, Sampson Wright, made the great leap forward when, following the Gordon Riots in 1780, he obtained permission to raise a part-time force of 68 men, armed with cutlasses, to patrol the streets at night. Like all

Bow Street officers up to this point, these men were not uniformed. He also revived the Horse Patrol on a permanent basis with government funding in 1783.

Uniformed policing started from Bow Street in 1805, when the chief magistrate, Richard Ford, started a new Horse Patrol, 52-men strong, with two Inspectors. They were dressed in blue greatcoats and trousers over spurred Wellington boots, and the famous red waistcoats that gave them the nickname 'Robin Redbreasts'. They were armed with pistols, handcuffs and truncheons, and they were an immediate success, clearing the outskirts of London of highwaymen and remaining in being until they were absorbed into the Metropolitan Police as the Mounted Branch in 1836.

In 1806 a Bow Street Foot Patrol was introduced to watch the streets at night. Its numbers were increased to about 100 in 1821, and the following year, Sir Robert Peel supplemented the nightly patrols with a regular daytime patrol wearing red-waistcoated uniforms like the Horse Patrol. These men, sometimes called the 'Dismounted Horse Patrol', were not referred to as Bow Street Runners. The latter were not (as is sometimes claimed) nicknamed 'Robin Redbreasts', and they continued to serve in plain clothes until their dissolution. Their reputation was extremely high, and the fees they were paid enabled some of them to amass considerable fortunes.

The Bow Street Runners' and Patrols' basic pay of a guinea a week was adopted for the constables of the New Police force in 1829. The officers attached to Bow Street to manage the Office and its court, like the other magistrates' Police Officers, remained under the jurisdiction of the magistrates, and not the Metropolitan Police Commissioners, until 1839. Some of the Foot Patrols were offered transfers to the New Police. The Horse Patrol was handed over to the Metropolitan Police in 1836. The Bow Street Runners remained the country's only permanent recognized detective force (Peel's police being explicitly preventive), until the Police Act, 1839 ordered their disbandment and the transfer of all officers still attached to Bow Street to the jurisdiction of Rowan and Mayne if they wished to continue serving and were found fit. Several Bow Street Runners joined the Metropolitan Police, most

notably Inspector Nicolas Pearce, founding senior officer of the Detective Branch.

BRADFORD, SIR EDWARD RIDLEY COLBORNE, BT., GCB, GCVO, KCSI

(1836–1911) Commissioner, 1890–1903. Son of a clergyman. Educ. Marlborough. Joined 6th Madras Cavalry, East India Company, 1853. Active service in Persia, 1856–7, and in latter part of Indian Mutiny. Col. of Horse and Political Agent, West Malwa, 1860. Mauled by a tigress (or leopard) and lost his left arm, 1863. Thereafter rode to pig-sticking, etc., with reins between his teeth. Superintendent of Operations against thugee, dacoity, and sedition, 1874. Chief Commissioner Ajmir, 1878, where established municipal government. KCSI, 1885. Secretary, Secret and Political Dept, India Office, London, 1887. Conducted Prince Albert Victor, heir presumptive to Queen Victoria, on tour of India, 1888–9. Commissioner of Metropolitan Police, 1890–1903. GCB, 1897. GCVO and Bt, 1902.

Appointed Commissioner in 1890, Bradford's urgent task was to restore a sense of stability after the Black Monday, 1886 and Bloody Sunday, 1887 riots, and the swift removal of three Commissioners in four years (Sir Edmund Henderson, Sir Charles Warren and James Monro). For this he proved perfectly chosen. His years in the Indian army and proven personal courage gave him authority in command, while his experience in crime prevention, administration and the Indian Civil Service Political Department gave him an understanding of the civil service and the need for discretion. He was in general an easy-going, amiable man; Evelyn Ruggles-Brise, Ministerial Private Secretary in the Home Office, summed him up by saying that if you couldn't get on with Bradford, you couldn't get on with anyone. Bradford ran Scotland Yard for 13 peaceful and almost incident-free years, during which the reputation of the police rose steadily. Press relations were untroubled for almost the only decade in the force's entire history and the policeman achieved his desirable status as a welcome and familiar part of the townscape. Crime figures fell to their lowest ever in 1899.

Nonetheless, Bradford had to impose himself

firmly on coming into office. He had not been at his desk many hours before complaints about pay and conditions reached him, and within a week he had to quell the Police Strike, 1890. But with that successfully settled, the Police Act, 1890 healing the running sore of uncertain discretionary pensions, and new pay scales rapidly offered by the Home Office, the force settled back into a period of general contentment.

The newly established London County Council took over certain onerous police duties, smoke abatement and the inspection of common lodging houses being high among these. It would have liked to take over the Met lock, stock and barrel, arguing that its ratepayers met most of its costs. Bradford and the Home Office successfully resisted this claim (as did their successors until the 1997 proposals for a new Greater London Authority under the newly proposed Mayor of London), with the primary argument that the capital of the nation and the empire required policing that was not merely local, and the secondary observation that the boundaries of the Metropolitan Police District and the London County Council were not the same.

Then, as Bradford became the first Commissioner to occupy the splendid New Scotland Yard on the Embankment (the Norman Shaw building), he declared that it was time for 'a period of recuperation'. He visited every station in the Met, letting the men see his face and listening politely to what they had to say. No Commissioner before had ever done this, not even the great founders Rowan and Mayne or the amiable and emollient Henderson. Financial restrictions prevented Bradford from bringing the force up to the strength he knew to be necessary, but he compensated by varying the beats to ease the pressure of patrol duty. He took advantage of the relative understaffing to improve the educational standard of recruits, since he could afford to be more selective, having fewer places to fill. He also carried out the Commissioner's duty to care for his men's welfare through the equipment and services provided: he built more stations; improved the quality of accommodation in section houses; completed the telegraph linkage of the divisions; extended the use of bicycles; encouraged police sporting activities; and even

introduced a lighter-weight uniform for summer.

Bradford cut a fine figure on parades, resplendent in cocked hat and gold braid, riding straight-backed and one-armed. His force grew equally late-Victorian and Edwardian. Music-halls were less inclined to pillory policemen as rogues and bullies. Divisional Police Balls became famous occasions when the local gentry would mix with the Chief Constables and patronize the Superintendents.

SIR EDWARD BRADFORD.

Bradford's momentum slowed in this idyllic period for the police. His force was generally unwilling to introduce telephones, one Sergeant notoriously complaining that they would allow the public to ring them up. The typewriter did not replace the clerk until Bradford had himself been replaced. But in the end, the unique acceptance of the Commissioner and his force as much-loved and admired institutions of Edwardian England can best be measured by Bradford's retirement honour. Lucky, perhaps, to be a Knight of the Royal Victorian Order and holder of an important office at the time of a corona-

tion, he was the first of the only three successive Commissioners to have their knighthoods raised to baronetcies.

BRANCHES Administrative sub-divisions of Departments.

BRITISH TRANSPORT POLICE A police service wholly independent of the conventional Home Office police services, deriving from the private forces established by railway companies when they were founded, and who were responsible, *inter alia*, for signalling before mechanical systems were devised. The BTP are responsible for preventing and detecting crime on the railway system, including the London Underground, and for investigating rail accidents. The Metropolitan Police retain the closest liaison with the BTP, especially with regard to crime on the Underground. Such famous cases of the 1840s as those of Daniel Good, or John Tawell (the first murderer arrested by use of the electric telegraph) were resolved by the cooperation of the Met with what were then known as 'the Railway Police'.

See also Sir William Horwood.

BRIXTON RIOTS, 1981 The first really serious riots of the 20th century, and the first entailing substantial burning and destruction of property since the formation of the Metropolitan Police.

At this time, Lambeth Borough Council's representatives had left the Lambeth Police Liaison Committee because senior officers had made it clear that consultation did not entitle the Committee to determine policing policy. A serious increase in street robbery caused the District Commander to institute a plainclothes operation known as Operation Swamp 81, which resulted in a significant number of black youths being stopped and searched. This intensified the resentment of a group who already frequently protested against and obstructed police actions on the street.

On Friday 10 April, PC Margottia (L 643) tried to assist a black youth who had been severely stabbed by other black youths. The young man, thinking he was being arrested, broke away with the encouragement of three other youths. Two more policemen caught up with him, gave him first aid, and summoned an ambulance by radio. Before it could arrive, a crowd of black youths hustled him out of police protection and dispatched him to St Thomas's Hospital by car. Thereafter the policemen who had tried to help the boy had bricks and bottles thrown at them, four police cars coming to their aid were attacked and damaged, and over the hour-and-a-half the disturbance lasted, six people were arrested and six police officers injured. In the meantime, false rumours spread and escalated that the police officers had refused to help the injured young man, that they had tried to prevent him from being taken for treatment, and that they had inflicted his injury themselves.

There was, therefore, great tension in the district the following day when the Operation Swamp searches were continued. The serious riot was triggered by the action of two young PCs who saw a man putting something in his socks, and searched him on suspicion of carrying drugs. Though he protested (truthfully) that he was a minicab driver who kept his money in his socks for safety, they proceeded to search his car on the suspicion that his money might have come from drug dealing, and walked round it to check the tax disc and licence plates. To the normal (in Brixton) small crowd which had gathered to harass them, this appeared to be provocative authoritarianism, and a man who was leaning on the minicab and refused to get out out of their way was arrested after a scuffle, and taken to a police van. Violence immediately broke out. The van was stoned and rocked. The officers radioed for support, and seeing a uniformed constable stagger out of the crowd clutching his stomach, radioed the misinformation that he had been stabbed. (He had been hit by a missile). They then drove away.

Several police vans, including one with dog-handlers, arrived at the scene, and a number of officers confronted an angry crowd which partially blocked the road and threw missiles at them. Senior officers were surrounded by articu-

late spokesmen with complaints. Violence escalated, and eventually centred on Railton Road, where the police only regained control after many buildings and cars had been set alight and the Fire Brigade had been attacked.

The original arrest took place at 3.30 p.m. and the rioting and looting continued until 10.00 p.m. The numbers injured were 299 police and at least 65 civilians; 61 private vehicles and 56 police vehicles were damaged or destroyed; 28

A ROOFTOP PHOTOGRAPHER DOCUMENTS THE 1981 BRIXTON RIOTS AT RAILTON ROAD.

premises were burned and another 117 damaged and looted; and 82 arrests were made. Molotov cocktails were thrown for the first time on mainland Britain. Television news reports showed the riot in progress. There had been no such event in England in living memory, and recriminations began immediately.

Even with heavy policing and a visit from Sir David McNee and Home Secretary William Whitelaw, there were minor disturbances the following day. After this things settled down, and Lord Scarman was appointed by Mr Whitelaw to hold a Public Inquiry (Scarman Report 2). As McNee objected, the report had to concentrate on the policing rather than the underlying causes of the riot. But Scarman's report made sufficiently clear that the riot was an outburst of violence against the police; that local community leaders and the police should share the blame for a breakdown in communications; and that the police needed to be better organized for riot control. It also

made clear the extent to which increasing unemployment coupled with discrimination against the black community in a variety of ways were vital contributory factors.

Important practical lessons were learnt from the experience, which were applied in later riots. The incident was, however, a significant introduction to a bitterly politicized and polarized decade which was to prove extremely difficult for the Met.

BROADWATER FARM RIOT

1985 riot on a housing estate in Tottenham during which PC Keith Blakelock was killed.

On 5 October, four police officers went to search the home of Mrs Cynthia Jarrett in Thorpe Road, Tottenham as her son Floyd was in custody at Tottenham police station for giving a false name when found in a car with an inaccurately made-out tax disc. The visit caused panic among some of the occupants, and Mrs Jarrett, who had a weak heart, collapsed and died despite their best efforts to resuscitate her.

The following day, when community leaders and the Jarrett family went to the police station to complain about improprieties in the entry to the flat, they were told that the matter was in the hands of the Police Complaints Authority and the Detective Constable who had led the search could not be immediately suspended, despite the family's claim (subsequently rejected by the inquest jury) that he had pushed Mrs Jarrett, causing her death. A small crowd started a demonstration outside the police station and broke its windows. At 3.15 p.m., two Home Beat Officers attached to Broadwater Farm Estate were attacked and seriously injured by a brick-throwing crowd, one of them having his spleen ruptured by a piece of paving stone thrown on his back when he had fallen. Following a protest meeting where responsible community leaders proposing a motion of complaint were shouted down, a police inspector driving past Broadwater Farm was attacked and had his car window smashed by two youths on a motorcycle, and a police van answering a 999 call on the estate was surrounded, attacked and severely damaged by a mob with machetes, bars and knives.

At this point, senior officers responsible for riot control preparations were based at Wood Green Police Station, the District Headquarters. By the time their first support groups with riot gear had been sent to the estate, the mob had put up barriers and prepared petrol bombs. Because of fears that a booby-trap lake of petrol had been created inside the estate, and the need to bring in reinforcements, cordons of police officers in riot gear with long shields were forced to withstand prolonged attack from rioters until the estate was restored to order some hours later. Some riot shields were damaged by gunfire directed against police lines.

At 9.30 p.m., a fire was seen in a newsagent's on the first floor 'deck' of Tangmere block, and attempts to support the firemen trying to put it out led to the murder of PC Keith Blakelock. Thereafter, as the news of Blakelock's death spread through the mob and rain started to fall, the violence slowly died out without the police having recourse to the plastic bullets of the Tactical Firearms Unit, whose use had been authorized by Sir Kenneth Newman.

It was the most traumatic of all the London riots of the 1980s for the Metropolitan Police. Matters were made worse when the future MP for the district, council leader Bernie Grant, tactlessly said the police received 'a bloody good hiding'. Despite the widespread perception that Broadwater Farm was a poor black ghetto which rose against police persecution, there were white and Asian youths among the most active rioters, and just over half the residents of Broadwater Farm were white. The incident resulted in a review of senior officers' training in public order tactics, the introduction of armoured Land Rovers, and the preferred tactic of 'early resolution' by faster-moving police units with short as well as long shields.

BULL RING DISORDERS, 1839 Chartist demonstrations in Birmingham which were not satisfactorily policed by an inexperienced Metropolitan Police contingent.

When the Chartists (who demanded working class parliamentary representation) summoned a National Convention in Birmingham in 1839, the authorities called on the only existing police force in the country to suppress any public demonstrations. Superintendent John May of A Division took 90 men to Birmingham, and ordered a mass meeting in the Bull Ring to disperse. Since no magistrate had given the order or read the Riot Act, and the Metropolitan Commissioners' jurisdiction did not extend to Birmingham, its legality was doubtful and the crowd was merely provoked. May then ordered a baton charge, and the Chartists successfully overpowered the police, who had to be rescued by a body of soldiers in the vicinity.

In renewed hostilities a few days later the police gained the upper hand, but left a rankling grievance. When May and 50 of his contingent returned to London, the remaining 40 were again worsted by the crowd and once more had to be rescued by the military. In the end, locally drafted special constables took over policing the Convention, and the Metropolitan officers returned to London with their reputation diminished.

The lesson of Coldbath Fields had been learned. There was no loss of life, and no convincing allegations of police brutality. But the Met were not drafted out of London to control political assemblies again until the 20th century.

BUSH, WP SGT ETHEL VIOLET (B.1916) One of two first Metropolitan Women Police awarded George Medal following injuries received decoying a violent sexual offender, 1955. Also received Commissioner's High Commendation and award from Bow Street Police Fund of £15. Joined Met, 1946 after wartime service in the WAAF. Sgt, 1953. Retd, 1971.

Several women had been attacked in Fairfield Path, Croydon, when Sgt Bush volunteered to join the many policewomen who acted as decoys for the assailant, early in 1955. He had seriously injured WPC Kathleen Parrott in March, and on 23 April approached Sgt Bush from behind and hit her over the head, making a wound that required 11 stitches. Nevertheless, Sgt Bush seized his coat and tried to hold him, but fell so that he escaped on this occasion. When he was finally caught, Sgt Bush and WPC Parrott were among nine women who were able to identify the 29-year-old labourer. Sir Anthony Hawke said from the bench of the two policewomen, 'I cannot imagine higher courage than you showed along that footpath', and in making the Bow Street award, Chief Magistrate Sir Lawrence Dunne observed, 'If anyone can imagine a finer story in the history of the Metropolitan Police, I shall be pleased to hear it.'

BYNG, FIELD-MARSHAL JULIAN HEDWORTH GEORGE, GCB, GCMG, MVO, 1ST VISCOUNT BYNG OF VIMY (1862–1935) Commissioner, 1928–31. Educ. Eton. 10th Royal Hussars, 1883. Served against Osman Dijna in Suakin, 1884. Raised and commanded South African Light Horse in Boer War, Winston Churchill serving as his mounted aide-de-camp, 1900. Col. of 10th Hussars, 1902. Commanded army in Egypt, 1912. Led 3rd Cavalry at Battle of Ypres. Organized successful withdrawal from Gallipoli at Suvla Bay and awarded KCMG, 1915. Commanded Canadian Corps and captured Vimy Ridge, 1916. Awarded KCB. Commanded 3rd Army at Battle of Cambrai, with first successful use of tanks, 1917. KGCB and Baron Byng of Vimy,

VISCOUNT BYNG OF VIMY. A PORTRAIT IN OILS COMMISSIONED IN 1934 AT A COST OF 30 GUINEAS, COLLECTED BY SUBSCRIPTION FROM SENIOR OFFICERS.

1919. Governor-General of Canada, 1921–6. Retired, 1926. Commissioner of Metropolitan Police, 1929–31. Retired again and given rank of Field-Marshal, 1932.

Whereas Sir Nevil Macready's Commissionership was an interlude in a very full career, Lord Byng's was a postlude when he expected to be nursing a weak heart and emphysema through peaceful retirement. But following the Macmillan Committee Report, and the Irene Savidge and Sergeant Goddard scandals, morale in and public esteem for the Met were so low that the government offered the Commissionership to eight candidates who all turned it down, before Byng took it on as a matter of public duty. He was personally encouraged in this by his friends John Buchan and Rudyard Kipling, and by the reported request of another old acquaintance, HM King George V. His job, he knew, was to restore the Force to being (in his words) 'a happy family'.

Despite his well-known good humour and simplicity of character, which had made him loved by the men he commanded (especially the Canadian 'Byng Boys'), the prediction of his appointment led to renewed protests about 'militarizing the police' from Labour politicians, notably George Lansbury and the young Emmanuel Shinwell. The people's party also objected to his aristocratic descent. When the Labour party became the government after the general election eight months later, Byng immediately offered his resignation to the new Home Secretary, A. J. Clynes, saying with typical modesty, 'I really am the most readily sackable person in the world, so please don't hesitate.' Clynes wisely refused to sack him. And when, like his successor, Byng found himself accused of making senior appointments from army colleagues, he promoted Sir George Abbiss the second Assistant Commissioner to rise from the ranks.

As a start to boosting morale in the force, Byng made visits to let the officers see him. He was already immensely popular as a war hero, and his personality rapidly won the affection of the Force, which called him 'Old Bungo', a nickname he had held since schooldays, and by which the King addressed him. He was quickly led into chatting amiably and with real interest about their families and personal lives. He proved so much more than approachable when looking at the Mounted Police that his driver had to draw him away from interminable matey chinwagging with three ex-Hussars.

To restore good relations with the press he called a meeting with Lord Riddell, chairman of the Newspaper Proprietors' Association and other proprietors' representatives where, with typical direct openness, he asked for fair play – honest reporting of genuine misconduct, of course, but not an ongoing daily search for every petty allegation that could be added to a cumulative campaign of abuse which was demoralizing the force. The proprietors accepted Byng's plea and the anti-Met crusade was halted; the police were hardly mentioned for three years. Byng's famous 'genius for making friends' started making friends for Scotland Yard.

Rather surprisingly, Byng proved a considerable reforming Commissioner in his short three-year term. He did not, like Macready or Trenchard, thrust his reforms forcefully on the service or steer them through personally. He hated paperwork, which he called 'garbage', and simply refused to be bothered with it. He loved a quiet life, especially in the Essex countryside. (Nobody, it was said, could lean on a gate and do nothing so perfectly contentedly as Lord Byng.) So he put up suggestions and delegated their execution to others. He had beats reorganized, with patrols linked by bicycles and motor cars so that excessive walking was reduced. He also instituted the practice of varying beats regularly, much to the chagrin of local criminals who had become accustomed to timing their break-ins to the predictable absence of the police patrol. He started London's chain of police boxes through which the public and the beat policemen could quickly contact a station. He strengthened the Flying Squad and had it equipped with improved radio communications as well as 'nondescripts' and Q-cars, which were at first queried as 'espionage', but were ultimately accepted as a means of combating crime when perpetrated by the gentle warrior Bungo. He popularized the use of the term 'war on crime' to describe the work of prevention and detection and set up the first Scotland Yard Information Room to act as a quasi-military communications centre.

Nor did he neglect the other aspects of policing. When the speed limit on urban traffic was (disastrously) abolished for a short time in 1930, Byng set up 'courtesy cop' traffic patrols with orders to issue polite advice and cautions in most cases, only reporting serious offences. This defused a situation in which a horrific increase in motor incidents looked likely to set the motoring public and the police at each other's throats if every infringement of every guideline in the new Highway Code was taken to court.

He was successful in defending his Force against cuts that might have followed from public expenditure economies in the great slump. In particular, he argued cogently for the retention of the Mounted Police – not from an old cavalry-man's sentimental attachment to horses, but from a practical policeman's recognition of their value in crowd control.

By the autumn of 1931 his health would no longer allow him to continue as Commissioner. He was approaching 70, and it had long been necessary for him to winter in the milder climate of South Africa or the south of France (whose cosmopolitan sophistication he loathed). Although rising crime figures were reawakening some press criticism of Scotland Yard, The Times recorded his 'complete restoration of public confidence in the police force and the force's recovery of confidence in itself.' Of all Commissioners, he was the one who was most definitely loved, and his irresistible personality revealed itself best in the well-known story of his office telephone. Despite starting to link the constables on the beat with police boxes, Byng personally hated the telephone and was displeased to see an array of them installed on his desk in Scotland Yard. 'What are those things for?' he asked his secretary, Miss Drysdale. She told him they were for him to talk to people such as the Home Secretary. He didn't want them, he grumbled, but he finally agreed to let one remain, provided it never rang but was only for him to make outgoing calls. So Miss Drysdale fielded all incoming calls and told him who wanted to speak to him. This worked for a few months, and then, predictably, the Commissioner's telephone bell was inadvertently sounded. Byng instantly summoned Miss Drysdale, and said 'Drysie! That thing's gone off! I knew it would! Do something about it!'

C DIVISION Originally the St James's Division subsequently described as West End. The Division always included Piccadilly Circus, the northern end of the Haymarket, Leicester Square, Mayfair and Soho. At different periods it has also also embraced Covent Garden and Tottenham Court Road.

Although one of the smallest Divisions territorially, this has always been one of the most important to police. Leicester Square was the favourite central London venue for duelling. The concentration of theatres and places of entertainment (including, until 1872, the notorious Panton Street night houses) attracted visitors spending money on leisure pursuits. They in turn attracted pickpockets, confidence tricksters and street prostitutes. By the 1850s, these last already patrolled an estimated 1.6km (1 mile) of streets, fanning out from the Haymarket. One hundred years later the patrol had become 11km (7 miles), with a heavy concentration around Piccadilly Circus and Soho and a spread into the Shepherd's Market area of Mayfair. 'The girls of Piccadilly' were an internationally scandalous object of tourist attention, until the Street Offences Act of 1959 swept them under the carpet. But their presence ensured that West End Central would hold the Met's most experienced officers dealing with vice, and Soho would remain a centre of strip clubs, drinking clubs, sex shops and pornography shops, all requiring constant police attention.

Additionally, Piccadilly Circus's role as 'the hub of the Empire' made it the centre of the noisy Boat Race night disturbances from the 1890s to the 1930s. Later, the presence of the American Embassy in Grosvenor Square ensured that C Division was kept busy handling demonstrations against the Vietnam War. Had C Division included Trafalgar Square and Whitehall (parts of A Division), it would have been responsible for nearly all the major political public order episodes in the Force's history prior to the 1980s. When Bow Street was added to the Division in 1965, all three of the British Monopoly board's orange set (denoting famous police stations Bow Street, Vine Street and Great Marlborough Street) were in C Division. Its major importance was recognized as the plans for Borough policing were drawn up, Commissioner Sir Paul Condon

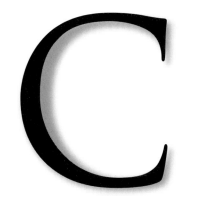

noting that Westminster (A, B and C Divisions) could be headed by a Deputy Assistant Commissioner rather than a Chief Superintendent, like the London Boroughs.

All these factors made service in the Division a memorable experience for many officers. Women Police Officers Joan Lock and Carol Bristow (see Bibliography) both mentioned service in C Division at the start of their careers as important training in dealing with disorderly conduct. Divisional Reunions for retired officers started in 1960. An excellent short history of the Division, and of the centre of London from 1829 to 1985, was compiled by former Deputy Commander W. C. F. Best QPM.

See also Clubs and Vice Branch, Street Offences Squad, Toms Squad.

CAD Computer Aided Dispatch. The present method of passing information electronically between Divisions and Scotland Yard, Divisional control rooms being sometimes referred to as CAD Rooms.

CADETS The Metropolitan Police Cadet Corps was set up in the 1960s in order to address recruitment shortages, and in particular to provide a means of attracting school leavers who would be attracted to the Police Service but who could not yet join as Police Constables because of the age limit of 19 (later 18½). The Commandant, Colonel Andrew Croft, was a much-loved man who provided inspirational leadership to a generation of young people. In the 1990s the Cadet Corps was eventually disbanded.

'CANTEEN CULTURE' Police jargon for the ethos and outlook of (especially) constables and Sergeants who socialize in station and section house canteens. Usually characterized as macho, cynical about senior ranks and the policy directives handed down from above, rather more conservative than the average citizen, tending to see moral and legal problems in simple black-and-white terms with a preference for a strongly punitive penal system, and frequently aggrieved about pay, prospects, the criminal justice system, and public perception of 'the job'. But additionally, contains an immense sense of pride and duty in being the guardians and protectors of the weak and innocent, especially those characterized as 'old dears' and 'dear old boys'.

The pressures of long and unsociable hours and the stress of being expected to take control of threatening situations at any time tend to compact some officers into very tight and loyal teams, in whose eyes, the above attitudes are sensible realism based on day-to-day experience.

CARS AND MOTOR CYCLES The first motor vehicle bought by the Met was a Vauxhall Cabriolet for the use of the Commissioner in 1903. Apart from the Flying Squad's pioneering vehicles and special requirements, the first cars widely used on general patrols were Jowett 7.04 cylinder tourers, bought between 1927 and 1931. Morris Cowleys, Armstrongs, Austins and Fords were tried in the following year, before the famous black Wolseleys, fitted with bell-shaped gongs and illuminated blue 'Police' signs in postwar years, became the most familiar police car. They were purchased in ranges from 14 to 20hp between 1932 and 1951, and Wolseleys continued to be purchased for the next 20 years, but with an increasing admixture of other British cars. Today the commonest Area patrol car is a white Rover 827i.

The policy of buying British motor cycles was also followed for as long as the industry allowed. The traffic patrols used BSA 4.93 solo and combination cycles in the early 1930s. Triumphs took over to a great extent at the end of the decade, and remained the best-known police motorcycle until the 1960s. Today it is necessary to go outside the UK and buy BMWs for police purposes.

CASS, MISS ELIZABETH (B.1864) Sempstress arrested for soliciting. In 1887, Miss Cass came to London from Stockport and found employment as a live-in forewoman at Mme Mary Anne Bowman's needlework establishment in Southampton Row.

On Jubilee night, after Miss Cass had been at Madame Bowman's for three weeks, she and Mme Bowman and Mme Bowman's niece went out in the evening to watch the display. Miss Cass became separated from her companions on the way home and traced a curious route, coming to Regent Street quadrant (Oxford Circus) and walking up to All Saints, Langham Place, where she turned round, returned to the quadrant, started east along Oxford Street and then made her way back again. Either in Oxford Street (as he said) or Regent Street (as she said), PC Bowden Endacott (Warrant No. 59281) arrested her and charged her with disorderly conduct. By his account he had watched her walking with a fair-haired girl in Regent Street, and then saw her approach three different gentlemen, the last of whom complained to him that 'It really was too much, being interfered with by these women.' (This rather formulaic 'complaint' occurs in the testimony of other constables making arrests for soliciting in other cases at the time). Endacott told her he had seen her walking the streets around the quadrant several times during the previous six weeks. Miss Cass denied it, saying at first she had not been in London, and later correcting herself to say she had only arrived in London six weeks previously, and had not before gone out at night. Later still she admitted she had once been in Regent Street on her own.

At the police station Miss Cass asked for Mme Bowman to be sent for, saying she would prove her innocence. Miss Cass was bailed on Mme Bowman's recognisances, and the following day the magistrate accepted Endacott's description of Miss Cass as a common prostitute who had been plying for trade in the area previously. She was dismissed with a warning.

Mme Bowman (who ran the risk of being seen as a procuress if the case stood unchallenged) wrote furious letters of protest to the authorities, and Sir Charles Warren held a formal inquiry to decide whether disciplinary action should be taken against Endacott. A volunteer witness, Mme Picard Pietra, claimed to have seen Miss Cass with the fair-haired girl approach a gentleman before she was arrested. Miss Cass's barrister, Mr Richard Grain, brought out that Mme Pietra had herself been thrown out of her lodgings more than once because 'men annoyed her' and her landladies suspected her of immorality. Sir Charles angrily defended Mme Pietra from the chair, while the police solicitor, Mr Wontner, was obviously shocked that such an unreliable witness had been allowed to testify. The whole case was confused by the definite existence of a Miss Violet Cass who had been dismissed from Marshall and Snelgrove in 1884 for using her position to make the acquaintance of gentlemen, and certainly seemed to have led a very immoral life. There was also the possibility that there was some other unidentified streetwalker bearing a strong resemblance to Miss Elizabeth Cass.

When the Home Office received the report of Warren's inquiry, Principal Private Secretary Godfrey Lushington thought Endacott should be charged with perjury. Mme Bowman accordingly brought a private prosecution, which was heard before Mr Justice Stephen in September. When Miss Cass was cross-examined, it became clear that police attempts to prove her immorality had uncovered nothing against her or Mme Bowman in London, though Miss Cass had enjoyed a dubious association with a married man behind his wife's back in Stockport.

The judge dismissed the case without hearing Endacott's defence. The only witness to support Miss Cass's story was a draper's assistant, and he had not watched her long enough to know whether she had or had not accompanied a fair-haired girl in Regent Street and approached any men. Even if her story were true, there was no evidence to suggest that Endacott deliberately perjured himself rather than making a mistake.

In 1906, Sir Howard Vincent informed the Royal Commission, 1908, that Miss Cass had subsequently been found to have led an immoral life and to have been pregnant at the time when Endacott arrested her.

The case was socially important, as Victorian critics of the police had long feared that they would abuse their powers by blackmailing prostitutes or harassing honest women who happened to walk through red light districts. The repercussions led ultimately to the situation which obtains today: a woman will only be charged with soliciting after she has received two cautions and had her name entered on the Prostitute Index.

CATERING DEPARTMENT Tracing its origins from a Police Order in February 1888 instructing 'Messes to be established', the foundations of the present highly professional service were laid by Col. Reg Owens (Director of Catering 1961–86), who joined the MPS after a distinguished career in the Army Catering Corps. The service employs around 900 civil staff providing nearly nine million meals a year from 130 units. The Operational Catering system can spring into action almost instantaneously. The system's first hot meal was a breakfast on the morning of Sir Winston Churchill's funeral in 1965. Snacks or main meals are provided in temporary premises to support the policing of about 500 events a year. The Notting Hill Carnival requires about 30,000 meals over the weekend; in 1997 25,000 meals had to be provided four days afterwards for the funeral of the Princess of Wales.

A POLICE CANTEEN IN THE 1940s.

The MPS Central Production Unit established by Col. Owens produced frozen meals for 25 years until the commercial market was able to cope. The Service also has a top-class banqueting capability and has frequently provided for royalty and senior politicians as well as retirement parties for junior staff. See also Teapot One.

CATHOLIC POLICE GUILD Formed in 1913 by a group of Catholic officers who frequently found themselves meeting after mass at Westminster Cathedral. Open to police officers across the UK, its best-known function is the annual Requiem Mass for all dead police officers. It is always extremely well attended, and the mass has been celebrated by Cardinal Hume.

Despite fears that the CPG represented some form of mutual aid group for career acceleration under the Catholic Commissioner Sir Edward Henry, it is not a secret society, and has never felt either competitive with or hostile to Freemasons, although obligations of faith may prevent Catholic officers from joining Freemasonry.

CENTRAL CASUALTY BUREAU A separate area within the Central Communications Complex to deal exclusively with enquiries from relatives and friends of people who may have been involved in major incidents or disasters. It was established in 1957 after the Lewisham Train Crash, and is staffed only when such incidents have occurred. It was opened during many of the PIRA bombing campaigns. Other examples of incidents when the Bureau was opened are the King's Cross Underground fire (1987), the Marchioness river disaster (1989) and more recently the Southall train crash (1997). It is capable of responding to incidents outside the Metropolitan Police District if necessary.

CENTRAL COMMUNICATIONS COMPLEX Established in 1984 at New Scotland Yard to replace the old Information Room, Map Room and Telegraph Office. It is fully computerized, electronically linked to Divisions by means of CAD, to the international Telex Network and to the Police National Computer. It is the call handling centre for all emergency calls made in the Metropolitan Police District. The appropriate

police response and deployment is made upon receipt of such calls. The Complex currently processes approximately 1.5 million emergency calls in a year, and also comprises the Message Switch Office, Central Traffic Control and Special Operations Room which deals with the control of major incidents, demonstrations and certain police operations. It will also take control of the initial stages of a major incident.

CHALLENOR, SGT HAROLD GORDON, MM, (B.1922) Policeman diagnosed as paranoid schizophrenic and made infamous for 'planting' evidence; one of the most notorious cases of malpractice ever exposed in the Metropolitan Police.

Elementary education only, his father refusing to let him take up the Watford Grammar School place he was offered. Engineer apprentice, Scammell Lorries, 1936; then orderly, Leavesden Mental Hospital, 1936–9. Driver and general labourer, De Havilland Aircraft, 1939–41. RAMC, 1941–3, serving in North Africa. No. 62 Commando, then SAS, 1943–6, serving in Sardinia; behind enemy lines in Italy, France and Germany, and on counter-terrorist duties in Palestine. MM,

CENTRAL COMMUNICATIONS COMPLEX, NEW SCOTLAND YARD.

1944, for extremely brave and difficult escape from Italian POW camp. Iron and steel worker, 1946–51. Joined Met, 1951. Beat constable V Division (Mitcham). Aid to CID in Battersea and Tooting. CID, 1956. Flying Squad, 1958. Sgt, 1962, and transferred to West End Central Station. Suspended from duty and charged with conspiracy to pervert the course of justice, 1964. Found unfit to plead and committed to Netherne Mental Hospital at Her Majesty's Pleasure. On his discharge in 1967 worked briefly as an industrial radiographer; then as a legal clerk; finally, until retirement, as an iron and steel worker. Published memoirs, 1990.

On 11 July 1963, plain clothes police teams headed by Challenor arrested several protesters outside Claridge's Hotel who were demonstrating against the supposedly pro-Fascist connections of Queen Frederika of Greece, currently on a visit to England. Two young men and six juveniles were charged with carrying pieces of brick to throw at 'Queen Fred', even though two of the juveniles were on their way home from playing tennis and had not participated in the demonstration.

Art teacher Donald Rooum was detained in cells without bail, and as a member of the National Council for Civil Liberties was able to pass his suit direct to their solicitor the following morning with the absolute guarantee that these were the clothes in which he had been arrested, and that he had not had any opportunity to tamper with them. Forensic examination found no trace of brick dust or scratches on the lining of his pockets, which disproved Challenor's evidence. Moreover, the three pieces of brick supposedly retrieved from Rooum and two of the juveniles (whom he did not know and who were arrested separately), proved to fit together into one brick. Despite Challenor's suggestion that this might mean the three had met and conspired together before the demonstration, the magistrate recognized a 'reasonable doubt', and dismissed their cases.

After questions in Parliament and an internal police enquiry carried out by Detective Superintendent John Du Rose, all eight of the defendants were officially cleared and had any fines they had paid refunded, together with substantial compensation to Rooum and three others. Challenor and three young officers under his command at the Claridge's demonstration were put on trial for conspiracy to pervert the course of justice. Before the case could be heard it was declared that Challenor was mentally ill, and when the jury heard evidence from distinguished psychiatrists that he had been (in the words of one) 'mad as a hatter' for years, he was detained at Her Majesty's Pleasure in the mental hospital where he was already being treated. The other three officers received prison sentences of three and four years.

DETECTIVE SERGEANT
HAROLD 'TANKY' CHALLENOR.

Challenor's mental illness seemed to have erupted at a suspiciously apposite time to spare the Met full public examination of his misdeeds, but the psychiatrists were unanimous that his childhood with a mentally unstable drunken father who abused him physically, followed by exceptionally traumatic wartime experiences, had indeed led him to delusions and the belief that outrageous actions were fully justified. Nevertheless, the public was concerned that colleagues had noticed nothing more than 'excessive zeal', increasing deafness, an overexcitable manner, and fatigue from overwork. Evidence was also tendered that Challenor had abused prisoners he was questioning and planted offensive weapons on them. It was also alleged that though not habitually corrupt, he had on occasions dropped charges or concealed incriminating evidence in return for smallish sums of money.

Challenor's memoirs evince a useful amnesia which means he can now remember nothing about the one case fully proven against him – Rooum's. But they also make it clear that during the war he acquired habits of violence under pressure, lying quickly to avoid trouble, and undertaking serious and dangerous tasks while very drunk (which, by choice, he often was).

Scotland Yard did not publish the results of Du Rose's enquiry, and apparently wished to perceive Challenor as a unique 'rotten apple' whose forceful personality and unfortunate mental illness had unhappily but fortuitously corrupted three junior officers. This somewhat ostrich-like response to a major scandal proved very bad for public relations, until Sir Robert Mark's forceful acknowledgement that malpractices did occur, and that he was determined to root out and discipline offenders, finally restored confidence.

CHAPLAINS In the 1870s, Commissioner Sir Edmund Henderson directed all stations to accept visits from members of the London City Mission. Subsequently the role of Chaplain to the Metropolitan Police became a full-time pastoral curé, with salary and housing provided by the Diocese of London and expenses by the Met. The Met is one of only three forces in England to employ a full-time chaplain, and a network of part-time volunteer clergy under his direction cover the Areas and Divisions. It is hoped to extend the service to non-Christian faiths.

CHARGING STATION Any police station with a custody suite for the charging of prisoners.

CHARTER The Metropolitan Police Charter was published in eight languages under the title Our Performance on 30 September 1993. It promised a quality 24-hour service to uphold the law and respond to emergency telephone calls, maintaining a reassuring visible profile on the streets and sensitive treatment of victims of crime. It committed officers to a courteous, honest and open approach to all members of the public, regardless of 'sex, colour, race, sexual orientation, religion or disability'. It guaranteed fairness to arrestees, and encouraged the policy of more staff wearing name badges.

It sets itself the high target of winning 100% satisfaction from the public, and sets the following more precise targets and expectations:

90% of 999 calls to be answered within 18 seconds

85% of urgent incidents to be attended by an officer within 12 minutes of their being reported

60% of direct line calls to officers to be answered within 30 seconds

90% of letters from the public to be answered within ten days, giving names and telephones of appropriate contacts where necessary

75% of callers at police stations to be attended to without delay

90% of victims of traffic accidents to be fully satisfied with police attention

90% of crime victims to be fully satisfied with police attention

80% of callers at police stations to be fully satisfied with police attention.

CHARTIST DEMONSTRATION, 1848

The movement demanding the 'People's Charter' (essentially universal manhood suffrage and the opportunity for working men to be represented in Parliament without fear of victimization) passed under the demagogic control of Feargus O'Connor in the 1840s. Since O'Connor had recommended 'physical force' Chartism (violent revolution), the 'respectable classes' were extremely frightened when he announced his intention of rallying a huge body of supporters to march from Kennington Common in April 1848 and present a 'monster petition' to Parliament. It was well remembered that Lord George Gordon's assembly of anti-Catholic protestors to march from St George's Fields to Parliament had led to four days' unbridled rioting in which enormous damage was done.

The government therefore made plans to prevent the march. The police were detailed to man the bridges and prevent the Chartists from crossing them. At least 150,000 special constables were enrolled, the largest number ever assembled. They were placed under the command of Earl Grey, while a military back-up was commanded by the Duke of Wellington.

The size of the force successfully intimidated O'Connor and his lieutenants, who cancelled the march and delivered the monster petition in three cabs. It was rejected by Parliament, partly on the grounds that it included large numbers of obviously spurious signatures and joke names.

The incident confirmed that pre-emptive policing was a more effective way of maintaining public order than letting a crowd get out of hand and then sending a magistrate to read the Riot Act and turn armed troops on them.

CHEQUE AND CREDIT CARD FRAUD UNIT – ORGANISED CRIME GROUP

Formerly SO1 (5) Branch, reorganized 1996. Investigates organized non-cash payment fraud where the crime affects financial institutions located in London and there is either sophistication in the system used or the principals identified are involved in organized crime and where

there is potential for substantial financial gain to any person or serious financial loss to any person or organization.

CHIEF CONSTABLE Rank lying between Superintendent and Assistant Commissioner, introduced in 1886, and given to the four District Officers or District Superintendents who had been placed in command of the Districts (1) in 1869. In keeping with Commissioner Sir Edmund Henderson's hope that the rank would be available to officers who had been promoted from constables,

THE CHARTIST DEMONSTRATION ON KENNINGTON COMMON, PHOTOGRAPHED IN 1848 BY WILLIAM KILBURN.

as well as ex-army men and other appropriate 'gentlemen' from outside, he appointed Chief Superintendent Robert Walker as one of the first District Officers. The equivalence of the title Chief Constable to that of the heads of provincial constabularies could be justified on the grounds that many Metropolitan Divisions, let alone the four Districts, were larger than many provincial constabularies, and the responsibility of commanding them was concomitantly greater.

In 1889 it was decided to appoint a Chief Constable in the CID. By this time Sir Charles Warren wished to reverse Henderson's policy, and appoint all Chief Constables from the 'offi-

cers and gentlemen' class. Somehow Adolphus Williamson circumvented this, and became the first detective Chief Constable (as he had already been the first titular Chief Inspector and Chief Superintendent). Thereafter the CID rank was held by two successive gentlemen (Melville Macnaghten and the Hon. Trevor Bigham), there being a gap of five years between them, and another gap of ten years before F. P. Wensley received his well-deserved promotion to the rank.

In the meantime, James Olive had reached the position of Chief Constable in the Uniformed Branch in 1918, the decisive move towards his appointment as the first Assistant Commissioner to rise from the ranks, and in 1923 Superintendent A. E. Bassom (see under Traffic Police) became the first Director of Traffic, with the rank of Chief Constable.

The creation of the rank of Deputy Assistant Commissioner in 1928 ultimately rendered the rank of Chief Constable superfluous, and it was abolished in 1946.

CHIEF INSPECTOR Rank introduced in the CID in 1868 as part of Commissioner Sir Edmund Henderson's structural reforms. It seems that Adolphus Williamson was accorded the title prior to his promotion to Superintendent in 1868, thus asserting his priority among Detective Branch officers. When Henderson promoted him to Superintendent and made it clear he was the actual and not merely titular head of the Branch, he also promoted three of the six Detective Branch Inspectors, Clarke, Palmer and Druscovich, to Chief Inspectors, as Williamson's chief lieutenants. Tragically, all three would stand in the dock at the Trial of the Detectives.

In 1869 the rank was effectively introduced on the Divisions as the Inspectors were graded in classes 1 to 4. In 1933 it was decided that each Division should have two Chief Inspectors: a Chief Inspector (Crime) and a Chief Inspector (Administration). Both were actually administrating officers, the Divisional Chief Inspector (Crime) being drawn from either uniformed or CID ranks, and not replacing the Divisional Detective Inspector. At the same time, Chief Inspectors were posted as Staff Officers to assist District Superintendents. In 1949, Sub-Divisional Inspectors were regraded Chief Inspectors.

CHIEF SUPERINTENDENT Rank introduced in 1949, initially for commanders of Divisions, since many Sub-Divisions were now large enough to demand an officer of Superintendent rank in command. The title was used by Adolphus Williamson as early as 1880, but like the title 'Chief Commissioner' seems to have denoted nothing more than that he was de facto the highest officer in the CID.

It had been in process of being phased out as a formal rank since 1995, but it is currently used as a recognition of seniority.

CHILD PROTECTION TEAMS Special teams of officers working on a Borough basis under the direction of Detective Inspectors. A scheme in Bexley in 1987 pioneered joint investigations with social workers in order to ensure

that police investigative skills brought better information to cases of suspected child abuse, and that police were not called in by social workers until too late. CPT officers attend case

MAJ-GEN SIR WYNDHAM CHILDS.

conferences and are specially trained to interview children who may be below the age when their evidence would normally be accepted by the criminal courts. A significant proportion of the Met's detective expertise is dedicated to Child Protection teams, whose enquiries invariably entail much liaison with Social Services Departments. Prosecution and conviction of suspects is less a criterion of their success than

establishing the truth and preserving the interests of child victims.

CHILDS, MAJ-GEN SIR (BORLASE ELWARD) WYNDHAM, KCMG, KBE (1876–1946) Assistant Commissioner C, 1921–8. B. Cornwall, son of a local solicitor to whom he was articled until the Boer War. Entered Duke of Cornwall's Light Infantry as Captain, 1900. Posted to India, Ceylon and (after cessation of hostilities) South Africa, where served under Sir Nevil Macready who frequently thereafter had him posted to his staff. Accompanied Macready to Wales in the Rhondda Valley Miners' strike, 1910, where also became acquainted with Winston Churchill and Sir John Moylan (Receiver, 1919–31). 1911–14, General Staff at the War Office. 1914–18, staff officer with BEF, and then under Macready in Adjutant-General's office, with frequent responsibility for military tribunals and mutiny cases. KCMG, 1918. Posted to Ireland at various times during the troubles, and made responsible for Sir Roger Casement's imprisonment in the Tower. KBE, and joined the Met as AC C, 1921. Retired, 1928. High Sheriff of Cambs, Hunts & Ely, 1922–46.

Childs' retirement from the army on pension in 1921 was timely for his old comrade-in-arms Sir William Horwood, who was finding Sir Basil Thomson personally unacceptable as AC C. The Home Office discreetly asked Childs if he would mind serving under Horwood, whom he had outranked in the army. Childs, a man whose opinionated bluffness seems to have contained not a shred of self-importance, had no objection whatsoever.

As Thomson's successor, Childs continued his active opposition to Communism but none of Thomson's other anti-leftist campaigns. In the Rhondda Valley, Childs had disliked the mine owners even more than Macready did, and unlike Macready, liked many of the strike leaders and sympathized with the aims and causes of the strike. He encouraged soldiers under his command to play football with the strikers, a policy which would be revived in the General Strike. He also liaised regularly with strike leaders to ensure that they were not carried away by misapprehensions about troop movements.

In the aftermath of the Police Strike, 1919, he was quicker than Macready to understand the men's valid grievances, and he welcomed the Police Federation as a necessary substitute for the Trade Union which he agreed would be inappropriate in a disciplined force of men. So while, as AC C, Childs bent all the CID and Special Branch power he could muster against the Communist Party, its front organizations and the illicit activities of Soviet diplomats, he always respected the rights and freedoms of English socialists and Trade Unionists who accepted the ballot box. Nor was he deceived by the Zinoviev letter (supposed Soviet directives to the British Communist Party, forged perhaps by members of British Intelligence with the successful intention of discrediting Ramsay MacDonald's first Labour government).

Much credit for the successful policing of the General Strike in London must go to Childs, especially in the light of his experiences in Wales in 1910. When a group of pre-Mosley Fascists offered themselves as auxiliary police, he advised them to remove their black shirts, and warned them that if they came near areas that needed policing, he would withdraw the Metropolitan officers and turn a blind eye while the strikers beat them up.

One of Childs' most laudable deeds came about when his investigations uncovered the over-zealous malpractices of a junior detective. Disallowing the excuse of noble cause corruption, Childs prosecuted the man and saw him sentenced to jail. However, throughout the period of the sentence, Childs personally paid the ex-officer's wife the equivalent of his police pay from his own pocket.

Childs left the police at almost exactly the same time as Horwood, sharing the Commissioner's generally disparaging view of the press campaign against overactive policing in Hyde Park (see Macmillan Committee, Irene Savidge) and convinced that the Police Appeals Act, giving officers the right of appeal to the Home Secretary against wrongful dismissal, meant the end to all good discipline. Though his own disposition

seems to have been sunny, and his more blinkered opinions were not remarkable for his times, his presence as a rather old-fashioned military man in the highest echelons of the force probably contributed to the demoralization which Lord Byng was brought in to reverse. See also Arcos Raid, Lee Commission.

CHOIR There have been numerous Metropolitan Police Choirs since the founding of the Police Choral Society as a branch of MPAA in 1945, with the aims of stimulating an interest in good music and harmony, providing an active interest for MPAA members too old for continuing sporting activity, and the promotion of an annual music festival. The charming scene of a station house off-duty choir practice in The Blue Lamp reflects the reality of a large number of Divisional Male Voice Choirs in postwar years, which competed for a cup presented by Supt Fred Archer, founder-chairman of the Choral Society. In addition there was a very large women's choir which gradually dwindled away until it folded in the early

1960s, and a Commissioner's Office male voice choir which frequently sang as a mixed voice ensemble with the women's choir at the Annual Concerts.

The Central (male voice) Choir was formed from the Choral Society in 1955, as the Divisional choirs were clearly flagging. It has appeared under a variety of names since then, including the 'Service Choir', 'Metropolitan Police Combined Choirs', and 'Metropolitan Police Choral Society'. Today it calls itself the 'Metropolitan Police Male Voice Choir', and is the group most often thought of as the 'police choir'. It plays a central part in the Annual Concert and has performed for charities, in music festivals, in the open air, in churches and cathedrals, and most notably at the funerals of serving officers, especially those who have died in the performance of their duties. It is capable of an extremely versatile repertoire, ranging from

THE METROPOLITAN POLICE MALE VOICE CHOIR IN 1992.

comic song and Gilbert and Sullivan to the most demanding sacred music. The choir's history is the subject of a book by ex-Chief Superintendent Leslie Stowe MBE.

CHRISTIAN POLICE ASSOCIATION

National organization promoting non-denominational fellowship among Christian police officers, with opportunities for witness both inside and outside the Service.

Founded as the International Christian Police Association in 1883 by Miss Catherine Gurney with *On & Off Duty* as its journal, the Association grew rapidly and at its peak 200,000 copies of the journal were distributed. The ICPA always made it clear that membership conferred no career advantage. Miss Gurney travelled abroad and encouraged the formation of Christian Police Associations in different parts of the Empire. Although the word 'International' was dropped from the CPA name in the 1950s to avoid confusion with the secular International Police Association, ties of fellowship with overseas Christian police groups are still maintained, these having expanded rapidly during the 1980s and 1990s with new groups being formed in many countries throughout the world.

To celebrate its centenary in 1983 a Thanksgiving Service was held in the Guildhall in the City of London and attended by several hundred delegates from the UK and around the world. In 1988, in association with the Gideons International, the CPA started placing New Testaments in all new recruits' rooms in the accommodation blocks at Peel Centre and this has continued ever since. In 1994 a publicity campaign called 'Met Mission' was launched, involving a mailshot of 46,000 letters to every member of the MPS, inviting them to publicity evenings at which the aims and objectives of the CPA were presented. This resulted in an encouraging increase in the membership.

On the approach to the year 2000 a '999' rally was planned for 9 September 1999, with representatives from the Police, Fire and Ambulance Services to be invited to share in a joint celebration of Christian witness.

CHRISTIE, JOHN REGINALD HALLI-DAY (1898–1953) Multiple murderer whose case had implications for police work, in conjunction with the case of Timothy John Evans, hanged for the murder of his daughter in 1950.

On 24 March 1953, the new tenant of a ground floor flat in Notting Hill found three concealed bodies in the kitchen. Police then found the body of Mrs Ethel Christie, wife of the former tenant, under the floorboards of the front room, and the remains of two more women buried in the garden. A widely publicized search began for Christie, who had disappeared four days previously. On 31 March, PC Thomas Ledger saw Christie on Putney Bridge and arrested him. It was embarrassing to the Met that despite a criminal record including one murderous assault on a prostitute in 1929 he had been a Wartime Reserve Constable until 1944, and had killed his first known victim at that time.

Christie's case, though sensational, was relatively straightforward. He was a sexual inadequate who rendered his victims unconscious before ravishing and strangling them. It is not known why he killed his wife.

It struck many people as suspicious that, three years earlier, 20-year-old Mrs Beryl Evans from the top-floor flat of the same house had been found strangled with her baby daughter Jeraldine in the outhouse laundry room behind Christie's flat. Her husband Timothy had been convicted of their murders after making a completely unprompted confession to having disposed of Beryl's body down the drain outside the house.

At his own trial Christie confessed to having killed Beryl, though he denied having killed Jeraldine. Subsequently he halfheartedly withdrew this confession, claiming that he had had the impression that his defence of insanity would be helped by increasing the number of his victims.

An inquiry conducted by Mr John Scott Henderson QC concluded that Christie's confession to murdering Beryl was false, and Evans had been properly hanged. But Ludovic Kennedy's account of the two cases, *10 Rillington Place*, published in 1961, argued that injustice had been perpetrated and an innocent man hanged. Kennedy's book raised several important questions about policing, including:

1. How did a man with Christie's criminal record come to be a WRC?

2. Did the police plant a stolen briefcase in Evans's room to give them an excuse for arresting him?

3. Did Detective Chief Inspector George Jennings and DI Black intimidate Evans into making

Surname *CHRISTIE.* O7732

Christian Names *John Reginald*
(Halliday)

Warrant No. W.R.

Division *X.*

Station *X. D*

Date of Joining 4–4–39 1–9–39.

Resignation *Pay to 28.11.43 Po 26.11.43*
28.12.43 Po 31.12.43

M.P.-17559/5,000 April/1939

5– 43– 3896

LEFT: J. R. H. CHRISTIE'S OFFICIAL RECORD CARD AS A METROPOLITAN POLICE WAR RESERVE CONSTABLE.

BELOW: MRS ETHEL CHRISTIE'S BODY WAS FOUND UNDER THE FLOORBOARDS OF 10 RILLINGTON PLACE. THIS SCENE OF CRIME PHOTOGRAPH SHOWS THE LOCATION OF THE BODY.

confessions at Ladbroke Grove Police Station? Did they keep him up half the night and then falsify the times of their reports?

4. Did they treat ex-policeman Christie favourably as a witness in Evans's case?

5. Did they blacken the character of a harmless, educationally subnormal man with a penchant for self-dramatizing lies by suggesting that he was habitually violent and dishonest?

The opening of the MEPO and Home Office papers on the case in 1994 supplied interesting answers to these questions, thus:

1. It is unfortunate that a man like Christie was accepted as a reserve constable on his own

unchallenged claim to have no convictions. It is, however, understandable in the circumstances of the wartime manpower crisis, which would have required checking 24,000 card-indexed records to guarantee the purity of all specials and reservists drafted in. It would not happen today, with computerized records.

2. Witness statements show clearly that Evans and Beryl dishonestly accepted the brief-case from friends of Beryl's, knowing full well that it was stolen by those same friends.

3. Nothing in the very full records supplied by Jennings to his Chief Superintendent suggests any impropriety or the cover of any impropriety whatsoever on his or DI Black's part. It appears that the press report that Evans was 'helping the police with their inquiries' into the small hours of the morning misinterpreted the fact that he was being held in custody overnight.

4. This case, among others, led police to be wary of ex-policemen questioned as suspects, given that their knowledge of police procedure may help them to frame convincing answers. There was, on the other hand, no sensible reason to believe Evans's sudden accusations against Christie, given that he had presented himself to the police, unannounced and uncalled for, to make his initial confession. The only curious fact revealed by the official documents is that the street had, for some time, been suspected of housing an illegal abortionist, and a watch had once been placed on No. 10. (This, of course, might be taken as evidence supporting Evans's claim that he believed Christie attempted to carry out an abortion on Beryl, and Kennedy's speculation that Christie used the false claim of having expertise in abortion to lure women back to his flat.)

5. Both the case papers and independent research by the authors indicate clearly that Evans was far more violent and deliberately dishonest than is suggested by Kennedy's book. It seems certain that Sir Ludovic was innocently misled by Evans's family, who had no doubt in 1950 that Tim had murdered Beryl and Jeraldine, and then, when Christie proved to have been a murderer, made the very understandable over-correction of sanctifying Tim and repressing the distressing fact that they once thought him guilty.

CID Criminal Investigation Department. Successor to the Detective Branch, and ever since its formation the normal term for plain clothes police detectives in the UK. Founded as Department of Crime under solicitor J.E. Davis, 1877, following Trial of the Detectives.

Founded by Howard Vincent on 8 April 1878 following Trial of the Detectives. Initially Vincent, as Director of Criminal Intelligence, was directly responsible to the Home Secretary, an anomaly which was corrected on the appointment of James Monro to succeed him as Assistant Commissioner (Crime), but which led to friction when Monro tried to reassert his independence of the Commissioner. Since Monro's resignation in 1888, it has never been questioned that the CID is under the authority of the Commissioner.

Vincent's study of continental police methods, and his adoption of a direct translation of the French title *Directeur des Recherches Criminelles*, aroused some initial fears that he might introduce suspect continental investigative methods such as spying, the use of *agents provocateurs*, or very long remands in custody to secure confessions. But although he and some of his successors openly envied the French their freedom from *habeas corpus* and their right to search private premises without a warrant, the steady hand of Superintendent Adolphus Williamson at the head of the detective police prevented him from overstepping acceptable bounds.

Vincent inherited a small body of detectives in Scotland Yard, with others in the Divisions under the command and control of Divisional Superintendents. His new Department proposed for the first time the formal establishment of permanent Divisional Detective sections who would liaise with the central Branch at Scotland Yard. The 60 Divisional Detective patrols and 20 Special Patrols commanded by 159 sergeants and 15 Detective Inspectors would be an improvement on the occasional plain clothes or 'winter patrols' of two working on a monthly shift system in the Divisions. Back in Scotland Yard, the old Detective Branch was remodelled with one Superintendent (Williamson) commanding three Chief Inspectors and 20 Inspectors, and an office staff of six Sergeants and constables.

The CID were granted slightly higher rates of pay than uniformed police, and could claim a number of allowances. While Vincent successfully used his personal charm to overcome grumblings from uniformed officers, he left in place a situation which could lead to unharmonious competition and an undesirable belief on the part of CID officers that they were inherently superior to the uniformed branch. It became a Met tradition that CID officers normally remained in the CID for the whole of their careers until Sir Robert Mark's interchange system and Sir Paul Condon's tenure system were implemented to introduce an element of Divisional uniform service.

In 1883 Vincent set up the Special Irish Branch which, as Special Branch, would become the first of the multifarious specialized squads and units spun off from the CID. By the end of the century, the Special Branch was pioneering protection duties.

The establishment of the Fingerprint Bureau in 1903, coupled with the emergence over the next two decades of the notable forensic advisors Sir Bernard Spilsbury and Robert Churchill, respectively refining pathological and ballistic evidence, led to Scotland Yard's CID becoming world-famous for its successes in solving headlined murder cases. Fingerprinting led to the development of the Photographic and Graphic Branch, and a hugely improved collection of Criminal Records. Detective Superintendent Frank Froest, and DCIs Walter Dew, Charles Arrow, John Kane and Frederick Fox were appointed by Home Secretary Herbert Gladstone in 1907 to be available to smaller forces lacking well-equipped CIDs when they were confronted with major cases. Thus this self-styled 'Murder Squad' formalized the practice of having a pool of senior detectives ready and waiting should outside authorities wish to 'call in Scotland Yard'.

In 1918 and 1919, two proposals first mooted by Chief Inspector F. P. Wensley were put into practice. The Flying Squad was formed, and the 'Big Four' Area Superintendents were each given command of detective work in a quarter of the MPD. Both proposals were successful in their aim of overcoming the territorial restrictions of Divisional policing, and the Flying Squad went on to pioneer motorized policing and wireless communications, two innovations with implications reaching far beyond detective operations.

From the 1920s to the 1960s, the CID enjoyed very high popular approval. The press reported favourably on their investigations, and there were no great unsolved cases such as Jack the Ripper's to encourage denigration of Scotland Yard's detective capabilities. Assistant Commissioner Sir Ronald Howe played a major part in resuscitating Interpol after WWII and started a new specialist body, the Fraud Squad, to work with the City of London Police in combating white collar crime.

Howe's successor, Sir Richard Jackson, had the support of Commissioner Sir Joseph Simpson in establishing half a dozen more CID specialist units, the most important of which became the Criminal Intelligence Branch. For a number of years the Murder Squad beloved of the press really existed formally at Scotland Yard, but CID squads also started specializing in motor vehicle crimes, Art and Antiques thefts and forgeries, Obscene Publications and Drug trafficking.

In the last two lay hints of problems to come. The 1960 *Lady Chatterley's Lover* trial showed that there was no longer a public consensus as to what was or was not obscene, and the worldly-wise detective officer who claimed to be shocked by material that could deprave and corrupt others (but not himself), would not be granted universal approval; and the irresponsible use of 'recreational' drugs by celebrities suddenly created a new situation wherein a substantial part of the younger generation were habitually breaking the law.

Nor was the CID done any favours when the courts handed down swingeing sentences on the Great Train Robbers, widely perceived as having minimized their use of violence, and therefore to be less culpable than rapists and sadistic criminals who drew shorter terms of imprisonment. The vicious intimidation accompanying the crime was generally overlooked, and the fact that many of those involved had in the past used savage violence when it suited their ends was largely unknown. The devoted officers who

gave immense energy to trying to recapture the dangerous and habitual criminals who escaped could be portrayed as vindictive thief-takers rather than servants of the public trying to check a threat to peace and safety. In an era when the Kray twins socialized with fashionable celebrities and criminals were too often seen as glamorous, the CID was in no position to rebut cynical reactions when the Obscene Publications Squad Corruption cases broke over their heads. A number of experienced crime-fighters resigned in disgust when the measures taken to combat corruption seemed like a withdrawal of support for their ruthless ways of pursuing dangerous professional criminals. (Indeed, the regulations subsequently introduced by PACE would make it impossible today to hold the Krays and their associates in custody for long enough to ease the fears of the witnesses they had previously intimidated.)

Yet even the severest estimate, that made by Sir Robert Mark, showed that five out of six CID officers were absolutely reliable. Mark himself felt that the major successes scored by the CID against terrorists and organized crime proved that morale had been actively improved by weeding out rotten apples by the shelf-full. The prosecutions of corrupt officers revealed that some of their colleagues were men of quite outstanding courage and integrity who resisted all pressures from above to collaborate in malpractices, and some of those caught up in corruption had ironically been extremely effective in catching criminals.

The supergrass operations brought a massive increase in prosecutions for armed robberies, although the cynical habits of mind engendered in the 1960s and 1970s have rarely allowed the CID to win credit for this as they did in the 1940s when the Ghost Squad achieved similar results.

In 1985, many of the former CID squads and branches became Specialist Operations. Some, for example Fingerprinting and Photography, had passed to Civil Staff some time earlier. However, with the immensely powerful addition of computerized crime information to the detectives' armoury the work of the CID remains as effective as it has ever been, even though understaffing remains so severe a problem that all officers are still handling case-loads at least half as

large again as they should be for optimum success in detection – a fact which tends to be disregarded when, months after the event, lawyers discover investigation errors.

In the 1970s the press recalled a major commercial lesson of the 1920s: corrupt police officers sell newspapers, if not as widely as sensational murderers. One general consequence has been for the CID to maintain a lower profile. Uniformed officers, as often as not, issue the appeals for witnesses to come forward or make the regular appearances on television programmes such as *Crimewatch*, while books of memoirs which made an officer such as Fabian of the Yard a household name and his CID a revered body are quietly discouraged. Though the press may prefer to highlight investigations that show 1% of officers meriting investigation, the other 99% of the CID carry on with the good work of detecting the perpetrators of crime without fear or favour.

CITY OF LONDON POLICE Independent police force at the heart of the Metropolitan Police District whose square mile of territory does not come under Metropolitan Police jurisdiction. Today, with 825 officers, it is the smallest in the country. Prior to the provincial force amalgamations of the 1960s, it was the seventh largest.

As the City Fathers already had efficient uniformed patrols of constables on their streets in 1829, they did not feel the need to be included in Peel's New Police. It was only when the New Police had proved their value and the government threatened to bring the City under their jurisdiction at the time of the Police Act, 1839, that the Corporation of London hastily reorganized its constables into a force modelled closely on the Met, with similar ranks, uniforms and stations.

Today the City Police remain independent and responsible to the City of London Police Authority. Uniformed constables and Sergeants are readily distinguishable from the Met by their coxcomb helmets with the coat of arms of the City of London as a badge. When flat or riding caps are worn, City officers are recognizable by their red and white chequered bands, just as their armlets when used are red and white rather than black and white. It was long a matter for good-natured teasing that the City adopted its height requirement from the Guards and only accepted officers of 5ft 10in and above, while the Met accepted men from 5ft 8in when a height qualification existed.

Relations between the forces are cooperative and marked by friendly competitive rivalry. Metropolitan Commissioner Sir Joseph Simpson's last letter, written from his deathbed thanking the City Commissioner Sir Arthur Young for his force's support at the Grosvenor Square Demonstration, catches the tone well:

> Dear Arthur,
> Please excuse crumpled paper but I'm in bed with a chest. Thank the City so much for coming trespassing with such welcome [sic – presumably 'effect' omitted] on Sunday.
> Ever yrs
> Joe

Some facilities, such as the riding school at Imber Court, are now used jointly by the two forces. The Fraud Squad was originally an entirely cooperative venture, drawing on the expertise of City officers whose territory included the financial heartlands of the Stock Exchange and Bank of England. The Control Room system of the Central Communications Complex is also a shared computer facility, so that both forces can be alerted to emergencies in central London, just as both forces routinely cooperate in policing large-scale demonstrations in London.

CIVIL STAFF Approximately 13,500 Metropolitan Police Service employees, graded and paid like civil servants as administrative and executive officers and specialist staff, in addition to industrial and support grades (messengers, cooks, cleaners, etc.) and approximately 1000 traffic wardens. They are the heirs of just four Commissioners' Office clerks headed by Charles Yardley and two clerks appointed to work for John Wray, the Receiver when the Force was founded. Prior to 1968 the Receiver's staff were responsible to him and not the Commissioner. Since then, the Commissioner has been the executive and administrative head of the entire Civil Staff as well as the attested Metropolitan Police Service.

Like their predecessors, today's Civil Staff are responsible for the orderly administrative and clerical running of the service. Large numbers of Civil Staff in the Finance and Personnel Departments therefore carry out duties similar to those of accountants and administrators in any other vast institution. Since the 1950s, however, certain responsibilities that formerly fell to CID officers are now undertaken by Civil Staff. They staff, for example, the Fingerprint Bureau and Photographic and Graphic Branch and supply all Identification Officers. Although the change was resisted by such stalwart detective specialists as Superintendent Fred Cherrill of Fingerprints, it has proved entirely satisfactory. The perception that an attested officer's powers of arrest were not necessary to individuals who collected and compared fingerprints, or photographed scenes of crime, or noted and collected evidence there, proved entirely correct. Cherrill would be proud of the way his old department has maintained the high standard he set, and although their contribution is made at specific points of investigations, Civil Staff in these sections and the Forensic Science Laboratory may justifiably be described as detectives establishing the significance of clues in the detection of criminals.

Just as Yardley and Wray were crucial to the success of the early police, so today's Civil Staff are an essential part of the Metropolitan Police Service. One of the most important tasks of the Plus Programme was to ensure that they were regarded as a vital part of London's police, both by themselves and by their police colleagues.

CLARK, PC GEORGE (1826–1846) Warrant No. 22098. Murdered on duty, with suspicion attached to brother officers.

In 1846 PC Clark (313K) was posted from Stepney to Dagenham village, which had only recently been added to the extended K Division. The arrival of police was not welcomed by local smugglers, and it was suspected that some Dagenham officers were accepting bribes to cast a blind eye to smuggling. Clark was sent to the station as an incorruptible young officer.

On 30 June, six weeks after Clark came to Dagenham, Sergeant William Parsons, patrolling the beats on horseback, reported that

POLICE NOTICE SEEKING INFORMATION ABOUT THE MURDER OF PC GEORGE CLARK, 1846.

the PC had not shown up for his appointed meeting at 3.00 a.m. Three days later Clark's body was found in a field a quarter mile away from his beat. He had been battered, stabbed in the throat and scalped.

At the inquest Parsons repeated that he had seen Clark at the appointed place at 1.00 a.m. and missed him at 3.00 a.m. However, later evidence indicated that Parsons himself had missed his duty that night, and amid a cloud of suspicion he and two other officers were charged with perjury and three more were dismissed from the Force. Parsons eventually succeeded in escaping from detention and was never seen again.

Twelve years later, a farmer's wife claimed that three men, including her late husband and brother-in-law, had carried out the murder when Clark caught them trying to steal corn. The only survivor of the trio was George Blewitt, and despite his strenuous denials, Detective Sergeant Jonathan Whicher, sent from Scotland Yard to handle the case, arrested and charged him. Blewitt was acquitted because no corroboration of the woman's statement could be found, and because she described a throat-cutting murder very different from the way in which Clark had died. The murder of PC Clark remains an unsolved mystery.

CLERK SERGEANT (OR SERGEANT CLERK) A grade above Section Sergeant in the early years of the Force. The Clerk Sergeant was responsible for book work at the station house and would also have such internal duties as dealing with correspondence and administration. The necessary educational skills for this work made rapid promotion to Clerk Sergeant an early sign of a potential high-flyer's career in the days before promotion depended on examinations.

CLERKENWELL BOMBING Terrorist act during the Fenian campaign in 1867, permitted by one of the worst instances of inefficiency in the whole history of the Met.

In September 1867, two men were arrested as vagrants in Manchester and proved to be Fenian subversives. They were remanded in custody by the magistrates, but the Black Maria conducting them to prison was attacked by about 30 Fenians commanded by 'Captain' Kelly and 'Captain' Richard O'Sullivan Burke, who sawed open the roof, shot the police sergeant guarding the men, and set them free.

In London, Detective Inspector James Jacob Thomson recognized Burke and an aide called Casey walking through Bloomsbury and arrested them, a feat which inspired Henry Whiting to start his philanthropic donations to the police. Burke and Casey were held in Clerkenwell Prison, and on 11 December the Dublin Police wrote to Scotland Yard that an attempt to rescue them was imminent. Commissioner Richard Mayne disregarded it. The following day, a policeman on duty watched without interest as a group of men dragged a barrel to the prison wall in Corporation Row, lit a fuse, and then dragged the barrel away again when the fuse smouldered and went out.

On 13 December the men repeated the attempt, with better luck. Their barrel of

CLERKENWELL PRISON AFTER THE EXPLOSION IN 1867.

gunpowder caused a tremendous explosion which destroyed 55m (60yd) of the wall and several houses opposite. It killed six people immediately and injured another 126, of whom six more died in hospital. It would have killed Burke and Casey had not the prison governor taken Dublin's warning seriously and kept the men out of the exercise yard beside the wall.

Scotland Yard's astonishing excuse for its inactivity was that they were informed the Irish intended to blow the wall *up* and not *down*, which led them to believe they should be looking for a sapping operation underground. The Home Office gave Mayne the well-earned rebuke that he had made a damned fool of himself, but in recognition of his past services declined to accept his resignation.

CLUBS AND VICE BRANCH
(CO 14) Originally the Clubs Office of C Division. From about 1930, uniformed officers from Vine Street on plain clothes patrols to identify brothels and, if possible, charge the holders of the rent books. They did not arrest street prostitutes, as for some years following the Sergeant Goddard case this duty was confined to officers in uniform.

After the opening of West End Central Station, the Office consisted of 24 uniformed constables and five Sergeants, two Inspectors, a Detective Constable and a Detective Sergeant, all under the command of a Chief Superintendent with a Superintendent as his Deputy. The Office had the duty of supervising and controlling all places where gaming and prostitution occurred, and commercial sex outlets such as pornographic bookshops, sex shops, peep shows, strip clubs, nude encounters, saunas and massage parlours, as well as certain licensed premises. In 1995 a reorganization led to the Clubs and Vice Unit being placed in the portfolio of No. 1 Area Assistant Commissioner.

Prior to that, references to 'the Vice Squad' may mean the Clubs Office, may describe tempo-rary *ad hoc* duties of C Division officers (for example the 'Tom patrols' or Sergeant Goddard's responsibility for clubs' supervision), or may refer inaccurately to the Obscene Publications Squad.

COLDBATH FIELDS RIOT
Public meeting of dissident working-class democrats in 1833, prohibited by the government, with the consequence that heavy police intervention caused a short but violent disturbance in which PC Robert Culley was killed. Notable for inquest and sessions juries' controversial expressions of dissatisfaction with the police.

HOME OFFICE NOTICE BANNING THE COLDBATH FIELDS PUBLIC MEETING IN 1833.

Following the Reform Act of 1832, an organization calling itself the National Union of the Working Classes was formed in London, comprising 1000–2000 men. Noting that it was avowedly republican, and fearing that it intended violent revolution, the Whig government had police spies infiltrate it (see Sergeant Popay) and reacted strongly when the NUWC called a public meeting on Coldbath Fields, a patch of waste land in Clerkenwell, roughly where Mount Pleasant Sorting Office now stands. Placards advertising the meeting at 2.00 p.m. on 13 May declared that this was 'The only means of Obtaining and Securing the Rights of the People'. Home Secretary Lord Melbourne decided that the placards expressed an intention of illegal action and ordered Police Commissioners Rowan and Mayne to stop the meeting. The Commissioners noted that preventing it from taking place at all would prevent honest citizens from going about their lawful business, so Melbourne and Permanent Under-Secretary Samuel Phillipps indicated that an illegal action would start when speakers addressed the meeting or flags were exhibited.

Rowan took personal command of the arrangements. He directed each Division to make up to 100 uniformed men and two in plain clothes available and arranged to have a section of the Life Guards standing by at their barracks. Their commander, Col. de Roos, accompanied him to Coldbath Fields.

By 1.30 p.m. on 13 May, 300–500 people had gathered in the area. Rowan had placed a military officer in a builder's yard to report the approach of NUWC committee members who were meeting in the Union Tavern (on the site of the pub of the same name in King's Cross Road today) and their anticipated support group of banners. He directed Superintendent John May that when the meeting commenced he was to lead the A Division men down Calthorpe Street to arrest the leaders and confiscate the banners. C Division and then F Division should follow as reserves if the meeting did not immediately disperse, and D Division should support A Division by approaching from Gough Street. The men were to march in the roadway, allowing clear access along the pavements for the crowd to disperse peacefully, and the route across Coldbath Fields to Bagnigge Wells Road should also be left clear.

At 2.45 p.m. a wagon left the Union Tavern bringing six speakers to start the meeting and halted at the junction with Gough Street. A popular agitator named Mee climbed the railings and started his address, whereupon Union men with banners marched in to support him. Mee's evident intention was to be law-abiding, for he asked the men to take away the banners, and when they refused, ordered that at least they take the heads off their pikes. Then Mee saw the men from A Division advancing down Calthorpe Street and made off across Coldbath Fields to Bagnigge Wells Road. There followed a furious scuffle of 5–10 minutes' duration before the crowd broke up, whereafter a body of police moved on to the waste ground to prevent any groups from reassembling. When C Division joined the fray, George Fursey made a murderous assault on Sgt Brooks, the only incident in the riot to come to trial. The whole occasion would probably have been dismissed as unimportant and possibly a triumph for police peacekeeping had not PC Robert Culley been killed in the affray.

At his inquest there was copious evidence from spectators that the police had not adhered to Rowan's directive that there was to be no violence and no use of staves except in self-defence. A number of uncommitted bystanders and some women had been attacked with truncheons as they tried to leave the vicinity, and the police sweeping out over Coldbath Fields had given the impression that there was no escape route for peaceable dispersal. Col. de Roos, importantly, remarked that although the crowd was 'disreputable' and in his opinion capable of turning ugly, they were peaceful and good-humoured until the police opened hostilities.

Culley's inquest and Fursey's trial for assault and attempted murder were marked by contradictory testimony. Police and demonstrators hugely exaggerated the numbers of people opposing them. (In fact there were probably about 300 men involved on each side.) No policeman saw any colleague use any unnecessary violence. No demonstrator saw any of his fellows do anything but defend themselves against unprovoked assault. One policeman and one demonstrator each shouted 'You bloody bugger!' at an opponent. But the inquest jury's obviously illegal verdict of 'justifiable homicide', and the acquittal of Fursey despite the clearest evidence (which he did not contradict) that he had made a potentially lethal assault on Sgt Brooks sent a clear message to the authorities that large sections of the respectable public were not willing to have the right of orderly public meeting curtailed by police action, and in consequence a Parliamentary Select Committee was appointed to enquire into the affair.

Its report exonerated the Commissioners and noted that the police had not inflicted any injuries on any members of the public comparable to those they had themselves sustained. It concluded that the initial police force was commensurate with the violent response they encountered when trying to remove the flags and arrest the speakers, but it criticized them for pursuing stragglers unduly and so passing beyond the control of their superintendents. Melbourne and Phillipps, whose over-reaction to the proposed meeting, subtle language when instructing the Commissioners and testifying to the Select Committee and cunning refusal to put any orders in writing were largely responsible for the contretemps, got off scot-free.

COLE, PC GEORGE (C.1856–1882) Murdered policeman whose death contributed to the campaign for constables on lonely beats to be armed. Joined the Metropolitan Police, 17 January 1881 (83N Warrant No. 65227).

On 1 December 1882, PC Cole intercepted young Thomas Henry Orrock attempting to break into the Dalston chapel where the Orrock family worshipped. PC Cole arrested him, but on the way to the station Orrock fired a pistol and escaped. PC Cole pursued him whereupon Orrock fired again. Cole fell but then resumed the chase through a dark and foggy night. A later shot killed PC Cole. The case is remembered for the dogged determination with which Frederick Cobb (Warrant No. 62248, later promoted to Sergeant), pursued the clues of Orrock's hat, dropped in the road at the murder scene; his almost illegible name scratched on his abandoned chisel by a knife-grinder; and the practice bullets he fired into a tree on Tottenham Marshes. His efforts brought the murderer to justice and the gallows two years later.

But Cole's death had more importance for the Met in that, coupled with the murder of PC Atkins and the attempted murder of PC Patrick Boans in 1883, it led to constables on the outer Divisions being permitted to carry pistols on beat duty at night. See under Firearms.

COLE, INSPECTOR JAMES ARTHUR, KPM & BAR (FL.1940) The only Metropolitan officer, and one of only six UK officers, to earn a bar on his King's Police Medal for Gallantry. Joined the Metropolitan Police 3 October 1927 (D50, Warrant No. 116839).

On 26 May 1929, at 1.00 a.m., Constable Cole was summoned to a burning house at 50 Molyneux St, Marylebone. Smoke was billowing from the windows, and people could be heard shouting for help inside. PC Cole immediately went into the building and made his way to the top floor, where screams could be heard. It was impossible to see through the smoke, but by feeling around the room he located a man, two women and a child. He took the child in his arms, directed the adults to clasp tightly to his belt, and guided them down the stairs to the safety of the street. Then, with a colleague, he immediately re-entered the building to make a thorough search of the top floor, but by this time he was exhausted, and collapsed. His colleague helped him out.

By 1943, Officer Cole was a Sub-Divisional Inspector stationed in south London. On 12 August, police were called to a house in Barry Road, East Dulwich, where a mentally disturbed man armed with a shotgun refused to be removed to hospital during the afternoon. At 5.40 p.m., Inspector James Price arrived, and tried to engage the man in conversation while another officer went up a ladder to enter the house. The plan failed. The man saw what was going on, and fired at both officers. Shortly after this his sister arrived, and was allowed to go into the house to reason with him. This failed, too, and the sister was held hostage.

The local Home Guard then proffered a tin of tear gas capsules, which had to be heated and placed on a tray in the hall. This failed when the man fired at the tray, scattering the pellets and nullifying their effect.

At 8.30 p.m. Inspector Cole arrived, and the police tried to rush the man. This too was unsuccessful, as he fired his shotgun wildly at them. When the army arrived with tear gas, they created a diversion. Under this cover, Inspector Cole and Special Inspector Leslie Howard Terry climbed through a window into the locked room where the man's sister was held, and released her.

Further tear gas proved ineffective, as it collected downstairs, affecting the police more than the man upstairs. While the besiegers waited, the man fired shots at anything heard moving down-

stairs. Finally a tear gas bomb was lobbed through the window into his room, where it landed on the bed. As it went off, Inspectors Cole and Terry rushed the room from the stairs. They heard a shot as they attacked the door, and inside they found their man had shot himself.

Inspector Cole received a bar to his KPM. The other two officers received KPMs for Gallantry, and all three received awards from the Bow Street Police Fund.

COLLATOR Officer (usually uniformed constable) responsible for maintaining and cross-referencing Criminal Intelligence from station books, files, records and local information reports in Divisional Police stations, together with maps and mugshots. Now given the official title Local Intelligence Officer. See also Spykanedy.

'COLONEL ROWAN'S CAGE' Press nickname for mobile detention van used by the

Detective Branch in the 1840s to hold pickpockets arrested at race meetings.

COLQUHOUN, PATRICK (1745–1820)

Magistrate and co-founder of the River Police.

Educ. Dumbarton. Orphaned and emigrated to America, 1760. Returned to Glasgow as a merchant, 1765. Studied the cotton trade and promoted British cottons in Brabant and Flanders. Lord Provost of Glasgow, 1782–3. Founded Chamber of Commerce. Became JP. In 1792 became stipendiary magistrate under the Middlesex Justices Act, sitting first at Worship Street, Finsbury; thereafter at Queen's Square, Westminster. In 1795 published *A Treatise on the Police of the Metropolis*, which explained various crimes and misdemeanours and suggested remedies. In 1800 he published another treatise on the commerce and police of the River Thames, a subject of which he was acutely aware as a resident of Wapping. This work was praised and cited by *The Times*, the government, and even the King. The University of Glasgow made Colquhoun LL.D. in 1797. He met John Harriott in 1798, and forwarded Harriott's plan and costings for a River Police through the West India Company to the government. When the West India Company agreed to pay for 80% of the scheme, the government approved it and on 11 June 1798, Home Secretary the Duke of Portland wrote to ask Colquhoun to become Superintending Magistrate of the Marine Police until further notice, while a substitute replaced him at Queen's Square.

In July that year, Colquhoun and Harriott began police operations. The Marine Police Office in Wapping High Street housed the magistrates' court, administrative offices for a force of about 200 constables and quay guards, and temporary lock-up rooms for prisoners. On the first day of the force's existence, Harriott led some constables to arrest coal-heavers with a boatload of stolen coal, and Colquhoun tried them. It was characteristic that he cautioned them without imposing a sentence. Both men believed that crime was best prevented by making criminals' detection and arrest a near certainty.

Within five days *The Times* was commenting favourably on the fitness of Colquhoun to super-

A COLLATOR, NOW KNOWN AS A LOCAL INTELLIGENCE OFFICER, PICTURED AROUND 1975.

intend a force which held out so much promise for commercial prosperity. Within a few months, the quay guards, constables and surveyors of the Marine Police had swept the traditional bands of mudlarks and thieves away from the wharves and the foreshore.

Losses by theft in the first year of the Marine Police's existence were one-fiftieth of those in previous years. No felonies occurred on ships which employed Colquhoun and Harriott's constables, but 2200 misdemeanours were discovered by the police and punished by the magistrates. Colquhoun was personally congratulated by Lord Penrhyn, the chairman, on behalf of the board of the West India Company. They presented him with a piece of plate worth £500 and the Russia Company added another worth 100 guineas. The Royal Navy thanked him personally for sending Marine Police sailing cutters to put an end to thefts from their stores, and at this Harriott wrote peevishly that he had been as much responsible for the action. Colquhoun's greater diplomacy and grace led him to harvest most of the praise for the successful foundation of the force; indeed, until Geoffrey Budworth's account of the River Police in 1987, most historians of the police (with the honourable exception of the Dictionary of National Biography and the right and proper exception of the Thames Museum curators) underestimated Harriott's larger and longer-lasting role.

In 1798 Colquhoun prepared a Bill which Jeremy Bentham presented to parliament. This would have made the force a permanent body for the next seven years, had not the combined jealous forces of City of London aldermen and the Customs Service succeeded in suppressing it. In his speech introducing the Bill, Bentham pointed to one of Colquhoun's great claims to fame: his refusal to take any payment for his work on the Marine Police. 'His services have been gratuitous . . . he has fed the establishment out of his own pocket.'

In 1800 Henry Dundas succeeded in carrying the Bill through parliament, and shortly thereafter Colquhoun returned to the bench at Queen's Square, leaving the Marine Police under

PATRICK COLQUHOUN, MAGISTRATE AND CO-FOUNDER OF THE RIVER POLICE.

the direction of Harriott for the next 16 years. He continued to sit as a magistrate until 1816, when he retired. Four years later he died, having given away most of his money to charities. A memorial was placed in St Margaret's, Westminster, commemorating his many acts of kindness and generosity.

COMETS (MPSSA) The Metropolitan Police Civilian Officers' Sports and Social Association (formerly the Comets Club).

Founded in 1931, Comets publishes a quarterly journal, *Metwork;* holds an annual dinner to bid farewell to the outgoing council, and presents a Trophy to the individual who has done most for the administration or organization. It organizes social and sporting events and group activities under the following sections: Amateur Radio, Angling, Badminton, Dragon Boat Racing, Dramatics, Football (men's, women's and 5-a-side), Golf, Great War Society, Road Running, Shooting, Squash, Steel Band, Table Tennis, Weight Training, Wine Appreciation, ARO Social Club, Cobalt Square Social Club, DMS Social Club, Eighth Floor Social Club, Forensic Science Social Club, Jubilee House Social Club, PIB Social Club and Regency Street Social Club.

COMMANDER Metropolitan Police rank lying between Chief Superintendent and Deputy Assistant Commissioner. The lowest rank of Chief Officer, conferring membership of the Association of Chief Police Officers. Held to be the equivalent of Assistant Chief Constable in a provincial force. Introduced in 1946 when the metropolitan rank of Chief Constable was seen to be superfluous or too weightily titled since the prewar promotion of the four Chief Constables heading the Districts (1) to Deputy Assistant Commissioners. The rank of Commander met the need for a grade marking out officers commanding especially prestigious and sensitive Branches such as the Flying Squad or Special Branch, or holding similar responsibilities which seemed to outweigh those of the newly formed Chief Superintendent rank for officers in charge of large Divisions.

When restructuring was under discussion in 1993 (see Sheehy Report), it seemed possible that the rank might disappear as the tier between Assistant Commissioners and Superintendents seemed overloaded. In the event it was the Chief Superintendents and Deputy Assistant Commissioners who were to be phased out as formal ranks, as Assistant Commissioners took direct command of the Areas.

The Commanders' Association was formed at the time of the Newman Reforms as a body to represent the interests of officers holding the rank. The rank of Deputy Commander has also been used for a short period.

COMMERCIAL CRIMES INTELLIGENCE BUREAU Unit within the Support Group of the Fraud Squad (SO6), established 1968 but renamed Departmental Intelligence Unit in 1998. Because SO6 is the largest fraud squad in the country it voluntarily keeps the National Fraud Index. The DIU is also the focus of intelligence liaison with many financial regulators and government agencies.

COMMISSIONER The Commissioner of Police of the Metropolis is the force's administrative, executive and operational head. The posts of Commissioner, Deputy Commissioner and Assistant Commissioner all lie in the gift of the Crown (i.e. the appointments are made by the Sovereign on the recommendation of the Home Secretary, to whom the Commissioner is responsible).

The exact legal nature of the Commissioner's operational responsibility was never spelled out until Lord Denning's judgment in *R. v. Commissioner of Police for the Metropolis* ex parte *Blackburn 1968*. Lord Denning's decision was that Metropolitan Commissioners and provincial Chief Constables were only answerable to the law itself for the way in which they chose to enforce the law. The Commissioner is not subject to orders from the Home Secretary, though the Home Secretary may require a report from him or demand his replacement in the interests of good policing.

Originally Peel's Police Bill proposed three joint Commissioners. All were to be executive magistrates, with the authority to swear in constables and direct them in their duties, but with no powers to try offenders. Peel's hope was that he would find men akin to Irish magistrates who were accustomed both to yeomanry command and administering the law. In the event he settled for two Commissioners: a soldier, Charles Rowan, and a lawyer, Richard Mayne. Both were sworn in as executive magistrates, a practice which was followed with all their successors until the Administration of Justice Act in 1973. When Rowan died and Mayne found it impossible to collaborate comfortably with his successor William Hay, the decision was taken to have one Commissioner only in future.

The early Commissioners' relations with the Home Office tended to be stormy when dyed-in-the-wool bureaucrats or radical Home Secre-

taries were in place, and after the retirement of the first Receiver, John Wray, there were long-running power struggles with the Receiver's Office. These problems were finally resolved when Sir Joseph Simpson became Commissioner, and established good relations with the Home Office. At the same time it was seen that the equality and autonomy of the Receiver's Office was an anachronistic anomaly. The Receiver was made a part of the Commissioner's establishment with an assumed status similar to that of the Deputy Commissioner, and the Commissioner became absolute head of the entire operational and administrative establishment of the Metropolitan Police, attested and civilian.

Prior to 1958, Commissioners were invariably appointed from outside police ranks, or in three cases, by the promotion of Assistant Commissioners brought in at AC or Chief Constable rank from long service as Indian Civil Service

Police Officers. Of the first 16, eight were soldiers, three were ICS Police Officers, two were Air Marshals, one was a lawyer, one was a Home Civil Servant, and one was an ex-soldier employed for 18 years in the Australian and Home Office Prisons Departments. Some Commissioners tended to recommend colleagues from their own former spheres of life for senior appointments or as their successors. James Monro, for example, twice submitted his resignation when opposed in recommending former 'old India hands' for senior posts. Sir Nevil Macready enlisted and was succeeded by his former army staff officer Sir William Horwood. Lord Trenchard brought in Air Vice Marshal Sir Philip Game to succeed himself.

Since 1958, all seven Commissioners have been full-time career police officers with the experience of having commanded another British police force. Until 1972, the Commissioner was expected to be able to ride a horse, and to do so on parade occasions. Sir Robert Mark did away with the formal requirement, though he and all subsequent Commissioners except Sir David McNee have taken to horseback on occasion. On the retirement of Sir Paul Condon the post was advertised for the first time.

The title Commissioner is exclusively used by the Metropolitan and City of London Police Forces, and the title of Scotland Yard's chief is simply 'Commissioner of Police of the Metropolis', not 'Chief Commissioner', although Jonathan Whicher addressed reports to the 'Chief Commis-

COMMISSIONERS COMMEMORATING THE BICENTENARY OF THE BIRTH OF SIR ROBERT PEEL ON 4 FEBRUARY 1988 AT NEW SCOTLAND YARD. FROM LEFT TO RIGHT: SIR DAVID MCNEE, SIR ROBERT MARK, SIR PETER (LATER LORD) IMBERT, SIR KENNETH NEWMAN, BUST OF SIR ROBERT PEEL.

sioner' in 1860, possibly answering an earlier need to distinguish between Mayne and Hay. The Departmental Committee, 1878 used the term, as did Sir William Harcourt (Home Secretary, 1880–5), and James Monro in some of his correspondence, probably to distinguish the Commissioner from the Assistant Commissioners. All other forces are headed by Chief Constables, a title once used in the Met for the rank between Superintendent and Assistant Commissioner.

COMMISSIONER'S ANNUAL REPORTS
Published since 1869. Important accounts of the size, actions, cost, expenditure and state of the Force. The most famous is Lord Trenchard's report of 1932, in which he laid out his philosophy of policing and detailed ideas for improving the Metropolitan Police. Different Commissioners have decided for themselves how far to follow his example, how far to voice complaints about underfunding or express pride in the Service's achievements, and how far to present a straightforward balance sheet of expansion or contraction; rising or falling crime figures; approved and completed innovations.

From 1869 to 1920, the reports were quarto booklets, possibly illustrated by graphs, the prose

only broken up by subject headings and tables. From 1921 until 1984 the size was reduced to octavo. Thereafter Sir Kenneth Newman introduced more eye-catching reports, laid out like company prospectuses with photographs and varied type and page layouts. Today the reports are glossy colour brochures, with detailed reports from the different portfolios.

COMMISSIONER'S FUND
Monies for the support of the Police Orphanage, Seaside Home, and similar institutional charities.

Originally collected by requests for donations from wealthy firms and individuals at the behest of Lord Trenchard when he decided that the activities of ticket Sergeants were undesirable and put a stop to the police Minstrels' concerts and other entertainments which had raised money for the charities from the 1890s to the 1930s.

COMMISSIONER'S OFFICE
The headquarters of the Metropolitan Police Service. Today, New Scotland Yard, 10 Broadway, London SW1H 0BG. 1890–1967, New Scotland Yard, (the Richard Norman Shaw Building) on Victoria Embankment. 1829–90, Whitehall Place.

Uniformed constables and Sergeants stationed at headquarters wear identifying numbers beginning CO where Divisional officers carry their Divisional letters. See also Back Hall.

COMMUNITY AND RACE RELATIONS BRANCH
A Branch has existed since 1968 to coordinate and develop policy in relation to community relations. A7 Branch was a very influential part of Headquarters for a significant period; nowadays the role is fulfilled by CO20-24. The Met has been in a unique position by being the only London-wide agency for many years, and the London-wide contacts with important opinion-formers and other agencies have often taken place at Headquarters level. See Racial and Violent Crime Task Force.

COMMUNITY CONSULTATIVE GROUPS
More properly Police and Community Consultative Groups. Important semi-formal committees

of councillors, local volunteers and police liaison officers at which the different perspectives of the Met and (especially) ethnic minority communities can be compared, with the hope of each side coming to greater understanding of the other. They form an important part of the consultative process between local Divisions and the public about policing issues and priorities. They were set up after the Scarman Report and formalized by Section 106 of PACE.

COMMUNITY LIAISON OFFICER A vital cog in Community Policing, Community Liaison Officers do exactly what their title suggests. They make formal contacts with community leaders, consultative committees, Neighbourhood Watch organizers, schools and other interested members of the public at Divisional or Borough level.

The genesis of the system was a 1936 order that all Divisions should appoint a Sergeant to visit schools and give lectures on road safety. This proved so successful, with several of the Sergeants coming to know local children as they grew up, that Chief Inspectors were appointed on Districts (2) to have responsibility for the Juvenile Bureaux, which responsibilities naturally extended to liaison with Social Services, other agencies and community groups.

The Newman Restructuring abolished the Waldron Districts and gave Divisional Chief Superintendents a much wider remit to consult with local communities, a measure which, together with sector policing, brought about far more contact with local communities, often through Neighbourhood Watch groups, than CLOs could have achieved on their own. Nevertheless, CLOs, usually of Superintendent or Chief Inspector rank, remained the main point of inter-agency cooperation, especially with Social Services, regardless of changes at the top of the old Districts or Divisions.

With the demise of the Waldron Districts, CLOs were attached to Areas. Increasingly, however, they are appointed as Borough Liaison Officers, utilizing a natural point of contact through local authorities which leads to their being essentially associated with Divisions.

Local authorities invariably value the services of CLOs highly – sometimes more highly than that of local Divisional senior officers. This is partly because they provide a single easy and constantly accessible means of contact with the Police Service, and partly because they have more time and continuity to develop contacts with the community groups.

COMMUNITY POLICING Techniques of policing aimed at integrating the Service more fully into the local communities it serves at Divisional level. The phrase was coined in America when the Detroit riots of 1967 and other major disturbances had shown that a serious confrontational situation existed between the police and deprived (especially ethnic minority) communities. Rapidly adopted and developed by the Metropolitan and other British police forces, where falling manpower had led to substantial use of panda cars at the expense of beat patrols, and the attempt to rectify this by Unit beat policing had already led some officers to de facto specialization in community contact.

Basically, Community Policing embraces three main strands. Home Beat Officers or permanent beat officers are personally integrated into the communities they patrol and can represent local feelings and give information to rapid response and relief officers or to senior officers. Outreach programmes (schools visits, instructional lectures, visits to old people's clubs and youth activity schemes), put the police perspective to interested or at-risk groups and accustom them to police officers as a familiar and unthreatening presence. Cooperative programmes (such as Neighbourhood Watch, or police and Community Consultative Groups) provide a two-way communication process which tends to clarify the public's view of problems and priorities and promotes crime prevention. This leads to a better understanding of the police resources available, and at the same time the public perspective feeds back into the police planning process. When the police are seen to respond to locally identified problems, the flow of information tends to increase and leads to greater community involvement in solving problems.

Community Policing is by and large proactive, whereas rapid response is by definition reactive to criminal or emergency situations. Social activities like police-sponsored youth clubs or youth football teams represent a very slow and indirect way of trying to ensure that young people ingest responsible social standards from an early age. The inevitable failure with some hard cases may be seen as being well balanced by the lasting successes. Community policing is often seen as the viable alternative to 'hard' or enforcement-orientated policing, though all police recognize that intransigent minorities of evildoers exist who are themselves determined to achieve their ends by force, and who can only be controlled by force majeure. It is worth stressing that Community Policing is not a mere exercise in image-enhancement for cosmetic purposes. Community Police officers are actively engaged in crime prevention and the gathering of information, especially from the 'respectable' class of citizens whose local knowledge can help in the control of petty crime (e.g. vandalism, pilfering, or the small-scale distribution of cannabis on the streets) where a more traditional habitual criminal 'snout' can be of little assistance. People often feel the need to know an individual police officer well before imparting even straightforward information about wrong-doing.

It is unfortunate but undeniable that Community Policing lacks the compulsive newsworthy interest of major crime and disaster stories, so that press reporting inevitably overlooks the constant and dedicated work of Home Beat and Community Liaison Officers, and the public may be left with the impression that the police are usually racing to crime scenes or swinging batons at rioters. A crime or a disaster prevented is not news. Failures in prevention are. Community Policing which aims to be an open and friendly face the police show the world is hardly ever remembered when most people think of the police, yet it is now seen as being of vital importance.

COMPLAINTS The Police Act, 1964 laid an obligation on all Chief Officers to record complaints. Nevertheless, easily accessible statistical records of the number of complaints made against Metropolitan Police officers do not appear to have been published until the formation of A10 Branch (Complaints Investigation Bureau) in 1972. (See under Sir Robert Mark). Since then a summary of the categories of complaints made against Met officers has been contained in each year's Commissioner's Annual Report.

Complaints were certainly received and dealt with from the earliest years, however. Commissioners Rowan and Mayne dealt personally with all the complaints that came to them, and encouraged the public to make their grievances known. Letter books preserve their and their successors' responses and delegated responses to many hundreds of complaints each year.

The Royal Commission, 1908 invited complaints about specific instances of misconduct by police on the streets, especially wrongful or violent arrests. Of 300 letters they received, only 90 were specific complaints as opposed to generalized criticism, and only 19 fell within the terms of reference they had stipulated. Nine of those complaints were upheld. Since the police had made a total of 74,590 arrests on the streets in 1905 alone, the proportion of reprehensible conduct was obviously insignificant, though nearly 50% of the precisely focused complaints which the Commission was empowered to examine scrupulously and independently proved justified.

In 1973, 5869 complaints were received; in 1998–9, 4570. Approximately 3% were upheld and followed by disciplinary action.

COMPLAINTS INVESTIGATION BUREAU
The internal disciplinary body within the MPS is CIB 1, which arranges hearings at Disciplinary Boards. If a hearing finds against an officer CIB 1 organizes the appeal proceedings which are then heard by the Commissioner, or an Assistant Commissioner. CIB 2 investigates the most serious and high-profile complaints against police officers, while Area Complaints Units investigate the vast majority of the remainder. Investigating officers are drawn from both uniformed and CID ranks, so that there is sufficient expertise within the Branch. CIB 3 maintains an ongoing watch on the service to uncover and weed out corruption. In this it continues the excellent tradition pioneered by Chief Superintendent Ray Anning who was in charge of

Discipline Office, (in those days A3(1) Branch), when Robert Mark was Deputy Commissioner. Ch. Supt Anning then became Commander of A10 Branch (Complaints Investigation Bureau).

Despite widespread public perception that investigation of the police by the police is an unsatisfactory answer to the traditional question *Quis custodes ipsos custodet?* (Who will police the police themselves?), those Commissioners who have acted most strongly against corruption (Sir Robert Mark and Sir Paul Condon) have entirely agreed that only police investigators can avoid the danger of being bamboozled by corrupt officers who know the ropes and might manipulate the system. Nor, since Mark's day, has anyone been able to point to any failure in zeal and integrity on the part of the CIB. The CIB is as disappointed as anybody else that strict Home Office guidelines and stringent legal protections against wrongful conviction mean that disciplinary action is not taken more frequently and with quicker outcomes, but police officers have become used to recognizing that a criminal justice system must not convict on a basis of suspicion, and neither should a disciplinary system which can take away an officer's rank or livelihood. The possibility of officers under investigation being discharged by virtue of medical disability is also a source of frustration, especially since the very length of investigations can severely affect the health of an officer subject to such proceedings. The independent Police Complaints Authority ultimately has the power to insist on a disciplinary tribunal, and this can constrain procedures which might otherwise be applied more promptly by senior officers in complaint cases, as was foreseen by Sir Robert Mark at the time of his resignation.

In the meantime, the possibility of a Disciplinary Board represents a very real Sword of Damocles hanging over the heads of officers tempted to abuse their position. All police memoirs indicate that it is something officers dread and nobody takes lightly.

COMPUTER CRIME UNIT Small but increasingly important section of the Fraud Squad (SO6).

Formed in 1984, the first (and only) such unit

in Britain, and one of the first in the world, the Unit has developed and run training courses on a national basis to help officers deal with computer-based evidence, and in 1994 joined an industry initiative to improve computer crime prevention. The Unit has developed expertise in dealing with 'hacking' and maliciously programmed viruses. Cases include the alleged unauthorized access of the Duke of Edinburgh's Prestel account; the 'mad hacker' Nicholas Whitely; the Eight Legged Groove Machine (8LGM); Dr Popp's Aids Diskette; the virus writer 'Black Baron' and the unauthorized access of US military systems by 'Datastream Cowboy.'

Difficulties in the law have been experienced. The first major case (*R. v. Gold and Schifreen 1988*) was overturned by the House of Lords on the basis that simple hacking did not constitute fraud or forgery. The Computer Misuse Act 1990 was subsequently passed, but the first important prosecution under that law failed to result in a conviction, despite the fact that hacker Peter Bedworth's activities had done £200,000 worth of damage to Central London Polytechnic's computer and crashed vitally important data on European cancer research being used by consultant surgeons all over the EU. Bedworth's plea that he was 'hopelessly addicted' to hacking persuaded a jury to acquit him of all charges.

Another notably successful detection by the Unit resulted in no conviction on the grounds that the suspect was mentally unfit to stand trial. They tracked down a consultant to the World Health Organisation who had attempted to blackmail banks and medical institutions all over the world by posting them a diskette purporting to contain information on AIDS, but which actually put a message on VDU screens once they played the diskette, warning that their hard disk systems would now be crashed if they did not send money to an address in South America to receive the necessary reprogramming data.

CONCERT See Annual Concert.

CONDON, SIR PAUL LESLIE, QPM (B.1947) Commissioner, 1993-
Joined Metropolitan Police, 1967. Selected for accelerated promotion. As Bramshill College

Scholar, educ. St Peter's College, Oxford (MA 1975). Inspector, 1975–8. Chief Inspector, 1978–81. Superintendent, Bethnal Green, 1981–2. Chief Superintendent and Staff Officer, 1982–4. Asst. Chief Constable, Kent County Constabulary, 1984–7. Metropolitan DAC, 1987–8. Assistant Commissioner, 1988–9. Chief Constable, Kent County Constabulary, 1989–93, responsible for setting up arrangements for policing the Channel Tunnel. Metropolitan Commissioner, 1993, at 46 the youngest since founding co-Commissioner Richard Mayne.

Sir Paul Condon's smooth rise through the ranks of the police from the time he was marked for accelerated promotion gave him a solid overview of the varied managerial responsibilities of senior officers. By the time he returned to Kent as Chief Constable, it was clear to informed observers that he was likely to become Metropolitan Commissioner in due course. It was also predictable that, knowing the ropes well from the inside, he would be concerned to keep the ship on a satisfactory course rather than change direction with radical innovations, and the best features of his two predecessors' terms of office were immediately reflected in his style of leadership. Sir Kenneth Newman's managerial priorities were retained and formally endorsed with Value for Money initiatives, while Sir Peter Imbert's approachability was happily reflected in his successor's quiet confidence at the press conferences and public appearances demanded by ever more thrusting news media. Visits to police stations and to individual officers increased, linked with a preference for informality.

The Home Secretary's annual objectives for the police were noted. The Metropolitan Police Service set its own parallel annual objectives, coupled with the standing requirements of the Police Charter, and measured their achievement through the Quality Performance Portfolio. Following the successful start-up and expansion of Operation Bumblebee, Sir Paul initiated Operation Eagle Eye. Where the postwar Met had been characterized by a constant plea for more officers and more resources to combat an accelerating crime wave, Sir Paul's sixth Commissioner's Report was able to boast that crime figures had fallen to their

SIR PAUL CONDON, PICTURED IN HIS STUDY WITH A PORTRAIT OF SIR ROBERT PEEL IN THE BACKGROUND.

lowest for the decade at the same time as the Met had successfully made more reductions in manpower than any other force.

In keeping with other public services, the Met looked for private sponsorship of certain programmes (like the Summer Action projects for young people, launched in 1994). The contracting out of certain Civil Staff services was undertaken.

The complexity of organizing the range of activities undertaken by police had grown to the extent that the Newman Restructuring had itself to be revised within 10 years. The Super Eight Areas were replaced by five. Smaller divisions were amalgamated and constantly scrutinized to see that they were at the optimum economic size. Specialist Operations remained much as they were, but Territorial Operations were divided into portfolios and allocated to five Assistant Commissioners, who each took responsibility for one-fifth of Area Policing as well. The organizational reshuffle was carried out without stridency and,

like many of Sir Paul's leadership initiatives, seemed to emerge democratically from the deliberations of Policy Board. Following the Blair government's creation of a new Greater London Authority with the advent of Borough policing, the five Areas were later reduced to three in 1999.

But early in his term of office, Sir Paul took one very private decision, shared with very few others, which was to colour the last years of his Commissionership. It has been suggested that, as a young constable, he had been disgusted by the malpractices he observed on the part of CID officers prior to Sir Robert Mark's reforms. Certainly, as Commissioner, he issued an early warning that noble cause corruption was not acceptable, and in 1994 he set up a covert operation to penetrate those parts of the Service which had particular opportunities for corrupt association with major criminals. In 1997 Sir Paul revealed to the press and to a Parliamentary Committee that he was increasing the size of the Complaints Investigation Bureau with a new branch, CIB3, to weed out corrupt officers. He believed there might be as many as 250 corrupt officers in the Met. Since this represented less than 1% of the total, he was obviously justified in saying he believed the overwhelming majority of his officers were honest. (Previous senior police officers asking business acquaintances just how many of their employees they thought they could trust, found that most large institutions thought that about 4% could be bent.) But 'rotten apples' in the police are invariably newsworthy, and Sir Paul's demands that he be allowed to remedy the situation stimulated a mixed response from the police professional associations, the press, and former officers who resented the likelihood of loss of reputation for some parts of the Service, while evidence could not yet be published.

Sir Paul noted that the huge profits of illicit drug dealing meant that huge bribes could now be offered to police. Whereas he, as a young officer, had once been offered (and refused) £5000 to duck out of making an arrest, attempted bribes of £80,000 or more were now possible. He also observed that Sir Robert Mark had resigned with the express fear that the disciplinary powers of the Commissioner and his Deputy were being eroded. This erosion was now so thorough that it had taken Sir Paul nearly four years to secure the dismissal of an officer who tried to blackmail a prostitute for money and sexual favours. Since the man was suspended on full pay while the laborious disciplinary procedures were followed, the taxpayer had shelled out £100,000 to keep a disgraced officer doing nothing at home. Sir Paul wanted 'the simple right of any supermarket manager' to fire an employee rapidly if he was caught fiddling. He wanted the 'double jeopardy' protection dropped which meant he could not bring disciplinary proceedings against an officer who had been found 'Not guilty' in court, for, as Sir Paul noted, unprofessional conduct deserving disciplinary action need not be criminal. He wanted to be allowed to make disciplinary decisions on the

civil law's test of the balance of probabilities, and not be compelled to find that infractions had occurred 'beyond a reasonable doubt', and he wanted accused officers to be refused the 'right to remain silent' while their cases were investigated, something which became especially important when the right had been altered under the criminal law.

The Home Office agreed that his demands were reasonable, as did most of the press. But the opportunity to print sensational stories harking back to the 1970s, and claiming that the Met was still notably corrupt, proved irresistible. Some commentators compared Sir Paul unfavourably with Sir Robert Mark, unaware that Sir Robert had written privately to him offering sympathy and support. Some Police Federation spokesmen felt duty bound to stand up for the privileges they had won for their members under disciplinary investigation.

Unhappily, this public rumpus was in full swing when the Macpherson Inquiry conducted its hearings. As this brought out that the heads of the Met might have too easily accepted assurances that the Lawrence family's complaints were misplaced, Sir Paul authorized the unprecedented issue of an apology through Assistant Commissioner Ian Johnston. He appointed the very experienced and senior officer DAC John Grieve, who had scored notable successes as head of the Anti-Terrorist Branch, to oversee the Met's investigations into racially motivated crimes. In his own evidence to the inquiry he repeated the apology to the Lawrence family; admitted that there was some racism in the Met, and indicated the important recruitment, training and supervision procedures that were being instituted to combat the disease.

Sir Paul's ambition to see the Met smoothly into the 21st century made him the longest serving Commissioner since Sir Joseph Simpson. His willingness to acknowledge malpractices and mistakes in the Service brought the Met some of the most screaming headlines since Sir Robert Mark's day. The Police Federation, necessarily defending its members as a body, could often be relied upon for newsworthy counter-statements. But like Mark's, Sir Paul's policy of openness made for better long-term public relations than

the alternative of grudging defensiveness. His commitment to resolving long-term problems affecting the organization made his period of office one of improved efficiency at a time of budget restrictions. The real merit of the Met came to be demonstrated through crime statistics and the more objective criteria favoured by the Inspectorate and the Audit Commission.

CONSTABLE The basic rank in the police force. Constables have wide powers of arrest and search to enable them to uphold the law, and were formerly officers appointed by magistrates *ad hoc*, or householders undertaking a rotating duty of serving for a year as the parish peacekeeping officer.

When Sir Robert Peel, Charles Rowan and Richard Mayne established the Metropolitan Police, they combined and enhanced the several ideas of the constable, and the Instruction Book 1829 stated that 'the first duty of a constable is always to prevent the commission of a crime.'

Although Commissioner Lord Trenchard and Secretary Howgrave-Graham rather despised lifelong constables as unambitious artisans who needed to be led by better (academically) educated men, the plain rank of Police Constable is regarded by many officers as 'the sharp end of policing', and the most important part of the Service. Had not thousands deliberately chosen to remain at this rank throughout their careers, the force might have collapsed many times when recruitment proved difficult.

The use of constables for administrative tasks has largely disappeared following a policy of employing Civil Staff wherever the powers and duties of a constable are not required.

CONVALESCENT HOME Popularly known as 'the Seaside Home', the Metropolitan and City Police Convalescent Home was established in Hove in 1890. Funded by contributions from all officers in police forces in Southern England, it has a counterpart for the North in Harrogate.

For several years the need had been recognized for a rest home for officers sick and injured on duty. The Police Convalescent Fund permitted resources to be used for sending officers to cheap hotels on the south coast, and in 1888 a house in Dover was retained exclusively for the use of convalescent police officers. Finally in 1890 the fund acquired and converted its own building for the purpose. The current home at Flint House, Goring-on-Thames, has comprehensive facilities for rehabilitation and counselling, in keeping with the demands of the modern Police Service.

COOKE, PC GEORGE SAMUEL

(1868–1893) The only serving Metropolitan Police officer ever to be hanged.

Joined the Met in 1888. Warrant No. 73717. Divisional No. B237. Lived in Bow Street Section House until, about 1891, met 21-year-old prostitute Maud Merton (or Smith, or Crowcher or, most probably as identified by her supposed mother and sister at the inquest, Maud Mary Locksley) in the Strand. They were a good-looking couple, attracted to each other, and set up house together, Maud adding the name Cooke to her various aliases. At least once they left lodgings after building up arrears of rent and quarrelling with the landlady. Throughout this period Maud continued to walk the streets. Cooke was not believed to be living on her immoral earnings, and claimed to have been trying to reform her. It may have been her refusal to abandon prostitution that led to their falling out, and in March 1893 Cooke declared his intention of leaving her. Maud retaliated by going to Bow Street Station and accusing him of putting her on the streets, living off her immoral earnings, and stealing money from her. Although her story was not believed, Cooke was disciplined for the indiscreet relationship by being transferred to X Division (Acton) and losing all leave for a month. He tried, nonetheless, to keep up distant friendly relations with Maud, visiting her a couple of times after she began cohabiting with a soldier named Adams.

In X Division, Cooke lodged with a married colleague, PC Robinson, in Silchester Road, Notting Hill. Through Robinson he met a lady's-maid to whom he soon formed an attachment, and the two considered themselves engaged, expecting to marry in October. News of this engagement reached Maud at about the same time as Adams found her in bed with a punter

and kicked her out. She turned up in Acton looking for Cooke, determined to break up his engagement or cause him trouble. On the night of Tuesday 6 June 1893, he was on duty at Wormwood Scrubs, patrolling the common around the prison. His beat partner, PC Kemp, was unfortunately recalled to the station to complete a report at exactly the time Maud caught up with him, between 9.30 and 10.00 p.m. She screamed at him, declared her intention of having him thrown out of the police, and fought back when he slapped her. Cooke, infuriated, felled her with his truncheon, then broke her skull with it as she lay on the ground, and stamped on her neck. Her body was found by a shepherd in the morning.

Cooke could give no convincing explanation for not having seen it himself when patrolling his beat. There were bloodstains on his uniform trousers and left boot. And, rather mysteriously, his landlady saw him bury a truncheon which he had illicitly obtained from an officer in A Division (and which, he claimed, was not the one he used in the assault), together with a whistle which appeared to have blood on it. Cooke quickly confessed, and although the coroner's jury felt he had been so strongly provoked that they contemplated finding no charge against him, and the trial jury, several of whom wished to bring in a verdict of manslaughter, made a very strong recommendation to mercy, the trial judge Sir Henry 'Hanging' Hawkins left no one in doubt that he would be making his own preference for severity known to the Home Secretary. Despite his fiancée's successful attempt to get the signatures of many brother officers and several common councillors and MPs on a petition for a reprieve, Cooke was formally dismissed from the police and hanged on 25 July.

CORONERS' OFFICERS The antiquity of
the coroners' role (believed to date from 1194) gives their inquests precedence over all other courts in commanding the attendance of police officers.

Coroners' officers have now been civilianized but remain employees of the Metropolitan Police in the MPD. They assist the coroner in his work of determining the identities of unknown dead

people, and the causes of deaths in which there is any reason preventing a doctor from signing a death certificate on his own authority.

CORRUPTION The most serious form of malpractice ever proven against Scotland Yard. The three important cases were the Trial of the Detectives (1877), Sergeant Goddard (1928) and the Obscene Publications Squad Corruption Cases (1977).

Although the cases were 50 years apart, and the men involved represented a minute minority of serving officers, Scotland Yard has never treated them lightly nor doubted that the occasional 'rotten apple' will taint many more if not checked. Since Sir Robert Mark's term of office as Commissioner it has been accepted that a permanent internal body (now the Complaints Investigation Bureau) is necessary to keep a constant watch for malpractices, and this is strengthened whenever serious cases are found to have escaped notice. The last occasion was in 1998, when Sir Paul Condon not only increased its strength by 30% – an additional 45 officers – but used a press conference to tell the public he was doing so. Such a public exhibition of dirty-linen-laundering would have been unthinkable in the years which allowed the three notorious cases to build up, and such publicity is in itself an important preventive measure against corruption.

In all three of the infamous cases, one or more officers were accepting bribes from criminals they were expected to be investigating with a view to prosecution. Because corruption inevitably implies an unsupervised or improper relation with a criminal, the use of informants is an associated topic, since seeking information is one of the few alternative explanations for close association with criminals. The term corruption is sometimes used to denote other forms of malpractice, not directly linked to avoiding enforcement of the law in return for payments. In some cases where the use of informants has led to officers being investigated, it has been clear that any impropriety in the association has not been motivated primarily for personal gain (cf. 'Whispering Squad' case, where allegations of an improper association with informants proved too insubstantial to be brought to court).

Nevertheless, since the 1970s, Scotland Yard has taken the question so seriously that the handling of informants is rigidly supervised. Since the publicized cases are inevitably those where officers are known or alleged to have evaded supervision, the public is unaware of the extent of this supervision, or the care most officers now take to ensure that their conduct is not only as near as possible impeccable, but can be proven to be so.

The majority of serious corruption cases occur when legislation prohibits some unacceptable recreational activity as a vice, and substantial profits are to be made by illicitly purveying it. Prior to the 1960s, this usually involved drinking or gambling at forbidden hours and places, and commercial sex other than the individual self-prostitution of women working on their own.

Since the Dangerous Drugs Act 1965, the massive profits attainable from addicts by traffickers have attracted elements of international organized crime to the UK and, by the 1990s, encouraged a continuous undertow of press innuendo about alleged corruption.

COST OF THE METROPOLITAN POLICE

Gross annual expenditure for single years, selected by approximate quarter-centuries.

1829-1830	£194,126
1848	£437,441
1873	£1,118,785
1898	£1,812,735
1923	£7,838,251
1948	£15,601,263
1973	£95,000,000 (estimated)
1998–9	£2,033,000,000

(The Commissioner's Annual Report for 1973 did not include the gross expenditure figure, so the mean between the nearest reported totals has been given. It must be stressed that the huge jump does not represent any sudden profligacy. The vast expansion of services under Sir Joseph Simpson in the 1960s formed a belated financial 'catching-up' exercise of the kind Sir Harold Scott had vainly demanded, and which was clearly justified by the crime figures. Annual expenditure had reached the £90 million figure by the end of the 1960s.)

'COURTESY COPS' Short-lived system of traffic patrols introduced by Commissioner Lord Byng in 1930, following the Road Traffic Act of that year. This introduced pedestrian crossings and the Highway Code, and abolished the 20mph speed limit. The combination was immediately disastrous. Motorists could not see the crossings at a distance, and, travelling at irresponsible speeds, hugely multiplied road accidents. Many people were bemused by the array of guidelines and signals laid down in the Highway Code and felt it was impossible to memorize them. Relations between police and (especially) motorists became fraught.

Byng directed the Assistant Commissioner B to set up patrols on motorcycles whose sole function was to look out for and correct bad driving and foolish pedestrianism. They were not to bring charges for infringements of minor regulations, but to explain and advise politely, possibly issuing cautions.

Traffic patrols remained a part of the police armoury against urban chaos. Courtesy copping, alas, could not survive for long when confronted with the persistent selfishness, rudeness and deliberate disregard for sensible legal restrictions which are always evinced by a number of motorists. The chaos created by the Road Traffic Act was rectified by Transport Minister Leslie Hore Belisha in 1934, when he restored the speed limit (setting it at 30mph rather than 20) and identified pedestrian crossings by the amber beacons which quickly took his name.

COURTS DIVISION Constables were employed by magistrates' courts from the Middlesex Justices Act, 1792, and with their duties transferred to the Met under the Police Act, 1839, the courts themselves became known as Police Courts. Gradually over the 20th century the courts became independent of police officers for their administration. In the 1970s, court duty was recognized as a specialization comprising the guarding and escort of prisoners, the enforcement of warrants issued by the courts, and many other duties helping the interfaces between police, public and courts.

The enforcement of fines has now been progressively civilianized, with civilian enforcement officers carrying out many thousands of arrests each year when defaulters (about 300,000 a year) are delinquent in paying after having been granted 'time to pay' by the magistrates.

The Court Escort Service was introduced in London in 1994 and contracted out to Securicor. The move relieved the Metropolitan Police of a time-consuming function, but was reflected in adjusted budgets and reduced manpower. It also meant the end of the Prisoner Transport Service, which had been in existence since Victorian times, and had proved a model of efficiency with the use of cellular vans. See Black Maria.

CRIME FIGURES Crimes reported in the Metropolitan Police District in single years, selected by approximate quarter-centuries across the Service's history.

1829/1830	20,000 approximately
1848	15,000 approximately
1873	20,000 approximately
1898	18,838
1923	15,383
1948	126,597
1973	355,248
1998–9	934,254

While the 'post-war crime' wave is visible as a dreadful tenfold, rising to fortyfold increase in reported crime, it should be borne in mind that the frightening lawless state of the streets and public highways prior to 1829 (for which no statistics exist) has never returned. Prior to the formation of the Bow Street patrols, it was a certainty that any person of means travelling alone and unarmed through the streets at night *would* be robbed; that any young woman travelling on a lonely part of the King's highway was *likely* to be raped; that vehicles as secure as the King's or the Prime Minister's *would* sooner or later be stopped by highwaymen in the outer suburban districts and their royal or noble occupants relieved of money and valuables.

Moreover, in modern times the police encourage the reporting of crimes, so that at the very least a reasonable picture of crime patterns may be obtained. Insurance claims often make reports to the police obligatory, and certainly in motor vehicle crime cases, reports to the police are the only means of recovering stolen cars.

A COURT ROOM SCENE AT BOW STREET, 1808.

In 1997–8 the total number of recorded crimes fell below 800,000 for the first time since 1989. Domestic burglaries averaged 25.6 per 1000 households (2.6%), and violent crimes averaged 11.2 per 1000 population (1.1%).

CRIME PREVENTION OFFICERS Introduced as specialist officers on Divisions in the 1960s, giving free advice on improving security to households and businesses. Under Sir Kenneth Newman their role was expanded to refine ideas for reducing criminal opportunities by the design of new buildings and developments; they also encouraged community crime prevention schemes like Neighbourhood Watch. Today crime prevention also considers street lighting, public house management, the design of housing estates, and other ways of reducing fear and making crime more difficult.

CRIMESTOPPERS National police initiative, started in 1988 with strong Met input, to encourage the public to report information about crimes to the police, using a publicized freephone number and knowing that anonymity is guaranteed.

Since the scheme started, the number of offences cleared up thanks to Crimestoppers has increased annually. In 1998, 12 arrests for murder, 42 for robbery, 66 for burglary, and 358 for drugs offences were made in the Metropolitan Police District as a result of people telephoning information to 0800 555 111. In addition, £695,085 worth of drugs were removed from London's streets, and stolen property worth more than £2.5 millions was recovered.

CRIME SUPPORT BRANCH SO2 OR ACSO'S SUPPORT BRANCH A Unit which provides Assistant Commissioner Specialist Operations, and his business groups, with the appropriate level of support information and advice in respect of administrative, financial, operational, secretarial, technical, transport, communications, personnel, training and Quality Assurance matters, in order to facilitate the proper discharge of their policing functions.

CRIMINAL INTELLIGENCE SO11 Originally Branch C11.

Started by Assistant Commissioner Sir Richard Jackson and Commissioner Sir Joseph Simpson in 1960 to collect, evaluate and disseminate information about prominent criminals and organized crime. Today the Directorate of Intelligence supplies information, analysis, research and support services to all branches of the Met and acts as a centre of expertise in relation to informants and intelligence. See also DC John Fordham.

CRIMINAL JUSTICE PROTECTION UNIT – ORGANISED CRIME GROUP A Unit within Organised Crime Group. Est. c. 1997.

Intimidation of witnesses and jurors has become so significant that the Government has created specific statutory offences. The CJPU is prominent in providing advice, support and positive action for not only the MPS but nationally and internationally.

It is also responsible for national training and best practice in the subject.

CRIMINAL RECORD OFFICE Strictly confidential listing of convicted criminals with their fingerprints, crimes and sentences. 1871 refinement of the Habitual Criminals Register which, prior to computerization, was the most useful way of securing information about a possible perpetrator's habits and methods. The CRO number stays with a serious convicted criminal throughout his life.

CRIPPEN, DR HAWLEY HARVEY

(1862–1910) Murderer whose case is cited in almost every history of Scotland Yard. Second arrest of a murderer by officer pursuing across the Atlantic in a faster passenger vessel. First case where detection was expedited by radio-telegraph. First case to bring pathologist Sir Bernard Spilsbury to prominence. Only case to supply the title for a Scotland Yard officer's reminiscences.

Crippen, for reasons unknown, poisoned his wife Cora (*née* Kunigunde Mackimotzki; better known by the stage name adopted in her unsuccessful music hall career, Belle Elmore), on or soon after 1 February 1910. Her friends were not satisfied with his claim that she had gone to visit relatives in America and died there, especially as Crippen's mistress and secretary, Ethel Le Neve, was seen wearing Cora's clothing and jewellery. When they reported the matter to Scotland Yard, Inspector Walter Dew questioned Crippen, and was satisfied with his explanation that Cora had eloped with a lover, and Crippen felt too humiliated to admit this. But Crippen panicked and fled with Ethel when Dew told him he would be returning to clear up a few points of detail.

A thorough search of Crippen's house uncovered nothing, until Dew found a loose brick in the floor of a coal-hole leading off the basement kitchen, and Cora's headless filleted remains were found buried there, wrapped in Crippen's pyjama jacket. The public search for Crippen and Ethel led the captain of SS *Montrose* to report by Marconigram that he believed his passengers 'Mr and Master Robinson', who boarded at Antwerp, were really Crippen and Ethel in disguise. The ship owners sent his reports to the press as well as the police, and the public followed the chase as Dew crossed the Atlantic on

CRIMINAL RECORD OFFICE IN THE NORMAN SHAW BUILDING (THEN NEW SCOTLAND YARD), 1946.

POLICE NOTICE USED IN THE HUNT FOR DR CRIPPEN AND ETHEL LE NEVE.

the faster ship SS *Laurentic* and arrested Crippen before he could land in Montreal.

Spilsbury's evidence was crucial in establishing from an old operation scar and a fringe of hair that the buried remains really were those of Cora Crippen. Crippen was convicted and executed. Ethel, tried separately as accessory after the fact, was acquitted. Dew entitled his memoirs *I Caught Crippen* (1938). How and where Crippen disposed of Belle's head and skeleton was never established.

Despite many writers' insistence on Crippen's meekness and Cora's shrewishness (leading ex-WPC Joan Lock to wonder whether male writers believe murder to be an acceptable way of dealing with dominant wives), Crippen's name headed the list of sinister murderers in the popular mind for the first half of the 20th century.

CRIS Crime Report Information System. Computerized database which replaces the old Crime Book, logging details of all crimes, victims, suspects and investigations in the MPD.

The largest customized computer of its kind in Europe, CRIS was proposed in the mid-1980s and was finally rolled out to all Divisions in 1996. This was partly because of a conflict between the computer experts' perceived need for a centralized system at a time when more independent localized Divisional policing was being encouraged, and partly because the manufacturers had difficulty in meeting the very large specifications proposed for a computer accessible from 1500 terminals across London. The system provides a powerful means of searching for suspects, property and linked crimes.

CS INCAPACITANT SPRAY First issued in 1997, following national trials. The spray uses a 5% solution of CS (Orthochlorobenzylidine Malononitrile) in the solvent Methyl Iso-Butyl Ketone (MIBK). The propellant is nitrogen. The spray, which causes irritation of the eyes, nose and throat, is used to incapacitate a person in circumstances where an officer is faced with violence or the threat of violence. It is not a gas but a discriminate 'streamer' spray which can deliver CS directly into the face of an approaching assailant.

All officers are given training before they are issued with CS sprays, which not only reiterate the warnings against unnecessary or indiscriminate use but also explain the correct aftercare procedures to administer to a person sprayed with CS.

CULLEY, PC ROBERT, (1806–1833) Murdered during the Coldbath Fields Riot.

Joined Met, 21 September 1829. Constable No. 95 C Division, Warrant No. 1044. Ht, 1.7m (5ft 8½ ins). Married, 1831, no children. Lived at Litchfield Street, Seven Dials. 1832–3 received at

POLICE DIGGING UP CRIPPEN'S GARDEN IN HILLDROP CRESCENT IN 1910. CHIEF INSPECTOR WALTER DEW IS ON THE EXTREME RIGHT.

least four gratuities. Died, 13 May 1833; buried 17 May, St Anne's Church, Soho.

During the affray that broke out in the attempt to halt the National Union of the Working Classes' meeting at Coldbath Fields on 13 May 1833, PC Culley was separated from his colleagues PCs Tom Flack (Warrant No. 7504), James McReath (Warrant No. 4837) and Samuel Acourt (or A'Court, Warrant No. 8218) as they proceeded down the right-hand side of Calthorpe Street toward Gough Street. Culley disappeared into a stone-throwing melée, saying, 'Now for it!' Almost immediately he reappeared, holding his chest, and said to Flack, 'Oh, Tom, I am stabbed, I am done.' Acourt said, 'I hope it's not serious, Bob. Try to keep up with the Division if you can.' But he and Flack were immediately distracted by two men attacking them. Culley staggered along Calthorpe Street and Gray's Inn Road to the Calthorpe Arms where he collapsed saying, 'Oh, I am very ill,' and died in the arms of the barmaid who called him a 'poor lamb.'

Culley's inquest opened on 15 May in the Calthorpe Arms, where his body still lay upstairs for the jury to examine. The jury were distinctly hostile to the police, and were particularly exercised that the Riot Act had not been read which, in their opinion, meant police intervention was an illegal assault. When, over the coroner's furious objection, they insisted on recording a verdict of 'justifiable homicide', they added a rider protesting that the Riot Act was not read, the police had been 'ferocious, brutal and unprovoked', and the Government had not taken proper precautions to prevent the incident. Though this verdict was promptly overturned by the Court of King's Bench, no verdict of 'wilful murder' was substituted, and the authorities left the matter in the hands of the Parliamentary Select Committee investigating the riot.

Culley was buried at St Anne's Church, Soho, on 17 May, his funeral sadly marred by the presence of a jeering mob. Mrs Lucy Culley, his pregnant wife of two years, was granted an unprecedented and well-deserved £200 by the government, whose panicky over-reaction to the NUWC had indeed made Culley an innocent victim.

The inquest jurors were feted by the public.

They were given testimonial dinners and river trips to Twickenham and Rochester. They were presented with silver medals, pewter medallions, inscribed goblets and a ceremonial blue silk banner. (This, with examples of the goblets and medals is now in the Museum of London. There are also Culley inquest memorabilia and artefacts at the Historical Museum.) Police historians have tended to describe them as ignorant and uneducated men who abused their moment of power. But their foreman Mr Samuel Stockton went on to become a highly respected vestryman and

BROADSHEET ACCOUNT OF THE MURDER OF PC CULLEY AT THE COLDBATH FIELDS DEMONSTRATION, 1833.

churchwarden. He and his fellows were in fact decent propertied tradesmen who explicitly deplored the purpose of the meeting, but deplored even more the unnecessary use of force by the police. Their 'perverse' verdict, though callously unfair to Culley, should stand with that of the famous jury in 'Penn and Mead' which established that an Englishman's 'jury of his peers' may override the legal opinions of a judge when, in their opinion, strict legality is enforcing injustice.

The subsequent press sympathy for Mrs Culley turned public opinion in favour of individual

police officers, and PC Culley's death thereby marks a significant milestone in police and public relations.

CUSTODY OFFICER Uniformed Sergeant in charge of the custody suite. Custody officers must be appointed so that there is always one on duty, 24 hours of the day. The Custody Officer has clear responsibilities set out under PACE which gives him authority even when the officer investigating a prisoner's crime is of a higher rank than Sergeant.

CUSTODY SHEETS Official record of prisoners with the details of their detention at a police station. Modern version of the former Charge Sheets.

CUSTODY SUITE Official term since 1985 for the cells, charge room and interview room/s in Police Stations. Under the permanent care of a custody officer.

CUTHBERT, SUPT CYRIL (1902–1984) Amateur enthusiast for forensic science who accidentally inspired the Metropolitan Police Forensic Science Laboratory.

Educ. Exeter Grammar School, where, allegedly, fagged for Oswald (later Sir Oswald) Mosley. Started, but did not complete, medical, then dental studies. Joined the Metropolitan Police on 26 May 1924 (A289, Warrant No. 112949) and subsequently served as a Clerk Sergeant and in CRO before becoming Liaison Officer for the Forensic Science Laboratory 1935–1939. Commandant, Isle of Wight aliens' internment camp, 1940–5. Supt, 1949. KPFSM Retd from Met, 1951. Secretary to St George's Hospital Medical School, Hyde Park Corner, 1956–70.

In later life, Cyril Cuthbert told an interviewer he never wanted to join the police and admitted that he had never made an arrest in nearly 30 years' service. Yet he holds a proud place in the annals of the Met, and his rise to Superintendent is proof positive that a successful police career does not depend on building up a strong numerical record of arrests.

As a young PC, Cuthbert was fascinated by

forensic science. He collected scientific books and instruments, took evening courses in chemistry and taught himself simple tests for chemical reactions to blood and the recovery of erased writing. Unfortunately his hobby found no favour with his immediate superiors, who felt that it distracted him from his clerical duties. He was ordered to restrict his attention to forensic science to his spare time, and to keep all his equipment permanently in the meagre accommodation of his section house.

In the 1930s he helped a colleague decipher the original writing on a document that had been tampered with, and the results were passed to Folkestone Police to help them with an investigation. When a senior officer in Folkestone asked Scotland Yard for a written statement from Mr Cuthbert of 'the Metropolitan Police Laboratory', Cuthbert was summoned before Assistant Commissioner Sir Norman Kendall and severely

reprimanded for exceeding his duties and leading another constabulary to believe in a non-existent laboratory. Folkestone's request was abruptly refused, but Cuthbert was nonetheless called to give evidence at Kent Quarter Sessions, and apparently given a lift in a car provided by the Chief Constable. The bench praised his skill and expertise and hoped it would be made known to the appropriate authorities. This commendation won him a further reprimand at Scotland Yard, which so disheartened Cuthbert that he would have resigned from the Force had it been economically feasible in the depression.

Fortunately, the commendation from Quarter Sessions came to the attention of Commissioner Lord Trenchard, who was impressed and demanded to be shown the 'laboratory'. Those superiors who had previously dismissed Cuthbert's efforts as detrimental to his proper duties were forced to order him to bring his equipment to his office,

METROPOLITAN POLICE BEING PUT THROUGH CUTLASS DRILL AT WELLINGTON BARRACKS IN 1867.

where they supplied him with a white coat to masquerade as the lab manager for the Commissioner's inspection.

The obvious inadequacy of Cuthbert's private property for the needs of the Metropolitan Force led Trenchard to start a lengthy correspondence with the Home Office, demanding the establishment of a proper Forensic Laboratory. When this was achieved, Cuthbert's contribution was not overlooked, and he was promoted and appointed the lab's Liaison Officer with Scotland Yard.

CUTLASSES Held in reserve in police stations for issue when required until the early 20th century. The last appearance of a police cutlass known to the authors was in 1910 at the Tottenham Outrage.

D'ANGELY, MME EVA (FL.1906) Prostitute whose discharge after arrest for soliciting provoked extravagant public indignation and led to the Royal Commission, 1908.

'Mme D'Angely' was arrested in Regent Street around midnight on 24 April 1906. She spoke little English and required an interpreter at the magistrate's court, where a M. René D'Angely testified that he was her husband and she had been waiting for him the previous evening. Divisional Inspector Alexander McKay (Warrant No. 75186) knew nothing against the couple who had only recently come to England, and Mr Denman the magistrate dismissed the case.

There was an immediate uproar in the press and Parliament, where radicals accused the police of wilful harassment of an innocent woman (cf. Miss Cass). Home Secretary Herbert Gladstone appointed a Royal Commission to investigate police conduct. Long before it reported in 1908, the D'Angelys had fled the country for Paris, bilking their landlord and abandoning the empty trunks they had brought as an appearance of luggage. The French police reported that Mme was a prostitute called Eva Clavell, and René, whose real name was Soubiger, was her ponce. They had lived on her immoral earnings in Algiers before coming to England, and were again doing so in Paris under the name of Dutiel. Both refused to return to England to give evidence to the Royal Commission which was deciding whether to order the police to make them an apology. The case was intrinsically trivial and unimportant, but is remembered as an outstanding example of the mischief-making propensities of sensational journalism and knee-jerk anti-police radicalism.

DEMEANOUR From the outset the founding fathers of policing by consent understood that the demeanour with which constables comported themselves towards the public was vital for the success of their endeavour. Sir Charles Rowan's military experience was valuable here. The army was accustomed to taking raw recruits in hand and transforming them into smartly turned-out men with upright carriage and commanding presence. To this end the original Instruction Book directed that policemen were

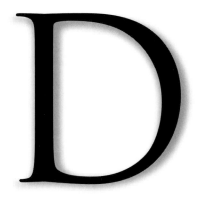

always to wear their uniform, and were to 'furnish themselves with new clothes whenever the Commissioners may direct.' The preliminary parade before patrols went on their beats were formal inspections, and from the swallow-tails of 1829 to the epaulletted white shirts of hot summer days in 2000, it has been taken for granted that a police officer on duty in uniform will be visibly clean and tidy.

WPC PATRICIA MULLIGAN HELPS CHERRY COUCHMAN ACROSS THE ROAD AT VICTORIA EMBANKMENT, SW1, c.1946 TO 1952.

The often-criticized drill which played such a large part in officers' basic training until the early part of the 20th century, and, though less central, continues to ensure officers' ability to move quickly and efficaciously in a body, also ensured that men carried themselves properly with an upright demeanour giving dignity to their public appearance at all times. Indeed, police officers' trained inability to slouch and shuffle sometimes made plain clothes officers all too readily identifiable, even when they adopted the deliberately grubby wear of dustmen or coalheavers by way of disguise. To this day, if lively activity is required, the physical fitness and alertness of young detectives on covert operations may suddenly distinguish them from the seedier denizens of the world of drugs whose sloppy appearance they have temporarily affected. The basic training regulation that when out of uniform, officers should normally wear sports coats and slacks, or equivalently respectable semi-formal female clothing, emphasizes the assumption that police officers will comport themselves with a degree of dignity at all times, and that this is professionally preferable to popular scruffiness.

The frequency with which 19th-century officers were dismissed or demoted for drunkenness looks comic to the casual student of discipline records today. Yet this was not a silly foible of Rowan and Mayne. 'The licentious soldiery' were not respected when they were not on parade or in battle. It was essential that police officers should not be similarly stigmatized, and Draconian severity was necessary to prove to policemen then (as to drivers today) that they themselves were not to be judges of how much they could take without impairing their efficiency.

Dignity, fitness, sobriety and physical size and strength suited the policeman for preventing disorder and, when necessary, making arrests. It was also necessary, however, that he should not intimidate, bully or nag. As early as 1754, Saunders Welch, who became High Constable of Holborn the following year, had recognized that watchmen and constables must at all costs avoid being seen as jacks-in-office. 'Let the service of the public be the great motive of all those actions which regard your office,' he wrote. 'This, properly attended to, will keep you from all officious,

wanton acts of power.' Rowan and Mayne issued the excellent and balanced instruction that a constable, 'must be particularly cautious, not to interfere idly or unnecessarily; when required to act, he will do so with decision and boldness; on all occasions he may expect to receive the fullest support in the proper exercise of his authority.'

There was, of course, trial and error in the early days. The murder of PC Joseph Grantham revealed that some members of the public viewed stopping a savage brawl on the streets as 'unnecessary interference'. It took some time before the calming influence of a firm, questioning, but not obviously bossy intervention became apparent. The slowly delivered, ''Allo, 'allo, 'allo! And what's going on here, then?' is familiar as theatrical parody of the deliberative constable, but the principle of using a confident but unhurried demeanour was always excellent. It avoids exacerbating tempers by introducing the officer as a new aggressive party, allows him or her a tiny breathing space to assess what is happening and how it is best dealt with, and, more often than not, it prevents a quarrel from developing into a fracas, or a brawl from spiralling to a serious disturbance. Today officers will normally avoid anything resembling the slow-moving caricatured bobby of old, yet will hope to find some way of defusing dangerous situations that matches modern ideals of clean-cut activity without suggesting a school prefect's novice delight in authority.

Matching the unhurried speech with which officers were encouraged to approach the public was the unhurried gait demanded by the beat. The dignified walk in the cheap, heavy, ill-made boots that replaced the original equally uncomfortable half-wellingtons was effective in warning evildoers to get out of the way quickly. This was desirable, as the general instruction was to prevent crime in preference to catching criminals after the event, but it also led to the perception of the policeman's plod. Today, beat officers may reasonably be seen to walk briskly about their business, or to comport themselves in an upright stroll with just a trace of spring in the step.

Rowan's general directive to the constable remains a model statement of ideal police demeanour: 'He must remember, that there is no qualification more indispensable to a Police Officer, than a perfect command of temper, never suffering himself to be moved in the slightest degree, by any language or threats that may be used; if he do his duty in a quiet and determined manner, such conduct will probably induce well-disposed bystanders to assist him, should he require it.'

DENNING, CHIEF INSPECTOR ELEAZAR (1828–1904)

House of Commons Inspector, 1860-88, in which role became a well-known public figure. Born Charlock, Dorset. Worked as a labourer. Joined the Met, 1846. Warrant No. 23680. Posted to Division F then served in A Division and J Division before returning to A Division in 1860 as House of Commons Inspector.

Eleazar Denning was the only policeman ever to be caricatured by 'Ape' in ordinary constabulary uniform for inclusion in *Vanity Fair*'s famous 'Men of the Moment' series. This called him 'the most prominent and reputable figure that the British Parliament has to show' (probably incautious drafting rather than a deliberate slight on, say, Mr Gladstone!) It mentioned his early service at Ascot and Epsom, and recorded that he was prominent in supporting the Police Orphanage and other good works, as well as being a Sunday School teacher. On the Speaker's orders, he was responsible for the regular ejection from the House of Charles Bradlaugh the atheist, who was repeatedly elected, but always refused to take the oath. Every Sunday Inspector Denning guarded seats in St Margaret's Church, Westminster, which were reserved for members although, as *Vanity Fair* dryly commented, they were never used.

DEPARTMENT OF TECHNOLOGY

Formed in 1992 by amalgamation of the Chief Engineer's Department and the Computing Services Department. The Department is responsible for the provision of technology services to all areas of the Metropolitan Police Service and is divided into three sections: Information Technology (IT) Communications and Transport.

The IT branches are responsible for the provision, maintenance and support of the majority of computer systems within the MPS. A major

CHIEF INSPECTOR ELEAZAR DENNING.

use of IT in the Met is in handling 999 calls, which are put through to the Central Communications Complex at New Scotland Yard, where they are typed into a mainframe computer with links to terminals in every Division and access to information on the Police National Computer.

The Communications branches provide radio and voice services with the MPS, and their remit includes maintenance and repair of all radios, transmitters, aerial sites and the entire MPS telephone network (MetPhone). The Transport Division has engineering responsibility for provision, maintenance and development of specialist vehicles, including all land and water vehicles and maintenance to the Air Support Unit. See also CRIS, Central Communication Complex, OTIS.

DEPARTMENTS The major administrative parts of the Metropolitan Police Headquarters from 1909 not to be confused with the territorial Divisions or Areas. Until 1986, Depts were lettered A, B, C and D (with occasional extra departments like L).

Under the Newman Restructuring the Departments became Territorial Operations (the Super Eight Areas), Specialist Operations, Management Support, and Personnel and Training. In 1995 the former Territorial Operations became Units managed from Headquarters by the five Area Assistant Commissioners, with CO numbers often relating them to the ACs' numbered Areas. There are also the Personnel Department, Finance Department, Solicitor's Department, Department of Procurement and Commercial Services, Property Services Department and Department of Technology.

The first reference to departments in the Commissioners' Office was in 1840, with the creation of three: the Correspondence, Finance, and Candidates' Departments. The personnel comprised either or both attested police and Civil Staff. Over the years as Departments and Branches changed, so did their staff composition. In the Receiver's office (composed entirely of Civil Staff), the term Department was not used until 1919, when the Accountants, the General and Contract, the Architect and Surveyors, the Engineers, and the Printing Departments were created. These continued until the merger with the Commissioner's Office Civil Staff in 1966.

The first specialized police department in Scotland Yard was the Detective Branch set up in 1842. In 1850 the Public Carriage Office was started, to manage the responsibility for licensing public carriages which was delegated to the Commissioner, and finally passed over to him in its entirety in 1860. In 1853 Colonel Paschal (formerly with the Public Carriage Office before it became a Scotland Yard Department) started the Executive Branch. He was a poor and inefficient manager, but his appointment was a sign of things to come, as administrative sections and subsections ramified. Howard Vincent's creation of the CID in 1878 paved the way for an Assistant Commissioner with responsibilities for an expanding but clear-cut and definable portfolio of operations. Not so his two previously established colleagues, loosely thought of as the Administrative and Executive (or Legal) ACs. In 1906, Sir Edward Henry listed the Assistant Commissioners' duties alphabetically as follows. AC Administration was responsible for Beats, Candidates, Complaints & Commendations, Clothing & Equipment, Discipline (including gratuities), Distribution of Manpower, Dockyards, Fixed Points, Mounted Police, Movements of Police, Protection of Public Buildings, Processions, Royal and Public Functions, Street Collections and Traffic Regulation. Apart from such Divisional matters as beats and fixed points, these obviously entailed complicated and varying types of administrative duty. But his unfortunate Executive colleague handled even more of a ragbag, to wit: Advertisements, Aliens, Betting in the Streets, Children's Employment, Costermongers, Disorder in the Streets, Disorderly Houses, Dogs Acts, Financial Questions, Gratuities (not connected with discipline), Insane Persons, Legal Questions, Liquor Laws, Lost Property, Military and Naval Deserters, Missing Persons, Motor Cars, Pedlars, Public Carriages, Stations and Stores, Summonses and Veterinary Preventive Measures. The AC Crime was relatively lucky. Only Gaming & Betting in Public Houses or Private Premises, Naturalisation and Missing Girls

distracted him from the business of detecting and preventing Serious Crime. (The Missing Girls came to him as probably connected with Procuring and White Slavery.)

In 1909 the three Assistant Commissioners were increased to four, and their respective spheres of responsibility became Departments labelled, like themselves, A (Internal Administration and Discipline), B (Civil, Financial and Legal Business, Traffic and Lost Property Office), C (Serious Crime, Special Branch and Convict Supervision), and D (Complaints from the Public, Disorderly Houses, Street Collections, Pedlars, Betting and Gaming, Fires, etc.)

In 1929 the Secretariat (Civil Staff, other than the Receiver's staff) became S Department, and took over from B Department responsibility for the Lost Property Office, and some of the financial and legal responsibilities, others of which were transferred to D Department (the legal section of which, for a time, was known as L Department), leaving B Department exclusively the domain of the Traffic Police. A Department was essentially the department of the divisional uniformed police.

The Departments were sub-divided into Branches which were themselves increased and redivided as the force expanded and more and more specialized operations came into being (especially under the CID or C Department).

Nonetheless, a fairly logical division of the non-Civil Staff Departments into A for Uniformed Police, B for Traffic, C for CID, and D for Training and Everything Else obtained, until external and internal policy imperatives gradually confused the clear lines. Externally, for example, the Equal Employment Act meant that by law Women Police could no longer be limited by a separate establishment. Internally, Sir Robert Mark's determination to check CID autonomy meant that serious crime-fighting units found themselves brought back under uniformed control. By 1986, the Departmental responsibilities were almost as confused as those Henry had sorted out. A Department handled Aliens Deportation, Animals, Charitable Collections, Community and Race Relations, Courts and Summonses, Crime Prevention, Diplomatic Protection Group, Divisional Operations, Firearms Licensing, Gaming Laws, Liquor

Licensing, Mental Health Matters, Obscene Publications, Police Dogs, Police Premises and their Security, Public Order, Radioactive Substances Index, River Police, Shotguns and Explosives, Special Constabulary, Special Patrol Group, Visiting Forces, and Young Offenders. B Department handled Air Support, Central Ticket Office, Communications, Fingerprints, Information Room, Juvenile Index, Missing Persons Index, National Identification Bureau, Police Gazette, Public Warnings, Traffic Patrols, Traffic Wardens, and Transport. C Division remained focused on serious crime, though it had lost the Fingerprint Bureau and Obscene Publications. D Department managed to concentrate on Personnel, Welfare, Recruitment and Training matters, though War Duties and Civil Defence looked like cuckoos in the nest.

The situation was sufficiently complicated by 1985 that Sir Kenneth Newman instituted a complete reorganization, re-forming C Department and all other Branches with force-wide operational responsibilities into Specialist Operations and the Uniformed and Traffic Branches in Territorial Operations, with Departmental status also going to Personnel and Training and Management Support. Other parts of the Force were organized as the Force Inspectorate, the Receiver's Department and the Solicitor's Department.

Finally, in 1996 as part of the Condon Restructuring, the Territorial Operations were changed to Headquarters (CO) administrative units, numbered according to the Area Assistant Commissioner (from 1 to 5) in whose portfolio they fell. Today these are

CO11	Public Order
CO12	Public Order Training
CO13	Mounted Branch
CO14	Clubs and Vice
CO20-22	Community Safety and Partnership
	Special Constabulary
	Wildlife and Charities
	Firearms
CO30	Criminal Justice
CO31	Courts Division
CO32	Forensic Medical Services
CO33	Language Services
CO41	Crime Policy Unit

CO42	CRIS Project
CO50	HQ Traffic
CO51	Central Ticket
CO52	Thames Division (River Police)
CO53	Air Support Unit
CO54	Specialist Dogs
CO55	Central Communications Command and Control
CO56	Communications programme
CO59	Policy Development Unit

DEPUTY ASSISTANT COMMISSIONER

Rank introduced in 1919, admitting valuable ex-officers from the army, like Col. Percy Laurie in a grade senior to Chief Constables. In 1933, four DACs, including the outstanding 'ranker' officer George Abbiss and the future Commissioner J. R. H. Nott-Bower, were created DACs in command of the Districts (1) (formerly posts carrying the rank of Chief Constable) while a further three DACs carried out duties in Scotland Yard. DACs continued to command Areas and head sensitive units in Scotland Yard, until it started to be phased out as a formal rank from 1995, it being deemed by the Sheehy Report no longer necessary for the two ranks of DAC and Commander to occupy the space between Superintendents and Assistant Commissioners once occupied by Chief Constables, especially as overall command of the Areas was transferred to Assistant Commissioners.

More recently, the title of Deputy to Assistant Commissioner has been given to some Commanders to reflect certain higher responsibilities.

DESBOROUGH COMMITTEE

Committee set up in the wake of the Police Strike, 1918 to make a final just pay settlement, and resolve the grievance about non-representation. Its generous pay settlement was anticipated by an immediate payment of £10, which undermined the Police Strike, 1919. Its report in 1920 offered satisfactory pay scales, and recommended the establishment of the Police Federation to represent officers below the rank of Superintendent on matters of pay and conditions. This finally destroyed the National Union of Police and Prison Officers (NUPPO). The result was

LIMEHOUSE CID INVESTIGATING DOPE SMUGGLING IN DISGUISE, c.1911.

regarded as a triumph by the authorities, but their satisfaction with Desborough allowed them to let pay slip badly behind the national average once more, leading to the manpower crises of the 1940s and 1950s.

DETECTIVE, THE

Occasional name used for the Detective Branch, especially in its early days.

DETECTIVE BRANCH

Name for the first permanent plain clothes branch established at Metropolitan Police HQ, Scotland Yard on 15 August 1842 in the wake of the Daniel Good case. Dissolved and reformed as CID following the Trial of the Detectives, 1877.

On the formation of the Force in 1829, Commissioners Rowan and Mayne and Home Secretary Peel were all quite clear that the principal responsibility of the police was the prevention of crime and the maintenance of public order, not the detection of criminals. The Bow Street Runners could still be employed for that purpose. Not until the Metropolitan Police Force was 13 years old, and the Runners had been disbanded for three, was the need for permanent official police detectives recognized, although in most

Divisions two officers patrolled in plain clothes every month to look out for pickpockets and prevent theft of produce from gardens.

The original Detective Branch was headed by former Bow Street Runner Inspector Nicholas Pearce, with Inspector John Haynes as his deputy. The other six detectives, all Sergeants, were Stephen Thornton, William Gerrett, Frederick Shaw, Charles Burgess Goff, Jonathan Whicher, and Sgt Braddick. There were rapid changes in the manning of the Branch, Pearce being promoted to Superintendent of F Division within 18 months and replaced by Inspector Joseph Shackell, who had himself been drafted in when Sergeant Goff was promoted out. Thornton and Whicher became the best known of the original Detectives. Thornton took a leading part in the pursuit of the Bermondsey murderers Mr and Mrs Manning, who killed a former suitor of Mrs Manning's and buried his remains in their kitchen.

In 1855 and 1857 the Branch scored two major coups which brought down the underworld empire of James 'Jim the Penman' Saward, barrister and master criminal who more nearly resembled Sherlock Holmes's enemy Professor Moriarty than any other historical British criminal ever has done. The first of these was the solution of the Great Bullion Robbery. The second was the exposure of the Saward gang's cheque-forging activities in Yarmouth.

Although other constabularies were steadily being created across the country, Scotland Yard was still the only force with its own detectives. The habit of 'calling in Scotland Yard' to help investigate major crimes therefore began, and was to continue until the Force amalgamations of the 1960s created large CIDs in all forces. Jonathan Whicher, in particular, became noted as a precursor of the 1920s to 1950s 'Murder Squad' of the CID.

In 1863 Inspector Frederick Adolphus Williamson began his 25-year innings as senior detective officer at Headquarters, and while he was more often criticized than praised by the newspapers he undoubtedly laid the foundations for the CID's years of triumph in the 20th century. The Detective Branch was immediately engaged in curbing the terrorist activities of the Fenians, a thankless task, as some of the ventures of well-organized, well-financed and highly motivated terrorists must inevitably elude detection, and these will be reported and remembered, especially if, as in the case of the Clerkenwell Bombing, they are accompanied by transparently incompetent policing. By contrast, police successes are quickly forgotten, or completely suppressed in order to protect covert investigators.

Though it was becoming apparent that detectives were needed in the territorial Divisions, Commissioner Sir Richard Mayne set his face against their introduction, mindful of the prejudice against political spies he and Sir Charles Rowan had so carefully laid to rest. One of Sir Edmund Henderson's first actions as a 'new broom' Commissioner in 1869 was to appoint detectives to the Divisions, with slightly higher pay than the uniformed force and a £5 p.a. clothing allowance in lieu of uniforms. Henderson's hope was that the (ultimately 180) detectives in the Divisions would prove to be men of higher than usual calibre. Sir Howard Vincent, however,

when he took over responsibility for the Metropolitan Police detectives in 1878, felt that Divisional Superintendents had deliberately put their most incompetent and least literate men into plain clothes, and used them as messenger boys.

Nothing of the kind happened at HQ. Here competence in foreign languages was recognized as hugely advantageous and Inspector Tanner's notebook of arrests shows how common it was for detectives to be sent abroad in pursuit of wanted men. A few officers were appointed on the strength of their educational or linguistic attainments and went straight into the Detective Branch. Notable among the multilingual detectives were J. J. Thomson and Nathaniel Druscovich (see Clerkenwell Bombing and Trial of the Detectives respectively).

Williamson ran the Branch with a light hand, despite a rather ponderous manner. He seemed to regard the detectives as friends, so he felt particularly let down when it transpired that men he had trusted took advantage of his preoccupation with Irish affairs to let corruption undermine the Branch. After the Trial of the Detectives which led to the complete reformation of the Detective Branch Williamson remained genial and encouraging, but the sense of comradeship which had so marked the tight-knit Scotland Yard Detective Branch was not recovered by the CID until long after his retirement and death, when it became particularly apparent again in the Flying Squad and some other Specialist Operations.

DETECTIVE TRAINING SCHOOL Section of the Metropolitan Police Training School at Peel Centre which offers a range of general and specialist courses to over 3000 students per year from the Met, other UK and overseas police forces, and appropriate armed services personnel.

The world's first specialized training programme for detectives was offered in 1936 and based in two old WWI huts on the Hendon Police College estate. Closed down during WWII, it was reopened in 1946, and moved to temporary premises in Knightsbridge. In 1961 it was accommodated in Peel House (2). Finally, in 1973, it returned to Hendon, with its own teaching rooms in the new purpose-built block which became Peel House (1) in 1974. Today it is based

in the new lecture block.

The School offers elementary and advanced training under five heads: General, Sexual and Domestic Offences, Forensics, Surveillance, and Fraud and Money Laundering. Sexual and Domestic Offences courses are important to uniformed officers as well as the CID, especially those women police who are frequently at the foreground of interviewing victims and children. Forensics courses include work in fingerprinting and photography, as well as scene of crime examination, all areas in which Civil Staff are involved with preliminary assistance in investigative work. Drugs courses give detectives information about the medical and psychiatric effects of illegal substances, as well as geographical and scientific information about their production and importation. Basic chemistry and physics show how forensic science can help an investigation, and give a proper understanding of how and why certain types of specimen should be sought and preserved for laboratory examination and analysis.

Until 1998 the School maintained its own Detective Training Museum. Shortly before the turn of the century, tight budgets and lack of space necessitated its closure. Some essential exhibits were retained in classrooms, some were taken by the Black Museum and the rest of the collection was sent to the Historical Museum.

DIPLOMATIC PROTECTION GROUP (SO16) Approximately 500 Authorised Firearms Officers providing a focused response to the needs of the diplomatic community in London, (which currently numbers about 10,000), and meeting MPS obligations under the Vienna Convention. Operationally, DPG provides armed uniform and plain clothes protection from terrorism to 160 embassies and high commissions, and a range of other sensitive premises with diplomatic status. DPG also protects the official Downing Street residence of the Prime Minister, New Scotland Yard and the private residences of diplomats, politicians and senior military staff at risk.

Residential protection for visiting heads of state and foreign ministers is provided in hotels and, more recently, DPG has undertaken the guarding of high-category prisoners and persons at criminal or terrorist threat in hospital. Support to the Firearms Unit (SO19) is available from DPG in armed crime operations, and the group invariably provides armed officers for all major state and diplomatic events, and at the venues of international conferences in London. The group maintains its own counter-terrorist search capability. Frequent liaison is maintained with Special Branch, Anti-Terrorist Branch and other Specialist Operations Branches, and externally with the Foreign & Commonwealth Office, Home Office and other government departments.

DPG operates from bases at Apex house near Trafalgar Square, Walton Street and Kensington. The group is armed with a variety of weapons, and its highly mobile nature ensures a rapid response in force to incidents at the premises it protects. The group maintains an index of all accredited diplomats, premises and vehicles in

A SCOTLAND YARD DETECTIVE MAKING AN ARREST WHILE DISGUISED AS A STATUE AT THE INTERNATIONAL EXHIBITION, 1862.

London. Since 1983 the DPG, Royalty Protection Branch (SO14) and Palace of Westminster Division (SO17) have come under the jurisdiction of the Commander, Royalty and Diplomatic Protection Department.

Dedicated DPG Inspectors liaise regularly and directly with the foreign missions for which they have specific responsibility, building trust and good working relationships. All missions are offered full security surveys, which they generally accept, and expert advice on the protection of staff and premises from terrorism and crime. Diplomatic staff new to London are given presentations about the MPS and the specific function of DPG, helping them to adjust their expectations about the role of police in Britain, which may be very different from those in their home states.

Since its inception, DPG has played a key role in several prominent events, including the Iranian Embassy Siege in 1981 (see also Trevor Lock), the Libyan Embassy Siege (see Yvonne Fletcher), and the unlawful occupation of diplomatic premises on numerous occasions. Although group members have never fired a shot in anger at these

times, three of its officers used their firearms effectively on street duty during the 1970s and 1980s. PC Peter Slimon GM was shot and injured in December 1972 by robbers when he went to his bank to draw out some money, and successfully shot two of them as they tried to make off in their getaway car. PC Stephen Peat assisted in the response to a bank robbery in Victoria and shot one of the robbers, who was thereupon arrested. And PC Gordon McKinnon, given permission to engage a suspect holding a hostage and moving around the area near Trafalgar Square, successfully shot the suspect and freed the hostage.

DIRECTORATE OF IDENTIFICATION (SO3 – IDENTIFICATION BRANCH) The Directorate of Identification comprises nine units which includes SO3.1 Fingerprint Bureau, SO3.2 Photographic and Graphic Services, SO3.3 PNC Bureau, SO3.4 Scientific Support College and the SO3.5 Directorate of Central Services. SO3.6–9 have Directorate support functions.

DISGUISE Use of men in plain clothes, or wearing butchers' or bakers' aprons to ask questions without arousing suspicion or to enter houses from which they feared suspects would flee on seeing a uniform, was used sporadically until the formation of the Detective Branch in 1842. Thereafter, detectives were divided in their view of the practice. Inspector Charles Frederick Field (Warrant No. 1332) favoured it. Charles Dickens portrayed him as 'Inspector Bucket' in Bleak House and indicated that it was highly effective. But Sergeant Jonathan Whicher (the model for 'Sergeant Cuff' in Wilkie Collins' *The Moonstone*) thought it was a silly waste of effort, and passed his views on to Adolphus Williamson. Quite the most extraordinary successful disguise of the early years was that of the officer who posed as a statue in the International Exhibition of 1862 and successfully arrested a thief.

Despite Williamson's general disapproval, detectives under his command continued to assume clothing associated with some civilian occupation from time to time when engaged on particularly difficult investigations. The Historical

Museum's photograph (see p67) of a group so 'disguised' shows that a serious and almost stagey effort was made to seem 'obviously' something other than a policeman. Chief Inspector John Littlechild recorded his preference for a butcher's apron and steel or a cabman's greatcoat, horsecloth, licence badge and whip. The widespread report that smooth-faced officers were dressed as women decoys during the Jack the Ripper scare, however, was flatly denied by Inspector Andrew Lansdowne in 1890. He reported that one young man acting on his own initiative tried it once, and it was not approved.

Inspector Maurice Moser (Warrant No. 61670), on the other hand, described himself as slipping in and out of various disguises with the rapidity of a quick-change artiste, once rushing back to his lodgings in Paris to disguise himself before returning to close surveillance of a suspect he had just confronted and talked with. Former Special Branch Sergeant Edwin Woodhall (Warrant No. 94985) believed that another of Moser's Paris operations was the most striking instance of disguise in the annals of the Met. On this occasion, Moser dressed as a French bricklayer and affected a limp, thereby luring out of his hiding place a Fenian suspect who was expecting a clandestine visit from a limping Irish confederate.

In the early years of the 20th century, Inspector Herbert Fitch's (Warrant No. 91520) Special Branch duties included passing himself off as a clumsy waiter at an International Workers' Movement dinner and knocking over papers belonging to Lenin in order to acquire an agenda of the meeting for police files.

Sir Basil Thomson, Assistant Commissioner (Crime) from 1913 to 1921, recalled an officer who disguised himself as a jobbing gardener to keep watch on a house; two others who dressed as labourers and worked slowly on a hole in the road to maintain their surveillance; and a quick-witted inspector who slipped off his jacket and placed himself in shirtsleeves behind a pawnbroker's counter to trap a known thief coming in with a stolen watch. And in 1913 George Cornish (then a Detective Sergeant, first-class) once put a plain clothes man in uniform to continue surveillance on a jewel thief who had spotted the heavy tail of four CID men watching him, but never suspected the 'bobby on the beat' strolling by.

By the interwar period, an 'unpolicemanlike' appearance for surveillance was often achieved simply by the use of plain-lensed spectacles and the employment of officers who barely reached the minimum height requirement of 173cm (5ft 8in), with a slight build that made them appear shorter. Women Police detailed to Vice Squad or decoy duties might have to acquire expensive evening wear for night-clubbing, or tarty clothes for standing among streetwalkers. They were also frequently asked to sit in plain clothes with surveillance officers on watch from cars to give the casual appearance of a courting couple.

PC Walter Raymond won the KPM for rescuing a struggling woman from her suicide attempt and carrying her to safety along a gutter 12m (40ft) above the ground. He had managed to approach her without causing her to jump by putting on a colleague's white traffic directing sleeves, wrapping a white towel over his head, and appearing at a window in this improvised disguise as a doctor.

Sergeant Harold Challenor, whose escape from a POW camp in Italy entailed dressing in woman's clothes, relates having worn a wig and one of his wife's dresses to accompany an informant to a pub where there were a number of bank robbers he wished to observe secretly. It is probable that his seniors would not have approved a situation in which, by his own account, he could be and was mistaken by at least one prostitute and one punter as a woman of ill repute.

Nowadays disguise is subsumed within the overall skills of surveillance and observation and does not extend beyond the adoption of clothing and appearance suitable for the operation.

DISTRICTS (1) 1869 grouping of the territorial Divisions into four large areas, each under the command of a District Superintendent (subsequently renamed District Officer; then Chief Constable). This was in response to the Commission of Enquiry set up after the Clerkenwell Bombing, which found there were insufficient senior officers to liaise between the Commissioner and the Divisions (essentially because of Sir Richard Mayne's refusal to delegate). In 1918, one of Sir Nevil Macready's reforms was insisting that three of the four District Chief Constables were stationed out in the Divisions, to make their liaison more efficient. In 1970, the Waldron Reforms renamed the four Districts Areas, a title they have retained.

(2) Name given to former and subsequent territorial Divisions between 1969 (the Waldron Reforms, which regraded former Sub-Divisions as Divisions) and 1985 (the Newman Restructuring, whereby the Waldron Districts were abolished, with the consequence that Divisional Chief Superintendents reported directly to their Deputy Assistant Commissioners, who were given greatly expanded Area Headquarters).

(3) The Metropolitan Police District (or MPD). The entire area covered by the Metropolitan Police Force: originally a radius of up to 11.2km (7 miles) from Charing Cross, embracing and containing the area then recognized as 'London', from Hyde Park in the west to Whitechapel in the east, and from the Angel, Islington in the north to the Elephant and Castle in the south, with the environs taken in wherever they might provide suburban shelter for criminals. Repeatedly expanded until, in 1999, 2038km² (787 square miles) covering Greater London reaching from Potter's Bar in the north to Kenley in the south, and Upminster in the east to Staines in the west. The exception is the City of London, which has its own independent force.

At the start of the 21st century, for the first time, the MPD is made identical with the metropolitan London local government boundaries. The outer suburban areas spreading into the edges of Hertfordshire, Essex and Surrey are returned to those County Constabularies. The purpose of the reform is increased direct political accountability to the Mayor of London and GLA, via the Metropolitan Police Authority.

DIVISION The basic unit of territorial policing in the Metropolitan Police, renamed Districts 1971–85 under the Waldron Reforms. See Districts (2).

Between 1829 and 1830, 17 Divisions lettered A to T were formed, embracing an area roughly 19km (12 miles) in radius from Charing Cross, and including parts of Kent and Middlesex. In 1829 each division was allocated a company of police which in turn was divided into sixteen parties of one Sergeant and nine constables. In accordance with classically educated 19th-century perception, letters I and J were not originally used, being seen as interchangeable in the Latin alphabet, and letter O was avoided as being open to confusion with the zero numeral. (But see O Division). Extensions of the MPD in 1865 led to the creation of new Divisions carrying down the alphabet to Y, and bringing in J to extend from Bethnal Green (in the former K Division) through the former N Division to the Barkingside area of Essex. The River Police were officially recognized as Thames Division. Z Division was formed in 1921, taking over the former Croydon Constabulary. The letter I was finally allocated to Heathrow and its environs.

In 1985, the Newman Restructuring introduced something like the Eight by Eight plan, with 67 Divisions and Sub-Divisions divided between eight Areas. This emphasized that the Division was the primary unit of policing, and placed each under the command of a Chief Superintendent. The Service Restructuring Exercise of 1995 reduced the number to 62 (with further fluctuations as the smaller Divisions became constantly vulnerable to amalgamation to save management costs) and the number of Areas to five. The whole traditional system was replaced by Borough Policing under the package of Greater London reforms introduced by the Blair government at the end of the 20th century.

DIVISIONAL INTELLIGENCE AND INFORMATION UNITS
Units set up under Sir Kenneth Newman to coordinate the Divisional planning process and hold management information. They included the Collator so that crime trends and information could be integrated with other information. See also 'Spykanedy'.

DIVISIONAL LETTERS OR CODES
Letters of the alphabet used to identify Divisions. The first series ran from A Division (Whitehall)

DIVISIONAL NUMBER AND LETTER ON THE TUNIC COLLAR BEFORE THE INTRODUCTION OF OPEN-NECKED TUNICS WITH EPAULETTES. THE NUMBER IS ALSO SHOWN ON THE HELMET PLATE.

to Z Division (Croydon). The letter I was used for Heathrow Airport. TD was used for traffic patrols until the Newman Restructuring. Between 1969 and 1986 the same single letters identified the Districts (2) as Divisions were renamed.

After the Newman Restructuring there were two letters identifying each Division, the first representing the letter of the former District (2) and the second the Divisional Station: thus CX = C for former C district, X for Charing Cross.

DIVISIONAL NUMBERS
Identifying numbers allocated to all officers on their posting to a Division, and now worn on the epaulettes of uniformed constables and Sergeants. The number comprises the Divisional letters followed by the digits of the officer's personal number.

Commissioner Sir Edmund Henderson's cancellation of the petty restriction denying policemen the right to wear beards stipulated that, when worn, they must not obscure the divisional number (originally embroidered on tunic collars).

The Police Federation has, from time to time, indicated that they would like them to be abandoned, but the public is assumed to value this means of identifying all officers on duty should they wish to report, favourably or unfavourably, on their activities. The alternative of an obligatory nameplate has been rejected on the grounds of exposing officers to the threat of intimidation since their home address could be established more easily.

DIVISIONAL STATION
Alternative title for a police station which also accommodates the Divisional Headquarters.

DIXON OF DOCK GREEN
Popular BBC Television series, running from 1955 to 1976. Its 376 episodes constitute the longest-running police series on television. Revolved around the central character of PC (from 1961 Sergeant) George Dixon, played by Jack Warner, a role he had created in the film *The Blue Lamp*. Essentially

concerned itself with the policeman's on-duty and professional character, giving a very positive and benign image of both. This fitted well with the public's approval of the 'bobby on the beat', though by the time the series reached its last years, the sentimental characterization (typical of the wartime and postwar 'united community' attitudes of the 1940s film-makers who created the original Dixon) had come to seem unconvincing.

DOCKS Prior to WWI, Metropolitan police station charge rooms were equipped with iron docks in which arrestees were placed to face the station officer's desk and be charged. These were frequently resented, and led to disputes and occasional struggles. Complaints about the docks were made to the Royal Commission, 1908. Commissioner Sir Edward Henry abolished them, and Walter Hambrook (subsequently first head of the Flying Squad) observed that the simple change to the request 'Please take a seat' effected a major and lasting reform in charge-room manners. An example of a station dock is held at the Historical Museum.

DOCKYARDS Apart from special wartime duties, the Metropolitan Police held responsibility for patrolling

POLICING THE CHATHAM DOCKYARDS IN THE 1890s.

Royal Naval Dockyards outside the Metropolitan Police District for differing periods from 1860 on, and for Woolwich Dockyard from 1841–1926. The release of officers from Woolwich, Rosyth (policed since 1914) and Pembroke Docks in 1926 made up the manpower urgently needed later that year to police the General Strike.

In addition, Metropolitan officers policed Chatham Docks until 1932, Portsmouth until 1933 and Devonport until 1934.

DOG SECTION Branch CO54 Specialists Dogs (i.e. 'sniffer dogs') is an operational command unit, based at Nine Elms. The more familiar German shepherd 'police dogs', though trained at Keston, which is part of the Training Branch designated P9(6), work with their handlers under the Operations OCU of each Area. The term 'Section' emerged without deliberate thought and has survived by tradition (cf. Youth and Community Sections for another widespread territorially based group using the collective noun).

The section started experimentally with three Labradors in 1946. Col. De Chair, No.1 Dis-

trict's Chief Constable, was its original head and Captain W. B. Kent, former Chief Instructor of the Army Dog Training School, was provisionally appointed for a year as expert adviser and director of training. His provisional appointment was renewed for another year, and another, after which it was clear that the Dog Section had proved its worth and was here to stay.

Col. de Chair was succeeded in 1950 by Captain Rymer-Jones. By 1952 the public was aware of the Labrador Ben's prowess, and in 1956 this was compared with that of the German Shepherd Rex III. (See Police dogs for the various

breeds used.) When the Keston Police Dog Training Establishment was set up in 1954, there were
120 operational Metropolitan police dogs. In
1959 Mr T. E. Mahir AC D took over, enjoying
the strong support of Sir Joseph Simpson who,
when Chief Constable of Surrey, had been an
enthusiast for police dogs, kept his own hounds,
and successfully introduced Dobermanns and
German shepherds to that force. Simpson found
a Metropolitan Dog Section of 182 dogs. It had
risen to 240 by the time of his death in 1968.
Today it stands at 298 German shepherd dogs
and 30 springer spaniel 'sniffer' dogs who are
based at Nine Elms.

Dog-handlers are volunteers with at least two
years experience in uniform. They are screened
for the suitability of their homes, since they will
be allocated 12-week-old puppies to make part
of their family if they pass a two-week aptitude
testing course.

Dogs are trained by their handlers at the
same time as handlers are trained by instructors.
Both visit Keston monthly for regular health and
aptitude tests. The dogs learn normal obedience
to commands; proceed to master tracking over
different terrains; then are taught to search buildings or open spaces and bark when they have
found the object they are looking for. Finally
comes criminal man-management. They have to
learn to chase and control a fugitive or a small
group. If possible, the dog will circle the arrestee
or arrestees to keep them in place while the handler shouts directions. If this proves impossible,
the dog jumps to seize the right arm in its mouth.
It learns to do this while under threat from sticks,
or guns. The training method is essentially based
on kindness and reward, never on physical punishment. The total training lasts for about a year,
and costs something in the region of £6000.

Since 1958 it has been agreed that dogs
should not police political demonstrations. They
are inappropriate for crowd control in all but the
least threatening situations. Crowds can overrun
dogs, and dogs can panic members of crowds.

Sniffer dogs, tails wagging enthusiastically,
can successfully search a building in half an hour,

GERMAN SHEPHERD DOG WITH HANDLER UNDER THE
STATUE OF QUEEN BOUDICCA AT WESTMINSTER BRIDGE.

POLICE WOLSELEY 14 HORSEPOWER CARS ON THE SKID PAN AT PEEL CENTRE, c. 1945.

whereas a whole team of officers might take several hours. And the dogs do not disarrange places where there is nothing concealed.

The dogs are often brought to sieges or to support cordons surrounding premises where dangerous criminals have taken cover. See also Queenie, Yerba.

DOMESTIC VIOLENCE UNIT Est. 1988. A small team of officers who follow up reports of violence between spouses or partners with a view to giving better support for the victim, and better information about various forms of legal action, should the victim wish to proceed with it. See also Vulnerable Persons Unit.

DOWLING, VINCENT GEORGE (1785–1852) Journalist, who esteemed himself the originator of the plan for a London police force. Wrote for the *Star*, *Observer* and *Day*. Edited *Bell's Life*, 1824–52, and from 1840 issued *Fistiana*, the annual survey of boxing news.

Between 1812 and 1829 he wrote to successive Home Secretaries Sidmouth, Peel and Lansdowne, and published letters in *The Times*, the *Observer* and *Bell's Life*, recommending the establishment of a system of policing. In 1834 he made the claim to the Parliamentary Committee on the Police that Peel's system was 'in letter and in spirit' exactly that which he had submitted to Lord Lansdowne.

DRIVER TRAINING SCHOOL The Metropolitan Police Driver Training School was established in converted aircraft hangars next to Hendon Police College in 1934. Commissioner Lord Trenchard called in Sir Malcolm Campbell, holder of the world land speed record, to advise on the necessary vehicles, garaging and equipment. In 1937, Mark Everard Pepys, sixth Earl of Cottenham, who had made a name for himself as a racing driver and published books about motoring, was appointed civilian adviser to the Force Driving School. He threw himself into the task with gusto, worked out new and improved standards of advanced driving based on the 'defensive driving' now taught universally by good driving schools, and devised training programmes which still lie at the heart of the

Hendon's courses. In recognition, the training track at Hendon is called the Cottenham Drive.

In 1970, the Hendon Training centre acquired an old sign-manufacturing building on Aerodrome Road, adjacent to the estate and just in front of Cottenham Drive and the skid pans. This was converted to a fully multi-functional driving school, with its own petrol supply centre, washing bays and garages as well as classrooms, workshops, canteen and assembly hall.

The driving school now offers a range of 20 different courses, from simple driving instruction in cars and light or heavy motorcycles for provisional licence holders to advanced vehicle inspection and accident investigation. All types of vehicles which a police driver may be called upon to use are maintained, from motor cycles to rigid HGVs and the Z-wagon. There are instructors' courses and courses on the working and inspection of lorry and coach drivers' tachographs as well as local introductory courses conducted in the student's projected working Area and refresher courses for experienced advanced drivers.

The famous skid pans, beloved of film makers for the spectacular effects they can produce, are actually used first and foremost to train drivers how not to skid, as well as how to regain control from a skid. They are surfaced with all the types of road metalling a driver may encounter in London, and kept slick by being permanently washed down with water and eco-friendly vegetable oil. The cars used on them are given over-inflated tyres devoid of treads.

'Hendon trained' was once used in motoring circles as the acme of praise for driving skill. It still deserves to be.

DRUGS SQUAD Established by Commissioner Sir Joseph Simpson in 1963 as one of his six new specialist crime-fighting units in C1 Branch. Duties passed to Area CID teams under the Newman Restructuring (1985). Supported by the Drugs Desk in Criminal Intelligence, SO11. From 1998, under the direction of the Drugs Directorate, a Commander, a Superintendent and three Inspectors.

Drugs were a relatively unimportant part of police work until the 1960s. It was legal (if foolish) to take habituating narcotics for recreation until the 1920s. The 'Brilliant' Chang case (see Sergeant Goddard) led to a Dangerous Drugs Act 1965, but did not encourage imitative behaviour. It did encourage sensational and inaccurate press stories about drug abuse and its results, which for nearly 40 years also inhibited popular use of marijuana, cocaine and the opiate derivatives. The National Health Act provided for registered drug addicts to receive treatment from their doctors which could entail a controlled supply of the drug to which they were addicted. This allowed them to earn a living satisfactorily, and may have contributed to the relative lack of professional drug traffickers making serious inroads into Britain.

In the 1960s the picture changed. A handful of irresponsible doctors persisted in overprescribing to addicts, which led to a small street sale of dangerous drugs. Influenced by irresponsible celebrities, increasing numbers of young

people discovered that marijuana did not have the frightening effects described in lurid stories, and so came to disbelieve all warnings about drug abuse. The pharmaceutical industry developed a broader range of tranquillizers, stimulants and other drugs with mind-altering effects, and a press campaign led to the Dangerous Drugs Act of 1967 which barred treatment of addicts by controlled prescription of their drugs, opening the door to international drug trafficking just at the time when organized crime in America was abandoning a policy of avoiding it. Since then, London's drug problem has expanded dramatically until, today, it is estimated that about 50% of robbery and assault is drug-related.

Metropolitan Police action against criminal drug dealing in London takes the form of intelligence gathering by covert investigators, followed by raids carried out by uniformed police, Territorial Support Groups, Authorised Firearms Officers and dog handlers. Covert officers characteristically present themselves as would-be buyers, thus avoiding the dangers of seeming to connive at the transportation of illegal substances. (Cf. 'Whispering Squad'.) Since crack cocaine joined heroin as a highly dangerous drug commonly bought, two of the Met's largest covert operations have been the prelude to drug raids: Operation Welwyn, which targeted the King's Cross area in 1991, and Operation Philosopher in Soho in 1999. The latter resulted in raids on 16 addresses and the arrest of 29 out of 30 people identified by the covert officers.

'DUE PROCESS' Shortened form of 'Due process of law'. One side of an ongoing debate about the best way for the police to secure necessary effectiveness and public confidence 'Due Process' or 'Crime Control'.

The 'Due Process' argument is that the public will prefer rigid adherence to the rules of the criminal justice system. This is seen as a guarantee against any suspicion of malpractices. Such thinking led to the replacement of judges' rules and other guidelines with the statutory PACE. Proponents of 'Due Process' maintain that any breach of rules should normally lead to acquit-

tal of wrongdoers in court, thereby forcing the police to adhere rigidly to the prescribed criminal justice procedures. The fact that police always stick to the rules, rather than trying to 'make the system work' should lead to greater public cooperation and willingness to give evidence in court to support prosecutions, and greater Government willingness to rationalize police powers when there is a demonstrated need. Thus Due Process, it is claimed, really offers more effective crime control than can be provided by those who claim that the end justifies the means by which a wrongdoer is deservedly convicted.

The converse view is that a system overweighted in favour of protecting the innocent perpetrates injustice by letting the guilty walk the streets to offend again. See PACE.

DUNNE, PC PATRICK (1949–1993) Policeman shot dead by crack cocaine dealers when going to investigate a reported disturbance.

Patrick Dunne trained as a maths teacher, and taught successfully for 18 years before joining the Met in 1990, attracted by community policing. On patrol in Clapham on 20 October 1993 he was advised that a disturbance had been reported in Cato Road. On going to investigate, he apparently interrupted a violent episode involving a gun or guns wielded by 'Yardies' (Jamaican drug dealers). When PC Dunne intervened, he was callously shot and killed on the spot.

The brutal murder of an officer whose entire life had been dedicated to service of the community in one way or another brought home to the public the intolerable new levels of violence and cruelty habitually employed by street drug dealers. The police were already aware that 57 crack-related murders had taken place across the country (mainly in the north and Midlands) in the space of three years. Nevertheless, the ruthless murder of an officer carrying out his duty sent a deep shock through the Service, and officers investigating the case were intensely frustrated when the DPP decided there was insufficient evidence to bring the three men they charged to court.

EAGLE HUT Large wooden structure erected during WWI by the YMCA as rest and recreation facility for American and Canadian servicemen. Sited between Aldwych and the Strand, where Bush House now stands. Taken over by the Metropolitan Police and continued to be used at first as rest and recreation facility; later as temporary overflow accommodation for training recruits in the aftermath of the war, when the flood of applicants was too great for Peel House (2). In 1934, transferred to Hendon Police College as one of two huts housing the Detective Training School. See also Battle of Bow Street.

ECHO (D.1993) Police horse injured by IRA bombing outrage.

At 11.00 a.m. on 20 July 1982, a bomb set by the IRA was exploded near Apsley Gate, Hyde Park Corner, with the intention of murdering and injuring as many as possible of a detachment of the Blues and Royals proceeding to guard duty in Whitehall. Three troopers and seven horses were killed by the 11kg (25lb) of gelignite encased in 13.5kg (30lb) of nails, concealed in a parked car.

PC John Davis, riding Echo as rear escort, was seriously injured by a nail embedded in his shoulder. Echo received severe wounds in the neck and abdomen. Both recovered, receiving hundreds of letters and cards from well-wishers, and a great many gifts of confectionery for Echo. Sugar lumps, carrots, apples, and the proceeds of £100 cash sent in were distributed among other horses at Imber Court.

When Echo returned to duty the following year, he was found to be suffering from stress in traffic. He was therefore retired to a horses' rest home in Aylesbury, where he died peacefully 10 years later.

EDGAR, PC NATHANAEL, (1915–1948) Aid to CID murdered on duty by a burglar he was questioning.

Joined Met, September 1939 (Warrant No. 128263). Divisional No. Y 807, performing normal duties at Muswell Hill Station. Rating, RN, 1943–6. Returned to Y Division on demobilization, serving as Aid to CID from time to time.

Twice commended by District Commander for arrest of thieves in 1947.

In January 1948, a sudden spate of housebreaking and burglary in Highgate, Southgate and Winchmore Hill led to the deployment of an extra squad of Aids to CID from the Y Division uniformed branch. PC Edgar partnered PC John McPartlan (Y 559) on 13 February, and at about 7.00 p.m. the two observed a man acting suspiciously in Wynchgate, and followed him to Oaklands Avenue, where they lost sight of him. At 7.20 they separated to search the Oaklands Estate.

At about 8.15, several people in Wade's Hill heard three shots, and looked out in the road without seeing anything. However, Mrs Elizabeth Laing and her brother Mr James Baillie, out walking in Broadfields Avenue, Winchmore Hill, saw a man running from Wade's Hill immediately after the shots, and on going to investigate found PC Edgar lying in the garage driveway of No. 112, groaning and bleeding. A local doctor hurried to the spot and administered morphine to PC Edgar, whom he found to have been shot twice in the right thigh and once in the lower abdomen. He then accompanied him in the ambulance to the North Middlesex Hospital, where PC Edgar died at 9.30 p.m.

His notebook contained one fresh entry that read, 'M[r] Thomas (Donald), 247 Cambridge Road, Enfield, BEAH 252/7.' The figures were an Identity Card number, war-time Identity Cards remaining in use while postwar rationing continued. It was quickly established that this entry described Donald George Thomas, a 22-year-old who had deserted from the army shortly before the end of the war, served two years'

imprisonment when caught, and deserted again on being released and returned to his unit.

The public appeal for information as to Thomas's whereabouts was the first to use the formula that he was 'urgently wanted to help the police with their inquiries', rather than the potentially prejudicial statement that he was wanted for murder. In response, Mr Stanley Winkless of Camberwell reported that his wife had left home three weeks previously, and he believed she had gone with Thomas. When the Press Bureau persuaded national newspapers to publish a picture of Mrs Winkless, a Mr and Mrs Smeed who kept a boarding house in Clapham told War Reserve PC George Searle (L 103) that they believed Thomas and Mrs Winkless were among their lodgers. WRPC Searle telephoned the Information Room and kept watch on the Smeeds' house, 16 Mayflower Road, until the arrival of an area patrol car with three constables. When Inspector William Moody (L Division) joined them, he, WRPC Searle, and Constables Dennis Wheeler (L98) and Robert Hide (L 359), went quietly upstairs with Mrs Smeed as she knocked on Thomas's room door. When Thomas came to the door they burst in and grappled with him to remove the loaded .33 Luger automatic pistol he pulled out from under the pillow.

Thomas was convicted of PC Edgar's murder, but as the House of Commons was debating the abolition of capital punishment at the time his death sentence was commuted to life imprisonment. The case played its part in the debate and contributed to the short-lived 1957 Homicide Act, which reserved capital punishment for certain specific types of murder only, including murder by shooting, and the murder of a police officer or prison officer in the course of their duties.

PC Edgar's death at the hand of a young tearaway (albeit when serving in plain clothes) inspired the plot of the film *The Blue Lamp*, whence the occasional suggestion that he was 'the original' of *Dixon of Dock Green*. In 1998, on the 50th anniversary of his murder, a plaque to his memory was placed in Muswell Hill Police Station on the initiative of his brother, Mr David Edgar, who was an ardent supporter of the police on the Greenwich Police Consultative Group. Mr

A YOUNG LADY OFFERS A SWEET TO PC ROSE ON 14 JANUARY 1920, WHEN LORD ROSEBERY FORMALLY PRESENTED INSCRIBED WATCHES OR MEDALLIONS TO OFFICERS INVOLVED IN THE EPSOM SIEGE.

Edgar was willing to pay for the plaque himself, but this seemed inappropriate to the local police, and funds were raised after an appeal to the Police Federation and the Friends of the Metropolitan Police Museum.

'EIGHT BY EIGHT' Restructuring of Areas and Divisions recommended by PA Management Consultancy in 1968. This would have replaced the existing 23 Divisions and their Sub-Divisions, and divided them between eight Districts, each divided into eight Divisions. It was never introduced exactly, but Sir Kenneth Newman's Restructuring in 1985 was extremely similar.

EPSOM POLICE STATION SIEGE, 1919
Riot by Canadian soldiers in which a policeman was killed.

On 17 June 1919, Major Bird, commanding the Canadian Army Convalescent Centre at Woodcote Park, telephoned Epsom Police Station to warn the duty officer that about 300 men had gone into the town for the evening, some-

thing which had caused friction with local residents in the past. Between 9.00 and 9.30 p.m., police were called to the Rifleman pub in East Street, Epsom, where they ejected Canadian servicemen who were causing a disturbance and arrested Private McDonald of the Canadian Army Service Corps. As four constables took him back to the police station on Ashley Road, Driver Veinotte tried to intervene, so they arrested him, too. About 20 Canadians followed them, threatening to release the prisoners, but they dispersed after some argument. Inspector Pawley locked the men in the cells which were in a yard beside the very attractive police station, a two-storey Victorian country villa with a railed front garden, and held men from the day shift in the station to reinforce the night shift in case of trouble.

After an hour's peace and quiet, a bugle call sounding 'Assembly' was heard, and a lot of shouting ensued. Inspector Pawley telephoned Woodcote Park, asking Major Bird to send forces to collect the prisoners. He also telephoned surrounding Divisions asking for strong police reinforcements.

Major Ross from Woodcote Park arrived on the scene and found about 400 men, mostly armed with sticks and fence palings, shouting a demand for the prisoners' release. A small cordon of police officers stood in front of the building. Major Ross told the men to go home, and said he would take charge of McDonald and Veinotte. The rioting soldiers ignored him, and started throwing stones at the police station windows. Ross and the police retreated into the station, whereupon the mob battered down the garden railings and smashed every pane of glass in the front of the building. As a few reinforcements arrived, climbing over garden walls and entering furtively through the rear of the building, Major Ross was smuggled out by the same way. By now some of the soldiers had forced their way into the side yard and jemmied open a cell door to release one of the prisoners.

After a consultation with Station Sergeant Thomas Green (V87, Warrant No. 80417), Pawley led the 15 officers under his command out in a baton charge. They cleared the garden but were forced back by the weight of numbers on the

street, and retreated into the station again. When they were inside, they realized that Sergeant Green (who was wearing civilian clothes) was no longer with them. He had been struck down by a heavy blow across the head. Some of the Canadians moved him into a nearby house, and from there he was sent on to Dorking Road Infirmary, where he died early the following morning.

Major Ross now returned to the station and made it clear to the men that he would take charge of the prisoners. A bugle sounded again, and the rioters withdrew. The whole affair had lasted about an hour, and well after it was over, 100 police reinforcements arrived from Surbiton and Wandsworth on bicycles.

Nine men were arrested to be put on trial for riot and manslaughter. In the event, no evidence was brought against two who were able to prove that their presence in Epsom was nothing to do with drinking and rioting. Bugler Todd, who was believed to have started and finished the affray with his signals, succeeded in persuading the court that he had only sounded 'fall in' on Major Ross's request. A military policeman called McAllan was acquitted after testifying that he had been leaving as soon as he saw the nature of the disturbance, but was hit over the head. The other five were convicted of riot but cleared of manslaughter and imprisoned for a year. Epsom was declared out of bounds to Canadian troops, and the Canadian Red Cross made one of the first large donations to the fund set up for Sergeant Green's widow.

The 24 police officers who had held the fort were rewarded with gold watches and chains presented by Lord Rosebery (a resident of the Division). Hundreds of policemen from all over London came to Sergeant Green's funeral. He had been a very popular man, with 24 years' service and the expectation of retiring the following year. More than 1000 people lined the route to pay their respects.

In 1929, Allan McMaster, who had been one of the five imprisoned rioters, was arrested by the police in Winnipeg and confessed that he had killed Green, hitting him over the head with an iron bar wrenched from a cell window. Winnipeg cabled the information to Scotland Yard, but since McMaster had already been tried and acquitted of Green's manslaughter, there was no action that could be taken. He died in 1939.

ESDA See Forensic Science Laboratory.

EVANS, SUPERINTENDENT JAMES (1779–1856) Longest-serving member of the River Police.

Joined the Marine Police as an assistant surveyor on its formation in 1798; promoted to surveyor, 1801. Chief Boat Surveyor, 1821–39. On the absorption of the Marine Police by the Metropolitan Police he became Superintendent, commanding Thames Division until his retirement on full pension in 1848. He had served an unbroken 50 years in the River Police and he

EPSOM POLICE STATION, DAMAGED BY RIOTING CANADIAN SOLDIERS IN 1919.

handed over its command to his son, Superintendent John Christopher Evans. In 1853, Charles Dickens found his portrait hanging in the charge-room of Thames Division's headquarters at 259 Wapping High Street.

EVEREST, DET SGT FREDERICK (B.1877)

Carried out largest single-handed arrest in the history of the Met. Joined the Metropolitan Police, 16 January 1899 (Warrant No. 84785) after being employed by his father in Sutton, and made a Detective Constable in 1902.

In August 1914, Sergeant Everest was in Special Branch on port duty in Folkestone Docks. On learning of the outbreak of war he signalled the Chief Constable of Folkestone that able-bodied Germans were hastening to the continent to take up arms. He recommended stopping them on the Sunday after War was declared. The Chief Constable demurred, believing that another four days had to be allowed for repatriation. But, with guarded permission, Everest acted on his own initiative. He persuaded the railway authorities (with difficulty) to stop the boat train and allow him to segregate physically fit German and Austrian men from women, children, the old and infirm, and other nationalities. Then, with the Kaiser's and Emperor's potential conscripts penned up on the docks, he sent the boat train on its way, and summoned soldiers from Shorncliffe Barracks to take over the (still unbroken) record 250 prisoners he had arrested. His temerity won him instant promotion to Detective Inspector.

EXPLOSIVES OFFICERS

Bomb disposal experts, recruited from former members of the Royal Army Ordnance Corps (now the Royal Logistics Corps) and attached to the Civil Staff. They are respected and admired throughout the Service for their undoubted courage and heroism in their lonely and exposed role in making safe the bombs left by murderous terrorists.

Protected by safety helmets and suits which only serve to ward off fragments, the 'bomb doctors' take charge of the immediate vicinity of a suspected dangerous explosive device, and risk their lives every time they proceed to investigate

ILLUSTRATED SUNDAY HERALD, MARCH 2, 1924.

250 FUGITIVES TRAPPED BY ONE MA[N]

Record Single-handed Coup that Earned Immedia[te] Promotion for C.I.D. Officer: Bold and Ingenious Mov[e]

To arrest 250 men on one's own initiative, and in the face of grave doubts as to t[he] advisability of the course on the part of one's immediate chief, is an adventure which f[ew] officers in the police service would care to risk.

That was a bold step that was taken, three days after the war broke out, by Dete[c]tive-Inspector Fred Everest, then a sergeant at Folkestone, now just retired from Sc[ot]land Yard after a quarter of a century's service.

The story of his exploit, which has hitherto been hidden from the public, forms one of the most daring records of individual enterprise in police history (writes an *Illustrated Sunday Herald* Special Commissioner). It was the biggest haul ever effected by one officer.

It was on the Sunday following the declaration of war that the coup was made. Realising that able-bodied Germans were hastening back to the Fatherland to take up arms, Mr. Everest, a sergeant in the Folkestone C.I.D., approached the local chief constable and suggested prompt action. That officer, however, after consulting the emergency instructions issued from headquarters, decided that four more days must elapse before such drastic steps as the sergeant proposed could be taken. Sergeant Everest placed a different interpretation on the orders, and obtained his chief's permission to act at his own discretion, though no assistance was given him

Sergeant Everest's next step was to try to persuade the railway officials to stop the boat train

INSPECTOR EVEREST.

between the Junction and the Harbour stat[ion]. Again obstacles were placed in his way.

"It has never been done before," one of [them] protested. Eventually the detective had his [way] —after promising to take full responsibility.

The plan was to stop the train just before [the] terminus, at a point where a huge iron door st[ood] as a protection against the tide. A numbe[r of] wooden barriers were erected to shut off a[ccess] to the boat side.

When the train arrived Sergeant Everest [sta]tioned two ship stewards, who spoke Ger[m]an: Austrian, at the barrier to examine passports. British subjects and neutrals diverted round the barrier to the boat side, all the physically fit German and Austrian were shepherded into an enclosure bounde[d by] the iron door on one side and the sea on [the] other. Their womenfolk were allowed to pro[ceed.]

At a signal from the sergeant the boat ste[amed] out, and the imprisoned men began to sho[w an] ugly temper. There was no help available [and] Sergeant Everest telephoned to the nearest [camp] —Shorncliffe—and asked for some troops, [who] speedily arrived and took over the prisoners.

On news of the coup reaching headquarter[s the] Chief Commissioner's personal thanks were [con]veyed to Sergeant Everest, who was immedi[ately] made an inspector.

He once saved Mr. and Mrs. Asquith from [the] attentions of a crowd of angry fishwives in [——]shire, and was himself pelted with bags of [flour] and red ochre by the infuriated women.

and, if possible, dismantle it. Two were killed in the course of the 1972–98 IRA terrorist campaign: Captain Roger Goad GC BEM, killed instantly by a bomb he was starting to handle in Kensington Church Street in 1975, and Mr Ken Howorth GM, killed by the explosion of a bomb in an Oxford Street Wimpy Bar in 1981.

In addition to dismantling or detonating terrorist devices under controlled conditions, explosives officers may also be called to deal with unexploded WWII bombs and ordnance discovered in the Metropolitan Police District. They were originally employed by the Forensic Science Laboratory.

EXTRADITION AND PASSPORT UNIT – ORGANISED CRIME GROUP

A unit in the Organised Crime Group which, since the restructuring of 1996, has carried out the duties

PRESS REPORT OF DETECTIVE SERGEANT EVEREST'S MASS ARREST OF ALIENS IN 1914.

of the one-time A3 Branch for Aliens' Deportation, together with those of the former C1 Branch handling Passports and Commonwealth Immigrants.

This unit facilitates all extradition requests seeking the arrest of any person thought to be located within the United Kingdom, Channel Islands and the Isle of Man.

Its other responsibilities are to investigate allegations of a serious and complex nature involving passsport and immigration offences where the level of criminality is highly organized, to facilitate removal of illegal immigrants where requested by the Home Office and to facilitate overseas requests for judicial assistance.

FABIAN, DET-SUPT ROBERT HONEY
KPM (1901–1978) Born 1901 in Ladywell, Robert Fabian joined the Metropolitan Police on 11 July 1921 (Warrant No. 111858), went to West End Central, and soon joined the CID.

Awarded no fewer than 40 Commissioner's commendations, he became most famous for his exploit, in 1939, of pulling to pieces an IRA bomb in Piccadilly, for which he was awarded the King's Police Medal.

His formidable reputation as an investigator, largely based in the West End, included his involvement in 1926 in catching the killer of Charles the Acrobat, the leader of a French vice gang. He later solved the murder of Alec Antiquis, killed during a jewel robbery off Tottenham Court Road, by tracing a ticket found in the lining of a raincoat.

After his retirement in 1949 he became involved in broadcasting, wrote two books about his career and was the subject of 39 'Fabian of the Yard' films.

FAIRFAX, DET-SGT FREDERICK WILLIAM,
GC (1917–1998) Hero of the Bentley and Craig incident, at which PC Sidney Miles was murdered.

Born in Westminster. After elementary education, worked as a bank messenger until joining the Met, 1936. Warrant No. 125235. Posted to L Division (Lambeth). 1940–5, served with the Royal Berkshires, attaining rank of Captain. 1946, rejoined Met, posted to Z Division (Croydon). Transferred CID, 1947. Sergeant, 1952, and transferred to C Division (Westminster) following the Craig/Bentley incident. George Cross, 1953. Returned to Z Division, 1954. Long service and Good Conduct Medal, 1958. Retired, 1962.

Fairfax was shot in the shoulder by Craig but continued in his attempt to arrest him, finally walking straight towards him until Craig ran out of ammunition. Commissioner Sir Harold Scott visited him in hospital the next day and found him remarkably modest about his courage in facing down a wildly dangerous armed criminal after he had been wounded. In fact, Fairfax was far more concerned about Sidney Miles's death, and the consequences for his family.

Constable Fairfax was immediately promoted to Sergeant for his part in the affair, and

received the George Cross in the next honours list – the highest of the five awards earned by policemen who contributed to the arrests of Craig and Bentley.

For subsequent attempts to denigrate Sergeant Fairfax's good name, (along with those of PCs Harrison and MacDonald) in the interest of overturning their evidence against Derek Bentley, see under PC Sidney Miles, PC Claude Raymond Pain. In 1998 the Court of Appeal quashed Bentley's conviction for murder on the grounds that the trial judge had not conducted the trial fairly.

FEDERATION
Police Federation: representative body for all officers below the rank of Superintendent, authorized to put the position of Constables, Sergeants and Inspectors in discussions and negotiations over pay and conditions of service.

Formed by the Act of Parliament with the approval of Commissioner Sir Nevil Macready in 1919, the Federation was deliberately fashioned to out-manoeuvre NUPPO, the unapproved Union of Police and Prison Officers which had called the successful Police Strike, 1918. In the hope that the Federation would prove amenable to management control, it was forbidden to be a Union, to ally itself with the TUC, to call strikes or initiate any other industrial action, and to intervene in disciplinary matters. In the hope that it would be further weakened, Macready's proposal of separate Branch Boards for the three ranks was adopted.

The aim of destroying NUPPO was achieved. By law, no other organization is permitted to undertake the Federation's function. But the Federation did not prove a toothless watchdog: from time to time it annoyed management by vociferously putting rank and file opinion, although it has never attempted to exceed its powers by calling for industrial action. Without attempting to interfere in disciplinary matters, it provides legal aid and advice to members facing disciplinary proceedings, and its representations have played an important part in securing protection for officers against disciplinary action without strong proof of justification.

Membership is compulsory but subscriptions are voluntary: there are approximately 26,000 members in the Metropolitan Branch. Representatives of the Constables', Sergeants' and Inspectors' Branch Boards come together in the Joint Executive Committee whose decisions become Federation Branch policy. All major stations have a Federation Rep, who looks after the local and individual needs of members much as a union shop steward or rep would.

FENIANS
Nineteenth-century Irish Nationalist terrorists organized in 1858 as the Irish Republican Brotherhood in Ireland and in 1867 as the Clan na Gael in America. The name derives from old Irish 'Fianna', legendary Irish warriors whose name became an Irish term for soldiers.

Their activities in the MPD included the Clerkenwell Bombing, the Scotland Yard Bombing and a plot to plant a bomb in Westminster Abbey at Queen Victoria's Jubilee Service of 1887. This last was completely foiled by excellent covert work masterminded by James Monro, Robert Anderson and Adolphus Williamson. Anderson and Monro also monitored legitimate and constitutional Irish Nationalist MPs' associations with American Clan na Gael members who raised money for the various terror campaigns. Though the clandestine surveillance was both necessary and useful, it contributed to Scotland Yard's unpopularity with radical journalists in the late 1880s, who saw it as a threat to civil liberties.

The activities of the Fenians led to the formation of Special Branch (initially the Special Irish Branch) as the first specialist operational Sub-Division of the CID.

Bureau, and he in turn was ably supported by Detective Sergeant Charles Stockley Collins and Detective Constable Frederick Hunt. These officers were originally posted to the Anthropometry Department within Scotland Yard and were trained by Henry to put into practice his system of classifying, filing and searching sets of fingerprints. The system immediately proved so successful in confirming the identities of convicted and habitual criminals that the Department was expanded by the addition of five more officers within a few months. The Commissioner, Sir Edward Bradford, then terminated the practice of sending police officers to 'observe' convicts entering prison with a view to memorizing their appearance for identification purposes. At this stage, the taking of fingerprints was the responsibility of the Prison Service. Scotland Yard merely held them as records, catalogued them on the Henry system, and made the necessary matching comparisons for identification purposes.

The conviction of the burglar Harry Jackson in June 1902 showed that the use of fingerprints was to become even more famous as a method of detection. The only evidence against Jackson was his dirty fingermarks on the window sill of a house in Denmark Hill from which he had stolen billiard balls. Prisoner identification, however, remained the principal use of fingerprinting and by the end of 1902, 1722 matches had been made establishing prisoners' identities: 400 more than had been achieved in six years of Bertillonage as used in the Anthropometry Department.

When Edward Henry became Commissioner the following year, his successor as Assistant Commissioner (Crime), Melville Macnaghten, encouraged Fingerprint Bureau officers to accompany divisional detectives seeking out pickpockets at the Epsom Derby. Taking and searching their fingerprints established the identities of habitual offenders so successfully that fingerprint officers from Scotland Yard went to the races regularly for the next few years to carry out this task.

The Stratton brothers' conviction for murder in 1905 led to some controversy, the medical profession tending to feel that doctors, and not

FIELDING, SIR JOHN (1721–1780)

Blind magistrate who established the model for the first Police Divisions.

SIR JOHN FIELDING.

In addition to perfecting and establishing his brother Henry's Bow Street Runners, Fielding published a weekly list of wanted criminals which his successor renamed *Hue and Cry* – the basis of the *Police Gazette*.

FINGERPRINT BUREAU SO3(1)

This Branch of the Directorate of Identification holds a collection of about 300,000 sets of fingerprints (3,000,000 individual fingerprints) which are rapidly accessed and retrieved by computer for purposes of comparison by Civil Staff fingerprint experts using visual display technology. Staff also have access to the Police National Computer and the National Fingerprint Collection of approximately 4,750,000 sets of fingerprints (47,500,000 individual fingerprints) which is managed by the National Fingerprint Office, part of NIS, the National Identification Service, which extends the search and comparison of fingerprint records with fingermarks from crime scenes.

The Fingerprint Bureau was founded on 1 July 1901 by Edward (later Sir Edward) Henry who had been appointed as Assistant Commissioner (Crime) a few months earlier. He selected Detective Inspector Charles Stedman to head the

policemen, should undertake all fingerprinting. But the Fingerprint Bureau (as the Department was already being called colloquially) was winning Scotland Yard its reputation as the greatest detective force in the world, overtaking the Paris Sureté, whose lead in blood typing was offset by its continuing reliance on Bertillonage. William Pinkerton, who with his brother had taken over direction of the famous Private Detective Agency from their father Allen, called the Fingerprint Bureau 'one of the most marvellous departments I have ever examined'.

In 1908 Detective Inspector Stedman retired, and DI Collins became Head of the Bureau, which had been made an independent branch the previous year, as opposed to being a subsection of the Habitual Criminals Register. In 1913 the police were given the right to take fingerprints when they charged a suspect (given the permission of a magistrate). This had the beneficial effect of allowing a prisoner's previous convictions to be put before the bench at a first hearing, instead of waiting for a long investigation while he was remanded in custody. It also meant that a great many more prints were added to the records, since Prison Guidelines prohibited taking fingerprints from convicts sentenced to less than one month's jail. Defendants who received non-custodial sentences did not have their prints recorded. However, the larger collection became too unwieldy for satisfactory accessing for crime detection as the Henry system classified complete sets of fingerprints rather than individual prints. In 1918 there were 300,000 criminals with their prints held by the Criminal Records Office, but not one crime that year was solved by fingerprint evidence.

Collins addressed this problem by using a very successful code he devised in 1921 for sending fingerprint data by telegraph. His new system for identifying single prints remained in use for eight years, though it was itself handicapped by a cumbersome search process. In 1928, Detective Chief Inspector Harry Battley, who had become Head of the Bureau, started work with Detective Sergeant Fred Cherrill to perfect the new method of single fingerprint classification, using a magnifying glass marked with concentric rings, and noting the relative positions of fixed recurrent points in the five general types of pattern found in fingerprints. Adding codings for ridge counts between the points, and classifying known offenders by types of crime, ultimately produced a reliable and impressive system under which Scotland Yard could determine within 24 hours whether a print sent for comparison was on their records. Battley's book *Single Fingerprints* was published by HMSO in 1930.

Cherrill, who subsequently became Head of the Bureau (1938–53), left a reputation as the greatest of all fingerprint officers. Fascinated by the fact of fingerprints ever since seeing his own, as a child, in the floury dust of an old mill, he had an unerring eye for the easily overlooked mark and an astonishing memory for prints he had seen more than once, so that he could often recognize familiar villain's prints on the spot, and only refer back to the records for confirmation.

Fred Cherrill was skilled at the deductive work required of fingerprint officers, estimating from its position on a particular object just which finger of which hand was likely to have left its mark. Even without clear prints to guide him, he was able to assess accurately that the indistinct marks impressed on the throat of Mrs Evelyn Hamilton, first victim of Gordon Cummins, the 'blackout ripper', were made by a left-handed man. His textbook *The Fingerprint System at Scotland Yard* (published by HMSO) replaced Henry's *Classification and Uses of Fingerprints* as the basic manual on the subject. During his 33 years with the Bureau he personally investigated the fingerprint details of practically all the most famous criminal cases between 1930 and 1953 and he testified in nearly all the great murder trials. He was thanked by J. Edgar Hoover for the help he gave FBI agents in Europe, and he enjoyed a cup of tea with mass murderer J. R. H. Christie when looking for fingerprints around the bodies of Beryl and Jeraldine Evans in Rillington Place. His retirement a year or so earlier than was absolutely necessary contradicted the expectation that he would stay with the work he loved until the last possible moment. It was prompted by his deep distaste for the decision to replace attested detective officers with Civil Staff in the Fingerprint Bureau. He was proud to be a policeman and knew he would have continued to serve in the Met even had he not had the good luck to win appointment to the bureau handling his personal passion.

The decision to civilianize the Bureau was taken in 1951: ironically the 50th anniversary of its foundation, when its first head, DI Stedman, sent a cheery note to the reunion dinner regretting that he was too infirm to attend without a couple of nurses. But at the same time extreme manpower shortage, aggravated by the inadequate Oaksey pay settlement, led Sir Harold Scott to look for all possible means of keeping experienced and trained police officers doing the basic work of policing and relieving them of any duties which could be undertaken by civil staff. In Cherrill's opinion this was tantamount to inviting the armed services to accept civilian technicians to replace the Royal Engineers, and although it took 28 years for the last attested officer to be phased out of the Fingerprint Bureau, Cherrill declined to oversee the start of the process.

It did not, however, lead to any diminution of the bureau's excellence. New and complex technical processes for making latent prints visible were developed. (See Fingerprinting.) In the early 1960s Detective Superintendent Gerald Lambourne (who served the Bureau with the dedication of Cherrill) masterminded the computerization of the National Fingerprint Collection. This dealt with the problems of slow, manual search and retrieval, posed by a collection of 1,813,156 fingerprints interrogated daily by approximately 550 inquiries. In 1970, 'LIFTS', finger and palm marks developed by application of aluminium powder and lifted on to clear plastic by means of special adhesive tape for preservation purposes, became acceptable as evidence before the courts.

Before he retired as the Bureau's Head (1975–80), Commander Lambourne introduced a glove print identification system which proved successful as evidence of a criminal's presence at a crime scene. Commander Paddy O'Neill was the last attested Head of Bureau, 1980–1.

In 2001 the Bureau celebrates its centenary. The Civil Staff will justifiably congratulate themselves on having maintained the great reputation established by their attested predecessors.

FINGERPRINTING Vital means of positive identification of individuals, resting on each person's uniquely different patterns of papillary ridges following the lines of sweat glands and pores on the balls of fingers and thumbs (as, indeed, over the entire palms of the hands and soles of the feet and balls of the toes). Often alleged to have been used before the Common Era by Chinese potters to 'sign' their work, but modern studies suggest that this was not the case: the fingerprints found in Chinese pottery were made accidentally.

In 1823, anatomist Professor Johann Purkinje published a paper suggesting that fingerprints were unique to individuals, and offering a descriptive classification which was too compli-cated to be of any practical value. In 1859, Indian civil servant William Herschell (later Sir William, grandson of the astronomer of the same name) routinely took the fingermarks of native pensioners as receipt 'signatures' to prevent fraudulent claims. With a large file of fingerprints, and checks on his own prints over a period of four years, he came independently to the conclusion that each man's fingerprints were unique and did not alter over the years. So, more intuitively, did Dr Henry Faulds, who used a set of sooty fingerprints left at a scene of crime in Japan to clear a suspected burglar. Faulds's article on the subject in *Nature* attracted the attention of Francis Galton, who used Herschell's data and his own studies in 1892 to establish on a scientific basis that fingerprints retained their unique details unchanged from birth to death. Galton estimated that the odds against any two individuals having identical sets of fingerprints – even identical twins – were 1 in 64,000 million. And in 1895 Galton devised a new system of classification. Unfortunately this was still too complicated for practical use, though he did realize that fingerprint patterns could be divided into three obvious varieties, 'arches', 'loops' and 'whorls', with a fourth variety, 'Composite', which was a combination of two or more of the others.

POLICE OFFICERS DEMONSTRATE THE TAKING OF FINGERPRINTS IN AROUND 1930.

The Troup Committee of 1893 recommended that fingerprints be included with anthropometric records which it felt Scotland Yard should keep. But there was still no effective way of sorting through the mass of recorded fingerprints to find matches with a suspect's.

In Calcutta in 1896, Edward Henry, Inspector General of the Bengal Police and a member of the Indian Civil Service, conferred with Galton while on home leave, and on his return to India, with assistance from two of his most able officers, Hemchandra Bose and Azizul Hacque, worked out a really practicable system of classification. (This is fully explained in Fred Cherrill's *Cherrill of the Yard*, and very clearly with diagrams in Sir Harold Scott's *Scotland Yard*.) Within the 1,024 possible combinations of ten paired fingers with or without loops and arches in each one of each pair, Henry then subdivided further by such details as the direction in which a loop, arch or whorl sloped, and the numbers of ridges between the centre of the loop and the base angle of the delta.

Henry's system, described in his book *Classification and Uses of Fingerprints* (1900) was adopted by the Government of India as a textbook, and when his home leave in 1900 coincided with the Belper Committee's sittings, he was able to demonstrate the superiority of his system to Bertillonage.

After his appointment to Scotland Yard and establishment of the Fingerprint Bureau in 1901, his system quickly proved its worth. Pickpockets arrested at Epsom on Derby Day normally gave false identities and claimed to be first offenders. Henry's classification system meant that 29 of the 54 arrested and fingerprinted in 1902 could be shown from the fingerprints with their anthropometry records to have previous convictions, and the number of prisoners over the year whose previous convictions and true identities were established from the records more than trebled the previous year's.

Accurate identification of men with criminal records was and is the primary purpose of maintaining fingerprint records, though fingermarks are also important clues for detectives. As statisticians have calculated that the odds against any two people having matching sets of fingerprints are actually 1 septillion (1,000,000,000,000, 000,000,000,000) to 1, the system is very reliable. Moreover it is cheap and easy to carry out. An ink pad, clean paper, a magnifying glass, and

THE SYSTEM OF IDENTIFYING CRIMINALS BY FINGER-PRINTS.

MORE INFALLIBLE THAN FACIAL IDENTIFICATION: SCOTLAND YARD'S REGISTRATION OF CRIMINALS' FINGER-PRINTS.

AN ILLUSTRATED PRESS ACCOUNT OF THE FINGERPRINT SYSTEM, PUBLISHED IN THE ILLUSTRATED LONDON NEWS.

a classifier who does not require any previous scientific training are the only prerequisites for building up a collection.

The fingerprints held on record are rolled and plain impressions. The finger being printed is rolled from edge to edge so as to reveal the maximum area of fingerprint pattern. Immediately after the rolled impressions have been taken, the plain impressions of the left and right hands are taken. The simultaneous imposition of the unrolled fingers of each hand are taken in boxes below those of the rolled impressions. These are to ensure that officer error does not lead to any mistake as to which fingerprint belongs to which finger.

When it was found in 1906 that identifiable fingerprints can be taken from dead bodies, an important means of tracing the unrecognizable or anonymous victims of accidents and disasters had been established.

Fingerprints at crime scenes fall into three categories: impressions in some soft surface (such as putty or drying paint), a mark left by a finger dirtied with blood, oil, or some other transferable substance, and 'latent' prints, left simply by the sweat on the finger, and sometimes initially invisible. To make the latter visible at the scene of the crime, fingerprint powders were traditionally used. Dark graphite powder enhanced prints on light non-absorbent surfaces (like white gloss paint). A grey powder was used on dark gloss surfaces, glass or silver. It was called *Hydrargyrum cum creta* – Latin for 'mercury with chalk' – which it literally was, one part of mercury by weight being pounded with two parts of chalk by a pestle and mortar. Simple powdered chalk was used on gold, which would have been adversely affected by the mercury. When enhanced, the fingerprints were traditionally photographed *in situ*, and enlarged pictures taken for examination.

Porous materials bearing latent fingerprints (untreated wood, paper, etc.) had to be taken back to the laboratory and treated with chemical reagents which reacted with certain constituents in sweat to leave a visible mark (for example iodine fumes which react with grease content, ninhydrin which reacts with amino acid, or silver nitrate which reacts with chlorides). After the discovery of ninhydrin in Sweden in 1954, it was found to be the most efficient of all porous-sur-

face print developers, and virtually replaced the others. To develop latent fingerprints on plastics, which do not respond well to powders, silver nitrate or ninhydrin, a process for the vacuum deposition of thin films of metal was developed, either a single deposit of lead or deposits of silver or gold followed by zinc or cadmium producing the best results. Heavy-duty coloured adhesive tape (often used to wrap axe handles, gun-butts, explosive devices and the like) can be developed by placing articles in an airtight chamber with radioactive sulphur dioxide. This does not render latent prints visible, but it allows them to be developed on X-ray films after being placed next to them for a predetermined period of time. Embossed or water-saturated papers can also have fingerprints brought to light by being treated with silver deposits which, if still not clear enough to photograph, may be placed in a radioactive developer solution and imaged on X-ray films in the same way.

'Lifting' latent fingermarks by transferring powder impressions on to sticky tape (like a less strongly adhesive sellotape) was for a long time forbidden in Scotland Yard. It was felt that judges and juries would not be convinced that the marks were genuine if they were not demonstrably photographed *in situ* or produced on objects where they still showed up. But in 1970, when the number of objects in store threatened to overwhelm available space at Scotland Yard, and there were not enough photographers to see that every single fingermark at a crime scene was photographed *in situ*, lifting prints became standard practice, and the actual lifted finger and palm marks are now produced in court as evidence. Coupled with direct reaction photographic exposure of lifts from their transparent tape (cutting out the negative stage), this is estimated to have reduced the cost of fingerprinting evidence by 75%.

The likelihood of fraudulent production of prints is negligible, since as in all cases where 'framing' by police technicians is postulated, the number of people necessarily involved in any such conspiracy would make it completely impracticable.

In 1974 the Fingerprint Society was founded in Britain, and now comprises 2839 members from law enforcement agencies all over the

world. In 1995 the Society raised funds for the expensive and honourable task of restoring Sir Edward Henry's dilapidated granite grave.

In 1979, on the 150th anniversary of the Metropolitan Police, the Queen and the Duke of Edinburgh had their thumbprints taken for a commemorative certificate.

FIREARMS Although Britain's unarmed police are a matter of national pride, and envied by many countries whose police habitually carry visible sidearms, firearms have always been maintained as a part of the Metropolitan Police supplies for emergencies and certain special duties. Between 1884 and 1936, constables in the outer Divisions were permitted to carry revolvers on ordinary night beat duty if they wished and were given their Superintendent's permission. Since 1967, special training has been given to selected officers, and today there are about 2000 Authorised Firearms Officers, of whom about 50 are Specialist Firearms Officers of the Firearms Unit.

At the Force's foundation in 1829, 50 flintlock police pistols were included in the initial requisition. In 1836 the Bow Street Mounted Patrol became the Metropolitan Mounted Police and retained their pistols and cutlasses for the next 30 years. In 1839, when the River Police were amalgamated with the Met, their blunderbusses were turned in, but pistols were retained at Wapping to be drawn when needed for special guard duties.

In 1868, following the Clerkenwell Bombing, 622 Adams's Breech Loading .450 revolvers were supplied from army stores in the Tower of London, and passed to Divisions to be kept under lock and key by Superintendents.

The murders of PCs Atkins and Cole in 1881 and 1882, and the attempted murder of PC Patrick Boans (PC 519V, Warrant No. 67807, promoted to Sergeant on 1 November 1883 without having to pass an examination and given a £10 reward) by two burglars who shot their way out of arrest in 1883 led to a press campaign to arm the police. In the still pertinent words of the *Evening Standard*, 'It is not only foolish but absolutely cruel to send Policemen to combat men possessed of revolvers, without any arm

AN OFFICER WITH FIREARMS SEIZED BY POLICE.

enable them to defend their lives.' Reports from Superintendents that constables had no wish to be armed proved to be severely distorted by those same Superintendents' unwillingness to be held accountable for any mishap with firearms. Sir William Harcourt (1827–1904), the political bruiser of a Liberal Home Secretary, confirmed his own suspicion that constables felt very differently when he insisted that they be polled, and 4430 out of 6325 officers serving night beats in the outer Divisions asked for revolvers.

A total of 931 Webley 'Metropolitan Police Revolvers' were ordered to replace the old Adams's, and sent out to the Divisions. At the same time, formal pistol training was given to officers who expected to carry them, though neither the training nor the revolvers were satisfactory by modern standards. Both caused a number of accidents, and the Webleys remained in service until 1914, by which time the majority were defective and dangerous. Strict regulations governed the use of revolvers, whose issue and return at the beginning and end of duty had to be entered in the Occurrence Book, which recorded every significant incident on the Division. They were to be worn in holsters on the right of the belt, in front of the truncheon, and were only to be taken out for the same right of self defence as any civilian member of the public enjoyed at that date.

Different Divisions made different use of the new privilege. N Division (Islington and Stoke Newington), whose Superintendent had been vociferously opposed to firearms for patrols, had only two applicants, presumably because constables feared his hostility. Y Division (Highgate and Wood Green), on the other hand, sent 110 constables for pistol training with the Middlesex Rifle Volunteers, and 311 men out of 519 in R Division (Greenwich) asked for pistols.

On 18 February 1887, PC Henry Owen (P161, Warrant No. 52206), became the first Metropolitan policeman to fire a revolver while on duty. He fired six shots in the air to waken the inhabitants of a burning house in Keston Village, after shouting, hammering on their door, and blowing his whistle had failed to rouse them.

By 1893 the fashion for carrying handguns on night duty in the outer suburbs was dying out, and many of the pistols were returned to the

other than a short club. If the law will not protect the Police by heavy penalties from armed resistance, they should at least have weapons to

Receiver's store. In 1904, two serious accidents at the range led R Division's Superintendent to inspect newly issued weapons very carefully, and return the majority for grave defects. This led to a recall of 324 weapons for refitting. At the same time, the Receiver discovered that many Divisions were holding far more pistols than the inventories suggested. In New Scotland Yard itself, 27 revolvers had been officially issued. Yet CO returned 68 to store and retained 25! In all this bad record-keeping, the Met had somehow lost three revolvers which were never traced.

After the Siege of Sidney Street had exposed the Met's incompetent marksmanship and inadequate weaponry, 1000 .32 Webley & Scott self-loading (colloquially 'automatic') pistols were ordered, and delivery was taken in 1912. Yet when the war broke out in 1914, 281 of the dangerous old Metropolitan Police Revolvers were brought out of retirement and reissued.

In 1920 they were replaced by 300 new pistols. By this time the .32 automatics purchased in 1911 were also becoming dangerous, and many would fire even when the safety catch was on. New pistols were purchased, and issued to men mounting road blocks and guarding important buildings during the IRA scare of 1921. Attitudes to their maintenance and their whereabouts were somewhat blasé under Commissioner Sir William Horwood and AC C Sir Wyndham Childs, who vaguely thought it 'a good idea' to have pistols around, as there were 'plenty of Irish gunmen still knocking about London'. PC Arthur Thorp (later Chief Superintendent i/c the Fraud Squad) recalled being sent to guard a building at this time with a loaded Webley pistol, although he had no idea how to use it. In the 1920s, a policeman committed suicide with a pistol he had abstracted from his annual firearms practice, and R Division lost another gun without trace.

Lord Trenchard standardized the issue of firearms to 10 pistols with 320 rounds of ammunition per Divisional Station, 6 pistols with 192 rounds per Sub-Divisional Station, and 3 pistols with 96 rounds in each Sectional Station. Sir Philip Game finally ended the right of outer Division officers to carry handguns on night patrols, and issued ancient Canadian WWI rifles as well as additional pistols for duties during WWII. Their

use was explicitly restricted to guarding vulnerable properties against sabotage and important police stations against enemy invasion. The police were not to be used as an additional fighting force in the case of invasion, though armed motor patrols, especially in unbuilt-up areas, were authorized to assist in the arrest of enemy parachutists.

ARMED POLICEMAN ON DUTY GUARDING PUBLIC BUILDINGS DURING THE GENERAL STRIKE IN 1926.

The murder of PC Sidney Miles by Bentley and Craig in 1952 led to exaggerated press reports of a high-powered gun-battle on the rooftops with 'police marksmen' firing back at the robbers.

This led to the speculation 40 years later that Miles had been accidentally killed by 'friendly fire'. All such claims are nonsense. There were no police marksmen at that date, and the pistols drawn from Divisional HQ did not arrive until after Miles's death. Nevertheless, the case led to a re-examination of the Met's armaments, 15% of which were found to be dangerously defective. Lengthy discussions finally resulted in Special Branch and Royalty Protection duty officers being issued with Beretta automatics to wear in shoulder holsters, and new .38 Webley and Scotts with 100mm (4in) barrels being supplied to Divisions.

The Shepherd's Bush murders in 1966 proved a turning point. A little earlier, 100 variegated weapons surrendered in a public amnesty for unlicensed firearms were found to have drifted semi-officially into police use, of which 25% were defective and dangerous. When Harry Roberts, the armed murderer who had killed Sergeant Head and DC Wombwell was being hunted in Epping Forest, it transpired that few of the armed officers had any experience in handling their weapons, and one CID man, at great risk to his future enjoyment of life, had stuffed a loaded pistol with its safety catch off into the waistband of his trousers.

Thereupon Sir Joseph Simpson sent 10 officers for small arms training with the SAS, and as instructors attached to Branch D6 (Civil Defence, subsequently renumbered D11, PT17, SO19) they became the nucleus of the Firearms Wing, which would ultimately grow into the Force Firearms Unit. Sniper training with military instructors ensured that there would for the future be efficient police marksmen for appropriate situations. They proved their worth covering the Balcombe Street Siege.

Smith & Wesson Model 10 .38 six-shot revolvers were accepted as the standard sidearm in 1974. They had been continuously manufactured since 1899, and all glitches had been worked out. Glock 9mm Model 17 self-loading pistols, holding 17 rounds in the magazine, subsequently became the 'automatic' of choice, and all AFOs were given detailed and proper training in the use and safe maintenance of their weapons. This was the more important, as renewed IRA and other terrorist activity led to the (essentially preventive) posting of highly visible officers with carbines and flak jackets at Heathrow Airport. The Heckler & Koch MP5 Carbines they carried fired a 9mm bullet held in a 30-round magazine. Such carbines are preferred to rifles for crowd protection situations, because they are less likely to fire a bullet right through the main target to injure an innocent bystander. For the same reason, soft-nosed ammunition – not quite as intensely dangerous as the illegal hollow-nosed dum dum – is preferred to the full metal jacket. The Met's carbines are always fixed at single shot – there is no question of ever spraying targets with rapid-fire bullets. Rifles are only used by police marksmen in appropriate situations where the target has caused or is justifiably believed to be about to cause the death of innocent victims. Marksmen are armed with Steyr SSG Police .308 counter-sniper rifles, which may be fitted with telescopic sights and night image intensifiers. In all cases, officers are strictly instructed to use firearms only as a very last resort to save life.

The Stephen Waldorf incident of 1983 (coupled with incidents in other forces) led to much public questioning of police use of firearms. The principal lessons learnt by the Met were the need for thorough planning and briefing for firearms operations, a clear command structure, and the need to deal with the dangers of stress likely to affect individual officers' judgements under pressure. Two years later a team from D11 carried out the Met's first successful hostage situation resolution by a police marksman, rescuing five-year-old Carlene Charles from her distraught and besieged step-uncle who had killed her mother and started to attack the little girl with a bread-knife. Accurate shooting that enabled him to be arrested before he could cause more serious injuries to Carlene justified the expenditure of time and manpower on skilled weapons training.

The recurrent danger to patrolling police officers' lives whenever criminals take to using firearms means that whether or not police should be routinely armed is one of the commonest ongoing debates inside the force. The need to protect officers, either by arms or by really effective deterrent penalties, quite properly links this to the debate on capital punishment. Majority opinions within the force change from time to time, and tend to be sharply influenced by recent events and crime patterns. But perhaps the most significant statistic on the Met's intensified need for and economical use of firearms at the end of the 20th century came in 1987. In that year, Authorised Firearms Officers went out armed to more than 1750 incidents, and used their weapons just three times.

FIREARMS OFFICER The term almost invariably now means Firearms Officer attached to the Force Firearms Unit, although about 2000 officers are trained and authorized to use firearms (AFOs).

FIREARMS UNIT (SO19) Started in 1966 as the Firearms Wing of D6 (subsequently D11) Civil Defence and Communications Branch, following the traumatic Shepherd's Bush murders of three unarmed policemen. Originally 10 officers, given special training by army instructors, who then themselves became instructors to Authorised Firearms Officers. Today, approximately 50 Specialist Firearms Officers (SFOs) are divided into teams of seven constables under the command of a Sergeant.

'FIRM WITHIN A FIRM' Slightly misquoted phrase to describe former CID autonomy and improper networking within the Met, and consequent opportunities to escape investigation.

The Times Corruption Allegations (1969) are probably best remembered for the taped remarks of Detective Sergeant John Symonds in a conversation with a young thief from Peckham. They proved a shocking revelation of corrupt association taken for granted and apparently corrupt assistance promised in the most avuncular way, coupled with dismissive contempt for honest provincial police forces: 'Don't forget to let me know straight away if you need anything because I know people everywhere. Because I'm a little firm in a firm. Don't matter where, anywhere in London I can get on the phone to someone I know I can trust, that talks the same as me . . . If you are nicked anywhere in London . . . I can get on the blower to someone in my firm who will know someone somewhere who can get something done. But out in the sticks they are all country coppers aren't they? All old swedes and that.'

FIRST OF MAY GROUP Late 1960s anti-Franco terrorist group in London which carried out a gun attack on the Spanish Embassy and bombing attacks on the offices of Spanish banks and Iberia Airlines before disbanding and passing equipment and some members on to the Angry Brigade.

FIVE-A-SIDE FOOTBALL Annual competition for youngsters organized by the Community Safety and Partnership Portfolio as positive youth work. Financially sponsored by the Midland Bank. Started in 1979 with the strong encouragement of Commissioner Sir David McNee. Probably the largest ever five-a-side competition, the finals took place at Wembley Arena. An early example of a major tournament encouraging football for girls and young women. Terminated in 1991.

FIXED POINTS (1) Points on beat patrols where constables were required to meet their Section Sergeants to report occurrences and confirm that they were carrying out their patrols.

(2) Positions where, after 1870, officers were stationed in view of the public, with orders not to move from their post. This was Commissioner Sir Edmund Henderson's response to public perception that with the increase in London's population and housing density it was no longer possible to be sure that a policeman on beat patrol could be found within a few minutes anywhere in central London. By the end of 1871, 270 fixed points manned night and day had been established, a few of them furnished with fixed point boxes (like sentry boxes) which were themselves the forerunners of police boxes. Despite occasional snags (like the officer who refused to leave his post to come and investigate the discovery of one of Jack the Ripper's victims) the system proved successful, and was continued until the installation of police boxes made fixed point duty unnecessary, except for officers directing traffic at major crossroads. By the time traffic lights and mini-roundabouts had

obviated the need for police directing traffic, variations in the forms of patrol (Unit beats, panda cars), meant that the public no longer expected to find a police officer on foot readily available, and unless an officer is placed to limit access to a specific location (on diplomatic protection duty, for example, or at scenes of crimes under investigation) it is unlikely that posting to a fixed point will occur.

A curious side-effect of the fixed-point system was the stratagems undertaken by officers to avoid stiffness and circulatory problems caused by standing motionless for long periods. All kinds of surreptitious shuffling and muscle-tensing were employed, and it is believed that this included the curious minimal knees-bend-and-straighten which became a popular part of stock stage representation of uniformed policemen's demeanour.

FLETCHER, WPC YVONNE (1959–1984) Murdered by 'diplomats' from the Libyan People's Bureau.

Daughter of a Wiltshire timber merchant.

TRAFFIC POINT CONSTABLE SALUTING AN INSPECTOR IN THE LATE 1940s.

WPC YVONNE FLETCHER.

Joined the Met, 1977. At 159cm (5ft 2¾ in) tall she was said to be Britain's smallest police officer. On 17 April 1984, she was sent with a detachment of 30 officers to police St James's Square where a demonstration was to take place organized by Libyan dissidents opposed to Col. Muammar Gaddafi's regime and his public execution of two student critics in Tripoli. The Libyan People's Bureau, staffed since February by Gaddafian extremists rather than orthodox diplomats, had warned the police that they intended counter-measures, but nobody expected that this would exceed the counter-demonstration in support of Gaddafi that arrived. The police kept the hostile groups apart on opposite sides of the road with crash barriers and their own physical presence.

Shortly after 10.00 a.m. the People's Bureau started playing loud amplified music to drown the shouts of the 75 or so masked anti-Gaddaffi demonstrators. At 10.18, shots rang out from the bureau's first floor, injuring several demonstrators and fatally striking Yvonne Fletcher in the back. She was rushed to hospital, but died soon after arrival. Her police hat and four men's helmets remained in the roadway, shown repeatedly on television news and in newspaper photographs over the next 11 days, during which time armed police held the occupants of the bureau in the longest police siege ever maintained in London, while negotiators and diplomats tried

to persuade the occupants to give themselves up. On the eleventh day, shortly before Yvonne's funeral, a young policeman ran out under the guns to retrieve her hat.

Despite the wish of the entire country to see the murderers brought to justice, and the government's severance of all diplomatic relations with Libya when Gaddafi made a posturing pretence that he was disgusted by Britain's refusal to let his 'diplomats' come and go, it was felt that the law of diplomatic immunity could not be overturned, even in this extreme case. And so, despite some press protest, the murderers were allowed to leave England on the day Yvonne was buried. The case led to the institution of the Police Memorial Trust at the instigation of Michael Winner, and a memorial in St James's square was unveiled by Prime Minister Margaret Thatcher.

In 1999 the Libyan government apologised for the incident.

FLYING SQUAD Essentially concerned with the detection and prevention of armed robbery and related professional crime, about 180 CID officers, with branches at Tower Bridge, Finchley, Barnes and Rigg Approach, Leyton, divided into small squads of about 12 mixed Detective Sergeants and constables, each squad commanded by an Inspector. The expert drivers, crucial to the work of the Squad, are drawn from outstanding

'THE BEDSTEAD': A 1923 FLYING SQUAD CROSSLEY TENDER WITH ITS RADIO AERIAL RAISED.

INVICTA 4.5 LITRE TOURER AS USED BY THE FLYING
SQUAD AROUND 1930.

uniformed police drivers, and are given the honorary title of Detective Constable while they serve with the Squad.

The Squad is not confined territorially to working within Divisions or Areas. They respond to radio reports of serious armed robberies from Scotland Yard (as do Divisional response cars) and arrange ambushes and arrests to prevent robberies whose planning has been reported by informants. Many of the squad, which includes women, are Authorised Firearms Officers. They wear a distinctive tie with the squad's swooping eagle logo.

Originally 'the Mobile Patrol Experiment' (1919–20). From c.1921 accepted the nickname 'Flying Squad', as a small unit of Branch C1, Central CID. Reorganized and enlarged throughout the 1920s. In 1929, with the Home Secretary's approval, given an establishment of 40 officers under a Detective Superintendent of C1 Branch. In 1948 given independent status as Branch C8. 1978–81, merged and renamed Central Robbery Squad. Thereafter officially accepted as the Flying Squad. Nicknames: 'Heavy Mob', 'the Sweeney'.

The Squad was formed on a one-year experimental basis by Commissioner Sir Nevil Macready in October 1919. Inspector Walter Hambrook was given command of 12 detectives with a roving commission to travel from place to place in the MPD, maintaining surveillance for crime on the streets from a horse-drawn canvas-covered Great Western Railway van with spy-holes cut in the side. On seeing known housebreakers or pickpockets, they were to leave the van and proceed on foot to make arrests if the occasion warranted. When not travelling and surveilling from the van, they were to frequent known criminal hang-outs in pubs and clubs, maintaining observation on the clientele and cultivating informants. All members of the Squad were known to have excellent contacts with and knowledge of criminals in their own Divisions. Thus a small group of officers combined to pool their knowledge and enjoy metropolis-wide familiarity with the underworld 'faces'.

The experiment was deemed a success, and extended. The Mobile Unit was held to have contributed greatly to the 7% fall in all kinds of thefts in the MPD, and its future was assured. Thereafter it expanded steadily. In 1920, two large Crossley tenders were bought from the demobilized Royal Flying Corps to replace the horse and wagon, though such thieves as had acquired cars for the newly invented 'smash and grab' raids could easily outrace the lumbering Crossleys.

In 1923 a radio transmitting station was installed on the roof of Scotland Yard and receiving apparatus set up in one of the Crossleys. The transmission was in Morse code and the vehicle had to stop to receive it. The aerial was a cumbersome contraption on the van roof, which slowed the vehicle down and earned it the nickname 'the bedstead'. But the value of directing the mobile unit from Scotland Yard proved itself immediately, and the second Crossley was also given its 'bedstead'. For camouflage purposes, the aerials could be lowered flat to the roof when not in use.

With ex-naval radio operators managing the wireless telegraphy in the vans, and ex-RFC drivers expertly handling the two improved Crossleys that were added to the fleet, the squad started to develop the ethos of tough armed service-type camaraderie which would characterize it over several decades. In 1927 it became truly 'flying' at last, when the Crossleys were supplemented by Lea Francis convertibles with good acceleration to a top speed of 75mph. The drivers were given special training at Brooklands motor racetrack. The Lea Francises, which used a series of interchangeable number plates and varied colours to prevent criminals' recognizing them, were dubbed Q-cars by the press, and the name stuck for unmarked proactive CID patrol cars. In 1929 the six expert drivers of the squad agreed that a slightly heavier vehicle would be useful, as the Lea Francises were vulnerable to ramming by villains in cars with stronger chassis, so Invictas capable of 90mph were purchased.

Wensley, as Chief Constable, rated their integrity so high that he selected the squad's commander, Chief Inspector 'Nutty' Sharpe, to put things straight in the Sergeant Goddard corruption case. Sharpe and his team evidently found the duty of raiding night clubs somewhat *infra dig*, and although they enforced them, were not convinced of the usefulness of laws prohibiting the sale of alcohol after certain hours, or the exhibition of mildly erotic cabaret. (Cf. Lee Commission.) According to Sharpe's and other memoirs, the squad was developing a curious intimacy and sympathy with 'decent' old-fashioned professional criminals, who would fist-fight or cudgel their way out of trouble if they could, but never used knives or guns; who were unresentful of justified arrests, and bore no malice when rules were slightly bent to ensure convictions in 'a fair cop'. This paid dividends in the cultivation of informants, and the squad's clear-up rate of serious crime was so impressive that it acquired extremely high status, and was perceived by itself and others as the *élite* branch of the CID, matched in the public eye only by those members of the Murder Squad who handled high-profile cases.

In 1935 the squad acquired the fleet of Railtons, capable of 100mph and exceptionally fast acceleration from stop to 60mph, which became their best-known vehicle. When demobbed criminals, anxious to return to their improper professions, accelerated the postwar crime wave, the Flying Squad was able to use its contacts in the press to sidestep Commissioner Sir Harold Scott's respect for austerity economies, and successfully campaigned for replacement of the Railtons, which had become worn out. Since then the squad has used a mix-

ture of car makes offering different types of high performance and reliability.

The short-lived but highly successful Ghost Squad was formed from members of the Flying Squad. Successes such as the Battle of Heathrow kept the Squad's prestige and reputation for fearless willingness to combat violent villains immensely high for the next 15 years, but questions were asked about their possibly improper relations with gangsters when neither Jack 'Spot' Comer nor his assailant Albert Dimes were convicted following their 1955 public knife fight in Frith Street, Soho. (In fairness to the Squad, it was not asked to participate in the arrests, and the case in court was muddied by a retired clergyman who was suborned by the gangsters to give perjured evidence which the jury accepted out of respect for his cloth.) The police recovered ground two years later when the work of Flying Squad detectives Tommy Butler and Peter Vibart secured the disbarment of lawyer Patrick Marrinan for improper association with Spot's rival Billy Hill, who had employed Dimes.

Given their knowledge of the underworld, the squad played some part in the gangbusting operations of the 1960s, and was largely responsible for the capture and conviction of most of the Great Train Robbers. A special 'Dip squad' with a roving licence to pursue pickpockets was established and scored a lot of convictions.

But its prestigious standing in the Force was starting to arouse resentment and scepticism. Why, it was wondered, had the Squad not been at the heart of the operations against the Krays and the Richardsons? (Actually, because such long-running retroactive investigations never fell within their remit. Flying Squad members were called in to assist with the arrests.) Why didn't Squadmen share their informants' intelligence with Divisional detectives, who were, in the end, pursuing the same criminals for the same reasons? (Some did, as a matter of fact. Others carried their miserliness with information to the extent of refusing to share it with fellow Squad members.) Membership of the squad has always required the courage and confidence to deal with violent and unorthodox villains, but has not always been to everyone's taste. DI Albert Wickstead was sceptical of the flexible, informant-dri-

ven methods of the squad and their relative freedom from protracted enquiries. Nevertheless, Wickstead deliberately drew several members of his special gangbusting squad from former Squadmen and had some serving Flying Squad officers seconded to his command.

The squad suffered, by association, an immense loss of prestige when its former Commander, Kenneth Drury, was charged with corrupt association with Soho businessman Jimmy Humphreys in the Obscene Publications Squad Corruption cases. The proceedings dragged on for five years, keeping the Squad's shame in the public eye. Many people thought that Sir Robert Mark's witticism, 'A good police force is one that catches more crooks than it employs' was directed at them. And for at least a decade thereafter, convicted criminals thought it well worth having a go at accusing Squad and other London police officers of 'fitting them up'. The press gleefully reported these charges, which culminated in the Operation Countryman investigation.

In 1978 the Flying Squad apparently disappeared, as it was merged with the special *ad hoc* robbery squad set up to deal with the supergrass investigations, and C8 was renamed the Central Robbery Squad. The 'Dip squad' was with difficulty persuaded that its time was over and forced to undertake other duties. But by 1981 the sentimental appeal of the old name revived, and C8 has been the Flying Squad ever since. Moreover, Commissioner Sir David McNee decided that enough was enough, and with the full approval of the A10 corruption investigation unit, the house-cleaning Assistant Commissioner C, Gilbert Kelland, and the outside support of the Director of Public Prosecutions Office, he took the conduct of Operation Countryman out of the hands of those provincial officers whom he believed to have started accepting any cock-and-bull story put forward by a disgruntled crook. While some cases of malpractice may have been evaded thereby, most observers agreed that far more mischievous cases of self-interested slander by villains were suppressed, and the Flying Squad started to look up again.

The use of supergrasses brought the squad a renewed run of major successes, and in many ways laid the foundations for the Squad's modern effectiveness against armed robbery. By the early 1970s, bank robberies and the routine use of firearms had started to become prevalent, and had replaced the older 'smash and grab' techniques. The Great Train Robbery of 1963 glamorized the image of the robber and across London there was a sharp increase in armed crime. During the 1960s the interior designs of banks seemed to make robbery easier for a period, and the abolition of capital punishment in 1965 probably removed a deterrent to the use of guns.

A £130,000 raid on the Wembley branch of Barclays Bank led to the first supergrass, one Bertie Smalls. In the late 1970s Detective Chief Inspector Tony Lundy made further refinements to the technique when he arrested David Smith and other professional armed robbers in northwest London. In the face of overwhelming evidence gained through patient intelligence-led investigation and surveillance, Smith made full and frank confessions to his entire criminal career and agreed to give evidence against his associates. This led to other members of the gang doing the same, and a large number of professional criminals were arrested, charged, and in most cases convicted and given lengthy prison sentences.

Perhaps the most spectacular, and dangerous, part of the Squad's work is the 'pavement ambush' where armed robbers are arrested in the act. Operation Yamato resulted in an armed robber, Kenny Baker, being shot dead by police in November 1990 at Woodhatch, Surrey, and Operation Char saw two armed robbers killed after they had shot at police when they were trapped trying to rob a post office in Harrow in 1987. But it is only rarely that police use firearms against bank robbers. Usually, speed and surprise win the day.

The Flying Squad has a proud history and is, without question, one of the most successful police squads in the UK. However much 'soft' policing may come into fashion as preferable to 'hard', there will always be a need for a strong and determined force like the Flying Squad, whose service to the public is directly confronting ruthless, greedy and violent criminal gangs.

FORDHAM, DC JOHN (D.1985) Officer killed while undertaking surveillance duties in connection with the Brinks-Mat robbery. Joined the Metropolitan Police in 1968 after service in Auckland City Police, New Zealand. Served at Bow Road, and joined CID 1974. Received four commendations over the next 11 years, and consistently refused to take promotion examinations in order to stay at 'the sharp end'.

In 1981, Fordham volunteered for a small unit of CII Criminal Intelligence which underwent special training with the SAS and the Royal Ulster Constabulary to undertake surveillance under conditions of extraordinary difficulty or physical hardship. Described by one senior officer as 'Britain's most experienced and best-trained surveillance operator', he shone at the work, once remaining up to his neck in water for 48 hours to keep observation.

In 1985 Fordham and DC Neil Murphy were directed to enter the property of Kenneth Noye, a receiver of stolen goods believed to be a principal in handling the bullion from the Brinks-Mat robbery. The 8 hectares (20 acres) of grounds around Noye's house at West Kingsdown, Kent, were surrounded by high barbed wire-topped walls and accessible only through electrically controlled gates. Rottweilers ran loose in them, but police dog handlers observing them via a hidden video camera assessed them as harmless domestic pets which should prove tractable if offered the yeast pellets Fordham and Murphy carried. Fordham and Murphy's function was to enter the grounds in camouflage costume and keep observation in case the occupants made an attempt to escape or to dispose of evidence when a large party of officers with search warrants entered the gates.

Tragically, the assessment of the dogs proved inaccurate. They scented Fordham and Murphy as soon as they entered the grounds, and surrounded them, barking and snarling. Murphy reported 'Dogs hostile' over his personal radio, and withdrew back over the wall. Fordham stood his ground, and reported, 'Someone out, halfway down drive, calling dogs'.

According to Kenneth Noye, he and his wife and a visitor, Brian Reader (who, like Noye, was subsequently convicted of handling the Brinks-Mat bullion), heard the dogs, and he seized a large kitchen knife he happened to have handy, and a shotgun, and went to investigate. Fordham, he said, was a sinister figure in camouflage combat fatigues with a balaclava helmet, who attacked him without declaring himself to be a police officer. In self-defence, Noye claimed he stabbed him 10 times with the kitchen knife, and Fordham died.

Noye and his wife and Brian Reader were all charged with DC Fordham's murder. Mrs Noye's defence team had Fordham's body examined by pathologist Dr Iain West, who reported that the injuries were consistent with the unarmed officer's being restrained by one man while another wielded the knife. It was particularly significant that there were no defensive wounds on the arms or hands, and some of the wounds were in the back. But before the case came to trial the prosecution decided to drop proceedings against Mrs Noye, and so Dr West's evidence was never revealed to the prosecutors nor heard by the jury.

Noye stuck to his story of having acted alone, and the defence exhibited a large photograph to suggest that an unarmed officer in camouflage fatigues with a balaclava helmet was such a frightening figure that any reasonable householder might have stabbed him repeatedly. Disregarding Noye's aggressive remark at the time of his arrest, 'He shouldn't have been on my property. I hope he dies,' the jury accepted his claim that he 'stabbed and stabbed in blind panic', and acquitted him. The Metropolitan Police were deeply shocked by the result, which seemed to reflect a very unhappy state of public mistrust for authority in the 1980s.

After serving his sentence for receiving stolen property, and making compulsory restoration of £3 million to Brinks-Mat, Kenneth Noye became subject to extradition proceedings from Spain in 1998 as the suspect in a 1995 'road rage' murder.

FORENSIC SCIENCE LABORATORY In 1929, Arthur Dixon, then Assistant Secretary at the Home Office and a keen amateur microscopist, proposed setting up police training in microscopy, physiology and medico-legal problems. The CID relied at the time on the assistance of scientists outside the Police Service, and Sergeant Cyril Cuthbert (described in the early days of the Laboratory as a 'scientific police-man') had developed a private collection of sci-entific apparatus at Scotland Yard. A commit-tee on detective work recommended the establishment of regional laboratories in 1933. In February 1934 Lord Trenchard wrote to the Home Secretary proposing the establishment of a scientific laboratory at Hendon Police College, and the employment of a scientific expert, at an approximate salary of £1200 per year, with two assistants.

During Trenchard's search for the right per-son for the post, he consulted the Deans of the Medical Schools, and in April 1934 saw Dr Roche Lynch. Trenchard's file note records that the eminent doctor 'was dead against a Police paid expert to give evidence in police courts and said that the public would not accept such evi-dence, nor would the judges. He said that scien-tific research of dust etc. was no good, and that it would never be accepted in this country; that what was done in France as regards dust, hairs etc. would not go down in England and would be laughed at'.

In the event Dr James Davidson from the Pathological Department of Edinburgh Universi-ty was selected to become the first Director, and the Laboratory was opened on 10 April 1935 by Home Secretary Sir John Gilmour. The staff numbered six.

The terms of reference included assistance in investigation of individual crimes, keeping in touch with scientific developments at home and abroad, referring to existing experts outside the Laboratory when required, undertaking research and educating the Force on relevant scientific matters.

The workload soon developed into the examination of blood and semen stains, abor-tion equipment, stomach contents to identify poisons, identification of alcohol in drinks to assist nightclub cases, jemmy marks, identifica-tion of explosives and ballistics. By the end of 1937 the Laboratory had dealt with 620 cases, approximately half of which emanated from the Metropolitan Police. Some civil cases were also dealt with. In one such case the Laboratory assisted a bereaved family of Chelmsford to prove that a Mr Laurence had died from lead

GATHERING FORENSIC EVIDENCE AT THE SCENE OF A SUSPICIOUS FIRE.

poisoning in paint during his work.

In 1946 Dr H. S. Holden, who had headed the Home Office Laboratory in Nottingham, replaced Davidson, and within five years he had re-established the Laboratory for postwar busi-ness and doubled the staff. In 1947 he brought in the redoubtable Margaret Pereira and another sci-entist who attracted attention when called to court as an expert witness by always wearing yel-low socks for sex cases and red socks for blood grouping cases. The use of coloured clothing has modern-day echoes: scientists now wear differ-ent-coloured overalls to signify whether they are dealing with suspect's or victim's exhibits as one of a series of measures to prevent contamination of items by minute fibres.

The Laboratory expanded in scope, staff, space and reputation, and in 1949 moved to the New Scotland Yard Norman Shaw building.

In 1965 it moved to Richbell Place, Holborn, and in 1974 to the current premises, where it occu-pies five floors of the Lambeth Support Head-quarters. Mr Nickolls replaced Dr Holden in 1951, and was in turn replaced successively by Drs Walls, Williams and Sheard. Dr Davidson was the only medically qualified doctor, the oth-ers being scientists.

Since 1 April 1996 the Met Laboratory's 600 staff have become part of the 2000 strong national Forensic Science Service, which has five other laboratories located around the UK.

Over the years, the original concept of the Laboratory has proved its excellence time and time again. London has provided the volume and seriousness of crime problems which have not only allowed expertise to develop but also justified special research. Some aspects of the workload have varied as crime patterns have changed, but the Laboratory has invariably been at the forefront of investigative methods and has developed a worldwide reputation as a centre of excellence.

Analysis of blood has developed remarkably since the early days because of the work of Margaret Pereira and Brian Culliford. By applying the advances of medical research to the science of identifying very precise blood groups from dried stains, the probability of a stain belonging to a suspect could be reduced to a low frequency in the population. In Victorian times a detective would go to court and simply give an opinion from experience about whether blood found at a scene was human or not. There was no scientific body of knowledge to back up the detective.

EARLY DAYS IN THE FORENSIC SCIENCE LABORATORY.

Nowadays the highly discriminating technique called DNA Profiling is used. It was first developed by Professor Alec Jeffreys in the mid-1980s and can be used effectively on all body samples including hair and bone. Current research techniques are working towards being able to obtain a DNA profile from a single cell. One of the differences noticed by long-serving scientists at the Laboratory is the small size of many of today's samples. No longer does the typical body sample arrive in a large sweet jar!

The first DNA database was launched by the Forensic Science Service in April 1995, and by 1999 matches between crime scenes and suspects numbered approximately 500 every week. The National Database in Birmingham currently holds over 480,000 samples from suspects, and over 40,000 profiles from scenes of crime awaiting the matching profile of criminals whose samples have not yet been brought into the system. In a rapidly accelerating workload, it receives 4000–5000 mouth swabs a week nationwide. The Met Laboratory alone received 1900 DNA

matches in 1998–9. Many of those matches have helped solve burglaries, as the system is not confined to serious cases of violence.

Rape cases have always been an area where scientific analysis has helped police investigations. Semen found in rape victims has identified suspects accurately even when a number of men have been involved in one incident. In medical research generally, there is not the same need to know how long semen remains in the vagina or other parts of the body, and no data was available. Volunteers from the Laboratory staff therefore had to conduct their own extra-mural research so that reliable data could be contributed to scientific knowledge. A database was developed of samples which established previously unidentified links between crimes. The work of Dr Frances Lewington MBE was of crucial importance in training Forensic Medical Examiners in how to take samples in rape cases. She gave valuable help in developing Victim Examination Suites to improve the facilities available for rape victims.

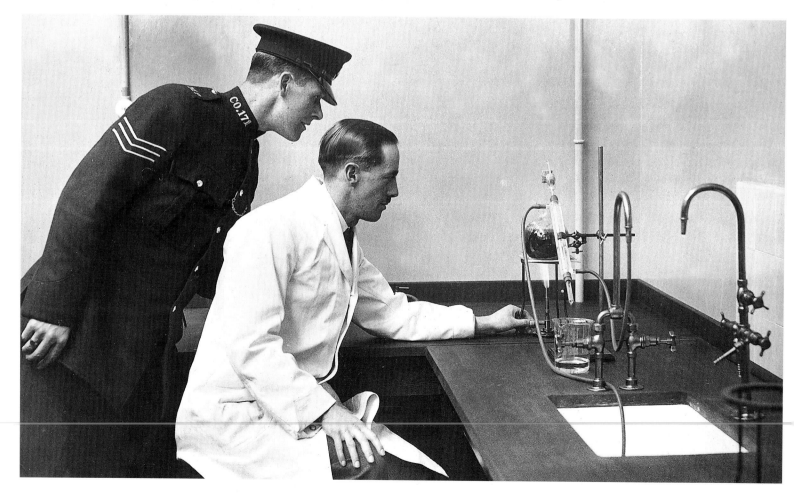

In violent sexual assault cases where no semen is found, the Laboratory techniques of analysis of fibres and hairs come into prominence. Many fibres can be matched because of the variations apparent in the dyes used to manufacture clothing. The same principle is applied to glass and paint samples. There is always some exchange from even the briefest of contact between two bodies, and the fundamental principle of Locard's Exchange Theory (whereby two bodies in contact with each other always leave behind traces on each other) has been proved many times.

GRIM, the glass refractive index measurement instrument which can determine the exact refraction of glass fragments for comparison with their possible sources, is one device developed by collaboration between the Laboratory, the Home Office and the manufacturers Foster and Freeman. The Laboratory also collaborated with manufacturers CAMSCAN to produce an automatic particle analysis system for the scanning electron microscope. Forensic Science laboratories worldwide have now adopted this. The Laboratory's *Biology Methods Manual* also became an established world reference book on how to analyse substances.

The developments of the Laboratory's techniques are also shown in relation to alcohol and the motorist. Before the Road Safety Act of 1967, the level of alcohol could be taken into account by the courts in determining whether a motorist's driving was impaired. The observations of the police doctor and the police officers about how the defendant could manage to walk along a white line, touch his or her own nose or perform other tasks was supported, when a sample was given, by the scientist who could relate the proportion of alcohol to a large number of other cases which had been submitted. There was no absolute alcohol limit for the motorist in those days, and scientists used to explain to judges their analysis by the equivalent number of pints of beer or measures of whisky drunk by the motorist.

The 1967 Act introduced compulsory samples from the roadside by means of Alcotest 80 devices. These contained a glass tube of crystals which would change colour progressively along its length according to the amount of alcohol in the motorist's breath. They were subsequently followed by blood or urine samples. By the mid-1970s they represented no fewer than 27,000 cases a year in London. Nowadays the workload has dropped to about 5000 a year, not because of fewer cases on the street, but because the Lion Alcometer roadside breath analyser is a more accurate screening device than the Alcotest 80. The Lion Intoximeter 3000 machine, introduced in 1983 at police stations, has drastically reduced the need for blood and urine samples. (They were due for replacement in the Met in 1998/9 by the new Intoximeter EC-IR.)

The actual analysis of a motorist's blood or urine sample has been refined by a gas chromatography process which takes only four minutes, providing a very quick response to any query where it is required to know how much alcohol is present in a person's blood.

The more recent concern over driving while under the influence of drugs is reflected in the Laboratory's involvement with monitoring the effectiveness of machines being developed for roadside drug testing. A screening test is currently available using sweat or saliva samples to provide a colour reaction visually similar to a pregnancy test, but full effectiveness will not be possible until a machine can screen for a number of different drugs in a rapid process. There will also be a problem of determining what limit of drugs in the body constitutes impairment, or whether a statutory limit should be set. Cannabis, for instance, may be detectable in the body for a number of weeks after consumption. Scientists are very properly reluctant to give opinions about interpretation and proof of impairment without research data. In the case of drink driving, the data came from the Grand Rapids Survey in Michigan, which found that at the level of 80mg of alcohol per 100 millilitres of blood, the probability of an accident was four times that when a motorist had no alcohol intake.

The drugs workload for the Laboratory has changed over the years. When drugs are mixed (or 'cut') with other substances it is sometimes possible to link samples as coming from the same supplier. There are always variations and unusual substances with which people are prone to experiment. The Purple Hearts of the 1960s have been overtaken by other amphetamines such as Ecstasy. Lysergic acid (LSD), which was once seen on sugar cubes, now comes impregnated in squares of paper, and cannabis typically only arrives at the Laboratory nowadays when there is a substantial amount seized from suppliers. Prosecutions for possession can now take place if all sides accept that the substance is indeed cannabis without the need for the confirmation by scientific analysis. Customs and Excise officers involved in detecting importers are likely to seize vast quantities of cocaine, heroin, cannabis and amphetamines in proportions beyond the imagination of a couple of decades ago.

Drugs are the driving force behind much income-generating and violent crime, perhaps most clearly in the use of firearms between warring drug dealers. The ballistics section has seen a steady reduction in the number of shotguns used in the robbery of banks, wages vans and similar situations, but they have been replaced by pistols and handguns. The section can tell the investigating officer whether a weapon fits a legal definition of a firearm, whether a weapon fired a particular bullet or cartridge case, and whether the gun could have been fired accidentally or not. The scientists can also help with bullet entry and exit wounds, trajectories and how far the victim might have been from the weapon. Some of the section's work comprises examining the unique scratch marks left by the rifling inside a gun's barrel, but scientific analysis also extends to the detection of discharge residues to prove a person has recently fired a gun.

Explosives have played an important part in the Laboratory's assistance to police. In 1949 Cyril Cuthbert, by then a Superintendent at the Laboratory, reported on a rare occasion when things went wrong in the Laboratory. Two men had been arrested in Barnet in possession of powder suspected of being explosive. As the scientist started to analyze the sample there was an explosion. This spread to remaining parts of the exhibits which had been left too close on the bench, and the scientist involved was badly injured. The experience led to changes in safety procedures.

FORENSIC BIOLOGIST EXAMINING DNA PROFILES.

The use of explosives to blow safes has now passed into the annals of criminal folklore, but scientific analysis of safe ballast regularly matched the contents of the interior of the safe door with residue found on a suspect's clothing. It was these non-terrorist explosive cases which led to the original employment by the Laboratory of two explosives officers, Don Henderson GM and Geoffrey Biddle MBE GM, in the early 1960s. They and their successors soon became a vital means of protection of the public in London from bombs left by the IRA and other terrorist groups.

Residue patterns are also important for the way in which other substances are projected. Blood splashes and droplets will be scattered according to scientific principles and analysis can lead to safe conclusions about the position of the suspect and victim, even when valiant attempts have been made to remove all traces of the crime visible to the human eye.

The Fire Investigation Unit provides scientific support for the investigation of the more serious of the 5000 offences of arson recorded each year by the Met, usually by the identification of fuels and solvents from the scene, and analysis of clothing worn by suspects. The Unit has a small-scale burning chamber for testing ignition sources, and access to larger specialist facilities at the UK Fire Research station.

The Serious Crime Unit, one of whose founder members was Mr Ken Creer MBE developed the use of lasers, light sources and chemical, physical and biological methods to reveal fingerprints and other marks, thus greatly increasing success rates both at the scenes of crime and in the laboratory. The attendance of scientists at the scene can very often add a valuable dimension to the investigation, a practice which has occurred in London far more often than elsewhere.

The Laboratory's Questioned Documents Section was set up in 1968, and in the first year of operation demand from the Metropolitan Police far outstripped expectations. What started with a complement of two scientists equipped with microscopes now employs around 15 specialists using a variety of dedicated equipment. A range of work is carried out including the comparison of handwriting and the examination of the output of office printers, photocopiers and typewriters. A number of developments in equipment and methods have kept pace with the changing nature of the work submitted; these include the Electro-Static Detection Apparatus (ESDA), Video Spectral Comparator (VSC) and Ribbon Analysis Workstation (RAW). The ESDA has acquired particular fame worldwide. It resulted from a collaboration between Mr David Ellen, the head of the Documents Section for many years, and Messrs Foster and Freeman, then from the London College of Printing. Foster and Freeman produced the ESDA equipment which allowed the minute impressions of handwriting on sheets of paper several layers lower in a pad to be made visible. This launched Foster and Freeman Ltd into manufacturing forensic equipment. The ESDA technique involves applying a high voltage charge of electricity to a piece of paper, and a mixture of glass beads and photocopier toner will then reveal impressions of writing made on earlier sheets of paper in a pad. Impressive results have been achieved in relation to plans and lists made by terrorists as well as in fraud cases.

Handwriting analysis comprises more than minute comparison of writing style and features; scientific analysis can reveal important detail about the type of ink and paper which has been used.

The degree to which scientific evidence has been universally accepted in the courts is an enormous tribute to the vision of those involved in the early days, and indeed to the professional observation and scientific integrity of the scientists who have made such a significant contribution to the criminal justice system.

FRAUD SQUAD (SO6) Originally the Metropolitan and City Police Company Fraud Department (C6 Branch), started in 1946 with Superintendent Arthur Thorp as its first commanding officer. This brought together the City of London Police's traditional expertise in complicated Stock Exchange matters arising on their patch and the Met's detective and criminal intelligence resources. It was the first fully integrated permanent collaboration between the two forces, and continued until the Serious Fraud Office was set up in 1987, whereupon the two London forces reverted to having their own Fraud Squads.

C6's early successes included stamping out a great many traditional business confidence tricksters practising 'long firm' frauds (establishing a reliable reputation for a dummy firm by making small orders and paying promptly, before making massive orders and welshing), 'share-pushing' (issuing worthless or fraudulently hyped shares), and the forgery and theft of rationing coupons in the 1940s. The squad's massive inquiry into Sidney Stanley's activities was underpublicized, as the Lynskey Tribunal received the major press coverage, and Stanley's flight abroad forestalled his trial, so that Scotland Yard and City Police officers were not required to give evidence of their work.

By the 1970s, massive frauds by major company directors were becoming complicated, and often involved other investigative bodies such as the Department of Trade and Industry. Additional uncertainties about legal decisions in relation to prosecution led to the Serious Fraud Office being established to prosecute such cases. The Scotland Yard Fraud Squad thereupon reverted to being a Metropolitan Police Unit (SO6), which supplies investigative staff to the SFO in appropriate cases. Famous City scandals such as the Guinness, Blue Arrow, Barlow Clowes and Maxwell cases were handled by the SFO assisted by SO6 detectives.

The Fraud Squad comprises about 140 officers, divided into seven operational teams, which deal with public sector fraud and corruption and a myriad other fraud offences including advance fee, bogus charities, false mortgages and investment frauds. Pro-active operations have increased to good effect. SO6 also has the only Fraud Prevention Office in the United Kingdom.

The Support group maintains a Departmental Intelligence Unit (see Commercial Crimes Intelligence Bureau) and a Financial Investigations Unit to receive and disseminate information compulsorily supplied by banks under the Criminal Justice and Drugs Trafficking Acts concerning suspicious large deposits which could be the proceeds of major crimes. SO6 also has a surveillance unit which may be called upon by any fraud investigation team, and a Crime Management Unit to receive information from the public.

The small Computer Crime Unit is increasingly important as hacking into company and government computers leads to serious espionage and sabotage, both commercial and political.

FRIENDS OF THE METROPOLITAN POLICE MUSEUM Founded in 1995 by Inspector Paul Rason as a support group for the Historical Museum, and with the particular ambition of securing a permanent home where the collection can be properly exhibited. They publish *Peeler* magazine and a newsletter.

FRONT COUNTER OFFICERS Early name for police officers undertaking duties now performed by their Civil Staff equivalent, Station Reception Officers.

GALLEYS Standard River Police rowing patrol boats, in use from 1798 to 1925.

Police galleys were 8.2m (27ft) clinker-built open boats with three thwarts for oarsmen and a seat in the stern for the Surveyor or Inspector, who steered with rudder strings. No written record has been found to prove the tradition that police galleys working above London Bridge were varnished, and below-bridge galleys painted black.

Surveyors (later Inspectors, first-class) were propelled by three men rowing randan (four-oared bow and stroke each plying a single oar while the third man on the centre thwart pulled

a pair of sculls). Sergeants (or Inspectors, 2nd and 3rd class) were denied the centre sculler and propelled by a pair.

The labour for two men of working these heavy boats against the tide in all weathers led to much sickness and premature retirement, as River Police were all too often literally worked to death. By 1921 it was recommended that oarsmen should be replaced by engines on patrol

THAMES DIVISION INSPECTOR ON THE QUAY AND TWO OFFICERS IN POLICE GALLEY AT WAPPING, 1890.

boats. This was not implemented until 1925, and the last police galley was finally sold off in 1931.

GAME, SIR PHILIP WOOLCOTT (1876–1961) GCB, GCVO, GBE, KCMG, DS Commissioner, 1935–45. Educ. Charterhouse and Woolwich. Joined Royal Artillery, 1895. Served in Boer War: Queen's Medal with 5 clasps, 1901–2. Staff College, 1910. Major with 4th Army Corps, 1914. Lt-Col and DSO, 1915. RFC staff, Brig-Gen., 1916. Air Commodore, RAF, 1919. Air Vice-Marshal commanding RAF in India, 1922. Air Council, Whitehall, 1925–9. Governor of New South Wales, 1930–5.

Though he was Lord Trenchard's personally chosen successor, Sir Philip Game was quite unlike the commanding and energetic 'Boom'. To start with, he was accident-prone. A broken knee-cap delayed his taking up office, and he was to break his leg three times while Commissioner. He was unassuming: a Commissioner who made frequent use of public transport instead of official cars. This may have been partly because he was a poor driver (though a fine horseman) and, as a man of the highest principles, unwilling to use a police limousine and chauffeur for his private movements.

More importantly, he was quiet and comparatively self-effacing – a 'listening' Commissioner. He dutifully listened to long submissions from the Police Federation and its Branch Boards, which Trenchard had treated with undisguised contempt. However much he disagreed with them, he was reluctant to make spot decisions, so that the Boards accepted it without demur on the rare occasions when he told them immediately that some proposal was impossible. He wanted to know what constables were thinking and feeling, and he made Sir George Abbiss his closest professional adviser and confidant, the only one of his Assistant Commissioners to have risen from the ranks. The results were wholly good. The force which Trenchard had left, as he said, 'sulky' recovered its good humour. In a decade when police pay had not been increased since the final Desborough reforms in 1921, and increases in pension contributions had actually eroded the net take-home, this paid dividends. The Federa-

tion realistically accepted that officers were lucky to have jobs at all in the Great Depression, and did not press for increases. Which was just as well, for, like Trenchard, Game did not press for them either.

Game was an administrator and a delegator. He wrote excellent letters and enjoyed doing so, and he lightened his Commissioner's Annual Reports with touches of humour. He gave people jobs to do and let them get on with them. Under him, 1935–9 was a period of relative calm for the Met after the tempest that was Trenchard.

Not that the streets seemed calm. Demonstrations by the unemployed always carried the risk of deteriorating into riots, and firm police control of them, added to memories of the occasional use of policemen as strikebreakers, made for shaky future relations between the Met and the left. To make things worse, Sir Oswald Mosley's Fascists deliberately provoked trouble in the Jewish East End, and then enjoyed their leader's ability to use his establishment credentials and have their right to 'peaceful' demonstration enforced by the police. The climax of this was the Battle of Cable Street, until at last the government took action and by banning Mosley's political uniforms took away half his attraction for many of his followers. On the credit side, Game had a policeman's son to liaise with when Herbert Morrison became the leading light of the Labour-controlled LCC, and both Morrison and the Communist Party's organizer for the unemployed, Wal Hannington, preferred witty and innocuous 'stunts' and photo-opportunities to mass demonstrations as a means of publicizing political protest.

During Game's term of office, the public was made increasingly aware of their potential for joining the police in the 'war on crime'. The wireless became an installation in almost every home, and BBC broadcasts of Scotland Yard's frequent requests for information and witnesses to come forward made Whitehall 1212 the best known telephone number in the land until 1937, when the 999 emergency call system was devised.

By 1938, Game had given full consideration to Trenchard's two revolutionary reforms: the Hendon Police College, and the system of short-term contracts. How much he was influenced by

Federation and rank-and-file detestation of the former is unimportant: neither was working properly. Trenchard's arithmetic had failed. Since the Police Pensions Act of 1921 had extended the period an officer had to serve before collecting a pension from 25 to 30 years, many of the 'old sweats' who were supposed to be replaced by bright young Junior Station Inspectors graduating from the college were well installed as Senior Inspectors and Superintendents. The ambitious high-flyers whom the college was supposed to attract with accelerated career prospects were going to have to wait in line for their promotions anyway. Also, by setting the age of entry to the college at 20, Trenchard had missed his chance to pull in bright young 'eagles' from the public schools. They had already made their career choices, and were not going to go back for more games and character-building in return for an inspector's cap when they were 22. Game proposed that entry by competitive examination should be suspended for the time being; that all candidates should do at least 12 months on the beat before they were admitted; and possibly the college should be closed until the promotion logjam had shifted. He politely notified Trenchard of his suggestions before submitting them to the Home Office, which mulled over the plans for two years, and then abruptly closed the college for the duration of the war.

Short term contracts (officially short service engagements under Section 4, Metropolitan Police Act 1933) had failed to attract many takers, and the principal beneficiaries had been provincial forces who welcomed trained and experienced officers from the Met, gleefully clutching whatever gratuity they had earned. They were abolished on 20 January 1939.

In 1939 the IRA made a surprise return to mainland terrorism in Britain with a bombing campaign. This was their first insurgence since the murder of Field Marshal Sir Henry Wilson in 1922. But the threat of a silly 'war' with romantic (if deadly) young Fenians was of little import compared with the major war threatening in Europe. Game was nearly 65 and his health was not good. He was ready to retire, but patriotically deferred doing so until the end of WWII.

His habit of delegation proved very effective

SIR PHILIP GAME. THE PORTRAIT WAS PAINTED IN 1939 FOR AN EXHIBITION BY THE ROYAL SOCIETY OF BRITISH ARTISTS.

his last Report by quoting the words he had seen written in the dust on a van, 'When a Doodle dawdles, duck', and when the war ended he was able to take his well-earned retirement having done his duty well. His memorial was a Boys' Club, started by Z Division in Croydon with his encouragement and named after him – a forerunner of the police cadets.

It has been Scotland Yard's good fortune (for one cannot believe it was Home Office foresight), that creative or radically reforming Commissioners have usually been followed by highly competent stabilizers who allow the dust to settle and the reforms to take effect. Rowan and Mayne succeeded by Henderson; Mark followed by McNee; Newman by Imbert. Perhaps, had funds allowed him to improve buildings as Trenchard did, Horwood would have been seen as an excellent successor to Macready. There can be no doubt that whether Trenchard be seen as tonic or emetic, Game provided absolutely the right convalescence to follow him and recruit the energies of a force which then entered its 'Dixon of Dock Green' phase.

GENERAL ORDERS The printed Standing Orders of the Force which, with the Instruction Book, constituted 'the Bible of the Met'. While it was not assumed that every conceivable contingency would be covered in two printed books, they laid down a pretty comprehensive account of an officer's duties and responsibilities. Adherence to their rulings was essential to avoiding disciplinary charges. Any officer offering himself for promotion would be expected to be instantly familiar with the General Orders from memory. Replaced today by the Instruction Manual and other specific desk manuals.

GENERAL REGISTRY Section of Records Management Branch (QPP3). Civil Staff, responsible for maintenance of files, records of circulation and storage of papers relating to policy, business, managerial and operational affairs and serious and interesting criminal cases. It does not hold papers relating to local matters dealt with entirely by individual Divisions. Normal government security codes and practices are followed and strict confidentiality guards

under wartime conditions. Although the police were initially a 'reserved' occupation exempt from military service, many officers wished to join the fighting forces, and in 1941, those who were TA or RNVR reservists were called up in any case. The force had been close to full strength (just under 19,000) when the war began. Special Constables and Wartime Reserve Police Officers

were rapidly enrolled to take up the slack, and police pensioners were recalled to duty. Although the force had fallen severely under strength by 1945 (to 12,000 men), the temporary wartime emergency was met by the volunteers and reservists.

Sir Philip endeared himself further to his men by visiting them on their dangerous patrols through the bombing raids. When Scotland Yard itself was hit by a flying bomb and his own office was blown apart, he was in the vicinity encouraging fire watchers and rescue workers. He echoed the cheery indomitability of Londoners in

the privacy of individuals on whom data is filed.

The General Registry places files into the classifications AC – Accidents, Claims and Compensation; AF – Accounting and Finance; CM – Communications; CR – Crime; CS – Civil Staff; DP – Computers; GN – General Matters; LB – Land and Buildings; OA – Office Administration; OG – Police Organisation and Administration; SS – Supplies and Services; TF – Traffic; and TR – Transport. Within each classification secondary numbers further identify the contents of the file, the year the file was opened, and the sequential number of the file. Routine procedures ensure the proper maintenance and storage of files, and the continuing ability to locate them rapidly or identify their last place of issue on request. When files reach a pre-determined age (normally 5 or 10 years) they are given a First Review, at which time a large number are destroyed, having outlived their administrative usefulness.

Two indexes are maintained to locate files: the Names Index, dealing with names appearing on registered papers, such as defendants, victims, officers, companies and police horses, and the Subject Index containing the titles and information on files that relate to general subjects and policy. A simplified subject index system known as the Tag Index was introduced as a short-term record in 1939, but the principal indexer's system was said to produce more cross-reference index cards than anything else. 'Corned Beef – see Spam' was one which staff frequently cited with amusement. Bomb damage during WWII affected the Names Index and caused temporary problems.

Special Branch records were removed from the General Registry after the war. The General Registry's Post Room also handles incoming mail addressed to Scotland Yard.

GENERAL STRIKE Called by the TUC on 3 May 1926 in support of the coalminers who were resisting pit-owners' demands that they accept reduced wages and work longer hours. A small minority of the Labour movement nursed the hope that this might be the prelude to revolution, while a small minority of the governing classes believed that it was a stalking-horse for a bloody *coup d'etat* engineered by Bolsheviks.

Prime Minister Stanley Baldwin kept his head, however, and TUC leader Walter Citrine had no stomach for a prolonged fight when the country did not come to an immediate standstill. As the government refused to cave in after six days, Citrine did, leaving the miners to struggle on alone to defeat.

The police earned plaudits all round for keeping the peace without provoking tension. It helped that the essential strike-breaking work of providing basic services was not carried out by the Met, but by an enthusiastic mixture of anti-socialist students, City gents and the unemployed. Many toffs who had always longed to drive a bus or a train got their chance, and proved far more dangerous than the strikers' pickets (as PC Frank Flood on traffic duty at Oxford Circus ruefully recalled. After several near-misses, one of the amateur bus drivers finally hit him and put him in hospital.)

The Metropolitan Police were especially fortunate that Assistant Commissioner Sir Wyndham Childs had served under General Sir Nevil Macready in the military force policing the South Wales Miners' Strike, 1910, and had there come to respect the miners greatly and to perceive the value of

maintaining good-humoured relations with strike pickets. Harmony was reinforced by sociable football matches, which were widely used in the General Strike to keep police and strikers interacting with each other amiably. Macready, too (Metropolitan Police Commissioner 1918–20) returned to the Metropolitan Police Service to head the 60,000 Special Constables sworn in in London. Though more overtly unsympathetic to unionized Labour than Childs, Macready had also learned sympathy for strikers' families in Wales. The leadership of the Met was not, therefore, disposed to treat strikers as if they were traitorous hirelings of the Kremlin.

The Specials were sent in larger numbers than the regular police to districts like the Docks where violence could be anticipated. It frequently took the form of overturning cars and lorries driven by strike-breaking volunteers. The practice developed of sending four or five specials to an incident under the direction of one regular police officer, and this continued in

POLICING THE GENERAL STRIKE AT COTTON STREET, POPLAR IN 1926.

the last couple of days of the strike, when disgruntled radical strikers sensing the TUC's defeatism and the strike's imminent failure tried to provoke a violent military response from the government as a last desperate fling for revolutionary victory.

When it was all over *The Times* commented on the sterling service rendered by the police, and opened a National Fund for them. A sum of £250,000 was raised very quickly, part of which went to building the MPAA clubhouse at Imber Court.

GHOST SQUAD Famous covert unit of four Flying Squad officers, formed in 1945 and disbanded in 1949.

The Ghost Squad was a purely intelligence-gathering unit, suggested by Chief Constable Percy Worth, developed by Assistant Commissioner C Sir Ronald Howe and put under the command of Detective Inspector John 'Charlie Artful' Capstick to collect information to combat the ramifying black market created by wartime and postwar rationing. The officers were required to cultivate criminal contacts and pass information received from them to colleagues who would conduct investigations and make arrests.

The Ghost Squad were rarely seen to be involved in overt law enforcement, and drove dirty and battered cars as a camouflage. Their worth was proved immediately, and in the three years and nine months of their existence, their work led to 769 arrests, the solution of 1506 cases, and the recovery of £253,896 worth of stolen property. Detective Sergeant (later Detective Superintendent) John Gosling was the only officer to stay with the squad from start to finish: its members were changed from time to time to prevent criminals from recognizing them.

The disbandment of the Squad at the height of its success was something of a puzzle to Gosling, and villains have been quick to pretend that they had successfully corrupted its members. In fact, the Ghost Squad members were returned

DETECTIVE CHIEF SUPERINTENDENT JOHN GOSLING OF THE GHOST SQUAD.

to Divisional duties at the time when manpower shortage was straining the police force to the uttermost, and Commissioner Sir Harold Scott was using every means at his disposal to deploy officers economically. In his own book on Scotland Yard, written after his retirement, Scott praised the Ghost Squad's work, and remarked that other officers were still using the same methods.

GODDARD, SERGEANT GEORGE (B.1879) Subject of the only substantiated serious financial corruption case in the late 1920s, when press reports alleged that malpractices were rife in the Metropolitan Police. Born in Guildford, and worked as a bricklayer before joining the Met in 1900. Warrant No. 86412. Posted to D Division (Marylebone), 1904. V Division (Wandsworth), 1909. Did not pass into CID as Sergeant, and transferred to S Division (Hampstead), 1910. Promoted Sergeant, C Division (St James's) 1913. Station Sergeant, 1925. Dismissed, 1928.

When Goddard was promoted Sergeant and transferred to Vine Street station, he was placed at the heart of the West End where illicit vices have long been commercially purveyed. In 1921 Sergeant Horace Josling accused Goddard of taking bribes from illegal bookmakers. In the investigation which followed *in camera*, Goddard succeeded in winning his case, and it was Josling who was required to resign from the Force.

But in 1928, with the press in full cry about the supposed improprieties being investigated by the Macmillan and Lee Committees, anonymous letters reached New Scotland Yard accusing Goddard of accepting bribes from West End club and restaurant owners who served drinks after hours, permitted gaming, promoted 'obscene' (mildly erotic) cabaret, and at worst, allowed their premises to be used for prostitution. The most important, signed 'Richetta', also accused a Chief Inspector (against whom nothing discreditable was ever established), and Richetta was one of many who named Mrs Kate Meyrick, proprietress of the notorious Cecil Club at No. 43 Gerrard Street, Soho, of lavishing money on Goddard in return for his casting a blind eye on her activities.

Chief Constable Wensley insisted on a thorough investigation of the charges, starting with a raid on 43 Gerrard Street by Flying Squad officers, led by Inspector Fred 'Nutty' Sharpe. The officers found various contraventions of the law for which Mrs Meyrick eventually went to prison for six months.

With this hard evidence that lawbreaking flourished in the demesne where Goddard had taken overall responsibility for policing vice, Wensley's investigators pressed further. They found that PC John Wilkin (Divisional No. 163C) had worked directly under Goddard to keep constant watch on suspect night clubs and restaurants. PC Wilkin confessed to accepting monies from Goddard which were represented as presents to him from the club owners. Promised immunity from punishment (apart from inevitable dismissal from the force), PC Wilkin agreed to testify against his Sergeant.

Enquiries then focused on Goddard's financial affairs. It was found that he owned a house and garage worth £2000, an expensive car, and two bank accounts totalling £2700. None of this could have been accumulated from his pay, but Goddard offered the explanation that he had been lucky in betting at the races, and had invested very successfully in a music company. When it was found that he held £12,000 cash under the false name Joseph Eagles in a safe deposit at Selfridges, the case against him was clear-cut. This was an astonishingly large sum in the values of the time. Goddard was suspended, dismissed and charged under the Corrupt Practices Act of 1906. He went to prison for 18 months, and a legal wrangle began as to the propriety of confiscating his ill-gotten gains. Mrs Meyrick stood in the dock beside him, and earned another 15 months. The Superintendent of C Division was reprimanded for negligence, fined, and transferred.

The newspapers jumped at the chance of pretending that the 'vice kings and queens' exposed proved the dangers of letting foreign immigrants come to London and practise their evil ways, citing, among others, the Chinese restaurateur 'Bril-

POLICE NOTICE DISPLAYED DURING THE HUNT FOR DANIEL GOOD.

liant' Chang, responsible for selling opium to two society girls who overdosed themselves and died, one of them being an habituée of Mrs Meyrick's club.

According to Harry Daly, Goddard and Wilkin also dressed in plain clothes to extort regular collections from street prostitutes with the threat of charging them out of turn if they did not pay up. Thereafter arrests for soliciting could only be made by officers in uniform until the War, and ceased attempts to extract bribes from prostitutes.

GOOD, DANIEL (1792–1842) Murderer whose escape prompted the formation of the Detective Branch.

Good, a philandering Irishman, worked as resident coachman at a merchant's house in Putney Park, while his common-law wife, Jane Jones or Sparks, took in mangling in Marylebone, and looked after his 11-year-old son by an earlier attachment formed on the Continent. At the same time, Good was pressing his suit with 16-year-old Susan Butcher in Deptford. In April 1842 Jane visited Good in Putney, where he killed her. Over the next few days he cut up her body and burned parts of it in the harness-room grate, probably distributing the soft organs in the river.

On 15 April he took his son Daniel to visit Susan Butcher in Deptford and give her some of Jane's clothes and belongings. On the way back to Putney he stole a pair of trousers from a pawnbroker's shop, and was seen doing so. PC William Gardner, guided by two shopboys, went to Putney Park to question Good and search the stables, and at about 9.15 p.m., in the straw of the last stable, he found 'Jane Good's' torso. Good fled the moment he saw Gardner touch the body, locking Gardner, the shopboys, the estate factor and his daughter, and his own son inside the stable. It was nearly midnight before a route paper started, slowly circulating the hue and cry around the police force.

The hunt for Good was further delayed because little Daniel Jr did not recognize the remains as his 'mother', and the police assumed they had found Susan Butcher's body. By the time they discovered that Good had run from Putney to Marylebone and absconded with Jane's belongings, he had disappeared again. For the next week, as the papers gleefully and critically reported, the police were always about two days behind Good, who went first to Spitalfields where his very first wife, an old Irishwoman called Molly, sold oranges on the pavement. She put him up for a day or two, and then directed him on to a niece he had never met in Rotherhithe. He stayed with her and her husband for a day or two, while the niece naively remarked on the peculiarity that he had the same name as the wanted murderer. And from there, after buying a secondhand suit of workmen's fustians, he completely disappeared.

One week later, Thomas Rose, an ex-policeman from Roehampton, recognized him working as an unskilled bricklayer's mate on a building site in Tonbridge. Good was arrested, tried, convicted and hanged in May.

There had been a completely unnecessary panic during the ten days he was missing, for Good was of no danger whatsoever to anyone after he killed Jane. Inadequate police attempts to make enquiries in plain clothes were reported, and it was observed that officers from outside H Division (Whitechapel) keeping belated watch on Molly Good's lodgings in Flower and Dean Street had awkwardly crossed the tracks of H Division officers doing the same thing. The wish for a detective force to *catch* criminals and not merely a uniformed force to *prevent* crime became so popular as to override the traditional fear of plain clothes police 'spies'. As the Bow Street Runners had been disbanded in 1839, the Scotland Yard Detective Branch was finally established, owing more to the Daniel Good case than any other cause.

GOULD INTERROGATION (1840) Prototypical example of successful but deceptive questioning involving induced self-incrimination, immediately discountenanced by the courts and Scotland Yard.

In May 1840 a potboy named Richard Gould was charged with murdering an Islington man named John Templeman in the course of a robbery. The case was lost, as circumstantial evidence proved that Gould had planned and profited by a robbery, but did not prove that it was Templeman's. Sergeant Charles Otway (Warrant No. 9211) thereupon took out a warrant for Gould's arrest on the burglary charge, and without telling Gould he held it, invited him to

give details of the crime, saying that now he could not be charged again with the murder he could tell all and claim the £200 reward offered for naming others involved. Gould promptly told a story of having committed the burglary with two accomplices, one of whom committed the murder, and Otway immediately arrested him. The court decided that the confession was inadmissible evidence, being self-incrimination procured by the false promise of a reward (though Gould was convicted on other and adequate circumstantial evidence and transported). Commissioner Sir Richard Mayne noted the legal and moral implications, and never again allowed Otway to be employed in detective cases.

GRANTHAM, JOSEPH (D.1830) First murdered Police Constable. Joined Met, 10 February 1830. Constable No. 169, S Division. Warrant No. 3170. Married; twins born to his wife the day before his death. Killed on duty 1830.

On 29 June 1830, PC Grantham intervened to stop two drunken Irishmen who were quarrelling in Smith's Place near Skinner Street, Somers Town (north of Euston) after one of them had been beating his wife. Both men and the woman then turned on him, knocked him down and kicked him. A kick in the temple from young bricklayer Michael Duggan led to his death a few minutes later. The coroner's jury cleared Duggan and concluded that Grantham brought about his own death 'by over-exertion in the discharge of his duty' perhaps a more outrageously callous expression of hostility to the new police than that evinced by the Culley and Fursey juries.

Sir Charles Rowan omitted to mention Grantham when reporting to the Select Committee on the Police in 1833, and described PC John Long as the first – and indeed at that date the only – officer killed on duty. His error was followed by most historians until John Price surveyed the early years of the Met in 1991.

GREAT BULLION ROBBERY Theft of more than £17,000 of gold bullion from a railway guard's van at Folkestone in 1855.

The Great Bullion Robbery was the most serious professional crime tackled by the early

Detective Branch. (Murder in England was invariably an amateur crime between 1842 and 1878; the hired assassin and the professional hit-man were unknown.) Like most great robberies (cf. the Great Train Robbery and the Brinks-Mat Robbery) success depended on an inside man. In this case the idea of stealing bullion transported by rail was conceived by a printer named Pierce who supplied the railway company with tickets. He corrupted a guard, James Burgess, and a clerk in the London Bridge Traffic Department, William Tester, who were able to keep him informed about the movement of bullion and the security arrangements. These entailed barred and locked boxes held in safes which were transferred in their entirety from the guard's van to the Folkestone–Boulogne ferry. Tester secured wax impressions of the safe keys when they came in for repair while a professional thief called Agar took impressions of the keys to the boxes, and when Tester reported that a shipment of bullion was to be transported the gang replaced the gold with lead shot and relocked the safes, so that the substitution was not discovered until the safes were weighed in France.

Experience today would probably have led to vigorous pursuit of the inside man or men, but in 1855 the detectives were baffled by the gang members' resolute silence. One year later, however, Pierce and Agar quarrelled over a large sum of money Pierce appropriated when Agar gave it to him to invest for a woman friend. At that point Agar turned Queen's Evidence and shopped his confederates. Inspector Thornton, Sergeant Williamson, Sergeant Smith and Sergeant Tanner were sent to round up the gang, who were all arrested and convicted.

One very important piece of information arising from the case was the involvement of James 'Jim the Penman' Saward who bought a quantity of the disposable ingots into which the bullion was melted. The conviction and transportation of this barrister of the Inner Temple in 1857 ended the activities of London's only 'Napoleon of Crime' ever, if the phrase implies an educated gang leader who, like Sherlock Holmes's Professor Moriarty, covers his activities with a respectable and learned professional career.

GREAT SCOTLAND YARD A small street running east from the northern end of Whitehall, parallel with Whitehall Place. The original Metropolitan Police Commissioners' Office (No. 4 Whitehall Place) backed on to it, and A Division was based there in the back of the building. In consequence, many visitors who wanted police assistance rather than a formal interview with the Commissioners came directly to Great Scotland Yard, and the name colloquially attached to the headquarters of the Metropolitan Police, especially as additional buildings in Great Scotland Yard were acquired to house branches of the expanding force. See also Back Hall.

GREAT TRAIN ROBBERY One of the last nationally headlined cases to be solved by 'calling in Scotland Yard', before amalgamations created regional forces large enough to undertake their own major investigations.

On 8 August 1963, the Glasgow to London night mail was stopped by a faked signal in Buckinghamshire, and men in balaclava helmets uncoupled the engine and high-value packages coach from the rest of the train, clambered aboard the engine, and beat down the driver who resisted them, causing him concussion and trauma. They forced him to take them forward another 1.6km (1 mile) to Bridego Bridge. There the robbers broke into the hvp van, intimidated the Post Office workers with axe handles and, forming a human chain, unloaded £2½ million in old used notes being taken for destruction at the Mint. After working for half an hour, the gang made off in a convoy of vehicles, leaving mailbags containing further huge sums, but escaping into the dawn before they could be detected. The audacity and skilled planning of the crime impressed the public as much as the huge booty (still the largest amount ever seized in used notes).

Buckinghamshire Police immediately called in the Yard. Detective Superintendent Gerald MacArthur went to Aylesbury and took charge of the local end of the investigation. Detective Chief Superintendents Ernie Millen and Tommy Butler started inquiries in London, for it was immediately apparent that this was the skilled work of highly professional thieves, almost certainly from the Metropolis, and a round-up of informants and villains with relevant 'previous' held out the best hope of tracing the thieves.

As it seemed certain that the large convoy had gone to ground reasonably near the scene of the crime, Superintendent MacArthur not only concentrated his search on lonely buildings in Bucks, he allowed the fact that he was doing so to be reported on the radio. As the police hoped, this panicked the thieves into making a premature departure from their hide-out, so that when a local shepherd reported strange goings on at Leatherslade Farm and MacArthur investigated, he found mailbags, tinned food, sleeping bags and other copious evidence that this was the roost from which the train robbers had flown.

While the farm was being combed for fingerprints, the first robbers were arrested in Brighton where a suspicious landlady (widow of a policeman) mistrusted two men who offered excessive advance payment in cash. Roger Cordery and his friend Arthur Boal (whom the robbers have always insisted was Cordery's companion after the event, and not a participant) were arrested, and Butler and Millen now knew they were looking for members of Jimmy White and Tommy Wisby's south London gang, who specialized in stopping trains with Cordery as their rather simple technical officer. (He covered green signal lamps with a glove and rigged up instead a red light bulb powered by an accumulator.)

Back at the farm, fingerprint evidence left on a few bottles, vehicles and a Monopoly set pointed to more members of the Wisby gang, and to north London criminal Bruce Reynolds and some of his confederates. Reynolds had, in fact, planned and directed the operation. Reynolds' associate Gordon Goody was suspected, but no fingerprint evidence was found to incriminate him. He was, however, brought to book by yellow paint on his shoes matching that with which one of the gang's vehicles had been repainted.

Despite the huge sums of money available to them, all but four of the perpetrators were arrested and brought to trial, together with the solicitors who had helped them acquire Leatherslade Farm. The 'inside man' from the railway or Post Office who must have identified the train carrying the money and certainly reported by telephone on its departure and progress has never been brought to book, however, and it was years before Reynolds was caught, when his money ran out and he returned to England. Tommy Butler delayed his retirement in the hope of catching Reynolds and the two train robbers, Charlie Wilson and Ronnie Biggs, who used their loot to engineer daring escapes from prison. Notoriously Biggs is still at large. He successfully defied Chief Superintendent Jack Slipper's attempt to secure his extradition on the grounds that he had fathered a child in Rio as by Brazilian law the parent of a Brazilian minor cannot be extradited.

At the time of the trial the train robbers made no attempt to accuse the police of falsifying evidence. Since then, Reynolds has claimed that the fingerprints must have been 'planted', since the police were on to the right gangs far too quickly and the thieves were professionals who never took their gloves off, while Biggs has produced an elaborate account of Goody's movements and footwear to suggest that the paint was put on his shoes by Scotland Yard to frame him. As the fingerprint evidence is still in the Black Museum, it will be perfectly possible for some future generation to carry out scientific re-examination which will show that nothing was planted. The criminals seem unaware of the huge numbers of people, including civilians, who would have to join a conspiracy to plant technical evidence. The speed with which the right gangs were identified was manifestly due to Butler and Millen's knowledge of the underworld and its informants. And Biggs seems sublimely unaware that his theory is contradicted by the absolutely scrupulous handling and examination of his own shoes and paint pots which he reports, and which proved conclusively that he had not painted the robbers' vehicle with materials in his possession.

Neither Scotland Yard nor the train robbers can glean much satisfaction from the loot. Only a small quantity was ever recovered, but the thieves either frittered it away (like Reynolds), lost it to dishonest 'minders', or had to pay immense quantities of it to people who helped their attempted or successful escapes.

AN INCIDENT AT THE ANTI-VIETNAM WAR
DEMONSTRATION IN GROSVENOR SQUARE, 1968.

GREENOFF, PC EDWARD GEORGE BROWN, KPM (1887–1917) Officer who sacrificed his life to save passers-by. Warrant No. 96389. Divisional No. 389K.

On 19 January 1917, Constable Greenoff's beat took him past the Silvertown Chemicals Works which, it was widely known, were used for manufacturing TNT during the war. As he passed, a fire broke out in the works which was obviously liable to cause a very serious explosion. People who were much closer to the fire than PC Greenoff made good their escape, but he stationed himself at a point where he could warn all passers-by of the danger. In consequence he was seriously injured when the TNT exploded, and died in hospital.

His heroism came to the notice of King George V, on whose suggestion an immediate posthumous King's Police Medal was awarded (see Appendix 3).

GROSVENOR SQUARE DEMONSTRATION/RIOTS Political demonstrations which led to accusations of deliberate violence by demonstrators and police.

American demonstrations against the Vietnam War, and the remarkable success of students and workers in helping to bring down De Gaulle in France, prompted British radical students to try to imitate their overseas counterparts. 'Sit-ins' called on a variety of pretexts at different universities coincided with repeated mass demonstrations outside the American Embassy in Grosvenor Square. Following the pattern set by the Committee of 100 at the Trafalgar Square Demonstration, 1961, protestors were bussed in from all over the country. However, whereas the Committee of 100's original supporters had been largely adult members of provincial peace organizations called out during the school and university vacations, the anti-Vietnam war demonstrators were largely drawn from students organized at universities for weekend demonstrations in term time. And many of them explicitly intended to provoke police violence. They succeeded sufficiently to allow other, more genuinely peace-loving students, to tell wry stories of having been manhandled or kicked, though such confrontations only occurred when demonstrators tried to leave their prearranged and stewarded route with the aim of storming and entering the embassy. They were probably for the most part unaware that had they succeeded in their efforts they would have been confronted by armed US Marines on what was legally American soil, and the police were concerned that there might be loss of life.

Many of the recurrent demos were nonetheless good-humoured. Their repetitive nature led police and demonstrators to join in singing 'Auld Lang Syne' at the end of one. But in the last and most extreme of the violent demonstrations on 17 March 1968, 145 of the 1399 police officers on duty were injured, and 295 of the estimated 7000 demonstrators were arrested.

The deployment of such large numbers of officers led to greatly improved logistical preparations. Ultimately the demonstrations were so familiar and so well-controlled that they no longer merited much publicity and came to an end.

GROUP OPERATIONS Group Operations comprises the pool of detectives stationed at New Scotland Yard in the Organised Crime Group from which Major Incident Teams are drawn to work on varied major enquiries of a complex nature and investigate other matters as tasked.

GRUNWICK STRIKE Longest-ever running violent industrial dispute requiring regular policing.

Compared with the great dock strikes or miners' strikes, the Grunwick dispute involved only seven Asian workers who walked out of an Anglo-Indian millionaire's small photo-processing plant in Neasden, and picketed the factory to protest against his refusal to let them join the white collar union APEX or pay them its nation-

ally agreed scale of wages. But in 1976 the country was already starting the political polarization which would culminate in the fierce divisions of the 1980s. Students, union members, Members of Parliament and ultimately huge crowds of picketers came to 'give support' and attack the police who helped the replacement workers' bus

CATHERINE GURNEY, FOUNDER OF THE CHRISTIAN
POLICE ASSOCIATION.

to exercise the right to enter the factory yard every day. The scenes were televised and a press photograph of a young policeman laid out (and subsequently hospitalized) by a brick in June 1977 illustrated the degree of violence facing the police. Eventually the Government set up an

inquiry and the heat was taken out of the dispute, which continued in a less public way for some years afterwards.

The dispute was an example of the difficulties created by mass picketing in narrow streets and the problems of balancing the rights of opposing workers in a bitter industrial dispute.

GURNEY, CATHERINE (1848–1930) Philanthropist and founder of the International Christian Police Association, the Police Institute and other charities. Daughter and granddaughter of philanthropic nonconformists in the family which invented the 'brachygraphic' system of shorthand.

In 1883 Miss Gurney was conducting Bible classes in Wandsworth and took an interest in the police officers who frequently escorted her across Wimbledon Common. When she offered one constable a tract, and he responded in surprise, 'Do you think policemen have souls?' she saw her mission to encourage active Christian fellowship and evangelism among the police. She started the International Police Christian Association immediately, with its journal *On and Off Duty*.

Five years later, after visiting an injured policeman in hospital who lamented his fall into insobriety and unbelief since joining the Met, she acquired a building near Charing Cross to supply a Police Institute, where officers could meet and socialize in decent surroundings with access to good books.

For many years Miss Gurney put in long days' work at the institute, administering the Association's activities across the nation and writing contributions to *On and Off Duty*. She cultivated the acquaintance of senior officers, notably Commissioner Sir Edward Bradford, and was one of the prominent figures behind the establishment of the Convalescent Home and the Orphanage.

She died in Hove, and her funeral was held in Harrogate. She left a thriving association and an element of Christian idealism which remains a leaven in the force.

HABITUAL CRIMINALS REGISTER Started by Commissioner Sir Edmund Henderson, in perhaps over-ambitious form, in 1869. Refined by Sir Howard Vincent, and ultimately subsumed in the Criminal Records Office. The Fingerprint Bureau was initially a Branch of the HCR.

HANDCUFFS Until the early 1980s, handcuffs were retained in limited numbers in police stations and on certain operational vehicles, and were issued on an *ad hoc* basis for specific operations.

In about 1982, officers were trained and issued with a pair of chain link handcuffs on an individual basis. In 1993 the chain link handcuffs were replaced as standard issue by rigid handcuffs which enable officers to apply the cuffs effectively with one hand and maintain greater control over a violent prisoner.

All officers receive training before they are issued with rigid handcuffs (or any other item of protective equipment). They are also required to undertake annual refresher training, and to report and record every use of force, including handcuffs.

HARDING, ARTHUR (B.1886) East End gang leader whose oral recollections dictated to social historian Raphael Samuel between 1973 and 1979 contain unique gossip about named H and J Division police officers and famous crimes in the years between 1900 and 1945, and an unusually frank set of underworld opinions on the Met. Particularly interesting personal reminiscences describe F. P. Wensley, and Detective Sergeants Rutter, Redman, Jack 'Jew Boy' Stevens, William Brogden and Harry Dessent. Harding's insinuation that policemen he came to like after their retirement (Stevens, Brogden and Rutter) shared his dislike of Wensley and Redman must be taken with a grain of salt, although he does offer useful confirmation of Wensley's recollection that Local Inspector Tom Divall did not originally want him in the CID or promoted to Sergeant. As a well-informed amateur 'barrack-room lawyer', Harding undoubtedly earned great police hostility by bringing a number of police malpractice cases before the Royal Commission, 1908 – some well-founded, but most

impudent and fallacious. By the 1930s, however, he had himself lost credibility with the underworld, and was reduced to becoming an informant for DCI (later Chief Superintendent) Ted Greeno of the Flying Squad.

HARRIOTT, JOHN (1745–1817) Magistrate and co-founder of the River Police.

Educ. Great Stambridge, Essex. Entered Royal Navy as midshipman. Post Captain, 1765. Transferred to Merchant Service, 1766, spending several months with Native Americans while travelling the world from the Baltic to the Indies. Joined East India Company army, commanding sepoys in battle, serving as judge advocate and chaplain. After injury returned to England via Sumatra and South Africa, 1780. Married and settled in Essex as wine merchant and farmer. Royal Society of Arts Gold medal, 1782, for reclaiming Rushey Island from the Thames estuary. Ruined by fire and flood in 1790 and emigrated to America for four years. 1797, designed and manufactured an engine, a windlass, a fire escape and a ship's pump which he sold to the Navy. Same year approached Lord Mayor of London (and Conservator of the Thames) Brook-Watson, the Elder Brethren of Trinity House and the Home Secretary, the Duke of Portland, outlining proposal with costings for policing the Thames to end theft and piracy from the Port of London. All ignored him until, 1798, he met Patrick Colquhoun, and let him take the plan to the authorities under the auspices of the West India Company. Portland promptly appointed Colquhoun Superintending Magistrate of the proposed Marine Police, and at the request of the

West India Company had Harriott sworn in as a JP and appointed Resident Magistrate (though he continued to reside at his house in Burr Street, near today's St Katharine's Dock).

The two men established a Magistrates' Court and Police Office in Wapping High Street, and recruited a small administrative staff to manage 30 quay guards, 220 ship's constables, and over 1000 registered dockers, whose supervised loading and unloading of vessels instantly reduced pilfering by 80%. They also organized five 'perambulating Surveyors' in galleys manned by 18 watermen to head off pirates attempting to raid moored vessels from the river.

Harriott's police force established its efficacy so quickly that within two years, Henry Dundas was able to carry an Enabling Bill through Parliament, guaranteeing its continuance for a further seven years with Harriott as chief magistrate and two other stipendiaries appointed to assist him. Harriott alone was to deploy and direct the quay guards and river constables. He was inclined to despise his magisterial colleagues for their lack of seamanship or military experience, and although he never quarrelled with Colquhoun (who left the Marine Police after the first two years) he resented the public's tendency to see Colquhoun rather than himself as the founding father of the River Police.

In 1810, two successive chief clerks whom Harriott dismissed for serious peculations tried to revenge themselves by assembling a list of 53 false and petty charges against Harriott, inscribed on a roll of paper 16.7m (55ft) long. Harriott was astonished that the investigating magistrates did not dismiss the case out of hand, and was indignant when he was suspended from duty and sent for trial before Lord Ellenborough in the Court of King's Bench. With typical high-handedness he did not prepare a detailed defence, and in consequence one charge was upheld against him: that he had not signed invoices for work done by his own pump factory to deal with the notorious seepage from the river into the basement of the Police Office. Despite the jury's recognition that this technical misdemeanour was committed with no corrupt motive, an officious Clerk of the Court recorded a guilty verdict in Ellenborough's absence and imposed a fine.

Harriott had to have his conviction overturned and his magisterial post restored to him by the direct intervention of the King on the Home Secretary's recommendation.

In 1811, when a gang of housebreakers terrified London by ruthlessly cutting the throats of two entire families as they lay sleeping in their

CAPTAIN JOHN HARRIOTT.

beds, the mainland watchmen and parish constables proved themselves totally incapable of finding out who had committed these murders, or of giving honest citizens any sense of security at night. Harriott earned a reprimand from the Home Office for offering a reward for information, over and above the official reward of £500 the government had offered. Harriott apologized, but avowed his determination to catch the murderers, and when his office received information that a

man named John Williams had been seen with one of the bloodstained weapons left behind in the first victims' shop, Harriott sent constables to arrest him at his Wapping lodging-house, the Pear Tree. Williams committed suicide in Coldbath Fields Prison which indicated that Harriott might well have caught the right man. No further attempt was made to find his accomplices.

In 1816 Harriott retired at the age of 71, suffering from cancer. The following year he stabbed himself to death in his bath at his home in Burr Street. The inquest jury brought in a generous verdict of 'death by natural causes', so that he was buried in the consecrated ground of St Mary and All Saints church at his boyhood home, Great Stamford, Essex.

The loss of his first wife and one of his soldier sons may have contributed to the abrasive manner which led so many contemporaries to prefer Colquhoun, though, as Geoffrey Budworth's history of the River Police demonstrated conclusively in 1997, Harriott was by far the more important of the two, both in the detailed plan for policing he had worked out, and for his dedication of almost the last 20 years of his life to the force. His firmness, integrity, determination to prevent crime, and insistence that his force must be sober and incorruptible made a major contribution to the success of the River Police which, in turn, made it possible for Sir Robert Peel to institute proper policing across London, 10 years after Harriott's death. And the example of Harriott and Colquhoun was evidently in Rowan and Mayne's thoughts as they planned and set up the Metropolitan police along similar lines to the River Police.

HARRISON, PC NORMAN, GM Officer decorated for participation in the operation leading to the arrest and conviction of Derek Bentley and Christopher Craig for the murder of PC Sidney Miles. Joined the Metropolitan Police, 12 June 1950 (Warrant No. 135799).

When DC Frederick Fairfax was shot by Christopher Craig as Derek Bentley tried to escape from arrest, PC Harrison tried to go to his colleague's assistance by making his way along the sloping roof of an adjacent house, his back to the slates and his heels in the guttering. Shortly after this Craig observed PC Harrison and fired two shots at him. It was impossible for him to present anything but a sitting target, so he returned to the ground.

When reinforcements arrived with keys to the building, PC Harrison was one of those who ran up the fire stairs to the exit door on the roof and pushed it open. Despite DC Fairfax's warning that the armed man was close by, PC Sidney Miles jumped out on to the roof and was immediately killed. As soon as DC Fairfax and PC MacDonald had cleared the body behind cover, PC Harrison jumped on to the roof and threw his truncheon at Craig, who immediately fired at him. Harrison then helped Fairfax push Bentley through the fire exit to be taken in custody by brother officers. For these gallant actions, PC Harrison was awarded the George Medal in the 1953 New Year Honours.

HAY, CAPTAIN WILLIAM, CB

(1794–1855) First Inspecting Superintendent and third Co-Commissioner.

Served in the Light Dragoons, Peninsular War and Waterloo. Subsequently on the Governor-General's staff, Canada. Joined the Metropolitan Police, 1850 as Inspecting Superintendent. 2nd Co-Commissioner, 1850. The eldest son of Robert Hay whose grandfather, Lord Alexander Hay, was fifth son of the first Marquis of Tweeddale.

Captain Hay's appointment in 1850 signalled that, despite Sir Robert Peel's ruling on filling senior posts by promotion from the ranks, there was to be a definite tier of 'officers and gentlemen' supervising and commanding the Superintendents. Hay's duties were not clearly defined, but effectively he became Assistant Commissioner, carrying out routine (but not operational) duties that Commissioner Rowan had previously performed. He was felt to prove particularly efficient in the preparations for the Chartist Demonstration of 1848, and when Rowan retired in 1850 he was appointed second Commissioner.

The Order appointing him clearly specified that he was to be second to Sir Richard Mayne, but within two years Mayne was complaining to the Home Office about 'the jarring of undefined co-ordinate authority', something that had never

been a problem in the 20 years he worked alongside Rowan. It is not clear whether this friction demonstrates Mayne's incapacity for delegating authority when he was a senior rather than junior commanding partner or Hay's tendency to act with ill-judged independence. The latter was instanced in 1852 when crowds at the Duke of Wellington's lying-in-state got out of hand, and it was reported that one or maybe two people had been crushed to death. The police were criticized, and Hay had a paragraph inserted in the newspapers to the effect that Mayne had ordered the arrangements. Whether this was to exculpate himself or to assure the public that the best possible authority had been in charge is not clear, but Mayne was furious.

Hay made matters worse the following year by submitting proposals for reorganization to the Home Office without showing them to Mayne. From then on, communication between the two Commissioners was distant and frigid. When Hay died in 1855 it was immediately decreed that there should in future be one sole Commissioner.

HAYES, SGT JOHN HENRY, MP

(1887–1941) General Secretary of NUPPO. Subsequently 'The Policeman's MP'.

Born Wolverhampton, son and brother of policemen. Joined the Met, 1909 (PC 443 S, Warrant No. 96535). Transferred from beat to Divisional Office, 1910. Sergeant, 1913. Elected to Metropolitan Police Representative Board, 1918. General Secretary, NUPPO, 1919, and resigned from the Met to become salaried union executive. Columnist for *Police Review*. Labour MP for Liverpool, Edge Hill, 1922–31. Vice-Chamberlain of the Royal Households, 1929. After losing seat, worked for Joint Council of Qualified Opticians and became Secretary of the British Optical Association until his death.

Hayes' rapid promotion from the beat marked his ability. Commissioner Sir Nevil Macready described him as 'the brain behind NUPPO' and claimed to have marked him down for promotion before he became the Union's General Secretary. Although Hayes only came to prominence after the successful Police Strike, 1918, he made an immediate impression by the moderation and good sense with which he pre-

sented the men's demands. He surprised the Desborough Committee by asking for an unacceptably large pay rise, but had the support of Sir Nevil in demanding the abolition of the 1s per day deduction from the wages of policemen off duty when sick. His worst mistake as a union leader was to apologize in the press for the 'militarization' which had led to 'police violence' in controlling a demonstration by discharged soldiers and sailors in 1919. As 20 policemen had been injured when the demonstration turned riotous, this announced to his members that he was more interested in his standing with the TUC than with them. He tried unsuccessfully to swing the Union Executive to a refusal of certain duties rather than the absolute Police Strike, 1919, but supported the strike loyally and incautiously with claims that the union would win a larger pay award than that granted by Desborough.

He continued to agitate on behalf of the unemployed strikers through his column in *Police Review*, and there and in Parliament took up questions of police pay and conditions. He entertained policemen weekly at the House while he was a member, and became known as 'the policeman's MP' – the only one until the Police Federation nominated the young James Callaghan their spokesman and political adviser in 1955. On his death, he was remembered with affection as a respected member of the Labour movement.

HAYTREAD, PC GEORGE (FL.1910)

Early recipient of KPM for making arrest despite suspect's attempt to shoot him. Joined the Metropolitan Police, 6 January 1908 (M 452, Warrant No. 95320).

From the first (see Tottenham Outrage) the KPM for Gallantry was seen as an award for officers who bravely disregarded the risk to their own lives presented by armed desperadoes. So many of the entries in Appendix 3: 'For Gallantry' record laconic citations for 'arresting an armed suspect who threatened the officer', that it is worth examining PC Haytread's meritorious conduct in greater detail as a good example. It is particularly interesting as a rare case in which a member of the public gave spontaneous assistance and was also decorated.

On 26 December 1910, PC Haytread was

patrolling his beat when he heard a police whistle and saw a man hurrying away from him. The constable set off after him. As soon as the man realized he was being followed he turned round and fired three pistol shots at Haytread. Undeterred, Haytread went right up to grapple with him, in spite of another shot being fired. The suspect then jammed his pistol barrel against Haytread's head and pulled the trigger. Mercifully, it failed to discharge.

Mrs Francis Maude Wright saw what was going on and hurried to PC Haytread's assistance. She hit the man in the face, seized PC Haytread's whistle and blew it, and went on hitting the man until she cut her hand on his teeth. By screaming at the top of her voice she attracted more assistance, leading to the suspect's arrest.

PC Haytread received the KPM for the tenacity and courage with which he pursued and arrested a suspect under desperate conditions. He also received a medal from the Carnegie Hero Trust, and £10 from the Bow Street Police Fund. Mrs Wright received the Albert Medal for going to his assistance and endangering her life.

HEIGHT REGULATIONS Minimum height requirement in 1829, 5ft 7in (170cm). Raised to 5ft 8in (173cm) in 1870 (except for Thames Division who were still permitted to recruit at 5ft 7in (170cm), and to 5ft 9in (175cm) in 1887. Reduced again to 5ft 8in (173cm) in 1912. Abolished in 1990 as discriminating against ethnic minorities. Women Police minimum height was 5ft 4in (162.5cm).

HENDERSON, SIR EDMUND YEAMANS WALCOTT KCB (1821-1896) Commissioner, 1869-86.

Educ. Woolwich. 1st Lt, Royal Engineers, 1841. Boundary Survey, Canada-New Brunswick, 1846-8. Comptroller of Convicts,

A RECRUIT'S HEIGHT BEING MEASURED BY INSPECTOR BERTHA CLAYDEN AT PEEL HOUSE IN THE LATE 1930s.

Western Australia, 1850-63. Lt-Col, 1862. Home Office Director of Prisons & Inspector-General of Military Prisons, 1863. CB, 1868. Metropolitan Police Commissioner, 1869. KCB, 1878. Resigned, 1886, and retired to private life.

On the death of Sir Richard Mayne, Assistant Commissioner Labalmondiére served as Acting Commissioner for several months, while a debate took place in the press as to whether his successor should be a military man or a civilian. Sir Edmund Henderson's appointment seemed tailor-made to meet the conflicting demands. A professional soldier, his occupation for 18 years had nevertheless been almost entirely civilian, overseeing prisons first in Australia and then from the Home Office. As a further advantage, he was virtually unknown to the public and would make his reputation, without prejudice, on his achievements as Commissioner.

He immediately found favour with the force by relaxing some of the petty restrictions imposed on them by Rowan and Mayne's generation-old regulations. He permitted officers to grow beards and moustaches, provided they did not conceal the Divisional Numbers on their tunic collars. He noticed that the prohibition on policemen engaging in political activity – a vital early safeguard against public suspicion of the force as an instrument of government tyranny – was preventing them from being numbered in the steadily increasing franchise, so he ensured policemen were given the right to vote, first in general and then in municipal elections.

He also embarked on a long-running struggle with Receiver Maurice Drummond to have police pay increased. Drummond was a bureaucrat, imbued with the Victorian belief that public money should be used as sparingly as possible, especially if it was being used to maintain the private living standards of public servants less well-off than himself. Henderson was only able to achieve a pathetic extra 3s. a week for Sergeants and 1s. for constables (bringing their respective pay up to £1.2s.0d and £1.5s.0d respectively), but he continued the good fight, incidentally setting off the tendency for Receivers to ally themselves with Home Office officials against the Commissioner which came to a head under Sir Charles Warren, and to some extent was always a potential tension until the Receiver was finally placed under the Commissioner's authority in 1968.

Despite Drummond, as a result of the Home Office Departmental Committee Report following the Clerkenwell Bombing Henderson found himself with extra funds to increase the strength of the force by 1350 more men. Even with this number, the beat system was inadequate to maintain the original intention of a uniformed policeman no more than 15 minutes away anywhere at any time. (The rapid expansion of London and the number of streets to be covered meant that an officer on beat duty walked 32km/20 miles on day patrols and 22.5km/14 miles at night). So Henderson devised the fixed point system, ensuring that policemen were available to the public as they required them.

He also carried out the Report's major recommendations. He improved the Detective Branch, increasing the Scotland Yard headquarters complement to 27, and deploying 180 detectives in the Divisions, all under the command of Superintendent Adolphus Williamson. He started a Habitual Criminals Register. (Though an advance on the Fieldings' old *Hue and Cry*, this was initially a failure because he was too ambitious in the amount of data he wished to include, but it ultimately led to the improved *Police Gazette*.)

The Departmental Committee had recommended more 'educated' senior officers in the upper echelons. Henderson therefore grouped the Divisions into four Districts, appointing District Superintendents to command them. One of them was a promoted Divisional Superintendent, it being hoped that the new rank would allow the best Superintendents to rise above the Divisional Police, and that ultimately the District Superintendents would take over some or all the responsibilities of the Assistant Commissioners. (Neither hope was realized until the 20th century.) The report also suggested Schoolmaster Sergeants in the Divisions to

SIR EDMUND HENDERSON.

improve literacy among constables.

Unhappily for Henderson, the Committee also decided that such pensions as existed were too generous and should be cut. Coupled with what Henderson already knew to be inadequate pay for the ranks, this proved explosive, and led to demands for a representative negotiating body, and the abortive Police Strike, 1872. Henderson dealt with the latter very competently, disciplining and dismissing the men involved, and then allowing most of them to rejoin the force, after being sworn-in and attested all over again. But the justified grievance that the men were not represented in pay negotiations dragged on until 1919.

The force lost ground in the eyes of the press as a consequence of the strike, but essentially Henderson succeeded in consolidating the public acceptance for the police that Rowan and Mayne had won without attracting more of the unpopularity that clung to Mayne in his last years. He played down the strike in his Annual Report, as he would the much bigger scandal of the Trial of the Detectives. He continued Mayne's policy of curbing unruly children in the parks by reiterating his regulation against bowling hoops, and adding new ones prohibiting tip-cat and catapults. This time the press did not mock the Commissioner – even when he ordered patrolling policemen to remove orange peel littering the footpaths. He gave attention to the unglamorous Public Carriage Office and saw to the provision of shelters for cabmen.

In 1873 he presided over the first two public complaints that the police were harassing respectable members of the public. (Cf. Miss Cass, Mme D'Angely, Irene Savidge.) Mr Belt, a barrister of Gray's Inn, was arrested for being drunk, but established to the satisfaction of the Bow Street magistrate Sir Thomas Henry that his eccentricities of manner were sober and normal (to him). And policemen attempting to arrest some guards officers for drunken misconduct outside the Argyll Rooms in Leicester Square became embroiled in an unseemly fracas with them, and would have faced charges of perjury had not the Duke of Cambridge as Commander-in-Chief stepped in to stop the proceedings. Henderson played down the incidents, but, possibly on Home Office advice, accepted the appointment of a Sheffield Stipendiary Magistrate as his legal adviser.

When senior officers in the Detective Branch were found to have been corrupted by the confidence tricksters Benson and Kurr in 1877, Henderson again minimized the importance of the affair in his reports. He made no attempt to interfere with Howard Vincent's creation of the CID, and raised no objection to Vincent's having access to the Home Secretary without consulting him. He was already busily engaged with trying unsuccessfully to have the Receiver made accountable to the Commissioner.

Busily for him, that is, for by this time Henderson was becoming much less active. He ignored the fact that his District Superintendents had become ineffective and two of their posts had fallen vacant. The Fenian bombing campaign that opened in 1883 led the Home Office to urge him to act strongly. Henderson put large numbers of constables on guard outside public buildings, and left serious action to Howard Vincent and his Special Irish Branch, and to Vincent's successor James Monro acting in concert with Dr Robert Anderson, the spymaster at the Home Office.

In 1886 Henderson's inactivity caught up with him when the Trafalgar Square Riot took place, and the absence of any competent senior officer to control it prompted the setting up of an enquiry. Henderson didn't wait to be pushed. He submitted his resignation immediately.

It was an unfortunate ending to a generally successful Commissionership. From the standpoint of history, it seems clear that Henderson's crucial task was to consolidate the acceptance won by Rowan and Mayne's creation, and this, by and large, he did admirably. He began by introducing the reforms and restructuring necessitated by Mayne's increasing isolation from his men and unwillingness to delegate. He went on to follow the principle that the thing worked and he didn't need to mend it. Masterly inactivity proved as good a way as any to deal with most press hullabaloos. When the force might have been justifiably shaken by the Trial of the Detectives, he did what he could to defuse the situation by unflappability, and allowed a more vigorous new broom to sweep as clean as he liked. When the Fenian bombings started, he was wise to let

the work of ending the campaign fall to those who could use covert policing and plain clothes infiltration without himself publicizing or openly endorsing such effective but unpopular and 'unEnglish' spying. His untimely resignation was lamented by London's cabmen, who presented him with a silver model of a hansom cab.

Of him it might be said, as it has been of many Prime Ministers: if he had only retired after five years in office instead of 10, he would have left a much higher reputation.

HENDON POLICE COLLEGE Established under the Metropolitan Police Act, 1933, in response to Lord Trenchard's perception of a need for specially trained officers, some with public school or university backgrounds. Opened by the Prince of Wales (later Edward VIII) on 31 May 1934. Closed September 1939 for the duration of the war, and never reopened in its original form, becoming the Metropolitan Police Training School in 1946.

Trenchard's belief that the Force would be improved if more officers came from the sort of backgrounds filling commissioned ranks in the armed forces was controversial. It was shared by some other Commissioners and Assistant Commissioners, but in general opposed by the rank and file, the *Police Review*, and the Federation. It had taken a long slow haul for constables to win the right to rise to Chief Constable (Adolphus Williamson, F. P. Wensley), and Assistant Commissioner (Sir James Olive, Sir George Abbiss). There would not be a Commissioner risen from the ranks for another 27 years. A few provincial constabularies had made the break and were willing to appoint Chief Constables (the provincial equivalent of Commissioners), from the best long-serving professional policemen – often Met officers. The Metropolitan rank and file were, frankly, fed up with a situation in which the highest offices in the Met were automatically handed out to ex-army and Air Force officers, prison commissioners, colonial civil servants and lawyers. It could also be argued that it lowered the status of Constable, and ignored the fact that a Police Constable's responsibilities are vastly greater than those of an army private. Despite the (fulfilled) promise that more than half the entrants to the new Police

College would be drawn from the ranks, the proposal was generally unwelcome.

Outside the Force, elements in the Labour Party shared and voiced the rank and file suspicion. The Police College, it was said, was pandering to militarism. It would create an 'unEnglish' officer caste.

But Trenchard was not easy to stop when he was determined. He acquired the Air Force base at Hendon with the old premises of the London Flying Club as existing buildings. A large area of the former aerodrome became sports grounds, in keeping with Trenchard's encouragement of physical fitness and good teamwork through voluntary sport. He proposed an ambitious building project (which got no further than the foundation stone laid by the Prince of Wales) and set up a 15-month course, following which Hendon graduates passed directly to the newly instituted rank of Junior Station Inspectors. His requirement that all students should include dinner jackets in their equipment evoked some derision, and seemed to confirm the widespread fear that this was 'class' education with a snobbish belief that some people were innately 'officers and gentlemen', and others were not. But in the five years of its existence, 197 young officers passed through its doors, many of whom were to achieve outstanding careers, including Sir Joseph Simpson, the first Metropolitan Commissioner to rise through the ranks from constable. As adjuncts of the College, the Driver Training School, Forensic Science Laboratory, Wireless School and Detective Training School were all opened between 1934 and 1936.

The Attlee government, with policeman's son Herbert Morrison as former wartime Home Secretary, had no hesitation in not renewing the 'experiment' after the war, despite the fact that Commissioner Sir Harold Scott was one of those who favoured special education and accelerated promotion for high-flyers, hoping that this would attract more recruits from public schools and universities. For the future, in-service training courses for senior ranks would be offered at a national rather than a Metropolitan Police College (first Ryton-on-Dunsmore, then Bramshill). The Hendon complex became the Metropolitan Police Training School, the basis of today's Peel Centre.

Trenchard's Forensic Science Laboratory and specialist schools survived the closure of his college, and flourish to this day. His perception of a need for senior officers who did not generally come from elementary education and artisan employment to climb laboriously through the ranks and wait for a Buggins' turn that might never come has been met by sharply increased recruitment of graduates, the release of many able officers to complete degree courses while serving, and new systems of accelerated promotion.

HENDON TRAINING SCHOOL See Peel Centre.

HENRY, SIR EDWARD, BT, GCVO, KCB, CSI (1850–1931) Commissioner 1903–18.

Born, 1850, Shadwell, Wapping, London, the son of an Irish Doctor. Educ. St Edmunds College, Ware, Hertfordshire, and University College, London. Accepted into the Indian Civil Service 1873 as an Assistant Magistrate Collector, later became Secretary and aide-de-camp to the Lieutenant Governor of Bengal and joint Secretary to the Board of Revenue. 1891 appointed Inspector General of the Bengal Police. Seconded to South Africa 1900 to organize the civil police in Pretoria and Johannesburg. On leave in London that same year gave evidence on the subject

RECRUITS STANDING BY A POLICE BEDFORD OB BUS AT THE HENDON TRAINING CENTRE, c.1950.

of Identification (Bertillonage and Fingerprinting) to the Belper Committee. Assistant Commissioner (Crime), 1901. Commissioner, 1903. Knighted 1906. Shot and wounded November 1912. Resigned following Police Strike, 1918. Bt. November 1918. Died, Ascot, 19 February 1931.

Sir Edward Henry was one of the great Metropolitan Police Commissioners. He, more than anyone else, set the Metropolitan Police Service on the path away from the beloved Victorian institution of gentleman amateur 'toffs' commanding humble, loyal, and rather comic policemen, and into the age of modern up-to-date professional policing. He restored morale, instituted proper training and added a fourth Assistant Commissioner as part of a new departmental structure which was to last for 50 years. It is ironic that almost every history of the police service puts these developments to one side and concentrates on his pioneering skills in developing a unique, workable fingerprint classification system, which became the backbone of Criminal Investigation Departments throughout the world.

When Henry was appointed Inspector-General of the Bengal Police he found that finger and palm prints were routinely used by the Presidency administration to prevent corrupt impersonation by illiterate native workers. The system had been pioneered by another English civil servant, Sir William Herschel, 40 years earlier but its major drawback, ever since fingerprints had been grouped into arches, loops, whorls and composites, was the difficulty of quickly sorting and identifying individual prints from a mass kept on record. Henry applied himself to the problem and worked out an infallible sequence of observations and calculations which made it possible for fingerprints to be easily filed, searched and traced through thousands upon thousands of others without prior scientific training. His monograph Classification and Uses of Fingerprints was published by the Government of India in 1897 and became a classic textbook. In 1900 when Henry gave evidence to the Belper Committee examining the relative success of Bertillonage and Fingerprinting he showed the greater reliability and accessibility of his method. His ability and experience were quickly weighed up and when Dr Robert Anderson resigned as Assistant Commissioner (Crime) the following year he was appointed in his place with the expectation that he would become Commissioner as soon as Bradford retired.

On 1 July 1901, Assistant Commissioner Henry established the first Fingerprint Bureau in the UK at Scotland Yard. Its primary purpose was to ensure that courts and prisons were not deceived by villains wanting to conceal their previous convictions. The public took note when it contributed to crime detection, bringing about the conviction of burglar Henry Jackson in 1902 and the execution of the Stratton brothers for murder in 1905.

AC Henry also brought the first typewriter into Scotland Yard other than those Registry had sensibly acquired for Civil Staff. Out went clerks laboriously drafting letter-book copies of the Commissioner's correspondence and in came the purple typed carbon copy. In 1902 Henry had a private telegraph run from Paddington Green Police Station to his home and in 1904 he had it replaced with a telephone. This was galloping into the technological age and once he became Commissioner, Henry showed that he meant business. By insisting that Divisional Stations were in telephonic communication with each other, he swept aside critics who were adamant that public telephone exchanges would be a security risk, and those that proclaimed, 'Why, we'd have all sorts of people ringing us up!' On an experimental basis at first, and then as a matter of determined policy, police stations could be reached by anyone with a telephone and directory and the fixed point police telephone box passed beyond the uneasy experimental stage at which his predecessor was prepared to leave it.

The technological age came to the police with a vengeance during Henry's time. The motor car's permitted speed was raised from 12 mph to 20 mph. For the first time since Sir Richard Mayne encouraged constables to be deferential towards their 'betters', the upper and middle classes faced humble bobbies who told them they were breaking the criminal law in the form of motoring offences. They didn't like it. They thought speed traps were unfair and unsportsmanlike. With the Metropolitan Police responsible for traffic policing in London, there was no way they could retain the undiminished affection of the bourgeoisie that Bradford had nurtured.

As Commissioner, Henry's first act was to deal with a public order problem Bradford had avoided. Large numbers of unemployed soldiers who had returned from South Africa formed begging processions on the streets and acted in a

SPY

SIR EDWARD HENRY.

threatening manner to passers-by when police-men were not in sight. Henry, simply by using regulations which prohibited street collections unless they were licensed by the police, caused the sturdy beggars to melt away.

Henry was able to increase the force strength by another much-needed 1600 officers and he also squeezed money out of the Home Office for four new section houses and additional married quarters. In 1907 he rationalized the administra-tion into four departments under the four Assis-tant Commissioners: AC A to manage the uni-form branch's administration and discipline; AC B to be responsible for pay and legal business and increasingly, traffic; AC C to handle serious crime and security; and AC D to deal with com-plaints from the public and a ragbag of licensing regulations and minor offences, lumped together because there didn't seem to be anywhere else to put them. Subsequently the public complaints element would lead to AC D's department tak-ing over disciplinary and related personnel ques-tions from AC A.

In the same year Peel House was opened and trainee constables were at last trained in some-thing more than simple drill. Henry, however, had his share of problems. The Adolph Beck case blew up in the authorities' face just as he came into office, but it was generally recognized that it was none of his making and it quickly became known that his fingerprint system would have obviated the mistake had it been available. The Mme D'Angely case was another hot potato dropped in the Commissioner's lap but out of that came a Commission of Enquiry in 1908 which reported entirely favourably on street policing. Indeed, the Police were winning new favourable opinions as an increasingly popular press enjoyed more and more sensational crime reporting. It became clear that with fingerprint-ing and nascent forensic science the CID was solving more crimes than it had done in the past. Murder mysteries were no longer mishandled as in the Daniel Good case, or drawn-out failures as in the Jack the Ripper enquiry. The transatlantic arrest of Dr Crippen brought Scotland Yard international acclaim for the first time; the Stinie

Morrison case was a masterpiece of detection to all, except malcontents like John Syme who argued that Stinie had been framed; and the Morrison investigation, the Siege of Sidney Street and the Tottenham Outrage suggested that our brave men in blue were holding the line against vicious anarchist immigrant killers. Public order, however, especially with respect to labour disputes, gave Henry more difficulty.

The Government was entirely satisfied by the way the uniform police and Special Branch observed and handled the suffragette movement. The Rhondda Valley miners' strike of 1910 was firmly controlled when Winston Churchill as Home Secretary sent in the Metropolitan Police and the army to maintain order and the Met won plaudits from their outspoken future Commissioner, Sir Nevil Macready, who commented on their manifest superiority to the local police. Although minimum force was used to prevent the strikes from turning into riots, the use of outsiders and soldiers was deeply resented by the miners, and 'Tonypandy' remained a bitter word for many in the Labour movement who never forgave the Met or Churchill. The popular and successful dock strike of 1911 also set the police at odds with trade unionists. While responsible Labour leaders recognized the need for order to be preserved, they objected to policemen shifting cargoes from boats: everyone expected the army to carry out such strike-breaking labour. Few thought the police would be called upon to carry out this work when their primary role was to keep the peace without fear or favour between those who legitimately withdrew their labour and those who needed that labour completed by someone else.

On 27 November 1912 Henry was shot at three times and wounded as he opened the front door to his Kensington home. His assailant, Albert George Bowes, had been refused a licence to drive a 'mechanical stage carriage' as a result of a conviction he had received for being drunk and disorderly eight months previously. When Bowes was later convicted at the Central Criminal Court of his attempted murder, Henry, in keeping with his humanitarian spirit made a personal plea for mercy on Bowes's behalf and had his life sentence reduced to 15 years. Henry never

really recovered from his ordeal: the whole experience had been traumatic and the injury he had received caused him pain for the rest of his life. He became increasingly aloof and detached from his force, even though he succeeded in winning them the guaranteed weekly rest day they had long demanded and equally long been refused by Home Secretaries advised by Receivers and Home Office officials who insisted that it was out of the question to afford such an expensive privilege.

Henry was ready to retire and would have done so in 1914 had not the war broken out but as a matter of patriotic duty he agreed to continue because the Government's choice to replace him, Sir Nevil Macready, was required by the War Office to remain in post as their Adjutant-General. Henry's force lost manpower to the armed services and acquired additional wartime duties. Over 1000 reservists from the police were recalled to the colours and others were called away to guard docks and ammunition bases. Three hundred Metropolitan Police officers were summoned to teach parade drill to the raw recruits of the 'Contemptible Little Army'. Three thousand Special constables were enlisted to keep London policed and Henry put the *ad hoc* constables on a permanent basis.

In 1913 the unofficial National Union of Police and Prison Officers (NUPPO) was formed and as a result the Government decreed that any police officer joining a union or association without the Commissioner's sanction rendered himself liable to dismissal. Constable Thiel, as one of the organizers of the unofficial police union, was one of the first to be dismissed from the Met for such a grave breach of discipline. Although Henry was unable to raise the Force's pay to meet the wartime inflation, in December 1917 he managed to persuade the Government to increase substantially the bonus his men received. Not content with this, he went back to the Government midway through 1918 with proposals to advance again not only his officers' salaries, but also their conditions of service, including an up-to-date generous pension scheme which would be of special benefit to the war widow. Unfortunately time and the will of the Government were not to be on Henry's side.

Throughout 1918 Henry was ill advised by AC

C Basil Thomson, who claimed agitation for a police union was the work of a Bolshevist TUC who wanted to get hold of the Force and run a police state. His deputy, Sir Frederick Wodehouse, assured him that the bulk of the Force would never support strike action, but strike they did. On Tuesday 27 August 1918, while Henry was on leave and the Home Secretary, Sir George Cave, was at his West Country home, NUPPO served on the Government and the police authorities a written ultimatum consisting of four demands. Strike action was threatened if these demands were not met in full by midnight, 29 August 1918. The Government and Henry's deputy dithered, misjudged the feelings of the men and regrettably called their bluff.

At midnight, on Friday 30 August 1918, approximately 11,000 Metropolitan and City of London Police officers withdrew their labour. The following day, the Prime Minister, the Home Secretary and Sir Edward Henry met the strike leaders. The Prime Minister, fearing that the country was on the verge of 'Bolshevism' gave into all the men's demands except official recognition of the police union. In keeping with the feelings of Sir George Cave and four former Home Secretaries, Henry believed that an impartial police force could not and should not align itself to a trade union movement which could, at a moment's notice, call upon its membership to take industrial action of one kind or another. With the chance that the Police Union could become recognized by the Government in peace time, and with the offer to reinstate former Police Constable and union agitator Tommy Thiel, Henry felt let down and betrayed. His immediate offer of resignation was accepted by the Prime Minister.

On 25 November 1918, in view of his long and honourable service, the King conferred on Henry a Baronetcy, an honour he was pleased to receive as his son would inherit his title. It became a matter of bitterly ironical grief when Edward John predeceased him in 1930 at the age of 22. On Thursday 19 February 1931 Sir Edward Henry died peacefully at Cissbury, his retirement home in Ascot, Berkshire.

HILTON, BARONESS JENNIFER QPM (B.1936) First career Metropolitan Police officer to be created a life peer.

Born Nicosia, Cyprus. Educ. Bedales, 1948–54. After a few classes at the Sorbonne in 1955, and a few months social work in an East End settlement, joined the Met, 1956. Constable in H Division (Whitechapel), 1956–8, N Division (King's Cross), 1958–60. Promoted Sergeant, K Division (Newham), 1961. Awarded Sybil Hill Trophy for most promising WPS, 1963. Promoted Inspector, N Division (Islington), 1965. Bramshill Scholarship to Manchester University, 1967–71. BA in Psychology, 1970. MA, with thesis on black school-leavers' aspirations, 1971. Returned to Divisions at Cannon Row (A Division) and Hammersmith (F Division), 1971–2. Chief Inspector and Lecturer in Psychology, Bramshill College, 1973–4. Published autobiographical careers guidance book, *The Gentle Arm of the Law* in 1973, and with Dr S. M. Hunt *Social Experience and Individual Development*, 1974. Superintendent, Airport Division (Heathrow), 1977–8. Commander, NSY, from which point on the most senior woman officer in the Met, 1984. Acting Deputy Assistant Commissioner and involved in Equal Opportunities (Race and Gender) Initiatives, 1990. Retired, 1990, and created Baroness Hilton of Eggardon, taking her seat among the Labour peers in the House of Lords.

Lady Hilton's police career was consistently paradoxical. She entered the Met as a career alternative requiring no very high academic qualifications after failing her A levels and finding untrained social work made her feel too much of a middle-class 'Lady Bountiful'. Nevertheless, her cosmopolitan and public school background made her seem something of an upper-class academic in the 1950s police. And yet she revelled in policing the tough low life of Whitechapel and King's Cross, and won promotion to Sergeant in the shortest time then possible. The Sybil Hill Trophy explicitly marked her as a probable high-flyer, and she proceeded to march steadily up the promotion ladder. But the Bramshill Scholarship to Manchester, her taking a fourth year to complete an MA, and her authorship of two books marked her as an intellectual, and her subject, psychology, was somewhat suspect from the viewpoint of canteen culture. Her Diploma in History of Art was also something unexpected in the supposedly macho and sports-mad police force.

Sir Kenneth Newman's intellectual style of Commissionership was, however, one which recognized her talents, and in her own words, her career took off again. There were still paradoxes. She was a prominent member of the Howard League for Penal Reform, and shocked the Federation when her name and rank as Commander appeared high on a list of prominent supporters signing a full-page advertisement in the *Guardian* opposing the reintroduction of capital punishment. Yet she made the canteens' legitimate views known to the liberal intelligentsia, pointing out to the Howard League that overstressing 'soft policing' values and community relations could weaken necessary enforcement of the law and even demoralise parts of the service – even when she personally was playing an important part in developing community policing.

As Deputy Assistant Commissioner (Personnel), Ms Hilton examined 'equal opportunities' employment, which ultimately became the policy of the Met, though without the corollary of controversial implementation by 'positive discrimination'. Commander Hilton's experience was that pockets of sexist prejudice existed in the Met, especially in the CID, but rank was respected so deeply that this never involved insubordination. A woman officer's difficulties with prejudice would usually come from equals and seniors. She felt that being a woman had probably delayed her promotion to Commander, but only by one or two years.

And the force had changed over the time of

JENNIFER HILTON AS A CHIEF INSPECTOR AFTER WINNING THE QUEEN'S POLICE GOLD MEDAL ESSAY COMPETITION.

her career. She joined a Police Force with 168 graduates nationwide and retired from one with 7000. Her predecessors, Dorothy Peto, Elizabeth Bather and Shirley Becke, had necessarily devoted much energy to promoting the interests of women in the Met. Commander Hilton served those interests best by acting professionally as though her gender was not a matter to be taken into account.

On retirement, Commander Hilton took a couple of Open University courses on the history of culture. Her membership of the Labour Party had always been a private matter, so there was some surprise when she was elevated to the peerage and took the Labour whip. Her own view was that she proved to the Lords and the country, 'just by being there, that the police service is not the right-wing, macho, chauvinist organization people think it is'. Her maiden speech praised the police service.

HISTORICAL MUSEUM Correctly Metropolitan Police Museum, but colloquially referred to as 'the Historical' or 'History Museum' to distinguish it from the Black Museum (or Metropolitan Police Crime Museum) and other specialized Met Museums. A large collection of police memorabilia held in a warehouse at Charlton under the care of a Civil Staff curator and deputy curator.

Founded as the Bow Street Museum in 1949, when Chief Superintendent Arthur Rowlerson (Warrant No. 11137, retired 1952)) wrote to *The Times* asking for memorabilia to mount an exhibition to mark the bicentenary of Henry Fielding's appointing the constables who became the Bow Street Runners. An overwhelming response provided sufficient exhibits to be kept on display until, in 1967, Inspector Haggett wrote to Commissioner Sir Joseph Simpson suggesting that they form the basis of a Museum supported by a Force History Society. Both suggestions were approved. The collection was renamed the Metropolitan Police Historical Museum and ex-policewoman Mrs Audrey Sams was appointed its first curator. With the help of members of the Architect and Surveyor's Department she cleaned and converted the top floor of Bow Street, arranged displays and standing cabinets, and inventoried the collection. At the same time the Museums Advisory Board was set up to oversee first the running of the Historical Museum and later 'the Black' and the specialist museums as well.

In 1979, a temporary exhibition on the police at the London Museum led to a careful re-examination of the Historical Museum's artefacts and the recognition that some which had been thought originals were replicas. It also led to realization that there was sufficient interest to justify

finding new premises and opening a museum for the benefit of the public.

In 1983 the space in Bow Street was required for operational purposes. Oliver Green, curator of the London Transport Museum, carried out a feasibility study for a Metropolitan Police Museum on a site at Wapping, including selected exhibits from the Black Museum. The Metropolitan Police Museum Trust was formed, but there were problems in finding the right premises and obtaining Home Office support to open a public

museum. The collection was transferred to a warehouse in Brixton, and subsequently moved to another in Charlton. Although in 1990 the Curator (Richard Sharp) acquired academic qualifications in museum studies, throughout his time and to the present, it remained impossible to

(FROM LEFT TO RIGHT) THE RECEIVER, KENNETH PARKER, MRS AUDREY SAMS AND COMMISSIONER SIR JOHN WALDRON INSPECTING THE BOW STREET POLICE MUSEUM IN 1969.

display the collection properly, a situation the Friends of the Metropolitan Police Museum hope to see remedied.

The museum has an almost complete collection of original and facsimile constables' uniforms, showing all the changes made at different dates (and compensating for the one missing tunic by holding Jack Warner's TV *Dixon of Dock Green* costume); an extensive collection of appointments from different periods, and including much of the Abbiss Collection of truncheons; furniture and fittings from old police stations, including a station dock; a large collection of internal administrative documents covering the history of the force such as were not considered of sufficient public interest to be deposited in the Public Record Office; a broad sample collection of officers' operational books – notebooks, occurrence books, stop books, disorderly house books, habitual criminals books and the like; a collection of medals, awards and sporting trophies; a large collection of photographs, posters

OFFICERS ON FOOT PATROL IN THE 1940s.

and notices; books, including the Russel Gray collection; items too large for display in the Black Museum, such as the bath in which 'Brides-in-the-Bath' Smith drowned his last wife; individual examples of a beat wheel, a hand ambulance, a Cadbury's chocolate bar in a presentation box as distributed to constables lining the streets for George VI's coronation; and a ball-and-chain of uncertain provenance, but believed to have been in use in Nottingham until 1842.

HISTORY SOCIETY The Metropolitan Police History Society held its inaugural meeting on 6 March 1967 at New Scotland Yard. It was formed to increase the awareness of history and tradition among the Police Service and those connected with it. The Society holds regular lectures at New Scotland Yard on a wide range of interesting historical topics.

HOLMAN, PC ARTHUR (B.1911) Pioneer police dog-handler, and trainer of Rex III.

Joined Met, 1932. Served in H Division (Whitechapel). Transferred to W Division (Tooting), 1935, for alleged loitering and gossiping

with a fellow constable when on beat, a charge that was expunged from his record later when the witness was found to be of bad character. After WWII, served as Aid to CID carrying out covert operations for the Ghost Squad in Mitcham, Tooting and Balham. Responded to Scotland Yard request for volunteers with experience of dogs to train as handlers, 1950. On hearing that one of the available dogs was called Rex III, Holman decided he wanted it, as he had already owned two successive dogs called Rex. When he saw that Rex III was older than the normal 12-week puppy accepted by the police, he disregarded arguments that this would make him difficult to train, and accepted what he rightly saw as a formidably strong and intelligent animal.

Sufficiently dog-mad that once, when out shopping without Rex, he absentmindedly said 'Heel!' to his daughter, Holman proved an outstanding trainer, and Rex came to hold the highest reputation of any dog in the force. Rex and Holman made 125 arrests, and pioneered the use of the dog's nose for searches rather than simple tracking. After Rex's untimely death at the age of 8, Holman's book *My Dog Rex* gave one of the best accounts of the nature, training and uses of police dogs that has ever been written.

HOME BEAT OFFICERS (OR PERMANENT BEAT OR COMMUNITY OFFICERS) The operational heart of Community Policing. Constables assigned to particular residential locales (often housing estates) to carry out high-profile foot patrols with the object of making themselves familiar with and to residents.

The system originated with Unit beat policing, as a counter-balance to panda cars, aiming to recover the major benefits of the traditional 'bobby on the beat', with the added advantage of integrating the police into local communities, especially those of ethnic minorities who feel distanced from the Met, and those where local needs require effective policing of vandalism, pilfering and juvenile disorder or sustained community contact.

The system has always operated with a great deal of discretion. Home Beat officers sometimes lived on their beats and were entrusted with so much responsibility that they could book on duty and off again without attending the police station at all. At Area and Divisional levels, senior officers with managerial roles make locally informed decisions as to the amount of Home Beat policing that is desirable. They may or may not aim at the (almost unattainable) 'full geographical coverage', and may or may not formalize the system with tiers of Community Sergeants and Community Inspectors to organize and direct the Home Beats. The Home Beat officer on patrol is equally given considerable discretion. No set timings determine their procedure along the beat. This allows them to stop and converse with the public. Whereas the old-style beat policeman was expected to maintain a courteous but definite distance between himself and members of the public (see demeanour), Home Beat officers are encouraged to become intimate – often on first-name terms – with their more valuable contacts. Through information from shopkeepers and long-term residents they may come to know the identities and habits of local petty offenders. If they are retained on duty in the community for long enough, they may observe children growing up, and know from early personal observation which of them are in danger of brushing with the law. They can encourage and sustain the growth of Neighbourhood Watch schemes, which will invariably mean good contacts once a local organizer and committee are in place.

The work can be extremely difficult where entrenched distrust of the police has become a normal community value, but sometimes Home Beat officers have won the trust of suspicious neighbourhoods by being perceived as distinctly different from officers more concerned with law enforcement. Home Beat policing has to be measured by different standards from the alternative reactive relief policing, wherein officers are sent on patrol with the direct purpose of imposing the law by firm enforcement and the arrest of criminals, or answer rapid response calls to react to reported incidents or crimes being perpetrated by people with whom they may be unfamiliar. Home Beat officers have to encourage a positive attitude to the law and the police. They may have to foster a sense of community where there has been none previously. Yet if a Home Beat officer interprets the befriending role too liberally, the job of law enforcement becomes concomitantly

more difficult. The best Home Beat officers have used their specialized local knowledge to deliver a real and lasting impact in reducing crime and misbehaviour.

The system is unpopular with those who favour firmly authoritarian policing as a response to socially disruptive delinquency, and may not understand that Home Beat officers are always there to uphold the law. Nor are matters made easier by the fact that Home Beat officers can always be switched to relief at a moment's need (especially when urgent major incidents occur, cf. Keith Blakelock). Since the system has become increasingly accepted, it has sometimes become a stepping stone to promotion, and sometimes (giving its intelligence-gathering role) transfer to CID. Such career advances almost invariably mean a shift to a new Division, or less locally based responsibilities, thus breaking the continuity of contact with the community.

HOME SECRETARY From the time of Peel's Police Act, the authority to whom the Commissioner is responsible for the running of the Metropolitan Police. The Home Secretary's concomitant responsibility is to recommend to the Crown names for Commissioners and Assistant Commissioners, and he may require their resignation. The power to enforce the Commis-

SATIRICAL CARTOON CALLING FOR THE DISMISSAL OF HOME SECRETARY SIR HENRY MATTHEWS FOR INCOMPETENT HANDLING OF POLICE AFFAIRS AND THE JACK THE RIPPER INVESTIGATION.

sioner's resignation has only been overtly used against Sir Edward Henry, and then on the calculated political orders of Prime Minister Lloyd George (See Police Strike, 1918). Nonetheless, Sir Edmund Henderson jumped before he was pushed, and Sir Charles Warren was encouraged by an almost insulting letter to tender a resignation that was gratefully accepted. A Special Tribunal in 1992 considered alleged improprieties by Assistant Commissioner Wyn Jones which led in 1993 to Home Secretary Michael Howard advising the Queen that his Royal Warrant should be withdrawn.

Lord Denning, Master of the Rolls, ruled in a 1968 case brought against the Commissioner by an MP who wanted him to enforce the Gaming Act more stringently, that the Home Secretary's powers did not extend to ordering the Commissioner how to manage the police, though he could demand a report from him at any time, and he could dismiss him in the interests of good policing.

The Home Secretary has nevertheless always been an important adjunct of the Metropolitan Police, answering questions in Parliament about their conduct and influencing their practice by guidelines and directives issued in the form of Home Office Circulars, and by the power of approval over certain items of expenditure. Home Secretaries are also highly visible whenever the police become a political issue, and a number have played a significant part in the history of the Met.

Sir Robert Peel's reputation as the greatest of all Home Secretaries rests almost entirely on his establishment of the New Police force. But within a year the Wellington government lost power to the Whigs, and Lord Melbourne succeeded Peel as Home Secretary. Melbourne was a moderate – he had served in Tory administrations under Canning and Wellington – but he was not above playing skilful politics with the New Police in the days of their early unpopularity. Too shrewd to give way to calls for their immediate abolition, he nonetheless distanced himself from them at the same time as he used them. This became most apparent in the Coldbath Fields Riot. Lord John Russell, who became Home Secretary when Melbourne became Prime Minister, was also realistic but cool. He knew the police were essential, and his confirmation of their position in the Police Act, 1839 was decisive in ensuring that there would be no future serious attempts to abolish the Met: rather their excellent example was to be imitated across the country. But typically, Russell permitted rather than ordered the shires and boroughs to establish police forces. He refused to consider Peel's and the Commissioners' ideal hope for a nationwide police force directed from Scotland Yard. In this he reflected the Whigs' love of liberty and fear of continental-style policing without consent.

In 1855, Palmerston, who like Melbourne was a moderate Whig and happily served or supported moderate Tory administrations, held office as Home Secretary for a short period. And like Melbourne, he used the police adroitly rather than openly, urging them to suppress the demonstration against Lord Robert Grosvenor's Sunday Trading Bill, and distancing himself from the result when the Hyde Park Riot, 1855 ensued.

The Derby-Disraeli governments' Home Secretary, Spencer Walpole, proved as inconsistent as his Whig predecessors, instructing Sir Richard Mayne to ban the Reform League's Manhood Suffrage Demonstration of 1866, and then receiving a delegation from the League and apologizing for Mayne's incompetence when this show of oppression deteriorated into the Hyde Park Riot 1866. Happily the public was not completely misled, for once, and the following year Walpole was forced to resign. Subsequent Home Secretaries usually resorted to Commissions of Enquiry to give a more comprehensive, but delayed, account of police crises to the House of Commons. Thus no Home Secretary was held responsible for the lack of police action leading up to the Clerkenwell Bombing, or the Trial of the Detectives, or the Miss Cass affair, the three great police scandals of the late Victorian period.

In fact the next Home Secretary with great impact on the police was Sir William Harcourt, a robust and ebullient political heavyweight, who introduced birching for juvenile offenders and oversaw the suppression of the Fenian bombings in the early 1880s. Harcourt deserved his reputation as the greatest Home Secretary for many decades, and firmly defended the Met when Gladstone himself advanced the belief that London's police might best be managed by placing them in the hands of local politicians. Harcourt sturdily insisted that the national duty of protecting London's national public buildings against bomb outrages simply could not be carried out if the police had to be answerable to vestrymen (the predecessors of Borough Councillors), whose libertarian sympathy with Irish Nationalist demands, he felt, would encourage them to obstruct necessary police operations. Despite sporadic attempts to bring the Met under local authority control, especially after the founding of the London County Council in 1889, the idea effectively dropped out of the political agenda for 100 years.

During the Jack the Ripper scare, supposed police incompetence was used as a weapon to try to secure the resignation of the unpopular Conservative Home Secretary Sir Henry Matthews. It was also held against him that his mishandling had led to the resignations of two Metropolitan Police Commissioners (Warren and Monro) in less than three years.

H. H. Asquith's successful tenure of the Home Office from 1892 to 1895 was of importance to the Met because he re-established the right to hold public meetings in Trafalgar Square, despite its lying within the 1.6km (1 mile) radius of the Palace of Westminster wherein Sessional Orders prohibited obstruction while Parliament was sitting. In the later Liberal government which Asquith headed, Winston Churchill was a notable Home Secretary from 1910 to 1911. His use of Metropolitan officers to police the South Wales miners strike and his personal involvement with the Siege of Sidney Street were generally seen at the time as marks of his unreliable flamboyance rather than brilliance. His reprieve of Stinie Morrison, however, was a measure of his ability to read papers carefully and come to wise conclusions.

Sir Edward Shortt, Lloyd George's Home Secretary from 1919 to 1922, was another decisive figure. His firm rejection of the nascent police union NUPPO was generally welcomed. Shortt could not tolerate being exposed as underinformed in Parliament, and this had unhappy consequences for Mrs Sofia Stanley when she briefed Lady Astor MP for her successful defence of the Women Police as they lay under threat of abolition as an economy measure.

Sir William Joynson-Hicks, Baldwin's Home Secretary in the 1920s, courted popular puritanical support at the expense of the Met by leaving in place the unenforceable Street Gaming Act of 1906, the unpopular licensing laws which encouraged officers to 'spy' on private clubs, and the ready interpretation of serious works of art and literature as 'obscene'.

When Herbert Morrison became Home Secretary in the WWII coalition, a policeman's son was, for the first and only time, in authority over the Met. Possibly for this reason, but more probably because he was preoccupied with organization of the Home Front, Mr Morrison made little impact on the police. His successor, Chuter Ede, on the other hand, was extremely popular with the Force, probably because he followed the lead of Commissioner Sir Harold Scott who, as a civil servant with neither military nor police experience, sensibly played himself in by listening to what his senior officers told him. Thus the abolition of Trenchard's Police College met a grievance of officers who came up through the ranks from working-class origins, and the harmless action of holding a fashion parade to select new uniforms for the women police freed them from the longstanding tendency to imposed frumpishness.

The most distinguished Home Secretaries of the Conservative governments from 1951 to 1964 were Sir David Maxwell Fyfe and R. A. Butler. The former robustly supported the general police wish to see capital punishment maintained, especially in the light of the deaths of PCs Nat Edgar and Sidney Miles. Unfortunately, he gave hostages to fortune by over-confident assertions that it was impossible that an innocent man ever could have been or ever would be hanged under English law. Mr Butler, characteristically, directed sticky police questions away from himself into the laps of committees of inquiry.

During this period, James (later Lord) Callaghan was the Police Federation's spokesman in Parliament, which led to great hopes that he would prove an admirable Home Secretary from the Met's point of view. When Callaghan succeeded Roy (later Lord) Jenkins in 1968, he gave strong support to Sir Robert Mark's anti-corruption sweep. As an ex-Chancellor, he did not find it possible to make the generous upward revision of pay which most officers felt was necessary. (Roy Jenkins' historic tenure of the office of Home Secretary was noted for the liberalization of laws persecuting adult homosexuals and serious art with erotic content. But apart from his final abolition of capital punishment, he did not essentially affect the Met except insofar as he oversaw the force amalgamations of 1966 which were coupled with the reorganization of local authorities in London and the MPD's being given further pieces of Essex to police.)

Jack Straw, Home Secretary at the end of the century, found himself with Metropolitan police questions back in his dispatch box as the Blair government decided that the 10-year experiment of doing without a metropolis-wide tier of local government had failed. With the proposal to create a new elected Greater London Authority and, for the first time, an elected Mayor of London, came the decision that the new democratic cre-

ations and the Metropolitan Police Authority should contribute a greater input to MPS policy than had been the case previously. Those who hoped that Home Office control would be entirely ceded to local politicians were disappointed that the final power of appointing and (if necessary) dismissing Commissioners would remain in the Home Secretary's hands.

HORWOOD, BRIGADIER-GENERAL SIR WILLIAM THOMAS FRANCIS GBE, KCB, DSO (1868–1943) Commissioner, 1920–8.

At the age of 20 he obtained a commission in the 5th Lancers. Adjutant, 49th Regimental District, 1900–2. War Office 1902–10. Chief of London and North Eastern Railway Police, 1911–14. Deputy Assistant Adjutant-General, War Office, 1914–15. Provost-Marshal, GHQ, British Expeditionary Force. Joined the Met 1918 as Assistant Commissioner A, and Deputy Commissioner. Commissioner, 1920. Retired, 1928.

When Sir Nevil Macready brought his former staff officer into the Met it seemed that he was sensibly calling in the one former wartime colleague who had relevant experience as pre-war head of the LNER Transport Police. And Macready's trust in Horwood was so great that he made his appointment as Commissioner a virtual pre-condition of his own acceptance of the transfer to command the troops in Ireland.

Although Horwood's term as Commissioner was marked by the extremely successful policing of the General Strike, for which the Met along with other police forces received high commendations in the press, he left the force with much lower morale and public esteem than he found. Unlike his four predecessors, Monro, Bradford, Henry and Macready, he made no attempt to get to know his men at the outset by visiting the stations and hearing opinions from men 'at the sharp end'. A clerk in his office recalled him as 'an unattractive man who mistook arrogance for leadership. I never saw him smile or return a courtesy, and his attitude towards his job seemed to be one of distasteful necessity.' The force returned his contempt by disdainfully nicknaming him 'The Chocolate Soldier' when a paranoid lunatic named Walter Tatam nearly assassinated

him with some poisoned chocolates sent through the post. Similar parcels had been received by other senior policemen, but Horwood was the only one who injudiciously sampled them (thinking them a birthday present from his daughter).

The sobriquet underlined the doubts about 'militarization of the police' which were expressed at this time by left-wing politicians. It was echoed by some officers who were concerned that Horwood continued Macready's bad habit of appointing old comrades-in-arms to senior positions. Sir Basil Thomson's wish to become personally involved in pursuing revolutionaries with Special Branch probably impressed Horwood no more than Labour Home Affairs spokesman Arthur Henderson, but Horwood's role became an issue when questions were asked in the House after Thomson's resignation. And Thomson's replacement as Assistant Commissioner C by another military anti-Communist, Maj-Gen Sir Wyndham Childs, worried senior policemen, especially when yet another army officer, Lt-Col Carter, was brought in as Deputy Assistant Commissioner. It seemed that too many influential and senior posts were being reserved for former military comrades.

The Met felt Horwood let them down when he made no attempt to resist a government demand that police pay be reduced as a public economy under the 1922 'Geddes Axe' expenditure cuts. Beating Geddes over pay was an early success of the Police Federation. Horwood, after one lame letter of protest, yielded to Geddes' other demand and suspended recruiting, allowing his uniformed force to be reduced by 5% (about 1000 men). The Met would have been seriously undermanned for the General Strike had not the government decided in 1925 to hand back policing of naval and military establishments to the Admiralty and the War Office. Almost overnight, 1300 policemen were restored to general duties, and the force was almost at full strength when the strike came.

Horwood failed to provide clear leadership when the press (headed by the *Daily Graphic*, but including very responsible newspapers) started warning in 1923 that stories of police misconduct abounded in London. Horwood's response in his annual report was to reply sniffily that

SIR WILLIAM HORWOOD VISITING THE METROPOLITAN AND CITY POLICE ORPHANAGE c.1923.

force, which had to pay £500 compensation to an Indian Army major whose case had been handled without due care and judgment or regard for General Orders.

Then the Irene Savidge scandal broke. Only the determination of Chief Constable Wensley saved the force from the humiliation of having constables sacked for perjury they had not committed and the Yard's internal enquiry discredited by partisan politicians. Horwood actually made things worse by declining to postpone his retirement, so that it seemed (falsely) as though he was leaving in disgrace and by his leaving confirmed that he had allowed the force to deviate into serious malpractices.

This impression was heightened by the Sergeant Goddard scandal which blew up at the same time. Here was indubitable evidence that the blackmail and bribe-taking allegations Horwood derided had some foundation. When his replacement was sought, Home Secretary Sir Herbert Samuel referred publicly to the need for a man to 'restore that confidence to police and public which I have been told on both sides of the House – particularly by the late Home Secretary – have been missing for a time.' It was a harsh, if oblique, rebuke to a would-be administering and building Commissioner who had been denied on economic grounds the funds to make the improvements he wanted. The judgment of some historians has been harsher still, holding Horwood responsible for tolerating the growth of those malpractices in the CID which culminated 40 years later in the Obscene Publications Squad Corruption cases. Horwood can hardly be blamed for letting Wensley's CID have its head in a decade when successful high-profile murder investigations – Ronald True, Henry Jacoby, Norman Thorne, Patrick Mahon, Browne and Kennedy – were the best publicity coming Scotland Yard's way.

HOSTAGE AND EXTORTION UNIT – ORGANISED CRIME GROUP The Unit was reorganized in 1996 to transfer certain duties from SO10 Crime Operations Group.
The Unit's role is to provide the MPS with a co-ordination of policy, strategy and practical issues relating to hostage negotiation, crisis

writers in 'the less reputable journals' seemed 'obsessed with the idea that blackmail and the acceptance of bribes are not uncommon, and that the higher authorities neglect to deal with the offenders . . . Nothing could be more unfair and exasperating to the members of the Force'. This aloof detachment achieved nothing. Over

the next few years the press took up cases where members of the educated public were charged with drunkenness or indecency in Hyde Park, and revived the old complaints that respectable citizens were being harassed. (Cf. Miss Cass, Mme D'Angely). A parliamentary committee under Hugh Macmillan MP heard Horwood speak dismissively about gossip in clubs and his wish that people who made complaints about the police could be made to organize vigilance committees and police public morality in the parks themselves. But he did not win exoneration for the

management, kidnapping and extortion. It is also the central liaison point both nationally and internationally for advice, guidance, training and operational support.

HUE AND CRY Weekly listing of crimes and wanted criminals, published from Bow Street

POLICE GAZETTE – THE FORMER HUE AND CRY IN 1830.

and circulated to magistrates across the country.

Sir Sampson Wright, Chief Magistrate at Bow Street, established it as *The Weekly Hue and Cry* in 1786, an expansion and improvement on Sir John Fielding's *Weekly or Extraordinary Pursuit*. It actually appeared twice a week and gave descriptions of criminals and stolen property, with some account of the examination of suspects at the Metropolitan magistrates' offices. The back page was devoted to army and navy deserters.

With the name changed to *The Public Hue and Cry* it continued until the formation of the Metropolitan Police, whereupon its function was taken over by the *Police Gazette*.

HYDE PARK RIOT, 1855 Peaceful demonstration by London tradesmen which was exacerbated by Government action, and led to recriminations against the police.

In June 1855, Lord Robert Grosvenor, Protestant son of the Marquess of Westminster, introduced a puritanical bill in the Commons to prohibit all forms of trading on Sundays. A small group of London traders gathered in Hyde Park on 24 June to protest, and jeered at the carriages of the gentry, who were assumed to support Lord Robert. At the same time, handbills were distributed advertising a meeting of the 'Leave-us-Alone Club' in the Park for the following Sunday, 1 July. Home Secretary Lord Palmerston unwisely ordered Commissioner Sir Richard Mayne to ban the meeting, and the press gave wide publicity to the ban as part of their ongoing attack on Mayne.

In consequence, a mob of 40,000 assembled in the Park, looking forward to a little trouble, and the intended peaceful rally never took place. The mob started throwing stones at carriages beside the Serpentine, whereupon Superintendent Samuel Hughes (Warrant No. 5383), commanding the 450 men standing by, ordered a baton charge in which several people were knocked down and 49 policemen were injured.

Some of the crowd retreated to Lord Robert's house in Park Street, where they shouted insults but offered no force. Superintendent Nassau Smith O'Brian (Warrant No. 8375), commanding a reserve, led an unacceptably violent baton charge to disperse them. Seventy-two arrests were made, including innocent passers-by. All were crushed into the inadequate cells at Vine Street Police Station.

The government set up a Royal Commission into the incident, and the press displayed bias by reporting the lurid claims of the public and passing over the evidence of the police. In the event the Commission exonerated the main body of police, but Hughes and O'Brian were reprimanded and six constables were dismissed. Mayne appeared to regard the whole business

as unimportant, but it was another example of the unpopularity liable to be wished on Scotland Yard by the political orders of Home Secretaries in relation to demonstrations in an age before responsibilities for banning demonstrations were clarified by the 1936 Public Order Act.

HYDE PARK RIOT, 1866

A serious riot provoked by the Home Secretary's decision to ban a meeting of the Reform League. The first occasion since the founding of the Met that troops had to be called in to restore order.

Agitation for an extension of the franchise after the failure of Lord John Russell's 1866 Reform Bill was led by respectable law-abiding politicians like John Bright and John Stuart Mill, who founded the Reform League, and after a number of peaceful rallies in Trafalgar Square, called for a mass demonstration with bands and banners in Hyde Park. The new Conservative Home Secretary Spencer Walpole was worried, and ordered Commissioner Sir Richard Mayne to ban it. It has been suggested that, given the temper of the times, the sensitivity of the cause, and the size of demonstration proposed, this was a far more defensible action than the earlier banning of the demonstrations which grew into the Coldbath Fields Riot and Hyde Park Riot, 1855. Nonetheless, as is always liable to be the case, banning the demonstration simply increased publicity which attracted more numerous and less orderly demonstrators, and deprived the police of a legitimate structure to control.

Mayne, on horseback, took personal command of 3200 policemen, a far larger contingent than had contained the Hyde Park riot 11 years earlier. At Hyde Park Corner, the respectable Reform Leaguers yielded to a strong police cordon, abandoned the attempt to rally in Hyde Park, and made their way to Trafalgar Square to listen to a speech by John Bright. But the mob who had joined them stayed to tear up the railings and fight with the police. Twenty-eight policemen were disabled for life, and many more, including Mayne, were injured. With blood streaming down his face, the Commissioner had to concede that he had lost control and send for the Guards to restore order. It was the first time since the formation of the Metropolitan Police that the military had been called in to suppress a riot. It was the first occasion to be nicknamed 'Bloody Sunday', and Mayne was blamed for it. He offered his resignation, but Walpole refused to accept it, grateful, perhaps, that Mayne had put himself forward as scapegoat, and the intervention of troops obviated the need for a further enquiry into the incident.

It is noteworthy, however, that despite the huge size of the defeated police contingent, *Punch*, for the first time, sided with them against the demonstrators, depicting a lone injured policeman confronted by a frightening, howling mob.

THE HYDE PARK RIOT, 1866: THE MOB PULLING DOWN THE RAILINGS IN PARK LANE.

IDENTIFICATION OFFICERS New grade introduced to replace Scenes of Crime Officers. Identification Officers are trained fingerprinting personnel who are able to eliminate the fingerprints of householders at the scene of a burglary, and who use their expertise to ensure the best possible quality of fingerprints and other physical evidence retrieved from crime scenes.

IMBER COURT Central Training Establishment of the Mounted Police and an Area Sports Club.

Former manor house of Thames Ditton at East Molesey, Surrey, with estate of approximately 32 hectares (80 acres). Acquired by the War Department in WWI, and sold in 1919 to a Major Smith, who sold part of the land for an industrial estate. Sir Percy Laurie acquired the remaining property from Major Smith, and established the Mounted Branch's Central Training Establishment, with stables, classrooms, accommodation and administrative buildings. When the City of London Police Mounted Branch was formed after WWII, it shared the training facilities.

Part of the estate was used as a sports ground by the newly formed Metropolitan Police Athletic Association (MPAA), and when a surplus was found in the National Fund following the General Strike, the money was devoted to building a clubhouse for the MPAA, which was opened in 1930.

IMBERT, SIR PETER MICHAEL (B.1933) Later Lord Imbert, QPM JP. Commissioner, 1987–93.

Son of a Kent farmer. Educ. Harvey Grammar School, Folkestone. National Service in RAF. Short period working in local government, with mixed aspirations to become either the youngest Town Clerk in the country or a great conjuror before he joined the Met, 1953. Attached to Bow Street station, 1953–6. Special Branch, 1956–73, where learnt shorthand and Russian. Deputy operational head of anti-terrorist squad, 1973–6. Visited the Continent investigating terrorist groups like the Baader-Meinhoff gang, and lectured around the world on terrorist hostage-taking and negotiation tactics. As a Detective Super-

intendent, he was principal negotiator at the Balcombe Street Siege, 1975, an incident which brought him into the public eye for the first time, and marked him as a potential high-flyer. Asst Chief Constable, Surrey Constabulary, 1976. Deputy Chief Constable, 1977–9. Chief Constable, Thames Valley Police, 1979–85.

The youngest Chief Constable in the country, Imbert allowed the BBC to make the fly-on-the-wall documentary *Police*, and incurred some criticism from junior officers when it exposed the extremely unsympathetic questioning of a rape victim by detectives. Imbert was, he admitted, shaken. But he was justifiably impenitent, noting that the revelation led to changed and vastly improved handling of rape victims by Thames Valley Police and throughout the country.

Returned to the Met as Deputy Commissioner, 1985–7. Commissioner, 1987.

The striking contrast between Sir Peter Imbert and his coolly cerebral predecessor Sir Kenneth Newman was instantly apparent in the number of anecdotes circulating about Imbert which testified to his geniality and informality. He loved to recount his first arrest. The suspect, a young tearaway contemplating a smash-and-grab raid in Sicilian Avenue, actually said, 'It's a fair cop, guv,' when PC Imbert found his half-brick and cautioned him. Back at the station, the Sergeant registered disbelief on hearing this, and warned Imbert the magistrates would never accept it. Imbert never again heard the trite for-

THE MOUNTED BRANCH STABLES AT IMBER COURT, NEAR THAMES DITTON, SURREY.

SIR PETER (NOW LORD) IMBERT.

mulaic confession beloved of fiction writers. As Deputy Chief Constable in Surrey, driving home from a function in evening dress, he found a gang of Hell's Angels overwhelming a constable and threatening to smash up a Little Chef on the Hog's Back. Imbert, using his well known negotiating skills, persuaded them to move out of the county. On another occasion, he directed traffic in evening dress when he came across an accident scene. As Chief Constable of Thames Valley, when his car broke down on an official occasion,

he simply arrived on the pillion of one of his motor cycle outriders. And on hearing that WPC Jane Kirby had complained that the top brass had lost touch with the sharp end of policing, he accompanied her on patrol in King's Cross for an hour and a half, and then invited her into his office to see what his work actually was.

For nearly two years as Commissioner he enjoyed an extraordinary honeymoon with the press. Journalists could find no one with a bad word for him, and Imbert himself deliberately directed a BBC team to two people he knew disliked him, so that they could get a fully rounded picture. Disgruntled hard left opponents of the

police were reduced to muttering that there must be something sinister and 'imperialist' about a man who dedicated himself to anti-terrorism and mastered Russian.

In 1988, however, he revealed to the *Evening Standard* that he was concerned that PACE (the Police and Criminal Evidence Act, 1986) threatened the experienced copper's discretion to act on a hunch, citing his own casual suggestion, when a Detective Sergeant at the Special Branch Unit at Dover, that Customs should cut open a car whose three student occupants seemed to him vaguely suspicious. The action resulted in the discovery of a consignment of explosives. He also criticized the right of suspects to remain silent without the court's being allowed to draw any inferences. These opinions, probably held by a majority of police officers, drew down the wrath of doctrinaire civil libertarians. Dedicated critics of the police hoped in vain that he might be discredited when it came out that during his time in Special Branch he had been one of the officers sent from Scotland Yard to interview the 'Guildford Four' in prison after they had been sentenced, but his involvement was connected with obtaining information about terrorism rather than being directly connected with the prosecution case.

Imbert had always acknowledged his respect for Sir Robert Mark, and said that his own ambition was to see the London bobby's image enhanced and police officers' integrity respected. With this in mind, he commissioned management consultants Wolff Olins to prepare a report on the Met. When it appeared in 1989, it made fundamental criticisms of the overall unity and corporate identity of the Metropolitan Police. Imbert thereupon set up the PLUS programme, which resulted in an integrated programme of change specifically aimed at the attitudes and behaviour of all staff of the Metropolitan police. He created the Central Staff to reinforce accountability and information on the performance of Areas and Divisions. He rationalized the Departmental structure under the Receiver, and generated a corporate commitment to organizational improvement. The Met became the Metropolitan Police Service, rather than a Police Force.

In 1990 he suffered a severe heart attack and was off duty for six months. His deputy, Sir John

Dellow, served as Acting Commissioner. In 1992 he was again hospitalized for a hernia, and the following year he retired. He remained energetic but approachable to the end of his career, his staff taking the liberty of pasting his name and address in his spectacle case because he so habitually left his spectacles on restaurant tables after reading the menu.

In 1994 he was created Deputy Lord Lieutenant of London and in 1998 succeeded Field

IMMEDIATE RESPONSE VEHICLE OUTSIDE THE FORMER CHARING CROSS HOSPITAL, NOW CHARING CROSS POLICE STATION.

Marshal Lord Bramall as HM Lord Lieutenant of Greater London. As Lord Lieutenant he also accepted the appointment of Keeper of the Rolls for the Justices of the Peace for Greater London. He was created a life peer in 1999, taking the title of Baron Imbert of New Romney in the county of Kent. These are distinctions which reflected credit in the Police Service for producing such a well-respected leader. Lord Imbert was introduced into the House of Lords on 23 February 1999 and made his maiden speech some seven weeks later, typically on the sensitive subject of the Stephen Lawrence Inquiry (see Macpherson Report.)

IMMEDIATE RESPONSE VEHICLE A patrol car whose general patrol duties are overridden by the requirement that it respond immediately to any reported incident occurring in its vicinity. The ideal aimed for is response to a high-priority emergency call within 4 minutes when IRVs are patrolling a Division. In practice, traffic conditions and the need to break off any encounter started in general patrol may delay this. The MPS Charter standard is to arrive at priority calls (approximately 700,000 a year) within 12 minutes 85% of the time. The Met usually achieves 88–90%, which is no mean feat in London traffic.

INFORMANTS From the Bow Street Runners to the present day, a basic and essential element in crime detection; equally, an ever-present test of an officer's discretion and integrity. Since an informant is an associate of criminals, he may be assumed to join them in their crimes on occasion. The police officer has to make finely judged decisions about whether to pursue ruthless investigations into minor crimes he has reason to believe his informant may have committed, thereby loosening his hold on the major crimes he hopes his informant will help him foil. Whether an officer's relationship with an informant is publicly perceived as corrupt or not will usually, in the absence of firm evidence, depend on the public's attitude to the police at the time. Charles Dickens provides a notable example. He mistrusted the Bow Street Runners, and took their association with known criminals to be evidence of probable corruption. He liked the Scotland Yard Detective Branch (especially Inspector Field), and took his easy and authoritative informality with criminals from whom he sought information as evidence of his shrewdness and detective skill.

Paying informants for their information also invites public criticism. Chief Inspector John Littlechild recorded in 1894 that officers in his day had to pay informants out of their own pockets, which made rewards a vital addition to normal pay. But paying them from a public fund may invite questions about rewarding thieves for practising dishonour among themselves. Littlechild also distinguished carefully between 'information received' (offered by informants), and 'information obtained' (by looking for it).

Protection of informants from revenge by those they have betrayed is another duty that may fall to the police. Detective Superintendent John Capstick of the Flying Squad once caught his informant participating in a robbery about which he had tipped him off. Had Capstick accepted his presence among the ambushed villains as a matter of course, it seemed certain they would deduce that he was the 'snout' who had given them away, so Capstick pretended to be outraged at seeing a man who was giving him constant trouble, and proceeded to administer such a savage beating to the informant that squadmen and villains alike

were dumbstruck. It would be absolutely prohibited today, but it probably saved the man from murder or maiming.

With the age of the supergrass, the informant entered a new era of protection, with police assistance to start a new life in a new place under a new identity once he had completed any sentence handed down to him – in spite of which the original supergrass, Bertie Smalls, was soon back in London undisguised after being placed in a witness protection scheme.

To protect operational officers, a well-established routine ensures that transactions are recorded and approved under supervision at all stages, though reduction in the number of senior officers and the sheer workload may lead to short cuts. The rule of disclosure of everything to both Crown Prosecution Service and defence lawyers (and thus defendants), however, may lead to all informants being warned that they may be required to give evidence. See Crimestoppers.

INFORMATION TECHNOLOGY TRAINING SCHOOL Part of the Peel Centre Metropolitan Police Training Complex. Accommodated in Farrow House.

The IT Training School has developed from Lord Trenchard's original school for police car wireless operators and dispatchers (set up in Scotland Yard in 1934, and transferred to Hendon after the opening of the Police College). During the post WWII period it was renamed the Wireless and Telecommunications School, and then simply the Telecommunications School, until the importance of computer technology both for sending and receiving information and messages by VDU, and replacing such former intelligence banks as the Information Room and Map Room at New Scotland Yard led to its stressing IT training for both police officers and civil staff as its primary purpose.

The Command and Control System, one of the world's largest, still demands expertise in radiocommunication and good procedure in control room management. At the same time, Computer Aided Dispatch (CAD) is now taught and used, and students learn how information from the Police National Computer can be accessed and circulated.

Computer-assisted crime-fighting is taught as students master the basics of many of the most modern operational systems, including HOLMES and CRIS. All aspects of policing benefit from efficient handling of resource information.

INSPECTING SUPERINTENDENT Effectively Assistant Commissioner from 1840 to 1855. A rank commanding Divisional Superintendents and subordinate only to the joint Commissioners. Held only by Captain Hay and Captain Labalmondiére, and abolished when the number of Commissioners was reduced to one and the rank of Assistant Commissioner was created.

INSPECTOR Second supervisory rank in the police.

In Rowan and Mayne's straightforward plan of 1829, an Inspector would command the Sergeants and constables in a station and himself be commanded by the Superintendent in charge of the several stations comprising a Division. Over the course of time the ablest and most reliable Inspectors would be promoted to Superintendent; their places would be filled by promoted Sergeants. So, in theory, the rank structure remained until Sir Richard Mayne's death in 1868. By that time London's population had expanded so much that Sub-Divisions were larger and more administratively demanding than the original Divisions created in 1829. There were not enough Inspectors to go round all the sub-divisional stations, and the men themselves were recognizing Station Sergeants at posts where no Inspector held the formal seniority. Divisional Superintendents, too, needed help with administration from the most experienced Inspectors, over and above the Inspectors' formal primary duty of running stations. Sir Edmund Henderson met the problem by breaking the rank up into classes. There were Chief Inspectors, and 1st and 2nd class Inspectors: Divisional and Sub-Divisional. In 1878 the Station Sergeants began a short-lived period of being ranked as 3rd class Inspectors.

Divisions were also given plain clothes Local Inspectors to head their CIDs. This rank, which was ultimately labelled Divisional Detective Inspector, became an important testing ground for officers who would be transferred to Central CID, with the possibility of becoming Chief Inspectors or Superintendents. Frederick Abberline made his reputation as H Division (Whitechapel) Local Inspector from 1878 to 1887. Superintendent Percy Savage (DDI, F Division, Paddington, 1917–24) and Superintendent Walter Hambrook (DDI, S Division, Marylebone and Hampstead, 1920–8) both regarded DDI as the most rewarding position in the police, and except for the increased pay and prestige, regretted their own promotions to Chief Inspector and Superintendent. The DDI, they observed, was normally autonomous on his own patch, had the full range of interesting cases to oversee, and could concentrate on investigations of his own choosing.

INSPECTORATE For many years the Metropolitan Police has maintained its own Inspectorate to ensure that standards are upheld. This pioneered thematic inspections and the publication of good practice, and these things were in turn adopted by HM Inspectorate of Constabulary, which did not have jurisdiction over the Met.

In the 1990s, Commissioner Sir Peter Imbert invited HMI to conduct periodic inspections of the Met, and the Police and Magistrates Courts Act, 1995, formally extended their jurisdiction over the Met.

INSTRUCTION BOOK Constantly revised and updated version of Sir Charles Rowan's and Richard Mayne's 'General Instructions.' Issued to all officers, it itemized and explained the major statutes under which police held powers, the laws they were expected to enforce, and the way they were to carry out their duties. All officers were expected to know it in detail and to be able to justify their actions by reference to it. Largely replaced today by the computerized Instruction Manual. The Manual was born in the PLUS programme, which tried to get away from rigid instructions to make more room for common sense, and to adopt plainer language.

INTERNATIONAL POLICE ASSOCIATION A fraternal organization dedicated to uniting in service and friendship all serving and retired members of the police service world-wide. Formed in 1950, with Metropolitan Police Chief Superintendent Peter Matthews (later Sir Peter, Chief Constable of Surrey Police) as IPA British President.

Several Divisions of the Met were extremely active in IPA and organized study groups and outings. X Division, notably, with Commissioner Sir Joseph Simpson's encouragement and blessing, followed trips to Germany and Italy with a 1962 official tour of Canada and the USA comprising 133 officers and their families, led by Chief Superintendent Matthews. At the time such transatlantic tours were unusual, and this one resulted in the presentation of the New York Police Department Honour Legion Medal to Sir Joseph, on a return visit by 165 American officers, and the emigration of several Metropolitan officers to the USA or Canada, including X Division's IPA secretary, who was head-hunted by Pinkerton's Detective Agency.

INTERNET The Metropolitan Police website (http://www.met.police.uk) went online in 1996 and contains a wealth of information about the Service, including the Commissioner's Annual Report, appeals, press releases, daily news, crime statistics and history. The online appeals have resulted in the arrest of several people wanted for very serious crimes, the first entry being for Brahim Aderdour, who was wanted for a 1995 murder and arrested in 1998.

The site is updated regularly and provides an international forum for publicity and communication, encouraging a greater degree of understanding of the organization and its aims.

INTERPOL International Criminal Police Organisation. With headquarters and a permanent secretariat in France, Interpol brings together police forces from over 50 different countries in a clearing-house for the exchange of information about international criminals, and arranges regular assemblies at which senior members meet each other and learn to assess and trust their different organizations. Interpol does not investigate any cases. It supplies data from a register of criminals to investigating officers, and circulates descriptions of crimes committed, wanted criminals and unidentified bod-ies in the hope that useful information may come in from abroad. It offers advice and assistance in extradition cases. It only deals with universally acknowledged crimes (murder, theft, arson, etc.), and is particularly careful never to assist in the pursuit of political criminals. For this reason the Soviet Union and all Warsaw Pact countries except Yugoslavia withdrew from membership, as did South Africa under Apartheid. Most of Interpol's business concerns obvious boundary-crossing offences: drug and bullion smuggling, international movement of counterfeit currency, and various major frauds and swindles.

Each contributing country sets up a National Central Bureau (NCB). Britain's was at New Scotland Yard until the establishment of the National Criminal Intelligence Service in 1993. Now the Metropolitan Police maintains liaison officers from each of the Areas, the Organised Crime Group, the Fraud Squad and the Directorate of Criminal Intelligence.

Founded in Austria in 1923 as the International Criminal Police Commission, Interpol was nearly eclipsed by the Nazi regime in Germany, which proposed to take over the organization after the Anschluss had forcibly united Austria with Germany. After the outbreak of WWII, Interpol was distorted into an Axis instrument under Reinhard Heydrich, feeding information from occupied Europe to the Gestapo. It fell to dedicated Belgian, French, Scandinavian and British senior officers, who remembered Interpol's pre-Hitler usefulness, to revive it and restore its credit in 1946. The name was changed from Commission to Organisation in 1966, to signal the permanency which seemed to have been achieved at last, especially after Robert Kennedy as US Attorney-General in 1961 nominated the Treasury to be America's NCB after many years in which doctrinaire isolationism had kept the USA out. The long-serving Director Raymond Kendall was a Special Branch officer from New Scotland Yard.

See also Sir Richard Jackson, White Slavery Branch.

IRA The Irish Republican Army, most prominent of the organizations calling the Bomb Squad and Anti-Terrorist Branch into being.

The IRA effectively continued the Fenians' work after the failed Easter Rising of 1916. British reaction to that incident shocked the Irish people when the Rising's 16 idealist leaders were executed. So whereas the Fenian Irish Republican Brotherhood had been the unpopular extremist wing of the Nationalist movement, committed to violence, it became possible from 1919 for an underground 'Irish Republican Army' to command the mass support required for successful guerrilla activity against an occupying power. In 1921 after Partition, the majority of the IRA became the soldiery of the Free State; a minority continued to call themselves the IRA and instigated the new state's vicious civil war. In London, they showed their determination to continue terrorist acts against the British mainland when Reginald Dunn and one-legged Joseph O'Sullivan gunned down Chief of Imperial General Staff Sir Henry Wilson outside his Belgravia home.

The 1920s and early 1930s, however, were a relatively peaceful time for mainland Britain, Irish Nationalists being taken up with the bitter internal wrangle over the ceding of the six counties. In 1939 there was a short-lived bombing campaign in London and the Midlands. This was brought to a rapid end by WWII, a struggle which engaged so many loyal Catholic Irishmen in the British Army that even the fanatically anti-English De Valera could go no further than neutrality to avoid assisting the Allies.

In the immediate post-war period the IRA was relatively inactive. It re-emerged in 1972. It had not practised serious street warfare for a long time, and when the province exploded after paratroopers killed 13 Catholic civilians on Bloody Sunday, 1972, the old 'official' IRA had to compete with the breakaway young 'Provisionals' (PIRA) who welcomed violence. An official IRA attempt at mainland competition with a car bomb in Aldershot killed five women cleaners, a gardener and a Catholic priest. The old guard were horrified by the folly of their actions, and swiftly renounced violence. PIRA then effectively became the IRA, and conducted the bombing campaign that tried to terrorize mainland Britain for the next 27 years.

Their campaign opened badly, with small cigarette-packet firebombs hidden in London stores, and the immediate arrest of the 'Uxbridge Eight' whose first car bomb outside New Scotland Yard was spotted by Special Patrol Group constables Stanley Conley and George Burrows and dismantled before most of the bombers had started their flight from Heathrow, where six of them were arrested on the spot. Despite the successful detonation of two other car bombs, the Met hoped they had nipped the terror campaign in the bud. They were wrong. Carrier bag bombs led to terror campaigns in the mid-1970s and 1980s, inside and outside London. But over the years the Anti-Terrorist Branch secured some notable successes to offset against the memorable MPD explosions in Hyde Park, 1982 (see Echo), Harrods in 1983, and Canary Wharf in 1994, and murders including those of MP Airey Neave by the parallel Irish National Liberation Army, and of journalist Ross McWhirter. The Balcombe Street Siege ended with the arrest of one of the most dangerous bomb-planting teams, and right up to the time when the former provisional IRA leaders heading Sinn Fein appeared to abandon violence and gesture politics in favour of negotiation, the Met continued to expose bomb factories and arrest terrorists.

In the course of this, the most sustained terror campaign ever opposed by the Metropolitan Police, four uniformed officers and two bomb disposal experts were killed, attempting to save the public from injury.

IRANIAN EMBASSY SIEGE Internationally famous incident, in which the best siege control methods of the Metropolitan Police failed to prevent Khuzestanian separatist terrorists from murdering a diplomat and so justifying an armed intervention by the SAS. Notable for the heroism of PC Trevor Lock GM.

On 30 April 1980, six heavily armed terrorists forced their way into the Iranian Embassy in Kensington, using automatic gunfire which smashed glass, fragments of which cut open the face of PC Lock, the uniformed Diplomatic Protection officer on duty. Twenty-six hostages, most of them Iranian, but including an Indian, a Pakistani, a Syrian and four Britons, were held hostage inside the Embassy.

The terrorists demands were for the release of 99 political prisoners in Iran, recognition of Khuzestan's claim to national identity with an end to the government terror campaign against secessionists, and an aeroplane to take them and their hostages to safety after their demands had been met. Commissioner Sir David McNee consulted Home Secretary William Whitelaw and the Foreign Secretary about this situation involving diplomats. The Thatcher cabinet supported his decision not to accede to the terrorists' demands.

Police control of the scene was made more difficult by the controversial nature of the Ayatollah's Islamic Republic. Muslim fundamentalists gathered at the cordon to demonstrate. Others, outraged by the Ayatollah's holding 90 US diplomats hostage in the American Embassy in Teheran, mounted a counter-demonstration. Deputy Assistant Commissioner John Dellow allowed both demonstrations to picket peacefully as long as they could stay in place, but refused to allow individual demonstrators to return once they had left the scene. Meanwhile the embassy was covered by police marksmen, and the classic siege management techniques were brought in: negotiators to try to talk the terrorists into giving themselves up peaceably; a psychiatrist from the Maudsley Hospital to give advice; hi-tech equipment to monitor the terrorists' movements and conversation inside the building; and the Catering Department's mobile canteen 'Teapot One' to provide subsistence for the police on permanent duty.

During the six days of the siege, six hostages were released, including a pregnant woman and a BBC correspondent who was taken ill. On the last day the terrorists threatened to start killing hostages at regular intervals if their demands were not met, a threat which was taken seriously. At 6.42 p.m. shots were heard from inside the building and at 6.46 the body of an Iranian diplomat was pushed out of the front door. At 6.56 Sir David requested and received permission from the Home Secretary to order the SAS to take over the operation. At 7.24 the SAS attacked the building and successfully freed all the hostages, killing all the terrorists except one.

It was an internationally admired success for British law enforcement, but it was a matter of great regret to John Dellow and his team of negotiators that their patient exertions had not led to a more peaceful ending.

'JACK THE RIPPER' CASE

'JACK THE RIPPER' CASE Famous murders which provoked an intense press campaign against the Met and were remembered by several officers as a major crisis for the force.

The press reported hearing from H and J Division detectives that the murder and mutilation of Mary Ann Nichols on 31 August 1888 might be connected with the multiple stabbing of Martha Tabram a few weeks earlier. As the *Star* and the *Pall Mall Gazette*, both radical evening papers, were already criticizing the Met in general and Commissioner Sir Charles Warren in particular for Bloody Sunday, 1887, the scandal of unsolved murders was grist to their mill. The police were accused of shirking their duty of serious crime prevention in favour of harassing the unemployed (whose weekly demonstrations were the subject of regular *Police Orders*) and spying on Irish Nationalist politicians. When a third murder occurred a week later the rest of the press joined the Radicals in criticizing the police.

The double murder on 30 September and the publicity given to the supposed confessional letters signed 'Jack the Ripper' ensured massive coverage, with demands for Warren's and Home Secretary Henry Matthews's resignations. Warren was further criticized, first for failing to use dogs to hunt the murderer, then for allowing

himself to be pursued in trials when bloodhounds were brought in, and finally for the erroneous report that the dogs had been lost when they were needed. When his resignation was accepted on the day the last murder was discovered, the press wrongly assumed he had been sacked for failing to catch the Ripper.

The Met's policy of withholding information from the press was contrasted unfavourably with the City of London Police's willingness to talk to journalists, and Chief Constable Williamson and Assistant Commissioner Robert Anderson both came in for criticism. In published memoirs, Anderson, Melville Macnaghten, Walter Dew, F. P.

Wensley and John Littlechild all recalled the outstanding importance of the case, as did Warren and James Monro in remarks recorded by their families.

The original Jack the Ripper letter and postcard were exhibited for many years in the Black Museum, from which they were removed at some time (probably by Macnaghten). The letter was returned anonymously to Scotland Yard in 1987, carefully studied by detectives and scholars, and then deposited with other MEPO papers in the Public Record Office.

JACKSON, SIR RICHARD 'JOE' (B.1902)

Secretary to the Metropolitan Police who went on to become Assistant Commissioner (Crime).

Born, 1902 in India, son of the leader of the Calcutta Bar. Educ. Eton, Trinity College, Cambridge, and the Middle Temple. Called to the Bar, 1926. Joined Director of Public Prosecution's staff, 1933, by his own account largely because it offered financial security and release from the heavy overheads of private practice at the bar. Joined the Metropolitan Police Civil Staff as Secretary, 1946. Assistant Commissioner C, 1953. Executive Committee of Interpol, 1958. President, 1960. Retired, 1963, and joined the board of Securicor.

As Secretary, Jackson sat on the Home Office Working Party under Sir Arthur Dixon which

THE LETTER WHICH GAVE THE WHITECHAPEL MURDERER THE NAME 'JACK THE RIPPER', AND THE ENVELOPE IN WHICH IT WAS POSTED.

GROUP PHOTOGRAPH OF OFFICERS, FOUR OF WHOM
RECEIVED AWARDS FOR THEIR INVOLVEMENT IN THE
ARREST OF CHRISTOPHER CRAIG AND DEREK BENTLEY.
(LEFT TO RIGHT) PC HARRISON GM, CHIEF
SUPERINTENDENT GILES, DC FAIRFAX GC, CHIEF
INSPECTOR MORRIS, PC MACDONALD BEM, PC JAGGS GM,
INSPECTOR FLEMING.

recommended the introduction of team (or Unit
beat) patrolling, and the civilianization of C
department (CID)'s Correspondence and Fingerprint departments, and the Criminal Records
Office. He served on an advisory committee in
Malaya, making recommendations for the
strengthening of the Malay police during the
emergency. But as he himself said, he was not by
nature a bureaucrat, and it was something of a
relief to him to move sideways into the Assistant
Commissionership (Crime) when Sir Ronald
Howe was promoted to Deputy Commissioner.

Jackson was struck by the fact that both he
and Howe were barristers who had served in the
DPP's office before coming to Scotland Yard.
And they shared many attitudes. Jackson established Branch C9, the Metropolitan and Provincial Police Branch (known irreverently as 'the
Home and Colonial'), for liaison with provincial
CIDs. He shared Howe's enthusiasm for co-operation with other forces and agencies, and came to
share his belief in direct recruitment of highly
educated CID officers without uniform experience or the general height requirements. After
Howe's retirement, Jackson took on his role as
principal Scotland Yard liaison with Interpol.

After his own retirement Jackson became a
strong advocate of the maintenance and later the
reintroduction of capital punishment.

**JAGGS, PC ROBERT JAMES WILLIAM,
BEM (1925–1978)** Officer decorated for his

part in the action leading to the arrest of Christopher Craig for the murder of PC Sidney Miles.

PC Jaggs was among the reinforcements
summoned to Barlow & Parker's warehouse in
Croydon on 2 November 1952. By the time he
arrived, Christopher Craig had already shot and
injured DC Frederick Fairfax, and killed PC Sidney
Miles. Despite knowing that this armed gunman
was on the rooftop boasting of his willingness to
kill policemen, PC Jaggs made his way to his colleagues' assistance on the roof by climbing the
drainpipe. He was fired upon as he arrived, but
his presence enabled DC Fairfax and PC Norman
Harrison to take Craig's accomplice, Derek Bentley, off the roof to be given into custody.

PC Jaggs was awarded the British Empire
Medal for Gallantry in the following New Year's
Honours.

Tragically, after his retirement he suffered a
breakdown, and he died in the street in Balham

after being evicted from his lodgings in April 1978.

JOB, THE Fortnightly in-house newspaper of the Metropolitan Police. A 16 or 20pp tabloid, usually in black-and-white, it covers news from around the MPD. Wide-ranging topics include operational stories, new initiatives, best practice ideas, letters from readers and sport. Material is gathered and researched by *The Job* team from a variety of sources in addition to their own network, such as the Press Bureau, Area Press Officers and Portfolios. Special issues are produced for major new initiatives or events. Distributed free across the Met, and to press and community leaders, it is also available by subscription and via the Internet on the Met's website.

It has been produced for the Met by outside agencies since it was launched in 1967, originally by Broadstrood Press Ltd and since 1996 by Barkers Trident Communications. It is assembled by a managing editor, deputy editor, and two reporters with an office close to the Press Bureau in New Scotland Yard. The same team produces *Inside Job* and *The Link*.

THE JOB, THE METROPOLITAN POLICE IN-HOUSE JOURNAL.

JOSLING, SGT HORACE ROBERT (1890–1941) Officer whose career was sacrificed to his integrity.

Worked as a schoolteacher before joining the Met, 1912 (D 119, Warrant No. 101504). Compelled to resign, 1922.

In 1921, as a Sergeant at Vine Street Station, Josling requested a private interview with Commissioner Sir William Horwood and reported to him that Sergeant George Goddard had invited him to participate in accepting gifts of money from bookmakers and others. Since Goddard had just been given overall responsibility for suppressing brothels and disorderly houses and ensuring that nightclubs adhered to licensing, gaming and decency laws in the very sensitive West End Central section, the charge carried serious implications. Horwood referred the question to the Home Office, which held a secret inquiry,

and refused to make public its findings. The lamentable outcome was that the case went back to the Met, and Josling was arraigned before a Disciplinary Board and charged with making false accusations against a brother officer. The Board found against him, and the Commissioner's Office demanded his resignation. Josling returned to teaching, becoming a village schoolmaster in Shropshire. It was noted at the time that this meant a substantial cut in pay from the relatively generous Desborough Committee scale of police emoluments.

The *Police Review* and ex-Sergeant John Hayes MP, wiser than the Home Office, continued to believe in Josling's innocence (and so, by inference, in Goddard's guilt), and they were proved spectacularly right in 1929 when Goddard was sentenced to 18 months' hard labour for taking huge bribes from West End club owners. Hayes promptly raised the matter of Josling's dismissal in Parliament, and the Home Secretary Sir William Joynson-Hicks, apparently grudgingly, had a letter sent to Josling which offered his reinstatement in what were described as 'cold and formal' terms. Josling refused, but he was in the Strangers' Gallery in Parliament to hear Home Secretary 'Jix' announce that he was to be awarded £1500 compensation. And his village rejoiced for him; Josling returned home to find flags hanging from all the windows and a triumphal arch erected in his honour.

At the time of his death in 1941, a number of Metropolitan Police officers travelled to Shropshire to honour him at his funeral.

JUNIOR STATION INSPECTOR Short-lived rank introduced by Lord Trenchard to be given graduates of Hendon Police College. Since the minimum age of entry to the college was 20, he anticipated having a number of 22-year-old inspectors in the force. Abolished in 1939 by Sir Philip Game when it became apparent that the planned accelerated promotion of young highflyers was not going to work.

JURY PROTECTION See Criminal Justice Protection Unit.

JUVENILE BUREAUX Formed in 1968 to allow police and other concerned agencies – Social Services, the Probation Services, Local Education Authorities – to cooperate in monitoring and cautioning young offenders. Subsumed by the Youth and Community Sections in 1984.

JUVENILE INDEX List of 'stray or missing' juveniles – a vital reference to missing children or children's previous brushes with the law – held in SO3(3). Started as the A4 Index by Dorothy Peto after the passing of the 1933 Children's and Young Persons' Act when she was Superintendent of A4 (Women's Branch). Mr Howgrave-Grahame, head of the Civil Staff, thereupon channelled all information about missing or wayward girls through the women police. Names are removed from the list when children reach the age of 18.

KESTON Metropolitan Police Dog Training Centre, based in 2.8 hectares (7 acres) of land near West Wickham, Kent. Opened, 1953, with Sergeant Peter Matthews (later Sir Peter, Chief Constable of Surrey) as Station Officer. Prior to this Keston was a Metropolitan Police wireless station, and dogs were trained at Imber Court. Interpol wireless facilities remained adjacent to the kennels while the Met was the Interpol National Contact Bureau.

In 1954 a new, but not perfect, range of kennels was opened by Sir John Nott-Bower (see also Rex III). Financial stringency (see under Sir Harold

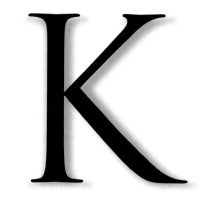

Scott) prohibited the lavish opportunities available to Sir Percy Laurie in opening the Mounted Branch Training School. Subsequently much improved quarantine, breeding and veterinary clinical facilities were opened. As with horses at Imber Court, dogs are trained to be impervious to crowd noises, bands, missiles and so forth.

Dogs are bred at Keston before being sent out

POLICE DOG AND HANDLER AT KESTON TRAINING ESTABLISHMENT.

to make their homes with their handlers. The annual dog show demonstrates skills they have learned in training, rather than looking for over-bred visible 'points'. See Dog Section.

KING, PC CHARLES (FL.1855)

The police Fagin. Prosecuted with PC Jesse 'Juicy Lips' Jeapes in 1855 for larceny and receiving. King took advantage of his plain clothes duties in prosperous Victorian C Division (St James's) to organize boy thieves. He trained them in pocket-picking, pointed out the likeliest targets, and kept a sharp look-out on their behalf while they were at work. When convicted, King was transported for 14 years. Jeapes was acquitted, but dismissed from the force.

The first Metropolitan policeman convicted of serious criminal corruption (as opposed to sacked for accepting petty drinks), King also appears to be unique in having organized and controlled his own gang of felons rather than being bribed or blackmailed into association with hardened criminals.

KING'S POLICE AND FIRE SERVICES MEDAL

Formal title of the 'Police Medal' between 1941 and the accession of HM Queen Elizabeth II. Appearance and conditions of award up to 1951, as for the King's Police Medal.

KING'S POLICE MEDAL

Instituted by Royal Warrant in July 1909 in response to popular demand for some fitting way of honouring the officers who displayed outstanding courage in the Tottenham Outrage. The Warrant also enabled the award to be made to firemen who displayed outstanding courage, and to officers who had given generally distinguished service, under the following heads

1. Conspicuous gallantry in saving life and property, or in preventing crime or arresting criminals; the risks incurred to be estimated with due regard to the obligations and duties of the officer concerned.

2. A specially distinguished record in administrative or detective service.

3. Success in organizing Police Forces or Fire Brigades or Departments, or in maintaining their organization under special difficulties.

4. Special services in dealing with serious or widespread outbreaks of crime or public disorder, or of fire.

5. Valuable political and secret services.

PC JOHN ABBOTT, AWARDED THE KING'S POLICE MEDAL IN 1921 FOR ARRESTING A DANGEROUS ARMED LUNATIC.

6. Special services to Royalty and Heads of State.

7. Prolonged service; but only when distinguished by very exceptional ability and merit.

No more than 140 were to be awarded across the Empire in any given year, of which no more than 40 were to be awarded to officers serving in the UK, Channel Islands and Isle of Man.

Provision was made for a dated silver bar to be added to the suspending riband in the case of a second award. After 1934, the bar was changed to a laurel. On the riband, a small silver rose denotes possession of the bar. (See Inspector J. A. Cole.)

Provision was also made for the withdrawal of the medal for subsequent misconduct or criminal activity. No Metropolitan Police recipient of the award for gallantry has ever had it withdrawn.

The appearance of the medal was essentially as it is now, except that the suspending riband bore no centre stripe until 1916, and from 1933 the riband and ribbon bore additional narrow red stripes in the centre of the silver stripes if the award had been made for gallantry. Between 1934 and 1950, the words 'For Gallantry' or 'For Distinguished Service' were added as appropriate. The renaming of the medal the King's Police and Fire Services Medal in 1941 made little practical difference, as recipients were not officially permitted to use the letters KPM (or QPM) after their names until 1969.

The first awards, gazetted in January 1910, included medals for F. P. Wensley (for distinguished service), and for three of the officers at the Tottenham Outrage, including a posthumous award for PC Tyler.

The Home Office defined gallantry very carefully. The KPM (and its successors, the KPFSM, QPM and QGM) have never been a compensation for injury or even death. It was necessary for officers attacked by armed and dangerous criminals to have known that they were dangerous and proceeded to take conscious risks, or continued to confront them despite being threatened or injured. Nor was the KPM a simple lifesaving medal. Fires, traffic, or the Thames had to threaten the officers' own lives if they were to be decorated for rescues.

The citations between 1909 and 1941 give interesting snapshots of changing social and criminal life in London over the first half of the 20th century. An anarchist outrage leads to the institution of the award. Runaway horses constantly demand prompt heroic action until WWII, but one nearly collides with an electric tram in 1912, and another hits a motor lorry in 1934. As the World War approaches its end, surely the last old-style poacher takes the last potshot to injure a policeman caught up in the war with landowners.

The motor car running board becomes a springboard for various acts of gallantry in the interwar years. Some officers leap on to runaway horses' backs from moving cars. Others engage in daring fist and truncheon battles with motorized fleeing gangsters. The disastrous libertarian experiment of abolishing speed limits between 1929 and 1934 leads to several injuries, some permanent, as officers fling themselves at children who stray into motorists' paths. A cement lorry driver loses control on Barnet Hill and threatens to plough into crowds coming to the fair; a policeman gives up his life to scatter as many pedestrians as possible before he is crushed.

Guns make an appearance in support of professional crime after WWI, though after 1909 no Metropolitan policeman is shot dead for 40 years. The doyen of interwar criminals, the safebreaker, makes an appearance in 1933. Smash and grab raiding, however, only shows up toward the end of the decade: it was, perhaps, a slightly up-market car-owning criminals' activity when it was first invented in about 1921.

The short 1939 IRA mainland bombing campaign wins KPMs for two officers (one of them 'Fabian of the Yard'), who dismantle live bombs (the forerunners of the supremely courageous Explosive Officers). And all the time, policemen are plunging into the Thames to rescue swimmers, suicides, and suspects, and repeatedly entering burning buildings to extract trapped occupants with no more protection than a handkerchief over the mouth.

Of the 505 KPMs awarded For Gallantry in the British Isles, a disproportionately high 223 were earned by Metropolitan officers. A tribute to the courage and gallantry of the Force, it also undoubtedly reflects the heavy traffic density of the Metropolis, the presence of a fast, treacherous, easily accessible river, and the existence of a large quantity of jerry-built, fire-dangerous, densely packed housing in the early years of the century, all features lending themselves to disaster situations which encourage quick thinking and selfless action. Cornish or Cumbrian or Connemara or Kirkcudbright policemen would, no doubt, have shown equal gallantry were their social circumstances similar. The Royal Ulster Constabulary, and before them the Royal Irish Constabulary, have received a like disproportionately high number of decorated officers whenever political troubles called for unusual police courage.

There were always many more medals for gallantry awarded to police officers than to firemen, almost certainly because the inherently dangerous nature of fighting fires makes a fireman's 'conspicuous' gallantry beyond the obligations of duty harder to assess. See also Appendix 3.

KRAY, REGINALD (B.1933) AND RONALD (1933–1995) Extortionists and receivers of stolen goods whose conviction was a triumph over planned and persistent intimidation of witnesses.

One of the two highly publicized operations against organized crime of the 1960s (the other being that against the Kray twins' rivals the Richardson brothers of South London). By sheer violence, the Krays terrorized small club owners in the East End and acquired property to become club owners themselves. When they spread to the West End, they were taken up by aristocrats who

apparently thought it glamorous to associate with them. Lord Howard of Effingham joined their circle, and Lord Boothby asked questions on their behalf in the House of Lords. A number of show business personalities were also seen in their company.

In fact, Ronald was actually paranoid (he died in Broadmoor), and Reginald had the unstable habit of shooting at gang members when he lost his temper. Ronald's notorious murder of rival gangster George Cornell in the Blind Beggar public house, Whitechapel Road, was openly perpetrated in front of witnesses whom he knew he could terrify into silence. Reginald's murder of minor gang member Jack 'the Hat' McVitie, who had failed to carry out a 'contract' on their behalf and boasted of having double-crossed them, was

almost equally undisguised. Detective Chief Superintendent Leonard 'Nipper' Read of the CID organized a very secret task force based outside New Scotland Yard which made the patient investigations that resulted in the arrests of the twins and all their criminal associates, and their detention in a police station for a considerable period to allow witnesses the reassurance to make statements.

The Krays' peculiar (and foolish) love of the limelight, and their wish for the good opinion of the society they preyed upon, was further exhibited after their life sentences with a recommended minimum of 30 years were handed down in 1969. With the assistance of their brother Charlie, they authorized and assisted in writing books claiming that their criminal activities in the East

THE POLICE ESCORT FOR THE KRAYS AT BOW STREET MAGISTRATES COURT, MAY 1968.

End served to control rapists and 'granny-bashers'. They approved the sale of T-shirts bearing fashionable photographer David Bailey's image of them. They even tried to improve their image with the criminal fraternity (which referred to them as 'thieves' ponces') by boasting of thefts they claimed to have carried out themselves in their young days.

It is a depressing mark of the changes in social ethos faced by the Met to reflect that hardly anyone remembered Darby Sabini, the immensely powerful extortionist of the interwar years, when he died, yet Ronald Kray's black-plumed funeral was treated as an East End and media event.

LABALMONDIÈRE, LT-COL DOUGLAS WILLIAM PARISH, CB (1815–1893) Assistant Commissioner, 1856–88 and Acting Commissioner, 1868–9.

Descendant of an aristocratic French family with sugar plantations in the West Indies. Educ. Eton and Sandhurst. Passed out head of the list with exceptional honours and joined 83rd Foot. Served in Canada, 1837–8. Carried dispatches during the Canadian mutiny, and promoted Lieutenant. Captain, 1844. Special duties in Ireland under the Poor Law Commissioners during the famine, 1848–9. Retired on half-pay as Lt-Col, 1850, and sold his commission 10 years later. Joined Met, 1850, as Inspecting Superintendent. Decorated for services at the Great Exhibition, 1851. Attended Queen Victoria to Paris, 1855. Assistant Commissioner, 1856. Acting Commissioner on the death of Sir Richard Mayne, December 1868, until the appointment of Sir Edmund Henderson, February 1872. Retired, 1888.

Labalmondière was the second and last Inspecting Superintendent – an 'officer and a gentleman' to oversee the Divisional Superintendents. He immediately demonstrated that this might be expensive by indenting for a horse valued at £30, when the allocation for new mounts was £25. When he was appointed Assistant Commissioner with responsibility for internal discipline (his colleague Captain W. C. Harris having responsibility for equipment), he was formally required to make quarterly inspections of every station and section house in half the Metropolitan Police District. Such tours of duty lasted 19 days and entailed travelling 692km (430 miles). A gig was found more convenient than horseback for these journeys, and Labalmondière received a further allowance for gig hire and tolls. Nonetheless, he continued to use his £30 brown mare for daily duties until, in 1858, he concluded she was worn out, when he indented for, and acquired, a new horse valued at £42.

He was the first successor to Rowan and Mayne, the founding Commissioners, but only acted in Sir Richard Mayne's place for three months. He played a major role in settling the

A RARE PHOTOGRAPH OF LIEUTENANT COLONEL LABALMONDIÈRE.

Police Strike, 1872, and appears to have been in every way a valuable and reliable asset to the Met as it passed from the experimental to the institutional stage.

LADY ASSISTANT TO THE METROPOLITAN POLICE See Eilidh MacDougall.

LANTERNS, LAMPS AND TORCHES

Simple oil lamps were issued to night patrols from the inception of the Force. Thomas Joyce and Son supplied them, manufactured them with the famous 'bull's-eye' lens, and cleaned them and trimmed the wicks daily for a charge of fivepence ha'penny (2p) per lantern per week. They were necessary, but expensive. Patrols could wave or flash their lamps in the direction of adjacent beats, summoning assistance without recourse to the noisy rattle whose use at night was only permitted in cases of life-threatening emergency. In 1833 the Commissioners ordered Superintendents to stop men from extracting unused oil at the end of their shifts, and appropriating it for their personal use. In 1840 they ordered patrols not to flash their bull's-eyes at riders, since they frightened the horses. In 1844 they cancelled the contract with Thomas Joyce and replaced their lamps with the Hiatt (of Birmingham) bull's-eye which, with occasional modifications and improvements, remained the night patrols' basic light until 1885. In that year the Dolan and Co. (Vauxhall) 'Crescent' lamp was approved for use by the Force.

The oil lamps were hot, smelly and dirty. They tended to leave filthy deposits of paraffin on the tunic when worn on the belt. The rectangular 'leather guards' issued in 1885 could themselves become saturated and soil the uniform. It was a great blessing when George Wootton, Assistant (Chief) Engineer in the newly formed Engineer's Department, invented a 4-volt electric lamp accumulator which came into use in 1920. In 1924 the improved Wootton Lamp with 2-volt accumulator was introduced. Its lens could be focused to project either a broad general or narrow and intense beam.

In 1949 the Wootton lamps were replaced by dry battery electric lamps. In 1962 these were replaced by cylindrical electric torches, which have remained the preferred portable light for night patrols. See illustration on p185.

LAURIE, BRIGADIER SIR PERCY, KCVO, CBE, DSO (1880–1962)
Deputy Assistant Commissioner i/c Mounted Police. Subsequently Assistant Commissioner.

Educ. Harrow. Joined Royal Scots Greys, 1902. Lt-Col, 1917. DSO and six times mentioned in dispatches, WWI. Joined Met, 1919, as DAC and Head of Mounted Police. Assistant Commissioner, 1933. Retired, 1936. Assistant Chief Constable, War Department Constabulary; then UK Provost Marshal, WWII.

More than anyone else, Sir Percy Laurie made the modern Metropolitan Mounted Police an ornament to the London streets and a superb spectacle on parades (where his own outstandingly beautiful white horse Quicksilver became familiar to horse-lovers) and in displays.

On his appointment, Sir Percy obtained 43 horses surplus to wartime requirements from the Army, and thereafter bought all horses for the Mounted Branch himself, phasing out surviving prewar multi-coloured mounts and acquiring all browns, bays, greys, chestnuts and blacks. In 1921 he planned and oversaw the building of Imber Court with completely up-to-date and innovatory stables that were the most sanitary and best accommodated to horses' needs that had ever been seen. He had the riding school built with a sprung floor and large mirrors at each end.

He included such traditional cavalry exercises as tent-pegging and lemon-slicing in officers' training, which made a dashing contribution to the Imber Court Horse Show (which he started) and the Branch's entries at other competitions. At the Tattoo for the Met's centenary in 1929, Sir Percy on Quicksilver led the Mounted Police team which gave a spectacular demonstration of formation riding in combination with a team of Police Motorcyclists.

Sir Percy wrote the Mounted Branch's training manual, and introduced the long baton to replace the short truncheon in mounted control of public disorder. During the General Strike he authorized the formation of a temporary Special Mounted Police Constabulary, and after its disbandment at the end of the strike, formed a body of Mounted Specials.

Always a keen sportsman, he was the founder of the Metropolitan Police Athletic

SIR PERCY LAURIE ON QUICKSILVER, THE LEADING HORSE ON THE RIGHT. BEHIND HIM IS PC GEORGE SCOREY, THE HERO OF THE 1923 WEMBLEY CUP FINAL.

Association (MPAA), which he chaired from its inception until his retirement. He was also chairman of the Police Orphanage. On his retirement in 1936, he was piped out of Scotland Yard and cheered by a crowd of officers.

After Sir Percy served his country well during WWII there was a sad report in *Police Review* that he had been fined for ration book offences in 1943.

LAW, DET. SGT ALBERTA MARY LAW, KPM (B.1914)
First woman to be awarded the King's Police Medal (1947).

Joined Met, 1939. Sergeant, 1944. CID, W Division, 1945. P Division, 1947. Resigned with Exemplary Certificate of Conduct, 1947.

Following a number of exceedingly violent robberies from women on Tooting Bec Common by a man who snatched handbags and carried out savage assaults at the same time, Sergeant Law volunteered to act as a decoy. The thief attacked her from behind, threw her to the ground and hit her viciously about the head with a bottle before seizing her handbag and running away. He inflicted sufficient bruises and shock to leave her unable to resume her duties for the next two weeks. Nonetheless, she recovered herself sufficiently to give chase until the man was arrested by a nearby male officer. She received

£15 from the Bow Street Police Fund in addition to High Commendation and the KPM.

Between the incident in January 1947 and the award of the KPM in September Sergeant Law married, which is why some authorities always state that the first woman KPM was Sergeant Watts. Mrs Watts resigned from the force shortly after receiving her medal.

The KPM (already officially named the King's Police and Fire Services Medal since 1941) was reserved for officers who died as a result of their gallant actions from 1950 onward, and Mrs Law is in fact the only woman officer in the UK to have received the award. But cf. WP Sergeant Bush and WPC Parrott, who both received the George Medal which, with the BEM, effectively replaced the KPM after 1950.

LAZENBY, SUPERINTENDENT J. (FL.1834)
Wrongfully dismissed on political grounds in what has been called Rowan and Mayne's darkest hour.

Served in Peninsular war. D Division, 1829–34. In 1831 he was charged with mishandling Divisional funds for housing and carelessly retaining K Division papers sent to him in error. Rowan and Mayne found these claims unproven, but agreed that he had been drunk on duty one night. He was only reprimanded for this in the light of the extremely high character he bore and the outstandingly good performance of his duties.

In 1834 he was wrongfully dismissed, over Rowan and Mayne's dignified protest, on the order of Whig government ministers hostile to the new police force. Lazenby was falsely charged with covering-up Inspector Wovenden's alleged rape of prostitute Ruth Morris in the cells. Following this incident, Rowan and Mayne issued orders that in future any charge of felony brought against an officer was to be reported to a magistrate without waiting for the Commissioners to be informed.

LEE COMMISSION Royal Commission on Police Powers and Procedure, 1928–9, Cmnd 3297. Chaired by Lord Lee of Fareham.

Set up in response to the kind of complaints investigated by the Macmillan Committee. Wisely eschewed listening to individual complainants (which had vitiated the Royal Commission, 1908), but listened to general evidence. Several witnesses mentioned the Helene Adele and Irene Savidge affairs; also the questioning of Patrick Mahon (executed in 1924 for the murder of his mistress in a holiday chalet on The Crumbles, Sussex), which was held to have been unduly lengthy. All officials questioned denied that 'Third Degree' interrogation was ever practised by the British police, which the Commission accepted.

The Commission gave serious consideration to the operations of plain clothes police who visited night clubs accompanied by women and bought drinks after licensed hours to prove that offences had been committed. All authorities affirmed that such covert activity was essential if the officers were not to be identified immediately as police observers. They insisted that it was impossible to control clubs by giving the police statutory powers to enter and inspect them without warrants, as such powers would also extend to such haunts of the establishment as the Carlton and Reform Clubs. The secretary of the National Vigilance Association urged that

restraints on drinking and gambling should be maintained and, if possible, tightened.

The role of women police was considered seriously. Sir Wyndham Childs gave bluntly offensive evidence that policewomen were not, in his opinion, attractive enough to 'look the part' in nightclubs. Therefore he sent women who 'were the part' to accompany officers. (This apparently meant *demi-mondaines* and prostitutes.) Sir Wyndham also made it clear that he wanted policewomen's duties to be restricted to emollient social work and he did not think they needed powers of arrest. Miss Mary Allen, Commandant of the Women's Auxilliary Service, recommended that policewomen should always be responsible for interviewing women, and that they should be employed properly as detectives (in which role Sir Wyndham specifically thought they were useless). At this time Miss Allen (later discredited as an eccentric pro-Fascist), was treated with great respect, although some of the committee suspected that her recommendations were merely intended to create work for women. Miss Dorothy Peto sent in unsolicited written recommendations along the same lines as Miss Allen's.

The Committee recommended that more women police should be employed. It categorically disapproved of officers being sent in plain clothes to nightclubs, especially as they were given expenses for buying drinks, but otherwise they gave the police a clean bill of health, noting that most complaints arose from the fact that, *pace* the National Vigilance Association, the laws restricting off-course betting and drinking outside licensing hours were out of harmony with public opinion. The remedy lay with Parliament, not the police.

LESBIAN AND GAY POLICE ASSOCIATION Organization of approximately 300 members established informally by a group of Metropolitan officers in 1990 with the stated objects:

1. To work towards equal opportunities for lesbians and gay Police Service employees.

2. To offer support and advice for lesbian and gay Service employees.

3. To work towards better relations between the police and the gay community.

LAGPA is a group recognized by ACPO and the Home Office.

LEWISHAM RIOT First occasion on which plastic shields were used by police.

In 1977 the National Front declared its intention to hold a march through Lewisham on 17 August – a deliberately provocative racist act in an area with a large black community. There had already been several clashes between National Front and Socialist Workers' Party activists in the neighbourhood, and an *ad hoc* 'All Lewisham Campaign Against Racism and Fascism' declared its intention of preventing the march. Strong church and political pressure was brought on Commissioner Sir David McNee to ban the event. With the full concurrence of Mr Justice Flynn in the High Court and Home Secretary Merlyn Rees, Sir David concluded that the obnoxious

THE FIRST USE OF PROTECTIVE SHIELDS BY POLICE OFFICERS WAS AT LEWISHAM IN 1977.

nature of the National Front's ideology did not give him the power to do so, and it would be a dereliction of his duty to try to force the march to take place somewhere else. The law only supported banning a demonstration on grounds of police being unable to control it, rather than on any political considerations about the abhorrence of demonstrators' opinions.

A local clergyman (more as a threat than a warning) advised Sir David that missiles had been prepared for the occasion. Mindful of the previous year's Notting Hill Carnival disorders, Sir David supplied the officers on foot with plastic shields. They were needed. Both factions hurled missiles at the police, who were also squirted with ammonia from water pistols; 270 police

officers were injured, as against 60 members of the public. A total of 210 arrests were made, and much public and private property was damaged.

Following this incident, Sir David banned all demonstrations of any kind for two months, and the violent confrontations between Fascist and left-wing groups died away.

LEWISHAM TRAIN CRASH Major incident which led to the reform of police emergency service practices.

The Lewisham train crash was one of the most serious rail accidents to occur in Metropolitan Police history, and a classic example of the difficulties of mounting a rescue operation with no advance notice. It played a seminal role in establishing firm principles for dealing with major incidents.

At 6.21 p.m. on Wednesday 4 December 1957, at Parks Bridge junction near St John's Station, the 4.56 p.m. steam passenger train from Cannon Street to Ramsgate collided with the rear of the stationary 5.18 p.m. electric passenger train from Charing Cross to Hayes. It was already dark, and thick fog had reduced visibility to about 9m (30ft). The force of the impact caused a rail bridge over the line to collapse, and another electric train from Holborn Viaduct to Dartford stopped with its front portion on the collapsed overhead bridge.

Without personal radios, which had not yet been introduced, the police had to organize road traffic diversions, control points, and liaison with the Fire Brigade, Ambulance and other emergency services. The railway line could only be reached from the nearest roads by climbing a very steep embankment, and the incident, while strictly speaking on R Division, was very near the boundary with P Division so that police operations were commanded from two control points. The local police station, Blackheath Road, suddenly became overrun by officers dealing with casualties and logistical problems, and the sheer number of police vehicles attending the scene was at one stage threatening to impede the ambulances. The number of officers dealing with various aspects of the incident rapidly rose to about 120.

The final death toll was 90. Another 92 people were seriously injured, and 85 casualties were treated in hospital and sent home. It took until about 10.30 p.m. for the last live casualties to be removed from the scene, and railway traffic was not resumed on that section of the track until a week later.

Following the Lewisham crash and a training exercise the following year, Superintendent Peter Matthews (later Sir Peter, Chief Constable of Surrey Police) made the recommendations which led to properly equipped mobile Incident Vehicles, a proper casualty index system, local

THE LEWISHAM TRAIN CRASH, 1957, SHOWING PART OF ST JOHN'S STATION.

major incident boxes of special equipment and stationery, and regular training in major incident procedures. See Rail Accidents.

LIBRARY The Library was established in 1921 when a memorandum was issued stating, 'There are scattered throughout the office and in the charge of no one in particular, books and documents which are of great interest to those dealing with matters relating to police work . . . The Commissioner directs that such books and documents should be taken over by an official specially charged with the duty, catalogued and made available for issue to responsible officials on demand.'

At one time the Library was known as the Commissioner's Reference Library but is now termed the Metropolitan Police Library. Its 15,000 books cover all aspects of policing within the MPS and nationally. This encompasses both current and historical information. The library also focuses on official publications such as Parliamentary Papers and Home Office documents, and has a comprehensive collection of quick reference books. It is housed within New Scotland Yard.

There are three other libraries within the Metropolitan Police Service: the Technical Library, the Peel Centre Library and the Solicitors' Library.

LOCAL INSPECTOR The original title given to Divisional Detective Inspectors. See under Inspector.

LOCAL INTELLIGENCE OFFICER Modern term for Collator.

LOCK, PC TREVOR JAMES, GM (B.1939)
Hero of the Iranian Embassy Siege.

Joined the Met, 1965. Diplomatic Protection Group, 1975. George Medal, 1980.

On 30 April 1980, PC Lock was posted to fixed point duty outside the Iranian Embassy in Kensington. He was in uniform, armed with a .38 Smith and Wesson revolver concealed under his uniform jacket.

Shortly after 11.00 a.m. he was inside the Embassy building, where he had been invited for a cup of coffee while he checked the incoming mail. This saved his life. Had he been standing outside the building, he would have been automatically shot down by the group of six Arab terrorists who stormed into the building firing automatic weapons which shattered glass, fragments of which cut PC Lock's face open. At pistol point, he and others in the entrance hall were herded into back rooms where the 26 occupants of the Embassy were to be held together for six days in separate rooms segregating men from women. When searched and patted down, PC Lock succeeded in concealing his pistol by demonstrating the papers in his pocket which created the bulge over it.

For the next six days he evinced exemplary courage and quiet authority. He sat in a chair rather than sleeping on the floor, explaining to the terrorists that it was his job to keep watch over the other prisoners' safety. He did his best to keep all involved calm, and intervened when a diplomat called Lavasani (later murdered by the terrorists) provoked their leader by declaring his personal fanatical devotion to the Ayatollah Khomeini. Lock's reassuring presence was known to the police negotiators, and when he

PC TREVOR LOCK GM.

sensed that the terrorists were growing dangerously edgy, he contributed his own classic summary of the Metropolitan Police's siege philosophy 'The police will not attack you as long as you do not hurt or kill any hostages. They will wait 10 years if they have to, if it would mean a peaceful end to the siege with no bloodshed.'

Tragically the terrorists ignored this sensible advice, bringing down on themselves the SAS assault within 40 minutes of their killing a hostage. After being rescued from the building, Lock learned that his ordeal had been steadily reported on television news and he was a national hero. He won the George Medal, the Freedom of the City of London, and special mention by name in a resolution passed by the House of Commons.

LOGO The Metropolitan Police Service logo was introduced as part of the PLUS programme to make the corporate identity more consistent. In formal situations, the armorial bearings are used.

LONDON POLICE PENSIONER Quarterly journal of the London Branch of NARPO, and a great source of anecdotal history, reminiscences, notes and queries on police officers and police practices. First published 1971.

LONG SERVICE AND GOOD CONDUCT MEDAL Instituted in 1951 for officers with 22 years' continuous and exemplary service.

LOST PROPERTY OFFICE Opened at 21 Whitehall Place, 1881. Responsible for property found on the streets and in cabs licensed by the Public Carriage Office. Moved to New Scotland Yard (1) in 1891. Transferred to Lambeth, 1926. Now Penton Street, Islington.

LUCAN, RICHARD JOHN BINGHAM, 7TH EARL OF (B.1934) The disappearance of Lord Lucan on 7 November 1974 is well known. He left behind him letters saying that he had seen a man attacking his estranged wife in the basement of her house; had gone to her aid, only to realize that she thought he had been the assailant. He declared his intention of 'lying doggo' for a while. The discovery of his abandoned car containing a US mailbag identical to the one holding the body of Lady Lucan's nanny, Sandra Rivett, in the bloodstained basement kitchen of her house, made it certain (as the coroner's jury agreed) that Lord Lucan was involved in a murder. Circumstances suggested that his wife might have been the intended victim – she was of similar age and build to Miss Rivett. It seemed that either Lucan or an assassin he had hired had mistaken Miss Rivett for Lady Lucan on the deliberately darkened basement stairs.

Scotland Yard has no secret knowledge of Lord Lucan's probable fate or whereabouts. The police are divided, like the rest of the world, and cannot decide whether his abandoned car indicates that Lucan committed suicide (in which case, how did he hide his body? Even sinking himself in the Channel would have left an abandoned or reported missing boat) or whether the numerous sightings reported from around the world (and especially the South African border) indicate that he managed to escape, and has been lying doggo ever since – in which case, who has been financing this bankrupt and inept gambler?

From the police's point of view, the shocking revelation of the case was the indifferent attitude of some of Lucan's circle of aristocratic gambling friends. Far from expressing regret about Miss Rivett's death, some of them made silly jokes about it. Far from trying to help the police with their enquiries, some boasted of their willingness to help Lucan escape if they could. And far from supporting Lady Lucan after her traumatic experience, some expressed snobbish disdain for her.

'LUMPS' Term adopted (for colloquial purposes only) by Metropolitan Police Secretary H. M. Howgrave-Grahame, in despair at trying to put forward a rational description of the Branches, Departments and other administrative units in Scotland Yard, and the reasons for their amalgamating one particular interest or activity with another.

LAMBETH ROAD LOST PROPERTY OFFICE c. 1930.

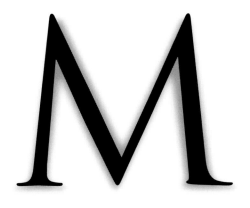

MACDONALD, PC JAMES, GM
Officer decorated for his participation in the operation leading to the arrest and conviction of Christopher Craig and Derek Bentley for the murder of PC Sidney Miles. Joined the Met on 25 July 1938 (M97, Warrant No. 127068). For his courage and determination, he was awarded the George Medal in the next New Year's Honours.

MACDOUGALL, (LORNA) EILIDH LOUISA, MBE (FL.1907–1947)
Pioneer sex statement-taker and manageress of the Police Home.

A social worker in the Lambeth district at the time when the White Slavery Bureau was at its most active, Miss MacDougall was among a number of women occasionally called in by the police to obviate the mutual embarrassment felt when policemen had to take statements from young women and girls concerning sexual abuse. Miss MacDougall interviewed foreign women held in a shelter she ran in three rooms at 198 Lambeth Road while they awaited repatriation. In 1907 she wrote to Commissioner Sir Edward Henry and Home Secretary Herbert Gladstone recommending that such interviewing should always be conducted by a woman. Her point was taken, and in 1912 she was appointed 'Lady Assistant to the Metropolitan Police', statement-taker from women and girls in all cases involving indecency for the entire MPD.

In 1910 the Receiver took over 198 Lambeth Road as a refuge for girls who could not be returned to their homes following indecent assaults, and Miss MacDougall was given charge of it. Thereafter it was generally known as the 'Police Home'. In 1914 Miss MacDougall used her family's friends and influence to collect the money from which the Mary Leaf Fund was started to help victims of sexual abuse.

Until 1922 Miss MacDougall continued as the sole Metropolitan sex statement-taker. Thereafter Inspector Lilian Wyles was appointed to take the statements north of the river. Had Miss MacDougall wished, she could herself have been sworn in and appointed Inspector in the CID, but she did not really approve of policewomen and she did not like Inspector Wyles, so she preferred to remain a civilian.

By 1928 the Police Home was costing the Police Fund more than the Receiver thought it justified. Miss MacDougall and Miss Ellen Leaf, principal trustee of the Mary Leaf Fund, tried to raise more money to fund it which, with a contribution from the Prisoners' Property Fund, allowed it to stagger on for a couple more years. But by 1932 the authorities agreed that the Home would have to be wound down, and Miss MacDougall was invited to retire. Not being a Metropolitan policewoman, Miss MacDougall was not entitled to a pension, but her outstanding and ground-breaking contribution was recognized, and the Home Office made funds available to pension her. She was also awarded a well-deserved MBE.

In 1933 the decision was taken to close down the Home, transfer its clients to private accommodation in Lambeth, and wind up the Home Fund that Miss MacDougall and Miss Leaf had accumulated in 1928. Scotland Yard thought Miss MacDougall and Miss Leaf were satisfied with the arrangement, but this proved not to be the case when Miss Leaf grew too old to manage the separate Mary Leaf Fund, and Miss MacDougall complained personally to Sir Philip Game that the Receiver was 'a machine' who had let the Home run down without soliciting further funds. In 1947, internal memoranda showed that the administrators were still suffering from Miss MacDougall's wish to keep some inappropriate control over the Mary Leaf Fund.

MACMILLAN COMMITTEE
A 1927–8 Parliamentary enquiry into the conduct and management of the police, chaired by Hugh Macmillan MP, and prompted by a succession of newspaper complaints that innocent courting couples were being harassed by prurient police officers in Hyde Park and respectable citizens were being wrongfully charged with drunkenness. The Committee's final report exonerated the police in the overwhelming majority of cases, but found that one arrest of an Indian Army major had been mishandled. He was awarded £200 compensation.

Unhappily for Scotland Yard, the clean bill of health offered by the Committee (like the subsequent Lee Commission) was immediately followed by the Irene Savidge and (much more serious) Sergeant Goddard scandals.

MACNAGHTEN, SIR MELVILLE, CB (1853–1921)
Assistant Chief Constable, CID, 1889–91. Chief Constable, 1891–1903. Assistant Commissioner (Crime), 1903–13.

Educ. Eton. Overseer, family tea plantations, 1873–87. Scotland Yard career, 1889–1913. CB, 1908. Published memoirs *Days of My Years*, 1914.

James Monro's determination to appoint Macnaghten Chief Constable (CID) in 1888 was the

SIR MELVILLE MACNAGHTEN,

final bone of contention between himself and Sir Charles Warren. It was the start of a very successful career, although Macnaghten never won the respect of his immediate chief, Assistant Commissioner Robert Anderson, and at one point almost transferred to the uniformed branch when relations between them grew fraught.

He was fortunate to become AC (Crime) just as Sir Edward Henry's introduction of fingerprinting was bearing fruit. Macnaghten's memoirs give interesting, if sometimes inaccurate, accounts of the most sensational cases of his day. (On his retirement Macnaghten seems to have retained interesting Jack the Ripper and Crippen case papers as souvenirs, which were only returned anonymously to Scotland Yard in 1987.) Though the *Police Review* commented that the real work of his department was done by the professionals from the ranks, those rankers bore the warmest memories of him as a kind and caring chief. Sir Basil Thomson said that in addition to his astonishing memory for criminals and their crimes, he knew 'the official career of every one of his seven hundred men and his qualifications and abilities'. Chief Constable Wensley said he 'managed to win and keep the respect and devotion of all kinds of men in all ranks of the service' and called him 'a very great gentleman' whose friendship he was proud to have enjoyed to the end.

MCNEE, SIR DAVID, QPM (b.1925)
Commissioner, 1977–82.

Educ. Woodside Senior Secondary School, Glasgow. Office boy, Clydesdale Bank, 1940–3. Rating, RN, 1943–6. Glasgow City Police, 1946. Marine Division CID, 1951. Sergeant, 1962. Inspector, Glasgow Flying Squad, 1964. Special Branch, then Senior Command Course, Bramshill, 1966. Deputy Chief Constable, Dunbartonshire County Constabulary, 1968. Chief Constable, Glasgow, 1971. On merger of Glasgow Police with most of Argyll, Dunbartonshire,

SIR DAVID MCNEE.

Lanarkshire, Renfrew, Bute, Ayrshire and parts of Stirlingshire, Chief Constable of the resulting Strathclyde Police, 1975. Joined Met as Commissioner, 1977. After his retirement from the force, joined the board of a number of public companies including Clydesdale Bank, Forte Hotels and Express Newspapers, and published memoirs, *McNee's Law*, 1983.

The fourth Metropolitan Commissioner to have risen from the beat and the second to have come to his position from a career in the provincial forces, Sir David McNee was the first to have served entirely in Scotland and the first to have a working-class background. He had 16 years' experience as a constable before promotion to Sergeant, which was rather earlier than the norm for local CID officers at the time but an unusually long period 'at the sharp end' for a high-flyer, who would normally start acquiring management and supervisory experience by much earlier promotion. He had not been greatly impressed by the Senior Officers' Short Course at Bramshill, and believed that academic theory should have been more closely aligned with operational policing realities. Unlike Sir Robert Mark, however, who had headed one of the smallest City constabularies in Leicester (500 officers), McNee's Strathclyde with 7000 and a complementary civilian staff was the second largest in Great Britain, and had pioneered the efficient use of computers to organize police work. He was also to introduce the first police-owned helicopter unit in the Met.

Despite suggestions that Mark's deputy, Sir Colin Woods, might be appointed, McNee was given a thorough introduction to Scotland Yard to make the transition easier. He was warned by responsible representatives of the Police Federation that pay had slipped so far behind private sector wages that a strike was a real possibility, even though the police were debarred from striking by the Police Act, 1919. Happily the Edmund-Davies pay review was in the pipeline, and that element of police morale was fully satisfied. The Met was particularly pleased that McNee stood up strongly for the London weighting which recognized its officers' heavier duties and responsibilities, and the expense of living and travelling in the capital.

McNee's reforming actions were very much as might have been expected from a Strathclyde professional policeman who learned his job on the streets and accepted the organizing opinions of businessmen rather than academics. He took action to improve the computerization of the force. He noted that the proposed reorganization of the Force into the Super Eight territorial Districts each containing eight subsidiary divisions was causing great anxiety among police and public, who feared among other things that up to 60 police stations would be closed. Nor would it have increased the number of constables on the ground. McNee therefore dropped the scheme, which had been nicknamed RUFUS (for Reorganisation of Force Structure), and made more modest changes. He decentralized authority in the force, giving District Commanders more power to act without reference back to Scotland Yard. He reinstituted the post of Metropolitan Force Inspector, seeing that Mark's clean-up had to be followed by continuous monitoring of standards. He did everything he could to get more police back on the streets – the popular ideal of 'bobbies on the beat'. He scrapped panda cars in the centre of London, and ultimately got 1500 more officers on the pavements. He managed to increase the manpower of the force from about 22,500 to 26,500 officers, and strengthened the CID by about 3500 officers in keeping with his feeling that crime control was one of his highest priorities. The level of crime was held in check in 1978 and decreased in 1979 despite the overall trend for annual increases.

But although his term of office coincided with a worrying increase in street crime (mugging) and armed robbery, Sir David was more consistently faced with high-profile public order problems. The Grunwick Strike was under way when he became Commissioner, while the Notting Hill Carnival the previous year had seen the first use of improvised police riot shields. In 1978 the IRA started a new terror campaign, three years after the Balcombe Street Siege had apparently taken out its principal mainland active unit. Confronta-

tions between the National Front and the Socialist Workers Party became a regular problem on London streets. The death of Blair Peach and the Lewisham Town Hall National Front meeting led McNee to take the considered decision to ban marches and demonstrations from time to time, a policy that had been generally eschewed since Sir Joseph Simpson only succeeded in attracting more participants to the Trafalgar Square Demonstration, 1961. McNee's selective policy of banning all marches and demonstrations in selected areas for short periods proved successful, although Monsignor Bruce Kent and the CND protested when their plan for a peaceful meeting was prohibited under an order actually intended (successfully) to prevent Fascists from holding a provocative march through Jewish and ethnic minority parts of Deptford. McNee wisely realized that he simply could not let his police be put in the situation of the Battle of Cable Street, fighting the literal physical battles of a cause that was deeply repugnant to the majority of peaceable citizens (including himself).

The Brixton Riots of 1981 were his worst public order experience. McNee realized that the term 'Operation Swamp' had become hopelessly associated with police harassment of young black men, and he ordered that operations were not to be given titles in future. He recognized that the time had come when the police would have to stockpile riot gear, including offensive as well as defensive weapons. He was determined, however, that the Special Patrol Groups should never become a squad whom the public hated as the French did their CRS (riot police).

He was justifiably annoyed by the Government's directive to Lord Scarman that his enquiry should be into the *policing* of the riots. This, as he saw, took the spotlight firmly off political action (or inaction) over many years and several administrations which had contributed to the deteriorating social situation in Brixton. Mrs Thatcher won his admiration, however, by her genuine concern for the many police officers injured in the riots, and her firm declaration that the rioters were simply criminals. McNee felt that Home Secretary William Whitelaw should have supported the police more forcefully, though with characteristic spiritual generosity he

continued to like and admire Whitelaw as he had his Labour predecessor, Merlyn Rees.

With the exception of Grunwick and the IRA campaign, most of the public order problems centred on racial tension fomented by the Fascist movements, contributing to the seething discontent of unemployed black youth. McNee was aware of this, but, possibly underestimating the reactions of black people, made the calculated decision to allow Assistant Commissioner Gilbert Kelland's annual report on crime in 1982 to include the observation that a disproportionate number of young black men had been convicted of street robbery and violent theft. The hope was that the overwhelmingly respectable majority of the black community would bring pressure to bear on the tiny minority of criminals in their midst and improve a situation which was being exploited for evil purposes by white racist agitators. It may even have enjoyed a temporary success. At any rate, street crime figures fell for a short time. But the presentation had become too controversial, despite Kelland's and McNee's firm observation that mugging represented a minuscule proportion of crime in London, and black criminals were a minuscule minority in the black community. As McNee came to see, with hindsight, the social situation of the black community needed to be recognized, although not in such a way as to excuse the commission of offences. His final conclusion, in which he found himself in agreement with the very different Chief Constables of Manchester and Devon and Cornwall, James Anderton and John Alderson, was that the publication of crime statistics was of limited value at best, and could be positively harmful.

Probably the most significant incident operationally was the Iranian Embassy Siege. McNee was very firm that the terrorists would not be allowed to leave the building, and the subsequent resolution of the siege by the SAS led both to world-wide admiration of the Met's siege management techniques and a real deterrent against a repetition of this type of incident in London.

His recommendations to the Royal Commission on Criminal Procedure 1981 were immediately pilloried in the press. His wish to strengthen the controversial 'Sus Laws' led to wide publicizing of his nickname 'The Hammer' (bestowed by the 1960s Scottish *Daily Express* headline, 'McNee Hammers the Underworld', when he stamped on strong-arm enforcement by unlicensed money-lenders in Glasgow). Now newspapers accused him of 'Hammering Too Hard'.

These public utterances suddenly made McNee a controversial figure. The hostile publicity surrounding Operation Countryman reversed the earlier correct impression that he was sensibly seeing through the clean-up of Metropolitan Police corruption initiated by Sir Robert Mark, but it was not generally realized that many long-standing dubious grievances were being recycled as complaints of corruption, sometimes being channelled through politicians. McNee gave the Countryman enquiry members personal support so that they had the access required to do their job, and made a significant contribution personally in supporting hard disciplinary punishments when circumstances demanded it. There was enormous publicity over Michael Fagan's entry to the Queen's bedroom. The Commander of A District retired. McNee also sought the resignation of the Queen's Police Officer when it was revealed that he had for some years enjoyed a personal relationship with a man who was a male prostitute. Neither incident pointed to anything seriously wrong with the Met, but both were treated as significant examples of serious incompetence. All this led to the misconception that McNee was retiring early in response to left-wing and newspaper criticism. This was quite untrue. His original appointment had been for five years, to be reviewed at the end of that time. He had been asked by Home Secretary Willie Whitelaw to stay on until his sixtieth birthday, but refused, feeling that five years was roughly the right length of time for anyone to hold the post (as, indeed, had been the case with every Commissioner since Sir John Nott-Bower, with the sole exception of Sir Joseph Simpson) and the succession had been well-planned for many months.

A 'policeman's policeman' with some of the conservatism and much of the downright commonsense of the section house canteen, McNee was, perhaps, unfortunate to be Commissioner at a time when society was starting to polarize as the postwar political consensus ('Butskellism') was falling apart. Harsh and illiberal attitudes on

the left and right were taking over among intellectuals as well as street-fighters. The days had long gone when, as Deputy Chief Constable of Dunbartonshire, McNee could appreciate the worth of solid old-fashioned Communist Party members as well as Conservatives on his Police Committee, all of whom believed in the firm but unauthoritarian maintenance of law and order. His strong support of the police Five-a-Side Football competition was an endearing response to the need for getting kids off the racially troubled streets. In troubled times, as some of his critics recognized when he retired, McNee had provided a steady hand at the tiller. He had introduced some long overdue technology, made some sensible structural changes, and manfully carried on Mark's clean-up of a temporarily suspect police force.

MACPHERSON REPORT Cmnd 4262. Report of public inquiry under Sir William Macpherson set up by Home Secretary Jack Straw in 1998 to investigate the policing of the Stephen Lawrence murder investigation. Published February 1999.

At about 10.30 p.m. on 22 April 1993, Stephen Lawrence and his friend Duwayne Brooks were looking for an approaching bus at Well Hall Road, Eltham, when a gang of five or six white youths suddenly attacked them, and one stabbed Stephen twice. Duwayne Brooks made a 999 call to summon an ambulance, and two passing couples (one of them an off-duty policeman and his wife) did what they could to support Stephen. A police patrol reached the scene before the ambulance, and Duwayne Brooks, who was extremely distraught, swore at them and demanded an ambulance instead. The police officers, noting that Stephen was in the correct recovery position, did not attempt to render first aid, and the seriousness of his injuries was not apparent to them. In fact, two main arteries had been severed, and nothing could have saved Stephen's life. He was pronounced dead in hospital after doctors had tried to revive him for nearly half an hour.

Territorial Support Group officers responded to the emergency call, but the newly arrived officers did not obtain a coherent statement from

Duwayne Brooks or give proper attention to his observation that the assailants had run away down Dickson Road. By the time CID officers arrived on the scene, Duwayne Brooks had been taken by police car to the hospital.

Stephen's parents, Neville and Doreen Lawrence, complained of insensitivity in the way they were told of their son's death, and both they and Duwayne Brooks complained about various aspects of the police handling of the case, including the fact that members of the murder squad appeared improperly to investigate Stephen's background and that police did not respond to demands from the Lawrences' solicitor. Local action groups were extremely concerned that this murder was only the latest in a series of unprovoked violent, sometimes lethal, and often racist assaults carried out by a gang or gangs of white youths in the district. Many people were subsequently offended that several junior officers investigating the case refused to agree at the Inquiry that Stephen's murder was necessarily a racist assault.

A variety of sources named a number of youths living in or near the area as being responsible, and surveillance (albeit without a back-up response) was mounted on a flat used by two brothers. Unfortunately, the Lawrences and their solicitor were left with the impression that their information was being disregarded. The perseverance of Mr and Mrs Lawrence ensured that their complaints made a strong impression on the public. Two weeks later, when the South African leader Nelson Mandela visited the Lawrences and gave them his support, the police arrested four of the named youths, charging two with being involved in another serious assault. The magistrates did not proceed with the charge against two in the Lawrence case, and the Crown Prosecution Service decided there was insufficient evidence against the other two.

A subsequent internal review, which the Inquiry found to be flawed, reported that all steps to trace suspects had been taken. The Lawrences complained to the Police Complaints Authority. An investigation by Kent Police concluded that there had been no racism hindering the investigation, but the arrests should have been made earlier.

Scotland Yard put a new officer in charge of the case, and he successfully installed a covert camera and microphone in a flat used by the suspect youths, revealing them making appalling racist remarks, and showing off how they would stab people with knives while imagining the killing of people from minority groups and 'coppers'. At the inquest on Stephen Lawrence, the five suspected youths made no answers to questions and the jury ascribed the murder to 'five white youths'.

Mr and Mrs Lawrence proceeded to bring a private prosecution which failed on the grounds that Duwayne Brooks' identification evidence, based on momentary glimpses as he ran away, could not safely be put to the jury, and the fibres found on Stephen's body matching the clothing of one of the suspects were stated by the forensic scientists to constitute 'weak evidence'.

The Macpherson report concluded, as the investigation by Kent police had done, that the decision not to arrest the five suspects while there was only limited evidence against them had been a serious strategic mistake. It criticized actions taken at the original scene of crime investigation, the surveillance mounted on the home of two of the suspects, and the fact that other possible clues were not followed up. The murder inquiry had been seriously understaffed, and the officers had been inadequately trained on the HOLMES computer.

While accepting that not all Metropolitan Police officers were racist, a significant thrust of the report was undoubtedly to point out that persistent unwitting attitudes led to stereotyping, insensitive and thoughtless or ill-informed treatment of black people which could justifiably be called racist. It therefore changed the definition of 'institutional racism' from one which specified racist policies to one which recognized unconscious attitudes, with the result that an organization failed to give a proper service to ethnic minorities. Sir Paul Condon accepted this definition.

The 70 recommendations of the report went well beyond suggesting improvements in police practices. Identifying the problem of racism as one endemic in society and not peculiar to the police, it made far-reaching proposals for radical changes in the criminal justice and education systems. See Racial and Violent Crime Task Force.

MACREADY, GENERAL THE RT HON. SIR CECIL FREDERICK NEVIL, BT., GCMG, KCB (1862–1953) Commissioner, 1918–20. Staff Officer to Chief Commandant of Metropolitan Special Constabulary, 1926.

Son of the great Victorian actor William Macready. Educ. Tavistock Grammar School, Cheltenham and Sandhurst. Lt, Gordon Highlanders, 1883. Staff-Lt, Military Police, Egypt, 1884. Active service in South African War, at Siege of Ladysmith, 1900. Asst Adjutant-General, the War Office, where helped form Territorial Army, 1907. Successfully commanded troops in Rhondda Valley coal strike, forming unfavourable impressions of both coal-owners and trade union leaders, with the exception of one ILP member, 1910. Felt sorry for strikers and (especially) their families, but successfully prevented their rioting by restricting the size of their pickets and moving would-be ambushers on with gentle bayonet prodding in the bottom. Acquired great respect for the Metropolitan Police involved in riot control. Sent by Home Secretary Winston Churchill on further strike-policing duties in Salford and London. Placed i/c Northern Ireland troops at the time of the Curragh Mutiny, 1914. Disgusted by Asquith's complaisantly permitting the mutiny to succeed, although he recognized that firm action could lead to a 'bloodbath'. Eighty years of trouble in Northern Ireland might just have been avoided had he been permitted to try and nip Orange insurgency in the bud. Attracted Asquith's favourable notice, and earmarked to replace Sir Edward Henry as Metropolitan Commissioner, but the outbreak of WWI kept him as War Office Adjutant-General. Persuaded with difficulty by the Prime Minister's personal appeal to leave the War Office and become Metropolitan Commissioner before the war had ended, as Churchill had told Lloyd George and George V that Macready was the man to stop the rot revealed by the Police Strike, 1918. Returned to the army and sent to command the troops in Ireland, where, despite a military ruthlessness that would have preferred to shoot every single man involved in the Easter 1916 uprising, his personal humanity with regard to innocent civilians stopped a very black period in Britain's history from being worse than it was. His courageous, personal, unannounced and unescorted attendance at a conference of Sinn Fein and IRA leaders helped bring about the truce of 1921. Macready oversaw the peaceful withdrawal of British troops from Southern Ireland before his retirement in 1923. The following year he published his memoirs, *Annals of an Active Life*, and returned briefly from retirement to police service as staff officer to the Commandant of Special Constabulary during the General Strike.

A fine amateur actor and singer, Nevil Macready could have made his name on the stage. He went into the army instead because his famous father had always detested his profession and would have been heartbroken to see his son follow him in it. As can be seen from the above, Sir Nevil Macready's term of office was unique among Metropolitan Commissioners' in being but a brief and successful interlude in a life consistently packed with action, excitement and achievement. Had he served longer, some commentators feel he would have proved one of the great reforming Commissioners, though others think his penchant for robust action would have led him into pitfalls once he had completed the specific task for which he was appointed, and others again see him as using the Met opportunistically as a way-station in his career, and devoting almost all his energies to the sheerly negative function of crushing NUPPO.

The positive view would be that he was expected to settle the discontent which had led to the successful Police Strike and to ensure that NUPPO was never again in a position to bring the policing of London to a standstill. Macready approached it with a pre-conviction that the Union was an undesirable 'Soviet'. As had been the case in South Wales, he admired the ordinary strikers and was personally concerned about the hardship the strike brought to their families. But with the single exception of Sgt Jack Hayes, he despised their leaders as stupid and inflammatory revolutionary agitators, and while his strategy was to give them enough rope to hang themselves, his tactics were often influenced by the exasperation he felt with their intemperate demands.

He had little respect for Sir Edward Henry,

though like him, and indeed like Sir Edward Bradford, he started his term by making himself known to junior officers, in contrast with the outgoing Commissioner's relative aloofness in his last years. Two inspectors, whom he sent for to wish them well on their retirement, shocked him when he learnt he was the first Commissioner either had spoken to in 35 years of service. He used constables and Sergeants as lines of information about feeling in the force, where Henry had relied upon Superintendents. He abolished the system of punishing men by levying heavy fines which were deducted from their wages over a period of months or years, a long-term demoralizing form of discipline. He abolished the 1s (5p) a day deduction made from pay when an officer was on sick leave: the influenza epidemic of 1918 showed that this caused unnecessary hardship. He was an effective, bracing speaker and addressed audiences of constables, always explaining his position without offering compromises.

Thus he was in a strong position to act against NUPPO when its domination of the first Representative Board set it on a collision course to challenge him for control of discipline. Explaining his decision to divide the Board into separate tiers for constables, Sergeants and Inspectors, he pointed out that a Sergeant who lost an argument with a constable on the Board would be less than human if he didn't remember it, resent it, and feel tempted to misuse his rank if he came across that constable on duty. Men who had started listening to him with suspicion ended by cheering him lustily.

He treated Union representatives with his own type of spontaneity. He hung *Daily Herald* posters saying 'Macready Must Go' behind his desk in Scotland Yard to amuse himself and embarrass Union deputations. But when he learned that the NUPPO Board had written over his head to the Home Secretary with the innuendo that he would deliberately hold up official information sent for the Union's benefit, he lost his temper completely, and after beating on the locked door of the room where the Board was in session, informed them that he would never again receive a deputation from a body which dared to accuse him of duplicity. And, to the

astonishment of NUPPO, he was as good as his word.

When the Desborough Committee accepted his three-tier structure for the new Police Federation and reaffirmed that Union membership and striking were prohibited, Macready, in concert

SIR NEVIL MACREADY.

with Sir William Nott-Bower, the City Police Commissioner, made preparations for the strike both knew would be attempted. Macready's informants from the ranks had correctly advised him that no more than 15% of the men were in favour of striking once the Desborough backpaid £10 had been assured. Macready was thus able to rely on his prepared resistance to heavy picketing to ensure that there was no repetition of 1918. He warned the men that striking would be rewarded with instant dismissal and no possibility of reinstatement, and he warned the Cabinet that he and Nott-Bower would both resign if they were made to take back a single striker.

Nevertheless, it was typical of the man that

he wrote a favourable reference for every unemployed striker who asked for one, just as his attempt to persuade Constable Spackman to leave the union and accept reinstatement before the strike owed as much to his knowledge of the sad future awaiting an unemployed ex-strike leader as to the political advantage he would gain if the martyr came down off the cross voluntarily.

With the labour and representation question settled, Macready's reforms were largely structural. He created the rank of Deputy Assistant Commissioner and replaced the operetta dress uniforms of the Assistant Commissioners with a sensible pattern on the lines of army officers' tunics. He took away inspectors' ceremonial swords, noting that men without military training were liable to trip over them. He renamed Henderson's District Superintendents District Chief Constables, and once again turfed them out of New Scotland Yard to live and work in their Districts, giving them cars instead of gigs to travel round London. When he realized that his appointment of his former staff officer, Brigadier-General Sir William Horwood, to one of these posts was causing disaffected mutterings about 'militarization' and army cronies, he promptly promoted Chief Superintendent James Olive, who had served his way up from beat constable. And he made the erroneous claim that Olive was the first Chief Constable to have risen from the ranks (cf. Adolphus Williamson) adding the correct prophecy that there might one day be a Commissioner so risen. He also formalized the *de facto* situation that the AC A (in this case Horwood) was Deputy Commissioner.

By confirming the standing of the Metropolitan Women Police Patrols he ensured the future of women police, though his claim to have 'invented' them was more colourful than accurate. His refusal to allow Margaret Damer Dawson's Women Police Service members to serve with his force unless they resigned from hers was put down to the observation that the WPS was tainted by old suffragettes, with whom the men might find it impossible to work. As this was almost equally true of the National Union of Women Workers' Women Special Police Patrols whom he, like Henry before him, accepted, one suspects another reason, hinted in his asides about 'vinegary spinsters' and his wish to transfer all policing of prostitution and brothel-keeping to the women. In Egypt, Macready had reduced venereal disease in the armed forces by licensing prostitutes and compelling their regular medical inspection. This was exactly the policy of the old Contagious Diseases Acts in England which had led Josephine Butler to start the women's movement. And Miss Damer Dawson had joined it, with the additional hope that official opposition might end all prostitution. Fortunately for Sir Nevil, the women in his force were unaware of his man-of-the-world attitudes, for they too had almost all become policewomen in the hope of eliminating prostitution around armed forces' barracks. His bluff manner discomposed them from time to time, but he was on the side of their existence and generally determined to see women police maintained against constables' hostility, and that satisfied them.

Sir Nevil never had the chance to advance the other great structural reforms his commonsense administrative ability recommended to him. It would have fluttered the dovecotes hugely had he started a campaign to end the 'anachronistic' City of London Police and absorb it into the Met. Nor would provincial police forces have been delighted by his reviving that old dream of Peel and Mayne – a national police force controlled by Scotland Yard.

Sir Nevil had an extremely bluff and breezy way of expressing very positive old-school paternalist attitudes toward his men and all women. Nor did he conceal his distaste for almost all politicians, any social theory that smacked of Marx, all pacifists, and any capitalist who wasn't a transparently benign and Pickwickian employer. This can make him sound ludicrously dated and old-bufferish from the standpoint of the 21st century. It was a breath of fresh air in 1918; the voice of a new generation that was determined to break with the stuffy pomposities and frigid class superiority of the late Victorian and Edwardian bourgeoisie.

MALPRACTICE The most serious police malpractices exposed at Scotland Yard have been the two corruption cases of 1877 and 1977 (see Trial of the Detectives and Obscene Publications Squad Corruption Cases). There is a whole range

of possible malpractice. At the most serious end, the motivation is the personal greed and dishonesty represented by bribery and corruption. In other cases malpractice is still wrong, and punished accordingly, but the motive may be short cuts or a view about 'just desserts' for an individual suspect, sometimes involving the abuse of a police officer's powers or knowledge (see noble cause corruption.)

Sir Robert Mark, responding to the Bar Council's allegation that police malpractices were occurring, agreed that this was not only so but it always would be the case. The forms cited were unacceptable police interrogation, improper offers of assistance in return for confessions, excessively violent arrests, police perjury (including the 'verbals'), and planting evidence. Though not approving of any *per se*, Mark's irritation with the Bar Council's failure to put its own house in order led him to say too little about the reasons for all the above. The public demands protection from thieves and violent criminals. For lack of evidence 'beyond a reasonable doubt' (especially as 'doubt' may be interpreted by persuasive lawyers) the police are often unable to secure convictions, despite strong belief and suspicion. If they claim, therefore, to have found stolen property on the person of an arrested thief, when in fact they found it 100 metres away where he had dumped it in flight, they are arguably committing 'pious perjury' in the public interest. If a busy young arresting officer at some public disorder hands over an offender to an older colleague before returning to the fray, and the older man saves time by bringing the charge and claiming, without altering the facts, that he made the arrest, the court would still be informed of the offence.

Yet these things may be the first step down the primrose path leading to the old interrogation method described in the 1930s as 'Hit first, ask questions later.' Clever crooks who find that attacking police probity is their only defence can create the situation described to one of the authors by a distinguished QC: courts where everyone is lying, and defence counsel find themselves unhappily compelled by their instructions to embarrass relatively honest policemen on behalf of totally dishonest villains. Attempts to rectify the situation

by judges' rules or PACE can create trial situations where procedural niceties will let the guilty escape – and then the press and public complain that there is a 'crime wave', or that vulnerable sections of the public are not protected by police.

Ex-Sgt Harry Daley's memoirs indicate that minor malpractices (the acceptance of small regular bribes from street bookmakers, for example), were routine in the 1920s, and sharply reduced in the 1930s. He attributes this to example and precept from the top, citing the replacement of Commissioner Horwood by Commissioners Byng and Trenchard. His observations prompt the curious reflection that since the press forms public opinion on a basis of official statements from Scotland Yard, satisfaction with the police may be highest when Commissioners like Horwood and Simpson pay more attention to crime control than to flourishing malpractice, whereas Commissioners like Mark and Condon who publicly root out malpractice and corruption are wrongly seen as presiding over unusually delinquent forces. See Complaints Investigation Bureau.

MANAGEMENT AND DEVELOPMENT SCHOOL Part of the Peel Centre Metropolitan Police Training complex.

In addition to the routine Sergeant's exams, and further internal Met training and refresher courses for Sergeants and Inspectors, the Management Development Unit offers courses for officers up to the rank of Chief Superintendent, as well as induction courses for officers transferred from other forces and training for Royal Parks Police, Negotiators and Community Liaison Officers. There is also a one-day course on the treatment of prisoners for all Civil Staff entering the Complaints Investigation Bureau.

MARINE POLICE OFFICE RIOT, 1798 An attempt to destroy the River Police within three months of their formation.

On 16 October 1798, Patrick Colquhoun and John Harriott fined two coal-heavers and a waterman's boy £2 apiece for stealing coal. At 8.30 that night, about 100 of the men's friends gathered at the Marine Police Office in Wapping High Street, armed with sticks and cudgels.

Colquhoun and Harriott, supported by no more than six or seven constables, loaded and distributed pistols and fired down at the mob, who were tearing up cobblestones and throwing them at the doors and shutters, as well as trying to set fire to the building.

One rioter was killed immediately, and the mob retreated. Colquhoun and Harriott came on to the steps of the office, where Colquhoun read the Riot Act. The mob ignored this, but regrouped to attack again, this time using their own firearms. An officer standing by the magistrates was shot through the hand, and Gabriel Franks, a Marine Police registered stevedore, was killed. Harriott thereupon led a furious charge against the rioters and drove them back, killing four more and wounding several others. The police were then reinforced by a civilian militia, and by 11.00 p.m. the rioters had dispersed. It is the only example of rioters being killed by gunfire by a police force in Britain.

The staunchness of the tiny band of River Police was important in demonstrating from the outset that policemen would not be intimidated or overcome by a rioting mob. Had they failed at this point, it is unlikely that Sir Robert Peel could have found parliamentary support for forming a peace-keeping Metropolitan Police force.

In June 1999 a Thames Division boat was named after Gabriel Franks.

MARK, SIR ROBERT, GBE, QPM (B.1917)
Commissioner, 1972–7.

Educ. Wm Hulme's Grammar School, Manchester. Trainee carpet salesman, 1935–7. Joined Manchester City Police, 1937. Manchester Special Branch, 1940. Regional Police Office, 1940–2. Royal Armoured Corps, 1942–5. The Control Commission, Germany, 1945–7. Manchester Special Branch, 1947–51. Chief Inspector, Administration, 1952. Superintendent, 1953. Chief Superintendent, 1955. Ryton-on-Dunsmore Police College, Superintendents' short course, 1956. Chief Constable, Leicester City Police, 1957. Home Office Standing Advisory Council on the Penal System, and Mountbatten Committee on Prison Security. Joined the Met, 1967, as Assistant Commissioner D (Personnel & Training). Transferred to AC B (Traffic), 1968. Deputy Commissioner, 1968. Com-

missioner, 1972. Retd, 1977. Author of *In the Office of Constable*, 1978.

Robert Mark was appointed to the Met by Home Secretary Roy Jenkins, probably because the Home Office felt that a new broom from outside was needed in the Yard. Sir Joseph Simpson almost certainly did not want Mark in his force. When Mark asked Jenkins if he had consulted the Commissioner and whether he agreed to his appointment, Jenkins replied diplomatically, 'He has loyally promised to abide by my decision.' Five months previously, it was thought, Simpson had advised against Mark's appointment as Chief Constable of Manchester. Since many officers at Scotland Yard tended to look down on provincial police officers, Mark's appointment over their heads (probably on the recommendation of Lord Mountbatten) was resented by other of his colleagues, and his early years in the Met were, by his own account, somewhat lonely. On first arriving in London he could get no help from colleagues in finding housing, and City of London Police Commissioner Sir Arthur Young offered him the use of a flat in Wood Street Police Station when he was house-hunting.

As AC D, he abolished assessments for less than £50, having calculated that the cost of fighting appeals against these petty charges for lost or damaged equipment outweighed tenfold the money recovered. He reversed traditional policy by allowing widowed officers with children to remain in Married Housing. He recommended improved pay scales for staff at the Police Convalescent Home and the Police Friendly Society.

His switch to AC B (Traffic) came when the management consultancy team reporting on organization (the Waldron Reforms) recommended that AC D should be the senior AC – an obviously inappropriate position for the most recent recruit.

Before Mark had mastered the Traffic work, Simpson died, and the new Home Secretary, James Callaghan, asked Mark to consider himself a candidate for his post. Mark refused, realizing he had not been in the Met long enough to be effective, but there was no doubt that the Home Office wanted him, as an outsider with a fresh vision, to take command as soon as possible. It was agreed that since Deputy Commis-

sioner Sir John Waldron had only two years to run before his sixtieth birthday and retirement, he should be appointed, and Mark would become Deputy Commissioner.

In the event, Waldron remained for four years, during which time Mark became deeply frustrated by the Commissioner's unwillingness to entrust him with any serious duties. He was particularly galled by the restriction the Met placed on the Deputy Commissioner's responsibility for discipline and the fact that all investigations into crime, even when committed by police officers, were the responsibility of AC C (Crime). This unique Metropolitan tradition (going back to Howard Vincent) rested on the assumption that only detective officers had the experience to undertake complex criminal enquiries. Frustration rose to fury when Mark realized that the CID's investigation of brother-officers within C Department reflected a scandalous solidarity and unwillingness to carry out proper disciplinary proceedings. His annoyance, however, was put down to a professional bias against detectives and in favour of uniformed police by many of his colleagues, who did not seem aware that much of his time in Manchester had been spent in Special Branch. In the meantime, Mark took riding lessons, because when he became Commissioner he did not want to perpetuate the practice of making horseback appearances at special occasions and parades, but he equally did not want it to be said that this was because he could not master a horse.

Shortly before Waldron finally retired, Mark felt he had been given the go-ahead to establish uncorrupt discipline, and he set about planning A10 Branch (Complaints Investigation Bureau) to take all serious disciplinary investigations out of the hands of the CID. He was given support and encouragement by Sir James Starritt (later Deputy Commissioner) and Ray Anning (later the first Commander A10) and has been keen to give credit to many other officers who supported his policies.

As Commissioner, Mark was outstandingly the right man in the right place at the right time. *The Times* Corruption Allegations had led to deep suspicion of Scotland Yard's integrity, especially among influential newspapermen. The revelation that Commander Kenneth Drury, head of the Flying Squad, had gone on holiday with Soho businessman Jimmy Humphreys, leading to the Obscene Publications Squad Corruption Cases, confirmed the suspicion. Scotland Yard was in for a pretty consistently bad press in the 1970s.

Unlike his two predecessors, Mark was a willing and articulate public spokesman with a gift for telling sound-bites. He believed in being open with the press, even though this would mean occasional mistakes and misrepresentation. Moreover, he knew from his years as Deputy Commissioner that the public was right to suspect the CID's integrity in examining cases of police wrongdoing, and he was determined to change this. He knew, too, that the main body of the Force knew that things were amiss, and felt powerless to set them right. In consequence he had the satisfaction of knowing that he enjoyed a great deal of support when he took over and faced the challenge.

He immediately set up A10 Branch, giving the uniformed police absolute control over dealing with all complaints, and was able to point to its success, especially after he invited Philip Knightley to investigate its activities for the Sunday Times. He decided that the CID's higher allowances and more glamorous profile had led them to separate themselves undesirably from their uniformed colleagues which, in turn, had led them to become complacently tolerant of malpractices ranging from (at best) suspect policing methods and (at worst) the little 'firm within a firm'. To correct this, he summoned the Police Federation CID representatives, roundly told them that they represented what had long been 'the most routinely corrupt organization in London', and threatened to transfer the whole plain clothes force back to uniform and start again if they didn't change. When his remarks were leaked to the press, he received a congratulatory note from Home Secretary Callaghan saying, 'Quick, Decisive and Right! All I hoped you would do. Congratulations!'

Meeting public concern over the Obscene Publications Squad, Mark transferred their general duties to the uniformed police in A3 Branch. He created a special Vice Squad at West End Central station to police Soho prostitution,

porn shops and strip clubs, and ordered the ferocious but straight East End officer DCS Bert Wickstead to move to the West End commanding a special CID squad in pursuit of the leading pornbrokers.

He made two senior appointments to root out corruption. AC B, Colin Woods, who had no 'contamination' by the CID, was made AC C (Crime), and No. 4 Area DAC Gilbert Kelland, who had at one time worked at West End Central, was put in command of a small task force to

investigate and discipline suspect officers. During this period 470 officers were dismissed, disciplined, or took early retirement. Mark later noted that most of the CID were honest and welcomed his reforms. Even so, the number of policemen he claimed to have rooted out amounted to nearly one in six of the CID.

SIR ROBERT MARK.

Mark insisted that in future CID officers would never be promoted to the higher ranks unless they spent some time back in the uniformed branches. He justified this on the grounds that senior policemen had to see their job as part of an integrated force, not part of an essentially separate and superior organization. He placed the Detective Chief Superintendent on each district firmly under the authority of the District Commander, rather than the Area CID Commander or the C Department hierarchy in Scotland Yard. These moves caused intense frustration to many CID officers, especially those who had learned the detective job over many years of service. There were a number of accelerated resignations, but Mark had no doubt the price was worth paying.

Most of the corruption which caused the scandals took place before Mark became Commissioner, and the trials which resulted caused adverse publicity long after the events. But there can be no question that it was his firm action that restored confidence in the police, although the scandalous stories in the press ironically put him in command at a time when public suspicion was at its highest, and cynics were claiming that the police were corrupt from top to bottom. Equally ironically, as spokesman confronting this press attack, he was the first Commissioner to reverse the traditional policy of saying as little as possible to journalists. He drew editors' attention to the existence of the Press Bureau, and issued instructions that instead of cautiously deciding whether they dared say anything in public, officers should decide just what it was essential that they withhold. His own pungent remarks on the IRA terror campaign and the two sieges that occurred while he was in office (Spaghetti House and Balcombe Street) were directed to reassuring the public that the police were determined to contain these outrages.

In 1973 he was invited to give the Dimbleby Memorial Lecture, and seized the opportunity to point out that unscrupulous defence lawyers not only perverted the criminal justice system and cynically secured unjust acquittals for habitual offenders, but also encouraged police officers to engage in improper countertactics which could degenerate into willing falsification of evidence –

and these things made a mockery of the legislature and penological system's contributions to the rule of law. He also showed, by example and precept, that the traditional neutral silence of police officers was worth breaking if the public was being misled into believing that all was for the best in the best of all possible worlds, or if underinformed pressure groups sought to push through bad laws.

Mark's confrontational style seemed in the short term to justify the old policy of keeping heads below the parapet and waiting for storms to blow over. His public profile became higher and more controversial than any Commissioner's since Sir Charles Warren. He, as much as anyone, stirred up the public debate on hard or soft policing which subsequently raged between (especially) Manchester Chief Constable James Anderton and Devon & Cornwall Chief Constable John Alderson. By discounting the National Council for Civil Liberties as an unofficial, unimportant pressure group, he annoyed some of those interested in the problems of justice and penology, while by attacking 'bent' defence lawyers, adversary trials and the hitherto sacrosanct unanimous jury system he antagonized powerful sectors of the establishment. His wonderful soundbite when asked what he would do if a senior politician was held hostage in a siege – 'Ask 'em if they'd like a few more' – delighted the public, but hardly made him friends in high places. His robust man-of-the-world acceptance that malpractices had happened, did happen and would continue to happen despite the best police disciplinary efforts could be made to look contemptuous of civil liberties, yet in the end his openness paid off. His use of the Press Bureau and the media was imitated by other forces, and some splendid successes by the Anti-Terrorist Squad coupled with a determined stand against serious crime showed that morale had been restored and improved in a CID which no longer felt constrained by guilty awareness of corrupt practices.

Yet Mark's vociferous stand against the proposed Police Complaints Board superficially seemed diametrically opposed to his determination to weed out the corrupt investigation of CID malefactors by their CID colleagues. He was not,

however, merely voicing the traditional police view that only coppers understand coppering well enough to know when a complaint is justified. He firmly believed that Chief Officers should be accountable for discipline in their forces. He had restored full control of all disciplinary matters in the Met to the Deputy Commissioner, and detached the AC C from his former responsibility for criminal charges against police. He had persuaded Roy Jenkins to correct the oversight by which this authority was entirely transferred to the Complaints Board in the Bill leading to the Police Act, 1976. And he feared that the new authority would be too slow, cumbersome, unperceptive and legalistically technical in its proceedings to bring about the speedy discipline and dismissals which were proving their worth in Scotland Yard. He had the unanimous support of ACPO in this stand, and claimed this was the first time in his experience that ACPO had ever been unanimous about anything. When the Bill received its third reading and Royal Assent, Mark tendered his resignation rather than administer the Act (although, as he honestly admitted, he had also worked out that for pension reasons it was financially important for him to retire at 60). Hindsight suggests that he was perfectly correct in identifying a conflict between the need for speedy disciplinary action, best achieved by a Chief Officer with very strong unquestioned powers, and the wish for open justice to be seen to be done by an independent authority, which is hedged about with checks and balances and the law's delays.

His memoirs, appearing within a year of his resignation, seemed to stamp his controversial status indubitably. His trenchancy reached new heights. He criticized (from time to time) the Police Federation and Superintendents' Association, much of the press, the Law Society, the second Wilson government, the old CID, anyone who believed in a national police force, parts of the American constitution, barristers and jurymen. Although he was especially severe about politically motivated violence and the abuse of power, it became possible for his enemies in the police and press to portray him as a publicity-seeking 'swede' with a down on the CID.

But Mark was not the belligerent conservative authoritarian he sometimes made himself seem. Although no friend to any political opinion that strayed beyond the mainstream, he was keen to ensure that the policing of demonstrations clearly reflected the use of minimum force. He had visited Ulster in 1969 and come to the sophisticated conclusion that the province would remain ungovernable as long as a substantial minority rejected its separate existence and an intransigent majority wanted to continue reaping the fruits of gerrymandered government fixing, supported by a police force that he thought was poorly led at the time. His contempt for Harold Wilson was matched by his admiration for Roy Jenkins, even though he resigned in public disagreement with him over a point of policy. He showed himself a cheerful reader of Private Eye and the satirical poems of Roger Woddis. He would never have slipped into the kind of homophobic and extravagant utterances that blasted Manchester Chief Constable Anderton's alleged hopes of becoming Metropolitan Commissioner. His contempt for one-sided professionals in the 'race relations industry' must be offset against his support both of A7 Branch to improve community and race relations and the community liaison officers in all Districts to try to curb juvenile delinquency by influencing the young in schools.

Rightly described as Britain's best-known postwar policeman in 1976, his most enduring structural contribution, perhaps, was the easily overlooked institution of the Policy Committee (later the Policy Board), formalizing a proper managerial system of control within Scotland Yard's potentially autocratic system of vertical linear authority rising to the Commissioner. Externally, his campaign for majority verdicts finally succeeded in bringing about a beneficial effect on the administration of justice. But he will always be remembered first and foremost as the Commissioner who ensured that none of his successors could overlook the need for constant vigilance inside the force to discover and discipline policemen who allow apparently unimportant departures from perfect practice to grow into complacent malpractice and confident corruption. In the public eye, he was the man who cleaned up the Met.

THE CALLING CARD PRESENTED BY MATA HARI WHEN QUESTIONED AT SCOTLAND YARD.

MATA HARI (MARGARETHA GERTRUID MACLEOD, NÉE ZELLE) (1876–1917) Legendary supposed spy, interviewed at Scotland Yard but released for evidential reasons.

A Dutchwoman who made her name as an exotic dancer, Mata Hari had a track record for assuming exotic personae when she came to the attention of Military Intelligence in 1915. Past her prime as an alluring stage performer, she was accepting presents from lovers who included French officers in Paris and German officers in neutral Spain. When foul weather caused the passenger vessel taking her from Spain to Holland to seek shelter in Falmouth, she was invited to Scotland Yard, where Sir Basil Thomson interviewed her. He reported that she answered all his questions openly and frankly, and established that she was not a notorious German spy known as Clara Bendix. Nevertheless, Thomson reached the conclusion that she was a dangerous double agent, although he could not arrest her as she had definitely committed no offences in England and had not deliberately tried to land in Falmouth. After her return to France she was arrested, convicted and shot as a spy.

Historians today feel that the woman who falsely pretended to be of Eurasian descent and to have acquired the title Lady Macleod from her husband had brought needless trouble on herself by pretending to have influence and information she did not possess, and possibly accepting money which some of her lovers had unscrupulously taken from intelligence funds. She was a victim of the spy fever of the times.

MATRONS Also known as 'female' or 'woman' searchers. Employed at stations to search or tend to women in custody, should this become necessary. A Station Sergeant's wife was preferred for this role, should he be married. Inspector Maurice Moser (Warrant No. 61670) in 1890 refers to 'the Scotland Yard search woman'. Two permanent paid matrons were employed at Bow Street in 1897, and other central London charging stations followed suit.

Matrons were slowly phased out from 1922 with the introduction of women police, though former WPC Joan Lock recalls one still in service at West End Central station in the early 1960s, and further recalls that the Matron looked on and made facetious comments when WPC Lock had to make a manual search of a prostitute's groin to determine her sex. ('She' turned out to be a transvestite male.)

Matrons were employed at some courts by the Inner London Magistrates' Courts' Service. The Met employed them at outer London courts until the introduction of the privatized Court Escort Service in 1994, the last one, Kate Corcoran, leaving her job in 1996.

MATTHEWS, WPC ANNIE DOROTHY (1890–1966) First-generation policewoman who served for 30 years.

Originally a housemaid at Glamis Castle, Annie joined the Women Police Service, and in 1918 became one of the first unattested Metropolitan Women Police Patrols (WPP No. 17, Warrant No. 64). In 1920, she and WPP Annie Pomeroy (subsequently the first WPO to marry while in service), received a commendation for their part in helping two detectives arrest three cocaine traffickers. (Most probably the occasion described in several memoirs and committee reports, when an unnamed policewoman posed as a streetwalker and infiltrated the distribution of cocaine in the underground lavatories at Piccadilly.)

She resigned in July 1922 (the year of the

'THOSE DREADFUL POLICEWOMEN IN FUNNY HATS WHO BOTHER PEOPLE IN THE PARKS' (AGATHA CHRISTIE). SEE UNDER ANNIE MATTHEWS.

'Geddes axe' economies disbanding the patrols), but rejoined in December and was attested the following year (Warrant No. 179). She failed her sergeant's exam in 1925, and never re-sat it.

At 183cm (6ft) tall she was nicknamed 'Big Ben', and quickly became a familiar figure patrolling Hyde Park. Among her duties was preventing swimming in the Serpentine prior to 1930, and this activity so aroused the ire of a cranky member of the public that he pushed her into the water on one occasion. Annie, who could not swim, stood waist-deep in the Serpentine, shouting to her fellow patrol WPC Winifred Gould to hold the man, after which she scrambled out, arrested him and marched him to the police station.

After Annie retired in 1950, Lilian Wyles described her as 'the perfect policewoman' who 'embodied strength, wisdom and an immense charity in a rugged exterior'.

'MAYNE LAW, THE' Hostile nickname given to Commissioner Sir Richard Mayne's 1868 order that following an outbreak of hydrophobia unmuzzled dogs on the streets would be impounded and might be destroyed. This was authorized by Section 18 of the Metropolitan Streets Act, 1867. It proved hugely unpopular, and was rescinded when it was no longer apparently needed. However, when Commissioner Sir Edmund Henderson reissued the order a few years after Mayne's death, it aroused no comment.

MAYNE, SIR RICHARD, KCB (1796–1868)

First joint founding Commissioner, 1829–55; thereafter sole Commissioner, 1855–68.

Born in Dublin, son of Judge Edward Mayne. Educ. Ireland. BA, Trinity College Dublin, 1818. MA, Trinity College Cambridge, 1821. Called to the Bar from Lincoln's Inn, 1822. Second Magistrate (Founding Joint Commissioner), Metropolitan Police, 1829. Married Georgiana Carvick, 1831. CB, 1848. First Joint Commissioner, 1850. KCB, 1851. Sole Commissioner from 1855 until his death in harness in 1868.

On 2 July 1829, William Gregson, under-secretary at the Home Office, wrote to Mayne, then a rising barrister, that several members of the judiciary had warmly endorsed his candidature as one of the two magistrates to head the proposed new Metropolitan Police Force. The other, Sir Charles Rowan, brought the military experience of man-management and disciplining a body of men. Mayne would provide legal advice. Fourteen years younger than Rowan, Mayne would be the junior partner (and would prove the youngest Commissioner ever appointed), though the two men worked in such perfect harmony that it was not until after Rowan's death that it became apparent how useful the older man's steadying influence on his colleague had been.

The two men met in Sir Robert Peel's office on 6 July, and accepted their appointment at a salary of £800 apiece. A memo in Mayne's hand records, 'We commenced operations immediately.'

They had need to do so. In an astonishing 12 weeks, these two men turned the vague aspirations of the Police Act, 1829 into a disciplined body of 1000 men, recruited, drilled, uniformed, armed with truncheons, rattles and lanterns, and trained to know the beats they were to patrol by day and night.

Rowan and Mayne started their work making notes on a blank sheet of paper in an empty room in the Home Office. By the end of July they had been given 4 Whitehall Place, (backing on Great Scotland Yard) as their headquarters, and on 29 August they were sworn in as magistrates by Lord Chief Baron Sir William Alexander. Then, on 16 September, they themselves swore in their entire force of 1011 men at the Foundling Hospital, whose grounds in Lamb's Conduit

London Published Nov.ʳ 2ⁿᵈ 1868. by A. Farmer. 105. Long Acre.

CARRYING INTO EFFECT THE "MAYNE" LAW.
OR
(Copyright.)
How doth the little busy Bobbie,
Approve of all he meets;
And gathers 'Tiny', 'Vic' or 'Toby',
From all the London Streets.

'THE MAYNE LAW' – A CARTOON SATIRISING SIR RICHARD MAYNE'S MORE PEDANTIC INSTRUCTIONS IN RELATION TO BEAT DUTY.

Fields offered one of the few large open spaces with some privacy in London.

The *General Instruction Book* approved by Peel and issued to all the force was the work of the Commissioners. Rowan probably drafted the first half, laying down the structure and character of the Police. Mayne probably wrote the second, explaining the legal standing of a police officer and the basic criminal law he was expected to enforce. Thanks to Mayne, it has been clear and formal from the outset that English police officers do not have undefined authority to order fellow citizens about at the behest of the state. They start with very little more power than anyone else to arrest anyone they see committing a crime, and some additional power to detain and search anyone they have reason to suspect is contemplating criminal action (see Arrest). They are expected to know what constitutes crime under English law, and may not merely impose their own code of morality on others. They need a warrant from a magistrate to trespass any further on any fellow citizen's liberty and privacy, and that warrant will itself describe and limit their temporary increased powers. The Commissioners themselves exercised only the limited executive powers of magistrates. They did not exercise the judicial function and try malefactors brought before them – that was left to independent courts. And while the Commissioners personally heard all complaints against the police from the public and took disciplinary action if it seemed necessary, Mayne was at pains to advise that police officers could be charged with offences in the ordinary courts if the complainants so wished. This very careful separation of the Commissioners' policing powers from the judicial powers of other magistrates was important in ultimately allaying public fear that the new police force meant that unoffending citizens might be arrested and punished if they annoyed 'Peel's private army'.

Rowan and Mayne worked harmoniously with John Wray, who was appointed Receiver to handle the finances of the force, and they did not chafe at his having equal authority with them. They were comfortable in their relations with Charles Yardley, who headed their small civilian staff of three clerks, and with Superintendent John May of A Division who, as the senior uniformed officer at the station house attached to Scotland Yard, was their primary channel of communication with the force. But Mayne, whose personality was actually more rigid and potentially abrasive than his military colleague's, rapidly crossed swords with Samuel Philipps, the permanent under-secretary at the Home Office. There was room for disagreement in the vague terms of reference which made the Commissioners should be subservient to its officials. In Mayne's eyes, this meant submitting to pettifogging bureaucracy, and he disliked Phillipps on sight. Phillipps returned the feeling, and acrimonious letters between the two disfigured the files. In 1832, Phillipps concluded a long correspondence with Mayne, who was asking for clarification of the Commissioners' and other magistrates' precise judicial and executive powers, with the apparently contradictory observations that the Commissioners could make all the regulations governing the general and particular duties of the police, 'subject to the approbation of the Home Secretary'. The contradiction lay in the fact that the Whig Home Secretary Lord Melbourne's exasperating refusal to support 'his' Police Commissioners against attacks and encroachment by the Bow Street magistrate Frederick Roe was exactly what Mayne wanted explained by some clearly defined statement of their respective duties. Rowan dealt with the Home Office as tactfully and diplomatically as possible, but the personality clash rankled with Mayne and left an undercurrent of friction with Home Office civil servants which lasted for 60 years until Sir Charles Warren's resignation brought the matter to a head.

SIR RICHARD MAYNE.

In 1848, Mayne was made a Companion of the Bath. Since Rowan (who had held the CB for military services since 1815) was made a Knight Commander at the same time, there was a mischievous suggestion in the press that Mayne had been deliberately singled out as an inferior Commissioner. Fortunately the relations between Rowan and Mayne were far too good for this canard to upset them.

When Rowan retired in 1850, Mayne expected to become sole Commissioner. The Home Office, however, stuck to Peel's original idea that a military man should be one of the heads of the police, and they promoted Captain William Hay to the rank of Second Commissioner. In 1851 Mayne took personal command of the temporary Division formed for the purpose of crowd control and policing of the Great Exhibition. Hay was not only annoyed that this duty had not devolved on him, he took the extraordinary step of opening an acrimonious correspondence with Mayne, protesting. Such a thing had never happened in the 21 years Mayne had worked with Rowan.

Mayne's policing of the Exhibition was, in

ers directly responsible to the Home Secretary. Philipps thought 'Home Secretary' should be interpreted as 'Home Office', and the Commis-

fact, so successful that he was awarded the KCB and became Sir Richard. He himself praised Superintendent Pearce for his crowd control, but this unusual note of commendation to one of his staff was interpreted as a snub to Hay, between whom and Mayne coolness increased. The situation was resolved when Hay died two years later, and the Police Act, 1856 laid down that there should in future be one Commissioner (Mayne) with two Assistant Commissioners.

As sole Commissioner, Mayne was in fact becoming increasingly distant and aloof from both the public and his men. He lacked Rowan's ability to explain and conciliate, which had been so important in establishing the force in the teeth of a hostile public. *Punch* got hold of Mayne's standing orders, and jeered at his directive in 1859 that uniformed policemen were not to carry umbrellas on duty. Yet the Duke of Wellington had to issue the same order to Guards officers at Waterloo. Still, Mayne was in fact showing himself more of a martinet than Rowan had been. One of his officers later remembered that policemen feared and respected him – they did not love him.

The force had been founded in the very last year of George IV's reign, when drunken aristocrats out whoring might need as much policing as the London mobs. Rowan had insisted that the Force must treat all ranks in society with the same courtesy and firmness, without fear or favour. Mayne had survived into the starchy mid-Victorian era which took its public tone from Albert the Good and, for better or worse, he reflected that tone faithfully. His police came increasingly to protect the dull and tranquil kind of 'Queen's Peace' valued by the Biedermeiers and the bourgeoisie. He issued directives to stop children bowling hoops in public places or throwing snowballs in the parks. *Punch*'s rival *Judy*, which always mistrusted the police, screamed, 'How much longer is suffering London to put up with the imbecility of Sir Richard Mayne?' And, indeed, the young Mayne who wrote half the *General Instruction Book* would have recognized at once that the police were now being used to impose middle-class manners and not to prevent crime. Mayne tried to oblige Victorian taste, and inculcated in the force a defer-

ence toward senior officers and 'the gentry' which perpetuated radical and working-class suspicion of 'Peel's raw lobsters' for decades after they had clearly established their real social value.

He and the Home Office also inflicted another demoralizing class imposition on the force. Peel had envisaged a force drawn from the working classes and the non-commissioned sector of the army, wherein the ablest should be steadily promoted 'from below'. Only the two Commissioners were to be drawn direct from the 'gentry'. But the appointment of Captain Hay as 'Superintendent Inspector' had breached this rule, and his rapid promotion to Second Commissioner showed that promotion and recruitment to the highest ranks would be made on grounds of class rather than ability and experience. The expansion of the administrative level by the creation of increasing numbers of Assistant Commissioners made this a grievance for serving officers, and Mayne, a true Victorian, allowed it to fester. It was not to be addressed until the 1880s, and not to be resolved until the 1940s.

Mayne's last years in office were marred by two sad failures. The Hyde Park Riot, 1866 was the third major instance of a worried Home Secretary turning a planned political demonstration into a dangerous disturbance by trying to ban it. (Cf. Coldbath Fields, 1833, Hyde Park Riot, 1855). This time, Home Secretary Spencer Walpole let Mayne take all the blame as well as actual injury in the riot. He did, however, have the grace to refuse Mayne's offer of resignation.

The following year he again offered his resignation for the Force's astonishing incompetence in the Clerkenwell Bombing. Again it was refused, but he had to suffer the humiliation of having Philipps's successor, under-secretary Liddell, say, 'We told Mayne that he had made a damned fool of himself, but that we weren't going to throw him over after his long service.'

He deserved that loyalty. The force over which he presided started as 1000 men and had grown to nearly 8000. The area it policed had increased tenfold. The nation, which so mistrusted Peel's original idea, had insisted on its being copied in every town and shire across the country. When Sir Richard Mayne died on Boxing

Day 1868, tired and embittered by public obloquy, he deserved greater tributes than he received. Of course, his 39 years in office – the longest ever to be served by a Commissioner – were too long. The old autocrat of 72 bore little resemblance to the enthusiastic 39-year-old who had followed Rowan's lead and helped with the tactful and diplomatic face that weathered opposition. But he had kept the Force administratively sound, and clear of either corruption or the forms of political tyranny the country once dreaded. The Metropolitan Police of 1868 was a national institution. The policeman, like the postman and the engine driver, joined the universal British stereotypes of the parson, the clerk, the farmer and the squire – and this would not have been the case had Peel selected a less honourable, able and indefatigable second Commissioner than Richard Mayne.

MEPO The Public Record Office's classification for the Metropolitan Police archives it holds at Kew.

In the 1950s it was realized that since the Met is the direct responsibility of the Home Office, its records and archives (unlike those of every other Force in the country) are public property, and should be deposited with the PRO. The heading MEPO (sometimes MEPOL) was given to the 2–3% of Met papers historically important enough to be worth preserving. As records become inactive, they are transferred after vetting by the civilian review staff to see whether they are of any interest, and whether they should be temporarily closed to the public to protect the names of innocent witnesses and people involved in cases, national security, or current police operations that could be compromised.

METROPOLITAN POLICE DISTRICT (MPD) The entire area policed by the Metropolitan Police. Defined in the Schedule to Peel's Police Act as an area covered by a radius of up to 11km (7 miles) from Charing Cross, and containing 88 parishes, liberties and hamlets. The MPD has been steadily increased from time to time, and by the 1980s covered about 1813km² (700 sq miles), mostly within a 24km (15 mile) radius of Charing Cross and embracing the 32

MRS SOFIA STANLEY (SEATED, RIGHT) WITH (LEFT TO RIGHT) ASST SUPT ELINOR ROBERTSON, INSPECTOR CHARLOTTE DIXON AND SERGEANT VIOLET BUTCHER.

Staff Association, to be a representative and reunion body. The name was changed in 1998 to encourage the membership of short-term contract staff and others who had proceeded to different employment.

METROPOLITAN POLICE SERVICE The correct title of the Metropolitan Police since Commissioner Sir Peter Imbert's institution of the PLUS programme in 1990. The title was intended to emphasize to public and police alike the role of the Met as public servants helping the community and upholding the law with a proper regard for the quality of service. At the same time, like the armed services, the police should also be expected to use proper force at the proper place and time to secure the Queen's peace.

Although the PLUS programme formalized the title, the Report on the Anguilla operation 20 years earlier had remarked that in training up a new Anguillan Police Force, the Metropolitan Police Unit bore in mind their own commitment as a Service, policing by consent, rather than a Force imposing state policy.

There are 27,000 attested officers, supported by 13,500 Civil Staff, all under the command of the Commissioner of Police of the Metropolis.

METROPOLITAN WOMEN POLICE ASSOCIATION Social organization for present and former women police officers.

Prior to 1976, A4 Branch (Women Police) at New Scotland Yard assisted with functions such as reunions. When the Branch was dissolved, it was suggested that some provision should be made for women officers to keep in touch. An inaugural meeting was held on 9 December 1976 at Trenchard House and an address was given by Commander Daphne Skillern (Met 1949–80). It was proposed that an Association should be formed, and since then the Association has gone from strength to strength. There are now some 600 members, serving and retired, who live world-wide. Reunions, functions and meetings are arranged by the committee, and members are kept in touch by a quarterly newsletter.

METROPOLITAN WOMEN POLICE PATROLS The first Metropolitan Women

excluded from the MPD, and since 1889 the parks, with the exception of Hyde Park, have been separately policed. The British Transport Police are responsible for the main line railway stations and the Underground.

METROPOLITAN POLICE FORMER CIVIL STAFF ASSOCIATION Society whose membership is open to all former Civil Staff employees of the Met. Holds regular meetings, and publishes regular newsletters. Founded in 1986 by Senior Executive Officer Norman Fairfax as the Metropolitan Police Retired Civil

Greater London boroughs, nine present and former Urban Districts in the counties of Essex, Hertfordshire and Surrey, and one parish each in Essex and Herts. The Blair government planned to return those Districts to their county constabularies, and make the MPD coincide with the administrative boundaries of Greater London.

At all times, the City of London has been

Police. Formed in 1918 by Commissioner Sir Nevil Macready following a Home Office Select Committee's recommendation that the Met regularize the position of the volunteer Women Special Police Patrols and Women Police Service in London. Fifty women were inducted in the first year, and the full strength of 112 was reached by 1921. Neither sworn in nor given powers of arrest, the patrols were sent to police (especially) roads frequented by prostitutes, London being divided into three areas for the purpose, with Sergeants Grace Russell, Patty Alliott and Lilian Wyles each commanding and placing the patrols on the streets in one of them. Overall Superinten-

dent of the Women Patrols was Mrs Sofia Stanley, with Mrs Elinor Robertson, formerly of the Women's Forage Corps of the Royal Army Service Corps, as Assistant Superintendent. In 1920 Mrs Robertson's title was changed to Chief Inspector, and Sergeants Wyles and Dixon were promoted to Inspectors.

In 1922 the stringent government economy measures known as the 'Geddes axe' proposed abolishing women police entirely. Twenty of the patrols survived, but were now sworn in and given powers of arrest. By 1930 their numbers had so increased and their usefulness been proved that they were formed into the Women's

Branch with a promotional structure and ranks similar to that of the men.

MIDDLESEX JUSTICES ACT, 1792 An Act establishing seven new Police Offices and giving statutory recognition to their model, Bow Street. Three stipendiary magistrates and six constables were attached to each. The magistrates were paid £400 a year and the constables 12s a week. The magistrates' duties were executive, in the

THE FIRST METROPOLITAN POLICEWOMEN ON THE STEPS AT KING CHARLES STREET, SW1. MRS STANLEY IS STANDING IN THE LEFT FOREGROUND.

management and command of the constables, and judiciary in trying offenders brought before them.

The new offices were Great Marlborough Street, Queen Square, Hatton Garden, Worship Street (Finsbury), Lambeth Street (Whitechapel), Shadwell and Southwark. In 1798 the Marine Police Office at Wapping was added to their number. In 1821 Marylebone Lane Police Office was created to meet the increased police needs of the Oxford Street neighbourhood.

MILES, PC SIDNEY GEORGE (1910–1952)

The only police officer to receive the posthumous KPFSM for gallantry in the years between 1951 and 1954 (at which point it was superseded by the QPM).

Joined the Met, 1930. Warrant No. 119962. Posted to Z Division (Croydon). Divisional No. 550Z. Married with no children. Commended by Commissioner and Justices in 1941 for work in a case of larceny and receiving. Defence Medal and five years' police war service chevrons, 1945. Long Service and Good Conduct Medal, 1952.

PC Miles was the officer murdered in the notorious Bentley and Craig Case. The gazetted citation for him and the other officers decorated on that occasion gives the best brief and accurate account of the incident:

Shortly after nine o'clock on the night of 2nd November 1952, two men (Christopher Craig and Derek Bentley) were seen to climb over the side gate of a warehouse in Tamworth Road, Croydon, and to reach the flat roof of a building about 22ft above. The alarm was given and Detective Constable Fairfax, Constable Harrison, and other officers went to the premises in a police van. At about the same time Constable MacDonald and another constable arrived in a police wireless car. Other police officers took up various positions around the building. When told that the suspects had climbed up a drainpipe to the roof, Detective Constable Fairfax immediately scaled the drainpipe. Constable MacDonald followed him but was unable to negotiate the last six feet, and had to return to the ground. Fairfax had reached the top and pulled himself onto the roof. In the moonlight he saw the two men about 15 yards away behind a brick stack. He walked towards them, challenged them, and then dashed behind the stack, grabbed one of the men and pulled him into the open. The man broke away, and his companion then fired at Fairfax and wounded him in the right shoulder. Fairfax fell to the ground, but as the two criminals ran past him he got up and closed with one of them and knocked him down. A second shot was then fired at Fairfax, but he retained hold of his man (Bentley), dragged him behind a skylight and searched him. He found a knuckleduster and a dagger which he removed. Constable MacDonald meanwhile had made another effort to climb the drainpipe and had almost reached the top. Fairfax helped him onto the roof and called to the gunman to drop his gun, but he refused and made further threats. During this time Constable Harrison had climbed onto a sloping roof nearby and was edging his way along towards the gunman by lying on his back on the roof with his heels in the guttering. He was seen and a shot was fired at him which struck the roof close to his head. He continued his journey, however, and another shot was fired at him which missed. Harrison then got behind a chimney stack and reached the ground where he joined other officers who entered the building, ran up to the fire exit door on the roof and pushed it open. Fairfax warned them that the man with the gun was nearby, but Constable MILES jumped from the doorway onto the roof. As he did so the gunman fired, and the Constable fell to the ground shot between the eyes. Fairfax immediately left cover to bring in the casualty and a further shot was fired at him. MacDonald also came forward and the officers dragged the shot Constable behind the fire escape exit. Constable Harrison then jumped out onto the roof from the doorway, and threw his truncheon and other things at the gunman who again fired at him. Constable Jaggs then reached the roof by way of the drainpipe and was also fired upon, but joined the other Constables. Fairfax, helped by Harrison then pushed his captive through the doorway and handed him over to other officers. Detective Constable Fairfax was given a police pistol and he immediately returned to the roof. He jumped through the doorway and again called on the gunman to drop his weapon. A further shot was fired at him but he advanced towards the man firing his own pistol as he went. The gunman (Craig) then jumped over the roof to the ground below, where he was arrested.

It is sometimes stated that PC Miles arrived at the scene with PC MacDonald in the police wireless car. This confuses him with a colleague, PC Leslie Miles. PC Sidney Miles was among officers called in subsequently as reinforcements.

The Home Secretary, Sir David Maxwell Fyfe, and a very large gathering of police officers, including Commissioner Sir Harold Scott, attended PC Miles's funeral at Croydon Parish Church. The incident, like PC Nat Edgar's murder four years earlier, confirmed public anxiety about the perceived rise of armed juvenile criminality, and the dangerous violence of 'cosh boys'. The tragedy would have aroused little or no public controversy, and the bravery of the officers involved would have enjoyed unqualified admiration, had the convention been followed of reprieving the confederate when the primary perpetrator could not, for legal reasons, be executed. In fact, while both youths were convicted, the 18-year-old Bentley, who had actually been under arrest at the moment of the shooting, was hanged. Craig, the under-age shooter, was detained at Her Majesty's pleasure.

Hanging the confederate while imprisoning the killer offended many people's sense of natural justice, and this led to the following ill-considered criticisms of the police:

1. Fairfax and other officers near the rooftop reported that Bentley shouted 'Let him have it, Chris,' as he was first apprehended. Since Bentley denied saying it, and Craig denied having heard it, it was alleged that the officers were lying.

2. The bullet which struck PC Miles was too damaged for ballistic evidence to prove that it had been fired from Craig's gun. It was alleged that it probably came from guns issued to police marksmen placed at nearby vantage points.

The weakness of the first point was demonstrated by protestors who offered the thin alternative excuse that the words meant, 'Hand over the gun, Chris.' Bentley's denial was worthless, since he denied everything that his limited intelligence thought might be incriminating. Nor was Craig's memory likely to be trustworthy, given the frenzied 20 minutes of the action, and the serious injuries he incurred immediately by jumping off the roof. The officers honourably reported remarks of Bentley's which were entirely favourable to him, and gave clear evidence that after DC Fairfax recaptured him he surrendered peaceably and took none of the opportunities which presented themselves to escape from arrest again.

The second point was a complete canard. There were no police marksmen present. The only firearms in the hands of the police were brought to the scene after PC Miles' death, and detailed research by Robin Odell and Christopher Berry-Dee subsequently established exactly when and from which chamber Craig fired the lethal bullet.

Bentley's family maintained an unremitting struggle to win him a posthumous Free Pardon, in the course of which the death of PC Miles tended to be overlooked, and the heroism of the other policemen on the roof was seriously defamed. Miles's widow subsequently remarried, and her husband, Mr Reginald Grasty, presented Miles's medals to the Historical Museum in 1977, and left £15,000 to the Widows' and Orphans' Fund on his own death in 1983. In 1994, officers and Civil Staff in Croydon

placed a granite plaque commemorating Sidney Miles' courage in the police station lawn.

In 1998, the Court of Appeal decided that Bentley's conviction was unsafe, on the ground that the trial judge's summing-up completely failed to put Bentley's defence fairly before the jury. The court said there was 'substantial evi-

PC SIDNEY MILES,

dence' of his guilt, but it was not overwhelming, as was the evidence in Craig's case. In view of Lord Goddard's bias, however, Bentley's conviction was set aside.

One voice stood out in a mass of media commentary about Bentley's case. Christopher Craig, long paroled and rehabilitated, offered a dignified statement of his deep regret for his actions and the suffering he had caused PC Miles's family, before going on to apologize further for the trouble he had brought on Bentley and his family. See also PC Claude Raymond Pain.

MINSTRELS Metropolitan Police concert party, raising money for police charities from 1872 to 1933.

Founded by 10 officers from A Division (Whitehall), including James (later Sir James) Olive, who was associated with it for the next 50 years. The Minstrel Troupe gave the standard 'Nigger Minstrel' entertainment of the period. Singers and musicians in evening dress and black-face make-up with banjos, guitars, trumpets, tambourines and bones performed instrumental solos and ensembles and sang negro spirituals, popular ballads and songs. Music hall artiste Clarkson Rose, the greatest pantomime dame of his day and founder of the popular south coast concert party *Twinkle*, wrote sketches for them.

Seats for the concerts were sold by uniformed 'ticket sergeants' who touted them from house to house and at business premises. This led to objections from Commissioners Sir William Horwood and Lord Byng, who saw that potential householders might feel improperly pressed in being solicited for subscriptions by uniformed policemen, and in this they were supported by the Metropolitan Federation Branch Boards who felt that ticket-selling derogated from the proper dignity of Sergeants. The Minstrels' defence was that the Orphanage, Convalescent Home, Widows' Fund and Relief Fund all relied heavily on donations from the concert profits. But when they confessed to Commissioner Lord Trenchard that the success of the concerts was entirely dependent on the door-to-door sales, he concluded that this meant the public were being blackmailed into buying something they didn't really want, and in 1932 he directed that soliciting subscriptions was to cease. To compensate the charities he opened the Commissioner's Fund. In 1933, the Minstrels closed down, several decades before their type of entertainment was universally discarded as offensive to black people. Over their 60-year lifetime, the Metropolitan Minstrel troupe raised £250,000 for their charities.

MONRO, JAMES, CB (1838–1920) First Assistant Commissioner (Crime). Commissioner, 1888–90.

Educ. Edinburgh High School; Edinburgh and Berlin Universities. Indian Civil Service (legal branch), 1857. Successively Assistant Magistrate, Collector, District Judge and Inspector-General of Police, Bombay Presidency. Resigned, 1884, and appointed Assistant Commissioner (Crime) Metropolitan Police the same year. Resigned, 1888, and for two months 'Head of Detective Service' before appointment as Commissioner. Resigned, 1890. Founded and ran Ranaghat Christian Medical Mission, 1890–1903. Retired to Cheltenham and other parts of England, following his son-in-law's movements.

The best-educated and most experienced lawyer among top-ranking Victorian Metropolitan policemen, and the only one with previous police experience, Monro's reputation has always stood high with brother-officers and historians of the police. His very short tenure of the Commissionership, like Sir Charles Warren's, has been blamed on the vacillations of Home Secretary Henry Matthews and the machinations of his Permanent Under Secretary, Godfrey Lushington. Until Monro's unpublished reminiscences were discovered in the 1980s, it was not known that his career in India had been studded with professional quarrels and threats of resignation on principle. Since then he has been described as a man with 'an elephantine memory for a grievance and an implacable impulse to self-justification', to which might be added an intolerable sense of self-righteousness. As he was at the centre of the friction which culminated in Warren's intemperate resignation, it seems possible that Monro should bear more responsibility than he has usually been given for the destabilizing appointment of three new Commissioners between 1886 and 1890.

He joined the Met in 1884 as one of the two additional Assistant Commissioners felt necessary to strengthen the command structure from the top. Monro's post was not brand-new, however. AC (Crime) was effectively a regularization of Howard Vincent's anomalous position as Director of the CID.

The problem immediately facing the new AC was the Fenian bombing campaign. Monro was successful in bringing it under control and putting most of its perpetrators behind bars or driving them out of the country by 1887. During this time he forged a strong alliance with Dr Robert Anderson, the Dublin lawyer who was overtly employed in the Home Office as 'political adviser' on Irish affairs, but actually controlled spies infiltrating the Fenians. Both men were Protestant millenniarists: they believed, that is, that the Second Coming of Christ was close at hand. Both believed that the constitutional Irish Nationalist Party was hypocritically conniving at Fenian terror. Monro and Anderson despised 'the wearing of the green', and Anderson certainly, Monro possibly, contributed anonymous articles using official secrets to the 1887 *Times* series linking 'Parnellism and Crime'.

Their great success came in the same year when Anderson's spies reported that American Fenians were making a collection for 'a pyrotechnic display' in honour of the Queen's Jubilee. The intention was to explode a bomb in Westminster Abbey while the Queen was at prayer. Monro discovered that the principal European conspirator was one of their own double agents, and sent Superintendent Adolphus Williamson to Paris to warn him that the plot was blown and he had better leave Europe. Subsequently Monro learned from H Division (Whitechapel) detectives that a suspect called Harkins was paying furtive visits to a sick man in Lambeth. Harkins was arrested and found to be carrying newspaper cuttings describing the movements of Irish Secretary Arthur ('Bloody') Balfour, whom the Fenians had sworn to murder. The Lambeth man, known variously as 'Cohen' or 'Brown', died, and Monro discovered that he had financed the terrorism in London. Rounding up a few more conspirators and charging them with possession of explosives, coupled with publicizing the death of Cohen or Brown, scared off any remaining would-be bombers, and London heard no more of Fenian terror until 1921.

But if the detective coup was remarkable, Monro's politicking in the covert world was no less so. When he came to office, he learned that the Special Irish Branch kept coming across apparent Fenian conspirators who turned out to be part of a Home Office spy system controlled by a man called Jenkinson. Monro was jealous for his territory, and complained to four successive Home Secretaries about Jenkinson's activities. He also implied that Jenkinson was not, by his rigorous standards, a man of integrity. Jenkinson for his part had little respect for Monro, Anderson or Williamson, but he lost the political struggle and resigned in 1887. Inspector John Littlechild's team, under Monro's control, known (finally) as Special Branch, ruled supreme and solitary as the covert force protecting security, and Monro kept it in being and under his thumb until he himself resigned the Commissionership in 1890.

With Jenkinson out of the way, Monro concentrated his fire on Commissioner Warren. It had been widely expected in 1886 that Monro would succeed Sir Edmund Henderson. The promotion would have been popular in the force, which respected Monro's professionalism. It may have rankled to have Warren brought in over his head. It certainly infuriated him that Warren dropped Henderson's policy of leaving the Assistant Commissioner (Crime) free to do what he liked, reporting only to the Home Secretary. The Special Irish Branch might be an Imperially funded venture outside the Commissioner's purview. The CID was not. Warren did not want to interfere with detective work, which didn't interest him as much as uniformed preventive policing, but as the man finally responsible, he wanted to know what his Assistant Commissioner was doing before he cleared it with the Home Secretary.

Monro protested that Vincent, as Director of CID, had enjoyed direct access to the Home Office. Warren wasn't interested in what had happened before the Directorship was translated into an Assistant Commissionership. Monro complained that, what with the Special Branch, he had too much work on his plate to be bringing everything to the Commissioner for approval. Warren encouraged him to give up the Special Branch work entirely.

Home Secretary Henry Matthews did nothing to sort out the imbroglio. Monro may have disloyally leaked some of his grievances to his men. Certainly the rumour went round that he was protecting the CID from Warren's 'interference', which the detectives were sure would have proved malign. Warren's Annual Report made no mention of their work, and it annoyed the CID that there was no praise for the rapid fall in the crime figures which followed the end of the Fenian bombings and Monro's turning his whole attention to more normal villainy.

In 1888 Monro reached a final impasse with Warren when the Commissioner vetoed his candidate for Chief Constable of the CID. Both men threatened to resign if they didn't get their way. Henry Matthews avoided making a clear judgment. He accepted Monro's resignation and appointed Anderson Assistant Commissioner in his place. He retained Monro as director of Special Branch, and gave him an office in the Home Office with the title 'Head of Detectives'. He allowed Anderson and senior CID officers to consult with Monro behind Warren's back, and actively encouraged them to do so when the Jack the Ripper case overwhelmed the police. Monro, meanwhile, staked a fine defensive position on the moral high ground by refusing to take any salary for his services.

This paid off at the end of the year when Warren resigned. To general approval, inside and outside the force, Monro was appointed to replace him, the only dissenting voice being the *Star*, which accused him of having 'got up' the bomb scares, leaked the information to the *Times* which appeared in the 'Parnellism and Crime' series, and now been rewarded for disloyally intriguing against Warren. Which was a bit rich, coming from a paper that had been howling for Warren's head!

Monro was to last little more than 18 months, the shortest-serving Commissioner in the force's history. He policed the great dock strike of 1889 unobtrusively, and to the satisfaction of everyone except a few blimpish observers who would have liked the strike to be crushed, and a few pickets who objected to being restricted in the amount of intimidation they could use. He saw to the permanent removal of responsibility for Dockside and Quay policing from AC (Crime) to AC (Administration). He guided and helped Robert Anderson to such an extent that crime figures dropped steadily over the next decade. He made a good impression on journalists and inspired confidence.

Perhaps equally significantly, he seized a belated victory over Warren. He appointed Melville Macnaghten, the protégé Warren had vetoed, Assistant Chief Constable, with an obviously likelihood of rapid succession to the post he had been refused a year earlier when the ageing Williamson retired.

He quickly became embroiled with the Home Office. He needed more men, and said so. He reiterated Warren's complaint that the boots issued to patrolling officers were inadequate and actually harmful and objected, too, to the dreadful-quality uniform trousers. These were the sort of demands over which the Receiver and the officials were quite accustomed to evading and procrastinating.

But in 1890 Monro started two disputes which set him on a collision course. Assistant Commissioner Lt.-Col. R. L. O. Pearson died unexpectedly. Monro quite reasonably wanted to replace him by promoting Chief Constable Charles Howard. The Home Office preferred the idea of transferring one of their own high-flyers, Evelyn Ruggles-Brise. There was merit in both proposals. Pearson knew the ropes in Scotland Yard, but Ruggles-Brise, whether his superiors knew it or not, was one of the civil servants most capable of understanding the difficulties previous Commissioners had suffered in their relations with the Home Office. (See Sir Charles Warren.) Moreover, the translation of Anderson from civil servant to policeman was proving a great success.

But Monro dug in his toes. Only Howard would do. The intrusion of an outsider would demoralize a force which had been told some senior promotions were to be made from below – which seems a little disingenuous, coming from the man who had tried to put in Macnaghten over Williamson's head.

His other battle was of longer standing. He took up the men's grievances over pay and pensions. When Matthews announced that he was introducing a bill to improve these, Monro declared that Matthews' offer was inadequate, and, unlike Warren, he made sure the men knew he was fighting for them. When it seemed Matthews would not budge, Monro submitted his resignation. It was accepted on 12 June to take effect on 21 June. On 17 June Matthews' bill was published, and it met Monro's demands. The press wondered whether he had ever been told the finally proposed details, and suspected that Matthews had performed another wriggle to escape the criticism showered on his head for getting rid of two Commissioners in two years. But Matthews jauntily assured Parliament that he had not known Monro thought his original proposals were non-negotiable. And, by the way, he was accepting Monro's recommendation and appointing Howard Assistant Commissioner.

Monro got in one more jab before he left Scotland Yard for ever. He chaired a meeting of Superintendents on 18 June which flatly rejected Matthews' new proposals, although these were the ones Monro had himself recommended.

And so Monro left the force, his head held high – a hero to the men whose rights he had publicly championed, a hero to the press who saw him as the architect of vastly improved crime detection, and a thorn in the flesh of officialdom and senior colleagues who was adept at making them seem in the wrong.

He went back to India as a missionary, carrying medicine and the gospel to the far north. After his retirement back to England, he made one more public appearance when, in 1910, he denied Robert Anderson's claim that he had given him permission to publish anonymous articles in The Times's 'Parnellism and Crime' series. Historians re-examining the case have felt it likely that some conversation took place which Anderson understood to be tacit approval. Both men were certainly in complete agreement with the main thrust of the series, and it has been suggested on internal evidence that one piece might have been by Monro.

MORRISON, STINIE (OR STEINIE, OR MORRIS STEIN OR OTHER ALIASES, D.1921) Burglar convicted of murder, whose case was used to blacken F. P. Wensley's name.

On New Year's Eve 1910, the young and handsome burglar Morrison spent much of the evening in Whitechapel with a middle-aged receiver of stolen goods called Leon Beron. The following morning Beron was found, robbed and battered to death, on Clapham Common, 11km

(7 miles) away. Morrison, who was on parole, disappeared for a week, and when Wensley arrested him, apparently denied involvement in murder before it had been mentioned to him.

At his trial, clear and convincing evidence from his landlady that Morrison spent the night in bed was offset against uncertain testimony from three cabmen about taking first two men, then one, on a sequence of journeys from the East End to South London and back to North East London. But Morrison betrayed a guilty conscience about the time in the evening when he had unquestionably been in Beron's company, producing a blatantly false alibi which was totally exploded in court and ensured his conviction. Wensley believed an accomplice did the actual

STINIE MORRISON IN THE DOCK AT SOUTH WESTERN COURT, LAVENDER HILL, ON NEW YEAR'S EVE, 1910.

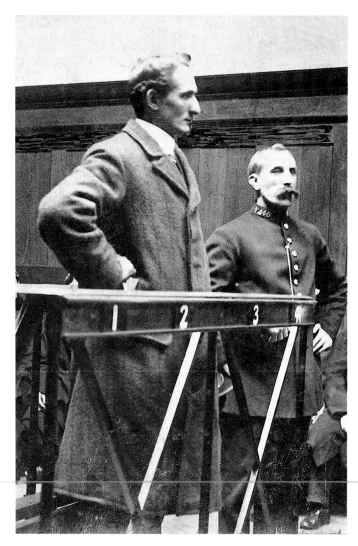

killing; Morrison may merely have 'fingered' Beron for abduction and robbery. Home Secretary Winston Churchill reprieved Morrison after studying the papers.

John Syme vigorously took up a defence suggestion that Wensley had in fact mentioned murder to Morrison before he himself used the word, and found a constable to testify that he had heard Wensley do so. The serious accusation that Wensley had 'put the verbals' on a man on a capital charge, and perjured himself to swear his life away, was investigated by a special committee, which heard from other officers in the room at the relevant time, and concluded that the constable supporting Syme was another unstable malcontent.

Nationally, the case (together with the Tottenham Outrage and the Siege of Sidney Street) tended to encourage the discriminatory perception of Jewish immigrants as criminals holding undesirable political views.

MOUNTED POLICE

Correctly, the Metropolitan Police Mounted Branch (CO13).

The Branch comprises 200 horses and 230 officers. The officers, like all other specialized police such as the CID and the River Police, must serve at least two years on ordinary uniform duties before volunteering for the branch. About five times as many volunteers as are needed put themselves forward. Twenty-five per cent of mounted police officers are women, a higher proportion than anywhere else in the force.

The officers selected for the Branch do not have to have previous equestrian experience. They are given a rigorous 22-week course of riding instruction, and are then sent out to one of the stables in the Areas as Mounted Police

Reserves, riding the mounts of off-duty officers for a probationary period before being entrusted with their own horses. Cavalry standards of smartness and polish are maintained. The uniform is topped by a navy blue riding safety cap with an identifying black and white checkered band. Visored caps like riot helmets may be worn when dangerous crowd situations are anticipated.

Normal duties entail roughly three-hour

patrols through the streets, followed by care for the horse and tack. It is held that working a horse for longer periods, except in the short term, leads to loss of fitness unless a compensatory supplement is administered in the diet. This, in turn, increases excitability.

The patrols are both crime preventive by their presence, and maintain a constant watch for any signs of breaches of the peace. Public order is the primary concern, and the horses can be used to best advantage in areas of heath and woodland. Otherwise, general traffic offences, rowdy misconduct, autocrimes and theft are the usual objects of vigilance. Up to half the Branch is likely to be on duty at football matches on Saturday afternoons during the season.

The horses, which can cost nearly £4000 each at today's prices, have to learn fearlessness

MOUNTED POLICE PATROL PASSING HORSE GUARDS IN WHITEHALL IN 1997.

in noisy traffic, and are trained to take for granted brass bands, pistol shots, missiles and lamentably (since the 1980s) petrol bombs. They learn to disregard loud noises at Imber Court, and are taken to 'Riot City' to learn to resist hostile crowds. The

missiles thrown at them are never harder than tennis balls. Petrol bombs are thrown near them, but never at them. They also learn how to advance at a near canter to disperse an unruly mob and clear a way for short shield riot serials to make arrests.

Frequently claimed as the oldest part of the Metropolitan Police, the Branch may date itself back to the two 'pursuit horses' acquired by the Fielding brothers at Bow Street in 1758 and Sir John Fielding's Bow Street Horse Patrol started in 1763. The history is, however, discontinuous as the patrol was allowed to lapse in the latter part of the 18th century, and only re-formed in 1806 (by which time the River Police had been in existence for eight years as the Marine Police). Nonetheless, the Mounted Horse Patrol was unquestionably the oldest part of the Met when it was incorporated into it in 1836, three years before the Marine Police joined.

At this point it comprised 68 constables commanded by four Inspectors and a Principal Inspector. They patrolled the rural suburban outskirts of London, keeping watch for malefactors (especially highway robbers), and courteously hailing travellers at night. They retained their arms – a pair of horse pistols and a sabre – and would continue to carry firearms until 1866. Their swords were not finally discontinued until 1925.

There was general fear of disorder by Chartist demonstrators after 1839, when the fiery demagogue Feargus O'Connor took over the movement demanding universal manhood suffrage. This led to the introduction of mounted police into central London, their value in crowd control being obscurely recognized, though not really put to the test, as the anticipated rioting never took place.

The glamorous uniform of greatcoats, leather stocks and scarlet waistcoats which had given them the nickname 'robin redbreasts' passed away with the original Peelers' tailcoats and top hats. The mounted policeman of the early 1860s presented the rather odd spectacle

of a helmeted bobby on horseback, with black-striped breeches disappearing into steel-spurred riding boots, a scabbarded sabre hanging from the saddle to his left, and a large pair of black leather pistol holsters across his mount's shoulders. In 1866 the Mounted Police were formally renamed the Mounted Branch, and lost their pistols.

On Bloody Sunday, 1887, the Mounted Branch were called in for the first time to support the cordon of police trying to control the crowd in Trafalgar Square. In the event their support was not enough to contain the riot, and a squadron of Life Guards was needed to clear the mob from Waterloo Place. But thereafter it was realized that crowd control was one of the most useful functions of the Branch. They could also be called upon to supply trained horses with no fear of traffic for ceremonial occasions in the city.

WWI might have ended the Mounted Branch. The cavalry-minded generals persistently hoped that one of their 'big pushes' out of the trenches could be followed by a decisive charge from the lancers or the dragoons, so many of the Met's horses were requisitioned for military service and the Branch was run down to a minimum strength. Yet 1919 brought a tremendous revitalizing spirit to the Branch when Col. Sir Percy Laurie took charge of it as Deputy Assistant Commissioner. He immediately bought 43 horses that were surplus to army requirements. Thereafter he selected the Branch's mounts himself, usually buying from studs in Yorkshire.

In 1920 Sir Percy acquired Imber Court as a training centre for men and horses. The supply of experienced cavalrymen from whom the Mounted Police had traditionally been recruited was drying up as cars and tanks replaced military horses, but Sir Percy retained the old cavalry style of training, and incorporated many of the more advanced exercises for his men. Superficially it might seem that the lancer's skill at precision spearing 'two rings and a tent peg' has little to do with the business of policing the streets, but in practice, as Sir Percy recognized, his constables had to be exceptionally skilled horse-riders if they were allowed to ride among unpredictable crowds of pedestrians. He

MOUNTED POLICE OFFICER IN TRAFALGAR SQUARE, 1951.

THE MPAA TUG OF WAR TEAM.

replaced the somewhat archaic helmet with a flat cap, strapped under the chin, and the 53cm (21in) truncheon carried in a spring-loaded case, which had been Mounted Police issue since 1912, gave way to a 91cm (36in) baton in a leather scabbard strapped to the nearside of the saddle.

The General Strike of 1926 and the mass demonstrations by the unemployed in the 1930s proved conclusively that, in the popular estimation, 'one mounted police officer was worth 12 constables on foot' when it came to controlling potentially riotous assemblies. The size and weight of the horse constituted a serious deterrent to violence, while the officer's elevation gave a clearer view of turbulent groups in the

mass of the crowd. The long baton seemed a formidable weapon, descending from above, yet its length was necessary to allow the rider to reach the culprit safely.

Economy measures after the slump of 1929 led to a determined effort to close down the Branch. Commissioner Lord Byng fought it off successfully, pointing to its vital role in preserving public order. This continued to be its most visible public role after WWII. The mass meeting in Trafalgar Square protesting against the Suez venture threatened to pour riotously down Whitehall. Mounted police easily dispersed the disorderly section of the crowd without inflicting injuries. The mounted police presence in the Grosvenor Square Demonstrations of 1968–9 brought fame to the Branch, while the Wapping pickets in 1987 were prevented from storming the International News Company building by mounted police controlled 'charges'.

In 1984, thanks to the exertions of Sergeant Chris Forester, Princess Alexandra opened a Mounted Branch Museum at Imber Court, exhibiting historic designs for uniforms and equipment, early veterinary equipment, trophies won by horses and riders, ceremonial swords, and photographs and memorabilia of the greatest occasions in the Branch's history. See also Echo, Quicksilver, Winston.

MPAA Metropolitan Police Athletics Association.

The principal formal MPS Social and Athletic Association, and an umbrella for a wide range of sporting and recreational activities. Founded in 1919, it now embraces 46 different sporting clubs, and such activities as the choir. Membership runs very high across the MPS, and membership is open to both police and Civil Staff.

MURDER BAG Cowhide Gladstone bag containing equipment needed by the officer in charge of investigating the scene of a murder. Two were retained in Scotland Yard from 1925, ready packed for immediate use when required. They contained rubber gloves, a range of magnifying glasses, instruments for measuring the depth of liquids, tape measures, test tubes and containers for holding samples of fluids, hair or materials for scientific examination, equipment for fingerprinting and for taking casts of footprints, first aid equipment, and stationery.

The murder bag came into being when Sir Bernard Spilsbury observed Chief Inspector Percy Savage handling decomposing pieces of Miss Emily Kaye's flesh with his bare hands after she had been murdered and dismembered by Patrick Mahon at his bungalow on the Crumbles. Horrified by the risk of sepsis, Spilsbury warned Savage that he should always be provided with rubber gloves for touching dead bodies, and the two then discussed with Savage's friend Dr Scott-Gillett the whole range of equipment to be brought to murder scenes.

'MURDER SQUAD' Despite books and newspaper articles detailing its supposed cases from Crippen (1910) to Donald Neilson, 'the Black Panther' (1975), most murders have been investigated by senior detectives on Districts or Areas, not Scotland Yard. Senior detectives in the Reserve Squad of C1 Branch did investigate serious crimes, usually murders, when called upon, often by other Forces or abroad. *See* Organised Crime Group Operations.

MUSEUMS Several are maintained by sections, branches or Divisions of the Metropolitan Police Service, and two, the Black Museum and the Historical Museum, are the responsibility of the Directorate of Public Affairs.

MUTUAL AID COORDINATING CENTRE See National Reporting Centre.

THE MOUNTED BRANCH MUSEUM AT IMBER COURT.

NARPO National Association of Retired Police Officers. Founded 1919 to safeguard the rights of members and promote measures for their welfare with particular regard to pensions. Now has 100,000 members nationwide, 14,000 of them in the London (Metropolitan Police) Branch. See also *London Police Pensioner*.

NEIGHBOURHOOD POLICING A pilot scheme to organize patrols with more focused community contact, introduced in 1982 under Sir Kenneth Newman. In the first instance it was a joint experiment with Surrey Police. The experimental sites included Kilburn, Brixton and Notting Hill Divisions and involved the traditional four reliefs concentrating their patrolling on their own quarters (Sectors) of their Divisions, and only responding to emergency calls from the other Sectors. Each Sector would thereby have a more dedicated team of officers with better local knowledge, and patrolling would become that much more concentrated on local problems.

Sector Inspectors had responsibility for all matters in their Sectors, including licensing and crime prevention schemes such as Neighbourhood Watch. They could adjust the hours of their officers beyond the eight hours for which each team had primary responsibility for patrolling the Sector. Uniformed officers on those Divisions would be predominantly attached to the Sector teams, rather than assigned to home beats or specialist duties on a Division-wide basis.

Inspectors' and Sergeants' accountability was sharpened because of their new geographic responsibility for a part of the Division, rather than rotating eight-hour shift responsibility for incidents across the whole of the Division. A number of other initiatives, such as Divisional Intelligence and Information Units, were pioneered as part of Neighbourhood Policing.

Under Sir Peter Imbert's PLUS programme, the system went Service-wide as the basic model, but was renamed Sector Policing to

reflect local discretion about the number and range of Sectors each Division would organize. Sector and Neighbourhood Policing both suffered from the conflicting demand of responding to immediate calls from incidents on other Sectors, which intruded on proactive preventive patrolling by reducing the number of officers available for it. As a result many Divisions were soon compelled to restructure and reduce the number of Sectors.

NEIGHBOURHOOD WATCH A successful crime prevention scheme introduced by Sir Kenneth Newman and adapted from an American idea. The schemes involve neighbourhoods of varying sizes forming a recognized geographic boundary, and marking that boundary with

1934 PHOTOGRAPH OF NORMAN SHAW BUILDING, NEW SCOTLAND YARD, FROM AN AUTOGYRO.

signs. Households taking part in the scheme display window stickers, listen to crime prevention talks, and support the principle of marking property with their postcode and house number to make it easier to recover and to deter thieves. Newsletters are distributed through local householders who act as coordinators for passing information about crime to and from the police.

The schemes soon became adopted nationwide, and a significant proportion of the MPD, particularly in owner-occupied housing, joined schemes. Insurance companies support the schemes and reduce their premiums in recognition of the beneficial effect. They also have value in supporting and developing natural community cohesion.

The principle soon led to similar schemes such as Business Watch and Pub Watch.

NEW SCOTLAND YARD (1) 1890–1967 Red-and-white brick Victorian Gothic purpose-built Police Headquarters on Victoria Embankment, SW1 adjacent to Cannon Row Police Station. Now referred to as the Norman Shaw building after the architect (1831–1912) whose *magnum opus* it was.

This famous and romantic building was the site of the unsolved Whitehall Mystery (1888) when a woman's torso was concealed in the cellarage by night while building was in progress. Its main gates provided a background in many police films, and it held the original telephone number WHItehall 1212. But its labyrinthine dark corridors and inadequate, cramped Victorian offices made relocation of the headquarters essential by the 1960s.

(2) From 1967: No. 10 Broadway, SW1 0BG, a plain aluminium-clad office block behind St James's Park Underground Station. Architecturally undistinguished, its most famous feature is the sign outside which performs over 14,000 revolutions every day.

Despite uniform corridors and a generally unexciting appearance, many of the internal facilities (Central Communications

Complex, Briefing Room, etc.) are excellent. The upper floors offer a spectacular panoramic view of London from the Houses of Parliament to the Post Office Tower, and make the best possible viewing point for appreciating No. 55 Broadway, the outstanding Art Deco building created as headquarters of the London Underground, incorporating St James's Park station.

NEWMAN, SIR KENNETH LESLIE, GBE, QPM, KSTJ, LLB, CIMGT (B.1926)
Commissioner, 1982–7.

Son of a Sussex builder. Left school, 1942, and took RAF apprenticeship at Cranwell, an institution instilling extremely disciplined habits. Wireless operator, RAF, 1944–6, serving in the Far East. After demob and return to England, joined Palestine Police largely (by his account) because policing in shorts in the sunshine seemed preferable to drab civilian life in drizzly London. With Zionist terrorism at its height, Newman's police career immediately propelled him into extremely serious public order problems, and his initial training included a strong paramilitary element involving use of firearms, and tactics for riot control. (Nonetheless, he was remembered locally for vehemently opposing cruelty to donkeys rather than for anything more contentious.) In 1947, seconded to Palestine Special Branch. On the disbandment of the Palestine Police in 1948, joined the Met, who sent a recruiting team to Palestine. At 173cm (5ft 8 in) he barely reached the Met's minimum height requirement, a fact which led to a good deal of jocularity from colleagues in his later career, and about which he sometimes joked himself. It also led to his facing a great deal of personal violence from louts who enjoyed starting fights with an apparently vulnerable beat policeman, and so, while on patrol from Bow Street Station, he learnt to take care of himself by self-defence. Married his childhood sweetheart in 1949, his outgoing and sociable wife proving a great support throughout his career.

After the (then) mandatory five years on the beat, promoted to Sergeant, and rapidly again to Station Sergeant, at which rank he proved himself a master of paperwork with an outstanding memory. Subsequently served as Inspector at West End Central Station with the Vice Squad: also planned and established the first traffic warden scheme in central London. Chief Inspector in Southwark, 1963–5. Superintendent and Chief Superintendent at Gerald Road Police Station, 1965–8. Involved in organizing policing of the Grosvenor Square Demonstration against the Vietnam War. After careful study of public order policing around the world (paying particular attention to the notorious 'police riot' scattering demonstrators at the Democratic Party convention in Chicago that year), the Met used very successful tactics that included the use of thousands of officers in close but non-aggressive proximity to the demonstrators, and the division of the attendant police into highly mobile units of 20 constables commanded by two Sergeants and an Inspector (serials). This operation marked him as a probable high-flyer. In his own time, Newman worked as an external student to acquire an Honours LLB. from London University, 1971. Promoted Commander, i/c Community Relations (then A7 Branch) in 1971 after spells as Divisional Chief Superintendent, second-in-command of D and then B Divisions.

In 1973, Mrs Newman noticed an advertisement in *Police Review* for the post of Senior Deputy Chief Constable of the Royal Ulster Constabulary, and wondered aloud 'What kind of nut would take a job like that?' only to learn that her husband had already expressed his interest in it. Home Secretary Merlyn Rees hoped that Newman would rise swiftly from Deputy to Chief Constable, and saw the promotion take place in 1976, when Newman contemplated applying for the post of Chief Constable in Northumbria. His appointment was not immediately popular in the province, as he replaced the first Catholic Chief Constable, Ulsterman Sir Jamie Flanagan, who had been trying to improve the image of the force in the community, some members of which saw it as a discredited organization with an overwhelming Protestant bias. Even the Rev. Ian Paisley, who might have been expected to welcome the ousting of a papist, objected that Newman was not an Ulsterman.

Newman introduced extremely successful methods of riot control, honing further the methods he had been taught in Palestine and improved for Grosvenor Square. Later he would remark that Northern Ireland's separation from mainland Great Britain made it a useful testing ground for police methods, a comment which inspired protests that Ulster folk were not police guinea pigs. When Protestant paramilitaries tried to bring the province to a standstill by enforcing a general strike in 1977, Newman's skilful police organization and courage prevented them from scoring a success such as they had previously achieved by intimidation, and it demonstrated the impartiality of the RUC.

At the same time he set up regional crime squads to gather intelligence and make arrests to forestall IRA terrorism. And, following the new Government policy of criminalizing the IRA and refusing to treat arrestees as political prisoners, he could point to a significant rise in convictions and detentions. In keeping with his constant insistence that the police must be apolitical and his experience in command of Community Relations, he encouraged unaggressive street patrolling, a non-retaliatory approach to political and sectarian hostility, and a more determined integration of the police with the people they policed. He streamlined the managerial organization of the force, and was widely recognized as having remedied a situation wherein the RUC tended to let the army play the major part in combating terrorism. It now offered a smoothly disciplined force in its proper place as a major element in law enforcement. He was knighted in 1978, and would later recall his time in Ireland as the most satisfying of his career.

But there was a downside. The anti-terrorist regional crime squads quickly came to see themselves as a police elite, and were accused of breaching suspects' human rights, particularly in Castlereagh. Newman was convinced that the complaints were part of an orchestrated attempt to denigrate the RUC (and indeed there was a definite propaganda campaign mounted against them). He insisted that the 'injuries' complained of were generally self-inflicted with the intention of bringing the police into disrepute, but he radically overhauled the complaints investigation system, and all allegations were scrupulously investigated and sent for independent scrutiny by the Director of Public Prosecutions. The

SIR KENNETH NEWMAN.

independent Northern Ireland Police Authority concluded that the complaints were grossly exaggerated, and the National Council of Civil Liberties – a pressure group invariably opposed to heavy-handed policing – praised Newman's approach. His departure from Northern Ireland was regretted by many when he was recalled to the mainland in 1980 to serve as Her Majesty's Inspector of Constabulary, and take office as Commandant of Bramshill Police Staff College.

Three years at Bramshill did not represent marking time for a man who was in some ways a natural academic. Newman was extremely interested in the efficient structure and organization of policing. (He was to become a Companion of the British Institute of Management.) As a lifelong reader of both the *New Statesman* and the *Daily Telegraph* he was well placed to estimate the neutral ground in politics, especially as he backed up these regular journals with occasional reading of *The Spectator* and *The Guardian*. A reader of *New Society* from its inception, he was well aware that the police did not function in a law-enforcing vacuum.

Not that he encouraged Bramshill to become a library-bound ivory tower. He actually owed

his appointment to the perceived need for a Commandant with 'street credibility' to inspire confidence in Chief Constables who were expected to second officers to the college. He set in motion the construction of premises for practical training in simulated serious operational situations such as sieges, civil disasters and complex crime investigations as well as public disorder scenarios (cf. 'Riot City'). He also introduced short 'carousel courses' delivering special skills training in areas of topical need. When his appointment as Commissioner of the Metropolitan Police was announced in 1982, few doubted that the Met was in for a managerial shake-up by the first Commissioner since Sir Charles Warren with a noteworthy intellectual background.

Newman inherited the Met at a critical time. Michael Fagan's breach of Buckingham Palace security and the potential embarrassment of a homosexual officer's heading the Royalty Protection unit had elicited strong press comment. The Scarman Report suggested that riot policing might have been better at Brixton, and The PSI Report roundly accused the Met of harbouring a small minority of racists, bullies and hard drinkers. Many people feared that Operation Countryman's failure to identify more than five officers deserving prosecution was a consequence of Met obstruction and cover-up, not evidence that Sir Robert Mark's campaign had virtually eliminated corruption. Such points, as Newman noted in his first Commissioner's Report, were fair criticism outlining matters for him to investigate and, if necessary, act upon. But he also observed presciently that the apolitical stance of the police was hard to maintain in the teeth of a systematic campaign of abuse such as occurred in parts of the ethnic and extreme left press. He would rapidly become a primary target of such vilification himself, one paper describing him as first and foremost an enforcer of 'imperialism' on the grounds that he had served in Palestine and Northern Ireland.

Within a few months of taking office, he confronted his first major public relations crisis, the Stephen Waldorf incident, which graphically illustrated the danger of fast-moving firearms incidents pressurizing officers into making mistakes. Less than two years later, the death of Mrs Cyn-

thia Jarrett and maiming of Mrs Cherry Groce, sparking off the Broadwater Farm Riot and Brixton 1985 Riot, produced renewed hostile reactions. Newman, named Communicator of the Year in 1984, had the misfortune to displease diametrically opposed critics inside and outside the force by his public responses to these events. Rank and file police, outraged by the murder of PC Keith Blakelock, were annoyed that he refused publicly to criticize the actions of under-trained senior officers controlling the riot. The left wing were equally outraged when he warned the citizens of London that plastic bullets might be used on the mainland if they continued to indulge in lethal rioting. It was Newman's clear view that the proper use of force to maintain public order should not be unrealistically withheld by inappropriate reliance on community negotiation techniques, although paradoxically, he more than anyone else initiated the policies of Neighbourhood and Community Policing.

To meet concerns inside the Force, he set up a working party, including representatives of the Police Federation, with a remit to review communication, organization and tactics for such occurrences. The outcome was the amalgamation of Special Patrol Group into Area-based Territorial Support Groups, 900-strong bodies of well-trained officers who could be rapidly mobilized and deployed at short notice, so as to obviate the situation where, in emergencies, sudden calls on divisional manpower led to the assembly of scratch groups of officers unused to working together in such situations. This, perhaps inevitably, was passionately resented by demonstrators in a politically divisive period, who were constantly frustrated in all their aims by the efficient deployment of what they saw as 'riot police'. The benefit to society as a whole became apparent at the end of the decade, when mindless 'football hooliganism' replaced politically motivated demonstrations as the major threat to public order.

Insofar as the Thatcherite decade represented a call to stronger and more efficient business management having little truck with sentimental tradition, Sir Kenneth was in a very positive sense the model radical Commissioner. His restructuring of the Force constituted the most fundamental

managerial change since its inception. The old plan of 'Eight by Eight' was revived, with the intention of making 'all-round' policing at Divisional level the force's centre of gravity. The famous Departments A, B, C and D disappeared. C Department, the internationally celebrated specialist CID in Scotland Yard, became Specialist Operations. Other centrally managed operational policing functions became Territorial Operations. A new strategic, community-based role for Chief Superintendents seemed, for a time, to threaten the continued existence of the rank of Commander.

And senior officers were expected to acquire formal planning and business management skills. Some were borrowed from America, like Policing by Objectives, and Problem-Orientated Policing. It was no longer enough to note that crime figures were down and arrests up on the previous year. Targets, achievement plans and budgeted projections allowing for predictable change were

demanded. Value for money (though not yet an expressly stated policy) would be expected. 'Proactive' rather than 'reactive' policing was encouraged, to anticipate problems and forestall them. The language of senior policing became increasingly that of the financial and business world, but it was based on a new and far more objective analysis of policing priorities, and recognition of the need to reduce the volume of unreported crime. The Commissioner's Reports ceased to be simple blue-covered octavo booklets giving the facts and figures as plainly as possible; they appeared in glossy quarto covers full of photographs, coloured charts and bullet points, like company prospectuses.

These changes were not universally popular within the force. Some senior officers felt that they had to devote far too much time to preparing reports and making estimates, when they wanted to oversee practical operations. The rank

CHIEF SUPERINTENDENT KENNETH NEWMAN (WEARING CAP) IN GROSVENOR SQUARE, 1968.

and file were not immediately impressed with the Commissioner's ongoing concern with Community Relations evidenced by his involvement of the public through Neighbourhood Watch and his efforts to improve community relations and increase the number of ethnic minority officers in the force. Nor did the quiet pipe-puffing geniality of his manner with visitors in the intimacy of his office come across in his public appearances. Although, like several of his reforming predecessors, he made special arrangements for regular visits to stations where he could test the opinions of Sergeants and Constables, some Metropolitan officers felt disconcerted by what they saw as his rarefied intellectual approach from on high. (Northern Irish constables, by contrast, had voiced 'sky-high respect' for his 'down to earth ability, oozing common sense'.) When his guidelines on police conduct (issued in 1985) drew attention to public misgivings about the influence of Freemasonry in the police, it seemed almost a piece of bloody-mindedness that Masonic officers should immediately inaugurate the St James's Lodge specifically for members of the Met (though the likelihood is that the proposal had already been mooted and steered through Masonic bureaucratic channels). The Guidelines themselves (*The Principles of Policing and Guidance for Professional Behaviour*) marked a new departure from traditional Standing Orders, listing 'Do's and Don'ts'. Sir Kenneth wrote the first 15 pages personally, and the booklet, placing police ethics in a constitutional context, paved the way for Sir Peter Imbert's PLUS Programme.

After his retirement, Sir Kenneth's services were snapped up by Bristol University as visiting professor. He also accepted a wide range of company directorships and became a trustee of four different charities. For some years commentators were unsure whether his reforms should be seen as a success or not. The unpopularity of paperwork with almost all officers and the evolutionary development of Territorial Operations and the Areas in 1995 masked the permanence of the managerial revolution, but with hindsight it is possible to see that he had a strong and lasting impact. The 'corporate' approach to police management superseded both the loyal militaristic sense of authority under the Crown which Rowan and Mayne set up, and the civil servant's sensitive response to government whims which Sir Harold Scott followed. Community Policing became the favoured form of 'crime-fighting' in residential districts of London, and initiatives such as Neighbourhood Watch and Victim Support Schemes became nationally accepted. Newman's restructuring of the Met led to much closer consultation with the public by local Divisions. The Neighbourhood Policing experiments gradually took hold, and were later formalized as Sector Policing, giving Inspectors and local police teams much more involvement with community problems. Intelligence-led criminal investigation and prevention was a Newman enthusiasm which became the policy of the service. Senior officers, up to the rank of Commissioner,

impress by their very unmilitaristic appearance. And Sir Kenneth's whole career reveals a man who tried to chart his way along the even-handed neutral ground of political theory, and who would never have been associated with any political label in a period of government by consensus rather than adversarial confrontation.

NEWMAN RESTRUCTURING The Force Organisation and Management Review introduced by Sir Kenneth Newman in 1985. In effect, the setting in place of a system whereby the modern managerial techniques Sir Kenneth wished to see applied to policing could be most efficiently carried out.

The most obvious change was the complete replacing of the old Divisions in their 24 Districts (2), and four Areas, by the Eight Areas plan proposed, but not implemented, at the time of the Waldron Reforms in 1969, and revived for consideration as RUFUS eight years later. At the same time Newman abolished Districts (2) and emphasized that Divisions were to be the fundamental unit of policing. The Divisional Chief Superintendent assumed an outward-looking role, ensuring that communities were consulted about policing issues, while the Superintendent concentrated on internal Divisional performance. A new role of Divisional Administration Manager was introduced for Higher Executive Officers from the Civil Staff. The duties of the HEO included responsibility for traffic process, which was subsequently moved back under police officers' control when Criminal Justice Units were introduced under the Service Restructuring Exercise, 1995.

Sir Kenneth also abolished the old lettered Departments A, B, C and D. He placed responsibility for all Operational Policing in Divisions and Areas under one Department (Territorial Operations); C Department, the former CID, was essentially replaced by Specialist Operations. The formation of Management Support Department and Personnel and Training Department also modernized the structure at Headquarters.

NICKELL, RACHEL (1969–1992) Murder victim.

Rachel Nickell was sexually assaulted and

stabbed on Wimbledon Common in July 1992 by an unknown assailant. The file on her case remains open.

In 1994, 31-year-old Colin Stagg was charged with the crime, but the case was dropped after the judge, Mr Justice Ognall, had rejected all police evidence based on covert interviews in which Mr Stagg was implicitly offered sexual favours in return for a confession (which he never made). The judge further observed that identifying a suspect on the basis of a theoretically assembled 'psychological profile' was fraught with dangers.

The case was the first since the Gould and Titley cases (1840 and 1880 respectively) in which the bench firmly discountenanced a new method of investigation pursued by the Metropolitan Police.

NINE NINE NINE (999) The world's first number for automatically telephoning the emergency services, introduced in London in 1936.

Prior to 1936, the Metropolitan Police could only be telephoned through WHItehall 1212 (connecting to the Scotland Yard exchange), or through the number of a local police station. A disaster in 1935 suggested the urgent need for a system whereby telephone operators could identify and prioritize callers dialling 0 (the exchange) and asking to be put through to one of the emergency services (Ambulance, Fire or Police). Five women died in a fire in Wimpole Street while their neighbour was unable to get through to a switchboard jammed with calls. A Parliamentary Committee looked into the question, and found that of 91,604 emergency calls made in the first six months of 1936, 56,724 were for the police. The Information Room in New Scotland Yard was taking 8000 emergency calls a month.

The General Post Office, which ran the telephone service, proposed that an easy three-digit number should automatically trigger a special signal and a flashing light at the exchange, directing the operators' attention to the emergency. An end or penultimate digit on the ring dial was proposed, so that it could be found by touch in darkness or thick smoke. 111 was rejected because it could be accidentally triggered by tapping the handset on faulty equipment (for which reason none of the three-letter area exchange codes used 1); 222 would connect with ABBey exchange via the digit hole 2(ABC); 000 was impossible as the first 0 would immediately make an unprioritized operator call; so 999 was inevitable.

The system came into operation on 1 July 1937, covering a 19km (12 mile) radius from Oxford Circus. On 8 July, the *Daily Sketch* reported that Mrs J. S. Beard of Hampstead made the first 999 call, which led to the police catching a burglar her husband had seen and was chasing. The claim was immediately disputed by other readers who claimed to have called 999 on 2 or 3 July. Whoever called first, the system received 1336 calls in the first week.

In November of that year the handling of all calls via the Information Room started, and a year later 999 calls were introduced outside London (in Glasgow) for the first time.

NOBLE CAUSE CORRUPTION A term used at one time to describe breaking the rules of procedure, or the law, in order to make sure that suspects did not escape prosecution because of small gaps in evidence or administrative failings not connected with a wider sense of justice.

Police officers have a duty to pursue and bring to justice those who break the law, and have a strong desire to see the full truth of incidents given to the courts. The criminal justice system has its own rules to protect the accused from unfair prosecution and to exclude evidence, however, and these are now supplemented by PACE and other provisions of a liberal democracy for ensuring that prisoners have rights such as access to legal advice at police stations. Sometimes there was a temptation to 'make the system work'.

In the inevitable cut-and-thrust of combating street-wise arrogant criminals, fully aware of their legal rights, the examples commonly given of noble cause corruption were giving evidence of a caution being given when the wording was not correctly stated or omitted; falsely putting details into administrative records of a prisoner's custody record or duty sheets to correct minor errors; tricking a prisoner into making a true

confession; inducing a prisoner to confess by the promise of bail; or adding to a prisoner's statement to ensure legal completion of an offence.

Nowadays technology and procedures adopted in custody suites have brought an end to the opportunity for such practices. Tape-recorded interviews, date- and time-stamped notes of evidence and the automatic right of prisoners to legal advice before interview have all brought strict regulation into the system, sometimes at the expense of spontaneous discussion and confession between arresting officer and prisoner.

These issues need to be carefully distinguished from efforts to test the legality of some methods of crime detection, such as the fictitious shop operated to 'receive' stolen goods by thieves who were then successfully prosecuted (see Operation Herring).

Attitudes to noble cause corruption have differed through the years. In the 1950s Detective Chief Superintendent John ('Charlie Artful') Capstick was described as administering a savage beating to an informant in order to protect him from revenge attacks if he had been identified as his informant. Nowadays he would undoubtedly have been prosecuted or disciplined, and all the malpractices are strictly forbidden simply because of the undesirable precedent they create by justifying breaches of rules or the law.

NODDY BIKES Lightweight Velocette motorcycles introduced experimentally for beat patrol officers on 19 September 1955 as part of Commissioner Sir Harold Scott's 'make-do and mend' policies to extend the use of constables when the government refused to increase available resources. It has been suggested that the nickname derives from Enid Blyton's children's books ('Little Noddy' drove a little car, and 'PC Plod' walked). It derived from the reinforced helmets

A 'NODDY BIKE' IN USE.

the officers received, so that their appearance marked them as patrolling beat police, instantly distinguishable from the flat-capped traffic police. Since they could not raise their hands to salute Inspectors while riding, they nodded, and the helmets earned the nickname originally as 'noddy helmets'. The water-cooled engines of Noddy bikes made them suitably quiet for night-duty use. They were phased out from 1969, being largely replaced by Panda cars.

NODDY BOATS Small duty boats used by the River Police in the years following 1967 for patrolling the non-tidal Thames between Teddington Lock and Staines. Inadequately powered for coping with flood waters, they were occasionally thus nicknamed by analogy with Noddy Bikes.

NORMAN, PC PERCIVAL, KPM (FL.1924) Officer awarded the KPM for Gallantry after stopping a runaway horse in Sloane Square.

Joined the Met 31 December 1923 (B513, Warrant No. 112531)

Until the 1930s, a very high proportion of the KPMs awarded for Gallantry went to officers who stopped runaway horses in the streets. Laconic entries in Appendix 3 'For Gallantry' give little idea of the dangers they accepted by spontaneously reacting to the crisis, so PC Norman's meritorious conduct is described here as an example.

At 7.30 in the evening of 23 July 1924, PC Norman saw a horse attached to an unattended coal cart in Eaton Terrace take fright at something and bolt towards Sloane Square with its bridle trailing. PC Norman raced after it until he could grab the front of a shaft with one hand and clamp his other over the horse's nostrils (the usual method of halting a runaway horse and cart). With both hands occupied thus, he was dragged for about 46m (50yd) before the horse collided with a lamp post, knocking him to the ground. (Similar collisions caused broken ribs, back and abdominal injuries to other policemen, sometimes leading to their being permanently invalided out of the force.) Notwithstanding, PC Norman chased the horse again, and again managed to get hold of it, hanging on until he brought it to a stop despite its making another jarring collision.

PC Norman received the KPM for Gallantry in the New Year's Honours List of 1925, one of 39 Metropolitan Policemen so honoured for tackling runaway horses between 1909 and 1948.

NOTT-BOWER, SIR JOHN REGINALD HORNBY, KCVO KPM (1892–1972) Commissioner, 1953–8.

Son of Sir William Nott-Bower, Commissioner of the City of London Police. Educ. Tonbridge. Joined India Police Service by competitive examination, 1911, and posted to United Provinces. Returned to India Office, London, on special duties, 1921. Superintendent, UP, 1923. KPM for conspicuous bravery in arresting armed criminals who shot him in the arm, 1931. Joined the Met as District (1) Chief Constable, 1933. Pro-

moted Deputy Assistant Commissioner the same year. CVO, 1937. Assistant Commissioner, general administration, 1940. Seconded to Austria as Inspector-General, Public Safety Branch of British Control Commission, 1944-46. Deputy Commissioner, Metropolitan Police, 1946. Kt,

SIR JOHN NOTT-BOWER.

1950. Commissioner and KCVO, 1953.

A lifelong policeman and also the son of a policeman, yet with his public school background and polo-playing expertise definitely 'an officer and a gentleman', Sir John Nott-Bower's appointment declared firmly that the Conservative Churchill administration was not going to continue its Labour predecessor's experiment of 'civilianizing' the police by appointing a mandarin Commissioner who had never worn a uniform. On the other hand, Nott-Bower's administrative skills had proved admirable during the war when

he was a highly efficient Assistant Commissioner (Admin), and his return from secondment to Austria had been keenly anticipated in the upper echelons of the force, where his only fault seemed to be an intolerable enthusiasm for dragging his colleagues into rubbers of bridge.

Unhappily his energy had run out by the time he became Commissioner. The golden 'Dixon of Dock Green' days were not yet over, and there seemed really to be little reason why he should reform, challenge or seriously refurbish the force he had inherited.

He remained a keen horseman, and took great pleasure in overseeing the practicalities of the Mounted Police Branch and buying their horses. The establishment of a Research and Planning Branch was a good idea, and the centralization of Traffic Control was a logical response to the increase in car-ownership. C9 Branch, Metropolitan and Provincial Regional Crime Squad, was a move in the right direction of proper liaison with other forces, but it was an inadequate response to the sudden and accelerating leap in crime figures, which had at last started to fall in the last two years of Sir Harold Scott's Commissionership. Nott-Bower amiably deplored, but he did not act. His successor would create no fewer than five new crime-fighting branches.

Equally, Nott-Bower did nothing to agitate for improved pay and conditions for his officers. The result, as is inevitable with any public service dependent on Treasury money, was that police pay fell so far below the rates of inflation and comparability with private sector wages that PCs were once again as badly exploited as nurses always are. In consequence, recruiting was difficult and the force remained under strength.

With Fabian of the Yard rivalling Dixon as the public image of the police, the CID and the prestigious Flying Squad were allowed to carry on in their time-honoured manner. This was inappropriate to the post-war society. Though professional criminals (always a tiny and unrepresentative section of the populace) were becoming more violent, respectable society was becoming far gentler. Some of the powerful detectives of

Nott-Bower's force saw this as 'going soft', a mark of the moral corruption of the times. In the year of Nott-Bower's retirement, ex-Commander Leonard Burt, recently retired head of Special Branch, wrote memoirs in which he lamented the passing of the cat o' nine tails and the birch; deplored the relative comfort of modern imprisonment and the imposition of shorter sentences; insisted that physical punishment by men strong enough to inflict it was the only way to control criminal bullies; and decried psychologists who 'explained' criminality and did not agree with him that homosexuals were depraved. None of these opinions would have been out of place in 1935, but by 1958 they indicated that some senior detectives were getting out of touch with the historical drift of society. Nott-Bower's Conservative mentor, Home Secretary Sir David Maxwell-Fyfe, seems to have come to feel that more was expected of Nott-Bower than he was giving.

It is a telling comment on him that his obituary in *The Times* said more about his activities as a prefect and athlete at school than as Metropolitan Police Commissioner. In the end, the sad epitaph on Nott-Bower's Commissionership is to be found in the words of a Superintendent, quoted by police historian David Ascoli as saying sympathetically that he was a nice man when what was needed was a bit of a bastard.

NOTTING HILL CARNIVAL

By far the largest public order commitment of the Met, the Carnival is now firmly established as a famous Afro-Caribbean cultural celebration which can attract more than a million people to crowd the streets of West London on the last Sunday and Monday of each August. The public order and crime prevention problems tended to increase year by year, with 1976 seeing police officers attacked by missiles and having to resort to dustbin lids for protection.

The 1985 event was the turning point for improved management of the event. DAC Paul Condon persuaded the moving music floats to accept a route which has now become standard, thus avoiding the intense crushing caused by random processions trying to pass each other on crowded streets. Static sound systems were also put under better control, and street trading and the sale of alcoholic drinks brought into a proper licensing system. But the most important development was the emergence of a more formal organization, which attracted sponsorship. This in turn has led to a number of years of steadily improving events, less crime and more enjoyment. The safety of the public remains the key issue of police concern, simply because of the risks inherent in so many people being crammed into confined spaces.

NOTTING HILL RACE RIOTS, 1958

In 1958 tensions rose between the immigrant West Indian community in Notting Hill and white racist youths. The West Indian community's perception that the police did not take their complaints of racial assaults seriously or act on them led to confrontations, some hostile demonstrations, and the fear that there would be serious black vs white rioting if something was not done.

The situation was apparently resolved when very positive action was taken about a gang of 10 youths who committed serious assaults, with sticks, iron bars and at least one knife, on six inoffensive West Indians in four separate incidents between 2.00 and 5.00 a.m. on 24 August. A report was radioed to all patrol cars, and at 5.40 a.m. PCs Wilding and Knight, driving along the Uxbridge Road, saw the assailants' small black Singer packed with white youths. They pursued it and frightened the youths away from their car, and although they were unable to catch them when they escaped into the White City housing estate, with the car as a lead, eight of them were arrested before the day was out. The investigating team worked 20 hours without stop, took a three-hour break, and resumed work to arrest a ninth youth the following day. The tenth, known only as 'Paddy', a stranger who had joined the gang at the outset of their night's misdeeds, was never identified and traced.

NOTTING HILL CARNIVAL, 1991.

The nine were given severe four-year jail sentences, and it was hoped this would ease racial tensions. Assaults stopped, but relations of mutual confidence between the police and the black community were never properly established, there being faults on both sides.

NUMERICAL STRENGTH In 1829 the founding Commissioners Rowan and Mayne commanded a force of 1011 men, 8 of whom were Superintendents, 20 Inspectors, and 88 Sergeants. By the time of Mayne's death in 1868 the force had expanded to more than 7000 men. When his successor, Sir Edmund Henderson, resigned 18 years later it had almost doubled again, to 13,115.

After that, it grew more steadily until on the outbreak of WWI the authorized strength was 22,048, although secondment to dockyard duties, municipal corporations, and hire by private individuals meant the actual strength was 19,129. The war sharply reduced this figure, which stood at 18,728 in 1919, and had only crept up to 20,000 by 1931, when Lord Trenchard took over from Lord Byng. Nor could the energetic Trenchard keep a force at full strength. It had slipped back to 18,846 by 1939, and emerged from WWII well under strength at 15,387. Three thousand of those were quickly lost, as they were War Reserve Officers or pensioned officers called back to duty for the duration.

By 1958, Sir Harold Scott and Sir John Nott-Bower had brought the figure no higher than 16,661. Sir Joseph Simpson managed the necessary large-scale postwar expansion in the end, leaving a force 20,539 strong when he died in 1968. That slowly rose to nearly 24,000 by the time Sir Kenneth Newman took office in 1982, and actually rose to 28,000 by the early 1990s. After this manpower economy measures under Sir Paul Condon started bringing the figure down again to approximately 26,000 at the end of the century.

NUPPO National Union of Police and Prison Officers. Short-lived police union, set up as a result of the agitation started by Inspector John Syme. It called the successful London Police Strike, 1918, but was destroyed the following year by the abortive national Police Strike, 1919.

In 1913 John Syme advertised the formation of a Metropolitan Police Union in *Police Review*. The paper's editorials pooh-poohed the idea, but Syme enrolled members clandestinely and ran the 'union' as a secret society whose members, identified by number only, faced instant dismissal for breach of regulations if they were found out. In 1914 he raised the title to National Union of Police and Prison Officers and tried to recruit members in the provinces, but membership stood at no more than about 200 when Syme went to prison for the second time in 1917.

During his incarceration, active Met policemen took over the running of the secret society, and discovered that Syme's management had been chaotic. They also realized that his obsession with his own grievances and increasingly eccentric means of protest brought the union into disrepute. Syme emerged from prison to find himself voted off the executive. Firebrand agitator PC James Marston became the Chairman, and popular Boer War veteran PC Tommy Thiel (147T, Warrant No. 90866) the Provincial Organiser.

Sympathetic Labour politicians tried to persuade Commissioner Sir Edward Henry to recognize the union, pointing out that its constitution prevented it from striking. Henry, however, was sure the no-strike articles would be rescinded in time of a dispute, and he believed the TUC hoped to take over the police whose use as attempted strike-breakers rather than mere peacekeepers in the successful and popular 1912 Dock Strike had been hugely resented.

In 1918, the Chief Constable of Manchester sent Scotland Yard correspondence from Thiel trying to recruit members in the north, and Thiel was dismissed from the Force. The union promptly demanded his reinstatement, as well as a desperately needed pay increase for men who were suffering serious hardship owing to wartime inflation and government parsimony. Henry and his Assistant Commissioners, taking their soundings from better-paid and relatively elderly Superintendents, concluded wrongly that pensions were a more serious grievance than pay, and that there was no urgency in responding to the union's demand. While Henry was on holiday the union (as he had predicted) rescinded its

no-strike commitment and laid down an ultimatum to Assistant Commissioner Wodehouse, which was peremptorily refused. The immediate result was the hugely successful Police Strike, 1918, winning policemen all over the country a generous and well-deserved pay rise.

Under the Lloyd George settlement, policemen were allowed to join NUPPO, though it was not to interfere in matters of discipline, should not supply representation for policemen on criminal charges, and would not for the duration of the war be the recognized negotiating body on matters of pay and conditions. Membership jumped from 200 underground Metropolitan policemen to nearly 50,000 out of a 60,000 strong force across the country. NUPPO could now collect dues and circulate its *Journal* freely. Marston and Sergeant Jack Hayes resigned from the police to become full-time salaried union employees, and when the Representative Board promised in the strike settlement was set up, Metropolitan NUPPO members won almost every seat, and nominated a NUPPO-dominated executive.

However, the new Commissioner, Sir Nevil Macready, was determined to break the union, which he regarded as a 'Soviet'. He called new elections for a restructured Representative Board with separate tiers for Sergeants and Inspectors who (he rightly expected) would be more moderate than constables. NUPPO called on its members to boycott the election, which only resulted in its having almost no candidates for the new Board so that it lost power. All the union really gained from the new election was a token martyr in PC Spackman. At the same time, provincial members expressed strong dissatisfaction with the union's Metropolitan domination, and Marston lost his position as chairman.

The Desborough Committee's decision to extend Macready's three-tier structure nationally in the Police Federation spelled the end for NUPPO. Marston wrongly assumed that his popularity in London would bring the men out for the Police Strike, 1919. In the event, not a single man from his own station, Loughton, heeded his call. NUPPO collapsed as quickly as it had arisen, and Marston joined the Communist party, finding employment with ARCOS until his dismissal for drink-related unreliability.

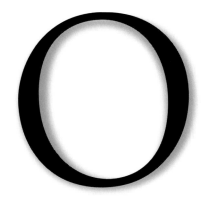

O DIVISION Because of the possibility of confusion with the numeral zero, there is no territorial O Division, for which reason the fictitious Division of television's police series *The Bill* carries the letter.

But on at least two occasions, 6 May 1935 and 12 May 1937, there was an actual O Division of sworn-in constables with correct uniforms and their Divisional numbers on their collars. The shortage of officers to police the Silver Jubilee procession of George V and the coronation procession of King George VI meant that recruits at Peel House were administered the Oath of Allegiance and given specially made uniforms. For the Silver Jubilee procession, the new O Division constables were sworn in at Scotland Yard a couple of days earlier. For the coronation processions, their successors took their oath at 4.30 a.m. in the boot-room at Peel House. Both groups paraded to the Mall, where they stood behind the Guards lining the route until 4.00 p.m.

The Silver Jubilee's O Division were within a day of passing out and being posted to Divisions. They spent the evening removing the Os from their uniforms. The Coronation Day O Division were allowed to wear the uniforms home, and retained them long enough for a photograph of their short-lived Division to be taken.

OAKSEY COMMITTEE Home Office committee on police pay, reporting in 1949, which recommended small increases and a £10 token London weighting (comparable to that paid to teachers and civil servants) to compensate for the higher cost of living in the capital. As a good civil servant, Commissioner Sir Harold Scott (who had recommended the London weighting) gave the increases a cautious welcome. They were, in fact, completely inadequate. Police pay had slipped so far behind private employment rates that the manpower shortage increased at a headlong rate, and a further 20% pay rise within two years still failed to bring about the necessary improvement. The Committee also recommended the greater use of Civil Staff.

A LATE VICTORIAN SCENE IN LONDON WHEN MANY OFFICERS WOULD HAVE TAKEN THE PRE-1886 OATH.

OATH OR AFFIRMATION The oath taken by all Metropolitan Police Constables when they are sworn in runs as follows:

I, - -, being appointed a Constable of the Police Force of the Metropolitan Police District, do solemnly, sincerely, and truly declare and affirm that I will well and truly serve our Sovereign Lady, Queen Elizabeth, in the office of a Constable, and that I will act as a Constable for preserving the peace, and preventing robberies and other felonies, and apprehending offenders against the peace, and in all respects to the best of my skill and knowledge, discharge the duties of the said office faithfully and according to law.

Prior to the 1886 Promissory Oaths Act, the form used was:

I SWEAR, that I will well and truly to the best of my knowledge and ability act as a Constable for the Metropolitan Police district and within the Royal Palaces of Her Majesty Queen Victoria and Ten Miles thereof for preserving the Peace and preventing Robberies and other Felonies and apprehending offenders against the Peace; and that I will well and truly execute such office of Constable and all powers and duties which I may be authorized or required to execute by virtue of an Act of Parliament passed in the Tenth Year of the Reign of His Majesty King George the Fourth for improving the Police in and near the Metropolis, or by virtue of an Act of Parliament passed in the Third Year of the Reign of Her Majesty Queen Victoria for further improving the Police in and near the Metropolis. So help me God.

After 1861, a further oath was required of Metropolitan Police assigned to guarding the Royal Dockyards and Military Stations (which could be as far afield as Devonport or Pembroke) extending their constabulary powers to a radius of 24km (15 miles) of the facility they were guarding.

Technically the modern form is an affirmation, not an oath (though the two carry exactly the same weight and penalties in law). Once the oath has been taken, the historical 'Office of Constable' as an official peacekeeping officer is still held by the policeman as he is promoted, hence Sir Robert Mark's entitling his memoirs *In the Office of Constable*.

OBSCENE PUBLICATIONS SQUAD CORRUPTION CASES The most sensational of the police scandals marring the 1970s, and arguably the very worst moment in the history of the CID, when two former heads of the Obscene Publications Branch, a former head of the Flying Squad, and a former CID Area Commander were all convicted of taking bribes from Soho pornographers (though the latter had his conviction quashed on appeal because the trial judge had inadvertently misdirected the jury).

On 27 February 1972, the *Sunday Mirror* revealed that Commander Kenneth Drury, head of the Flying Squad, had been on holiday in Cyprus with Jimmy Humphreys, a well-known Soho businessman and pornography merchant (b.1930; educ. approved school, Borstal and prison; repeated convictions for theft and receiving, 1950–8). Drury's claim that he paid his own way and the two men were looking for escaped Great Train Robber Ronnie Biggs convinced nobody, and he was suspended, resigning before a Disciplinary Board could hear his case.

In articles in the *News of the World*, Drury claimed that Humphreys had been his paid informant, an accusation which infuriated the vain and self-important Humphreys. He in turn told the paper that he had never given Drury information or received money from him: rather, he had lavished expensive entertainment on him.

In April 1972 Sir Robert Mark became Commissioner and in November began replacing the CID officers in the Branches with uniform officers and civil staff. The following year he

appointed DAC Gilbert Kelland to form a small *ad hoc* Anti-Corruption Squad (Inspector Ronald Hay and Sergeants James Sutherland and James Bilby), to root out the corruption in the old Obscene Publications Squad and the apparent connection of some former Flying Squad members with leading pornography merchants.

Kelland reactivated proceedings against Humphreys for conspiring to have his wife's former lover, Peter Garfarth, 'striped' (his face slashed with knives or razors). Humphreys was arrested in Holland and extradited, eventually agreeing to testify against some of his former CID collaborators. It appeared that No. 4 Area CID Commander Wallace Virgo, in collaboration with DCS Bill Moody, operational head of the Obscene Publications Squad, had extorted bribes totalling at least £13,000 from leading Soho pornographers, with additional heavy weekly pay-offs.

Between 1969 and 1972 very close links were established between dealers in the pornography business and a number of one-time OPS and Flying Squad officers. An old Reptonian pornographer was lent a CID tie to accompany DCI George Fenwick, effective operational head of OPS 1970–1, to Holborn Police Station and select what he wanted for redistribution from a mass of confiscated pornographic material. DCI Anthony Kilkerr and four other officers revealed that Fenwick and other senior officers had tried to compromise them when they were constables in the OPS by forcing small sums of money on them. Kilkerr was so distressed that he threw the money away unexamined on St James's Park underground station and made successful efforts to have himself transferred to other duties.

'Big Jeff' Phillips, the most successful of the early pornographers, told the press before his suicide in 1975 that the Dirty Squad had been receiving £250,000 a year, to which he personally contributed £15,000. Allowing for probable exaggeration, it is nonetheless clear that this was the most serious corruption ever exposed in Scotland Yard.

In the end Kelland's squad investigated 74 officers and saw 40 of them leave the police force. Eight were dismissed following internal police disciplinary proceedings (one of which was not connected with corruption by pornographers); 13 were charged with offences and sentenced to a total of 96 years' imprisonment; the rest retired or tendered voluntary resignations (as some of those convicted had done, leaving the question of their pensions a matter for serious administrative consideration).

The seniority of the men involved with the pornographers was the most shocking aspect of the affair. The Head of the Flying Squad, Kenneth Drury, resigned under a cloud before being sentenced to eight years' imprisonment. His fellow-Commander Wallace Virgo got 12 before his conviction was quashed. It was testified that Detective Chief Superintendent Bill Moody (12 years) said he was going to organize the collection of bribery 'as it had never been organized before', and even collected £100 'transfer fees' from honest officers who wanted to leave his corrupt squad. The personal tragedy was that huge sums of money destroyed the reputations of men with distinguished careers, but in Sir Robert Mark's opinion, Kelland's team carried out the finest piece of detective work in the history of the force.

OBSERVATION Sometimes used interchangeably with surveillance, but the two may be used distinctively with surveillance indicating a constant watch including following the person or persons surveilled, whereas observation more usually denotes watching one position from a fixed point. Surveillance is also used to describe maintaining a protective watch over a person believed to be under some threat. Observation is more likely to be carried out in pursuit of information.

The word 'observation' may also be used to describe an early method of identifying convicted criminals by having detectives make monthly visits to London prisons and 'observe' the intake of recent convicts, attempting to memorize their faces. The practice was dropped shortly after the formation of the Fingerprint Bureau in 1901 offered an infallible means of establishing quickly whether any arrested or convicted person had previous convictions under another name.

It may, nevertheless, still be useful for officers to surreptitiously observe the faces of known or suspected but unconvicted criminals who are not recorded on photographs held by a Local Intelligence Officer.

According to Inspector John Littlechild in 1894, 'Observation and information are the detective's two best weapons.'

OCCUPATIONAL HEALTH DIRECTORATE Branch of the Personnel Department employing 104 specialists, other Civil Staff, one police officer and a wide range of medical specialists on sessional contracts. Their principal role is concerned with maintaining a healthy workforce in a healthy workplace, and their services range from specialist advice to management and staff on fitness to work, health and safety risk assessment, health education and a Trauma Support Programme. First Director appointed 1991.

OLDS, PC PHILIP MICHAEL, QGM (1952–1986) Police officer paralyzed in the course of duty who became an icon of courage for paraplegics.

Son of Police Sgt Philip Olds, Advanced Driving Instructor at Hendon. Educ. Hampstead Comprehensive School. Police cadets, 1969–71. Joined Met, 1971. Posted to Vine Street station (C Division) thereafter X (Ealing), B (Chelsea) and D (Paddington) Divisions. Award from Bow Street Fund and Commissioner's high commendation for risking his own life and saving a brother-officer's in preventing a suicide from the top of Swan & Edgar's building (now Tower Records) in Piccadilly Circus, 1973. Selected for traffic police, 1974, and posted to Alperton.

On 23 December 1980, PC Olds was on patrol in a car driven by PC Laurie Howarth when he got out of the car to buy cigarettes in Hayes. As he did so, two armed men in balaclavas ran out of the shop. PC Olds drew his truncheon and approached them to make an arrest, realizing at the last moment that one of them definitely intended to shoot him at pointblank range. He turned sideways to present a smaller target as Stuart Blackstock fired a filed-down dumdum bullet which punctured his lung and broke his spine, causing instant and permanent paralysis from the chest down. Then one of the two, probably Blackstock's accomplice Leslie Cooke, kicked PC Olds savagely in the eye, and the two men only backed off when Olds warned them that 23,000 policemen wouldn't rest until they were caught if they killed him, while PC Howarth radioed for help. For this episode, PC Olds received £200 from the Bow Street Police Fund and the Queen's Gallantry Medal.

The jury reduced the charge against Blackstock from Attempted Murder to Wounding with Attempt to Resist Arrest. The judge passed a life sentence in any case, but the conviction for the lesser offence appeared to contribute to the frustration which caused PC Olds' early death. (Seventeen years later, Cooke was stabbed to death while brawling outside a Hayes pub.)

A Cabaret Dinner, sponsored by many well-known companies, clubs and individuals, raised £10,000 to help PC Olds with the equipment and training he required to continue an independent life. In the remaining five years of his life, PC Olds became a well-known public figure, strongly supporting a number of charities and taking a leading part in action on behalf of the handicapped. He successfully and extraordinarily pleaded a case to be allowed to continue working as a police officer, even though he would obviously be unable to return to street duties at any time. He worked in traffic control, and was training as an instructor of recruits at Hendon at the time of his death.

OLIVE, SIR JAMES WILLIAM, KBE (1854–1942) First officer to rise from the rank of constable to Deputy Commissioner.

Joined the Metropolitan Police in 1872, Sergeant in 1877, Inspector in 1886 and then moved rapidly through the ranks until Chief Constable in 1918, Assistant Commissioner, 1920 and Deputy, 1922 until his retirement, 1925. CBE 1920, KBE, 1924.

With nearly 53 years' service, Sir James Olive may have been the Met's longest serving officer ever. His dedication to the Force was universally recognized, and his steady promotion paved the way for a fully professional force without the supposed need for a top tier of 'gentlemen' from the armed services or with public school backgrounds.

As head of the River Police, 1903–5, he carried through a reorganization to improve efficiency which so impressed his seniors that he was made Superintendent of X Division, one of the largest in the Force. When Commissioner Sir Nevil Macready appointed him Chief Constable this counterbalanced Macready's perceived, and to some extent resented, practice of filling the top ranks of the Met with his old army staff officers (see Sir William Horwood, Sir Wyndham Childs). At this date it was still exceptionally rare for a Superintendent to be promoted to the rank, despite the declared hope of Sir Edmund Henderson in the 1880s that it might be a level at which 'gentlemen' from the outside mixed on equal footing with officers promoted from the ranks (cf. Adolphus Williamson, F. P. Wensley). Olive's appointment as Assistant Commissioner was a true pointer to the future, although it would be 10 years after his retirement before another 'ranker officer' succeeded him (see Sir George Abbiss).

But the precedent had been set. When Olive retired with the standing of Deputy Commissioner in 1926, the principle of promoting professional police officers to the highest ranks was far from being unthinkable, as it had been when Olive joined the force. Indeed, in the very week of Olive's retirement, Sgt Jack Hayes MP embarrassed Home Secretary Sir William Joynson-Hicks in the House of Commons by exposing his evasiveness in admitting that the bad old system was being maintained, and Olive's replacement was to be Admiral Sir Charles Royds rather than a police officer. The fact that Royds proved a good and loyal Assistant Commissioner did not compensate the rank and file for the loss of an AC who knew what it was to be one of themselves. Olive had been a founder member of the Police Minstrels, performed with it for many years, and wrote sketches and lyrics for its concerts for the last 30 years of his service. He was further affectionately remembered as a truly dedicated patron and supporter of the Orphanage.

OPERATION AIRLINES Little-known but entirely successful Anti-Terrorist Branch activity

during the early 1990s which foiled persistent and well-planned Provisional IRA attempts to cripple London by destroying its power supply.

SIR JAMES OLIVE.

OPERATION BUMBLEBEE Joint police and public campaign against burglary conducted across the Metropolitan Police District since 1993. Stickers, leaflets and Yellow Page telephone listings encourage the public to photograph and mark their valuables and to take proper precautions to secure their premises. Roadshows exhibit stolen property recovered and invite the public to identify it. And police raids on targeted burglars 'sting' them.

In its first year, Bumblebee reduced burglary figures in London by 13%. By the end of the decade Londoners were less likely to be burgled than the inhabitants of any other large English city.

OPERATION EAGLE EYE Campaign against street robberies, which are seen by the public as the most serious threat to them in certain areas. Launched in 1995, following the striking success of Operation Bumblebee. Dedicated officers using high-tech video and surveillance equipment, CCTV and computer software maintain intelligence on street crime and criminals and circulate it across the Service. Liaison with British Transport Police monitors robbers known to travel to London to commit their crimes. Victim support and transportation is given a high priority, as are good practice in relation to witnesses and self-protection against repeat attacks. School involvement programmes, along with the local authority, business and community groups' partnership with the Met in providing Summer Youth Programmes, make an effort to give young people positive activities and goals as an alternative to criminal street-life.

Although Eagle Eye has not had the dramatic success of Bumblebee, it has checked the continuing rise in street crime to the point that the MPS feels it may have turned a corner.

OPERATION HERRING CID covert operation in which an apparent jeweller's and secondhand shop was actually fitted with concealed video cameras and staffed by plain clothes police officers, who received stolen jewellery and credit cards while the vendors were filmed

without their knowledge.

Important because the Appeal Court (*R. v. Christow and Wright*, 1992) determined that this was a completely legitimate means of obtaining evidence, and not entrapment (cf. Gould, Nickell, Titley). It was evident to the court that the existence of the shop could in no way be held to have induced or persuaded the thieves to carry out thefts they would not otherwise have done.

OPERATION ORDERS Special documents setting out the logistics of police arrangements to deal with demonstrations and ceremonial events.

OPERATIONAL COMMAND UNIT (OCU)
A Division, Area Headquarters Unit, or other operational unit, usually commanded by a Chief Superintendent, and with delegated operational, managerial and budgetary control over its own resources.

The term was introduced in the Service Restructuring Exercise, 1995, and is a variant of 'Basic Command Unit', the form used by many provincial forces in the 1990s to denote Sub-Divisions which became independent of their previous Divisional Command Structures and reported direct to Assistant Chief Constables.

Since Operational Policing (embracing public order and civil emergencies as well as traffic control) may be used as a term differentiating it from Criminal Investigation, Areas have both Crime and Operational OCUs.

ORGANISED CRIME GROUP An operational command unit within 'SO' Specialist Oper-

THE FRONTAGE OF THE METROPOLITAN AND CITY POLICE ORPHANAGE, STRAWBERRY HILL, TWICKENHAM. IT WAS DEMOLISHED IN AUGUST 1971.

ations, formed in 1996 from the former SO1 Branch, SO8 Branch and SO10 Branch.

See under Art and Antiques Unit, Cheque and Credit Card Fraud Unit, Criminal Justice Protection Unit, Extradition and Passport Unit, Flying Squad, Hostage and Extortion Unit, Paedophilia Unit, Specialist Operations, Stolen Vehicle Unit, War Crimes Unit.

ORPHANAGE AND METROPOLITAN AND CITY POLICE ORPHANS' FUND
Although a privately run Home for Police Orphans existed at Brighton from 1865, Commissioner Sir Edmund Henderson took the

initiative in raising subscriptions to open the Metropolitan and City Police Orphanage in Twickenham in 1870. Henry Whiting was a leading benefactor. A weekly subscription of 1d, later raised to 3d (approximately 1p), was levied on members of the Force, and when the Minstrels started, their contributions became the Orphanage Fund's largest regular receipts.

But within 10 years it was clear that no building could house all the dependants of dead policemen, and widows were given direct payments from the fund to support their children. By the time the Orphanage closed in 1937, 2807 boys and girls had passed through its walls – but 5194 widows had received grants in respect of over 10,000 orphans.

In fact, the Home had become an uneconomic way of distributing charity, for which reason the Trustees were given permission to close it and redistribute funds directly to the parents and guardians of police orphans. By the time the centenary of Sir Edmund's foundation was reached, more than 14,000 children had benefited, and the charity continues its good work today.

The Secretary of the fund, which is entirely separate from the Widows' Fund, may be contacted at 30 Hazlewell Road, London SW15 6LH.

OTIS Operational Technology Information System, commenced in 1993.

Internal Scotland Yard computer network with terminals in all Divisions and Areas, and at Service Headquarters, carrying information which needs to be circulated around the entire Metropolitan Police Service.

A CLASSROOM SCENE AT THE ORPHANAGE.

PACE Police and Criminal Evidence Act, 1984.

This put into legal effect the broad recommendations of the Royal Commission on Criminal Procedure chaired by Sir Cyril Philips in 1977. It introduced time limits for police detection of suspects, reduced the power of police to set up road checks, codified police powers of arrest, and clarified the powers of stop and search (see under 'sus laws').

PAEDOPHILIA UNIT – ORGANISED CRIME GROUP Formerly Obscene Publications Squad in C1 Branch then transferred to A3 Branch (latterly TO13 Branch). The functions concerning videotapes and the abuse of children became the responsibility of SO1(4) while the remainder was devolved to the Clubs and Vice Unit at West End Central Police Station.

The unit is now part of the Organised Crime Group and investigates paedophiles and the associated production and distribution of child pornography within the Metropolitan Police District, although these investigations often widen to a national or international scale. The unit also deals with the investigations of computer pornography.

PAIN, PC CLAUDE RAYMOND (1908–1992) Officer present at Barlow & Parker's Warehouse, Tamworth Rd, Croydon on the night PC Sidney Miles was murdered, who was later alleged to have made statements seriously undermining testimony given by DC Frederick Fairfax and PCs Norman Harrison and James MacDonald.

Worked as a cable jointer before joining the Met, 1929. Warrant No. 119044. Posted to J Division (Bethnal Green). Transferred to H Division (Whitechapel) in 1933, then Z Division (Croydon) in 1936. Earned three commendations for good work in theft cases.

PC Pain was a dog handler who accompanied DC Fairfax, PC Harrison and PC Allan Beecher-Brigden in a van to answer the 999 call advising that two men had just climbed over the warehouse fence. The officers arrived to find the men (later known to be youths Derek Bentley and Christopher Craig) were on the roof. PC Pain and his dog remained in the road to intercept them should they try to escape, as did several

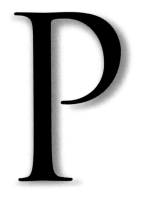

other officers, while Fairfax and two colleagues made their separate successive ways to the roof.

Nearly 40 years later, author M. J. Trow reported statements by PC Pain alleging that he had ascended to the roof by means of a rickety ladder, and had been within earshot when Fairfax first apprehended Bentley. According to Trow, Pain insisted that Bentley had definitely not made the incriminating remark, 'Let him have it, Chris', thereby inciting Craig to start shooting. Trow was refused access to the MEPO file on the case. In the light of what Pain told him, he believed that Scotland Yard must be covering up evidence that testimony against Bentley had been falsified, and he speculated that when the file was opened, PC Pain's original deposition might well be found to have gone missing.

In fact, the deposition is still on the file, and it shows that Pain reported at the time that he had been in the road at ground level throughout the incident, in no position to hear what was or was not said on the rooftop. It is not known how his later misleading misrecollection came about.

PALACE OF WESTMINSTER DIVISION (SO17) A Division whose 'territory' comprises the Houses of Parliament. Its services are actually hired from the Metropolitan Police by the Palace of Westminster authorities.

The Division's main objectives are:

1. To provide for the safety of peers, Members of Parliament, staff and visitors.

2. To prevent unauthorized access to the Palace of Westminster.

3. To safeguard the buildings and their contents from damage.

4. To prevent theft.

5. To prevent disorder or obstruction within the precincts of the palace.

These objectives are discharged after consultation with Black Rod and the Serjeant at Arms, who have overall responsibility for security at the Palace of Westminster.

Uniformed police preserve public order – at first sight an easy task, as the surroundings are conducive to respectful quiet – but the very nature of Parliament means that threats of disorderly protest and unauthorized entry are a constant concern.

A Search Unit carries out important sweeps of the buildings and car parks before Parliament sits, using sniffer dogs to hunt for explosives. The tradition of searching the cellars for gunpowder goes back to Guy Fawkes and 1606. The continuing urgency was underlined in 1979 when the INLA succeeded in murdering Airey Neave MP by attaching an explosive device to his car while it stood in the Members' underground car park below Old Palace Yard.

In addition to the Palace of Westminster, the Division is responsible for the security of the Norman Shaw Building (the former New Scotland Yard on the Embankment), which contains MPs' offices.

PANDA CARS Small saloon cars introduced in 1965, at a time when pandas at London Zoo featured regularly in the press. Initially an experimental part of Unit beat policing, they provided mobile non-urgent patrols in combination with Home beat officers, and collators, all linked by the newly introduced personal radios. The cars were painted white and Bermuda blue, which led to their nickname. The name was phased out partly because the Met adopted the corporate style of white vehicle with a red body stripe as begun under Sir David McNee, and partly because of the trend towards using Immediate Response Vehicles.

PARROTT, WPC KATHLEEN FLORA (B.1916) One of the first two Metropolitan Women Police awarded the George Medal for bravery in 1955. Left GPO telephone service to join the Met in 1951. Served in Z Division (Croydon). Resigned, 1956.

KATHLEEN PARROTT GM AND HER SON OUTSIDE
BUCKINGHAM PALACE ON 22 NOVEMBER 1955.

Large numbers of policewomen volunteered to act as decoys in Fairfield Lane, Croydon, where a man was attacking women early in 1955. On 7 March, WPC Parrott was seized from behind and forced to her knees, and felt herself starting to lose consciousness. Hitting the man with her torch she broke his hold and rose to her feet, where she pulled off the scarf concealing the lower part of his face, and noted his appearance before he ran away. WPC Parrott was on sick leave for five weeks following the attack, but immediately volunteered for the same decoy work when she returned to duty, and was able to identify the man at his trial. 'I cannot imagine higher courage than you showed along that footpath,' said Common Serjeant Sir Anthony Hawke from the bench to WPC Parrott and to WP Sgt Bush, who had suffered assault in the same operation. They were Highly Commended by the Commissioner, and received £15 from the Bow Street Police Fund and the George Medal.

In November, WPC Parrott received a further commendation from her Area Commander for arresting a 'flasher' when she was off duty. Early in 1956 she passed her Sergeant's exam, but she resigned at the end of the year without taking up a promotion.

PEEL CENTRE Metropolitan Police Training Centre: probably the largest and most comprehensive police training centre in the world. All recruits to the MPS undergo an 18-week residential basic training course here. The Peel Centre also maintains the Metropolitan Police Driver Training School, Detective Training School, Information Technology Training School, Management and Development School, and Traffic Warden Training School.

The site was developed by Claude Grahame-White as the London Aerodrome, London Flying Club, and Grahame-White Flying School and was taken over by the Air Ministry as an Air Force base in 1926. Lord Trenchard acquired the property freehold for his Hendon Police College in 1934, and established the principle (unbroken ever since) that the greater part of the old airfield should be kept as sports fields. Originally the Hendon site had the additional function of being one of the sports grounds Trenchard established for the four Districts (today's Areas). Subsequently No. 2 Area acquired its own sports ground at Bushey, but rugby, soccer, hockey and cricket pitches, a running track and an athletics field still dominate the Hendon site.

In 1935 hangars were converted to house the newly formed Driver Training and Wireless Schools. In 1936, two old WWI huts accommodated the nascent Detective Training School. After the wartime closure of the College, during which time no instruction at all took place, the centre reopened as the Metropolitan Police (or Hendon) Training School, with the basic training of recruits at its heart. Specialist detective, driving and telecommunications instruction started again. In 1968 when the old Peel House police training centre in Regency Street, Westminster was closed, Hendon took over all responsibility for basic training, and the courses for Sergeants' and Inspectors' promotion exams. (Senior ranks may attend courses at Bramshill National Police College.) On 31 May 1974, HM the Queen formally opened the Training School under the new title Peel Centre.

PEEL HOUSE (1) Since 1974, the principal administrative building at the Peel Centre, Hendon. Though not then named Peel House, the building was also the main teaching block at the centre, 1968–73.

(2) From 1907 to 1968, the Metropolitan Police Basic Training centre in 105 Regency Street, SW1P 4AN.

A six-storey building on the corner of Regency Street and Causton Street, Peel House was opened as the first police training school in Britain on 14 October 1907. It was expanded in 1909 then turned over to Dominion troops as an Overseas Club during WWI. In 1918, part of the building was reclaimed for training Metropolitan Women Police Patrols.

The postwar expansion of the force with new recruits was such that additional accommodation in Aldwych was taken: the Eagle Hut, where Bush House now stands.

In 1923 Peel House started to offer Staff College courses for senior overseas police officers. In 1928 it ran courses for the Sergeants' and Inspectors' promotion exams, and after temporary closure on the outbreak of war in 1939 it reopened to train the 12,000 volunteer War Reserve Constables who enlisted.

In the postwar period it shared responsibility for residential basic training with the former Hendon Police College, and continued to offer senior non-residential courses. From 1961 it housed the Detective Training School. Finally in 1967 its functions were entirely taken over by Hendon, which usurped its name for its own main admin and teaching block in 1974. 105 Regency Street now houses the Personnel Department and continues to offer training to Civil Staff. Although the name Peel House can still be seen in paint on the brickwork at the back of the building, it is now always referred to as Regency Street.

PEEL, SIR ROBERT, BT. (1788–1850) Home Secretary and founder of the Metropolitan Police.

Born in Bury, Lancs, son of calico-printing manufacturer. Educ. Eton and Oxford. B.A. (double first), 1807. MP for pocket borough of Cashel, 1809. Under-Secretary for War and the Colonies, 1810–12. Chief Secretary for Ireland, 1812–18. MP for Oxford University, 1817. Home Secretary, 1822–7. Resigned in opposition to Catholic emancipation. Home Secretary and

Leader of the House of Commons, 1828–30. MP for pocket borough of Westbury, 1829. Suc. bt., 1830. MP for reformed constituency of Tamworth, 1833. Prime Minister, 1834-5, and again, 1841–6. Thereafter in opposition until his death after a fall from his horse.

As Chief Secretary for Ireland, Robert Peel at the age of 26 formed the Irish Peace Preservation Police to maintain order in rural districts. These forerunners of the Royal Irish Constabulary were nicknamed 'Peelers' 15 years before the word came into use in London. As Home Secretary, in 1822 he set up a Select Committee to consider the state of the existing Police Offices, watchmen, constables and Bow Street patrols, and began to contemplate some form of centralization. By 1826 he was outlining a plan for six police districts to cover a 16km (10-mile) radius from St Paul's, excluding the City of London. The following year he resigned his office when Canning, the new Prime Minister, attempted to remove Catholics' political disabilities. However, on Canning's death in 1828 he returned to the Duke of Wellington's cabinet, and with a Prime Minister sympathetic to the idea of a disciplined quasi-military police force in London, he appointed a new Select Committee dominated by his chosen nominees, and began drafting the Metropolitan Police Bill of 1829 (see Peel's Police Act) to carry out their recommendations.

He made the brilliant appointment of the military Col. Charles Rowan and the barrister Richard Mayne, and gave them a virtually free hand to establish the force much as they saw fit. On 20 July he wrote approving their establishment of a force of 895 constables, 88 Sergeants, 20 Inspectors and 8 Superintendents, supported by a Civil Staff of one Chief Clerk with two assistants.

Peel stressed that the principal duty of the police was to be crime prevention (rather than detection). But his decision to retain final authority in his own hands, making the Commissioners and the Receiver directly responsible to the Home Secretary, engendered the charge that he had created 'Peel's private army', or 'a bodyguard for

RECRUITS ENTERING PEEL HOUSE IN REGENCY STREET IN THE 1930s.

the government'. The nicknames 'Peelers' and 'Bobbies' which quickly came into use were intended to be uncomplimentary to both him and the police. 'Peel's Raw Lobsters' was another term of abuse in the press. The wave of initial public hostility makes it surprising that Peel's Police Act went through Parliament with scarcely any opposition.

Peel's proposal that senior uniformed ranks should be 'filled from below' and not brought in from the higher social classes has been more or less followed to this day and, indeed, improved by abandoning the practice of appointing Commissioners, Assistant Commissioners and Chief Constables from outside (usually army officers, civil servants or lawyers). Peel himself said that he accepted low pay for the men as he did not want any policeman feeling superior to the job or his colleagues. For the same reason he insisted that commissioned army officers should not be appointed as Superintendents (though there were a few early breaches of this ideal. Cf. Capt. William Hay.)

Sir Robert Peel is commemorated in the Met by the training schools' names (Peel House, then Peel Centre); by a bronze statue that was originally erected in Cheapside on Peel's death, transferred to Postman's Park off Little Britain in 1952, and acquired by the Hendon training school in 1973; and by an excellent marble bust by Matthew Noble acquired in 1917 and displayed on the stairs of Norman Shaw's New Scotland Yard. Since the transfer of headquarters to Broadway, the bust has been held in the Historical Museum from which it is brought out for special occasions.

PEEL'S POLICE ACT (1829) Act 'For Improving the Police in and near the Metropolis' which in fact established the Metropolitan Police. The Act contained a long preamble setting out the need for gathering the scattered bodies of constables, watchmen and patrols under one authority, but gave very little detail as to how this was to be done. Two executive magistrates were to be authorized to establish a single force covering a 7-mile (11.2km) radius from Charing Cross, divided into six Divisions; they should appoint stipendiary magistrates in police offices in each Division; and they were to be directly responsible to the Home Secretary. Further details were left to them.

PENSIONS A Superannuation Fund for the Metropolitan Police was established by the Police Act, 1839, supported by a 2½% contribution from wages. Unfortunately this was inadequately costed, and the Fund was bankrupted in 1849.

For the next 40 years police pensions were a major source of discontent. Since there were no general old age pensions, parsimonious Victorian civil servants treated the benefit as a valuable and expensive perquisite which justified keeping police pay low. Nor were the pensions automatic. They were only awarded following a certificate of satisfactory service from the Commissioner, and a certificate from the Chief Medical Officer that disability justified the payment of superannuation. Thus they became, in effect, discretionary pensions when the fund had dried up. The men were understandably furious that officers who suffered severe and lasting injuries on duty could be adjudged still fit to find other employment of some kind, and refused pensions. Dismissal meant loss of pension with no restoration of the accrued contributions. ('There goes his pension!' is still a Met comment on an officer seen to behave reprehensibly in public.)

Commissioners Henderson, Warren and Monro all took the matter up strongly with successive Home Secretaries, until the resignation of the last finally led to the Police Act, 1890, which established automatic pensions of half pay after 25 years service, and discretionary pensions at lower rates for officers who resigned on medical grounds after 15 years' service or at any time following injury. When the Bill was before Parliament, it was claimed that very few officers would take up their pensions immediately they had completed 25 years' service as most would feel themselves still fit for duty and prefer to draw full pay until they were

too feeble for duty. In practice, the very fatiguing beat and point duties, the potentially disabling labour of the River Police oarsmen, and the attraction of employment as security officers in the private sector meant from the outset that the overwhelming majority of policemen

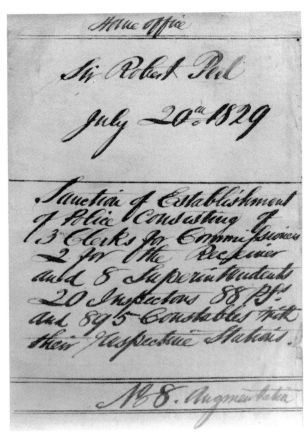

PEEL'S ORIGINAL INSTRUCTIONS ESTABLISHING THE METROPOLITAN POLICE AND SETTING OUT SALARY LEVELS.

claimed their pensions as soon as they could.

The Sheehy Report (1993) recommended that pensions should only be payable after 40 years' service. This was roundly criticized for effectively requiring constables to perform rotating shifts through 24 hours and other arduous duties until the age of 60 before being allowed a pension. In 1997, after a period when officers who joined in a recruitment peak had achieved 30 years' service, the Home Office started a consultation exercise about changing the pensions regulations and proposed to lengthen the qualifying period and alter the arrangements relating to ill health pensions and injury awards which were seen as becoming too costly. This roughly coincided with

a report noting that public service employees (civil servants, teachers and police officers) averaged 10 days' absence from work through ill health per year, compared with 6 days for private sector manual workers. The notion that this might be improved by changing the regulations rather than the conditions of work seemed attractive to the Treasury.

Inspector John Spratling (1840–c.1934) became well-known in the course of his long retirement for boasting that he had drawn more in pension than he had done in pay. However, his record must have been been exceeded by Inspector Lewis Keaton of the River Police, who drew his pension from his retirement in 1917 until his death at the age of 100 in 1970. These two are balanced by officers who die very shortly after retirement.

PEREIRA, MARGARET, CBE, BSC, CBIOL, FIBID. (B.1928) Leading forensic serologist and forensic science administrator whose career started in the Met Forensic Science Laboratory.

Daughter of an engineer, and married to an engineer. Joined Met Forensic Science Laboratory staff, 1947. BSc and promoted Experimental Officer, 1953. Became an expert witness in 1960, the first woman to achieve this status in the British Forensic Science Service. Joined Home Office Forensic Science Service in 1976 and rose to become Controller, 1982–8. Retd, 1988.

Margaret Pereira enhanced blood grouping with procedures that are followed worldwide. She held the top job in UK Forensic Science, controlling all six Home Office laboratories, yet in retirement, she still remembered her successful battles against sexist opposition in the Met Forensic Lab of the 1950s as her great achievement. She had joined the laboratory staff in 1947 without imagining that a great career lay ahead of her. She accepted encouragement to take her BSc, and then found when she graduated that she was not to be appointed Scientific Officer – the normal grade for good honours graduates – but was held back as an Experimental Officer. The reason was fear on the part of her superiors that she would not prove competent if called upon to give testimony in court. Women, they thought, would break down and weep under cross-examination. For some years Miss Pereira suffered the frustration of doing the basic work of preparing evidence and then coaching less experienced male colleagues to present it to the court.

When she finally won promotion and started giving perfectly competent testimony, she encountered a new setback. Male lawyers were embarrassed by hearing evidence in sex cases from an unabashed woman expert. One judge complained directly to Scotland Yard about having to listen to a woman describe taking anal and penile swabs in a case where the defendant pleaded not guilty to a charge of buggery. Apparently the judge used the unfortunate expressions that the court was unable to 'probe' the case with 'penetrating' questions because of his embarrassment!

The consequence, from Miss Pereira's point of view was entirely satisfactory. She was taken off what she described as 'boring sex cases', and concentrated on the work on blood grouping which was to bring her international fame. She studied the ways in which the Rhesus antigen factors and enzymes in blood cells could be used to refine the simple grouping into A, B, AB and O which had been known since 1901. In 1966 the press hailed her work with Brian Culliford as having established 'blood fingerprinting'. This was a slight exaggeration: typing was not refined to the point that every individual could be said to have unique blood until DNA testing established this for all an individual's body cells, unless the individual had an identical twin. But evidence that particular blood could only have been shed by one in so many million of the population, if taken with other evidence about the shedder's whereabouts, should cover most eventualities beyond the legal test of 'reasonable doubt'.

During her time with the Met, Miss Pereira was involved in the setting up of new laboratories in each of the MPFSL's moves: from Hendon to New Scotland Yard (1) in 1949; to temporary quarters in Richbell Place in 1965; and to its pre-

sent purpose-built accommodation in Lambeth Rd in 1974. Her technical and organizational experience in the Met fitted her for the administrative appointments at Home Office establishments, through which her meteoric rise brought her to the highest Forensic Scientific post in the country. She was awarded a CBE for services to forensic science in 1985 and was President of the Forensic Science Society 1991–3.

PERSONAL RADIOS Essential part of the appointments of officers on patrol, linking them immediately with the Divisional Control Room, so that the patrol can summon assistance or be directed to a point where police presence is required.

The possibility of personal radios or radio-telephones to supplement whistles and telephone boxes was mooted in the 1930s. Chief Inspector Kenneth Barrington Best, a former naval com-

A POLICE OFFICER USING 'METRADIO' IN 1995.

mander, was inducted into the police in 1933 to take charge of all wireless operations, and the following year he toured the country investigating police wireless facilities in other forces. Brighton was experimenting with one-way pocket receivers with earpieces which enabled officers to hear calls at a distance of up to 9.6km (6 miles). Best recommended the establishment of regional wireless control centres to reach patrolling officers in the Metropolitan and Home

Counties districts, but apart from an abortive 1936 experiment with specially designed receivers for some police motorcycles, all operational developments in radio communications were confined to cars for the next 10 years.

In 1946 some personal radio transmitters were purchased from the Cossor Company, but it was another 20 years before technology had improved to the point that all patrols could be equipped with personal radios. Between 1966 and 1969 the process of establishing divisional radio control systems was completed, and all cars and beat patrols were linked to them with Stornophone VHF equipment. The force promptly nicknamed them 'batphones'. A few extra channels are maintained for the public order policing of crowds at major events, and some traffic wardens have also been given personal radios.

PERSONNEL DEPARTMENT Personnel Department is led by a Director of Personnel who is assisted by senior police and Civil Staff colleagues. The Department provides a strategic lead for the personnel function and a range of services such as staff planning, recruitment and pay bargaining. It supports a training infrastructure and protects the Service's interests particularly in matters of law, fairness, and health and safety.

PETO, SUPERINTENDENT DOROTHY OLIVIA GEORGIANA, OBE, KPM (1886–1974) First Superintendent of A4 Branch (Women Police).

Joined Met, 1930. Warrant No. 242. Supt, 1932. KPM, 1944. Retired, 1946.

Clerical assistant in St John's Ambulance Brigade. Joined National Union of Women Workers' Women Special Police Patrols in Bath, 1914. Appointed secretary to Mrs Flora Joseph, patrols organizer for Somerset, and sent to Southampton and London to broaden her experience, 1915. With Mrs Joseph and Bristol patrols' organizer Mrs Gent, negotiated with the

Women Police Service to set up joint training school at Bristol. Miss Peto visited Liverpool to see police and social workers' experimental projects with children and to oversee the Women's Police Patrols. She also visited London, where she patrolled Hyde Park for three weeks with Mrs Edith Smith, who became the first attested WPO (in Grantham) later that year.

Mrs Gent was appointed first principal of the Bristol Training School (BTS), with Miss Peto as her assistant. Miss Peto proposed a paragraph from the Liverpool Police Instruction Book as its motto, stating that helping the very poor and removing the children of the criminal classes from evil influences was true police work. Women were given physical training and taught ju-jitsu, and heard lectures on first aid and human biology. Margaret Damer Dawson of the Women Police Service withdrew her support in 1916, accusing the BTS of plagiarizing her ideas. However, she continued to take their trainees for policing munitions workers, though she maintained they required two further weeks' training at her own school in London. In 1917, Mrs Gent resigned for family reasons and Miss Peto became principal of the BTS, making a good impression on Under-Secretary Sir Edward Troup at the Home Office when she and Mrs Joseph visited to push for proper pay and pensions for women attached to the police. In 1918 the BTS supplied two women on the request of the Chief Constable of Gloucestershire, and noted his method of circumventing the Police Acts (which specified the swearing in of 'fit *men*') by swearing in women as 'fit *people*' to be Special Constables, and then transferring them, already sworn, to the full constabulary.

In 1918 Miss Peto asked the Home Office whether the new Sex Disqualification Removal Act, which admitted women as civil servants, jurors and MPs, should not apply to the police. The inability of officialdom to agree on this point led to Sir John Baird's setting up the Home Office Committee on Women Police which heard evidence in 1920. Miss Peto's recommendations to the committee were that women police minimum height requirements should not exceed

1.63m (5ft 4in), and that they should not be employed under the age of 27 as they were likely to be given more responsible immediate duties than male recruits.

In 1920, the BTS closed down. Without elaborating, Commissioner Sir Nevil Macready told the Baird Committee that the Chief Constable of Bristol had not had bad enough words to say about it! But Miss Peto was awarded the OBE for her work with the NUWW, and appointed unattested Lady Enquiry Officer to Birmingham City Police, changing the title to Detective Enquiry Officer in the first year. In 1924–7, needing a better salary after her father's death, she became travelling organizer for the National Council for Combating Venereal Disease. 1929, appointed Staff Officer in charge of Metropolitan Women Police for one experimental year. Although the post was on the Civil Staff, she succeeded in having herself sworn in before assuming office, and

SUPERINTENDENT DOROTHY PETO (IN TRILBY HAT AND TIE) IN 1937 WITH WPC SOPHIE ALLOWAY.

noted that for the very first time she really was a full member of the police. In 1930, her appointment was renewed for another probationary year, and she was asked to sit on the Police Council Committee drafting regulations on the employment of policewomen. In 1933 she refused to accept a further probationary year and was created Superintendent in charge of Women Police. The same year she recognized that the new Children and Young Persons Act denoted areas wherein

policewomen's work could be of the highest value, and thereafter insisted that all paperwork concerning children and young people should be channelled through A4 Branch (women police). She cultivated excellent relations with educational authorities and the juvenile courts, and had women appointed court officers and, where necessary, gaolers at central London magistrates' courts. She initiated the Juvenile Bus scheme to transport juveniles from remand homes daily. She built up the A4 Index of stray and missing girls, the basis of today's Juvenile Index, and rounded off the white slavery panic by supervising young women leaving the country on theatrical contracts. When the war broke out she made a point of inspecting shelters and underground stations where her officers were on duty. One of her last and proudest duties before her retirement in 1946 was leading the detachment of Metropolitan Women police in the Victory Parade.

While many women constables were more attached to her approachable and motherly predecessor and second-in-command, Chief Inspector Bertha Clayden, none ever questioned Superintendent Peto's dedication to police work and the women she commanded. 'She lived for the police' was a common observation, and she did more than anyone else to establish the women police as an indispensable part of Scotland Yard.

Her manuscript memoirs were handed to Norman Fairfax, Senior Executive Officer and historian of Scotland Yard, who deposited them with the Historical Museum in 1970. They were published by the 1992 European Conference on Equal Opportunities in the Police.

PHOTOGRAPHIC AND GRAPHIC BRANCH Founded 1901 as essential support for the Fingerprint Bureau. This followed 10 uncertain *fin-de-siècle* years in which the Met lagged behind (at least) the City of London Police in photographing crime scenes and victims in mortuaries, while Assistant Commissioner (Crime) Dr Robert Anderson exploited the myth that corpses' pupils retain the images they last saw to try to frighten a suspect into believing he had been captured on camera in his victim's eyes.

Subsequently civilized, hived off from the Fingerprints Branch, and acquiring the Graphics Section in 1988, the Branch now comprises 60 central photographers, technicians and administrative support staff, and 40 photographers on Area. In addition to fingerprint, scenes of crime, surveillance and public order photographs, the branch carries out studio work and, with 10 professional graphic designers, prepares publicity and educational material.

PIG CLUB The Metropolitan Police Pig Club was inspired by Sgt Harry Baker, who started keeping pigs in Hyde Park in 1940 as part of the wartime food production drive.

Sgts Freddy Allsop and Bob Sheppard of Chelsea Police Station followed his example, and with the help of PCs Arthur Robinson, Jim Cherrill and Bert Archer (respectively a former carpenter and two former bricklayers), built four sties on a building lot beside the station. Over the next five years 40 officers assisted in raising about 250 pigs and supplying the equivalent of five years' bacon rations for every man, woman and child in Chelsea. As breeders they could have kept half the output themselves, but in fact two were slaughtered every six months and divided among the members.

PITT'S POLICE BILL, 1785 Unsuccessful measure laid before Parliament in 1785 by William Pitt the Younger's first administration. It proposed appointing three Commissioners to command patrols of peace officers organized in nine divisions covering London, Westminster and Southwark. The Commissioners would have power over all existing parish constables, watchmen and beadles, and were to appoint paid Justices of the Peace at public offices in each division.

The aldermen in Parliament threw the Bill out, and Pitt's only further attempt to reform the police was the weak compromise of the Middlesex Justices Act, 1792.

Except for the inclusion of the City and the three extra divisions, Pitt's proposals were almost exactly those ultimately introduced in Peel's Police Act, 1829.

PLAIN CLOTHES Initially rejected in formative conferences as suggesting a political spy system. *Police Orders* for the Lord Mayor's Show, 1830, nonetheless directed that 10 of 'the most active men' were to attend in plain clothes, and the Lord Mayor's Show *Police Orders* for 1833 spelled out that 'Each Division will have two of their most active and intelligent men in plain clothes to apprehend thieves and pickpockets.' William Popay told the Select Committee on Fredk Young's Petition, 1833 that P Division had 'two patrols who are constantly in private clothes'. The Committee concluded astringently that plainclothes policing 'affords no just matter of complaint, while strictly confined to detect Breaches of the Law and to prevent Breaches of the Peace, should those ends appear otherwise unobtainable; at the same time the Committee would . . . solemnly deprecate any approach to the Employment of Spies . . . as a practice most abhorrent to the feelings of the People, and most alien to the spirit of the Constitution'.

In April 1837, the large detachment of uniformed police detailed to maintain order around St James's Palace on the occasion of a Royal Drawing Room was supplemented by 44 men in plain clothes. The same year, policemen in plain clothes were ordered to be present at the nomination of Members of Parliament for Westminster. From 1839 the plain-clothed Royal Palaces Division took responsibility for policing Buckingham, Kensington and St James's Palaces, and, when the Royal Family visited Scotland, Holyrood House and Balmoral. A plainclothes patrol drawn from A Division also mounted Royal Theatre Protection when necessary. Since these men's work was preventive and not detective, they were drawn from the uniformed police and not (when it was founded) the Detective Branch.

The enlargement of the Detective Branch in 1869 led to the placing of permanent plain clothes officers on the Divisions under Detective Sergeants. They were given £10 per annum clothing allowance, and were allowed travelling expenses up to 15s a day for any distance beyond a 4.8km (3 mile) radius of their station. Ten years later, the inadequacy of these allowances had become a grievance that had to be resolved. It

was also found that uniformed Station Inspectors often placed their most incompetent officers in plain clothes and used them as messengers. The foundation of the CID corrected these problems, until its separate, superior and more glamorous status became a problem in itself. Sir Robert Mark insisted that the route to the highest ranks would be closed to officers who did not vary their years in plain clothes with some return to uniformed duty. See also Disguise.

PLAIN CLOTHES PATROLS Beat constables who were required to patrol in plain clothes prior to the formal establishment of permanent Divisional detectives in 1868. (Mentioned by William Popay as already in existence in 1833.) Plain clothes patrol duty, often referred to as 'Winter Patrol', was taken in turns for a month at a time, and was most unpopular as there was no clothing allowance. It was also ineffective if the men were allowed to patrol their usual sections, as they were recognized there as policemen.

The continuance of plain clothes patrols in A Division to police public indecency in Hyde Park led to complaints of police prurience and harassment in the 1920s. (See Macmillan Committee and Irene Savidge.)

PLUS PROGRAMME A determined attempt to improve the Service's self-esteem, cohesiveness, relations with and perception by the public. Started by Sir Peter Imbert in 1989.

Plus arose from a report by the management consultants Wolff-Olins, delivered to the Commissioner in 1988. This declared that the Force operated in an atmosphere of 'shabby confusion', was losing the respect of the public and suffering from poor morale, largely because it had no clear identity. Sir Peter promptly set up a group to organize a series of seminars reaching out to every officer and Civil Staff member. He had already decided that the Metropolitan Police *Force* should be renamed the Metropolitan Police *Service*, in consonance with harmonious policing, which, in a democratic but multi-cultural society, could no longer claim consent by appealing to some generally approved authoritarian standards. Plus drew up the Common

A 1960s 'POLACC' INVOLVING A MORRIS COMMERCIAL VAN.

Statement of Purpose and Values and invited officers and Civil Staff to commit themselves to the ideal of public service this enshrined. It was a remarkable attempt to harness the best aspects of canteen culture solidarity to a more liberal philosophy, steered by quality management procedures and monitored by constant inspection. The programme was probably Sir Peter's finest achievement, and by the time of his retirement had significantly altered attitudes within the MPS.

'POLACC' Police jargon for an accident involving a police car. Any such incident must be investigated independently by the Area Traffic Department, and not the Division to which the officer involved is attached.

The word derives from an abbreviated version of 'Police Accident' used as the heading of a teleprinter message format.

POLICE ACT, 1829 See Peel's Police Act

POLICE ACT, 1839 Confirmed the establishment of the Metropolitan Police as a permanency and enlarged the Metropolitan Police District. Removed the executive function of magistrates in the Police Offices, and turned the offices into Police Courts with Metropolitan constables allocated to executing the magistrates' warrants. Compelled procrastinating boroughs and magistrates to disband or make over their peacekeeping officers (including the Bow Street Runners) to the Commissioners. Amalgamated the River Police with the Met as Thames Division. Gave the Commissioner powers to introduce temporary regulations for the maintenance of public order. Established the Superannuation Fund from a 2½% levy on the men's pay. Created Public Order Offences.

POLICE ACT, 1890 Settled the grievance over pensions which underlay the abortive Police Strikes of 1872 and 1890. It gave all officers the right to a half-pay pension without medical certification after 25 years' satisfactory service, and a modified pension after 15 years' service if an officer was discharged on medical grounds. Modified pensions were granted to all officers who had to leave the service because of injuries received on duty, and widows' and orphans' pensions or gratuities were introduced. The contribution remained 2½% of pay.

POLICE ACT, 1919 Implemented the improved pay and pensions conditions recom-

THE TRAFALGAR SQUARE POLICE BOX IN 1955.

mended by the Desborough Report, and established the Police Federation as a negotiating body, reiterating that police officers might neither belong to any other union or take strike action.

POLICE ACT, 1933 Implemented Lord Trenchard's major reform proposals. Established

Hendon Police College, introduced short-term contracts, created a fifth Assistant Commissioner, and debarred officers above the newly created rank of Junior Station Inspector from membership of the Police Federation. In the interests of accelerating promotion for Hendon graduates, it introduced a retirement age of 55 for officers up to the rank of Superintendent beyond which they could only continue in service by special dispensation. To this day this leaves the Met with a lower retirement age than provincial forces.

POLICE ACT, 1934 Enabled the Receiver to proceed with Lord Trenchard's plans for building new and refurbishing old station houses, section houses and canteens, and creating an extension to New Scotland Yard (the Norman Shaw Building).

POLICE ACT, 1946 Led to adjustments in the boundaries of the Metropolitan Police District in 1947.

POLICE ACT, 1964 Formally established the roles of Police Authorities, the Home Secretary and many aspects of Police Complaints Procedures, and gave the Home Secretary power to amalgamate Police Forces in England and Wales.

POLICE AND CRIMINAL EVIDENCE ACT, 1984 See PACE.

POLICE BOXES Large blue kiosks topped by electric lights. Each kiosk contained a telephone linked directly to the local sub-divisional police station and mounted in an external cupboard. Officers on beat patrol could report their whereabouts from them without having to make carefully timed meetings with their Sergeants at fixed points, and the flashing light could indicate to the patrolling officer that he was required to make contact with the station to receive an important message or instruction. The public had access to the telephones so that they could contact the police rapidly. Officers also had keys allowing them access to the boxes' interiors, which normally contained a stool, a table, brushes and dusters, a fire extinguisher, and a small (often very inadequate) electric fire. These were for the convenience of patrolling constables to make their refreshment stops in privacy and shelter, and also provided locales for Sergeants to receive reports and give instructions. The earliest boxes were made of wood; later ones were of concrete, which officers complained remained extremely cold, even when the electric fires were increased from 80 watts to 250 watts. (In later years there were no fires at all in some of the central divisions' boxes.) A replica police box is exhibited at the Peel Centre. A small 'police box' mounted in the plinth of a gas lamp in the southeast corner of Trafalgar Square was fitted with an external telephone cupboard and internal seat and shelf. The long-running children's science fiction television programme *Dr Who* featured a police box called the 'Tardis' which proved to be a futuristic time- and space-travelling machine with a large interior when the doctor and his companions used it.

Boxes were installed experimentally in Richmond and Barnes in 1928, and the following year Superintendent George Abbiss and Mr G. M. Trench, the Metropolitan Police Surveyor, visited Manchester and Salford, and reported favourably on the installation of boxes across the conurbation. They were gradually introduced across the Metropolitan Police District, Commissioners Byng and Trenchard installing most of them, so that the chain was effectively complete by 1937.

They played an important part in police work until the mid-1960s, when they were phased out following the introduction of personal radios. In 1997 a replica police box was erected at Earls Court, equipped with closed circuit TV.

POLICE COURT From the 1840s to the 1940s, the accepted term for magistrates' courts attached to Police Offices, on the pattern of the Middlesex Justices. The important and valuable change brought about by the establishment of Police Courts was that the police brought the prosecutions, thereby lifting a heavy burden of administration and expense from the public, who had previously been required to prosecute privately if they wanted to see charges brought for misdemeanours. A secondary benefit which officers greatly valued was the early experience they gained in giving evidence under the guidance of experienced court Sergeants, who managed the prosecution in cases which did not demand the services of solicitors.

In due course the term was replaced by 'Magistrate's Court.' Fear that a court was 'controlled'

GREENWICH POLICE COURT IN 1908.

by officers with a career interest in successful prosecutions came to outweigh recollections of the advance this represented over private prosecutions. In 1986 this fear grew to the extent that the Crown Prosecution Service took over all prosecutions from the police, whereupon the perception that insufficient prosecutions were initiated became the new public grievance.

POLICE DOGS In popular parlance (and the original Kennel Club registration of the breed), another name for German shepherd dogs, also then known as Alsatian Wolf Dogs and Army Dogs.

However, many breeds have been tried out for work as police dogs. The first Scotland Yard experiment was with bloodhounds, suggested for use in the hunt for Jack the Ripper (1888). Mr Edwin Brough, founder of the National Bloodhound Association, supplied two hounds, Barnaby and Burgho, for trials. They performed adequately following scent trails through the parks, and despite Mr Brough's warning that they might prove useless for tracking on well used city pavements, Commissioner Sir Charles Warren was trying unsuccessfully to persuade Receiver Richard Pennefather to acquire a dog or dogs when he resigned.

Despite the excellent olfactory system which made them famous as the tracker sleuth-hounds of the Tudors, bloodhounds are timid and will not attack the quarry they have traced. They tire easily, and are inclined to delicate health. The Met has hardly used them since 1888, though in 1998 certain rural police forces began experimenting with them again, as their better olfactory senses seemed more valuable than German shepherds' greater strength in the detection of country criminals.

The London and North Eastern Railway Police were the first force in the country to keep dogs officially, and they preferred Airedales. Their dogs proved particularly useful for rousting out tramps who hid in piles of timber at stations and goods yards. However, Scotland Yard was slow to acquire dogs. In 1910, the Commissioner's Office noticed that some constables in the suburbs were taking their dogs with them on night patrol. The following year the practice was officially approved, provided that the animals were under effective control. Four arrests made with the help of dogs over the next two years suggested that the practice was desirable as well as permissible.

A census in 1914 showed that 171 constables regularly took their pets on beat duty with them. The dogs comprised 48 labrador retrievers, 31 mongrels, 28 airedales, 18 collies, 14 Irish terriers, 10 sheepdogs, 9 fox terriers, 5 spaniels, 3 bull terriers, 1 great Dane, 1 Manchester terrier, 1 Welsh terrier and 1 Pomeranian. (The last must have been quite a spectacle, trotting beside a large policeman.) That amounts to one less

'NIGGER' AND 'TINT', THE FIRST METROPOLITAN POLICE DOGS, IN 1938.

dog than there were constables supposedly taking them, so either two constables shared one pet, or the force that in these years mislaid three handguns was living up to its reputation for inaccurate record-keeping.

WWI revealed that dogs were extremely useful to the armed forces as guards, as trackers, as defensive support in hand-to-hand fighting, and even as messengers. The Germans had developed the perfect breed for service purposes. The German shepherd was brave, agile and hardy. It was a good tracker, if not as good as a bloodhound. It was fast when speed was required, but responded well to training and did not set a pace that its handler could not maintain. It was intelligent and obedient.

But it was German. Acute hatred of 'the Hun' after 1918 inhibited any British force from adopting this ideal police dog. The attempt to win more affection for the breed by renaming it 'Alsatian' was vitiated by the addition of the words 'Wolf Dog'.

In 1934, Assistant Commissioner C Sir Ronald Howe reported on the excellent use of police dogs he had seen at the Interpol conference in Vienna. The Home Office set up a sub-committee of the Departmental Committee on Detective Work to consider the case for police dogs, and after two years deliberation, this rejected the view that German Shepherds should be imported. Instead, following the example of the South African Police, who crossed bloodhounds, Dobermanns and rottweilers to produce their approved police dog, it was decided to try and cross some pure British strains. Experiments were made on crossing Irish fellhounds with labradors and bloodhounds with otterhounds at a dog training centre which was set up at Imber Court.

Since perfecting a new breed would take some time, police forces were offered pure-bred labradors for the interim, and in 1938 the Met accepted two. Although it was felt their presence deterred housebreakers and reassured the public, their handlers did not think they really served any useful purpose, and Commissioner Sir Philip Game, who had never been enthusiastic about having a dog section, happily let them go on the outbreak of war.

Sir Harold Scott was much keener on the idea.

Encouraged by Col. De Chair, the Chief Constable of No. 1 District, he authorized the purchase of five labradors in 1946. They were sent to the outer Divisions, and they proved immediately effective in tracking thieves, making arrests, and bringing down crime figures where they were deployed. In 1947 the number of dogs was increased to nine, and they scored a major success when they were brought to Hyde Park and effectively eradicated the handbag snatching which A Division patrols had been unable to check.

The first German shepherd was tentatively brought into the service in 1948, and Smoky quickly proved his worth. By 1949 the strength was up to 12 German shepherds and seven labradors. In 1954 the Keston Police Dog Training Establishment was set up and German shepherds became the only breed used until springer spaniels proved their worth as 'sniffer dogs', enthusiastically hunting out drugs. Labradors have been brought back into the Specialist Dog Section to support the springer spaniel 'sniffers'. They are trained to scent out explosives. See also PC Arthur Holman, Queenie, Rex III, Yerba.

POLICE FEDERATION See Federation.

POLICE GAZETTE A descriptive catalogue of known and wanted offenders, which superseded the old Bow Street magistrates' publication *Hue and Cry*. See also under Sir Howard Vincent.

POLICE MEDAL See King's Police Medal, King's Police and Fire Service Medal, and Queen's Police Medal, all or any of which may at times be so described and gazetted (see Appendix 3).

POLICE NATIONAL COMPUTER (PNC) National computerized database, located within the Hendon Training School Site. It was introduced in 1974 by the Home Office to enable the police service to access the vehicle registered owners' records held by the Driving Licence and Vehicle Licensing Agency (DVLA) and to record details of stolen vehicles. Since 1974 the database has been expanded to include the details of all persons who have a criminal record, e.g. have been convicted or

cautioned, or have been reported as wanted or missing. The national Fingerprint collection can also be accessed through the PNC.

SO3-3 PNC Bureau was formed in 1991 to manage PNC records on behalf of the Commissioner and is now part of the Directorate of Identification. It is headed by a Superintendent and staffed by a total of 15 police officers and 137 civil staff. In addition, the bureau is also responsible for the Juvenile, Missing Persons and Prostitutes indices.

Access to the PNC facilities can be obtained by trained users through the Command & Control System, directly connected terminals and, most recently, through the OTIS system.

POLICE NOTICE A handbill or poster issued for public information.

POLICE OFFICES (1) The earliest magistrates' offices, predating the formation of the Metropolitan Police, with permanent constables in attendance under the command of the magistrates. See Middlesex Justices Act, 1792.

POLICE NOTICE DATED 16 MARCH 1910.

(2) Small police shop front premises with facilities for dealing with members of the public and a limited patrolling base, but few other facilities. Not necessarily open 24 hours a day.

POLICE ORDERS Regular directions with orders of the day or week, issued from the inception of the Force, at first handwritten, later printed. The first number, on the day the Force went out onto the street, contained a reiteration of Commissioner Rowan's insistence that officers on patrol were not to react to rudeness from the public. Over the years, the *Police Orders* came to carry increasing details of pro-motions, commendations, resignations, disciplinary actions, etc., so that today the Orders appear in five forms – *Notices* and *Personnel Notices* issued weekly; *Special Notices* issued *ad*

AN EARLY- TO MID-VICTORIAN POLICE OFFICE.

hoc; and *Commendations* and *Honours and Awards* issued quarterly.

POLICE RELIEF FUND A fund endowed by Henry Whiting in 1878 for the relief of officers suffering hardship. Distributed at the discretion of the Commissioner. See under Bow Street Police Fund for its origins.

POLICE REVIEW The most widely read police professional journal in Britain. Its original full title was *The Police Review and Parade Gossip*.

Founded in 1893 by Victorian reforming journalist John Kempster (d.1916). Kempster set the tone which has won the journal its continuing respect and readership: he resolutely put the case of the man on the beat rather than the official position preferred by Commissioners and Home Secretaries. With an inevitable concentration on Met matters in the early years, the *Review* campaigned for one day's leave a week; persistently included in the obituaries of Assistant Commissioners appointed from the 'gentlemanly' classes references to their dependence on Superintendents and Chief Inspectors promoted from the ranks; championed John Syme until his sense of personal grievance had become an eccentric obsession; guardedly reported on NUPPO and then supported the Federation. Ex-Sgt Jack Hayes MP contributed a regular column.

POLICE STRIKE, 1872 Abortive attempt at industrial action on 16 November 1872, in protest against the dismissal of PC Goodchild, the would-be secretary of a rank-and-file pay negotiating committee.

Discontent arose from the 1868 Home Office Departmental Committee Report on police pay and conditions following the Clerkenwell Bombing. This made inadequate recommendations for much-needed pay rises, and actually proposed a reduction in such discretionary pensions as were authorized. In the autumn of 1872, the radical MP Roger Eyken called a meeting of constables at the Cannon Street Hotel to discuss their grievances. It was agreed that a pay and conditions negotiating Committee should be set up to represent the men, and PC Henry Good-

POLICE REVIEW WITH ADVERTISEMENT FOR THE NEWLY LEGITIMISED NUPPO IN 1918.

child, (466P) was elected secretary. Strike action was firmly ruled out.

The Home Office responded very promptly to this threat, rushing through the considerably improved pay scales that Commissioner Sir Edmund Henderson had consistently demanded, but rather fudging over the future of pensions and how they were to be funded.

This might have defused the row, had not his Superintendents tried to bully Goodchild into giving them written details of his proto-Union's meetings and membership, and ordered him to transfer when he refused. Then Assistant Commissioner Labalmondière sacked him for insubordination when he asked to have the charges against him read out. Goodchild visited the six other members of the proposed negotiating committee, who agreed to support him with industrial action. That night, Saturday 16 November, 7 Sergeants and 173 men refused to go on duty. The Divisions involved were D (Marylebone), P (Camberwell), E (Holborn) and T (Kensington). The disruption of normal duties across the metropolis was slight, and order was generally restored by the Commissioner's Office promulgating the mendacious line that Goodchild's dismissal was wholly and solely because he had refused the order of a transfer, and this had nothing whatever to do with his proto-Union activities. Still, the public was deeply concerned that Bow Street police station should have seen industrial action. And Goodchild hired an omnibus driven by four greys, placarded with posters saying, 'Policemen on Strike', and drove it to Hammersmith Police Court where his fellow would-be unionist, PC John Brown (51T) was before the bench for refusing to go on duty, an 'offence' for which he was sentenced to a month in prison.

Henderson acted promptly and firmly to restore public confidence. He sacked all the strikers, but two weeks later reinstated all but Goodchild and a handful of others, with a fine of a week's pay and a reduction in rank wherever possible. He also required them to retake their oath. In this he foreshadowed the curious belief of some of his successors that taking the police oath lays a heavy and obvious moral burden on an officer never to combine with anyone else to make representations about his pay and conditions, no matter how outrageously inadequate they may be. The omen for the future was blandly disregarded by the authorities, who allowed non-representation of the junior ranks to fester until the Police Strikes of 1918 and 1919, and even thereafter sometimes treated the Police Federation and its Branch Boards with some contempt.

The press reaction was to withdraw some of the favour the force had at last been acquiring.

POLICE STRIKE, 1890 Threatened refusal to go on duty by 130 E Division constables and Sergeants in protest against the Home Office's and Commissioner's refusal to authorize a negotiating body. Followed by a so-called riot.

Extreme discontent had been fomented in the force by the discussion of pensions throughout the latter part of 1889 and the first half of 1890. There was a genuine grievance, exacerbated by Commissioner James Monro's making known his support for the men's case (in contrast with his predecessor Sir Charles Warren's confidential agitation on their behalf), and by the meetings called by H. F. Hyndman's Social Democratic Federation and other socialist sympathizers. In line with their policy in other trades and industries, the socialists identified the need for a union or negotiating body to represent the men, something against which the authorities set their face.

So when the Police Act, 1890 appeared to have met the pensions complaint, there remained a small nucleus of agitators in the force who (rightly) wanted to open the question of pay scales, which had not been improved for 18 years – since the Police Strike, 1872, in fact – and who (more controversially) wanted the establishment of a union. The new Commissioner, Sir Edward Bradford, accepted two petitions on pay, one signed by constables and Sergeants, the other by Inspectors, and agreed to forward the men's requests. But he was concerned that demonstrations continued, especially at Bow Street Station, and ordered that they should be stopped.

On Saturday 5 July, Bradford refused to meet representatives asking for the formation of a negotiating body on the grounds that there was no negotiating body and so they didn't represent anyone. This has appeared 'reasonable' to previous historians of the police, but seems to the authors like a frustrating variant of Catch-22. That night 130 men refused to go on duty until an Inspector promised to convey their demands, including the demand for a union, to higher authority.

Bradford acted firmly the following day. He had 39 ringleaders paraded individually and sacked. The rest of the protesters were transferred to other Divisions.

On Monday 7 July, the 39 sacked men met at the Sun Tavern in Long Acre and composed a telegram to the Home Secretary threatening a complete police strike if they were not reinstated. They discussed the possibility of knocking down the first man to go on duty from Bow Street Station. They were joined by socialist agitators with

THE POLICE STRIKE OF 1890: THE ROWDY
DEMONSTRATION AT BOW STREET.

pamphlets declaring that the time was ripe for revolution, and then by a mob with an even clearer conviction that the time was ripe for mayhem. Everybody sang 'Rule Britannia', and went to mill around Bow Street. Bags of flour and rotten vegetables were hurled at mounted police who came to control the situation. Drunken sacked policemen sat on the station steps until Assistant Commissioner Howard took the wind out of their sails by inviting them in. A basin of

water was flung over the mob out of an upstairs window beside the police station, and an exuberant fracas, hardly amounting to a riot, was taking place when two troops of Life Guards were called in, and quickly and quietly dispersed the crowd.

So ended the so-called strike of 1890, the second in the Force's history. But the need for a negotiating body did not go away, as the authorities found thirty years later.

POLICE STRIKE, 1918 The most serious of all the Metropolitan Police Strikes, which led to the Commissioner's resignation, and was rapidly settled by Lloyd George with immediate reforms and the hint of postwar recognition of a union.

In 1917, police wages had again fallen far behind the requisite for a decent standard of living, and the discretionary nature of widows' pensions or gratuities was an obvious irritant in time of war. Inflation meant that constables with families were suffering actual malnutrition as they spent their little available cash on food for their children, and many officers were in debt. The Home Office obstinately refused any improvement beyond occasional derisory 'bonuses'. The Receiver's office had prepared an actuarially approved plan for widows' pensions, but Home Office officials let it stagnate on their desks. NUPPO, the banned police union, was growing underground and was benefiting by the support and advice of three experienced trade union-sponsored Labour MPs, the London Trades Council and the *Daily Herald*.

Commissioner Sir Edward Henry and his intemperate anti-Bolshevik ACs Basil Thomson and Frederick Wodehouse were convinced that NUPPO was an unrepresentative Bolshevist organization, and the majority of the men were quite content that the Home Office was looking into the pay and pensions questions. They ignored the junior ranks and liaised with the force through Superintendents, whose pay scales were higher and whose primary concern was improved pensions.

When Parliament recessed in August 1918, Henry went on holiday to Ireland. The Home Secretary, Sir George Cave, was also on holiday in the West Country, and the union acted very swiftly. They sent a peremptory demand for recognition, an immediate pay and pension increase, and the reinstatement of their provincial organizer, PC Tommy Thiel (147T, Warrant No. 90866), who had been dismissed on the complaint of Manchester's Chief Constable that he had been recruiting members in the northeast. They declared they would call a strike at midnight if their demands were not met. Acting Commissioner Wodehouse peremptorily rejected

it, and then looked on with horror as midnight struck, and the men on night duty returned to their stations and picketed the day shifts. By noon on Friday 29 August, 6000 of a force of 18,000 had declared themselves on strike, and policemen on duty directing traffic were being jeered at as blacklegs until they gave up and joined their comrades.

Lloyd George dared not let the capital slip into anarchy with the war still undecided. He appointed General Smuts, the South African statesman who was Minister without Portfolio in the Imperial War Cabinet, to deputize for Cave. Smuts decided against seeing the Union leaders when they tried to meet him in the afternoon, on the grounds that they were not recognized representatives. He rapidly realized he had made a serious error of judgment. By midnight, practically the entirety of the Met had come out, and the following day the City of London Police responded with equal solidarity when the union executive called them out. Only the outer divisions had men still reporting for duty. Central London was without police, though policemen were visible everywhere, marching in plain clothes behind bands and banners and searching stations to roust out strike breakers. Troops had to be posted to guard government offices and important buildings. Lloyd George ordered an unwilling Home Secretary (summoned back from Burnham-on-Sea) to invite the union leaders to No. 10 Downing Street for discussions the following day.

Downing Street was packed solid with policemen out of uniform, who cheered their leaders as they arrived, and did not cheer Henry and Cave. To the extreme annoyance of the Home Secretary and the Police Commissioner, Lloyd George immediately stated that Thiel was thereby reinstated and promised immediate and substantial pay improvements. He said that it was not possible for NUPPO to be recognized in wartime, but promised that a representative body to put forward the men's views would immediately be set up.

When the meeting ended and the men had left, Lloyd George ordered Cave to secure Henry's resignation, though, knowing that nobody wanted the job of Home Secretary at that point, he refused to accept Cave's resignation at the same time. But he was as good as his word to the men. Standing Orders the next day increased constables' pay by 13s. There was also a war bonus of 12s, and a child allowance of 2s 6d for every child of school age. Widows were granted a weekly pension of 10s. The men's pension was raised to £1 15s 4d a week after 26 years' service. An organization to represent the men was to be set up forthwith. In the meantime, policemen were allowed to belong to NUPPO, provided it never tried to interfere with disciplinary matters and never called for withdrawal of labour, and NUPPO could put up candidates for the new representative body.

The strike ended immediately. It was a triumph for organized labour, which hoped that a National Police Union would soon become an affiliate of the TUC, and industrial strikers could hope for fraternal treatment from officers policing strikes. It was a triumph for Lloyd George's political sense: the rest of the 'management' team (except Smuts) would have insisted on Thiel's continued dismissal and dickered over the pay proposals, thus causing the strike to drag on. It was a triumph for the good sense of Londoners, who neither rioted nor looted except for one small incident involving one shop in the East End, and for NUPPO, which promptly expanded its membership to the point that it really did, for the time being, represent the police force. Its nominees secured practically all the seats on the new government-sponsored representative body.

But its leaders failed to grasp that politicians, practising the art of the possible, may change their positions very quickly as circumstances change. They wrongly assumed that Lloyd George's assurance that he would be available to them at any time meant that he would give NUPPO recognition after the war. Sir George Cave had, in fact, been at pains to announce immediately after the successful meeting that there would never be any question of a Police Union affiliated to the TUC, and police officers would never have a 'right' to strike.

POLICE STRIKE, 1919 The first and last attempt at a National Police Strike. Less serious in its immediate effect on the Met than the Police Strike, 1918, but ultimately decisive in preventing police officers from ever having a formal union or the legal right to withdraw their labour.

At the end of May, 1919, NUPPO, feeling threatened by their loss of control of the Metropolitan Police Representation Board coupled with Commissioner Sir Nevil Macready and Home Secretary Edward Shortt's manifest hostility to the union's existence, balloted its members to measure support for a strike on three issues:

1. A new pay claim

2. The reinstatement of PC Spackman, dismissed for excessive union zeal.

3. Recognition of the union.

An overwhelming 44,539 voted 'Yes' to striking – 10 times as many as the 'No' votes. Even so, Union General Secretary Jack Hayes doubted whether the 44,539 would willingly come out if called, especially as it seemed certain that the pay claim, which mattered most to the membership, was about to be granted rapidly.

In July, the Desborough Committee's proposed reforms were incorporated in a Police Bill which established the Police Federation, declared any other form of union illegal, and made it an imprisonable offence to cause disaffection in the police – effectively a prohibition on police strikes.

NUPPO was effectively wiped out. Opposition from a few Labour backbenchers was ineffective. Those members of the union executive who had resigned from the Met to become full-time union officials seemed about to lose everything. And relying on the ballot in the spring and general promises of support made by other union leaders at conferences, the executive called a national strike by the narrowest of majorities.

The result was a fiasco. John Syme, the union's founder, had presciently warned in Police Review that a strike would fail, because the immediate payment of £10 to every member of the force in anticipation of the backpaid Desborough rises had calmed the men's dissatisfaction; because the union had not the funds to maintain strike pay for more than a couple of days; because for all their brave words, the big unions would not rally to their support with sympathy strikes; and because Macready and Shortt had taken NUPPO's measure and knew

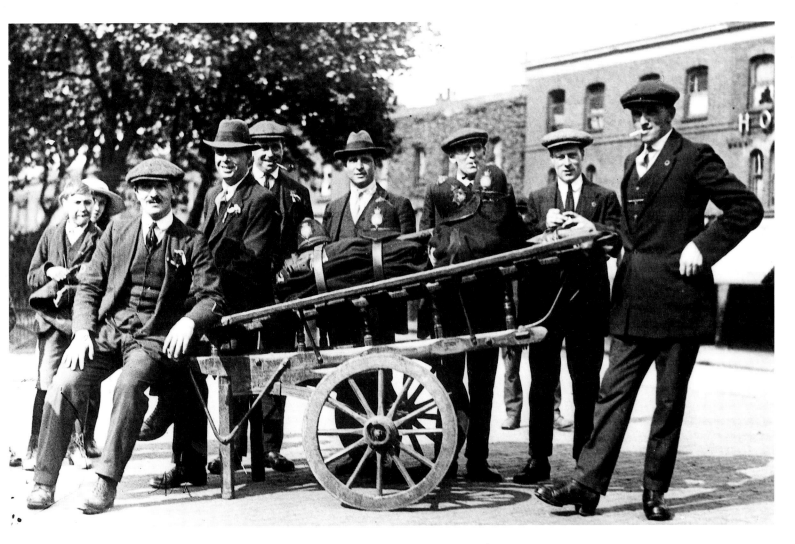

NUPPO MEMBERS AT POPLAR RETURNING THEIR UNIFORMS ON A COSTERMONGER'S BARROW AFTER DISMISSAL FROM THE FORCE, 1919.

they could beat them.

Syme proved right on every point. The £10 back pay satisfied all but the staunchest union supporters and the most aggrieved provincial forces. Although never required to produce strike pay for more than 1.5% of their membership, the union was soon out of funds. The only London fellow unionists to come out in sympathy were the Nine Elms branch of the National Union of Railwaymen, and they hurried back to work when advised by their executive. The only prominent Labour politician to support the strike was the much loved George Lansbury, outside Parliament as editor of the *Daily Herald* at the time. It was apparent that he hoped unionized police would never again help to maintain public order during industrial strikes, something more responsible Labour leaders perceived as dangerous. And the *Herald*'s wildly over-optimistic reporting of the strike probably encouraged a few more men to come out to their doom. Shortt and Macready had troops on standby to take over police duties in London if needed, and Superintendents and Inspectors had organized resistance to intimidatory picketing.

Worse still, half the NUPPO executive declined to join the strike, several of them resigning from the union as soon as it was called. Many loyal union branch secretaries were so horrified by a decision that was not in their members' interest they tore up their membership cards, returned all funds in their care to the Union HQ, and dissolved their branches. The 50,000 strong membership of NUPPO melted away overnight.

Nationally the effect was minimal: 2400 men came out from a national police strength of 60,000. There was some support in Birmingham, but most of the other provincial forces regarded the strike as a mistake and stayed on duty. There were, however, serious riots and looting on Merseyside. About half the force struck in Liverpool, whose aloof Chief Constable and reac-tionary Watch Committee had allowed many of the force's Sergeants and Inspectors to become infamous for their petty tyranny and savage discipline. About half of Birkenhead's force came out. In Bootle, 63 of the 77 men refused duty, and the borough was completely pillaged, as was the Scotland Road district of Liverpool. In Birkenhead rioters drank every drop of liquor in the Wheatsheaf Hotel, and stole the bar staff's clothing. The government actually had to 'send a gunboat' (a battleship and two cruisers) to restore order.

In the Met, 1056 of the 18,200 men struck. The most senior was an Inspector, an unstable religio-maniac who was certified insane three days later. Twenty-eight were Sergeants and the rest constables. All the strikers were sacked. Their desperate appeals for reinstatement, or at least the refund of their accrued pension contributions, were resolutely refused. The disorders in the north-east caused the public to look favourably on the prohibition of the union and police strikes, and only a few Labour MPs supported the unemployed strikers' cause, though some unions gave as generously as they could to help strikers' families. In 1924, when Labour came to power, Home Secretary Arthur Henderson set up a Committee to reconsider their case. Clement Attlee, as Mayor of Stepney, argued movingly on behalf of the Stoke Newington constables who had been ordered to march to a strike meeting at Tower Hill by their Inspector, who was confined in an asylum three days later. But the Committee could not reach a unanimous report, and the majority favoured doing nothing for the strikers except restoring accrued pension contributions to the wives of married men. When Attlee himself became Prime Minister and met a delegation of elderly men from the Association of Strikers, he cold-shouldered them and refused to give them any belated support or compensation.

History books declare that the Police Strike of 1919 proved the impossibility of ever seeing another. Nevertheless, whenever pay slips too far behind national averages, disgruntled constables discuss the possibility, complain that the Federation is not a proper union, and remember resentfully that the Labour movement let their predecessors down in 1919.

POLICE SUPPORT UNIT See Serial.

POLICING BY CONSENT The most important aspect of Peel, Rowan and Mayne's innovation.

It was a *sine qua non* for establishing the Metropolitan Police that the founders must somehow meet the fear expressed by the 1822 Home Department Committee that it would be hard to 'reconcile an effective system of police with that perfect freedom of action and exemption from interference which are the great privileges and blessings of society in this country.' Peel's riposte, uttered in a letter to the Duke of Wellington seven years later, was, 'I want to teach people that liberty does not consist of having your house robbed by organized gangs of thieves, and in leaving the streets of London in the nightly possession of drunken women and vagabonds.'

To gain acceptance by the public, the early police were instructed by Rowan and Mayne to tolerate a great deal of unprovoked abuse. The first directions on demeanour stressed that unruffled patience and courtesy were crucial characteristics of the successful police officer. One year later, Rowan reminded the men that, 'at a time when an attempt is being made to create a strong prejudice against them . . . they should do their duty with every possible moderation and forbearance, and . . . they should not furnish a just cause of complaint against themselves by any misconduct.'

On the streets such misconduct was caused by unprovoked physical assaults by ruffians and and, it is said, cuts from the whips of coachmen who obeyed their master's instructions. Nevertheless, the patience of the police, coupled with Mayne's subsequent encouragement of a deferential attitude to the middle and upper classes, led to their gradual acceptance. Upholding the law will never be a universally popular task, particularly when there is conflict between different groups within society, but it is possible to retain public respect and consent to the law being objectively enforced.

However long it may have taken, the establishment of an unarmed, publicly accepted body of law enforcement officers was an outstanding achievement. It is a matter for national pride that England set the pattern for a system which is now widely seen as one measure of a nation's liberty and democracy; and a matter for Metropolitan police pride that the Met was the force which took the hard knocks at the beginning and earned the consent.

POLICY BOARD Or Commissioner's Policy Board.

The supreme managerial committee of Scotland Yard, under the Commissioner, who is administrative, executive and operational head of the force. Comprises the Commissioner, Deputy Commissioner, Assistant Commissioners and Receiver. Senior staff (e.g. Director of Technology, Director of Public Affairs, Director of Personnel, Director of Property Services Department) also regularly attend.

POPAY, SGT WILLIAM SEWARD (OR STEWARD OR STEWART. B.1798) Dismissed with contumely (17 August 1833) for exceeding his duties when in plain clothes.

Born in Yarmouth, and worked there as a school-keeper. Subsequently a 'coal-meter', measuring shipments landed from colliers, which work he continued after joining the Met on 3 September 1831. Warrant No. 6778. Married with eight children, working in the Brixton area, he was promoted to Sergeant, P Division in March 1833.

In February 1833, Superintendent Andrew McLean of P Division ordered Popay to attend meetings of the Camberwell 'class' of the National Political Union of the Working Classes, which was agitating for universal manhood suffrage and other electoral reforms, and which frightened the authorities by calling for a National Convention such as had preceded the French and American revolutions. Popay posed as a painter with vehement anti-police opinions, and soon found himself accepted as one of the leading local revolutionaries. From this position he submitted reports to McLean which were forwarded to under-secretary Samuel Phillipps at the Home Office, and from him to Home Secretary Lord Melbourne. In May, a member of the NPU saw Popay chatting amicably with officers in Park House police station, and although he offered plausible excuses and attended the Coldbath Fields Riot in plain clothes, the suspicions of George Fursey were aroused, and following the riot and Fursey's trial where Popay appeared, 10 citizens of Camberwell petitioned Parliament against the use of police spies in plain clothes who acted as revolutionary *agents provocateurs*. A Select Committee was set up to inquire into the case, and it sat and reported alongside the Select Committee on the riot. Despite clear evidence that Popay had been acting with at least the connivance of the Home Office, and many parliamentarians' probable awareness that the use of spies and *agents provocateurs* to infiltrate dissident workers' movements long preceded the formation of the Metropolitan Police (most notably in the Cato Street Conspiracy of 1820), the Committee declared that the practice was 'most abhorrent to the feelings of the People, and most Alien to the spirit of the Constitution'. Popay was made a scapegoat. His conduct was declared 'highly reprehensible', and he was sacked.

PORTFOLIO From the 1995 Service Restructuring Exercise, the block of centrally managed Headquarters Branches under the responsibility of Area Assistant Commissioners. Grouped by themes such as public order, vice and licensing, 24-hour response, traffic, criminal justice and crime.

The principle was introduced to ensure that Headquarters Branches were always linked to an Assistant Commissioner who had responsibility for the realities faced by Divisions.

PRESS BUREAU The flagship of the Directorate of Public Affairs and Internal Communication (DPA), Press Bureau is one of the busiest organizations of its type in the world, and deals with many thousands of press and media enquiries from its computer-assisted 13th floor room at New Scotland Yard. Press Bureau has the capacity to monitor all the major TV and radio channels, and is seen at its busiest when a major incident occurs.

All this has developed from the press briefings introduced by Sir Nevil Macready in 1919 when S1 Press Branch was created with G Rivers-Bodilly, the Commissioner's secretary, as its head from 1919 to 1922. Shortly after WWII Sir Harold Scott appointed Percy Fearnley as Information Officer. This was the first time a professional from the media had been recruited by the Yard. In the 1970s Sir Robert Mark transformed the policy towards openness with the media unless there was a definite reason to the contrary.

Nowadays the DPA also arranges sophisticated poster and publicity campaigns to support major operations like Operation Bumblebee and anti-terrorist initiatives. It also manages the Met's Internet website (www.met.police.uk).

PRISONERS' PROPERTY ACT An Act of Parliament governing the disposal of property coming into police possession (which led to the

formation of the Black Museum). It provides a method for magistrates to give rulings on disputed ownership of property in police hands. Unclaimed property is sold by auction, and the proceeds form the Prisoners' Property Act Fund, which in turn is donated to charity.

PRIVATE SECRETARIES Prior to 1914 these were always male clerks provided for the Commissioner and Receiver only. At the end of WWI, the shortage of men and the numbers of women who had mastered shorthand and typing led Commissioner Sir Nevil Macready to transfer his male secretary to an Assistant Commissioner, and appoint a Mrs Brunskill. Thereafter, whether or not a male PS was appointed, there was always a female shorthand typist in the Commissioner's private office.

In the inter-war period, Assistant Commissioners were given Private Secretaries, who were usually male civilian executive officers with annual allowances to cover their increased hours and duties. They were expected to draft and type letters, and act as liaison officers between the ACs and their Heads of Departments. For dictated let-

ters, ACs were required to borrow shorthand typists from the pool.

In c.1966, AC B Andrew Way decided that he wanted a permanent shorthand-typist as his PS, and a senior police officer as his Staff Officer for liaison. This example was gradually followed by the other ACs. Private Secretaries are now the norm for senior staff.

PROPERTY SERVICES DEPARTMENT
Approximately 240 Civil Staff, including estate surveyors, architects, engineers, building and quantity surveyors and a small direct labour force to service areas of high sensitivity. Mainly based at Cobalt Square, the department manages the 500 or more sites and buildings owned by the Receiver on behalf of the MPS, the Inner London Magistrates Courts Service (ILMCS) and the Inner London Probation Service (ILPS).

It buys and sells properties, develops new

MISS EDITH ELLEN DRYSDALE, PRIVATE SECRETARY TO COMMISSIONERS HORWOOD AND BYNG. IN 1931 SHE MARRIED DEPUTY COMMISSIONER SIR TREVOR BIGHAM.

buildings, maintains the estate and manages other estate services, such as security guarding, cleaning, messengerial and reception staff, and reprographics.

It also provides various operational support services, including the deployment of pedestrian barriers, signs and traffic cones, the provision of temporary accommodation and feeding centres and a special 'forced entry' facility, as well as preparing plans and three-dimensional modelling for scenes of crime.

PROSTITUTE INDEX Computerized list of women who have been cautioned or charged for soliciting, managed by SO3 (3) PNC Bureau.

Required because, by law, a woman can only be charged with soliciting if she has been cautioned with the offence twice or convicted once during the previous 12 months. See Elizabeth Cass.

PSI REPORT (SMITH REPORT) Comprehensive research into relationships between the Metropolitan Police and the public commissioned by the Met in 1979, conducted by the Policy Studies Institute and published in 1983. Despite severe criticism of the organization of the Met and the attitudes of some officers, it found that police officers tended, if anything, to give additional consideration to black people in their dealings with them on the street.

PUBLIC CARRIAGE OFFICE Arguably the very oldest part of the Metropolitan Police,

since licensing the cab trade has its origins in an ordinance introduced in 1654 for the regulation of hackney coachmen in London. Coincidentally, the Hackney Coach Office was at Scotland Yard and the officers heading it were called the Commissioners of Scotland Yard. Their duty was to license all drivers and vehicles carrying the public for a fee. While the apparent defencelessness of passengers in strange vehicles might point to the need for public authorization and inspection, the real interest of the government originally lay in the revenue derived from collecting licence fees.

In 1850, however, duties regarding licensing of drivers were transferred to the Commissioners of the Metropolitan Police, and the Public Carriage Office was born. From 1869 it undertook licensing of cabs and drivers. In 1871 fare tables

THE OLD PUBLIC CARRIAGE OFFICE, LATER CID HEADQUARTERS, GREAT SCOTLAND YARD.

and small licence plates were displayed inside hackney carriages. A 6 mile (9.6km) limit, or a one-hour journey, was introduced in 1853 as the distance drivers were legally obliged to take passengers. The first mechanically propelled vehicle (electrically propelled) was licensed in 1897 and the first petrol-driven cab in 1903. The last horsedrawn hackney carriage was withdrawn in 1947. The PCO has maintained high standards of taxicab safety and reliability, and licenses the drivers only after ensuring their good character and their acquisition of the hard-learned 'knowledge' of London's streets and one-way systems. It is arguable that having the police rather than local authorities oversee 'the knowledge' contributed to the world-wide fame of London taxi drivers. The PCO was at first housed in headquarters, but transferred to Lambeth with the Lost Property Office in 1927, and since 1966 has been at Penton Street, Islington. See Traffic Police.

PUBLIC ORDER BRANCH (CO11) One of

the earliest duties for which Sir Robert Peel intended his New Police was the maintenance of Public Order in a metropolis which was barely 50 years away from the wildly destructive Gordon Riots. After a few hiccups (see Clerkenwell riot, Hyde Park riots) the civilian peace-keeping force proved extremely effective. The non-occurrence of the feared Chartist Demonstration, 1848 was a key incident.

Any crowd, especially a political crowd, may become a focus for public disorder. For this reason a permanent Public Order Branch is part of No. 1 Area Assistant Commissioner's portfolio. On winter weekends the Mounted Police and large numbers of foot police attend football matches to control the crowds. All officers receive elementary training at Riot City as part of their basic training. Major events like royal weddings and state funerals require special policing, for which the Public Order Branch may need the Central Communications Complex to activate the Special Operations Room. For the enormous operation of policing the funeral of Diana, Princess of Wales in 1997, effectively four fifths of the entire MPS was directly involved, and 2000 special constables were drafted in. Uni-

formed police had to line miles of streets to ensure free passage of the funeral procession from central London to the M1. All leave was cancelled for the whole of Special Branch, who had a special role in ensuring security. In the event, the huge and unprecedented operation was an entire success, and only six arrests were made throughout the day.

The Public Order Branch has maintained an Intelligence and Planning function since the Brixton Riots of 1981. In liaison with other police forces throughout the country, this tries to anticipate serious political or other disturbances and arrange police operations accordingly.

See also Notting Hill Carnival, Riots

PURDY, DETECTIVE SGT RAYMOND (1916–1959) Murdered police officer whose case aroused unwarranted sympathy for his killer.

Joined the Met, 1939. Warrant No. 128057. Posted to V Division (Kingston). Promoted Sergeant and transferred to F Division (Hammersmith), 1955. Transferred to B Division (Kensington & Chelsea), 1958.

On duty in Chelsea Police Station on 13 July 1959, Sgt Purdy joined DS John Sandiford in responding to information that Mrs Verne Schieffman, an American model living in South Kensington, was holding on the telephone a man who had obtained her name when robbing her flat and subsequently tried to blackmail her with the pretence of holding tapes and documents of her supposed activities. The call was traced to a telephone box at South Kensington Underground Station, where Purdy and Sandiford arrested the man, who escaped from their grasp on the street and ran into the hall of a block of flats in Onslow Square. There the detectives re-arrested him, and Sgt Purdy held him while Sgt Sandiford went to look for the porter. When Sgt Purdy momentarily turned his head toward Sandiford, the man drew a pistol and shot him dead, escaping once more.

His wallet and fingerprints, coupled with suggestions from informants, finally determined that he was Gunther Fritz Podola, a German-born immigrant from Canada with convictions for theft in that country. Five days later he was

traced to a small hotel in Queensgate, where Chief Inspector Bob Acott led a team of police to arrest him. Podola was locked in his room, and did not open the door when first summoned. Hearing a click on their second demand to be admitted, the officers assumed he was cocking his pistol, and charged through the door. Unfortunately, the click had been Podola's attempt to start unlocking the door. He was hit in the face by its edge with the full weight of the arresting party behind it, and was brought before the magistrates with a black eye and a severe state of concussion. Press pictures of him led to the immediate assumption that he had been beaten up by the police, and questions were asked in the House of Commons.

At his trial, Podola's counsel called doctors and psychiatrists to testify that he had been in a state of amnesia ever since Acott arrested him; that he could remember nothing of his original offence or the death of Sergeant Purdy, and was therefore unfit to plead. The jury was convinced by prosecution medical evidence that Podola was skilfully fabricating amnesia, and convicted him of Sgt Purdy's murder. Podola 'recovered' sufficient memory to mount an unsuccessful appeal, and was hanged.

Metropolitan Police relations with the liberal intelligentsia were not enhanced by the latter's evident concern for the 'rights' of an undoubted robber, blackmailer and murderer to the exclusion of Sgt Purdy's posthumous right to justice. The case contributed to a state of tension which had existed since the previous year, when the anti-capital punishment lobby furiously opposed the execution of 25-year-old Ronald Marwood, who stabbed to death 23-year-old PC Raymond Summers when he intervened to break up a fight between two delinquent gangs in Seven Sisters Road, Holloway. The tension was aggravated the following year when 18-year-old 'Flossy' Forsyth received immense sentimental sympathy on his execution for brutally kicking to death 21-year-old Alan Jee in a fit of fury that his delinquent gang's vicious attempt to rob the innocent passer-by in a lonely lane had secured them only 1/4d (7p). A commemorative plaque to Sergeant Purdy was unveiled inside Chelsea Police Station in February 1999.

Q-CARS Unmarked police cars, fitted with radio communications and carrying plain clothes police officers involved in dedicated proactive anti-crime patrols.

Originally a nickname devised by journalists in 1927 when the Flying Squad acquired its first fleet of Lea Francis cars (to supplement their four Crossley tenders) and proceeded to install concealed radio aerials in the hood struts and fit them with interchangeable number plates of varied colouring, so that they could not be readily identified by lawbreakers. The analogy was with WWI Q-Boats – warships disguised as merchantmen to deceive enemy submarines (or U-Boats).

The original Q-cars also carried illuminated 'Metropolitan Police' signs which could be shown on the windshield when they wished to make their official presence known. (Today unmarked cars carry 'Kojak' magnetic revolving blue lamps.)

When Divisions were given unmarked cars, their Q-Cars typically carried a Sergeant (from either uniformed branch or CID), a Detective Constable or Temporary Detective Constable, and a uniformed branch constable as driver, all in plain clothes. The cars were allotted letter and digit/s radio call signs, such as, 'Foxtrot One One'. (Cf. Shepherd's Bush murders for details of a Q-car and occupants on duty.)

QUEENIE (D.1983) Police dog killed in the Harrods' IRA bombing, 1983, and given the RSPCA's highest award.

Among the police called to Harrods at 12.45 p.m. on Saturday 17 December after the warning call received in Scotland Yard were dog-handler PC Jon Gordon (674X) from Uxbridge and his dog Queenie. Both were among the group preparing to examine the Austin car in Hans Place when it exploded.

PC Gordon was declared dead at the scene, where he was found to have lost a leg and suffered extensive burns, but he made a miraculous recovery in hospital, and despite the loss of his other leg and part of one hand was able to return to light duties in December 1984.

Queenie was so badly injured that she had to be put down. She was buried at Keston where she

had been bred, and on 3 August 1984 was awarded posthumously the Margaret Wheatley Medal, the RSPCA's award for intelligence and courage.

QUEEN'S POLICE MEDAL Circular silver medal bearing the sovereign's effigy on the obverse, and a robed figure with sword and shield representing 'Protection from Danger' on the reverse. The words 'For Distinguished Police Service' run round the circumference.

Originally awarded to officers who had performed 'acts of exceptional courage or skill at the cost of [their] lives, or exhibited conspicuous devotion to duty, as members of a recognized police force' within the Queen's sovereign territories. In 1954 it replaced, with the QFSM, the KPFSM which, following a Home Office circular of 1951, was already only awarded for gallantry in posthumous cases.

In 1977 the QPM for Gallantry lapsed entirely, being superseded by other awards. Seventeen had been awarded in the UK between 1954 and 1976, five of them to Metropolitan Police Officers (see Appendix 3). Although this closely matches the ratio of Metropolitan to other police on mainland Britain, it should also be noted that five went to members of the Royal Ulster Constabulary killed in the troubles. It is a sad commentary on the latter half of the 20th century that the two Metropolitan officers awarded posthumous KPMs prior to 1939 both sacrificed their lives in clearing members of the public away from the danger of serious foreseeable accidents (see PCs J. W. Thomson and E. B. W. Greenoff), whereas the five postwar posthumous KPFSM and QPM holders were all killed by criminals.

The QPM today is normally awarded to officers of or above Chief Superintendent rank who have rendered exceptionally distinguished service, but lower ranks can also qualify when they have distinguished themselves by a particularly successful piece of work. A conscious effort has been made to ensure that distinguished service is recognized at junior as well as senior levels.

QUEEN'S POLICE OFFICER Title given to the most senior ranking police officer on the Queen's Personal Protection Team. (See under Royalty Protection Branch.)

QUICKSILVER (1911–1936) Famous horse owned by Sir Percy Laurie and ridden by him and others on ceremonial occasions.

Grey gelding, foaled in Ireland and purchased by Army 'Remounts' in 1915. Selected by Lady Hunter-Weston for her husband, General Sir Aylmer, Commander of the 8th Corps, who found him rather lively and ill-disciplined for a parade charger. Knowing that Sir Percy Laurie coveted this very beautiful mount, Sir Aylmer promised Quicksilver should be transferred to him if he did not settle down. When the horse threw the general over its head while he was delivering a pep talk to a brigade, leaving him to complete his lecture from a seated position on the ground (but with his eyeglass still in place), an ADC telephoned Sir Percy with the message, 'Percy, the 'oss is yours. Ask no questions.'

Wounded at the Battle of the Somme, but recovered by November and present at the Battle of Passchendaele. Advanced into Germany, and repatriated from Cologne, 1919. Expeditionary Force, General Service and Victory Ribbons; Order of the Blue Cross, and one Wound Stripe.

Ridden successfully by Sir Percy at all subsequent state ceremonies and ceremonial parades, and lent to Field-Marshals Sir John French and Lord Cavan for Trooping of the Colour parades. Winner of the King's Cup for Best-Trained Police Horse, Richmond Royal Horse Show, 1920.

Retired with Sir Percy, 1936, and thereafter ridden by him to hounds with the Cricklade. Put down 1943 when back muscles atrophied. Commemorated by a poem in *Horse and Hound*.

RACIAL AND VIOLENT CRIME TASK FORCE Set up in August 1998 under DAC John Grieve during the Stephen Lawrence Inquiry (see Macpherson Report), to ensure that racial and violent crime is prevented, and that if it occurs it is recognized, investigated thoroughly to agreed quality standards, and is reviewed objectively so that lessons may be learnt from the experience. Codenamed Operation Athena.

RAIL ACCIDENTS High among the major incidents to which the police will invariably be called as an emergency service are rail accidents. Though there are fewer of them than there were in the days when railways were being built, and a government philosophy of *laissez-faire* militated against legislation to ensure passenger safety, the greater size and speed of modern trains can make accidents more serious disasters. Conversely, however, the technology which has advanced train performance also enhances the capability of the police to respond efficiently to emergencies. Simultaneously the Clean Air Acts which have eliminated the old London pea-souper fogs make it relatively unlikely that we shall see crashes like the MPD's worst-ever disaster at Harrow and Wealdstone (1952) or the Lewisham train crash of 1957 (90 dead and 92 seriously injured).

The Harrow and Wealdstone Station disaster drew attention to some of the possibilities for improving the police emergency service. At 8.19 a.m. on Wednesday 8 October 1952, the 7.31 train from Tring to Euston was pulling out of the station when the Perth to Euston express crashed into its rear. The Euston to Liverpool express then crashed into the wreckage from the opposite direction. A total of 112 people were killed and 154 were injured, of whom 91 were detained in hospital. Heroic rescue efforts were made without benefit of modern technology and support. A mobile canteen, for instance, did not arrive until 4.00 p.m. The police noticed that the Fire Brigade had access to modern 'walkie-talkie' portable radios, and it was recognized that additional telephone lines needed to be installed for such incidents.

The Lewisham train crash five years later caused fewer fatalities and casualties, but led to

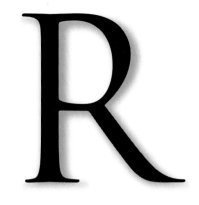

the greatest single series of improvements in police emergency operations.

The 1967 Hither Green crash, near St Mildred's Road SE6, saw the new facilities being tried and put to effective use. On Sunday 5 November at 9.16 p.m., the 7.43 passenger train from Hastings to Charing Cross became derailed at about 65 mph. The Mobile Control vehicle worked well, but it was found that it needed distinctive lighting at night. This led to the illuminated chequered roof lights being introduced on police control vehicles. The Central Casualty Bureau answered the hundreds of telephone calls

from anxious members of the public, but better links with local officers handling casualty information were identified as an improvement needed for the future.

The Clapham crash on 12 December 1988 which killed 35 people was blamed on faulty signal wiring. A helicopter from the Metropolitan Police Air Support Unit ferried medical teams to the scene, and a support system for the victims' families was introduced to help them understand the procedures following the accident, and sustain them in their bereavement.

RATTLES Means of summoning assistance or raising an alarm issued to police on patrol between 1829 and 1885.

One thousand rattles manufactured by Parker's of Holborn were ordered for the new police force in 1829. Their death-knell was sounded when they were tested against whistles in 1883, and found to be clearly audible over 400 yards (366m), and indistinctly audible for another 300

AERIAL VIEW OF POLICE AND EMERGENCY SERVICES AT THE CLAPHAM RAIL DISASTER, 1988.

yards (274m). A whistle was clearly audible for 900 yards (823m). In February 1885 whistles were issued to all patrolling officers, though rattles were still kept at stations and issued to night patrols for a couple of years. In April 1887 all rattles were called in and returned to the Receiver's office. The rattle then disappeared from official public life, though it would have made a comeback in 1940 had German bombing raids used gas, when it was to be the official warning. As long as they were used the term for sounding them was 'springing a rattle.'

RECEIVER Formally 'The Receiver for the Metropolitan Police District', the Receiver is in fact the financial manager of the Metropolitan Police – in legal terms the Treasurer of the Metropolitan Police Fund. The name derives from the duty of the original Receiver (John Wray) to 'receive' from the parishes of the Metropolitan Police District those monies raised on the rates for the maintenance of watchmen and constables prior to 1829.

The Receiver is appointed by and holds his office at the pleasure of the Crown. His legal status is that of a corporation sole with perpetual succession and with capacity by his official name to acquire and hold property of every description for police purposes, to sue and be sued, and to enter contracts on behalf of the Metropolitan Police Service. In other words, in the eyes of the law the entire property of the Metropolitan Police Service – police stations, cars, helicopters, New Scotland Yard, frogmen's flippers and whistles – is the property of the holder of the post of Receiver and must be bought and sold in the Receiver's name. Peel's police force was run by the triumvirate of two Commissioners and the Receiver. Nothing could be bought or sold and no contracts could be entered into without the Receiver's approval and cooperation. This had certain beneficial effects. The police *per se* were protected from the sort of corruption and contractual favouritism from the top which might seem unthinkable to Victorian gentlemen, but which easily creep into public finances without firm checks and balances. Commissioners Rowan and Mayne were insulated from the pressure that had to be brought to bear on the more recalci-

trant parishes to make them turn over funds prior to the Police Act, 1839. And as long as Wray was Receiver, the system worked perfectly.

Friction started from the moment of his retirement. First Mayne, then Commissioner Henderson found his successor, Maurice Drum-

JOHN WRAY, FIRST RECEIVER FOR THE
METROPOLITAN POLICE.

mond, difficult to work with, and when Richard Pennefather became Receiver the situation was exacerbated. Sir Charles Warren, accustomed to the full military authority of the General Staff, was exasperated by having to clear every order for necessary equipment with a stickling finance officer whose standing and authority were equal to his own. Conversely, 50 years later, Sir John Moylan, a Receiver with long experience of civil service methods, was quietly appalled by Lord Trenchard's habit of using the Home Secretary's promise of full financial support to pursue his demands for new buildings and facilities despite pleas that resources were limited. The possibility of conflict remained until 1968 when, following the recommendation of PA Management Consultants, the formal independence of the Receiver's Department was ended and the Commissioner was made Head of the whole Metropolitan Police Service.

By the end of the 20th century, the Receiver was a Grade 2 Civil Servant, holding a post that was once described as 'the best job in Whitehall'. He had become Director of Finance, with direct responsibility for the Finance, Property Services and Technology Departments, exercising certain functions which, outside London, fall to Police Authorities. With the consent of the Home Secretary he could issue a precept on the local Authorities making up the Metropolitan Police District. He has acquired responsibility for the financial and some support functions of the Inner London Magistrates' Court Service and the Inner London Probation Service.

The decision to replace the Receiver's role under the new Greater London Authority leaves a number of details to be worked out in the light of experience, taking into account not only the legal niceties of dealing with the Met's contracts and property, but also the relocation of those responsibilities for Courts and Probation.

RECORDS MANAGEMENT BRANCH Approximately 60 Civil Staff under the Quality Performance Portfolio, comprising the General Registry and Archives. Lead authority for all record management issues in the Metropolitan Police Service.

RED LION SQUARE RIOT, 1974 Incident leading to the first definite violent death of anyone but a police officer when the Metropolitan Police were restoring Public Order. (Cf. PC Culley for the first person to die during a Metropolitan Public Order operation, the Marine Police Office riot, and Bloody Sunday, 1887 for the first unproven allegation that a demonstrator or demonstrators subsequently died of injuries received in a riot put down by the Met.)

On 15 June 1974 the National Front, a Fascist organization, planned a short march culminating in a meeting at Conway Hall, Red Lion Square. An *ad hoc* counter-organization calling itself 'Liberation', but definitely including students from Warwick University and members of a body called the International Marxist Group, declared their intention of stopping them by force. It fell to the Metropolitan Police to try to preserve order and protect the Fascists' democratic right to hold their demonstration in an orderly fashion.

When the two groups reached the Square, Liberation made an immediate attempt to attack the National Front physically, and being restrained by the police attacked them instead. To end the pitched battle, the Mounted Police were called in, and in the mob's rush to escape, a bystander called Kevin Gately, who is not believed to have been a participant in either demonstrating body, was kicked or crushed to death.

An enquiry by Lord Scarman (not to be confused with his Scarman Report following the Brix-

ton riots) concluded that the International Marxist Group were essentially to blame, having initiated the violence by attacking the police. The Met ingested the crucial lesson, followed in all subsequent Public Order operations, that mounted officers should never drive back a large crowd without ensuring that it has good clear space into which it can escape safely.

'REFORMERS' TREE' The traditional starting point for many demonstrations, located in Hyde Park between Speakers' Corner and the Hyde Park Police Station. The original tree's location is now marked by a lamp post.

REGIONAL CRIME SQUAD A network of Regional Crime Squads coordinates investiga-

tion of serious crimes nationally. No. 9 RSC covered London and comprised Metropolitan and City of London Police officers until reorganized as the National Crime Squad in 1995.

RELF, RICHARD (1832–1915) The baby-farming investigator. Born Chatham. Joined the Met 1858; previously a musician. Warrant No. 37525. Posted to B Division (Div. No. 216), 1858–9. J Division (Div. No. 417) and W Division, 1859–1871. Sergeant, 1870. Inspector, 1872. Retired, 1883.

Relf's work on the Margaret Walters and Sarah Ellis case shortly after he had been promoted to Sergeant in 1870 led to his becoming the first Metropolitan officer semi-officially recognized as the force expert on a particular category of

HIGH HOLBORN, NEAR RED LION SQUARE, 1974,

RELIEF OFFICERS Originally the 'Relief' was the in-service term for the body of men on any patrolling officer's shift.

Today the term describes officers who patrol in cars or on foot from police stations to cover the basic operational demands of a (normally) eight-hour period of duty, as distinct from Home Beat Officers or other systems more closely associated with community policing. The relief officer's function and attitudes are sometimes held to represent 'traditional' or 'short-term' policing with enforcement of the law and the need to respond to calls taking priority over longer-term problem-solving. Thus excellent service by relief officers might be measured in a high arrest record, whereas successful community policing may result in reduction of crime and disorder problems.

Most would agree that longer-term prevention is highly desirable, but that a short-term response inevitably takes precedence when resources are in short supply.

RESERVE OFFICERS 'The Commissioner's Reserve' denotes officers from the Territorial Support Groups on stand-by to respond anywhere in London at short notice, with patrolling duties managed accordingly.

Until the 1960s, used as a term to describe the officer controlling radio communications from a station, sometimes supported by a second reserve officer who made tea, stoked boilers and ran general errands. For this reason the Control Room was for a time known as the Reserve Room.

In the late 19th century, officers of peculiarly imposing demeanour and appearance, who were the first to be called upon for ceremonial occasions. They received a small pay increment and wore the letter R after their Divisional Number.

Originally (1829) the reserve officer was the ninth man under the command of each Section Sergeant while the other eight were on their beats.

RESERVE SQUAD Until the 1986 restructuring of C1 Branch into Specialist Operations, the

crime. Baby-farming was the commercial practice of receiving unwanted infants either on the pretence of placing them for adoption or in a supposed nursery home, and deliberately underfeeding and overcrowding them in the interests of profit and at risk to their lives.

Relf's was neither the first nor the most notorious of the baby-farming cases. (The Tooting baby farm ran by a man called Drouet had been the subject of Charles Dickens' journalism ten years earlier, and Mrs Dyer, hanged in 1896, left the longest memory.) But Relf's successful detective work when 18 dead infants were found over a short period of time in Brixton led to Margaret Walters being the first person executed for murdering the babies left in her care, and he was presented with a testimonial by the Vicar of Christ Church, Camberwell, and called in on subsequent baby-farming cases in other divisions until his retirement.

title of the present Group Operations unit of the Organised Crime Group.

Not to be confused with Reserve Officers (above).

The 1920s to 1950s predecessors of the Reserve Squad were inaccurately called the 'Murder Squad' by the press, because sensational murder cases were crime reporters' preferred sustenance. The principle of having senior experienced detectives designated to deal with the next major case proved very effective, and is carried over in today's Area Major Investigation Pools as well as the Organised Crime Group.

REX III (1949–1956) Famous and decorated police dog.

Pedigree German shepherd, originally placed as a watchdog in the French Legation. Acquired by the Met, 1950, when the Legation installed electric alarms. Trained by his volunteer handler,

OFFICER TRAINING AT 'RIOT CITY'.

PC Arthur Holman, despite being older than the normal 12-week training age. The third Metropolitan police dog given the name Rex; oddly, the third dog named Rex that Holman had owned, too.

In 1951, Rex was called into court by a south London magistrate and commended for tracking and guarding three safebreakers who had broken into Dorman Long's offices at Nine Elms, and then evaded a squad of detective and uniformed police. This gave him his first newspaper coverage.

On 13 June 1954, PC Holman, Rex and two detectives went to arrest an army deserter. After being arrested, the man broke free and ran away. Rex was sent after him, but as he approached the man fired a revolver at him. He missed, and as he attempted to fire a second time, Rex jumped and caught his right arm. The man then managed to fire again, but Rex held him firmly until the detectives caught up to rearrest him. PC Holman called Rex off, and the instant his arm was free, the deserter ran away again. Rex was sent after him once more, but this time the man paused and aimed carefully before shooting at the dog. The

bullet grazed Rex's ear; the shock knocked him to the ground, and there were powder burns in his eyes which temporarily blinded him. But the time it took the man to aim allowed the detectives to seize him and hold him firmly under arrest.

Rex received a huge sympathetic postbag when the exploit was described in the press. He was awarded the Silver Medal of the People's Dispensary for Sick Animals and the Bronze Medal of the Canine Defence League. He was the first police dog to receive a CDL medal for bravery, and the medal from the PDSA was only the second bravery award it had ever made. When Keston Police Dog Training School was inaugurated that summer, Rex was used to 'open' it, standing beside Commissioner Sir John Nott-Bower as he formally cut the tape.

Rex pioneered 'sniffer dog' work by proving that he could detect drugs hidden in rooms, about people's clothes and in handbags, despite the masking scents of people, perfumes and tobacco. He was the first dog to succeed in tracing a person buried under fallen masonry (unfortunately too late to save a life).

In 1956 Rex was the first winner of the Black Knight Trophy, a gold cup for Police Dog of the year awarded by Lady Munnings, wife of Painter Sir Alfred, in honour of her Pekingese Black Knight. Rex was also trained to present a bouquet to Lady Munnings as she handed over the cup.

'RIOT CITY' Nickname for nine-acre Public Order Training Centre established at Hounslow Heath in 1980. 'Streets' providing a realistic environment for public order training, and 'rooms' which are to be searched for dangerous offenders. All officers are sent to Riot City to learn expeditious movement in Police Support Units, the use of shields and riot equipment, and efficient embarkation and disembarkation from specially adapted vehicles as part of their basic training. Mounted Police and Territorial Support Groups receive further specialist training, including the necessary tactics to deal with petrol bombs (for which hundreds of milk bottles are used every month in weekly exercises), other missiles, and specialist roles such as evidence gathering in riot situations and search techniques.

RIOT POLICE There are no dedicated Riot Police in England, though Police Support Units may be equipped with riot gear (visored helmets, protective clothing and shields) for serious public disorder incidents, and Territorial Support Groups receive a high level of specialized training for dealing with dangerous riot situations, among other things.

RIOTS In law, any assembly of 12 or more persons deliberately using violence to perpetrate breaches of the peace.

In practice, the kind of violent public disturbances the Metropolitan Police were specifically intended to prevent, most often caused by political demonstrations becoming inflamed and disorderly.

The Gordon Riots of 1780 developed from opposition to granting Roman Catholics civil rights. A huge drunken criminal mob seized the opportunity to rage through London for four days, burning and looting and causing untold damage. They were a lasting anxious memory for nearly 100 years, and fear of a repetition (especially following lesser riots in London in 1815), contributed greatly to middle-class support for the idea of a permanent police force.

The only effective control of a major riot was the use of troops. By law, once a magistrate had read the Riot Act ordering people to disperse, he could have troops fire on a disorderly crowd, and any resulting injury or loss of life was legally approved. Refusal to disperse was a crime punishable by the death penalty. By tradition, crowds were usually allowed one hour to disperse before the troops were sent in. But the growing agitation for Parliamentary reform led to mass meetings which were seen as potentially riotous by magistrates. When mounted soldiers were turned on a crowd in St Peter's Fields, Manchester in 1819, killing 11 people and injuring 600, the incident gained the name 'the Peterloo massacre'. One of Peel's aims was to avoid the use of the military in the control of civil disturbances.

The first serious political demonstration involving the Met was the Coldbath Fields Riot of 1833. An attempt at gentler crowd control deteriorated into the two-day Bull Ring Disorders of

THE BRIXTON RIOT, 1981. THE PUBLIC HOUSE PICTURED WAS LATER BURNT BY RIOTERS.

1839. But the art seemed to have been mastered when subsequent Chartist mass rallies passed off peacefully, and the demonstration against Lord Robert Grosvenor's Sunday Trading Bill (needlessly exacerbated into the Hyde Park Riot, 1855 by government attempts to ban it) was brought under control by 450 policemen, outnumbered 100 to 1. Then came the Hyde Park Riot, 1866 and troops had to be called in for the first time since the police were formed. They were present, too, at Bloody Sunday, 1887, and the Met was seemingly pitted by government against the deprived and the unemployed after the Trafalgar Square Demonstration and Riot, 1886 had toppled Commissioner Sir Edmund Henderson.

Mafeking Night, by contrast, could be described as a 'tolerated disorder', though the patriotic and often drunken demonstrators did not burn, loot or fight. There is a difference between a general exuberant celebration and an angry crowd with a grievance.

The militant suffragettes were neither in the traditional sense rioters, nor even crowds in need of control. Their politically motivated activities were intended to vent their grievance, sometimes regardless of the law, but the involvement of crowds in demonstrations was generally passive.

It became a matter of pride that the General Strike of 1926 led to no great clash between police and strikers. The great rallies of the unem-

ployed in the 1930s led to friction, but nothing deserving the name of a riot, perhaps because there was no focus for what later became known as mass picketing. The Battle of Cable Street, on the other hand, placed the Met in their most invidious position ever. Forced to defend Sir Oswald Mosley's legal right to hold a deliberately provocative Fascist march through the Jewish East End, they were routed by a mob of Jews and dockers, whose motives were unquestionably political and pro-democratic, and not mere troublemaking.

The early postwar years were singularly free from major unruly demonstrations. Even the monster rally in Trafalgar Square protesting against Sir Anthony Eden's Suez venture was easily contained by Mounted Police when some of the demonstrators tried to charge Whitehall and Downing Street. The Notting Hill Race Riots of 1958 were relatively small disturbances compared to those of the 1980s, but with the politically unimportant St Pancras Rent Riot of September 1960 there were signs which heralded two decades of ever-increasing political violence.

Large-scale demonstrations began with the Campaign for Nuclear Disarmament's annual marches to and from Aldermaston – good-humoured holiday occasions fronted by well-behaved celebrities and politicians. The Committee of 100 then escalated the situation by using the tactic of civil disobedience, and the policing of their Trafalgar Square Demonstration, 1961 shocked many respectable citizens who had generally disbelieved tales of police using excessive force. The 1967–8 Grosvenor Square Demonstration/Riots against the Vietnam War became increasingly violent as large crowds tried to overwhelm the American Embassy by sheer weight of numbers. Civil disobedience deteriorated to violent lawlessness, and finally this cost a life in the Red Lion Square Riot – the first time this had been the outcome of a political rally in London since 1887. But, like many 'Anti-Fascist' rallies of the period, Red Lion Square was essentially an excuse for a brawl between two opposing political factions who found extremist political labels

useful. The Grunwick Strike, by contrast, was a genuine industrial dispute, where weight of numbers, publicity, and mass picketing on a daily basis created policing problems. Secondary picketing gave the opportunity for troublemakers to join in and attack the police.

Meantime, recurrent disorders at the Notting Hill Carnival warned of troubles ahead in rioting directed against the police. These disturbances resulted in the first informal use of dustbin lids as shields to ward off missiles thrown at the police, and in the Lewisham Riot, 1976, proper riot shields were used for the first time.

The Brixton Riots, 1981 showed that a serious breakdown in trust between the police (among other agencies) and younger members of the black community boded ill for the future. But they were accompanied by riots in Bristol and Liverpool, and the Scarman Report concluded that inner city deprivation was the main cause.

The small-scale Southall Riot, notable for the death of Blair Peach, might have given warning about ethnic tension, but the circumstances of his death and whether it had been caused by police became the main issue.

But racial tension exploded horribly in the Brixton Riots, 1981 and the Broadwater Farm Riot. The latter was notable for the first murder of a police officer during a riot since 1833, and the first occasion ever on which rioters used firearms against the police.

The Miners' Strike (1984–5) was notable for the establishment of a National Reporting Centre (later the Mutual Aid Coordinating Centre), and the large number of police deployed on a national basis to combat mass picketing. The Wapping Pickets outside the News International

TRAFALGAR SQUARE IN THE AFTERMATH OF THE POLL TAX RIOT, 1990.

RIVER POLICE IN THE POOL OF LONDON.

company headquarters in 1986 would have been difficult to police under the best of circumstances, given the difficulty of directing the demonstration marches to a better location and meeting ground. Both disputes were manifestations of structural changes in the respective industries; both degenerated into occasions of noisy rioting; and both resulted in recriminations against individual officers on picket lines.

Finally the Poll Tax Riot was the first occasion since 1855 when a very wide range of opinions and backgrounds were represented in a very large demonstration against government policy. Despite an attempted sit-down at Downing Street, and attacks on police who tried to reroute the march around it, this might have passed off as a risky but acceptable assembly for political protest had not a small anarchist minority used

the cover of the demonstration for serious offences including arson.

Football brought a separate set of problems when sheer mischief-making riot for riot's sake began to be practised by hooligans. Elation or dissatisfaction with the result of a match had no real part in their wanton mayhem. Rather, the football matches provided a focus for a sinister hard core of violent trouble-makers to use the cover of a generally respectable sport to provoke fighting by minorities within the large crowds of genuine supporters.

See also Marine Police Office Riot, 1798.

RIVER POLICE Officially Thames Division (CO52; formerly TO29 and A10). Originally the Marine Police Office. All its stations along the river are in the CO52 Command unit, but use the letter U in their Divisional Codes.

'The River Police' is the universally used popular name for the Division which patrols the

River Thames, originally to prevent theft and piracy from vessels in the Port of London, today to deal with river-based crime and promote safety on the water. Founded in 1798, the River Police are the oldest patrolling part of the Met, the first police force introduced in London, and arguably the first police force in the world whose duties were entirely desirable crime prevention and peace-keeping with no extension into spying on opponents of government.

The Port of London was for 500 years the largest river port (and at times the largest commercial port of any kind) in the world. Prior to the construction of reasonably secure walled docks, vessels using the port were moored in tiers by open quays on the Thames, which made them vulnerable to theft. By the last decade of the 18th century this was organized on such a scale that total losses in 1797 were valued at £506,000. Seamen, dockworkers and junior Customs officers were all active in plundering what they could from cargoes, 'mudlarks' gathered on the foreshore around beached ships at low tide to collect any marketable or usable goods thrown over the side to them by men aboard, and pirates armed with guns and cutlasses plied the river between Greenwich and the Tower at night.

In 1796, Patrick Colquhoun, a merchant and magistrate, published an anonymous treatise on the Police of the Metropolis, explaining the various crimes and suggesting remedies. It was well received. Early in 1798 Colquhoun met the inventor and former sailor John Harriott who had worked out a scheme for just such a force, costed at £14,000 p.a. The two men combined their ideas, reduced the costing to £5,000 p.a., and with the support of the West India Company persuaded the government to give the scheme a trial. The Chancellor of the Exchequer agreed to find £980 of the cost and the West India Company supplied the remainder.

The largest element in the new Marine Police was the force of 220 constables and about 1000 registered dockworkers (lumpers) who could be hired to load and unload vessels. The lumpers were given uniform clothing which did not include pockets or the traditional docker's apron, long used for concealing stolen goods. The constables were not uniformed but, given the prevailing lawlessness, they were heavily equipped. Not only did they have the traditional watchmen's rattles, lanterns and truncheons, they were allowed hangers (60cm/24 inch curved swords) and firearms, and they were given cutlass and pike drill. The large numbers, however, were introduced gradually. The Marine Police opened with 35 gangs of 10 dockers apiece, each under the direction of two constables and one master stevedore.

The River Police proved immediately successful. A total of 2200 people were convicted of misdemeanours at Thames Court in its first year of existence, of whom 200 were imprisoned. Two Customs officers were hanged for helping sailors steal a load of coffee. The West India Company saved £150,000 compared with the previous year's losses.

Colquhoun and Harriott were worthy predecessors to Rowan and Mayne. Like the great founding Metropolitan Commissioners they were a complementary pair, Colquhoun having legal experience and diplomatic tact, and Harriott knowing seamanship and man-management, and having the driving determination to see his force succeed and survive over the 16 years he headed

SAVED FROM DROWNING: THE RIVER POLICE AT WORK IN THE 1930s.

it following Colquhoun's return to the land-based magistracy.

In 1800 Colquhoun published another treatise 'on the commerce and police of the River Thames, suggesting means for preventing the depredations by a legislative system of River Police.' This supported Henry Dundas's efforts in carrying an Enabling Bill through Parliament to confirm the existence of the Marine Police for a further seven years, with an increased budget of £8,000 and two stipendiary magistrates to assist Harriott. At the same time, the Marine Police's responsibility for registering and licensing the huge body of stevedores with their foremen and supervising constables was dropped. Henceforth bye-laws would control the activities of dock workers. When new docks were opened at Poplar the following year, the constables appointed to guard them were attached to Harriott's police force. In 1804 a cutter was purchased to operate below Greenwich and police

the river as far downstream as Sheerness. It was replaced by a large 18-ton cutter in 1808, which housed an inspector and eight constables for two-week tours of duty. When the Enabling Act came up for renewal in 1807, it passed without question.

After Harriott's retirement in 1816, the new Resident Magistrate, former naval officer Thomas Richbell, opened a second Police Office aboard the former warship *Port Mahon*, moored in the Thames alongside Somerset House. This, the first of the floating Police Stations, was to become the Upstream (and above bridge) station. The Thames Police Office in Wapping was the Middle Station, and hulks at Blackwall became the Lower Station until the building of a small house in 1894. By the time Peel's Police Act established the Metropolitan Police in 1829, these three stations controlled a fleet of 15 boats, three of which were always patrolling between Brentford and Deptford at any given time.

The 1839 Police Act recognized the success of Peel's creation, and consolidated it by amalgamating all peace officers within an enlarged Metropolitan District. By this Act, the Marine Police was subsumed into the Metropolitan Police as the Thames Division. They turned in their blunderbusses and hangers, but were given a hugely improved budget of £20,000 a year and were reissued with swords, which they carried until 1922, and were given a uniform. James Evans, who had been Master Boat Surveyor since 1821, became Superintendent of the new Division. Other surveyors were made Inspectors. Those whose rank was really equivalent to Sergeants in the Metropolitan Police became Inspectors, 2nd or 3rd Class, because it was felt their very wide Customs warrants to search and seize required this superior title, which remained a peculiarity of Thames Division until the 20th century.

Waterloo Pier was rented in 1873 in place of the old floating Upstream Station, and with a barge moored to it became the most familiar

River Police base actually on the water. In 1875 a Divisional CID of four plain clothes officers were sent out on patrols – a curiously ineffective measure, since the police galleys were instantly recognized by all watermen. The River CID was dissolved in 1917; then re-formed; and dissolved finally in 1975 to be replaced by a Divisional Investigation Officer, with uniformed support, to investigate and prepare the paperwork on all dead bodies discovered by the River Police, and refer suspicious cases back to the land-based CID.

Recovering dead bodies has always been a large part of the River Police's work. The *Princess Alice* disaster of 1878 (sometimes inaccurately described as the Woolwich Ferry disaster) was the worst accident ever to occur on the Thames, when the iron screw-propelled collier *Bywell Castle* ran down the flimsy paddle steamer *Princess Alice*, sending it straight to the bottom with the loss of over 600 of the 800 day-trippers it had been carrying back from the coast. The poor navigation which caused the accident led to the introduction of Thames navigation rules.

At the inquiry into the disaster, it was pointed out that the police galleys and cutters were inadequate: for modern conditions they needed steam-powered vessels to patrol the water. In the 1880s two were purchased. The habit of thinking 'above bridge' and 'below bridge' was of longstanding, and they patrolled respectively upstream and downstream of London Bridge. By 1898 the River Police fleet consisted of 10 steam launches and 28 oared galleys. As the 20th century began, experiments were made with petrol-and-paraffin engines to power the galleys. The first, constructed by River Police Sergeant Engineer George Mitchell, proved too weak to make its way under London Bridge against the ebbtide. The next, designed by Sir John Thorneycroft, was top-heavy, unseaworthy and liable to capsize. Sergeant George Spooner was drowned in 1913 after his Thorneycroft 'Handy Billy' failed to complete a turn against the tide below Southwark Bridge and was swept broadside under a barge. Thereafter a variety of custom-designed working motor-boats gradually replaced the old galleys fitted with engines.

Since 1910 the division has also maintained from one to three motor launches for very senior officers and ceremonial occasions. These are usually named after the founding fathers of the police. *Sir Richard Mayne* was the first, and others have included the *John Harriott*, the *Patrick Colquhoun* and the *Sir Robert Peel*. When three very handsome ex-RAF rescue launches were acquired for conversion in 1946, these ceremonial vessels acquired the nickname 'green parrots', because their hulls were painted bright green. And the nickname has stuck, even though their fibreglass successors are naval blue. Green Parrot crews are expected to have the diplomatic skills to attend VIPs and, on occasion, royalty.

The River Police expanded steadily until the mid-1970s, reaching its peak with 216 officers operating 33 motor boats from seven stations, from Erith to Shepperton. Retrenchment came very quickly with the collapse of the London docks. Hampton Station was reduced to a mooring after less than 10 years in service. Erith and Blackwall were closed before 1980, Barnes in 1994. And in 1991 Waterloo pier, the Thames-users' favourite River Police landmark and the world's only remaining floating police station, was reduced to a 'jump station', with two officers on duty to crew a rescue boat for anyone leaping off the bridge.

But with 131 officers crewing 6 fast patrol boats between Wapping and Dartford, 12 duty boats (the small Noddy boats), 2 rigid inflatables and the *Patrick Colquhoun* as 'Divisional Command Vessel', the River Police still play an important role for Thames users. Even though more pleasure than commercial craft now use the river, it remains a very busy waterway and the River Police still have the difficult, dangerous and distressing work of recovering about 60 bodies from the Thames every year. The 20th century's worst river accident was the *Marchioness* disaster of 1989, when the heavy dredger *Bowbelle* emerged downstream from Southwark Bridge to smash into the light pleasure boat's stern, sinking it instantly. Five police duty boats equipped with Morse teleflex, loud-hailers, searchlights, VHF radio and echo-sounders as well as first aid and resuscitation equipment rushed to the scene. They rescued 53 of the 87 survivors, and helped the m.v.*Hurlingham* rescue the remaining 34. The Underwater Search Unit

which had been attached to Thames Division HQ in 1964 had to dive and recover the bodies of the 24 passengers and crew trapped below decks, while the River Police recovered the remaining 27 bodies from the river. The work of finding and recovering decomposed bodies is recognized as unusual and unpleasant, and until recently search payment was always paid. This long stood at 6/8d (33p), but rose to £15.95 before its abolition in the 1990s.

The River Police are now the smallest of the Metropolitan Divisions. All officers are volunteers who have completed two years ordinary policing in uniform. They have to prove their ability to swim, handle a dinghy and tie basic seaman's knots and they are then given a year's training in navigation, boat-handling, radio operation and marine law. The Division evinces unusual solidarity and cohesion, even by the very close standards of the police. This is apparent in the activities of the Thames Police Association and the contributions to its journal. Much of their work is again combating pilfering, nowadays directed against the host of cabin cruisers and private pleasure boats on the river. Many officers and river-users regret the reduction of constant patrolling which offered much the same reassuring sense of security as beat duty on land, but managerial staff point out that a patrol boat answering a call for help can take two hours to reach the incident, whereas an inflatable transported by a van can be on the spot in 20 minutes.

The best summary of rivermen's attitude to the River Police was given by a retired lighterman and former holder of the Doggett's Coat and Badge who told an Inspector, 'They luvs yer, boy; they luvs yer.'

See also Tilts, Toe-Bags.

ROBERTS, DET SGT NORWELL, QPM (B.1945) First black police officer.

Born Anguilla, nephew of Hendon-trained Anguilla policeman. Brought to England as a child. Despite passing 11 plus exam, refused grammar school place on pretext he 'hadn't learned English ways'. Worked as university lab technician before joining the Met, 1967.

As the first black British police officer (an East African Asian from Coventry had been

PC NORWELL ROBERTS DURING TRAINING.

attested the previous year), Norwell Roberts attracted instant press attention, appearing on the cover of *Private Eye* and in newspaper articles in the southern USA states expressing shock at the appointment. Paul Condon, later Commissioner Sir Paul, was among his intake at Hendon, and was not among the small number who subjected him to racist tormenting. Some did, however, and Norwell Roberts' first few years in the police were among the unhappiest of his life. His property was damaged; he was subjected to insults; and a humiliating climax came when a passing officer in a patrol car shouted, 'Black bastard!' at him while he was on beat patrol in Covent Garden. Learning later of his miserable experiences, many officers of his generation who had known him slightly realized that they should have made more positive efforts to welcome him into the force, something finding fruit in the 1990s when Sir Paul Condon made intense efforts to excise racism from the Met.

At the same time, Norwell Roberts was subjected to abuse as a 'traitor' to the black community when he policed demonstrations. It was two years before another black officer was recruited and three years before they were joined by a third, so that Roberts was a very conspicuous figure in London in the late 1960s.

Transfer to the CID started a considerable improvement. Working on a bank robbery, he found himself among colleagues who accepted him. He had a very distinguished detective career, winning an outstanding commendation for the arrest of five contract killers in 1985, and two other commendations for covert operations with the Drugs Squad. He was in fact the first black undercover officer and was involved in numerous operations leading to many hardened criminals being brought to justice. He did a considerable amount of work against burglary artifice (gaining entry by deception) at Barnet and contributed to the formulation of the famous phrase, 'If in doubt, keep them out!' In 1996 he was awarded the QPM for 30 years' distinguished service with the Metropolitan Police. On his retirement in 1997 he received so many letters of congratulation and commendation that the Black Police Association opened a website to display them to the world.

He was certainly the first black officer in living memory. Interestingly a Superintendent Robert Branford (retired 1876) was apparently of mixed race, and a 1910 photograph arguably shows an officer of African descent at Chislehurst.

ROBERTSON, PC STEPHEN (1916–1941)

Policeman whose ghost is alleged to haunt Buckingham Palace.

The North Lodge of Buckingham Palace was bombed in an air raid in March, 1941. PC Robertson from Dagenham, a member of the Royalty Protection Branch, was on duty, and was crushed and buried under falling masonry. A rescue squad heard him tapping for help and dug him out, but he died on the way to hospital.

Subsequently mysterious scratchings were reported from the spot where he was trapped, and one observer claimed to have seen the ghostly figure of a policeman materialize and dissolve.

In 1998, after PC Alan Graham of the Royalty Protection Branch had researched the incident, his request that a memorial should be placed was granted. In the presence of Commissioner Sir Paul Condon, the Queen Mother unveiled a plaque to PC Robertson.

ROLLS OF HONOUR (1) The Metropolitan

Police War Memorial Book, containing the name of 1076 members of the Metropolitan Police who gave their lives in the World Wars, was deposited and dedicated in Westminster Abbey in the presence of King George VI and Queen Elizabeth on 27 July 1950.
(2) The Roll of Honour (see Appendix 4) recording the names of members of the service who have died since 1920 in the course of duties involving special gallantry or risks.

ROUTE PAPERS Means of communication

before the invention of the telegraph.

In the early years, when information requiring immediate distribution across the force was received at a station (say the commission of a major crime and/or the escape of the perpetrator), the station inspector drafted a note on a special form, to be carried by a reserve officer to the nearest station in the next Division. It carried printed spaces for each recipient to initial and endorse with the time of receipt before sending it on to the next Division. At the same time a copy or copies were sent out to Sergeants on patrol, and the next body of men coming on duty were informed. In this way, the whole force was told of emergencies over a matter of six hours or so.

Route papers were returned to Scotland Yard so that the proper circulation of information could be checked, and any officers failing to respond promptly could be reprimanded, while any who had acted with particular diligence and efficiency could be commended.

A useful representative collection of route papers and inspectors' reports on when they received them and how they dealt with them is to be found in the Public Record Office papers on the Daniel Good case (1842).

ROWAN, SIR CHARLES, KCB

(C.1782–1852) Commissioner 1829–50.

Born in Ulster, fifth of 10 sons of improvident Co. Antrim landowner Robert Rowan. Ensign, 52nd Foot, 1797; Paymaster and Lt, 1798. Captain, 1803; Brigade-Major, 1809. Major of 52nd Regiment, 1811; Brevet Lt-Colonel, 1812. Commanded a wing of his regiment at Waterloo, where wounded. CB, 1815. Retd. from army, 1822. First Magistrate (Founding Joint Commissioner), Metropolitan Police, 1829. KCB, 1848. Retd, 1850. Died at his home in Park Lane, 1852.

Charles Rowan preceded his elder brother William (later Field-Marshal Sir William) into his regiment, and both served in the Napoleonic Wars, in Sicily (1806–7), Sweden (1808), and from the Peninsula through France to Waterloo (1815). In the Peninsula he served under Sir John Moore and learned Moore's innovatory preference for humane rather than brutalizing discipline. He also learned Moore's 'Shorncliffe System' of using liaising bands of skirmishers instead of a solid phalanx as advance-guard or rear-guard. Both would be applied to the Metropolitan Police Force.

Rowan's activities between 1822 and 1829 are not known (though Sir John Moylan's *Scotland Yard* of 1929 records, without citing his source, that he was a magistrate in Ireland). On 2 May 1829, Sir George Murray, Wellington's former Quartermaster-General in the Peninsula, wrote from Downing Street to Rowan that his name was to be put before Home Secretary Sir Robert Peel on a shortlist of candidates to head the proposed Metropolitan Police Force. Peel originally offered the post of 'first of the two magistrates' to Lt-Col. James Shaw, who turned it down flat on 29 June, and might have proved less suitable than Rowan, since some years later he resigned the headship of the Irish Constabulary on the grounds that the judiciary wanted to usurp his authority. Just such a struggle would occupy the first five years of Charles Rowan's tenure of the Metropolitan Police Magistracy, which he was offered immediately, Peel having been advised by 'the highest Military Authorities' (probably Wellington and Murray) that Rowan had brought the 52nd Regiment 'to the highest state of discipline' when he was its colonel.

On 6 July, Peel introduced Rowan to Richard Mayne, 14 years his junior, a barrister who would be his close colleague for the next 21 years and supply the legal half of the military and legal team. The two accepted their posts and started work the following day, drawing up plans for the force of about 1000 men Peel and Parliament rather vaguely envisaged. Their draft plan was accepted by Peel on 20 July. Before they were sworn in as Justices of the Peace by Lord Chief Baron Sir William Alexander at his Grosvenor Square home on 29 August, they were already being described as the Police Commissioners, the title Pitt's Police Bill had proposed for the chief magistrates it wished to create.

During July, No. 4 Whitehall Place fell vacant, and the Commissioners were promptly moved into it as their headquarters. As it was altered and extended for police purposes, a residential apartment for Rowan was created upstairs.

The older and senior partner with experience in command and man-management, Rowan played the main part in devising the plan for six Divisions to police an area from the Angel, Islington in the north to the Elephant and Castle in the south, and from Whitechapel in the east to Hyde Park in the west. Each Division was divided into eight sections and each section into eight beats. The model was an army regiment divided into companies and platoons. The flexible beat system, by which constables would almost cross each other's tracks and could come to each other's aid, was directly borrowed from Sir John Moore's Shorncliffe system. But Rowan was aware that the public feared a bullying militarized police: the only rank whose title he borrowed from the army was Sergeant. His 'privates' took the name of the old parish constable; his senior officers took the titles of other parochial administrators – Inspectors and Superintendents.

Fear of militarization, balanced by fear of spying, led to intense debate about whether or not there should be uniforms for the police. On balance, the chiefs concluded that British loathing of unidentifiable political spies outweighed the threatening appearance of a uniform, which in any case would have a deterrent effect on would-be criminals when an identifiable police uniform appeared. Peel's original grandiose notion of scarlet and gold was wisely overruled in favour of the blue swallowtail and stovepipe hat, which came as close as possible to smart civilian clothes. Rowan's hand has been detected in this decision, though with characteristic modesty he did not lay claim to it when describing the uniform debates to the Parliamentary Select Committee of 1833. Similar anxieties about a 'gendarmerie' led to the original policemen's equipment being confined to rattles, truncheons and lanterns.

Nonetheless, Rowan was a soldier. Disciplined men, for him, meant drilled men. To the mingled amusement and alarm of the public, he had his recruits square-bashing in Old Palace Yard even before their uniforms had been supplied and they could march on to the streets.

Rowan probably wrote the first half of the magnificent *General Instructions* book and laid down the command structure and guidelines. As his greatest legacy to British policing, Rowan insisted on a high standard of personal conduct,

SIR CHARLES ROWAN.

unshakeable respect for the civil rights of all citizens, and the habit of courtesy to the public at all times. These were enforced by rigid discipline. Drunkenness was the first thing to be avoided at all costs. Drunkenness on duty meant instant dismissal: this, coupled with absenteeism, led to policemen being sacked before the force had even taken to the streets, and during the first two years of the force's existence, the commissioners dismissed and replaced half the entire manpower for these offences. Loitering in pubs and conversing with women there was also forbidden, as was conversation with prostitutes. Two policemen were sacked in the early years when they were found to have contracted venereal disease. Prevention of crime rather than detection of crimi-

nals was the force's first duty, and policemen were therefore prohibited from following the Bow Street Runners' suspect practice of associating with criminals to cultivate informants. Officers were warned against shouldering civilians out of their way on the streets, or even staring in people's faces if they were on duty at church services.

But while he was strict in using his Commissioner's authority to punish bad behaviour, Rowan was equally determined to follow Moore's principle that authoritarian treatment of unexceptionable behaviour must be avoided. Superintendents were enjoined to be firm and just but kind and conciliating to the men under their command, and they were expected to get to know them all personally. In the lower ranks, tantrums and swearing were not proper policemanly behaviour: one Sergeant was dismissed for flying off the handle when making a legitimate arrest. This was not conduct worthy of a policeman.

Rowan and Mayne's achievement was astonishing. Financial chief John Wray, appointed Receiver, took some weight off their backs, and their chief clerk Charles Yardley proved a tower of strength. Superintendent John May of A Division was conveniently close at hand, and was used rather as though he were an unofficial Chief Constable. But it was essentially Rowan and Mayne who, in a mere 12 weeks, assembled and set on the streets a working organization of 895 uniformed men armed with truncheons and commanded by 100 officers. Rowan and Mayne implemented the pay scales and interviewed recruits, drew up working orders for each day, designed, ordered and distributed uniforms and equipment, and found and furnished station houses. They personally swore the men in at the Foundling Hospital on 16 September. The men had learned the beats they would tour in alternating six-hour shifts before they went on duty at 6.00 p.m. on 29 September. The entire force was strictly enjoined to ignore unimportant mockery and deal firmly but courteously with serious hostility.

And the public were encouraged to bring any complaints about the police to the Commissioners. Rowan and Mayne dealt personally with an immense volume of complaints, always offering complainants the alternative of taking a policeman to court if they preferred.

Rowan tried to use the maximum tact and diplomacy in dealing with envious magistrates and parish vestries who did not like losing their own constables. He was patient when several parishes dragged their feet over sending him the lists of their constables he required, and Marylebone tried to postpone responding for a year. He silently swallowed the insult when some magistrates continued to use the Bow Street Runners in preference to the Metropolitan Police for a few years. He insisted on maintaining a strictly nonpartisan stance, even though the Tories who had created the force were far more sympathetic to it than the Whigs, who had opposed it, and the Radicals who were downright hostile, seeing it as an instrument of Tory oppression.

He took personal command of riot control as the Reform agitation increased disorder on the streets in October 1830. Knowing his men could easily be overrun by a larger mob, he started by ordering the police to practise passive resistance to a would-be violent demonstration at Hyde Park Corner on 28 October. The proto-Gandhian tactic was an immediate success, confusing the potential rioters and leading to the crowd's peaceable dispersal as they quickly lost enthusiasm for beating policemen who wouldn't fight back. But it was too demanding and risky a tactic to be maintained, and the baton charge replaced it the following month.

Rowan took personal command of the arrangements for policing the Calthorpe Street demonstration which deteriorated into the Coldbath Fields Riot. The Committee of Inquiry into that disaster heard that, 'The last words spoken by Colonel Rowan to those who alone were expected to take an active part in the affair, were to be cool and temperate, to hurt or strike no one unnecessarily, or unless they resisted.'

While the Parliamentary Select Committee on the Police was ruminating what actions should be taken with respect to the four-year-old police force, the government changed and the Whig Home Secretary Lord Duncannon ordered the Commissioners to dismiss Supt Lazenby and

Inspector Wovenden following a demonstrably false accusation that the latter had raped a prostitute in the cells. Rowan wrote a dignified letter in their defence on 6 November, but did not tender his own resignation as he and Mayne realized that the hostile Whigs could maim the new force if given the chance to replace them with apathetic Commissioners. This diplomacy paid off when the consequent Parliamentary Select Committee on the Police Report of 13 August 1834 made the firm recommendation that apart from Rowan and Mayne, the stipendiary magistrates should be stripped of the power to control police, and all their constables including the Bow Street Runners were to be transferred to or supplied by the Met, which should also extend its jurisdiction to embrace the City of London. Although these recommendations were not realized until 1839 (when the City hastily organized its own force to avoid being handed over to Rowan and Mayne), the grudging respect the Metropolitan Police had earned by its success in reducing crime sharply was acknowledged when in 1835 the Whig Home Secretary Lord John Russell yielded to Rowan's long-running plea that some definite commitment be made to pay policemen a fixed sum if they were injured on duty.

He did not, however, accede to Rowan's other bold recommendation, that a national police force should be established under the control of the Metropolitan Commissioners, even though this was supported by Edwin Chadwick the sanitary reformer. Fear of a politically controlled quasi-military force ensured that the subsequent borough and county constabularies would be introduced piecemeal, with no one man ever holding too much power over them.

The highest recognition of Rowan's achievement came in 1848 when, with the police generally accepted by the middle classes as a worthwhile institution, he was awarded the KCB. A few eyebrows were raised that Mayne was only given the CB at the same time, but Rowan was the older man and had always been the senior partner. Moreover his health was beginning to give way. In 1850 he retired, as well he might at the age of nearly 78. Two years later he died of cancer.

It is, arguably, scandalous that there is no official standard biography of Rowan, or, better,

of the partnership of Rowan and Mayne. If great Victorians who gave us the steam engine, the postage stamp and the electric telegraph are commemorated, along with several hundred local bigwigs and philanthropists and obscure generals, in London's proliferating statuary, how much greater is our inheritance from Charles Rowan, who, far more truly than Robert Peel, devised the true form of the British bobby, and enforced on him that respect for the public and freedom from jack-in-office tyranny which, at its best, has led to the foreign visitors' cliché, 'Your police are wonderful.'

ROYAL COMMISSION, 1908 Cmnd 4156.

Set up by Home Secretary Herbert Gladstone in 1906 to inquire into the duties of the Metropolitan Police with respect to drunkenness, disorder and solicitation in the streets. It responded to parliamentary pressure over the Mme D'Angely affair, and a complaint to the Home Office from Dr Maurice Gerothwohl FRCL and M. Henri Lavalette that they had been arrested on Boat Race night and charged with being drunk and disorderly, when they were simply trying to protest about the excessively forceful arrest of a young groom.

The Commission invited anyone with complaints against the police arising from alleged or actual offences on the streets over the past four years to submit them. They received 300 letters, of which only 19 fell within their terms of reference: offences against public order on the streets. They examined their 19 cases with scrupulous thoroughness, and found 9 officers guilty of misconduct and 4 who had made errors of judgment (usually station officers accepting charges they should have queried).

Mme D'Angely's case was hopelessly lost, the French police proving that she was definitely a habitual prostitute. Only one other lady came forward at first to claim that the police had wantonly charged her with prostitution. (Actually Mrs Braham's hysteria when she realized what was happening led to her being wrongfully charged with drunkenness.) The Commission appealed for more to come forward, and managed to unearth two further complaints, from members of such respectable classes that their evidence was heard in camera and their identities were veiled under initials. Mr Y, a young motor engineer, had gone by prearrangement to take a friend's mistress to supper in the West End. When she and her lady friend resisted arrest for soliciting, he urged them to go quietly; and accompanied them, protesting and offering bail, until he too was arrested for trying to help them escape. All three were bound over by the magistrate. Mr Y was obviously honest and gallant, but naive. Miss A and Miss B declined to appear before the Commission and have the certainty that they were common prostitutes rather than classy kept women exposed.

Mrs X's case was even stranger. The Spanish wife of a prominent naval architect from Balham, she had been his mistress for two of the six years they lived together. Since her marriage, she had taken to visiting Hampstead when he was away on business. There, she said, she gave French or Spanish or general conversation lessons to a French woman whose address she could not remember and had always refused to tell her husband. (Her testimony was voluble and persistently self-contradictory.) Travelling by bus on these occasions, she broke her journeys at Oxford Circus, where she was frequently seen soliciting. On being charged, she said (apparently truthfully), 'I don't do this for money. I do it for love.' The Commission believed that if the Hampstead 'French woman' and her French lessons had any existence at all, they probably concealed assignations with a male lover. The police were cleared again.

Two of the four drunk and disorderly complaints were really complaints that the arresting officers had lost their tempers and falsely charged men who annoyed them. These complaints were upheld. The respectable and sober Belgian professor's was not. Gerothwohl and Lavalette's excitability, the Commission found, justified the police in finding them disorderly, even though they were not drunk.

The complaints against police brutality included some fascinating cases. One officer had justifiably felled a brutal assailant with his truncheon, but then blotted his copybook by going on beating him where he lay. Another was found not to have hit the Post Office clerk he ejected

PUNCH APPROVES THE MET'S CLEAN BILL OF HEALTH FROM THE ROYAL COMMISSION, 1908.

from an alley in Clerkenwell, but avoiding the main complaint did him little good, as the Commission found that the clerk had indeed found him there *in flagrante* with a little prostitute (who, unusually, seemed to have touched the Commissioners by her simplicity). And an East End copper had savagely booted a streetwalker's favourite punter, permanently damaging his urethra, when the lady of the night refused to abandon her regular customer for a 'short time' round the corner with the policeman. The Commission thought the fight was about normal by Whitechapel standards, except that the victim was a bit pusillanimous in not standing up to take his lumps. And (improper though his con-

duct was), the policeman had not meant to inflict quite such serious injury. (Subsequently the Met and the courts took a less tolerant view, and both the PC and his Sergeant, who had failed to discipline or report him, were given jail sentences.)

This case, and several others, were brought before the Commission on the initiative of the young East End gang leader Arthur Harding, who also jumped at the chance to strike a blow at his old enemy Inspector Wensley, whom he accused of setting up a perjured case against him for hitting a constable who was arresting one of Harding's gang. Harding's complaint was rejected with contempt, as was the wickedly impudent claim of another two of his gangsters that a policeman to whom they had administered a vicious beating in a dark alley before he managed to lay one of them out with his truncheon had actually started an unprovoked assault on the man he arrested.

Given the complaints which set it off, the Royal Commission was a great waste of public money. But like most of the old government blue books, it provides a splendid quarry for the historian.

Also see under Complaints, and cf. Miss Cass, Docks, Lee Commission, Macmillan Committee, Irene Savidge, Sir Basil Thomson.

ROYAL PALACES DIVISION (SO15)

Now part of SO14 Royalty Protection Division. The direct descendant of the plain clothes division, established in 1839 to guard the royal palaces within the Metropolitan Police District. At that time the palaces all fell within A Division, (Whitehall)'s territory, and so A Division men assumed responsibility for them and for the Royal Parks.

In 1993 Royal Palaces Division amalgamated with Royalty Protection to form an enlarged SO 14 within Royalty and Diplomatic Protection Department. Approximately 265 officers, responsible for permanently policing Buckingham Palace, Kensington Palace, and St James's Palace and Windsor Castle. Officers also travel to and cover Balmoral Castle, Holyrood House and the Castle of Mey in Scotland when the Queen or other members of the Royal Family are in residence. Armed officers are placed both inside the palaces and in the grounds. Policing of Sandringham passed from the Metropolitan Police to Norfolk Constabulary in 1937.

In addition to placing uniformed police at fixed vantage points around the buildings and grounds, the Division maintains a comprehensive security system including video and electronic surveillance. There is a control room in Buckingham Palace which is permanently staffed by officers monitoring the security systems. The Division manages the rigorous pass system imposed on palace staff, visitors and contractors. The nature of the buildings and the royal family make perfect security impossible. Very large residences and castles with extensive gardens cannot be maintained as acceptable homes and at the same time securely exclude the uninvited well-wishers, paparazzi and persons of unsound mind who persistently want to intrude. The outer protective wall has been breached on several occasions. A boy called Cotton was found inside Buckingham Palace in 1838, and claimed to have lived there for a year. 'The boy Jones' gained entry to Buckingham Palace three times, and was caught and sent to prison on 3 December 1840. Released the following March, he was again captured inside the palace and ended up in Broadmoor. In 1982, Michael Fagan entered the Palace and penetrated to the Queen's bedroom. A little earlier two foreign girl tourists pitched a tent to bivouac overnight in the gardens. Following those incidents, a highly sophisticated system was introduced. Contingency plans include calling in aid the soldiers on guard at the palaces, whose presence is not merely ornamental or for the entertainment of tourists.

Aside from anxiety about possible terrorist attacks, the Division's most worrying recurrent duties are the large

social occasions which bring crowds of guests into the palaces: garden parties and investitures, or the Knights of the Garter celebrations at Windsor. These, like public order policing at processions and public ceremonies, are occasions when large numbers of Metropolitan Police officers are called upon for quite demanding extra duties, and carry them out with such unobtrusive success that they generally go unnoticed and unsung.

ROYAL PARKS POLICE Force independent of the Met with responsibility for Hyde Park and Kensington Gardens, Regent's Park, Green Park, Greenwich and St James's Park. Instantly recognizable by helmets topped with a short ball-ended pillar rather than a rose. Formed by the London County Council in 1896 with responsibility for all the above parks except Hyde Park, which passed from the Met to their jurisdiction on 1 April 1993.

ROYALTY AND DIPLOMATIC PROTEC-TION DEPARTMENT Amalgamation, for administrative purposes, of Royalty Protection Branch SO14, Diplomatic Protection Group SO16, and the Palace of Westminster Division SO17

HYDE PARK POLICE STATION, 1982.

including the Special Escort Group.

The Department was formed in 1983 by combining the Royalty Protection Department (as it was then called) with the Diplomatic Protection Group. It retained the former's headquarters in Buckingham Gate, and coordinated a tighter security system following Michael Fagan's entry the previous year.

ROYALTY PROTECTION BRANCH SO14 While SO14 Branch now embraces the Royal Palaces Division and the Special Escort Group, the Specialist Operation number was originally allocated to the approximately 80 Authorised Firearms Officers who act as Protection Officers to members of the Royal Family. All are uniformed branch officers in plain clothes.

The police have semi-officially supplied occasional Protection Officers for the Sovereign ever since two Bow Street Runners were allocated to accompany George III on his public appearances, following the mad housemaid Margaret Nicholson's attempt to stab him with a table-knife in 1786. Since the work was intended to prevent crime, and not detect it after the event, the plain-clothes work of protecting royal parties attending the theatre remained in the hands of uniformed officers from A Division, even after the formation of the Detective Branch in the 1840s. Royal Theatre Protection Patrols were partly selected for their manners and bearing, and were supplied with evening dress for the occasion if necessary. The several attempts on Queen Victoria's life, however, were normally made while she was driving in her carriage, and the uniformed police lining the streets might have been better briefed in relation to suspicious characters.

By the 1890s Special Branch had established a fine reputation for security policing, and the habit grew up of selecting royal Protection Officers from their number for a period. Patrick Quinn was prominent among the early royal Protection Offi-

THE 1882 ATTEMPT ON QUEEN VICTORIA'S LIFE BY RODERICK MACLEAN AT WINDSOR RAILWAY STATION.

cers, and may owe his unique knighthood while still a Superintendent to this position. In the early part of the 20th century, patriotism and the public's pro-monarchical affection for Edward VII, George V and Queen Mary were at such a high tide that Special Branch officers assigned to royal protection duties regarded the crowds as themselves essentially protective of royalty. The only attempt to assassinate Edward VII (and the last attempt on the life of a Sovereign) was made by the anarchist Spirido in Brussels, and Special Branch saw liaison with continental detective forces when royals travelled abroad as a major part of their duties. Xavier Paoli of the *Sûreté* was a particularly esteemed colleague.

Special Branch also made itself responsible for guarding visiting foreign royalty, and even after WWI, Inspector Herbert Fitch (Warrant No. 91520) acknowledged a continuing affection for the Kaiser and a concomitant lack of admiration for Marshal Foch. Prior to WWII it was acceptable for royal protection officers to publish memoirs with modestly intimate sketches of their principals as they knew them. (They could be relied upon to be extremely complimentary.)

Today the Official Secrets Act binds all officers, and they have proved more reliable than former royal household servants in preserving absolute discretion.

Until the 1974 attack on Princess Anne, warded off by Inspector James Beaton GC, it was still generally assumed that the popularity of the Royal Family guaranteed them against serious danger in this country. But that incident, and the assassination of Earl Mountbatten in 1979, led to considerable improvements in equipment and training (even though Mountbatten, not being in the direct line of succession, would not have warranted a Personal Protection officer in any case).

On first appointment to the Royalty Protection Branch, officers are allocated as either Personal or Close Protection Officers and kitted out by the Met with the necessary clothing (dinner jacket, white tie and tails, morning suit), though replacements have to be met from the officer's own resources. Three or four officers are allocated to each principal, so that round-the-clock protection can be afforded. When members of the Royal Family are known to enjoy demanding sports (such as skiing or riding) they will be allocated Personal Protection Officers for the occasion who can, if necessary, keep up with them. As well as protecting the Prince of Wales and his sons on the slopes, the ski-skilled Protection Offi-

cer may be extremely important in preventing (say) paparazzi from creating a dangerous situation through impetuosity.

Strict protocol is followed, as it is important that officers do not let themselves become so familiar with the situation that they cease to concentrate on their work of maintaining a guard. This means they must maintain a distance, even from younger royals who may wish to relax into greater informality. Equally, the officer must not let themselves be exploited as a personal servant. They are employees of the Metropolitan Police and not the Royal Family.

The Close Protection officers work with the Personal Protection Officers to support protection at large and crowded public occasions. Like Special Branch officers undertaking similar duties, they are likely to take up positions ensuring that they are providing discreet but effective coverage of their principals. They liaise with local police for intelligence about the local situation. They are trained in highly sophisticated First Aid, and carry medical equipment in their vehicles. They are trained in self-defence and the use of firearms. They are armed with standard issue Glock handguns, and may be in radio communication with the Special Escort Group support units. All Royal Protection Officers have to be prepared to shoot in the event that they see their principals' lives threatened. In practice, however, officers may well complete a long period of protection service and never draw their gun anywhere except at the range.

RUSSEL GRAY COLLECTION Nearly 600 volumes on true crime and police matters, assembled by Russel Malcolm Gray (1944–97), from the civil staff of the Archives Department who was responsible for vetting sensitive files and whose expertise on criminal history was recognized within the department. After his unexpected death in harness, his family consulted the Archives Department, which referred them to Camille Wolff and Loretta Lay of Grey House Books (crime book dealers). In the event all parties agreed that the collection should be kept together and presented to the Historical Museum, which now holds it as a memorial to Mr Gray.

SAVIDGE, (MARJORIE) IRENE (B.1905)

Acquitted co-defendant in a public indecency case, who accused the police of improper interviewing in a subsequent enquiry.

In April 1928 Sir Leo Chiozza Money, a former MP and close associate of Lloyd George, was arrested in Hyde Park with 22-year-old Irene Savidge, a valve-tester for the Standard Telephone and Cable Co. in New Southgate. The arresting plain clothes patrols, PCs Alexander McLean and George Badger, testified at Great Marlborough Street Magistrates' Court that Sir Leo had his hand up Miss Savidge's skirt and that she 'had her hand on his person'. On being arrested, Sir Leo said, 'I am not the usual riffraff, I am a man of substance. For God's sake let me go!' Sir Leo hired a battery of lawyers for his defence and denied all the officers' statements. The magistrates, displaying some bias in favour of a member of the establishment, declined to hear testimony from Miss Savidge, and did not press the interesting question why Sir Leo made a practice of wining and dining young ladies of limited education whom he encountered casually at clubs or in Great Windmill Street. They dismissed the case with costs against the police, and criticized the arresting officers. The Scotland Yard hierarchy was so appalled at this unusual procedure that they consulted the police solicitors in the vain hope that the case might somehow be reopened.

To deflect attention from the unfavourable publicity Sir Leo turned to friends in Parliament, who demanded that the arresting officers be charged with perjury. The Home Office ordered Scotland Yard to conduct an internal enquiry, and Chief Constable Wensley placed it in the hands of Chief Inspector Alfred Collins. Miss Savidge was fetched from her work for questioning at Scotland Yard by a police car holding Inspector Collins, Sergeant Clarke of the CID and Detective Inspector Lilian Wyles. She was not accompanied or supported by any friends, relatives or legal advisers.

Inspector Wyles was abruptly dismissed from the actual interview, Inspector Collins having consistently grumbled about the need to have a policewoman accompany Miss Savidge. His questioning mixed fatherly encouragement, such

as calling the girl 'My dear', with questions which she felt were suggestive and distressing. She had, for example, acquired a medical certificate that she was *virgo intacta*, to which Collins responded, 'There are several things you can do without really sinning: do not be afraid to tell us, we are looking after you.' He asked whether Sir Leo's fly was unbuttoned. He had also made her stand up to inspect her skirt length, and asked her the colour of her petticoat. During the tea-break, when they were forced to share teaspoons, Sergeant Clarke said lightly, 'Now, Irene, will you spoon with me?'

When Miss Savidge complained about her treatment, Sir Leo's friends in Parliament created a rumpus which successfully distracted the public investigation from Sir Leo's peccadillo and made the police the object of a highly publicized special investigation. Three MPs chaired the hearing, two of whom concluded that Collins had been misled into a too-fatherly manner because of Miss Savidge's youthful appearance, and that Sergeant Clarke's flippant remark was ill-considered under the circumstances. The minority report by Mr H. B. Lees-Smith declared that the police were lying. All three MPs recommended that a woman should always be present when any woman was being questioned on intimate moral matters, unless the interviewee expressly asked otherwise.

The case was seen as a crisis for Scotland Yard, given that the Director of Public Prosecutions was on standby to bring charges of perjury against certain police officers should the hearing go against them, and it led to conclusive acceptance of the principle that policemen should be

chaperoned by women officers or matrons if they questioned women about intimate matters.

But those who perceived the whole kerfuffle as Sir Leo's attempt to throw dust in the eyes of the public by attacking the police were justified five years later. In 1933 an anxious spinster got off a train at Esher and revealed to a porter that she had no idea where she was or how to get home. She had abandoned her journey because Sir Leo, whom she did not know, had pestered her before she boarded at Dorking, tried to molest her in a tunnel, and held her and kissed her passionately against her will. The Railway Police were luckier than the Met. Their prosecution of Sir Leo succeeded, costing him £3 in fines and 5 guineas in costs.

SCARMAN, LORD (B.1911)

Lord Scarman of Quatt, Salop. OBE. Lord of Appeal in Ordinary, 1977–86.

Author of two influential reports into policing in London. The first was his report (Cmnd 5919) into the demonstration at Red Lion Square which had led to the death of Kevin Gately, the first participant to die in the course of a demonstration in London since the Marine Police Office Riot 1798.

His second report was into the Brixton Riot in 1981 (Cmnd 8427). This set the tone of police and community relations for more than a decade in relation to the balance between suppressing crime and risking public disorder.

SCENES OF CRIME OFFICERS

Part of SO3 Branch which now comprises the Directorate of Identification, which has subsumed the photographic and fingerprint officers who undertake much of the SOCO work. The logic is that much of the evidence gathered by SOCOs and fingerprint officers aims to identify perpetrators while their traces are still undisturbed at the scene. They then require the backup of Scientific Support to examine and compare the materials they submit. Identification officers, trained additionally as fingerprint officers, have replaced many SOCOs. They are all civil staff.

SCHOOLMASTER SERGEANTS

Short-lived Divisional appointments started by Sir

PC GEORGE SCOREY ON BILLY, THE WHITE HORSE OF WEMBLEY.

Edmund Henderson in 1872, when he discovered a disturbingly high rate of illiteracy in the force. Discontinued within three years as impossible to organize adequately.

SCIENTIFIC SUPPORT COLLEGE The

Scientific Support College is part of the Directorate of Identification and provides fingerprint, forensic and photographic training to scientific support staff and police officers. It also provides advice to Area Training Units as required.

SCOREY, PC GEORGE ALBERT, (1882–1965) 'The Wellington of Wembley': a mounted policeman who became famous for saving the first Wembley Cup Final when the crowd invaded the pitch.

Born Bristol. Joined Scots Greys, 1898, and served 21 years, seeing action in the Boer War and Great War. Left the army with rank of Trumpet Major and many decorations, August 1919. Joined Met November. Warrant No. 107832. Posted to P Division (Lewisham). Joined Mounted Police, 1920. Allocated grey gelding Billy.

In 1923, PC Scorey was one of a detail of 10 mounted police on duty at the first FA Cup Final to be played at Wembley, between West Ham United and Bolton Wanderers. Wembley Stadium was filled with 130,000 spectators, and an estimated further 100,000 people were locked outside. When King George V arrived by car, PC Scorey and a mounted Inspector were detailed to escort the King to the Royal Box. The would-be spectators outside managed to force their way into the stadium and a huge crowd milled over the pitch, completely impeding the King's entry and making it impossible for the players to take the field. Many of the crowd were injured, and stretcher bearers were active throughout the afternoon. It was assumed that the match would have to be cancelled, but PC Scorey, controlling Billy with his knees, rode forward waving both hands to direct the crowd back. His manoeuvre was successful. His colleagues were able to ride after him, conduct the King to his box and the players to the arena, and clear the pitch. The match started 10 minutes late, and Bolton beat West Ham 2–0.

'Billy the White Horse of Wembley' and Scorey 'the Wellington of Wembley' became national heroes. They were invited to many galas and appeared at various Mounted Branch exhibitions, where their favourite manoeuvre was jumping over a fully laid dining table. They were recognized on duty at the General Strike in 1926, and a man shouted, 'Here's the bloke from Wembley. They've sent him to settle the strike like he settled the football crowd.'

In 1928, Scorey and Billy won the King's Cup for the best-trained horse, and they were presented to George V. In 1930 Billy died. The childless Scorey missed him deeply, though he grew attached to his replacement mount Highland Laddie. But it was Billy who had attracted the attention of the lady who became Mrs Scorey in 1922, and Scorey felt he was almost

THE NORMAN SHAW BUILDING (NEW SCOTLAND YARD 1890-1967)

one of the family.

In 1939 Scorey's eyesight had become so defective that he retired on a disability pension. He lived in Hove for the next 25 years, with one of Billy's hooves mounted on a shield in pride of place on his wall. But he was always at pains to point out that colleagues in the mounted and foot police had done as much as he to ensure the playing of the match, adding, 'I was never much interested in football.'

SCOTLAND YARD (1) Metonymy for the Metropolitan Police Service, as in *The Official Encyclopedia of Scotland Yard*.

(2) Metonymy for Metropolitan Police CID, as in, 'Scotland Yard has been called in'.

(3) Shortened form of New Scotland Yard, official name of the MPS headquarters since 1890, firstly at the Norman Shaw building on the Embankment, and from 1967 at 10 Broadway, London SW1H 0BG.

(4) Colloquial term soon adopted for the Commissioners' Office and Metropolitan Police Headquarters at No. 4 Whitehall Place from 1829 to 1890.

The general uses of the term Scotland Yard all spring from (4) above. 4 Whitehall Place backed on to a court called Great Scotland Yard, itself one of three streets retaining the words Scotland Yard. The name, according to the earliest surviving record (discovered in the 1970s after diligent research by Norman Fairfax, senior executive officer on the Civil Staff) derived from the fact that a man named Adam Scott owned the land in the early Middle Ages. The other school of thought is that this area, adjacent to the royal Palace of Whitehall (destroyed by fire in the 17th century) was used by the kings of Scotland and/or their ambassadors as an official residence when they visited the English court.

By 1887 the Police HQ embraced Nos 3, 4, 5, 21 and 22 Whitehall Place, Nos 8 and 9 Great Scotland Yard, Nos 1, 2 and 3 Palace Place, Great Scotland Yard, stables, stores and new office buildings in Great Scotland Yard, with the freestanding building in the centre of the Yard that had successively held stores, the Public Carriage Office and the CID offices. The habit of approaching police headquarters through Scotland Yard led to the name's superseding 'Whitehall Place' in popular usage, and the familiar title was retained in the two subsequent moves to larger and more suitable buildings when they were required.

See also Back Hall.

SCOTLAND YARD BOMBING The most embarrassing incident for the Met in the Fenian bombing campaign of 1883–5.

Late in 1883, Scotland Yard received an anonymous letter threatening to 'blow Superintendent Williamson off his stool' and dynamite all the public buildings in London on 30 May 1884.

On the predicted night, shortly before 9.00 p.m., the CID and Special Irish Branch headquarters were indeed successfully bombed, though no one was in the offices and only neighbours and a cabman were injured by shattered glass. The bomb was concealed in a cast-iron urinal on the corner of a detached building in the centre of Great Scotland Yard which had formerly been used as stores, and now housed the CID. The corner was blown away to a height of 9m (30ft) and a width of 4.5m (15ft). Williamson's office was completely destroyed, and the public house opposite, the Rising Sun, suffered extensive damage. The same night, bombs went off in the basement of the Carlton Club and outside Sir Watkin Wynne's house, and an unexploded bomb was found at the foot of Nelson's column.

The failure of Scotland Yard to protect its own offices, and the subsequent successful

GREAT SCOTLAND YARD AND (LEFT) THE RISING SUN PUBLIC HOUSE AFTER THE 1884 FENIAN BOMB ATTACK.

explosion of Fenian bombs under London Bridge, in the Tower of London and in the House of Commons the following year, did much to lower the reputation of the Metropolitan Police in the years running up to the Jack the Ripper case. In 1973 an IRA car bomb outside Scotland Yard was detected by Special Patrol Group officers and defused. The Met's success in preventing any further bomb outrages after 1885 was easily overlooked, just as, 100 years later, the success of Operation Airlines was generally unknown, while inevitably the successful IRA bombings were familiar to everyone.

SCOTLAND YARD ROSE A strongly scented yellow floribunda hybrid with a pinky-orange edge to the petals. Grows to a height of 1.2m (4ft). Bred by Messrs Harkness of Hitchin in 1992, but discontinued commercially two years later. Planted in beds outside New Scotland Yard in Broadway for some time.

SCOTT, SIR HAROLD RICHARD, GCVO, KCB, KBE (1887–1969) Commissioner, 1945–53.

Educ. Sexey's School, Bruton, Somerset and Jesus College Cambridge. Entered Home Office, 1911. Foreign Trade Dept, 1916–18. Secretary to the Labour Resettlement Committee, 1918–19. Home Office, 1919–32. Chairman, Prisons Commission, 1932–9. London Civil Defence Administration, 1939–42. Permanent Secretary, Ministry of Aircraft Production, 1943–5. Metropolitan Commissioner, 1945–53. Thereafter lectured and wrote, publications including *Scotland Yard* (1954) and *The Concise Encyclopedia of Crime and Criminals* (ed., 1961).

Late in 1944, Home Secretary Herbert Morrison summoned the Permanent Secretary to the Ministry of Aircraft Production, and astonished that bespectacled, pin-striped Civil Service mandarin by asking whether he could ride a horse. Sir

Harold Scott could, though he had not done so for a long time. Since he could meet the ceremonial requirement, he was told the government hoped he would accept Commissionership of the Metropolitan Police after the war. It seemed the Labour members of Churchill's wartime coalition were taking advantage of their general responsibility for home affairs to attack the 'problem of police militarization' which had been a bee in left-wing bonnets for 20 years. (A more cynical suggestion is that the Deputy Permanent Secretary at the Home Office lured Morrison into making the offer to Scott with an eye to ensuring that this very senior figure did not impede his own smooth route to the Permanent Secretaryship.)

And so came the unique experiment of setting an administrative grade civil servant the task of turning himself into a policeman. It was regarded with grave reservations in some quarters. In the entire history of the Met only Sir Richard Mayne had become Commissioner with no military or police experience, and of his successors only James Monro and Sir Edward Henry had never been in the armed forces. Some people doubted whether Scott could give the necessary leadership to a disciplined force of police. Others were sceptical about the quality of his horsemanship. (As the Commissioner who fell off his horse and had to be encased in plaster under his uniform, Scott remains a sort of naughty schoolboys' joke memory among historically minded old hands at Scotland Yard, even though he was not unique: Bradford, justifiably admired for riding one-armed, came off from time to time, and Sir Paul Condon was badly injured in a riding accident.)

Scott came to the job with the rather stagestruck eyes of a complete outsider. He held the general public's view of 'Scotland Yard' as first and foremost the greatest detective force in the world, and was surprised to find the CID comprised less than 10% of the whole. He went riding in Flying Squad cars, attended one or two major trials, and enjoyed cruising with the River Police. He got used to his police grey, Norton, and ultimately took great pleasure in riding, with cocked hat, gold braid and horn-rimmed spectacles, in front of the State Coach at the Queen's coronation, though two grooms stood by to catch him if he fell when mounting.

But he came, too, with the merits of a great civil servant – unusual merits for a Commissioner of Police. Perhaps uniquely in the history of Scotland Yard, Scott saw both sides of a case without difficulty, and accepted bureaucratic and policy defeats without either sulkily retreating to inactivity, or throwing grit into the machine by trying to fight old battles over and over. For the whole of his time at Scotland Yard he was bedevilled by seriously understrength manpower, a generally rising crime rate, and governments which, under conditions of postwar austerity, could not give him the money for the tools to do the job. Scott reported the fact every year in his annual reports. He may have been the only Commissioner with the statistical nous to observe that between £3 million and £4 million was saved by keeping the police under strength for 10 years after the war, while a balancing £4 ½ millions-worth of property was stolen in the Metropolitan Police District alone. However, his argumentative skills fell on deaf ears, so he sensibly got down to the policy he described as 'make-do and mend'.

He hung on to the War Reserve Specials as long as he could, and delayed allowing pensioners recalled 'for the duration' to return to their retirement for as long as possible. He abolished zones of promotion, which he felt encouraged some unnecessary resignations. He substituted competitive examinations, which might not always promote the most street-wise officers, but at least ensured that nobody felt passed over by reasons of favouritism or accident. He considered increasing recruiting by lowering physical or educational standards, and during his term of office turned as much clerical work as he could over to Civil Staff to free police officers for patrol duties. He made what was, in its own way, the revolutionary decision that fingerprinting should gradually be transferred entirely from police detectives to Civil Staff, thus initiating progress towards today's situation where Identification Officers are not expected to be attested police officers.

He rejected the idea of traffic wardens to ease the beat police officer's burden of handling parking offences, part of his reasoning being the characteristic observation that the physical health requirements could not be lowered without an increase in the cost of pension obligations. He

did, however, try to persuade courts to bunch traffic cases together on one day of the week to reduce the amount of time officers spent hanging around to give evidence, and he made adjustments to traffic patrols to try to ease the pedestrian police officers' traffic responsibilities. He experimented with the 'Aberdeen Scheme' (cf. Unit Beat) whereby individually allocated beats were abolished, and former sections were amalgamated and policed by between three and nine constables in contact with their Sergeant, who was in a car with a radio and could quickly transport officers from one place to another as they were needed.

He managed to make small increases in the Women Police and the CID, the latter being justified by the alarming postwar crime figures. Scott's term of office coincided with a quite remarkable number of sensational headline-making cases. The sexual sadistic murderer Neville Heath might have appeared at any period, as might the confidence trickster John George Haigh, who disposed of his victims in acid baths before forging powers-of-attorney to give himself control of all their property. But Donald Hume's murder of Stanley Setty was symptomatic of growing amorality reflected in the black market and the 'spiv' culture. Alex de Antiquis's murder by the young hoodlums Jenkins, Geraghty and Rolt illustrated lethal delinquency by juveniles, as did the tragic murder of PC Miles by Bentley and Craig. The Christie case, with its implications for capital punishment and aspects of police work, saw Scott behaving as a perfect civil servant. He cooperated with the Scott-Henderson enquiry, and thankfully accepted its conclusion that everyone had behaved properly and no innocent man had been or was ever likely to be hanged. He was fortunate to have retired before Ludovic Kennedy's magisterial re-examination of the case led to exactly the reverse conclusion winning general public acceptance.

He showed himself aware of the problems of victimless crime, laws that the public despised, and politicians' enthusiasm for increasing the number of fussy statutes and regulations. With diminishing degrees of enthusiasm he suggested that the law might be changed to save police the unpleasant and potentially demoralizing duties of hassling street bookmakers, gaming club proprietors, prostitutes and homosexuals. He favoured police having the discretion to downplay the enforcement of trivial, irrational and justifiably unpopular legislation.

He was at his best in weighing the pros and

challenging identification evidence at any future trial, he barred publishing photographs of Neville Heath when he was wanted for the murder of Margery Gardner. It would later be argued that this allowed Heath, using a different name, to murder Doreen Marshall. But Scott made no

respected, but he was quickly traced through a witness who recognized Mrs Winkless. In Christie's case there was nothing to lose and everything to gain by publishing his photograph: his unquestioned occupation of the 'slum mausoleum' at Rillington Place was the basic evidence against him, for which no identification witness was necessary.

Scott gave Ealing Studios all the help they needed in making *The Blue Lamp* as an all-round picture of police duties in the context of an exciting and tragic crime story. This paid huge dividends by engendering more than a decade during which the police basked in the favourable image created by Jack Warner as 'PC George Dixon'.

He made a small but significant improvement to uniforms by replacing the historic tunics with open-necked jackets over white shirts and black ties. Although some old sweats complained that the tunic was actually cooler on dog-days, when they were unofficially permitted to undo the collars, Scott was moving towards today's more rational and comfortable uniforming with short-sleeved shirts and belted trousers permitted as summer wear.

As far as funds allowed, he made small cosmetic improvements to the Met's ageing and war-damaged building stock, which suffered sadly from not having seen the completion of Lord Trenchard's ambitious building programme. In this respect, and with regard to his depleted force, Scott's critics felt that a more demanding figure like Trenchard would have been a better postwar Commissioner and would have insisted on having the money to rebuild his force, regardless of other social needs. But, noting that Attlee's Home Secretary Chuter Ede is almost the only one who has generally been approved by police officers as a true and understanding friend to the force, one must wonder how much this admirable state of affairs owed to Ede's being the only Home Secretary whose entire term of office gave him an experienced civil servant, knowing in the ways of ministers, as the Metropolitan Police's head and spokesman. Sir Richard Jackson, who was Metropolitan Police Secretary for almost the entirety of Scott's time at Scotland Yard, called him able, clever, modest, genial, broad-minded and a pleasure to work for – and

SIR HAROLD SCOTT AT THE HEAD OF THE TABLE, WITH OTHER SENIOR OFFICERS IN THE COMMISSIONER'S OFFICE, NORMAN SHAW BUILDING.

cons of releasing information to the press and accepting philosophically that one or another difficult decision might not always prove to have been the right one. To avoid defence counsel

mistakes over the murder of PC Nat Edgar. With the aid of his newly appointed Public Information Officer, P. H. Fearnley, he devised the classic form of words 'The police urgently wish to interview Donald George Thomas to help them with their inquiries', and he issued a photograph of the woman Thomas was believed to be living with. Thus all Thomas's civil liberties were

Jackson spoke as a former barrister and subsequent Assistant Commissioner (Crime), who was by nature more comfortable as a crime fighter than as a Civil Service administrator.

Scott had little idea that the force over which he presided would be remembered as representing a golden age of British policing. When coppers of later years were accused of intimidatory conduct and bending the rules, the 1950s image of *Dixon of Dock Green* would be recalled. Conversely, when undisciplined juveniles, supported by their irresponsible parents, made life a misery for their neighbours, everyone looked back with longing to the days when a friendly neighbourhood copper could give vandalizing brats a clip across the ear and break their catapults without being hauled up for assault and misappropriation of property.

SECRETARY Title of the Head of Civil Staff (excepting the Receiver's staff), 1919–68. Previously designated Chief Clerk. In 1968 the post was redesignated Secretary and Establishment Officer for a period. Most of the responsibilities are now undertaken within the Personnel Department or in other administrative roles.

Although the Receiver's Head Clerk was also given the title Secretary in 1919 (redesignated Secretary and Deputy Receiver in 1946), it was the heir of Charles Yardley who was generally perceived as 'Secretary to the Metropolitan Police'. He was held to be of similar status to an Assistant Commissioner. Thus Sir Richard Jackson, the only man to have made such a career move, observed that his transfer from the low-profile job of Secretary to the high-profile job of Assistant Commissioner C (Crime) was a sideways move and not a promotion. ˎ

SECTION HOUSES Accommodation for unmarried officers.

Undoubtedly a product of founding Commissioner Sir Charles Rowan's military background and concomitant expectation that 'the men' should be housed in barracks, conveniently placed for summoning them all to duty as they might be needed. The name suggests that he hoped to supply one to each section, an overambitious target, as it proved.

ELLIOT SECTION HOUSE, CRAWFORD PLACE, W1.

If station houses were not used to accommodate Station Inspectors, they might have upstairs rooms adapted as section houses. Alternatively (as in the case of the original Scotland Yard) a section house might be attached to the back or side of a station.

Until the 1930s, section houses provided extremely spartan accommodation. A bed, a fold-down table and an upright chair were the only furnishings. Regular inspections enforced quasi-military tidiness in the rooms; a section house was definitely not a home. From Sir Edmund Henderson to Lord Trenchard, almost every Commissioner undertook some increase in the comfort of section houses, and commented adversely on the outdated and inadequate accommodation he found in place. As late as the 1930s, ablutions were still simply a row of sinks and troughs, with no privacy and no running hot water. Trenchard provided reasonable comfort and modern conveniences with an excellent range of lounges and gymnasia, but still left in place kitchen facilities for those officers who did not wish to eat in the canteen.

Until WWII, roll-calls were taken to ensure that all section-house dwellers were 'back to barracks' by midnight. As late as 1968, section houses could be found which provided constables with cubicles whose privacy was only such as could be afforded by walls that did not extend to the ceiling, and bedrooms no more than 2.1m (7ft) across which barely contained a bed, a chest of drawers, and space for hanging uniforms.

Despite the relative discomfort, many officers from the 1890s onward held nostalgic memories of the camaraderie and horseplay of their probationary years in the section houses. They proved great centres for bonding the tight-knit *esprit de corps* of the Met, and often provided the base from which recruits ingested the shared outlook of 'canteen culture'.

In more recent years the number of section houses has reduced, along with the 'married' quarters, and officers are normally expected to find their own accommodation. A nucleus of section houses is retained, however, particularly in central London.

See also station houses, Trenchard House.

SECTION SERGEANTS Title used for Sergeants who commanded the patrolling beat or fixed point officers in Divisional sections, distinguishing them from the deskbound and senior Station Sergeants or Clerk Sergeants, who were not normally required to inspect outdoor patrols.

SECTIONAL STATION A small police station with limited facilities, under the command of an Inspector or Sergeant.

SECTIONS Areas quartering Divisions which, in the original establishment of 1829, could be divided into the beats of eight patrolling constables under the command of a Section Sergeant. Later came to be used to denote the patrolling sergeant's responsibility.

The word Section is also used to denote the entire Dog Section, for reasons of tradition rather than logic, and has been applied to the Youth and Community Section.

SERGEANT The first supervisory rank in the police, one step above constable. Roughly equivalent to army non-commissioned officers in that they are primarily responsible for overseeing and ordering the day-to-day work of constables.

The only military title adopted by founding Commissioners Rowan and Mayne, and a rank that is still marked by the use of the equivalent military triple chevron on the sleeve. Sergeants' quasi-'non-commissioned' status is also marked by their uniforms' including helmets and divisional numbers, unlike Inspectors who normally wear only caps. When the uniforms included duty armlets, Sergeants too were required to wear them.

There were originally 16 Sergeants to each of the Divisions, each Sergeant commanding nine men, eight of whom were officers on patrol and the ninth the reserve officer. Each Sergeant was responsible for a section of the territorial division (his 'manor'), normally divided into eight beats. The sergeants were normally the patrol inspecting officers who inspected constables on parade before they went on the beat, checked that they

were carrying their appointments, and marched them out of the station to their positions. They also patrolled the section themselves to ensure that constables were carrying out their duties.

Station Sergeants (a unique Metropolitan Police rank, phased out from 1973) were responsible for overseeing Section Sergeants and drew higher pay, as did Clerk Sergeants. The two grades of Sergeant were carried over as 'Sergeants, class 1 and 2' into the CID where beats and sections did not apply. Promotion to Sergeant depended on a non-police written examination until 1933, when a Civil Service examination in the 3 Rs, geography and general knowledge was set for all recruits, and passing this was held to fit the new constable for promotion to Sergeant in due course. Sir Harold Scott made promotion up to Inspector dependent on a specific Metropolitan Police competitive examination rather than recommendation from above. Subsequently the general educational exam was coupled with a law exam, until eventually the Met's competitive examination was abolished in favour of the current national police OSPRE (Objective Structured Performance Related Examinations) system, which combines knowledge of law and correct procedure with practical tests.

Like constables, Sergeants are at the 'sharp end of policing', and may be required to maintain higher standards of physical fitness than more senior officers.

See also Schoolmaster Sergeants.

SERIAL Small unit mobilized for public order operations and riot control. Usually comprising one Inspector, two Sergeants and 20 constables, who may or may not be issued with riot gear and shields. The Mounted Police use a serial comprising one Inspector, one Sergeant and 10 constables.

The familiar name has now been superseded by Police Support Units, comprising an Inspector, three Sergeants and 18 constables.

SERVICE RESTRUCTURING EXERCISE, 1995 The aim of the restructuring set in place by Sir Paul Condon when he was appointed Commissioner was to direct more resources into 'front-line policing', with officers on the spot

deciding whether Divisional, Area or MPD-wide operations were appropriate. To this end, lines of command to operations were drastically simplified. The buck stopped with the Commissioner MPD-wide. Assistant Commissioners commanded Areas, while Chief Superintendents commanded Divisions. The Area Assistant Commissioners also formed part of the Policy Board, thereby linking policy-making strongly to the Area dimension. Delegated control of budgets was promised to Divisional Commanders. Other senior officers at Area level supported the Assistant Commissioner, but did not have strict line management over OCUs.

Area Business Managers were brought into the Area Structure as Grade 7 Civil Staff to co-ordinate costed business plans. They soon became the contact and liaison point for all the Receiver's Departments, and even took over Personnel and Training responsibilities.

The reorganization coincided with the publication of the Sheehy Report and other police reforms set in train by Home Secretary Kenneth Clarke and subsequently implemented in part by his successor, Michael Howard. These national changes led to the ranks of Deputy Assistant Commissioner and Chief Superintendent being phased out, but practicalities soon meant that they reappeared as job titles rather than formal ranks.

The most visible restructuring change was the reduction of the Super Eight Areas to five. Each Area was placed under the command of an Assistant Commissioner, and each Area Assistant Commissioner also managed a portfolio of the former Territorial Operations. In addition to the five Area Assistant Commissioners (which entailed increasing their numbers by two), ACSO continued to command Specialist Operations, and the Deputy Commissioner's portfolio included a range of planning, inspectorial and disciplinary functions.

The Assistant Commissioners soon developed a very powerful role in the organization, and Areas assumed a far greater importance than the small coordinating function initially foreseen by Sir Kenneth Newman. The power over substantial budgets soon began to direct resources towards operational priorities rarely achieved before, and constructive competitiveness helped the process of improving Divisional and Area performance as indicated by management statistics.

SESSIONAL ORDER An Order from Parliament to the Commissioner at the beginning of each Session to keep the streets within 1.6km (1 mile) of the Palace of Westminster clear of obstruction and gatherings which are likely to result in disorder. The Commissioner then makes regulations under Section 54 of the Metropolitan Police Act, 1839, to give the instruction legal force on the streets. Thus demonstrations are routed away from Parliament Square while Parliament is sitting. Since the formation of the Metropolitan Police, there have been few occasions when demonstrations appeared likely to threaten the seat of democracy as did the Gordon Riots of 1780.

When one-way traffic was introduced around Parliament Square, Winston Churchill deliberately drove the 'wrong' way to the House of Commons, brandishing his Member's pass at the police on duty. In explaining his conduct to the Speaker he pointed to the Sessional Order's direction that the streets were to be kept clear of obstruction. As he never repeated the offence once he had made his point, the legal position has never been tested in the courts, who might not, in any case, have been able to hear the charge as it related to an MP at the time when he was arguably under the jurisdiction of the Speaker.

SEX STATEMENT TAKERS Miss Eilidh MacDougall (employed 1908–1930) and DI Lilian Wyles (employed 1921–1930) who heard the complaints of women members of the public who had suffered sexual assaults.

SHEEHY REPORT Report of Parliamentary Inquiry into Police Responsibilities and Rewards, published June 1993, chaired by Sir Patrick Sheehy and commissioned by Home Secretary Kenneth Clarke.

Unlike the Edmund–Davies Report, the Sheehy Report accepted the principle of comparison with pay rates in the private sector, and recommended that such direct comparability should replace broad general observations of underlying earnings increases across the economy as a basis for police pay revisions. The Committee noted that such comparability was now accepted as the basis for Civil Service pay revisions.

The Committee also recommended that overtime payments should be replaced by a job grading system, and many allowances that had become outdated should be scrapped.

It further recommended that outdated restrictions on police officers' rights to live where they pleased and take in lodgers if they chose should be scrapped. It recommended that the rank structure be simplified by the abolition of the Chief Inspector, Chief Superintendent, and Deputy Assistant Commissioner ranks. It recommended that retirement should normally be at the age of 60, and pensions should not normally be paid until 40 years' service had been completed, though retirement might be permitted on a reduced pension from age 55. And it recommended that police officers should be given performance-related pay with fixed-term contracts, and become liable to dismissal for unsatisfactory performance.

It has been suggested that this report became the greatest single cause of disharmony in the history of the Police Service since the Police Strike, 1918. The comparison index produced less generous pay rates than the existing Edmund–Davies formula. The proposed system replacing overtime was seen as crude, while the proposed contract and pensions conditions were distinctly disadvantageous to serving officers. Although the report recognized the extra pressures and expense of working in London and recommended a £4000 pay lead for the Met and City of London Police, it was in the end a comprehensive attempt to revise the pay and conditions of the Police Service which completely failed to persuade the Service of its merits.

SHEPHERD'S BUSH MURDERS Cold-blooded shooting of three unarmed plain clothes policemen making routine inquiries of the occupants of a motor vehicle, parked suspiciously close to Wormwood Scrubs prison.

At approximately 3.15 p.m. on 16 August 1966, Sergeant Christopher Head, Detective Constable David Wombwell and PC Geoffrey Fox, all attached to Shepherd's Bush police station, were routinely patrolling F Division (roughly covering the Borough of Hammersmith) in a Q-car with the call sign Foxtrot 11 (vocalized as 'Foxtrot One One', not 'Foxtrot Eleven'). In Braybrook Street, a one-sided crescent of houses whose north side is Old Oak Common and the open heath of Wormwood Scrubs, they saw a battered blue Standard Vanguard estate van parked, with three men sitting in it.

Since Wormwood Scrubs prison wall abuts directly on to the southern extremity of Braybrook Street, and escape attempts were sometimes made with the support of getaway vehicles, there was every reason for the policemen to ask the occupants what they were doing. It has been speculated that PC Fox, who had worked beats in F Division for many years, and was valued as an occasional Aid to CID driving Q-cars because of his wide knowledge of local villains, may have recognized the driver, a 36-year-old small-time criminal called John Witney. Alternatively, the policemen may simply have noticed that the van carried no tax disc. In any case, Sgt Head and DC Wombwell walked over to the van and Sgt Head asked whether Witney owned it and why there was no road fund licence displayed. Witney said he had to take the car for its MOT test before he could tax it. Head asked for his driving licence and insurance certificate and, observing that the latter had expired at midday, left DC Wombwell to take Witney's name and address while he walked round to the side of the van. Witney was asking Wombwell to give him a break, saying he'd been nicked for the same offence just a fortnight before, when Harry Roberts, sitting in the passenger seat, shot and killed Sgt Head without warning. Roberts, a dangerous criminal with several convictions (including one for the despicable robbery and mutilation of a 74-year-old man whose finger he had cut off to steal his ring), had formed the impression that Head was going to search the car. A woman friend had warned him that he would get a 15-year sentence if he was found carrying a gun, and on the spur of the moment Roberts decided to shoot his way out of possible arrest.

DC Wombwell ran back to the Q-car to take cover, but Roberts ran after him and shot him through the head. At the same time, Roberts

POLICE NOTICE FOLLOWING THE SHEPHERD'S BUSH MURDERS, 1966.

shouted some command to petty criminal John Duddy, who was in the back of the van, and Duddy ran over to the Q-car and shot PC Fox through the window as he tried to start up and pull away.

The two murderers piled back into the van, which Witney reversed rapidly down a side street and out on to Wulfstan Street, driving away at speed. Fortunately a passerby, thinking that a car racing away from the vicinity of Wormwood Scrubs Prison might be concerned with a jail-break, took down the number. This led to Witney's speedy arrest and the discovery of the van in a railway arch lock-up in Vauxhall. After pretending to have sold the van to an unknown man in a pub that day, Witney admitted that Roberts and Duddy had been with him and had shot the policemen. Duddy was traced to Scotland on information received from his brother. But Harry Roberts was at large for 90 days, camping out in

Thorley Wood, Hertfordshire. There was some indignation among the police that the £1000 reward offered for information while he was missing was substantially less than the sums offered for information in jewel and furs thefts.

The atrocious murders led to massive public sympathy for the police, and many calls for the restoration of the recently abolished death penalty. Assistant Commissioner C, Sir Richard Jackson, the head of Interpol, subsequently pointed out forcefully that armed robbery had suddenly increased after abolition; that professional thieves were violent men, even if they were as resourceful as the Great Train Robbers, and police and public needed the protection of some more serious deterrent than a 'life' sentence (which usually lasted no more than eight or nine years) if thieves were to be discouraged from carrying guns.

Six hundred uniformed police officers lined the way to St Stephen and St Thomas's church opposite Shepherd's Bush police station, where the three officers' funeral service was held. A

week later, a memorial service in Westminster Abbey was attended by Prime Minister Harold Wilson and Leader of the Opposition Edward Heath, with the Queen sending a representative. Thousands of police officers from every force in the country attended. More than 1000 members of the public who could not get tickets for the service stood reverentially outside the Abbey, and a collection was taken for the newly formed Police Dependants' Trust. The Braybrook Suite at Hammersmith Police Station was named after the officers in 1996.

SHERLOCK HOLMES The most famous of all fictional detectives was created in the year before the Jack the Ripper case. He maintained a serenely contemptuous attitude to Scotland Yard in the stories written by Sir Arthur Conan Doyle between 1887 and 1915.

After 1895 Scotland Yard regularly received letters seeking the equally fictional address of the detective (221B Baker Street), in one case from an East European police chief who wished to settle a bet that Holmes was not real.

SHIELDS Reinforced perspex items of riot equipment. Long (almost body length) shields enable a phalanx of officers to advance against missiles, but make swift advances against rioters more difficult. Consequently, smaller short shields, first used in 1976 at the Lewisham Riot, are now increasingly used by Police Support Units.

SHORT-TERM CONTRACTS System of recruiting officers to the police on 10-year contracts with the promise of a gratuity of one month's pay for every year served. Resignation with the gratuity was possible at any time, but it was not possible for the contractee then to return to the regular force. Introduced on Lord Trenchard's initiative in the Metropolitan Police Act, 1933 with the expectation that it would bring 5000 recruits into the force as 'new blood' over the next 10 years. Abolished in 1938 when it was clear that it was not working. Only a few hundred had taken the contracts, and many of them had soon departed to provincial forces with their gratuities.

"The Battle of Stepney"
Firing-Line of the Scots Guards

PART OF A SET OF POSTCARDS ILLUSTRATING KEY EVENTS IN THE SIEGE OF SIDNEY STREET.

See under Lord Trenchard and Sir Philip Game for fuller discussion.

SIEGE OF SIDNEY STREET Famous incident of 1911 when, with the approval of Home Secretary Winston Churchill, troops were brought in to assist the police in a gun battle with two members of a murderous gang of robbers.

Three City of London policemen were killed and two others wounded on 16 December 1910, when they attempted to arrest a gang of Latvian immigrant burglars breaking into a jewellers' premises in Houndsditch. The gang escaped into Stepney in the Metropolitan Police District, where their leader, George Gardstein, died of gunshot wounds accidentally inflicted by one of his confederates during their flight. A national hunt for the remaining gang members, including their supposed leader 'Peter the Painter', was reported in the press.

On 2 January 1911, Metropolitan Police received information via the City Police that two of the gang were sheltering in Mrs Betsy Gershon's flat on the second floor of 100 Sidney Street. By 4.45 a.m. on 3 January a combined force of Met and City Police had cordoned off the area and evacuated other residents. Mrs Ger-

shon's room could not be rushed as its door opened on to a narrow landing covering the topmost flight of stairs, where gunmen could have taken cover and picked off ascending policemen with impunity. The gunmen had taken away Mrs Gershon's skirt and shoes to prevent her from leaving the building, but she was permitted to go downstairs, where the police promptly rescued her.

At dawn, Inspector F. P. Wensley, commanding the H Division (Whitechapel) men at the

house, went with a handful of officers to knock on the door. Receiving no answer, he threw pebbles at Mrs Gershon's window, from which there immediately came a volley of pistol shots, one of which hit Detective Sergeant Ben Leeson. He was carried to an adjoining house, where the doctor who examined him ordered his immediate removal to hospital. It proved that the only way to carry him out of the line of fire was across the roof. Wensley, who was unarmed, supervised his removal, and remained on the roof until the stretcher party was clear, which led to the gunmen detecting his presence and pinning him down in a pool of icy water behind a parapet for half an hour.

Such arms as the police had, they brought with them – bulldog revolvers, shotguns, and rifles fitted with .22 Morris-tube barrels for use on a miniature range – but these proved completely inadequate for flushing out the gunmen, whose Mauser pistols were capable of rapid and deadly fire calibrated to 1000 metres. Commissioner Sir Edward Henry was out of town, but Deputy Commissioner Major Frederick Wodehouse was telephoned, and he gained Home Secretary Winston Churchill's permission to send for troops before himself going to Sidney Street to take command.

About 500 uniformed and Mounted Police were needed to keep back the crowd which gath-

"The Battle of Stepney"
Mr. Winston Churchill surrounded by Detectives and Armed Police

ered. At 10.45 a.m., 21 volunteer marksmen of the Scots Guards arrived from the Tower of London. Three were placed on the top floor of a nearby brewery building from which they could fire accurately into the second-storey and attic windows from which the gunmen (known to be Fritz Svaars and a man called Josef) had been shooting. The gunmen were driven down to the lower floors, where they came under fire from more guardsmen, placed in houses across the street. The remainder of the guards formed a prone cordon across Sidney Street, firing at the building.

Winston Churchill arrived just before midday to observe the battle, and decided that heavier artillery was needed. Before it could arrive, smoke was seen to be rising from the building, and one of the gunmen (almost certainly Josef) pushed his head through a window to see more clearly, and then fell back suddenly (almost certainly shot). Thereafter the rate of fire from Sidney Street slowed down considerably.

By 1.30 p.m. the building was well alight. The Fire Brigade arrived, but were forbidden by Churchill to extinguish the blaze. A Maxim gun supported by another 54 Scots Guards arrived from the Tower; a section of Royal Engineers came in from Chatham, and finally, at 2.40 p.m., a troop of the Royal Horse Artillery trotted up.

They were not needed. The last shots from 100 Sidney Street had been heard half an hour earlier. The fire had gutted the building and the roof had caved in. Firemen were at work to prevent damage to other buildings, when a wall collapsed, burying five people, one of whom died in hospital. Two bodies were found inside the building. One of the gunmen had been shot on the first floor, while the other had been overcome by smoke on the ground floor.

The City Police found that the gang's political commitments spanned the far left spectrum from Anarchism to Bolshevism, and they robbed on principle, feeling justified by their cause; the Met believed they were by now first and foremost simple burglars. Most of the surviving gang members and their women were rounded up over the next few months and put on trial. All but one woman secured acquittals or had their cases dismissed by the magistrates, and the woman's conviction was reversed on appeal. Such were the

difficulties faced by the police when magistrates and juries were confused by an array of non-English-speaking defendants and witnesses, who could only follow and contribute to the proceedings through interpreters. The failure of the police marksmen and their equipment was duly noted, and improved firearms were ordered with better training for officers. This was a very rare case of a Home Secretary taking police operational command decisions.

Family traditions often recall relatives who served in this operation, as is true of the Jack the Ripper case.

SIEGES AND SIEGE MANAGEMENT Situations when armed and dangerous criminals or terrorists are known to be taking cover and are known or expected to refuse to emerge peacefully. May be complicated further if the criminals hold hostages.

The Siege of Sidney Street (1911) took the police completely by surprise. Although the Gardstein gang had already killed three policemen and injured two others when fighting their way out of the interrupted Houndsditch robbery, nobody envisaged the two men in 100 Sidney Street opening a gun-battle and fighting to the death when they were surrounded with no possibility of escape. Nothing like it had ever happened before in the history of the Met.

Subsequent arrests of armed and dangerous murderers who had killed policemen (as in the earlier attempted arrest of Paul Hefeld after the Tottenham Outrage of 1909) show that the basic idea of encirclement and going in mob-handed prevailed for 50 years. Donald Thomas, the killer of PC Nat Edgar, was pinned down on his bed before he could (as he said he intended) go for his gun to kill the arresting officers. Gunther Podola, murderer of DS Raymond Purdy, was overwhelmed by the heavy policemen who smashed down his hotel room door, blacking his eye and concussing him with the force with which it hit him. Harry Roberts, leader of the trio perpetrating the Shepherd's Bush murders, was surrounded in his Essex hideout by an army of policemen with rifles, CS incapacitant canisters and police dogs, before the arresting officer aroused him by pointing a rifle barrel into his sleeping bag.

But the international outbreak of 'political' hijackings and kidnappings in the early 1970s led Sir Robert Mark to initiate serious discussions on the best way of handling any such situations that might arise in the Metropolitan Police District. Consequently the Met had the general outlines of a predetermined drill to follow when robbers held civilians hostage in 1975, and the outcome was the successful Spaghetti House siege. Debriefing after that operation led to refinements of the drill which paid dividends at the Balcombe Street siege in 1975. The Iranian Embassy siege (1980) was ultimately passed by the Met to the SAS in recognition that specially trained combat commandos were a better force to deal with totally intransigent desperadoes who had started to assassinate their hostages. The Libyan Bureau siege, following the murder of WPC Yvonne Fletcher (1984), was terminated by government fiat for diplomatic reasons, frustrating the completion of a Met operation or the invocation of the SAS.

Briefly, the siege technique is to surround and control the premises very obviously, making sure the suspect is aware that he is surrounded. To this end, loud-hailers, barking dogs, and visible armed police and marksmen may be used. If no hostages are being held, CS incapacitant gas may be brought in in readiness to flush out the suspect (especially if he is in a tactically commanding position, such as a door overlooking a short and narrow flight of stairs). Surrounding dwellings are evacuated, and the approach roads sealed to traffic.

At the same time, negotiators are brought in to try to persuade the suspect or suspects to end the siege peacefully. Means of communication with suspects – preferably by telephone – are established, but ideally telephones are controlled so that the suspects cannot make calls to numbers of their own choosing. Technological surveillance is brought into play where possible. If the siege is evidently going to last for some time, electricity, gas and water into the building are sometimes cut off, leaving the suspects dependent upon negotiating with the police to supply them with chemical toilets and other comforts.

Hostages complicate but do not determine the situation. A high priority is placed on their well-being and giving all possible reassurance to their relatives but it is always insisted that suspects' threats to or ill-treatment of hostages will never result in their demands being met, as this would simply encourage future criminals to take hostages. All police officers, including the most senior, know that rather than yield to terrorist criminals' demands, their colleagues will allow their lives to be sacrificed without hesitation should they be held hostage.

Firearms are only used in the last resort to save life, either of hostages (if marksmanship can successfully take out the suspect without injuring the hostage), or of the encircling police officers if the suspect is evidently determined to force a shoot-out. If suspects start to murder their hostages in an attempt to enforce their demands, the balance shifts towards terminating the siege by force, as in the Iranian Embassy case.

SILVER TOKEN Proof of identity issued to Commissioners, Assistant Commissioners and Deputy Assistant Commissioners in lieu of or addition to warrant cards. Introduced in 1919, Commissioners' silver tokens must be the very rarest items for collectors of police memorabilia to obtain. It also amuses cheeky members of the public (and police constables!) who are aware of them to know that, in theory, they might demand of the Commissioner of the Metropolitan Police, 'Show us your silver token!' if they pretended to be unfamiliar with his appearance from television or newspaper images.

SIMPSON, SIR JOSEPH, KBE (1909–1967) Commissioner, 1958–67: the first to have risen from the ranks and the third to die in harness. (Cf. Sir Richard Mayne, Captain William Hay)

Educ. Oundle and Manchester University Technical College (without completing degree). Joined Met, 1931, constable in Q Division (Wembley). In 1934, one of first intake by competitive examination at Hendon Police College. Instructor, 1936. Called to the Bar from Gray's Inn, 1937, and appointed Assistant Chief Constable of Lincolnshire the same year. Acting Inspector of Constabulary, Nottingham and Cambridge, 1939–43. Chief Constable of Northumberland, 1943–6; Chief Constable of Surrey, 1946–56. Rejoined the Met as

Assistant Commissioner B (Traffic), 1956. Deputy Commissioner, 1957.

Sir Keith Simpson's apparent triumph as the first Metropolitan Commissioner who had pounded the beat was marred, for some of his subordinates, by two things: he was an ex-public schoolboy (like practically all his predecessors), and he had gone through Trenchard's unpopular Police College for high-fliers. When, after the second reshuffle of top posts in his term of office, all four Assistant Commissioners, the Commissioner and his Deputy were

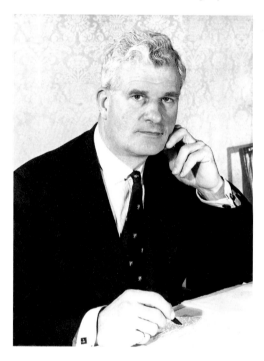

SIR JOSEPH SIMPSON.

alumni of Hendon, there was serious murmuring among some of the middle ranks, who feared their career prospects were blocked. The discontent was made worse because many officers wrongly believed that the Commissioner could make his own appointments to the top posts. (In fact, they were and are Crown Appointments made on the recommendation of the Home Secretary.)

Simpson's Commissioner's Reports were marked by forthright and challenging observations owing much to his lifetime's experience in the police, from bottom to top. He was willing to urge Parliament to repeal victim-free laws like the anti-gaming statutes, to release his officers from harrying street bookmakers at the expense

of combating serious crime. During his nine years in office he introduced five new crime-fighting branches: the Obscene Publications Squad, the Drugs Squad, the Special Patrol Group, the Scenes of Crime Branch and the Art, Antiques & Philately Squad. He enlarged and strengthened the Flying Squad. He introduced personal radios and, along with other Forces, utilized them to introduce the Unit Beat system, combining home beat officers with panda cars in most parts of the Metropolitan Police District. He reorganized the Special Constabulary, bringing them closer to the Divisional police. He introduced traffic wardens and fixed parking penalties to reduce the time his officers were spending on the unproductive pursuit and prosecution of parking offenders, and established a Traffic Branch which encouraged keen and skilled drivers to specialize in traffic matters. He improved recruiting, introduced the Cadets, and built up the strength of the Force. When he oversaw the move from the Norman Shaw building into the Broadway New Scotland Yard, he was able to report that crime figures had fallen for the first time in 13 years.

And crimebusting in the 1960s won the force some major triumphs. The confidence of the underworld was made clear to all in the Great Train Robbery but the professionalism of the police led to the arrest of almost all the robbers, despite their head start and vast funds. The South London Richardson gang was smashed and a start was made on bringing the Kray Brothers to book.

An efficient force, in Simpson's oft-repeated view, was a contented force. To this end he fought for (and won) pay improvements, and brought the married housing provision up to the Force's needs for the first time ever.

His decade in office was marked by increasing public order problems. Firm and swift action by the courts after the Notting Hill Race Riots had checked disorder by anti-immigrant thugs for the time being, but first the CND's annual Aldermaston marches, and then their successor the Committee of 100's Civil Disobedience rallies signalled a new mood of political intransigence. The sudden St Pancras Rent Riot of 21 September 1960 was a surprising revelation that normally law-abiding citizens were preparing to take to the streets with their grievances.

Sir Joseph was in a cleft stick. The government wanted him to suppress demonstrations on the streets. The huge numbers of officers required to do so resulted in his force becoming overworked with quite excessive overtime demands. There were demonstrators who wanted to start fights in the hope that 'police brutality' might win sympathy for their cause, and there were police who simply could not control their tempers. When the Challenor case occurred, the police needed a firm and disciplinarian spokesman to insist that malpractices would not be tolerated, and to reassure the public that Challenor's acquittal on grounds of insanity was not a clumsy whitewash. Sir Joseph was reserved and lacked the articulacy of some of his successors. He must bear some responsibility for overlooking CID excesses that mounted rapidly under his successor.

Nor was he welcoming to the vocal Assistant Commissioner wished on him from outside by the Home Office. Robert Mark respected Sir Joseph's integrity, but felt, with regret, that he never won his Commissioner's confidence.

Sir Joseph's untimely death was the result of overwork. By the time of his appointment it was widely felt that five years in the post was demanding enough for anybody, and there was some surprise in the force when he did not retire in 1964. Those who had hoped for consequent promotions sometimes shared their grievances with journalists.

In 1966 there were wholesale boundary changes in the Met, when Divisions were obliged to become aligned with London Boroughs. This put many police stations in the 'wrong' places in their territory. At the same time, the Met had to assume responsibility for a large part of what had been Essex. Sir Joseph took many decisions personally and so exhausted himself in trying to run his empire. He has, in consequence, sometimes been described as an ineffective or barely competent Commissioner. Nothing could be further from the truth. He was first and foremost a policeman. Every year he made a personal visit to an old pensioner from Q Division who had been his guide, philosopher and friend when he first went on the beat. He was known affectionately as 'Joe' at all levels of the Force, and met an enormous number of officers in the Met while he was Commissioner. He hated the paperwork and endless meetings that went with his post. Sportsmen recalled that he had been a notable rugby player, and as an athlete once defeated Olympic gold medalist Lord Burleigh at the hurdles. He was a reforming Commissioner whose low-key self-presentation and preference for Force-centred improvements led to better relations between Scotland Yard and the Home Office than had ever been known. His reforms were lasting, and it is the ultimate tribute to his success that it is now impossible to imagine a Commissioner being appointed who has not been a life-long professional police officer.

SOLICITOR'S DEPARTMENT Well-staffed solicitor's office which in 1935, during Lord Trenchard's Commissionership, was created to take over all the Met's legal business, including (in those days) preparing cases the police were to prosecute in the courts. Trenchard's abrupt decision deeply affected Messrs Wontner's, who had handled all the Met's legal affairs since the 1880s, and were understandably aggrieved to be unceremoniously dropped by their most important client, in whose favour they had set aside most other business. Trenchard was impenitent. It was more convenient and cost-effective to have the legal section in house, and it remains so.

Since the formation of the Crown Prosecution Service, the Solicitor's Department provides advice and representation in a wide range of matters involving operational policing but not prosecutions. It also deals with all Employment Tribunal work and employment advice. The Solicitor is responsible to the Commissioner and has a department of 40 lawyers and support staff.

SOUTH WALES MINERS STRIKE, 1910 The most important instance of a provincial strike in the early 20th century when Metropolitan Police were seconded to support overstretched county or borough constabularies. Also, as he not only sent in the Met, but sent troops to Tonypandy, control of this strike was long seen as an instance of Winston Churchill's impetuous tendency to over-reaction as Home Secretary.

A hundred Mounted Police and 700 constables on foot were sent from the Met to Glamorgan in November. Their most important encounter was with General Sir Nevil Macready, commanding the reserve forces. Neither policemen nor Macready anticipated that he would be their next Commissioner when he wrote in his final report on the strike, 'for tactful, firm, good-tempered handling of an angry mob so as to prevent, if possible, resort to force, the Metropolitan Police Officer stands out far beyond his country comrades'.

SOUTHALL RIOT Public disorder in which a demonstrator was killed, apparently by a blow from a Metropolitan police officer.

On Monday 23 April 1979, a National Front election meeting in Southall Town Hall evoked predictable violence. It was deliberately provocative on the part of the National Front to run a Parliamentary candidate advocating repatriation of immigrants in a largely Asian neighbourhood.

Despite requests from the local Indian Workers' Association, it was quite incompatible with democracy, as Home Secretary Merlyn Rees agreed, for the authorities to ban a small election meeting (no more than 60 people attended) called by a nominated and approved candidate, no matter how distasteful his personal ideology.

Following a technique recommended by Lord Scarman after the Red Lion Square riot, the police cordoned off the Town Hall and only admitted genuine visitors to the political meeting. There was a violent confrontation lasting about three hours between police and anti-Nazi demonstrators trying to break through the cordon. When the meeting in the Town Hall had passed off peaceably, the demonstration broke up.

Officers pursuing a group of Asian youths who had broken a policeman's jaw with a brick were halted by the discovery of Blair Peach, a New Zealand schoolteacher and member of the Anti-Nazi League, lying seriously injured in a side street. He was hurried to hospital, where he died; a blow to the head had fractured his abnormally thin skull. The injury's shape was consistent with its having come from an officer's truncheon, but the force of the blow suggested the possible involvement of a personal radio.

The internal Scotland Yard investigation identified several officers who could have been responsible, and sent the papers, including their suspicions as to the most likely culprit, to the Director of Public Prosecutions. He decided that their suspicions did not offer enough evidence to justify sending the matter to court. The Home Secretary decided that a public inquiry was not warranted, a decision which effectively prevented the Met from assisting the private inquiry held by Professor Michael Dummett (for which they were criticized).

The incident led to some reorganization of Special Patrol Groups (forerunners of Territorial Support Groups), and the insistence that their public order duties be given equal weight with their crime-fighting functions.

SPACKMAN, PC WILLIAM (D.1922)

Casus belli for the Police Strike, 1919.

Joined the Metropolitan Police on 30 November 1908 (B513, Warrant No. 96376). As NUPPO Branch Representative at Harefield Station, X Division, in 1919 Spackman wrote 'No action, W. Spackman, Branch Representative' on the notice his sub-divisional Inspector had posted announcing the second elections to the Metropolitan Police Representative Board, which NUPPO wanted boycotted. He was dismissed for this act of insubordination on 4 April, despite Commissioner Sir Nevil Macready's best efforts to persuade him to save his job by recanting and leaving the Union. The 'Spackman affair' became one of the alleged grievances cited to justify the abortive Police Strike, 1919.

SPAGHETTI HOUSE SIEGE

Six-day siege of armed robbers holding hostages which enabled prearranged siege tactics to be tried out.

On 28 September 1975, three gunmen led by Franklin Davies, a Nigerian, forced their way into the Spaghetti House Restaurant in Knightsbridge, where the managers of the chain assembled weekly to deposit their takings (totalling £13,000 at that time). Nine Italian staff members in the building were taken to the basement: a tenth escaped unobserved and gave the alarm.

Police immediately surrounded and cordoned off the area. The gunmen, who pretended to rep-

resent a 'Black Liberation Front', demanded safe release and an aircraft to fly them abroad. Sir Robert Mark, in consultation with the Home Office (since foreign nationals were involved), refused. Attempts were made to conduct hi-tech surveillance without the gunmen's knowledge. Dr Peter Scott gave invaluable psychiatric advice about the mental state of men cooped up under threat in uncomfortable conditions. Radio reports set out to demoralize the robbers with the insistence that their demands would never be granted (which was true), and the *Daily Mail* nobly suppressed a hard-won scoop at Sir Robert's personal request, concealing the fact that the police had arrested a man they believed to be a confederate of Davies. When a false message was sneaked in to Davies to the effect that this alleged confederate was being paid for selling information to the newspapers, it completed his demoralization, and the robbers emerged with their captives unharmed.

SPECIAL BRANCH SO12

The Metropolitan Police Unit concerned with national security. Just over 550 officers with about 140 Civil Staff. Special Branch has markedly more graduate officers than other units, and a slightly higher proportion of women officers than the CID as a whole. It comprises two Operational Command Units, one essentially concerned with counter-terrorist and counter-extremist operations, and the other providing security at international ports in London and protection nationwide to public figures and important foreign visitors who do not come under the aegis of SO14 Royalty Protection or SO16 Diplomatic Protection. In 1991 the Security OCU was one of the first major detective branches in Scotland Yard to come under the command of a woman officer, DCS Eileen Eggington QPM.

A group of four CID and eight uniformed officers were picked by Howard Vincent on 17 March 1883 as the Special Irish Branch. It was a response to the Fenian bombing campaign, intended to gather intelligence on Irish Home Rulers and their sympathizers in Parliament and the immigrant communities. Chief Inspector Adolphus Williamson commanded it, but as he had the further command of the whole CID, it came to be

headed by Inspector John Littlechild. Although its officers were outwardly indistinguishable from other CID men, their activities were financed directly from Imperial Funds, not the Scotland Yard budget. When James Monro became Assistant Commissioner and head of the CID, he kept it effectively separate from the rest of the CID under his personal control, and saw that it replaced a Home Office outfit which had been infiltrating Fenian groups. In 1888 the word 'Irish' was dropped from the Branch's title. Administratively it was 'Section D'. Colloquially it was 'the Home Office Crime Department', 'the Special Department', or 'Special Branch'. Monro and later Bradford kept it in being to keep an eye on anarchists and other left-wing revolutionaries, as well as the tiny handful of Indian nationalist students who threatened violence. In 1886, Special Branch members took over from A Division responsibility for Royalty Protection duties. The Branch vetted aliens entering the country, and was allowed to station officers at 13 ports outside the Metropolitan Police District on the west and south coasts. It gathered intelligence on Lenin and Trotsky's activities while they were in London at the beginning of the century. DC (later Det. Insp.) Herbert Fitch (Special Branch, 1905–26), with fluent French, German and Russian, hid in a cupboard and disguised himself as a waiter to listen to their propaganda speeches. At this point the Branch began to acquire a potentially sinister name for covert infiltration of political groups outside the mainstream – the sort of 'political police' activity Sir Robert Peel had always been at pains to say would not be undertaken by the Force. Fitch's subsequent racist and xenophobic memoirs (1933) certainly evince paranoid fear of foreign and left-wing organizations, and a wish for intolerably increased police powers and judicial penalties to contain them. But Fitch's explicit admiration for Mussolini's Fascisti, and express opinion that there was nothing to fear from Hitler's Germany, distances him from (for example) Sir Wyndham Childs and Lord Byng, and his frequent inaccuracy in describing well-known cases makes him an unreliable and unrepresentative commentator.

The great espionage scare of World War I restored Special Branch to popular favour, espe-

WINSTON CHURCHILL INSPECTING BOMB DAMAGE, ACCOMPANIED BY HIS POLICE PROTECTION OFFICER DETECTIVE INSPECTOR W. H. THOMPSON, AUTHOR OF *I WAS CHURCHILL'S SHADOW*.

cially as Assistant Commissioner Sir Basil Thomson was deeply concerned about spies and subversives. Special Branch was strengthened and became effectively closer to MI5 than to Scotland Yard. Throughout the war, the Branch was kept busy tracing, interrogating and arresting suspects brought to its attention by the Post Office, which monitored correspondence with known German espionage addresses in Holland. Thomson was horrified when 25 Special Branch men gave moderate support to the Police Strike, 1918, turning up for work but refusing to leave the briefing room on the day of the strike. Thomson saw the Bolshevik threat as at least equalling the threat from the Kaiser, and he equated any form of socialism with bloody Bolshevism. In 1919 he ran the branch experimentally as an entirely separate Department with himself as 'Director of Intelligence'. At this period the practice began of sending Special Branch officers obtrusively to Communist Party and left-wing extremist meetings, where they took shorthand notes and their visible presence often had the desirable effect of restraining the speakers' militant vehemence.

It reverted to being a branch of CID in 1922, and encouraged by Assistant Commissioner C Sir Wyndham Childs, who replaced Thomson, it continued the official policy of rooting out Communist (Bolshevik) subversion. (See the Arcos raid.)

Despite Lord Trenchard's sensible concern about the equal threat from the right in the 1930s, the lack-lustre National Governments of MacDonald and Baldwin were slow to endorse his recommendation that the Fascists' wings should be clipped by banning their uniforms, and the impression was allowed to grow that the authorities were more concerned with far left than far right activities. Special Branch, however, was monitoring right-wing extremist activities well before the outbreak of hostilities.

The Branch's contribution to World War II was considerably reduced by MI5's determination to have its own powers of search and arrest this time. To that end, DCI Leonard Burt, DI Reg Spooner, DS Jim Skardon and two other CID officers were seconded to the Security Service for

the duration, retaining their attestation. At the end of the war, Skardon remained with MI5 and became the notable interrogator who wrung confessions from Fuchs, the atom bomb spy, while Burt was posted to command of Special Branch.

The postwar years were initially much taken up with Cold War concerns, and Special Branch came under suspicion of keeping unnecessary tabs on left-wing Labour MPs. The activities of the CND from 1958, and anti-Vietnam War protesters in the 1960s, needed vetting not so much from a suspicion that they were dangerous spies, as to ensure that they did not provoke violent counter-demonstrations. (See Red Lion Square Riot.)

The Committee of 100, formed in 1961 with the avowed purpose of practising civil disobedience in opposition to nuclear arms, had to be kept under surveillance as its declared intention was breaking the law, no matter how high-mindedly and theoretically without violence.

The Portland spies (Harry Houghton and Ethel Gee, Konon Monody posing as Gordon Lonsdale, and Morris and Lena Cohen, posing as Peter and Helen Kroger) were genuinely acquiring and passing naval secrets to the USSR. They, like George Blake and John Vassall, were actually detected by the Military Intelligence Services, but Special Branch's police powers of search and arrest were needed to bring them finally to justice.

Bombing returned at the end of the decade with the anarchist Angry Brigade, to be followed in short order by the effective retirement of the Official IRA, and their replacement by the reckless and violent Provisionals (PIRA). From 1973 to 1998, Irish terrorism was once again a major concern for the Branch. In 1992, the government handed the lead responsibility for nationwide counter-terrorist intelligence-gathering over to the Security Service. Special Branch work in close partnership with them by continued gathering and exploitation of intelligence in London, as well as providing support for other police forces in Great Britain.

Until the 1990s Special Branch (like the Military Intelligence services) was rarely given official recognition as existing, and its administrative details and telephone numbers were not printed in reference books available to the public.

The Branch's responsibilities today include acquiring intelligence on terrorists and political extremists; dealing with espionage matters; conducting operations against terrorists and extremists involved in serious crime; delving into the financial affairs of terrorists and their organizations; enforcing provisions of the Prevention of Terrorism Act at the capital's ports; monitoring the threat posed to public order by subversive or other extremist groups; protecting VIPs and visiting Heads of State; and assisting other government agencies to counter the proliferation of weapons of mass destruction, subversion and sabotage.

A Squad has national responsibility for providing personal protection for certain politicians and other VIPs who are at threat from terrorist attack or other politically motivated violence. Members of the Squad are drawn from elsewhere in Special Branch following completion of the National Protection Officer course. The officers will normally be on the Squad for five years. By way of intelligence-led assessments, Special Branch is able to respond flexibly and also provides personal protection to visiting VIPs during official visits and major events held in this country, such as the Commonwealth Heads of Government Meeting held in Edinburgh in 1997, when protection was provided for 90 visiting heads of state, heads of government and foreign ministers. Although each officer carries a lightweight semi-automatic Glock pistol, the style of protection is intended, whenever possible, to be discreet and unobtrusive. This is achieved primarily by pre-planning and, where appropriate, the use of uniformed police support.

B Squad exercises a national role in Great Britain for the police service in respect of Irish republican terrorism. Its officers work in a close partnership with the Security Service to ensure that intelligence is exploited to the maximum to counter terrorist activity. They add the police perspective and provide advice for provincial forces on intelligence where police action may be necessary, and provide a range of assistance, information and resources to other forces for particular operations. During 1996–7 B Squad initiated the operations leading to arrests by SO13 Anti-Terrorist Branch of PIRA terrorist units planning to destroy public utilities which probably would have caused loss of life and would most certainly have had devastating effect on the capital's trade and commerce. B Squad operations have also led to the prevention of further PIRA operations planning bombing targets in central London and to the recovery of firearms and explosives, thus disrupting terrorist activity.

C Squad gathers, analyzes and exploits intelligence on domestic extremists who threaten public disorder and commit criminal offences. In the case of extreme left- and right-wing groups the principal concern is to provide intelligence to assist in the policing of demonstrations and counter-demonstrations. The assessment of threats to public order from animal rights and environmental extremists has now become a principal source of concern for the squad, replacing the traditional work against subversion.

E Squad combats the threat from international (but non-Irish) terrorism which affects the UK, in particular with regard to London. The Squad monitors international events and the political situation abroad in order to assess the public order implications and the possibility of politically motivated crime, such as terrorist attacks on dissidents in London or nationwide.

AUTHORITY FOR THE FORMATION OF THE SPECIAL IRISH BRANCH SIGNED BY DIRECTOR OF CRIMINAL INVESTIGATIONS, HOWARD VINCENT.

P Squad operates at London's international ports (Heathrow, Waterloo International, London City and the Port of London), collecting and disseminating intelligence on terrorist suspects and travelling criminals from among the 70 million passengers a year (1998). The Squad also works closely with HM Customs and HM Immigration Service in their respective roles of countering drugs smugglers and illegal immigrants. In addition, it plays a key role in the prevention of child abduction from the UK.

Sir Robert Mark found the Special Branch to be entirely unblemished by the corruption and corner-cutting that disgraced some of their colleagues. It is perhaps noteworthy that much of his own early police experience was with Manchester Constabulary Special Branch, and of his successors, Sir Kenneth Newman spent a short period with the Palestine Police Special Branch, and Sir Peter Imbert was a Metropolitan Special Branch officer for 15 years. Many other provincial Chief Constables have served with the Metropolitan Police Special Branch, which has proved a fertile nursery for the excellence leading to command.

SPECIAL CONSTABLES Attested constables who have powers of arrest and give unpaid service in support of the full-time uniformed police, undertaking similar duties – in the Metropolitan Police District, roughly 1000 men and 400 women. Area Commandants now work through Divisional Superintendents. Nicknamed 'hobby bobbies' by the press, although the 22 weeks' training and subsequent hours of work (usually between four and eight hours a week) mean that only those who are really committed can manage the time. Expenses and subsistence may be provided for certain duties, and uniform is supplied. Otherwise the Specials are making a voluntary sacrifice of their time for the benefit of the community.

The rank structure and uniform badges are Chief Commandant (four silver stripes), Area Commandant (three silver stripes), Divisional Officer (two silver bars), Sub Divisional Officer (one silver bar), Constable (Divisional letter and number). Special constables wear a flat cap instead of a helmet, but other than that their uniform is similar to that of the regular police.

A CEREMONY TO PRESENT LONG SERVICE MEDALS TO MEMBERS OF THE METROPOLITAN SPECIAL CONSTABULARY BY THE DUKE OF YORK IN OCTOBER 1921.

The Special Constables Act, 1831, empowered any two magistrates to appoint any number of Special Constables they deemed necessary to control a crowd and prevent 'tumult or riot'. The Birmingham Bull Ring disorders of 1839 proved that this might be preferable to sending a small body of Metropolitan policemen to handle crowds outside their own bailiwick. In London, the first major induction of Special Constables was for the Chartist Demonstration, 1848. The number then attested (at least 150,000: some authorities suggest 200,000) has never been exceeded, even in wartime. In 1867 Specials were attested as a response to the Fenian terror campaign. In 1887, over 6000 Specials were sworn in to help with the disturbances in Trafalgar Square that led to Bloody Sunday and in 1911 Specials were called up to police a rail strike, as it was slowly dawning on the authorities that using regular police as obvious strikebreakers aggravated what radicals already hoped was a revolutionary situation.

In all these cases the attestation of Specials was for a single *ad hoc* purpose, and they were disbanded and lost their powers of arrest as soon as the crisis was over. The outbreak of WWI led to the establishment of the Metropolitan Special Constabulary on a permanent basis. Until 1915 they performed principally Civil Defence and Home Guard-like duties and were most often organized into groups relating to their occupation or status. Thus businesses and Civil Service departments would often undertake the Special Constabulary duties of guarding their own vulnerable or sensitive buildings.

In 1915, the Specials were issued with uniforms and were given crowns and chevrons as badges of rank. They began to undertake crime prevention and law enforcement duties, going on beat patrol in place of regular constables who had joined the armed forces, and even in some cases patrolling in plain clothes on underground stations to look out for pickpockets. In 1919 it was realized that they could have a permanent role to play in peacetime.

They were not, however, universally popular with the public. Exactly why Marie Lloyd sang, 'You can't trust a Special like an old time copper' is not clear, but characteristically she represented an attitude that was common among the urban working classes. The Specials' malign reputation as strikebreakers received sympathy from within the Force when they continued to carry out duties during the Police Strikes of 1918 and 1919, though their attitude gratified Commissioner Sir Nevil Macready, who supported the idea of maintaining a permanent peacetime force of Special Constables.

From 1919 to 1934 a force of 10,000 called the Metropolitan Special Constabulary Reserve was kept in being. Those aged over 45 were known as the Auxiliary Reserve, and were only called out in emergencies. But when the greatest emergency of the interwar period arose, 61,000 men responded to the government's call for Special Constables to police the General Strike, 1926, and recruiting was suspended for some time.

In 1932 Sir Percy Laurie organized a 100-strong Mounted Division of Specials. Shortage of horses led to the number being reduced to 50 in 1938, and the Division was disbanded at the end of WWII. The MSC River Section proved longer lasting, and increased its strength from 50 to 100 in the pre-war years, finally acquiring its own boat in 1957.

A reorganization in 1934 gave the Metropolitan Specials the title they have retained: Metropolitan Special Constabulary. Efforts were made to recruit younger men, and they were given training in First Aid and emergency service that proved invaluable during the war. In 1938, following the Munich crisis, reservists were called to the colours, and the police lost thousands of men. The government immediately set in train plans to maintain police services in the event of war. Although policing was a reserved occupation, Special Constables were still liable for conscription. The government established the Police War Reserve, conscripting and enlisting men somewhat indiscriminately at first, so that a number of undesirable characters with criminal records or even warrants out for their arrest managed to become attested constables. Specials who became infamous after leaving the

service include William Joyce in 1927 (Lord Haw Haw, the Fascist traitor), and John Christie the mass murderer (WRC 1942–4). The 20,000 War Reserve Officers who flooded into the Met during the war were not technically a part of the MSC, although by 1945 Specials, WROs and regular officers were used interchangeably. For the duration of the war, Specials were allowed to volunteer for full-time service and receive pay. This caused some tension with regulars, who felt that inexperienced or underskilled officers were sometimes replacing them and sometimes receiving greater rewards. But as had happened in WWI, the excellent service rendered by the majority was recognized in the three George Medals and other decorations earned by Specials, and those who gave their lives or were injured on duty.

The Met hung on to its Specials and WROs for as long as possible after the war, as demobilization was slow and the force was depleted. By the end of 1945 the 11,000 men who could have been called upon during hostilities had reduced to 2000, but it was felt in 1949 that 9000 were needed to combat the crime wave. In 1950 women Specials were inducted for the first time, and in 1958 the MSC was brought under the direct control of Scotland Yard instead of being a separately administered body.

It is not easy to recruit police of any kind from ethnic minorities, and nearly 98% of the Specials are indigenous white people. Even so, the Special Constabulary is finding it easier to recruit ethnic minority officers than the regular service, and it is the hope of the Black Police Association, and, indeed, the Met as a whole, that this may be one way of improving the racial balance in the entire Service. The MSC can prove a useful testing ground for minority needs and aspirations. The first Sikh officer in London to be allowed to wear a turban on duty was Special Constable Harban Singh Jabbal, recruited in 1970.

Famous specials include Prince Louis Napoleon Bonaparte (later Emperor Napoleon III) in 1848, Jack Hulbert, the film star who was a Commandant in the 1940s and stationed at Vine Street police station.

SPECIAL ESCORT GROUP SO14 (2)

Forty advanced drivers and motor cyclists, most of whom have previously served in the Traffic Police. They have the duty of providing motor escorts for royalty, government ministers on certain occasions, visiting dignitaries and heads of state. They also escort the Crown Jewels and the royal art treasures whenever they have to be moved for cleaning, repair or display; high-value loads of gold bullion or cash; weapons being taken for destruction; and high-risk prisoners being moved to or from detention. They are equipped with five Rover 827 saloon cars, three Volvo T5s, three Range Rovers, one Sherpa Mini-bus, and 33 BMW RS 1100 motor cycles. Their cars are fitted with sirens of different tones, with a three-tone signal to warn traffic when a convoy rather than a single police car is approaching. In addition to reaching Class 1 in both Driver and Motorcycle training at Hendon, all officers of the group are trained in First Aid and the use of firearms. They undergo anti-terrorist ambush tactical training, and learn the high-speed turns and effective evasion techniques which constitute anti-hijack measures. When requisite they will carry standard issue Glock 9mm self-loading handguns, and for certain tasks will also carry Heckler & Koch MP5 carbines.

A special escort group was first put together in November 1952 to prepare for the occasion of

SPECIAL CONSTABLES BEING INSTRUCTED IN THEIR DUTIES FOR THE BLOODY SUNDAY DEMONSTRATION IN 1887.

SPECIAL PATROL GROUP OFFICERS AT THE BALCOMBE
STREET SIEGE, DECEMBER 1975.

Yugoslav President Marshal Tito's state visit the
following March. It is a tribute to the success of
Lord Byng's courtesy cop programme that the
notion of motorcycle outriders was acceptable to
Britain in this 'Dixon of Dock Green' period, when
dictators' motorcades and even armed American
'speedcops' bore a somewhat sinister image. The
acceptability was such that the group was re-
formed in June to participate in the Coronation
procession. Two years later, when it was put
together yet again for the visit of the Soviet leaders Bulganin and Khrushchev, it was realized that
'Special Escort' had better become a permanent
unit. In 1959 the Precision Team was created to
give demonstrations of formation riding, but has
now been disbanded.

Though the unit's headquarters are at Barnes,
and its duties require constant liaison with other
MPS units, its primary role is providing an escort
for the Sovereign, and so it comes under the command of the Royalty Protection Branch (SO14). The
Queen is customarily given an escort of four
motorcycles: other members of the royal family
have three. The lead motorcyclist is responsible for

ensuring that the escorted VIPs reach all engagements exactly on time. To this end they adjust
their speed up or down at certain precisely timed
and measured landmarks. (The device of faking
exact royal punctuality by hiding workmen in
public clocks to make them chime at the moment
the sovereign arrived was abandoned after
Richard Dimbleby revealed its use in a broadcast
commentary on the Trooping of the Colour.)

When security is the prime factor, the lead
cyclist or driver is able to select the route as they
proceed, using radio to communicate direction
changes to the other members of the escort.

In the half century of the Group's existence
no direct attack has ever been mounted on a passenger under escort, but an incident in Surrey on
6 August 1986 demonstrated vividly the heroism

that can be expected of the Special Escorts should
terrorists challenge them. PCs Alistair Thain and
Keith Wilkin were leading an escort accompanying the German President to Gatwick. As they
passed through Banstead on the Reigate Road, a
vehicle driving the wrong way down the dual
carriageway approached the convoy. Since it
made no effort to stop or pull over, PCs Thain
and Wilkin brought it to a halt by riding their
cycles directly in its path, both suffering severe
injuries in consequence. It proved that the driver
was an elderly man who had become confused by
the rather complicated one-way system and
intended no harm to the president, but PCs

SPECIAL ESCORT GROUP OFFICERS RIDING PAST
BUCKINGHAM PALACE.

Thain and Wilkin's selfless devotion to duty was warmly recognized by the German government, and they were both awarded the Iron Cross.

SPECIAL OPERATIONS ROOM Nerve centre for communication and control in major Public Order operations. Housed in the Central Communications Complex and staffed by Information Room, Traffic Control and Public Order officers, with liaison officers as and when required. Its computer system, METOPS, keeps track of resources and is part of the technological assistance which can also record images from police cameras and CCTV systems all over London. The room is usually referred to as GT, from its radio call-sign, M2GT.

The size and rank of teams manning the SOR will depend on the magnitude of the event being policed. The funeral of Diana, Princess of Wales was the largest Special Public Order operation within living memory, and the SOR was effectively monitoring and controlling 20,000 officers and 2000 Special Constables (including City of London Police) from banks of television screens.

SPECIAL PATROL GROUP Unit organized in 1961 to provide a centrally based mobile squad for combating particularly serious crime and other problems which could not be dealt with by local Divisions suffering from increasing shortages of manpower. The convenient presence of a disciplined, well-organized team soon brought the Group into increased use for the control of demonstrations, where their presence sometimes came to assume unwanted symbolic significance. Replaced by Territorial Support Groups.

SPECIALIST OPERATIONS Units carrying out policing functions which for one reason or another cannot best be handled by territorial Area officers. The general reasons are extreme specialization of the work; the large scale of the work; the spread of the work over territorial boundaries; the national importance of the work.

When Specialist Operations were set up under Sir Kenneth Newman's reorganization of 1986, they effectively took over many of the duties of the former C Department and its branches. ACSO holds many of the responsibilities of

the former Assistant Commissioner C (Crime). The scale and complexity of today's specialist squads is far greater than the eight-man Detective Branch of 1842.

(SPECIALIST OPERATIONS) MAJOR INVESTIGATION TEAMS (SOMIT) – ORGANISED CRIME GROUP Formerly the original Detective Branch, Central CID, C1 Branch and SO1 (1) Branch.

This unit of the Organised Crime Group deals with investigations which are beyond the remit of Areas and Divisions. These include active allegations of kidnaps for ransom, linked crimes or incidents with a national, international or pan-London element and other cases as directed by ACSO, for example government or judicial referrals.

These officers are the heirs of high-profile detectives like Jonathan Whicher in the 19th century and Robert Fabian and Reg Spooner in the 20th, who spent much of their time investigating murder on behalf of provincial forces when they 'called in Scotland Yard'. Since the creation of larger police forces in the 1960s, OCG is no longer likely to be called out on provincial cases.

FIELD MARSHAL SIR GERALD TEMPLER (LEFT) AWARDING 'SPIKE' HUGHES (CENTRE) AND EDGAR GURNEY (RIGHT) THEIR BRITISH EMPIRE MEDALS FOR DEVISING AND ESTABLISHING THE COLLATOR SYSTEM.

Former colonies may call them in from time to time and they have, for example, played a major investigative role in the separate murders of Julie Ward and Dr Robert Ouko in Kenya, and the murders of 'Pele' Paris and others in Barbados. Significantly, perhaps, these crimes were causing political repercussions which were best met by governments 'calling in Scotland Yard' in earnest of their bona fides, though by the same token this meant that none of the cases cited resulted in successful criminal convictions. In many other instances, however, SOMIT has brought cases overseas, or on British-registered vessels, to a successful conclusion.

'SPYKANEDY' In-force nickname for two PCs, Nevil 'Spike' Hughes, who dreamt up the collator system of local intelligence gathering in 1964, and Edgar Gurney, who helped him refine it and put it into practice at Carter Street Station in 1967. They assembled a Local Intelligence Room holding maps, criminal records, vehicle registrations and other data seen as likely to be serviceable in the investigation of Beat Crimes. The system proved so successful that it was imitated throughout the Met, and PCs Hughes and Gurney were awarded British Empire Medals for the excellence of their invention and their exemplary determination in pushing the project through without the funding and equipment that would have been made available to an initiative from a more senior position.

STAINES AIR CRASH On Sunday 18 June 1972 at about 5.10 p.m. a Trident 1 aircraft G ARPI owned by British European Airways, Flight No. 548 from Heathrow to Brussels, crashed shortly after take off on to meadowland owned by the Metropolitan Water Board on the south side of the A30 Staines by-pass near the Crooked Billet roundabout. One hundred and eighteen people on the aircraft, including six crew, were killed.

The first senior Metropolitan Police officer at the scene was Inspector Yalden, who had recently attended a special training course in aircraft incidents. The X Division Airport Incident Plan swung into action, and was made somewhat easier by the fact that most of the crash site had a natural boundary, there was no initial fire, and a purpose-built Incident Coach was readily available to help as a control post. It was one of the first examples of the use of tapes to hold back crowds, in this instance supplied by a City of London unit fresh from a training exercise. There was also a commendable degree of cooperation between Traffic Division and the neighbouring constabularies to implement traffic diversions.

It transpired that the aircraft's leading edge flaps had been retracted when it was flying at 174 knots at 533m (1750ft). It had stalled and then crashed tail first.

The rarity of such crashes does not remove the need for constant training, not least by the officers of Airport Division, now part of the Metropolitan Police Service, and there is a well-practised routine of implementing the initial stages of emergency procedures whenever aircraft report potential difficulties.

STANHOPE GOLD MEDAL Established by the Royal Humane Society in 1873 and awarded annually to the performer of the bravest deed reported to the society over the year. Twice won by Metropolitan Police Officers, in 1882 by PC John Jenkins, E Division, for rescuing a person in danger from Waterloo Bridge, and in 1992 by PC Lesley Moore, A Division, who let a scaffolder swing her across a perilous gap, five storeys above the ground, to land on a small dormer window's flat surface and give aid and assistance to a workman who had fallen 15m (50ft) on to the adjacent sloping roof. In a temperature of 12°C with 43mph winds, PC Moore covered the injured man with her tunic and pullover and stayed crouched on the dormer window for over an hour to support him until the fire brigade arrived to complete the rescue.

STANLEY, SIDNEY (B.1901) Confidence trickster whose activities, unravelled by the Fraud Squad, led to the Lynskey Tribunal (1948) and the biggest political scandal in England between the Marconi case of 1912 (when Lloyd George and other Liberal cabinet ministers were accused of using confidential government knowledge for 'insider dealing') and the Profumo affair of 1963 (when the Minister for War

was found to have enjoyed the favours of a *demi-mondaine* who also serviced the Soviet Military Attaché).

Stanley's activities were brought to the attention of the Fraud Squad when a football pool promoter complained that a cheque for £27,000 Stanley had handed to him was stopped by the bank on the grounds that it had been stolen from the firm whose account it purported to draw upon. In short order followed a complaint from the director of a women's store that Stanley, acting under cover of a company fronting for him, had offered to corrupt Board of Trade officials and acquire unjustified trade permits. Then the Board of Trade itself reported that it was hearing allegations of attempts to bribe its officials.

As normally happens when the press catches the whiff of a major political scandal, extravagant allegations involving all manner of notable personalities from business and government circles began to circulate. Prime Minister Clement Attlee announced that on completion of the Fraud Squad's investigations a public tribunal under Mr Justice Lynskey would enquire into the affair, concentrating in particular on four allegations that Stanley had corrupted officials to secure favours for businessmen.

In the event, the Fraud Squad effectively cleared almost all the 'big names' supposedly contaminated by association with Sidney Stanley, and established that he had never secured corrupt favours for anybody. He had made a great deal of money out of businessmen who were desperate to find their way round the restrictions placed on trade as part of the Attlee government's postwar recovery austerity programme; he had thrown parties and dropped names to suggest that he had influence in high government circles; but he had never delivered the influence he pretended to be peddling. The only dignitaries with whom he had any close connection were a former director of the Bank of England and Mr John Belcher, Parliamentary Secretary at the Board of Trade. Both had foolishly accepted relatively small gifts and favours from him. Neither had returned him anything more than information, but both were disgraced.

At the Lynskey Tribunal in 1949 Stanley, a Polish immigrant whose real name may have

been Solomon Kohsyzcky, proved himself an unscrupulous liar with a forceful personality and glib charm. He was transparently guilty of blatant fraud, and was committed for trial. He outwitted the plain clothes detectives maintaining surveillance on him to ensure that he did not jump bail and fled to the Continent, winding up in Israel where he published a fantastic story of having passed out of England by rail and ferry with a false passport in disguise as a senior army officer. In fact, as the Fraud Squad knew, he had secured secret passage to France by private car and yacht, through a man well-known to them and to HM Customs and Excise.

Stanley was a colourful rogue, whose lies, boasts and machinations amused and astonished the country. Though his prosecution would probably have proved successful the authorities did not try to have him extradited, probably because he had not in fact secured any corrupt breach of regulations, and his victims had generally invited their own defrauding in their willingness to circumvent them.

STANLEY, MRS SOFIA ('FIA') (C.1873–1953) Supervisor of the National Council of Women's Women Special Police Patrols, and subsequently Superintendent of Metropolitan Women Police Patrols.

B. Sofia Westlake in Palermo. Educ. England. Ran away from home in early teens: left Presbyterian church for High C of E, and became very young Head of St Mary's School, Poona. Trained as a nurse. Married Madras Railway engineer Herbert John Stanley, after return to England, c.1900. Nursed in London, Guildford and India, returning to England when Herbert lost use of legs. While living in Southsea, 1914, was visited by a former ICS police officer who stimulated her interest in police work.

Mrs Stanley then became a National Union of Women Workers' Women's Patrol Leader in Portsmouth. On moving to Mottingham, near Lewisham, she was appointed Supervisor of the National Council of Women's London Patrols in March 1917, quickly raising the number from 37 to 55 full-time women patrolling central London. Over the following year she wrote regular reports on her patrols' work for Commissioner Sir

Edward Henry, and drew his attention unfavourably to the competing activities of the Women Police Service. Shortly before the end of the War, when the Ministry of Munitions pressed the Home Office to establish official women police, Mrs Stanley was appointed Superintendent of the Metropolitan Women Police Patrols. She inducted 50 women within a year and reported favourably on the patrols' activities to the Home Office's 1920 Baird Committee on women police. She allowed a woman police patrol in plain clothes (possibly Annie Matthews or Annie Pomeroy, both of whom received commendations for a 1920 cocaine case) to infiltrate the Piccadilly streetwalkers and help break up their distribution of cocaine in the underground lavatories. She had brought the establishment up to the recommended 112 by 1922 when the public service economies demanded by Sir Eric Geddes ordered their immediate dissolution. Mrs Stanley and her senior officers immediately liaised with Lady Astor, the first woman MP to take her seat, who succeeded in forcing Home Secretary Edward Shortt to concede the continuation of a nucleus of 20 women. But Shortt was embarrassed when Lady Astor showed herself better informed than he was about the women's intentions, and during the negotiations Inspector Lilian Wyles broke ranks and complained about Mrs Stanley's tactics. This led to a disciplinary enquiry which concluded that Mrs Stanley and her lieutenants had disloyally intrigued against the Commissioner and the Home Office and subsequently lied about it. Mrs Stanley was made redundant and accepted a post with the RSPCA in Calcutta, where she was soon assisting the police in closing brothels and rescuing child prostitutes. She returned to England in 1939.

Mrs Stanley's close co-operation with Sir Edward Henry did much to ensure the future of the women police. She commanded mixed loyalties from the women who worked under her, however, and was unfortunate that the hostile action by the Home Office in 1922 led her into a position where she and her senior advisers could be made to look like schoolgirlish intriguers.

STATEMENT OF OUR COMMON PURPOSE AND VALUES One of the first outcomes of the PLUS Programme, the Statement runs:

> The purpose of the Metropolitan Police service is to uphold the law fairly and firmly; to prevent crime; to pursue and bring to justice those who break the law; to keep the Queen's Peace; to protect, help and reassure people in London; and to be seen to do all this with integrity, common sense and sound judgement.
>
> We must be compassionate, courteous and patient, acting without fear or favour or prejudice to the rights of others. We need to be professional; calm and restrained in the face of violence and apply only that force which is necessary to accomplish our lawful duty.
>
> We must strive to reduce the fears of the public and, so far as we can, to reflect their priorities in the action we take. We must respond to well-founded criticism with a willingness to change.

STATION HOUSES Originally the houses founding Commissioners Rowan and Mayne bought or acquired for police stations. Subsequently the term was likely to be used especially for Divisional Stations where accommodation was supplied, either for the Station Inspector, or by the addition of a section house.

Several surprising erections have been adopted as small station houses. A very poor equestrian statue of George IV which stood at the junction of Euston Road and Pentonville Road during the mid-19th century (and gave the former Battle Bridge area its present name of King's Cross) was supported by a large plinth whose interior was a small police station. Marble Arch and Wellington Arch, at the opposite ends of Park Lane, both contained tiny police stations, the latter even supplying a section house for 10 constables and War Reserve Officers in its bridge, and later becoming the central London Traffic Control Centre.

STATION RECEPTION OFFICERS Civil Staff who deal with the public at the front counters of police stations. Phased in to start replacing uniformed officers from 1990.

STATION SERGEANTS Originally a term denoting the senior Sergeant or Clerk Sergeant at a station, and differentiating him from the Section Sergeants who oversaw eight constables on their beats.

From 1890 to 1973, a rank unique to the Metropolitan Police, which replaced the short-lived rank of Sub-Inspector. The grade recognized that some stations were too large for one Station Inspector to carry out his duties without an assistant authorized to (for example) approve contentious charges, and some were so small that an Inspector's assumed skills and experience were wasted in posting him to it. A Station Sergeant's duties could include assuming the entire control of a small station, or deputizing for an Inspector at a large one. And, in fact, the titular rank was unofficially recognized by the junior ranks of the Force before it was given official blessing by the Commissioner.

When Sir Harold Scott made promotion to Inspector dependent on competitive examination, Station Sergeants were selected from those who had passed the examination, and Inspectors were selected for promotion from their ranks. The CID equivalent was 1st Class Detective Sergeant, who traditionally managed the allocation of crime investigations in the CID office on behalf of the Detective Inspector.

Station Sergeants and 1st class Sergeants were phased out from 1973, as the existence of their pay scale had placed a limit on provincial Sergeants' pay. William Palmer, the last to wear the crown and three chevrons, retired in 1980.

STOLEN VEHICLE UNIT Formerly Motor Vehicle Squad; originally C10 Branch (Stolen Motor Vehicles).

Started by Commissioner Sir Joseph Simpson in 1960. Now unit of Organised Crime Group.

Eighteen officers and 15 Civil Staff specialize in combating organized car theft. The unit comprises an Operational Arm, Intelligence Unit and Crime Reduction/Prevention Unit. An unmarked six-floor garage in Chalk Farm holds the cars they have recovered, and an aircraft hangar has been used to hold stolen JCB diggers.

Vehicle Examiners are specialist officers with a great knowledge of motor car construction who are skilled at identifying particular makes and years of cars, even after they have been doctored with cannibalized parts and disguised by having serial numbers altered.

'STOP BOOK' Police vernacular for Book 90, the register of persons stopped in the streets by officers under the provisions of the 'Sus Laws' (or the Vagrancy Act 1824), which had to be maintained at all stations. The name of the person stopped had to be recorded, and the legislation under which the stop was made. Abolished when PACE required only details of those searched on the street to be recorded.

STRATTON, ALFRED AND ALBERT (D.1905) The first British murderers convicted by fingerprinting.

On 27 March 1905, the Stratton brothers, a pair of thieves from Creekside, Deptford, robbed Chapman's Oil Shop in Deptford High Street and killed its elderly manager and his wife. Though local investigations quickly cast suspicion on them, there was no reliable evidence, since witnesses who had seen two men running away were unable to identify them, and Albert had destroyed his (presumably bloodstained) overcoat and boots.

But when the newly formed Fingerprint Bureau examined the shop's rifled cashbox, they found among prints left by the dead couple and a police officer who had handled it, one thumbprint left by Albert Stratton. On this evidence, the brothers were brought to trial.

The Bureau gave Mr Richard Muir, the prosecuting counsel, a thorough coaching in the fingerprint classification system developed by Assistant Commissioner Edward Henry. And in direct examination Muir had Detective Inspector Charles Stockley Collins give a very clear account of it to the court before exhibiting enlarged comparison photographs of the print on the box and Albert's thumbprint. For the defence, Dr John Garson, President of the Anthropometry Society and a former adviser to Scotland Yard's Anthropometry Department, gave positive evidence that the two prints were not the same, and accused the Bureau of incompetence. He was completely discredited when it was shown that he had written to both defence and prosecution on the same day offering his services without having made any examination of the prints. Although Mr Justice Channell warned the jury to weigh the matter very carefully before condemning two men to death on the slender evidence of one tiny thumbprint, they quickly brought in a verdict of guilty, and the Strattons were hanged.

Dr Henry Faulds, who had been trying for some years to establish his own pre-eminence in the field of fingerprinting, also worked with the defence, though he did not testify. After the trial he published claims that Collins' observations were inaccurate, and his own (undefined) 'measurements' proved that the thumbprint was not Stratton's. This led to correspondence in *The Lancet* demanding that fingerprinting should be taken out of the hands of the police and only doctors should be allowed to testify on the subject. Fortunately this advice was disregarded. The cashbox has been preserved in the Black Museum, and tests using modern resources have proved conclusively that Collins' evidence was absolutely accurate.

The Strattons' trial was the last time any defence in a murder case tried to dispute fingerprint evidence, and almost the last time it was seriously challenged in any British case of any kind. (But see under Great Train Robbery.)

STREET OFFENCES SQUAD Special group of 28 officers, formed in 1981 at West End Central station and provided with a transit carrier and a saloon car. The surprisingly large size of the squad points to the tragic existence of many marginalized men, women and young people frequenting the streets of central London.

The squad amalgamated former Vagrancy and Juveniles squads. While ensuring that homeless people and street prostitutes are not breaking laws or causing unacceptable offence to passersby, it is also concerned to see that these unprotected people are not themselves victimized or exploited by ponces, extortionists and drug traffickers. The squad collaborates with social work and other agencies concerned with the protection of juveniles. It is an interesting form of Community policing, reflecting the fact that officers in Central London have usually maintained humane and sympathetic attitudes to derelicts and prostitutes, even when compelled to arrest them and charge them with disorderly behaviour.

SUB-DIVISION A territorial command unit comprising a station or small group of stations within a Division, headed by a Superintendent and given its own Divisional letters.

SUFFRAGETTES The militant suffragettes whose 1905–1914 campaign to win votes for women entailed breaking windows, chaining themselves to railings, and threatening or abusing members of the government, presented an unusual Public Order problem for the Met. They were not, as a rule, dangerously violent. They did not incite mobs and rioting. But their activities in damaging property were clearly unlawful, and they relished the prospect of arrest to publicize their grievance.

It was an extreme embarrassment for a force of men who had won a reputation for respectful and decorous conduct towards the middle and upper classes, with definite gallantry in going to the assistance of ladies in distress, when they had to manhandle or carry screaming, squirming well-dressed little ladies who howled imprecations at them in impeccable English. There was the ever-present fear that they might injure themselves seriously; something the police were trained to prevent for any citizen. Furthermore, they adopted hunger strike tactics in prison. It was a relief to every one when the suffragettes shelved their activities for the duration of WWI, and many of them enrolled in the institutions which ultimately became the Women Police.

'SUPERGRASSES' Arrested criminals who offer to confess to all their undetected offences, name their confederates, and testify against them, in return for anticipated favourable treatment from the courts and a programme to protect them against revenge. The first was robber Bertie Smalls (see under Flying Squad), whom the DPP offered complete indemnity from prosecution for former offences in 1973, in return for giving evidence against 27 associates. The courts immediately insisted that complete

THE ARREST OF A SUFFRAGETTE.

indemnity should never again be offered, but subsequently also recognized the advantage of a 'tariff' of sentence reduction in return for information and testimony.

The supergrass system led to an immediate impressive upsurge in prosecutions, but it also led to some public criticism when it transpired that some supergrasses were enjoying relatively 'luxurious' accommodation in police cells to secure them against revenge in prison. There were doubts among some experienced detectives whether very much more by way of successful convictions was achieved than could have been secured by other methods of using excellent and well-managed informants. And in the climate of cynicism toward the end of the century there were doubts about the advisability of encouraging apparently generous 'deals' with calculating and impenitent criminals.

SUPERINTENDENT The highest rank below the Commissioners in Rowan and Mayne's 1829 Force. Superintendents commanded the Divisions, and were given quite detailed standing orders in the *General Instructions* book concerning their need to report regularly to the Commissioners' Office and (remarkably) treat the men under them kindly. Superintendent John May of A Division, being readily accessible to the Commissioners in Scotland Yard, immediately became their usual channel of information to the Force at large, and played a major role in early events marking him out as effectively (though

never officially) 'Chief Constable'. The title Superintendent (like Inspector, borrowed from the inoffensive civilians who oversaw parish schools, orphanages and the like) aimed at reassuring the public that the New Police were not a military body. It was Sir Robert Peel's wish that they should not be drawn from the ranks of commissioned army or naval officers, but replaced by promotion from below. The creation of Captain William Hay 'Inspecting Superintendent' in 1839, however, signalled the preference for having someone from the 'officer caste' as overall commander of the uniformed men.

On the introduction to the Met of the Chief Constable's rank in 1869 it was intended that the best Superintendents should be mixed with the superior gentlemen recruited from outside the Force. Only Superintendent Robert Walker secured the honour, and apart from Adolphus Williamson (promoted Chief Constable CID in 1888) Superintendent remained the highest rank acquired by anyone promoted up from constable until Sir James Olive. This grievance was well aired throughout the period in *Police Review*.

In 1995 the Service Restructuring Exercise drastically reduced the number of Superintendents in the Met from about 460 to 200. This left a markedly lower ratio of officers to exercise leadership at this level in London than elsewhere in the country.

SUPERINTENDENTS' ASSOCIATION
Police Superintendents' Association of England and Wales: the Staff Association and sole representative body of all police officers of the rank (including Chief Superintendents).

Formed after the Desborough Committee report, the first central Conference in May 1920 elected one representative to sit on the Police Council advising the Home Office, and a committee of eight to communicate direct with the Home Secretary. Metropolitan Superintendents, however, remained outside these arrangements until 1952, when the Association was re-formed with the Metropolitan and City of London Superintendents forming E District with a full-time Secretary. Each Area and CO Branch has an elected Chairman, Secretary and third member all of whom sit together as E District Executive.

By virtue of its independence and seniority, the Superintendents' Association can often make credible public statements explaining police actions which reflect the practical view of officers running Divisions.

A GROUP OF VICTORIAN SUPERINTENDENTS PHOTOGRAPHED AT THE POLICE ORPHANAGE FETE, 1876.

SURGERIES Small offices staffed at fixed weekly, fortnightly or monthly hours by Community Officers in residential areas, where the public can bring problems to the police. The analogy is with Members of Parliament's constituency 'surgeries'.

The system has rarely been widely used, but as with other symbolic aspects of Community policing is seen as making a positive contribution by assuring sceptical citizens that the police are a constant presence genuinely at their service.

SURVEILLANCE Full surveillance, involving surreptitiously following the person under observation, may be undertaken to acquire information, or to guard and protect some person or persons believed to be under threat. In the 1890s Inspector John Littlechild also recommended open and obvious surveillance on occasion. This may be used to alarm, embarrass or simply control and deter known and defiant criminals against whom there is insufficient evidence to make an arrest. The method was used very effectively to discredit the Kray twins when they were trying to establish their credentials with visiting delegates from American organized crime.

Before the establishment of the Detective Branch it was apparent that surveillance required plain clothes. Uniformed police watching the Spitalfields home of Daniel Good's ex-wife Molly in 1842 were forced to hide awkwardly in doorways and entries, and press mockery of their intrusive presence in the district encouraged the formation of a permanent Detective Branch.

There are now thorough training courses in surveillance methods, including changing from foot to public transport to private cars. Observation is the term used when an officer remains in a static location.

Observation from an indoor hiding place can have the most ludicrous appearance. Inspector Field told Dickens of the discomfort he suffered when hiding under a sofa in a gentlemen's club to catch a sneak-thief who was rifling overcoat pockets hanging from pegs. The hiding-place was so draughty that he had to tie a bandanna handkerchief around his face. Twenty years later, Andrew Lansdowne

cramped himself into a tiny lavatory and bored a spyhole to look for a thief in the home of a 'high official of state'. It was a long wait, and uncomfortable, but it worked. (It was a footman who filched valuables while the family were out.) Chief Inspector Littlechild recalled an occasion when a Police Superintendent, a Detective Sergeant, the father of a ward of court, and a family solicitor all hid in separate cupboards in a registry office, and emerged to prevent the ward's illicit nuptials with a fortune-hunter.

The most extraordinary example of detective hide-and-seek was related by Sergeant Harold Challenor. Wishing to mount surveillance on a house from a prostitute informant's well-placed window, he persuaded her to let him stay in her room provided he hid when clients visited. The only hiding place was under her bed, from which position Challenor gained much interesting information about his friend's professional life, though he suffered grievous discomfort when she was visited by a forceful 14-stone punter. The only advantage of the position was its proximity to the bidet, allowing Challenor on one occasion to creep out and relieve himself without the preoccupied client ever being aware of his presence.

SURVEYOR (1) (Obsolete) Senior uniformed rank in the Marine Police. Became Inspectors when amalgamated with Metropolitan Police as Thames Division.

(2) Civil Staff in the Receiver's Department. In the 1880s there was some disappointment that architect Norman Shaw was called in from outside to design the New Scotland Yard on the Embankment, as it had been expected that the Force Surveyor would undertake the work.

'SUS LAWS' Section 4 of the Vagrancy Act of 1824 empowering the courts to deal with offenders as incorrigible rogues who were 'suspected persons or reputed thieves loitering with intent to commit an indictable offence,' and Section 66 of the Metropolitan Police Act, 1839, empowering an officer to stop, search and detain anyone whose possession of property in the street gave rise to reasonable suspicion. Police officers were required to make written

entries in the Stop Book of all persons they stopped, citing the legislation under which they acted. The offence of 'loitering with intent to commit a crime' was extremely useful in preventing (for example) thefts from cars, and is legally different from a police officer's powers either to stop or additionally to conduct a search of a suspect in the street. Civil rights groups in the 1970s accused the police of using sus laws to harass young black men. After much acrimonious public debate the old Sus Laws were repealed and to some extent replaced by parts of the Criminal Attempts Act, 1981 and PACE. The powers to stop and search remain an essential part of the armoury against crime, producing a significant percentage of arrests and charges, but they are also still perceived as being disproportionately used against young black people.

SYME, INSPECTOR JOHN, (1872–1945) An officer who followed his controversial dismissal with an extravagant campaign against Sir Edward Henry and founded NUPPO.

A solicitor's clerk from Ayrshire. Joined Met, 1894. Warrant No. 79972. Constable B Division (B22). CO Division, 1896. Sergeant, 1899. Station Sergeant, V Division, 1901. Inspector, 1908. Reduced to Station Sergeant, T Division, 1909. Dismissed for insubordination, 1910.

In the small hours of 18 August 1909, two constables arrested two noisy drunks in Pimlico and brought them to Gerald Road Police Station to be charged with 'wilfully and wantonly disturbing Mrs Costa of 134 Warwick Street by pulling the doorbell and knocking at the door without lawful excuse.' Syme, the Station Officer on duty, was a pedant: a devout Presbyterian with an inflexible certainty about what was right and what was wrong, what was true and what was false. He also had a determination to be absolutely fair at all times which accorded ill with his precisian mentality. Mrs Costa had brought no complaint; nor had other residents of the street, although they volubly objected to the noise. Syme therefore refused the charge when the drunks gave the true excuse that they lived at the house in Pimlico and one was Mrs Costa's husband, trying unsuccessfully to get her to let them in. The arresting constables' names then had to be entered in the Refused Charges Book. This brought them severe reproof from the Sub-Divisional Inspector and Chief Inspector (Acting Superintendent), a pair of disciplinarian old sweats who resented Syme's unbending scrupulosity and his insistence that the constables should not be disciplined for wrongful arrest, since the drunks had not given them the facts. When Syme persisted, they transferred him to another station, with an adverse report agreed on all sides to be unreasonable, and including the very damaging claim (in 1909) that he was 'obviously too familiar with the constables'.

Syme protested to Commissioner Sir Edward Henry and proceeded to add general complaints about dissatisfaction at Gerald Road Station, arising from heavy-handed discipline. He was routinely suspended while his complaint and his seniors' counter-complaint against him were investigated, and he added his suspension to the list of complaints he forwarded to the Home Secretary when a Disciplinary Board recommended his reduction to Station Sergeant. When the Home Office refused to intervene, Syme threatened to raise the matter with his MP. He was thereupon dismissed from the force as impossibly insubordinate.

Syme's case was taken up by the *Police Review*, and attracted a good deal of sympathy. Winston Churchill, the new Home Secretary, offered him reinstatement as Station Sergeant, which would have provoked Henry's resignation had not Syme refused anything less than his return as an Inspector. Syme added Churchill's 'inadequate' offer to his list of grievances. In 1911 he wrote to Ramsay MacDonald threatening to assault Churchill and murder his former Sub-Divisional Inspector, for which letter he was sentenced to six months' imprisonment. On his release in 1912 he formed the 'John Syme League' and organized public meetings at which he distributed libellous pamphlets about the police. In 1913 he advertised the formation of the Metropolitan Police Union, although Regulations strictly prohibited any such body. In 1914 he expanded it to the National Union of Police and Prison Officers. Until the Police Strike, 1918, this consisted of no more than

a couple of hundred officers, mostly in London, who met clandestinely and secretly distributed a very few copies of their union *Journal*.

Syme was imprisoned again in 1914, for a libellous leaflet which claimed that the Met suborned perjury to secure Stinie Morrison's conviction, and again in 1916 when his speeches were held to breach the Defence of the Realm Act. On his release from prison, the other leaders of NUPPO realized that his obsession with his own grievances, his rancour against Henry, and his unpredictable attacks on all and sundry were making him a liability. Syme was voted off the executive of the Union he had founded, and became one of its bitterest enemies when it did not include his name among those of officers suspended or dismissed for union activities whose reinstatement was demanded in the 1918 strike.

From then on, he became increasingly eccentric and was repeatedly arrested and imprisoned. He threw stones and (once) a shell-case through the windows of 10 Downing Street. His speeches threatened politicians, policemen, even the King and Queen. Home Secretary Sir Edward Shortt said in 1921, 'The moment he is not being watched he is outside Buckingham Palace with a brick.' His repeated hunger-strikes in prison led to his being the last victim of the 'Cat and Mouse Act' (a measure for the temporary release from prison and re-arrest of hunger strikers) introduced by Asquith to deal with suffragettes. In 1924 the Labour government agreed to an official enquiry into his case. Two judges and the future Lord Chief Justice Rayner Goddard heard all the evidence, and found that Syme had been quite right to refuse the original charge against the drunks; quite right to defend the constables who brought it; quite right to protest about being accused of over-familiarity with them; quite right to accuse the Divisional Inspector and Sub-Divisional Inspector of fomenting discontent by their heavy-handed discipline; quite right to protest that they bullied men into giving false testimony against him before his disciplinary hearing; and quite right to say that his transfer did not (as the authorities pretended) meet the need to break up the personality clash between him and the Divisional Inspector, whom he would still encounter

at his new station. Yet nonetheless, they found against him, saying his transfer was not a punishment as he was not required to pay his moving expenses; his demotion was warranted because in one clause of one of his statements he had used emotive language when he rightly accused the Inspector and Sub-inspector of encouraging false testimony; and his final dismissal was justified because no disciplined force could let a man exercise his democratic right of appealing against its bad decision to Parliament!

Well might Syme find this final judgment against himself literally maddening. The disappointment overturned his unstable reason, and on his next (and thirtieth) imprisonment for uttering threats, he was found to be insane and transferred to Broadmoor, where he was treated for a year before being discharged. Labour MPs George Lansbury and Ellen Wilkinson, however, believed (wrongly) he was being penalized for standing up to the reactionary Home Secretary Sir William Joynson-Hicks, and they kept Syme's case high on the party agenda. The second Ramsay MacDonald government re-examined the case, and in 1931 Home Secretary J. R. Clynes reported that Syme had indeed been wrongfully transferred in 1909. The specious pretence that this was not a disciplinary action was treated with the silent contempt it deserved, and although a formal whitewashing remark absolved the civil servants who had handled the case, Syme was praised for his integrity and sincerity and granted his pension, backdated to 1909. Sympathetic MPs like Ellen Wilkinson and Fenner Brockway stopped him from making this victory into a new cause of grievance, and reopening his campaign with a demand for additional compensation for his lost career prospects!

For the last years of his life he continued to hang around Buckingham Palace, lugubriously advising young constables of their duties if they failed to make a note of his presence. But on his death he received a glowing tribute from the former MP, JP and internationally respected journalist Leonard Matters, who called him 'the soul of honour' and said he had 'never met a man of higher principles'.

TANNER, DETECTIVE INSPECTOR RICHARD (1831–1873)

Early detective whose notebook detailing arrests he made between 1856 and 1867 has survived.

Born Egham, Surrey. Worked as a clerk. Joined the Met, 1851. Warrant No. 3018. Posted to C Division (St James's). Transferred to A Division (Whitehall), 1854, and joined the Detective Branch. Sergeant, 1857. Inspector, 1863. Briefly shared with Adolphus Williamson general responsibility as senior officers in the Detective Branch. Retired, owing to rheumatism, 1869. Moved to Winchester and kept the Swan Hotel.

Tanner's fame in his own day was as the officer who travelled to New York and arrested Franz Müller, the first railway murderer. He was also well-known to the sporting gentry and aristocracy, having policed many race meetings in the late 1850s and early 1860s. However, his importance to historians lies in the preservation of his personal 'Prisoners' Apprehension' notebook at the Historical Museum. This lists 58 cases,

DETECTIVE INSPECTOR TANNER'S NOTEBOOK ACCOUNT OF THE MURDER OF MRS MARY EMSLEY BY JAMES MULLINS.

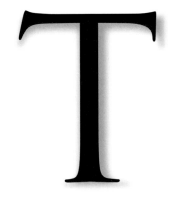

including Müller's, and gives Tanner's brief synopses of most of them, as well as stating when and where the prisoners were arrested, before whom they were tried, and what was the outcome. They include another famous case in which Tanner established that a murderer named Mullins had laid false information leading to the arrest of an innocent man for his own crime. They included cases peculiar to the period – the arrest of a prizefighter and a dog handler for arranging a boxing match, or the arrest of a man passing counterfeit sovereigns, with whom Tanner played bagatelle at a Holborn pub to observe him until he committed the offence. In

one extraordinary case he arrested an artist whom he believed to be well-known in his own right. The man had appropriated a number of paintings and artefacts from a gallery, apparently in order to make copies of them. When they were returned and the copies destroyed, charges were dropped. In many commonplace cases he arrested pickpockets and thieves and he once closed an illegal gaming saloon, but he never raided a brothel nor charged a prostitute with soliciting (though he arrested many for theft). 'Disorderly houses' and 'insulting behaviour' on the street, we infer, were matters for the uniform branch and below the dignity of 'the Detective'.

Tanner lists his awards and gratuities. The highest was £50, for going to Malta and arresting a Frenchman who had stolen opera glasses worth a total of £600. The lowest was 10s (50p) for arresting an army deserter. The Müller case won him £5 from the victim's family and £20 from the government. The Great Bullion Robbery brought him into collaboration with some very famous contemporaries – Adolphus Williamson and two of the early Detective Sergeants described by Charles Dickens.

TAPE-RECORDED INTERVIEWS

After experiments in the early 1980s, put into statutory form by PACE (1984). The Met's pilot scheme was followed by the introduction of specially equipped rooms for interviewing prisoners throughout London. The volume of interviews made tape storage a logistical problem and transcription time-consuming, but it was remarkable how rarely defence solicitors challenged (or even appeared to listen to) recorded interviews produced as assurance that prisoners' statements were correctly transcribed.

TEAPOT I

An imaginatively assigned radio call sign first used for the Catering Service's emergency response vehicle serving officers on duty in the Wapping area during the News International dispute in 1987.

TECHNICAL SERVICES AND DEVELOPMENT

Approximately 60 engineers and technicians in the Department of Technology who devise and develop crime-fighting tools and gadgets, such as tracking devices, night vision aids, surveillance equipment and so forth.

TEMPORARY DETECTIVE CONSTABLE (TDC)
Probationary position, held for (usually) two years by new members of CID before they were confirmed Detective Constables. Replaced the former post of Aid to CID and in turn replaced by Trainee Investigators.

TERRITORIAL OPERATIONS
Under the Newman Restructuring (1984–5), the Department supplying support and back-up services to the Area and Divisional mainstay local policing. They included (for example) Branches dealing with Mounted Police and dog-handlers, as well as central Traffic Police services. The whole operational system was commanded by ACTO (Assistant Commissioner, Territorial Operations).

Changed by Sir Paul Condon's Restructuring Exercise, 1995, which abolished the post of ACTO and the term Territorial Operations, and made five ACs responsible for a section of area policing and a portfolio of the HQ Branches apiece.

TERRITORIAL SUPPORT GROUPS
Uniformed officers with special training in rapid deployment, crowd control, search and evidence-gathering under hazardous conditions, surveillance and similar skills requiring physical fitness, physical courage and close disciplined teamwork. They are available as reserves for instant response, and may be based in Areas, or centrally as the Commissioner's Reserve.

Most familiar to the public as police support units in riot gear at major public order incidents. Nonetheless, they are neither the only police who may serve in such a way on such occasions, nor are public order duties their only responsibility. They may be called in to help on the ground at emergencies or serious traffic accidents. The death of TSG PC Nina McKay, assisting in the arrest of a mentally disturbed and dangerous suspect in 1997, is a useful reminder that TSG officers are female as well as male, and are involved in everyday incidents in support of Divisions policing local communities. They are not a relatively unaccountable riot police.

THAMES MUSEUM
Museum of River Police at Wapping. Established in 1976, the collection includes equipment and memorabilia relating to the history of the river and the formation of the Marine Police and Thames Division.

THAMES POLICE ASSOCIATION
Society formed in April 1956 and open to past and present members of Thames Division and attached Special Constables and Civil Staff. The association organizes social events, publishes the quarterly *Ogglers' Journal* (an 'oggler' being one who ventures on the 'oggin', naval slang for the sea) and has as its badge a shield showing a water-beetle on a background of wavy blue and grey bars, supported by dolphins and with a naval crown as crest. The motto is 'Primus Omnium 1798' (First of All).

THOMSON, SIR BASIL HOME (1861–1939)
Assistant Commissioner who wrecked his career and reputation on being arrested for public indecency with a prostitute in Hyde Park.

B. Queen's College Oxford, son of the Provost, who later became Archbishop of York. Educ. Eton and New College, Oxford, which he left for health reasons before graduating. In 1883 joined armed forces in Fiji; soon thereafter appointed Prime Minister to the aged King of Tonga's heir. In 1889 returned to England and started secondary career as a writer, mainly of his own memoirs and experiences. In 1896, called to the bar (Middle Temple) and appointed governor of a succession of prisons, and in 1908, Secretary of the Prisons Commission. In 1913, appointed Assistant Commissioner C and head of CID, Scotland Yard. Concentrated on anti-espionage activities during WWI, and played a leading part in the unsavoury circulation of the homosexual entries in Sir Roger Casement's diaries to ensure that the Irish patriot's international reputation as a philanthropist did not prevent his execution for treason. In 1919, awarded KCB and appointed Director of Intelligence at Scotland Yard (effectively head of Special Branch with direct responsibility to the Home Secretary). Became known as fanatical anti-Bolshevist, and extremely hostile to left-wing pacifist and internationalist groups and

individuals as well as markedly anti-Semitic. Sir William Horwood's insistence that he be brought back under the authority of the Commissioner led to Thomson's resignation in 1921 (cf. Sir Charles Warren and James Monro), and the resumption of his writing career with *My Experiences at Scotland Yard* (1922). But he appears to have hoped that he might be appointed Deputy Commissioner when Sir James Olive reached retirement at the end of 1925, and so succeed Horwood himself in 1928.

His hopes were dashed when he was arrested on Saturday 12 December 1925 sitting on park chairs in Lovers' Walk, Hyde Park in the company of 'actress' (and subsequently self-confessed prostitute) 'Thelma De Lava'. According to the uniformed arresting officers, Thomson made insinuations that charges might be dropped because of his standing, or he might be able to help their careers if they helped him. Thomson vigorously denied these allegations, and said they had misunderstood his remarks. At Hyde Park police station he signed his bail notice 'Hugh Thomson', later claiming that the station officer must have written it, mishearing his middle name 'Home'.

He and Thelma both failed to turn up at Great Marlborough Street magistrates' court on Monday, which was probably his greatest misfortune. He had gone to Bow Street in error, and might well have won the magistrates' sympathy had he appeared alone to plead his innocence. But by the time he appeared before the bench, defended by the leading barrister Sir Henry Curtis-Bennett, Thelma had made her own appearance, pleading guilty and accepting a £2 fine and binding over, although no details of indecency emerged beyond the fact that Thomson had his arm around her neck and they were kissing.

Thomson's defence was that he had gone to the park hoping to hear a Communist speaker (whose name he did not know), and to gather material for a book about prostitutes soliciting in the park. The speaker was not around when he got there, and Thelma had addressed him, apparently begging. He continued in conversation with her, hoping to learn more for the purposes of his book. He produced a former Home Secretary and the head of MI6 as character witnesses, but the magistrate regretfully pointed out that he had

SIR BASIL THOMSON.

never said a word about his alleged book to the police, which made his plea of innocence seem very lame. Sir Basil was found guilty and fined £5.

With extreme folly, he appealed and repeated his defence, adding a number of character witnesses. But this time Thelma was called by the prosecution and, again without going into detail, she testified that she and Sir Basil had indeed committed an offence after he had approached her and offered her money which she accepted. The appeal was rejected, and to the delight of all left-wingers, Sir Basil's reputation was in tatters and there was no further chance of his ever holding a senior police position again.

THOMSON, PC JAMES WARRENDER, KPM (D.1935)

Officer who sacrificed his life to save pedestrians. Joined the Met 29 October 1923 (PC 397S, Warrant No. 112399). At his death he left a widow and three children, the oldest of whom was six.

Barnet Fair attracted large crowds in September 1935, and PC Thomson was posted to direct traffic at the junction of the Great North Road, Barnet Hill, with Mays Lane. An adjacent

tram stop attracted pedestrians to cross the road continually, and full trams meant that many more stood in the roadway waiting.

At approximately 11.30 a.m. on 7 September, a heavy lorry carrying cement lost control on the hill, and headed straight for the crowd. PC Thomson spotted it, and held his position in its path, pushing people out of its way and shouting to the crowd to clear away. Many people were injured by the vehicle, but thanks to PC Thomson's heroic devotion to duty only four lives were lost, including, of course, his own.

He was posthumously awarded the KPM and a Memorial Certificate from the Carnegie Hero Trust. His case led to the introduction of the Roll of Honour (see Appendix 4).

TIGER

Privately owned Airedale police dog, reported as achieving the first canine arrest in the MPD.

In 1911, shortly after Commissioner Sir Edward Henry had confirmed that officers were permitted to take their dogs with them on their beats, Tiger was accompanying PC Cheeseman (17 V) on patrol in Richmond. The dog observed movement in a greenhouse, and Cheeseman stopped to observe the building. When a man came out with some flowers and ran away instead of answering PC Cheeseman's call, Cheeseman and Tiger gave chase together and caught the thief between them. Cheeseman received a Commissioner's Commendation and 7/6d (37p) reward for the arrest.

TILTS

Rectangular boat-aprons of waterproof material (oilskin or rubber) lined with serge. Issued to Surveyors and Inspectors in the River Police as essential for warmth and protection against spray as they sat in the sternseats of galleys. After 1902, when engined boats began to be used, all crew members were issued with tilts as they were no longer presumed to be warming themselves by rowing. (cf. toe-bags).

THE TIMES CORRUPTION ALLEGATIONS

Claims that Scotland Yard detectives were blackmailing criminals for money or information. Ultimately the articles led to two officers receiving prison sentences.

On 29 November 1969 *The Times* gave prominent front-page coverage to taped conversations which apparently recorded Det. Sgt John Symonds accepting £150 from a petty thief for getting him off a charge, and giving him warm avuncular advice to come back if he needed help because Symonds was a little firm within a firm in London, though there was little anyone could do about the provincial police, or 'swedes'. Perhaps most alarmingly of all, Symonds calmly warned the crook against blackmailers in the Met, telling him, 'We've got more villains in our game than you've got in yours, you know.' Det. Insp. Bernard Robson of C9 Branch, and Det. Sgt Gordon Harris of Brighton, on secondment to the Yard, were accused by the paper of being among such greedy blackmailing villains.

The case was important as the first in which an outside investigator (Frank Williamson, Her Majesty's Inspector of Police for the North East) was put in place to examine a complaint against the Met rather than leaving it in the hands of the CID.

In the end, Robson and Harris were sent to prison, while Symonds was eventually arrested in Spain. This was the first of the 1970s scandals which led to the appointment of Sir Robert Mark as Commissioner and his reforms of the CID.

TIPSTAVES (Singular is 'tipstaff').

Originally short hollow brass or wooden tubes for carrying documents. Their screw-on metal caps came to take the form of the monarch's crown when the papers were royal warrants, and the expression 'I'll crown you!' derives from the production of the truncheon-like tipstaff as authority for making an arrest. There was nothing, however, to prevent the arch-receiver and prototypical organized crime chief Jonathan Wild (1682–1725) from arming himself with an unauthorized tipstaff and using it to order the arrest and impeachment of thieves who refused to work for him.

Tipstaves were carried as identification by the Bow Street Runners. Peel's New police, ordered to wear uniform at all times and thereby identifiable, were given, but not required to carry, warrant cards. When the Detective Branch was formed in 1842 it was not at first recognized that its officers might need a permanent means of identification. In 1863 the detectives were directed to summon a uniformed constable if they ever entered a beer shop or public house so that their police authority could be confirmed. In 1867 they were issued with 15cm (6 inch) brass tipstaves, officially known as Warrant Carrying Cases. Uniformed officers of and above the rank of Inspector were given similar tipstaves in carrying cases. In 1870 the CID tipstaves were inscribed 'Metropolitan Police Constable in Plain Clothes'. In 1880 tipstaves were withdrawn.

TITLEY, THOMAS (FL.1880) Purveyor of abortifacients whose arrest and conviction led to Parliamentary questions and threatened Sir Howard Vincent's public standing by making him appear an employer of *agents provocateurs*.

In 1880, Bow Street police were informed that Titley, a young pharmaceutical chemist, was selling abortifacients. The information, however, was mere hearsay which could not be presented as evidence in court. Accordingly, local Inspector John O'Callaghan and Detective Sergeant Shriver employed a female searcher from Bow Street to pose as a client. Martha Diffey, wife of a police pensioner, pretended that her daughter had been impregnated by the young son of a house where she worked as a servant. Titley was suspicious of a letter she produced, supposedly from the putative father, and asked to see the girl or the young man. A detective from another Division, Sergeant Stroud was dressed up in fashionable clothes and given £25 to make a show of wealth. He described himself as 'Henry Williamson' (apparently a private joke on Superintendent Adolphus Williamson, the senior CID officer at Scotland Yard), and succeeded in obtaining ergot of rye and perchloride of iron for the remarkably modest sum of 4s (20p).

Titley was arrested and appeared in court in July. His counsel, Sir Edward Clarke, roundly abused O'Callaghan, Shriver and Mrs Diffey, though he carefully exculpated the Director of the CID, Sir Howard Vincent, who had overseen the whole operation, if he did not in fact personally mastermind it. The judge's summation condemned the officers' conduct, but warned the jury that it could not outweigh any evidence against Titley. He was convicted, with a strong

recommendation to mercy, and was sent to prison for 18 months.

The following day, O'Callaghan, Shriver and Mrs Diffey appeared before the magistrates charged with incitement to commit a crime. The case against them was dismissed on the technical grounds that the indictment had been improperly drawn up, and no further proceedings were taken. It has been suggested that this was a ruse to prevent Vincent's involvement coming out in court.

The press was quick to seize on the issue of entrapment, and Home Secretary Sir William Harcourt assured Parliament that the police would not generally resort to it in the future, though he pointed out that in a subsequent abortion case, the evidence had depended on the deaths of a mother and child.

TOE-BAGS (OR TOW-BAGS) Lined sacking leg-warmers used by River Police on patrol in galleys. The toe-bag ensconced a man warmly from his feet to his waist like a short, narrow sleeping-bag, and would be covered by a waterproof tilt or boat-apron if he was issued with one.

TOMS SQUAD C Division duty, especially prior to the Street Offences Act, 1959. Officers were required to arrest and charge prostitutes who lined the streets from Shepherd's Market in the east to Covent Garden in the east, and St Giles's Circus in the north to the Haymarket in the south. There were so many by 1959 that they were normally arrested on an unofficial rota system, and could usually expect to be charged and fined £2 every three or four weeks.

Early references to 'the Vice Squad' in central London usually describe officers carrying out this routine duty. They did not have the important social and Community policing duties of the later Street Offences squad.

See also Sergeant Goddard.

TORCHES See Lanterns.

TOTTENHAM OUTRAGE Murder of PC William Tyler (Divisional No. 403N) and 10-yr-old Ralph Joscelyne, and wounding of 21 other people by two 'anarchist' robbers trying to escape after a wages snatch.

Paul Hefeld and Jacob Lepidus were Latvian immigrants who stole the wages from Schnurrman's rubber factory on the corner of Tottenham High Road and Chesnut Road on 23 January 1909. The two stood at the corner armed with pistols and when the chauffeur-driven car carrying the wages clerk drew up they seized the leather cash bag and shot at the chauffeur and a passing stoker who grappled with Lepidus. The shots brought reserve constables William Tyler and Albert Newman (Divisional No. 510N) running from the police station on the other side of the High Road, and they started the long chase during which the anarchists would fire over 400 rounds at their many pursuers. Farcical moments peppered this tragedy, starting with the action of a housewife out shopping who saw Hefeld and Lepidus running from the police and threw a potato at them. A number of officers ran out from the section house attached to the station and joined the pursuit. Some seized their truncheons, several of them used bicycles, and one officer was seen to be riding a bicycle and brandishing a cutlass.

At the Mitchley Road Mission Hall PC Newman urged the chauffeur to try to run down the gunmen with the wages car. In response, Jacob and Hefeld shot and injured Newman and the chauffeur, shot and smashed the car's radiator water pipe, and shot little Ralph Joscelyne as he ran for the cover of the car. The boy was taken straight to hospital, but was pronounced dead on arrival. Police in the station now smashed open the locked firearms cupboard to bring pistols to the pursuit.

At the railway footbridge leading to Tottenham Marshes, PC Tyler took advantage of the wall cutting off Jacob and Hefeld's view to race over waste ground and catch up with them. 'Come on, give in. The game's up,' he said. Hefeld deliberately shot him in the face at point-blank range with his Bergmann automatic. Tyler bled to death in the scullery of a nearby cottage.

The gunmen then ran across the marshes, collecting an ever-growing band of pursuers, including footballers, labourers, duckshooters and gypsies. Shots were fired at them, but the light peppering of duckshot he received did not deter Hefeld.

ARTISTS IMPRESSION OF LATVIAN ANARCHISTS HEFELD AND LEPIDUS COMMANDEERING A TRAM IN CHINGFORD ROAD AND BEING PURSUED BY POLICE.

When the chase reached Chingford Road, it entered a moment of Keystone Kops absurdity. Jacob and Hefeld commandeered a tram, terrorized the three passengers and the driver, and made the conductor drive it when the driver hid upstairs. The police commandeered a tram going in the opposite direction and made it reverse after them, the occupants of the two trams firing ineffective shots at each other. At Kite's Corner the conductor got rid of his unwanted passengers by laconically warning them there was a police station round the corner. The gunmen tumbled out, shooting and injuring the old man who was the only surviving legitimate passenger on board. They commandeered a parked milk van, and immediately wrecked it by cornering too fast; next they commandeered a parked greengrocer's van but could not flog the horse into more than the slowest of ambles because they omitted to release the brake. They then abandoned the van and ran along a path beside Chingford Brook. When the path petered out, leaving them trapped by a high fence, Lepidus scrambled over it. But Hefeld was exhausted, and seeing he was about to be arrested, put his gun to his head and shot himself. He was taken to hospital, where he refused to speak until he died three weeks later with the uninformative remark, 'My mother is in Riga.'

Lepidus, meanwhile, ran into the nearest of a small development of cottages at Oak Hill, and frightened the housewife and two children into the lean-to scullery. When his pursuers reached the house he locked himself in a bedroom, and used his last bullet to shoot himself as PCs Charles Eagles, Charles Dixon (a CID officer) and John Cater broke in and fired shots through the door at him.

Sooty handprints on the kitchen wall suggested to the police that Lepidus had tried to escape up the chimney. They did not search the flue, however, and so missed the stolen wages bag, off whose £80 it is said that the occupants of the cottage lived very happily for some time after.

A collection of £1,055 was raised for PC Tyler's widow, and the interest from it was added to her police-granted pension of £15 a year. The King's Police Medal was instituted in recognition of the gallantry of those officers who had pursued the murderous pair, and Cater, Dixon and Eagles were the first recipients (see Appendix 3).

The outrage had a considerable influence on public and police perception of immigrants and the international left, and provoked some misplaced public anti-Semitism. This in turn influenced the Siege of Sidney Street and the trial of Stinie Morrison.

TRAFALGAR SQUARE DEMONSTRATION, 1961 Banned demonstration, whose heavy-handed police dispersal won militant left-wing activists undeserved support for subsequent violent demonstrations.

After three years of legitimate but apparently ineffective Aldermaston marches, a breakaway section of the Campaign for Nuclear Disarmament rejected its policy of consistent obedience to the law and proposed a campaign of Ghandian Civil Disobedience. The new 'Committee of 100' consisted mainly of little-known young agitators, but the elderly philosopher Bertrand Russell lent it his name, and to the accompaniment of huge publicity was given a short term of imprisonment in 1961 for inciting others to break the law.

The Committee thereupon insisted on going ahead with a CND rally planned for Trafalgar Square, actually delighted that the Home Secretary had encouraged Commissioner Sir Joseph Simpson to ban it by declaring the square temporarily closed to the public for the evening of the demonstration. This ensured massive press and television coverage for the tens of thousands of demonstrators bussed in from all over the country, and the 4000 police officers ringing the square, waiting to receive arrests in vans and buses parked nearby.

The demonstration was peaceful and initially ineffective. The police reacted impassively to taunts from a few demonstrators. The Committee of 100's hope was that all demonstrators would be arrested and clog the courts by all pleading not guilty, but the police only arrested those who drew attention to themselves and there were few scuffles as the demonstrators followed a directive to accept arrest with 'passive resistance' (relaxing limply on the ground so that they had to be carried away). By midnight, the majority of the demonstrators had given up hope of being arrested, and drifted home peacefully.

And then, with the television cameras removed, a body of police was ordered to clear the square and arrest all remaining 'passive resisters'. Just over 1000 arrests were made. Many of the arresting officers were tired, annoyed by the unwanted late-night overtime duty, and exasperated by silly taunting from sections of the demonstration. A few used unacceptable force in clearing the square. The incident led to adverse newspaper coverage about police behaviour in controlling and dispersing passive demonstrations.

TRAFALGAR SQUARE DEMONSTRATION AND RIOT, 1886 Brief riot and subsequent panic which forced the resignation of the Commissioner and his replacement with a military man. Sometimes known as Black Monday.

On Monday 8 February 1886 two rival radical organizations, the London United Workmen's Committee and H. F. Hyndman's revolutionary Social Democratic Federation, gave notice of their intention to hold meetings in the square on the same day. It was recognized that they might clash violently and an experienced Commissioner or Home Secretary might have ordered serious precautions, but there had been no grave public order problems in London since the Hyde Park Riot, 1866, two years before Commissioner Sir Edmund Henderson's appointment. The Home Secretary, Hugh Childers, had only taken office that week in the new Gladstone administration that was preoccupied with trying to introduce Irish Home Rule. The meetings were approved with arrangements for a small force of constables to police the square and a reserve of 563 men standing by. District Superintendent Robert Walker was appointed to maintain public order, but he was 74 years old and quite unfitted for such active service. He went in plain clothes to observe the meetings, lost touch with his men and disappeared into the crowd, where he had his pockets picked. The meetings passed off without incident, but when the speakers had left the square a crowd of 5000 streamed west along Pall Mall bent on mischief and a more fiery resumption of the meeting in Hyde Park.

With Walker mislaid in the square, a garbled message came to the reserve that there was trouble brewing in *The* Mall instead of *Pall* Mall. So they marched away to guard Marlborough House and Buckingham Palace, while a few hundred metres north of them the mob rushed unhindered along Pall Mall and St James's, smashing club windows as they went. Their meeting in Hyde Park inspired them to more mayhem, and in the early evening they raged back down Oxford Street, breaking shop windows and looting. At Marylebone Lane, Inspector James Cuthbert (attached to Marylebone Lane, C Division) was routinely parading a Sergeant and 15 constables to go out on patrol. When he heard a mob was approaching, he did not hesitate. He marched his men down to Oxford Street, and with a determined baton charge the 17 policemen scattered the crowd and ended the riot.

Two days later, in thick fog, word reached the Oxford Street traders that a new mob was assembling, and they hastily barricaded their windows and waited for an event which never took place. Scotland Yard was blamed for this panic, and it was even claimed erroneously that Henderson himself had issued the unnecessary warning.

Childers immediately set up a committee to report on the incidents, and despite having had earlier ministerial experience in the War Office and as Chancellor of the Exchequer, improperly appointed himself chairman to report back to himself. This indicated that he would not be taking any personal responsibility. Henderson took the hint that he was to be the scapegoat, and resigned. The circumstances of his going lent appeal to the idea of a more military Commissioner, for which reason Childers replaced him with Sir Charles Warren.

TRAFALGAR SQUARE RIOT, 1887 See Bloody Sunday, 1887.

TRAFFIC CONTROL Radio-telephone communications system within the Central Communications Complex, maintaining contact with patrolling officers in cars. The call sign for traffic patrols is 'Oscar'.

Central Traffic Control can deploy police resources rapidly to the scene of any incident. In adjacent offices at New Scotland Yard, the state of traffic on London streets is monitored and congestion is eased by the traffic light phases at busy major roads and at junctions being coordinated by computer.

TRAFFIC MUSEUM Established in Catford (South-east London) by Sergeant Ray Seal with the assistance of serving and retired police officers throughout the MPD and members of the public. A range of police cars and motor cycles of the types used by the Met since 1930 were collected, together with traffic police uniforms, photographs and memorabilia. It was officially opened by HRH the Duke of Gloucester on 24 April 1986. The collection has now been transferred to the Historical Museum.

TRAFFIC POLICE Nominally, the Metropolitan Police had power to 'control traffic' from the time they were established, probably because congestion and the general use and condition of London streets were already problematic. Still, the police did little more than move beggars on and keep crossing-places clear in 1829. The Metropolitan Police Act, 1839 instructed the Commissioners to make regulations 'from time to time' to prevent obstruction in the streets, but the Home Secretary, like the Commissioners, was more interested in their maintaining public order by controlling crowds and preserving the Queen's Peace by suppressing crime.

In 1841 came an ominous sign that the police were going to shoulder the burden of traffic regulation as the government became more interested in maintaining movement through the streets than squeezing revenue out of various sorts of vehicle owners. The Commissioners were required to fix the location of cab ranks. Col. Rowan shouldered the duty with glum resignation, but his co-Commissioner, Richard Mayne, fumed. He protested every step of the way that ordering traffic was no proper part of the duties of a civilian peace-keeping force – and he was only concerned with horse-drawn vehicles! But his protests were of no avail. When the Public Carriage Office was transferred to Scotland Yard in 1853, it might have seemed no more than typical 'dumping' from other government departments, which had already hived off guarding the dockyards to the new police. It was, however, more comprehensive than that. In 1869, all licensing functions for public carriages were transferred to the Commissioner, and henceforth the police would be held responsible for London's accelerating ability to grind itself to a standstill with an excess of potentially fast-moving vehicles.

London was as choked by horse traffic in the 1880s and 1890s as it is by automobile traffic today. It could take five hours to cross the somewhat smaller metropolis in the slower vehicles: nowadays an average speed for central London is 12–13 mph. The first appearance of the motor car seemed a move for the better. Cars did not leave droppings or urine wherever they went; they did not need haystands and water troughs in

TRAFFIC PATROL IN THE 1930s: A BSA MOTORCYCLE, COMBINATION AND A MORRIS COWLEY POLICE CAR.

inconvenient places; they did not collapse through being given excessive loads to draw up steep hills, or distress the public if they were maltreated by angry drivers, or run away in fear if a child bowled a hoop in front of them. They proceeded very sedately, governed by the 12mph speed limit of the Highways Act 1896. However, Commissioner Sir Edward Bradford did not believe that they would become popular, even when the 12mph speed limit was abolished.

In 1903, the year of Bradford's retirement, Parliament raised the speed limit to 20mph, and self-propelled vehicles started to replace horses. The change wasn't immediate. The Public Carriage Office licensed 19 motor taxis in 1905, when they were still seen as a novelty rather than a challenge to the 9000 hansom cabs. All had changed by 1910, when 6397 taxicabs took to the roads in London. In 1914 there were 7000 taxicabs and 200 hansoms. Indeed, adding in other sorts of horse-drawn public carriage (four-wheeled 'growlers' or 'clarences') there were only 1500 of them all told.

One immediate effect was the worsening of relations between the police and the propertied classes, who were the first to acquire private motor cars. Soothed by Commissioner Sir Richard Mayne's encouragement of deference from the

police, the middle and upper classes had no experience of the policeman as an authoritative figure of the law bearing down on them. Now they had cars, exceeding speed limits seemed natural – and the police dealt with them. Moreover, to prove the offence, the police had to time them over a measured distance, and since the policemen with stop watches kept discreetly out of sight of the motorists they were checking, their 'speed traps' were perceived as an unsporting, sneaky sort of spying. Bluntly, the middle classes didn't like observation and surveillance being turned on their own activities which their own kind in Parliament had made illegal. Kenneth Grahame's *The Wind in the Willows* and Rudyard Kipling's 'The Village that Voted the Earth was Flat', from the aesthetic liberal to the imperialist conservative ends of the spectrum, told the same tale: the motorist who exceeds the speed limit is a merry and lovable buccaneer, while the policeman who reports him is a dim-witted killjoy, subservient to mean-spirited magistrates. The Scotland Yard chiefs had not foreseen the public relations disaster ignited by the internal combustion engine.

MODERN TRAFFIC PATROL ON WESTMINSTER BRIDGE.

granted the rank which marked him out as 'Ace' among detectives.

The 1930 Road Traffic Act recognized the huge importance of the motor car in the modern world. It introduced the Highway Code and the pedestrian crossing and, less happily, the lamentable experiment of abolishing all speed limits. The Traffic Department responded by expanding and making permanent its experimental motor patrols with courtesy cops on motorcycles. Police drivers were selected by competition and graded. All were required to be on the look-out for drivers in difficulty, for traffic congestion which they could ease, and for driving offences. Their uniforms had white waterproof sleeve covers on the right arms, and the motorcyclists wore flat caps and booted or gaitered breeches; to maintain their balance, they saluted with a downward thrust of the right arm. The sleek but at times ungainly uniform led to their acquiring the in-force nickname 'Black Rats'.

The Traffic Department also installed experimental electric traffic lights on Oxford Street. They proved an instant success, and steadily increased over the next 40 years until they replaced the fixed-point traffic police entirely. The Hendon Driving School opened in 1935, bringing superlative standards of car control and roadcraft as the norm for police drivers.

Perhaps the most important key to the future of traffic policing was the establishment of separate garages, normally one for repairs and one for housing vehicles, in each of the four Districts (1). Central Traffic Control in B Department was very important, making great use of the Map Room to identify accident sites and areas of congestion, and organizing wireless cars for instant communication at major ceremonial events. It retained responsibility for servicing and maintaining the ever-expanding fleet of cars and motor-cycles. A Central Traffic Control room was established in the little police station housed in the Wellington Arch at Hyde Park Corner in 1956, moving to New Scotland Yard in 1962, and to the new building in 1967. Subsequent modernization, including dedicated map rooms and various kinds of televisual and computer-linked systems for monitoring traffic flow and noting activity on the M1 M11, M4 and M25 motor-

Commissioner Sir Edward Henry and Receiver Richard Pennefather acquired official cars for their own convenient transportation in response to the 1903 Motor Car Act. When Henry increased the number of Assistant Commissioners, and defined their departmental responsibilities precisely, B Department included traffic as part of a general portfolio called 'Civil Business', which included all the miscellaneous licensing. In 1919 everything except Traffic and Lost Property was shifted to a new Department L (for Legal), and until the dissolution of the Departments under the Newman Restructuring, B Department was one of the four main police departments at Scotland Yard.

The new Department under AC Frank Elliott was established on a firm footing by an unlikely partnership: the very decisive and active Superintendent A. E. Bassom of the Public Carriage Office, who devoted himself to a study of traffic problems and ways of policing them, and a very gentle old Civil Staff member, Mr Suffield Mylius, who was best remembered for dressing like a pauper and always wearing enormous hobnailed boots, yet whose tact and wisdom admirably complemented Supt Bassom's energy and enthusiasm. In 1923 Bassom's work won him a well-deserved OBE, and the even rarer distinction of being promoted to Chief Constable and Director of Traffic. This was just three years after James Olive had paved the way for officers from the ranks to reach the highest positions, and one year before F. P. Wensley was

ways, took place from 1984 onwards.

As on-street parking and related traffic offences occupied more and more police time in the years after WWII, pressure developed for the beat police to have greater powers of immediate action to deal with infringements, and some support from non-attested officials to relieve them of time spent charging and prosecuting illegally parked motorists. With the introduction of parking meters and yellow lines in 1957, the police were at last given the right to remove illegally and dangerously parked vehicles. Traffic wardens and fixed penalty notices were introduced in 1960, and administered as an adjunct of the Met, with the Central Ticket Office processing the penalties. Civilian volunteer 'Lollipop' men and ladies were recruited experimentally in 1949, and by 1966, with the support of Traffic Wardens at difficult times and places, had entirely taken over a duty that few police officers relished. On 4 July 1994, the London boroughs took over responsibility for Special Parking Areas and parking attendants, leaving the Met to concentrate on Red Routes with police officers and traffic wardens.

Since the Newman Restructuring in 1985, the major responsibility for Traffic policing has rested with Areas, who appoint their own senior staff and manage patrols. HQ Traffic and the Central Ticket Office (CO50 and CO51) are now part of the 24-hour Response and Traffic portfolio of Area Assistant Commissioner Paul Manning, and supply very important liaison with the Fire Brigade and Ambulance Service, as well as with public and private transport companies, coach firms, and tour operators. The Central Communications Complex and CAD system command technological means of observation, control and despatch beyond the wildest dreams of the hi-tech enthusiasts in Victoria Street in the 1960s.

The annual national Christmas campaign against drinking and driving has clearly struck a chord with most of the public and led to far greater sympathy for traffic policing than existed even 15 years ago. It is even possible that, except when speeding down motorways, a majority of motorists today recognize that the traffic police are there to help them when they encounter either individual difficulties or problems with traffic flow, and make a significant contribution to road safety.

TRANSFER The movement of an officer from one Division or Sub-Division to another. This will normally be a result of changing manpower needs, and may also be intended to broaden the experience and improve the career prospects of a young constable.

But it may have disciplinary implications. It is an easy administrative solution to problems caused by personality clashes, and it could be seen as an additional punishment if an officer were transferred following a disciplinary hearing. And in the early part of the 20th century it could be used as quite a heavy informal penalty for married officers, who might be required to find new houses and interrupt their children's education when shifted to distant divisions.

Regular transfers broaden an officer's experience, provide some respite from particularly difficult postings and can remotivate officers, but the need for continuity in serving local communities also has to be taken into account.

See under John Syme for the most contentious disciplinary transfer in the history of Scotland Yard.

TRENCHARD HOUSE Section house in Broadwick Street, Soho. Opened in 1940, replacing Charing Cross Section House.

Perhaps the first really comfortable and convenient housing for unmarried officers in the MPD: certainly the first in central London. The building contains useful function rooms and a gymnasium as well as accommodation, and the gym was used during the war for Star Celebrity Concerts, where Tommy Trinder, Arthur Askey and Jimmy Edwards frequently entertained officers.

TRENCHARD, AIR-MARSHAL LORD HUGH MONTAGUE, IST VISCOUNT TRENCHARD, GCB, OM, GCVO, DSO (1873–1956) Commissioner, 1931–35.

B. Taunton, son of a solicitor whose practice failed while Hugh was at school. The boy was hideously embarrassed that relatives had to pay for him to go to a military crammer. His educa-tion was so poor that the Dictionary of National Biography describes him as 'uneducated' when he arrived in India in 1893. He had failed entry to Dartmouth Naval Academy; failed entry to Woolwich Military Academy; twice failed entry to the militia; scraped through in 1893 and joined the 2nd Battalion, Royal Scots Fusiliers. Posted to India.

Seriously wounded in the Boer War. Major and Commandant, S. Nigeria, 1903–10. Served in Ireland, 1910–12. Learned to fly and joined RFC, 1912. Instructor and Assistant Commandant, Central Flying School, Upavon, 1913–15. Major-General and Commander of the RFC, 1915–18. Chief of Air Staff on formation of RAF, and created Bt, 1919. Appointed by Winston Churchill (War and Air Minister) to re-establish the RAF, which had been too hastily

AN OIL PAINTING (COMMISSIONED 1936) OF LORD TRENCHARD.

demobilized. Trenchard devised everything for the new service, down to uniform buttons. Air Marshal, 1927. Retired, Baron Trenchard, 1930. Commissioner, Metropolitan Police, 1931–5. Retired again, GCVO, Viscount Trenchard, 1935. Chairman of permanent advisory committee on the use of science for police purposes, 1934–8. Became Chairman of United Africa Co. and director of several other companies. Continued to advise, support and agitate on behalf of the RAF for the whole of his life.

'The Father of the RAF', who commemorated his birthday like the Sovereign's, Lord Trenchard, like Lord Byng, came to the Met with a national reputation already fully established. Like Byng, too, he had no great wish to take up a full-time post after he had retired, but he accepted this as a public duty, urged on by George V, who became a personal friend.

He was assured by Home Secretary Herbert Samuel that he would be given whatever financial support he needed. This was important, as the slump had led government to propose a swingeing 10% cut in the pay of all public servants, including, for once, Cabinet Ministers, judges and senior civil servants. The Police Federation, trusting Byng to support them, had at first restricted themselves to a cautious and moderate protest meeting in the Royal Albert Hall, but dissatisfaction was growing. The Branch Boards were sounding mutinous and leaking deleterious information to the press. The government secretly dreaded a repeat of the Police Strike, 1918, despite the technical illegality of such action. They quickly agreed that the police alone should have their 10% cut phased in over two years, and that the second 5% should be restored to them as soon as the economy permitted (which turned out to be 1940). This favouritism was manifestly unfair to teachers, the armed forces, and civil servants, but the Federation was still not satisfied. Consequently, the reason for appointing a Commissioner of Trenchard's great public stature was to instil discipline and ensure public confidence in the police.

He accepted the position for three years only, later accepting the King's request that he stay on for a fourth, but his short tenure of office proved the most intense period of radical reform the Met

has ever seen. And in calling Trenchard a controversial Commissioner, one is not politely remarking that his ideas were not always favourably received. There is to this day diametrical disagreement between those who think he was the greatest of all reforming Commissioners, and those who think he was only prevented by his successor from effectively destroying the morale of the Met.

A note Trenchard made listed the areas where he believed urgent action was essential. They were as follows:

1. Discipline was poor and there was discontent with pay and conditions in the ranks.

2. The Police Federation was holding far too many meetings.

3. Constables were patrolling outdated beats, some of which had been laid down in Peel's day.

4. There was no proper Statistical Branch to show the spread and prevalence of crime.

5. There was no map-room.

6. There was no scientific laboratory.

7. There was no welfare officer.

8. Sport and recreation facilities were inadequate.

9. Section houses and married quarters were appalling.

10. There were not enough supervisory ranks for the number of constables.

11. There was too much corruption.

12. There was too much tipping.

Trenchard set about to deal with all these problems. He was lucky that he had the support of the King and the Home Secretary against Chancellor of the Exchequer Neville Chamberlain, who detested his free-handed spending of public money. But beyond reporting that the men were dissatisfied with their pay cut, Trenchard did not do anything to improve their pay and pensions rights. He protected the 'privileged' phasing-in of their 10% cut when it seemed that other Cabinet Ministers might force the Home Secretary to withdraw his unfortunate pledge to the police, but there was strong feeling in the ranks that 'Boom' (who had acquired his nickname in the Central Flying School from his habit of bellowing commands at people) was no friend to constables and Sergeants.

Certainly he was no friend to the Police

Federation, but a Federation had been foisted on him by the Police Act, 1919. As he was entitled, Trenchard cut it back to the size granted it in the Act, which allowed 12 Federation meetings annually. The Federation had called 480 in one year! With the full approval of Metropolitan Police Secretary Howgrave-Graham, a great admirer, Trenchard treated the Federation as an ill-informed disruptive nuisance and barred it from taking any members above the rank of Junior Inspector.

Trenchard was wrong in imagining that any of the beats planned by Rowan for Peel remained, but he was right to feel that beats need constant updating and revision as building development changes districts. He did a certain amount of tinkering with section and Division boundaries, created a Statistical Department and established the Daily Crime Telegram, by which Divisions reported their crime figures to the Information Room. He upgraded that room considerably, linking it to radio cars in all divisions, appointing a Wireless Officer and adding Map Rooms. He created a Wireless Training School at Hendon, a Detective Training School, and a Police Scientific Laboratory. He added sports grounds to all the Areas and built excellent new section houses and new married quarters, which were indeed sorely needed by a Force which was still almost entirely housed in Victorian buildings. 'Nice things make nice people' was his pleasant defence of this budgetary increase. He planned an extension to Shaw's New Scotland Yard, which was equally needed.

He did little overtly about the corruption he had noted. Quite extraordinarily, this whirlwind of energy, discipline, rational restructuring, innovation and authority, seemed nervous of his own constables when it came to stopping them from taking 'drinks' from street bookmakers, prostitutes and publicans. The problem was so deep-rooted and endemic, in his opinion, that an open attack on it would instantly destroy Scotland Yard's prestigious reputation. Moreover, no law was broken if policemen accepted gifts in cash or kind from anybody they liked. Trenchard saw to the disciplining and dismissal of corrupt officers who were exposed through the normal channels, but he clearly saw and left unremedied a problem which festered until the boil burst in 1970. Nor did he succeed in checking the CID's steady growth into a higher-paid, more glamorous section of the force that felt superior to uniformed officers.

But it was in the question of excess constables and how the force was to be officered that his most famous, controversial – and short-lived – reforms were made. Trenchard's 1932 Commissioner's Report (the first that was based on his own experience and observations) is lastingly famous as the unique occasion when a Commissioner with a genius for administration put down for all to see and understand his philosophy of what the Met was doing and what needed to be done to it. It is the more amazing that this came (possibly at one or two removes) from the pen of Trenchard, since the 'uneducated' subaltern of 1893 remained pretty much an uneducated Air Marshal 40 years later. In the Air Force, his inability to compose or dictate a coherent document had become notorious, and his staff officer Philip Game earned Trenchard's approval and every one else's bemused admiration for his ability to take pages of Trenchard's incomprehensible gibberish and turn them into clear statements of what the Old Man actually meant. His letters were often from start to finish disjointed sentences that seemed to imagine the recipient was putting his own questions and points to which Trenchard was responding with casual saloon-bar phrases. Sometimes they completely baffled his secretary at New Scotland Yard, who brought them to Howgrave-Graham for him to interpret.

In 1932 Trenchard made clear his fears about long-serving constables. After a number of years, they would know that they had passed all chance of further promotion; they had simply to soldier on in the same old routine until they collected their pensions. Peel's old policy of promoting from within wasn't working. The majority of policemen were artisans from the working class and not leaders of men (Trenchard clearly had no real appreciation of what in later years came to be recognized as the status of the constable exercising a valuable role in London's communities) and very few had advanced beyond the rank of Superintendent since the formation of the force.

There were only 11 of the senior 800 officers whom Trenchard regarded as 'educated'. The Commissioner wanted a young and energetic force led by men who really were 'officer material'. Clearly, such ambitious young high-fliers would not come into a service which expected them to plod the pavements for 10–12 years, waiting for 'Buggins' turn' before they could become Sergeants.

Trenchard proposed two answers. The first was the Hendon Police College to catch the most able young constables, by competitive entry or recommendation for accelerated promotion, and to recruit well-educated young men from public schools, colleges and universities, all with the promise of immediate appointment to the newly created rank of Junior Station Inspector after their two-year course. The course itself would concentrate rather more on physical fitness and character-training than academics.

This was the scheme which turned the Police Federation, the Police Review and the Labour Party apoplectic with fury. It was, said Aneurin Bevan to Parliament, 'an entirely Fascist development, designed to make the police force more amenable to the orders of the Carlton Club and Downing Street'. Trenchard pointed to the opportunities for the ablest and most ambitious ordinary constables to rise quickly, but his class-biased view of desirable officers was exposed to public disdain when it was revealed that he required Hendon entrants to include dinner jackets, four dress shirts and patent leather evening shoes in their kit.

His second idea was still more military in its inspiration. He proposed short-term contracts for police officers, like the short-term commissions available in the army. Police officers could sign on for 10 years, and then retire with a gratuity. In that way the backlog of middle-aged men plodding their way on to their pensions would be reduced. He had no effective answer to the observation that it took about 10 years' experience to make a really good police officer and he would be losing officers just as they reached their peak of usefulness, nor did he foresee that these contracts would become a handy way for provincial forces to acquire fully trained and experienced officers who had learnt their trade at the Met's expense.

Trenchard was not lamented by the force when he finally retired in 1935. It had always been clear that 'Boom's' first love was the RAF and he just didn't think the Met measured up to it. He had never understood the pride some police officers took in *not* being even quasi-military, and his contempt for the rank and file marred his fine leadership qualities. Yet the police had benefited from the astringent experience of a Commissioner who had genuine new ideas and the will, energy and determination to see them carried out. His 10-year-old son described him as 'the Metropolitan Police Commotioner' when he first saw him in the braided uniform, and the slip of the tongue was prophetic. There had been nothing like it since Sir Nevil Macready departed in 1920. In the *Daily Express*, 'Beachcomber' commented that 'the monthly reorganization of the Metropolitan Police will take place weekly in future'. And on his retirement, even the hostile *Daily Herald* acknowledged that Trenchard had brought Scotland Yard 'to such a pitch that it began to work with the sureness of a machine'.

To make sure the machine went on running perfectly, Trenchard insisted that he must be succeeded by Sir Philip Game – 'the best staff officer I ever had'. He believed he had Game's explicit assurance that his great reforms would not be undone – particularly his two darlings, the short-term contracts system and the Police College. He never forgave Game's 'treachery' for abolishing the first as soon as it became clear it was not working, and letting the government close down the second as a wartime measure in 1939.

Whatever may be felt about Trenchard's reforms, the man's greatness was undeniable. The improvements in wireless communications, information, mapping, housing and canteen services that he introduced would have made the reputation of a Commissioner serving twice as many years, and his rather offensive wish to have more 'gentlemen' in the higher ranks must be offset against a genuine freedom from personal snobbery.

TRIAL OF THE DETECTIVES Notorious corruption scandal of 1877 which resulted in the reorganization of the Detective Branch into the

blackmail over an unsigned note he sent to an informant which might have been read as corrupt. Chief Inspector Druscovich was tragically caught when he backed a bill for his brother; was left with a debt he could not repay; and accepted Meiklejohn's fatherly invitation to borrow money from Kurr. Chief Inspector Palmer appears to have been duped into going along with his colleagues.

All four men stood in the dock. Williamson spoke up for Clarke's character, and he was acquitted. He had been lucky and he knew it. He resigned very rapidly. The other three all went to prison for two years (the experience hastening Druscovich's premature death). On their release, Palmer became a publican, and Meiklejohn set up as a private detective.

CID. Sometimes described as 'the Turf Club Frauds' or the 'Madame de Goncourt case'.

In 1877, a rich Parisian lady called Madame de Goncourt horrified her attorney by seeking to have £30,000 of her money released to be placed on a horse in England. It transpired that she had been the victim of two astute young confidence tricksters, Harry Benson and William Kurr. Both had experience in selling fraudulent racing tips, but with Benson as the brains and Kurr as the energy, they planned a complex and elaborate sting in 1877, printing a dummy sporting paper with false reports of an English punter whose 'system' was so successful that bookies would not take his bets. Therefore he would pay a small commission to French residents to place them for him in their own names. With a dummy bookmaker's letterhead to receive bets on non-existent races, and dummy cheques on the non-existent 'Bank of London' as the 'winnings' to be forwarded back to the imaginary English punter, Benson and Kurr had a nice little scam to persuade suckers that they, too, could make a fortune on the turf by adding their 'investments' to the English punter's. Madame de Goncourt was the perfect sucker.

Superintendent Adolphus Williamson put his

THE TRIAL OF THE DETECTIVES: (ABOVE) THE DEFENDANTS IN THE DOCK AT BOW STREET (LEFT TO RIGHT) INSPECTORS MEIKLEJOHN, DRUSCOVICH, PALMER AND CLARKE. (BELOW) MR POLAND, TREASURY COUNSEL, EXAMINES THE CONVICT BENSON.

brightest young multi-lingual Chief Inspector, Nathaniel Druscovich, on the job of fetching Benson back from Amsterdam where he had been arrested. Druscovich seemed to make surprisingly heavy weather of the job. Sergeant John Littlechild and two others went after Kurr, and were repeatedly foiled by his moving on just as they expected to arrest him. Finally they caught up with him in Edinburgh, and the two rogues and some lesser gang members stood trial and were convicted.

After which Scotland Yard started to wonder why their arrests had been so difficult, and Benson and Kurr started to talk. Inspector John Meiklejohn, a deeply corrupt character, had started accepting bribes from bookmakers and turf swindlers several years earlier. He had been in Kurr's pay since 1873, accepting sums of up to £100 to tip him off when his crimes were about to lead to his arrest. Chief Inspector Clarke, a contemporary and close friend of 'Dolly' Williamson's, was threatened with

The scandal nearly wrecked Williamson's career. Although his integrity was unquestioned his supervision of subordinates seemed wanting, and following the Committee of Inquiry, Howard Vincent was given his opportunity to reshape the Detective Branch.

TROUP COMMITTEE, 1894 Home Office special committee set up by Home Secretary Herbert Asquith to examine methods of criminal identification. The chairman was Home Office official Edward (later Sir Edward) Troup, and the other members were Melville Macnaghten and Major Arthur Griffiths, Inspector of Prisons. The committee heard evidence from Francis Galton, who had just published an account of fingerprinting, and visited Paris, where Alphonse Bertillon gave an enthusiastic account of his identification method. The Committee recommended that both methods be used at Scotland Yard, with fingerprints added to the cards recording Bertillon body measurements. Initially, however, the fingerprints were of little use because of the lack of a formal categorization system. The Troup Committee recommendations were finally superseded by the Belper Committee report in 1900.

See also Anthropometry Department, Bertillonage.

TRUNCHEONS Truncheons of male bamboo or lancewood (a tough, elastic wood from the West Indies and South America, much used by coachbuilders) were issued to the first constables

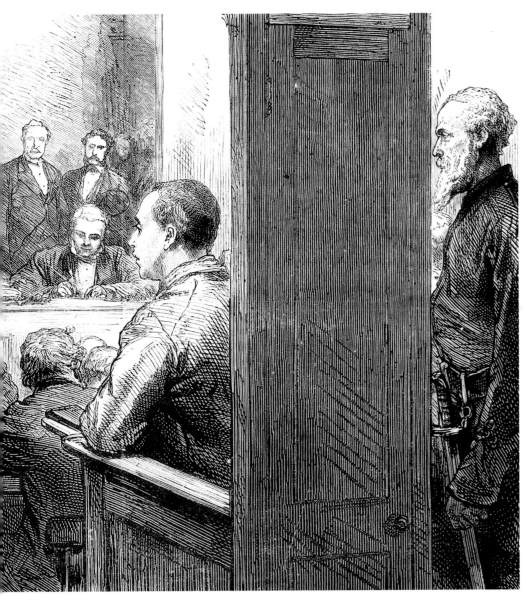

on the formation of the Met in 1829, to be carried in a swallowtail pocket of the uniform coat. They were 50.8cm (20 inches) long and were decorated with the Garter Coat of Arms and the letters MP in gold on red. In 1846 they were marked with each constable's Divisional Number. The length was reduced to 43.2cm (17 inches) in 1856, and existing truncheons were cut down to the new size, losing their ornamentation. Most officers made their own efforts to replace it, and many went further and created their own individual decorations. Mid-Victorian truncheons, therefore, never appear to be of uniform pattern. Spring-loaded truncheon cases to be carried on belts were issued in 1863 when the swallowtail coat was replaced by the tunic. In 1887 a truncheon pocket was introduced in the uniform trousers, and the cases were withdrawn. At the same time all truncheons were called in and a plain undecorated 38cm (15 inch) crocus wood truncheon with a leather thong at the handle end was issued to uniformed constables and Sergeants. Inspectors and CID officers received a slightly shorter 30.5cm (12 inch) model. From then on, all ornamentation of truncheons was forbidden. Lignum vitae was also occasionally used as the wood.

The Mounted Police were given longer truncheons for effective reach of unruly pedestrians. A 53.3cm (21 inch) truncheon was issued to them in 1912, and replaced with a 91.4cm (36 inch) leather-hilted truncheon in 1920.

In 1994, after a series of knife assaults on officers and lengthy field trials, amid some controversy a long, straight, acrylic baton was chosen to replace the traditional truncheon. The new baton varied in length from 56cm (22 inches) to 66cm (26 inches), and both solid and hollow versions were issued. The side-handled baton was rejected for use in the MPS because of the complexity of its use and the much increased training implications.

More recently the 'gravity friction lock' baton has replaced the acrylic baton as standard issue for most officers. This is a three-section collapsible baton made of hollow metal, and is a more practical piece of equipment for operational officers to carry than its predecessor. See also Baton Charge.

UNDERWATER SEARCH UNIT (POLICE FROGMEN) Formed in 1962 as a part-time unit, and so functioned for a year. Then made full time, and in 1964 based at Thames Division HQ. Comprises one Inspector, one Sergeant, nine constables and a civil staff driver with a three-tonne van to carry equipment and inflatable.

On average, the unit undertakes about 200 operational searches per year, occupying approximately 264 days. A typical year would find them recovering about 20 bodies, 12 firearms, 10 stabbing or cutting weapons, 15 cars, and a dozen motorbikes. Divers from the unit undertake searches in sewers and underground conduits and drains, including the regular search below St Stephen's Palace before the State Opening of Parliament, originally instituted after the Gunpowder Plot.

The remaining three months are devoted to recurrent dives in the Metropolitan Police area, logging everything observed on the bottom of rivers, canals, ponds and so forth, without removing it. The complete chart of submerged items thus maintained means that it is now often possible for frogmen to retrieve immediately some stolen or other evidential object thrown into the water months before detectives want it, or alternatively to state with certainty that no such object has ever been in the river.

UNIFORMS See Appendix I.

UNIT BEAT System introduced in 1967 by Sir Joseph Simpson following a nationally promoted reorganization of patrolling systems. An efficient development of the 'Aberdeen System' copied by Sir Harold Scott, made possible by the introduction of personal radios. Panda cars and motorcycles supplemented the limited number of Home Beat foot patrols, ensuring maximum Divisional coverage with sensitively selected areas where the visible uniformed officers on the pavement made their reassuring rounds. Ultimately largely replaced by sector policing. See Neighbourhood Policing.

'VICE SQUAD' Frequently mentioned in books and journalism as though it were a formally established Specialist Operations Unit, although until the establishment of Clubs and Vice as a part of No. 1 Area Assistant Commis-

THE RECENTLY FORMED UNDERWATER SEARCH UNIT AT KINGSTON IN 1962.

sioner's portfolio there was no permanent unit dedicated to vice work in the Met, except for C Division's Clubs Office and Street Offences Squad. References may be to Toms Squads, to the Obscene Publications Squad, or to the special *ad hoc* squad under Commander Bert Wickstead set in place by Sir Robert Mark to clean up the West End following the Obscene Publications Squad corruption cases.

Cf. 'Murder Squad' for another famous Scotland Yard unit that was only briefly so titled.

VICTIM EXAMINATION SUITE

Rooms set aside from 1985 for the more comfortable and sensitive treatment of rape victims.

VICTIM RECOVERY TEAM

Twenty-four hour team comprising 19 uniformed and five CID officers from Heathrow Police Station, organized by Inspector Gerry Jackson in 1987 to give urgent compassionate assistance to accident or disaster victims, especially by recovering and identifying bodies and relaying sensitive information to the next of kin, while maintaining a low profile and, as far as possible, an unobtrusive approach. The team's work was so successful that they were drafted to help Thames Division (River Police) with the *Marchioness* disaster, and were sent to Scotland to assist at the Lockerbie air disaster. On this occasion they may have been the first uniformed Metropolitan Police to carry out duties other than Royalty Protection in Scotland.

VINCENT, SIR CHARLES EDWARD HOWARD, KCMG, CB (1849–1909)

Founder of the CID.

Younger son of Prebendary the Rev Sir Frederick Vincent, Bt. Educ. Westminster and Sandhurst. Lt., Royal Welsh Fusiliers, 1868–73. Studied military organization in Russia and published *Elementary Military Geography*, 1872. On leaving the army entered the Inner Temple and read for the bar. Lt-Col., Central London Rangers (militia), 1875–8. *Daily Telegraph* correspondent in Russo-Turkish war, and called to the bar, 1876. 1877–8 studied continental police systems (especially French) and prepared report for Home Office Departmental Committee.

Appointed Director of Criminal Intelligence, Metropolitan Police, 1878. CB, 1880. Resigned, 1884. Conservative MP for Central Sheffield, 1885–1905. Member of London County Council, 1889–95. Kt, 1896. KCMG, 1898.

At the age of 28, before Howard Vincent had seriously settled to the practice of law, he saw an opportunity for a change of career: the Trial of the Detectives was evidently likely to lead to a shake-up in Scotland Yard. Vincent went to Paris to study the French detective police, and prepared a report with recommendations which he put through 18 drafts before sending it to the Departmental Committee investigating the scandal. His proposal for a semi-independent bureau modelled on the *Sûreté* with its own independent chief was put forward with an eye to his winning the appointment for himself.

In this he succeeded. He combined military experience with legal training – just the combination Sir Robert Peel had hoped to find for his first Commissioners, and one which would not recur in Scotland Yard until the appointment of Sir Wyndham Childs as Assistant Commissioner C in 1921.

Vincent was a young man in a hurry, not suitable as a Commissioner, but he could appropriately execute the shake-up needed in the Detective Branch. There was some public concern that Vincent's plans were based on the suspect French system, but in March 1878 he was appointed and started to form the new Criminal Investigation Department which was to become, in many people's eyes, synonymous with 'Scotland Yard'.

Vincent's post was slightly anomalous. He was given the status but not the position of an Assistant Commissioner. Like the Commissioner, he was responsible to the Home Office. Although the officers in his Department were directly subordinate to the Commissioner, Vincent was not. Conversely, he had no official authority to command his officers, not being officially a part of their Force or an executive magistrate with authority over constables. This awkward independence caused friction later when it had been corrected. (See James Monro.) Fortunately for the fledgling CID, Vincent and his Commissioner, Sir Edmund Henderson, were personally compatible

and rubbed along easily, and with the experienced and good-humoured Adolphus Williamson as the senior attested officer at his side, Vincent was able to implement energetic reforms, and accept needful restraint when it was advised.

Vincent's new Department was intended to consist of 280 officers, 254 of them to be based in the Divisions under 'Local Inspectors' (as the heads of separate Divisional CIDs came to be known). Though he had to make do with 260 men all-told for several months, within six years he had expanded the MPD-wide CID to 800.

His enthusiasm and energy could create problems. There was serious disaffection among elements of the uniformed police when he swiftly secured increased pay and allowances for his detectives. Vincent smoothed this over by personally charming the leader of the malcontents, but his policy left a potentially divided police force which would remain problematic until Sir Robert Mark's initiatives to restore equality with the uniformed branch 100 years later.

Nor were Vincent's detective suggestions always acceptable to authority. He was reprimanded for the excessive use of press advertisements in the hunt for criminals, something the Home Office regarded as undignified. The Titley affair occurred with his approval, reviving fears of the *agent provocateur*. He made a completely unsuccessful attempt to reverse Peel's policy of eschewing constables drawn from the 'officer and gentleman' class. Hoping to find detectives with higher educational standards and better linguistic abilities, he dropped the physical requirements for entry into the CID, and recruited six men from 'retired officers of the army and younger sons of gentlemen'. The experiment was a disastrous failure: five were dismissed from the force, and one was made to resign. Vincent later admitted that the only case he ever found proven against an officer for using police information to make money for himself was one of these 'gentlemen' (and he himself put the epithet in inverted commas when describing him). In principle it remained possible for the CID to directly recruit shorter constables with demonstrable educational advantages. In practice, physical height regulations were regarded as advantageous (until consideration of the effect on ethnic minorities caused their abolition), and a substantial period in uniform on the beat was the best practical education for a police officer.

Vincent was much more successful in initiating the collection of Criminal Intelligence. He improved the *Police Gazette* so that it became a really useful source of information about wanted criminals, disseminated around the Divisions. He established the Convict Supervision Office, with a 'Rogues' Gallery' of pictures of habitual offenders. Its major weakness was not his fault: as long as the prison service clipped convicts' hair and left them unshaven for considerable periods, they tended to look very similar in photographs, and could easily change their appearance when they had been released for a few weeks.

In 1882 he wrote a Police Code, which later became the Police Guide: a masterly summary of the laws officers needed to know, which, with regular revision and updating, remained a crucial police *Vade Mecum* for nearly 80 years. He founded the Special Irish Branch to maintain covert watch over the Fenians.

After six active years as head of the detective bureau Vincent resigned and entered politics, becoming MP for Central Sheffield. Parliament always looked to him for authoritative opinions on police questions when they arose and in the last year of his life he was heard very respectfully as a witness before the Royal Commission, 1908 on the police, although his observations were not substantially different from those of Sir Edward Henry and other senior officers.

During his period as Director of Criminal Intelligence there was little significant improve-

SIR HOWARD VINCENT.

ment in the crime figures, but the system he had put in place proved itself statistically as soon as the professional policeman James Monro took command of it. Monro and his successor, Robert Anderson, were always willing to acknowledge that Sir Howard Vincent's reforms were the basis of the CID which became famous and respected in the 1890s, and remained one of the most prestigious sections of Scotland Yard for many decades.

VINE STREET Famous central London police station.

Originally the St James's parish watch house at 10 Little Vine Street (later known as Piccadilly Place), it was taken over by founding Commissioners Rowan and Mayne to be the Divisional Station House for C Division. Rebuilt in 1868, and enlarged with married quarters and a section house in 1897. In 1931 the adjacent historic public house the Man in the Moon was taken over and turned into process and typing offices. Closed and used as Aliens Registration Office in 1940 when West End Central Station was purpose-built, it reopened in 1971 as the volume of central London work became too great for West End Central and Vine Street became an additional division. It was closed finally on 5 November 1997.

Abutting closely on Piccadilly Circus, Vine Street Station rapidly became one of the two best-known Metropolitan Police stations after Scotland Yard. The other, Great Marlborough Street, was already familiar as one of the offices established under the Middlesex Justices Act, and by the latter part of the 19th century these two stations were jointly responsible for charging the street prostitutes who lined the streets from the Haymarket to Langham Place. This was so important a part of Vine Street's function that in 1897 it became the first station required to have a matron permanently on duty, rather than calling one in as and when female searching was required.

In the same period, Vine Street became the station most heavily engaged in policing Boat Race night festivities. For this reason it features

in memoirs of the period, and is mentioned from time to time by P. G. Wodehouse's Bertie Wooster as a part of his undergraduate experience. Boat Race night arrestees formed a "Vine Street Club" in the inter-war period and would-be members sometimes surrendered themselves at the station with glasses stolen from a nearby pub. When the board game Monopoly was invented and a British edition was created using London street names, the orange set drew on streets famous for the police stations, and Vine Street was included (with Bow Street and Great Marlborough Street). Its closure in the 1990s, at roughly the same time as Bow Street Police Station's final retirement, marked the end of two of the oldest connections with Rowan and Mayne's original establishment.

VOLUNTEER CIVIL FORCE The Volunteer Civil Force was the forerunner of the Special Constabulary as we know it today. It was founded by Lieutenant Colonel William Mailes Power, at the instigation of Winston Churchill, then Home Secretary, on Trafalgar Day 21 October 1911. The members of this new Force later became known as 'Winston's Bobbies'. Their headquarters was located at Ruskin House, Rochester Row.

The Force was paramilitary and was armed. It proved its worth a year after its formation in the Great Dock and Transport Strike of 1912, which threatened to disrupt the country. When the 1914–18 war began, the Force contributed to the Artists Rifles Regiment and Power was the first Territorial Army officer. A thousand men from the Force were also sworn in as Special Constables to form the nucleus of the uniformed Special Constabulary organized by the State during the War.

VULNERABLE PERSONS UNIT Extension of Domestic Violence Unit facilities to other victims of irrational and passionate assaults, such as racial violence, homophobic assaults and so forth. Pioneered at Richmond Police Station in 1998.

WALDORF, STEPHEN (B.1956) Victim of mistaken identity and accidental shooting by police officers.

In 1982, officers maintaining surveillance to trace a dangerous armed criminal who had recently shot at and nearly killed a constable wrongly identified Stephen Waldorf as the suspect, intercepted the car of which he was an occupant in King's Road, Chelsea, and opened fire, believing that Waldorf was about to draw a gun. He was seriously injured but survived. The officers concerned were prosecuted, but acquitted since neither negligence nor recklessness could be proved.

Despite the considerable distress of the officers involved, and a public apology from Commissioner Sir Kenneth Newman, the incident contributed to a public perception of police becoming too ready to employ firearms, and was the catalyst for significant changes in the training and planning for the police use of firearms.

WALDRON, SIR JOHN LOVEGROVE, KCVO (1910–1975) Commissioner, 1968–72.

Educ. Charterhouse and Clare College, Cambridge. Joined Met, 1934. Seconded to Ceylon Police as Deputy Inspector-General, CID, 1944–7. Asst Chief Constable, Lancashire Constabulary, 1951–4. Chief Constable, Berkshire Constabulary, 1954–8. Rejoined the Met as Assistant Commissioner B (Traffic), at the instigation of newly appointed Commissioner Sir Joseph Simpson. Transferred to AC A (Uniformed Police) in 1963, at which point for the first (and only) time, all four Assistant Commissioners, the Deputy Commissioner and the Commissioner were alumni of Hendon Police College, a fact which received a mixed reception from officers who had not been so selected. In 1966, KCVO, a decoration personally awarded by the Queen in recognition of the policing of Sir Winston Churchill's funeral. Deputy Commissioner, 1966. Commissioner, 1968.

Waldron was widely seen as a stopgap Commissioner when Sir Joseph Simpson died unexpectedly in harness and it was thought that he would retire on his sixtieth birthday after two years in office. In the event, the upward revision of higher salaries introduced in 1970 persuaded

Home Secretary James Callaghan to offer Waldron a further year's extension to bring his pension up to the new rate, and the fall of the Labour government in the 1970 election brought a new Home Secretary, Reginald Maudling, who asked Waldron to stay another year to give him time to grasp the Met's requirements.

Waldron made significant management changes which had been recommended by a firm

SIR JOHN WALDRON.

of consultants who reported just before Simpson's death. He improved the comparability of London officers' terms of employment with those of provincial constabularies, upgrading and renaming several ranks to make them correspond more closely with their duties and responsibilities. He renamed the Districts (1) Areas, and the Divisions, Districts (2). Recognizing that his Deputy, Robert Mark, was being groomed for the succession, Waldron sat at one side to let him chair some meetings. Unfortunately, in the opinion of some observers, this tended to weaken the Commissioner's authority without strengthening his Deputy's.

The Times Corruption Allegations led to the Met's humiliation when Callaghan felt he had no alternative but to appoint an outside enquiry headed by HM Inspector of Constabulary Frank Williamson – the first time in its history the Met had been judged incompetent to sort out its own disciplinary problems. Waldron failed to protect Williamson from the reported Metropolitan hostility which triggered his early retirement from the Police Inspectorate. His loyal refusal to believe that subordinate colleagues could be tolerating malpractices exasperated Mark, as did his failure to back up the Deputy Commissioner over a matter of discipline in the CID. Finally Waldron made a disputed throwaway remark at a meeting which Mark interpreted as authorizing him to set up A10 Branch (Complaints Investigation Bureau) and start rooting out corruption.

In 1970, following a direct appeal from a WDC awaiting promotion to Sergeant, Waldron abolished the inequitable ruling that female but not male Detective Constables had to return to uniform duties for at least a year before they could be promoted.

Waldron enjoyed a major success with the meticulously prepared but unprovocative policing of the 'Red October' Grosvenor Square demonstration against the Vietnam War, robbing the organizers of the headline-grabbing riot some of them probably wished to promote. But a storm burst after his retirement, with the Obscene Publications Squad Corruption Case and its associated scandals, and journalists who had been affronted by Scotland Yard's management of the Times Corruption Allegations were happy to imply that his indifference to reported malpractices had allowed an evil to grow under his nose.

WALDRON REFORMS, 1970 Structural changes in the Metropolitan Police Force, following some of the recommendations of PA Management Consultants whose report was completed shortly after the death of Sir Joseph Simpson.

The report proposed far-reaching structural changes, many of which were not implemented until the Newman Restructuring because Sir John Waldron and the Assistant Commissioners recognized that the creation of the Greater London Council and the new London boroughs in 1963 had inflicted considerable disruptive changes in territorial policing, for which reason it did not seem appropriate to introduce wholesale restructuring until the dust had settled.

Nevertheless, the consultants' point was taken that lines of communication between New Scotland Yard and the Divisions were suffering bottlenecks from a proliferation of senior officers in charge of the Districts (1), and the difficulty of their liaising with Divisions. The report's radical proposal for eight Districts each containing eight Divisions ('Eight by Eight') was rejected. But the old Districts were renamed Areas, and the old Divisions were renamed Districts, with Commanders taking charge of them. This move was popular with the Force, as it recognized that Metropolitan officers frequently carried out duties which would have given them higher ranks in provincial Forces, and the Waldron Reforms were generally perceived as a much-needed effort to give Metropolitan officers parity with their provincial counterparts.

WAR CRIMES UNIT – ORGANISED CRIME GROUP Established in 1991 following passage of the War Crimes Act, which empowered the Met retrospectively to investigate alleged war crimes committed by British nationals or people now resident in Britain. A team initially of nine detectives, three uniformed constables and one Executive Officer, set up to investigate crimes sanctioned by the Nazis which violated the laws and customs of war.

By 1999, 81 suspects had been interviewed, in addition to 1,555 witnesses (1,327 of whom lived overseas) and 12,410 documents had been dealt with, many being historical items requiring certification.

In April 1999 Anthony 'Andruska' Savoniuk, a retired railway employee, was sentenced to life imprisonment for murdering Jewish people in 1944 in Domachevo, a town formerly in Poland, but now in Belarus. This was the first conviction obtained by the Unit, who had travelled to ten countries, interviewed 430 witnesses and submitted 90,000 pages of evidence for the case.

WARRANTS Literally warranties or guarantees that a magistrate has empowered a constable to encroach on the normal common law liberties of a citizen in the interest of law enforcement. On being sworn in and attested, every

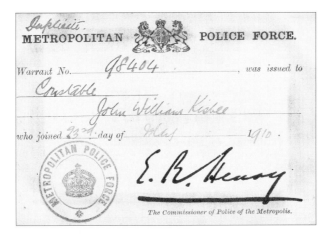

A 1910 WARRANT CARD.

police officer is warranted to hold 'the office of constable', with concomitant powers to arrest or stop and search as defined originally in the 'sus laws' and Police Act 1839, and modified in later legislation culminating in PACE.

If greater powers are needed, for example to arrest some person whose whereabouts are unknown and against whom there is strong suspicion that he or she has committed a crime, or to enter private premises to conduct a search, then magistrates grant the additional arrest or search warrants if persuaded by the police application. The magistrate may directly issue an arrest warrant for the arrest of some person who has (for example) failed to answer to his bail in court.

Colloquially, a 'policeman's warrant' usually refers to his warrant card, issued as proof of his identity and attestation after he has been sworn in. In the early years of the Force, officers may not have been required to carry them, as the uniform (which had to be worn at all times, on and off duty) was sufficient proof of identity. Nor, in days of widespread illiteracy, would a flimsy piece of printed paper have persuaded everyone that an officer in plain clothes was what he claimed to be. For this reason tipstaves were issued to the Detective Branch as 'warrant carriers'. In 1880, tipstaves were withdrawn and officers were required to carry their warrant cards.

WARREN, SIR CHARLES, GCMG, KCB, (1840–1927) Commissioner, 1886–8.

Educ. Cheltenham, Sandhurst and Woolwich. Lt, Royal Engineers, 1857. Served in Palestine and carried out archaeological research on which he later based three books, 1867. CMG, 1877. Active service in the Kaffir War, 1877–8. Lt-Col .and Chief Instructor, Army Engineering School, Chatham, 1880. KCMG after leading successful expedition in Egypt to find missing archaeological party, 1882. Sent to Khartoum with 2nd relief expedition for General Gordon; then successfully put down disturbances in Bechuanaland, for which GCMG, 1884. Military commander, Suakim, 1885–6. Metropolitan Police Commissioner, 1886–8. Returned to army following resignation, and played controversial part in the Battle of Spion Kop, 1900. Retired from the army, and devoted the latter years of his life to the Boy Scout movement.

Warren was the most unlucky of all Commissioners. He was appointed to bring military discipline to public order and was welcomed by the press in that role – but the same press damned him as soon as he did what had been asked of him. His regard for his men's welfare took an unglamorous form and his concern for uniformed policing did not go down well with a public that had become more interested in the CID. His constables and Sergeants found him aloof and only his Superintendents really appreciated him. He was unlucky in his Assistant Commissioners (Crime), his Receiver, and the Home Office officials with whom he had to deal; and supremely unlucky in the Home Secretary who ultimately accepted his resignation. The Miss Cass case ruined the successful policing of Queen Victoria's Jubilee. The Jack the Ripper case popped up when the press needed a stick to beat him; and finally his historical reputation came to rest with irresponsible writers on the Ripper who knew nothing of the history of Scotland Yard's press relations, and swallowed wholesale the claim that Warren proved the unsuitability of military men as police Commissioners. (In spite of which, his predecessors, except Sir Richard Mayne, his immediate successor and three later Commissioners were all soldiers.)

Sir Edmund Henderson's ignominious resignation after the Trafalgar Square Demonstration and Riot, 1886 led to the demand for another soldier to restore order to the streets. When in after years Warren had been generally written off as the most unsuccessful of all Commissioners, historians wondered, 'Why *this* soldier?' The answers should have been obvious. He had been given the KCMG for successful detective work in tracking down the murderers of Professor Palmer and his missing party of archaeologists, and the GCMG for restoring public order in Bechuanaland. He was, as the press immediately recognized, ideally fitted for the job.

He was also politically in tune with the Liberal government that appointed him. Though he loyally and professionally set aside all political bias in the exercise of his duties, privately he sympathized with Gladstone's approach to the Irish problem and regretted that James Monro running Special Branch was obsessed with spying on Irish Nationalist politicians. But that was of no service to him when Gladstone's administration fell after a few months, and the Conservative Lord Salisbury appointed Henry Matthews Home Secretary.

SIR CHARLES WARREN.

Matthews was a Roman Catholic and an Irishman, the first Catholic cabinet minister since the Reformation. As such he was indispensable to Salisbury at a time when the Irish question dominated politics. But Matthews was essentially a lawyer and not a firm administrator. Warren expected that as a military appointee he would be given quasi-military authority over his subordinates, and he took exception to Monro's belief that as Assistant Commissioner (Crime) he inherited the complete independence that Howard Vincent had enjoyed and Henderson had never minded. Matthews paid no attention to Warren's complaints, nor was he interested that Warren found the stringent financial control exercised by the Receiver intolerable, though this complaint had been voiced by all Commissioners since the passing of John Wray in 1860. The situation was aggravated by Permanent Under Secretary Godfrey Lushington, who seems to have politicked against the Metropolitan Police and was personally far friendlier with the somewhat raffish Deputy Commissioner of the City of London Police than with Warren, the intellec-

tual evangelical Christian. These problems underlay the whole of Warren's short term of office.

In the first flush of his popularity he gave two hostages to fortune. Accustomed to the flamboyant splendour of colonial administration, he had no intention of passing his life restricted to occasional dress uniform. Without seeking Home Office approval he adopted a variant of his military uniform. This flummery was a godsend to cartoonists when he became unpopular. And in his first Commissioner's Report he complained about the poor quality of boots and saddles issued to his patrols. This responsible concern about equipment which was actually injuring the feet of men with 32km (20 miles) to walk on the beat was later pilloried as a silly soldier's typical fuss about kit inspection.

But Warren was popular until the Lord Mayor's Show in November, when part of the crowd got out of hand and behaved riotously in Clerkenwell. Warren promptly reinstituted regular foot drill for all officers up to and including Inspectors. This again would later be attacked as obsessive militarism, but it meant his men could be moved quickly and easily for crowd control, and the policing of the Jubilee celebrations was hailed as a triumph – until the arrest of Miss Cass in the evening. This was exactly the sort of problem for which Warren was worst fitted. He wanted to be firm and fair, but had not the diplomacy to combine the two at the same time. So he acted firmly and unfairly against PC Endacott who had made the arrest, and, without apology, rescinded his judgment after investigating the case. The press understandably felt that unquestioned military discipline with a right-about-turn was inappropriate.

At this time, too, Warren and the police came under political attack. Mr Gladstone in opposition claimed that the police were not to be trusted in their interrogation of suspected Fenians. Socialist agitators held public meetings and circulated pamphlets voicing rank-and-file police grievances about pay, pensions and promotions, and Bloody Sunday, 1887 turned the Radical press decisively against Warren. Thereafter the unemployed continued to hold regular rallies in Trafalgar Square, and Warren issued regular orders for deployments of men to police these rallies. There were no further disturbances in 1888, but Warren got no credit for this. As far as the left was concerned he had declared himself the enemy of the poor, and could do no right.

In 1888 another reform led to Warren's first offer of resignation. The shortage of senior officers to liaise between Scotland Yard and the Divisions had not been solved by the creation of two extra Assistant Commissioners in 1884. Warren set about to reinstitute Henderson's system of District Superintendents which had fallen into desuetude. He renamed them Chief Constables, and a Home Office Committee (on which he sat), said they should be 'of good social standing' and usually army or navy officers. He also decided that the CID should be given a Chief Constable, who would effectively become the Assistant Commissioner's deputy and liaise with his men. Monro, an old India hand, wanted Melville Macnaghten, a young planter he had met in Bengal. Warren approved at first, but withdrew his approval when he learnt that during a riot, Macnaghten had been 'the only man in India who has been beaten by Hindoos' (Warren's words). Monro insisted. So did Warren. Monro threatened resignation. So did Warren. Henry Matthews wriggled. He accepted Monro's resignation, but placed him in the Home Office with the curious title 'Head of Detective Service' and continuing command of Special Branch. He established that Warren was willing to work with Dr Robert Anderson, the Home Office controller of spies infiltrating the Fenians, and he appointed Anderson Assistant Commissioner (Crime). The contentious post of Chief Constable was given to Superintendent Adolphus Williamson, the senior detective and effective head of the CID, who had been threatening his own resignation, and thus became the only man for the next 30 years to benefit from the original supposed opportunity for ranker Superintendents to better themselves. For some unfath-

omable reason the Home Office insisted that preparations for these changes be made in great secrecy, which led some officers to believe that Warren was spying on Anderson to undermine Monro.

Clandestinity was really the other way round. Anderson and Williamson were encouraged to liaise with Monro behind Warren's back, and did so when the Jack the Ripper crisis broke over Scotland Yard before Anderson had even set his office in order. The immediate press storm provoked Warren intolerably. He was criticized for refusing to offer a reward, when in fact he wanted to do so but was forbidden by the Home Office. He was criticized for not having enough police on the ground when he was submitting Whitechapel to swamping. He was criticized for paying too much attention to uniformed policing and not enough to the CID, which, like his fellow Sapper, Henderson, he was sensibly content to leave in the hands of professional detectives and spymasters. He was criticized for not using bloodhounds to trace the murderer; criticized for calling them in and letting himself be 'hunted' by them in Regent's Park; criticized for losing them when they were wanted, which he had not done. After his retirement he was to be criticized for letting them bite him, which never occurred either. The Met was compared unfavourably with the City Police, which was free to offer a reward, and

managed to look informative while actually being the more secretive force.

Stung beyond endurance, Warren responded with an intemperate article on 'The Policing of London' in *Murray's Magazine*. He made firm and relevant points about work that was being done, but he also attacked the public and press for being unhelpful, and encouraged Vigilante Committees, which police on the ground knew to be dangerous. Worst of all, he aired his grievance about not having unfettered control of the CID. This brought him a reprimand from the Home Office, which pointed out that he should not publish comments on his duties without first having them vetted by civil servants. The requirement was not unjustified. Warren's outburst had encouraged an anonymous 'PC' to publish an answering pamphlet voicing rank-and-file grievances about square-bashing and their constant duty to control or suppress working-class demonstrations with which they were in sympathy. But the tone of the memo was deliberately offensive, and Warren had had enough of interference by Lushington and his colleagues. He declared that if he were not allowed to defend his force against public attacks as he saw fit, he would resign. His resignation was thankfully accepted.

His going was announced on the day of the last Whitechapel murder, and the press wrongly believed he had been fired for failing to catch Jack the Ripper. Senior officers knew they were losing a good and efficient boss, and all the Superintendents in London went to his house to pay their respects and say how much they regretted his going. But the men had never loved him. They blamed him for their unsatisfactory pensions situation and for the continuing policy of instant dismissal for drunkenness. Typically, Warren was too loyal and professional to leak to them his fervent but ineffective attempts to get the Home Office to remedy these grievances. His best epitaph was supplied by Home Office mandarin Evelyn Ruggles-Brise, who said, 'Warren

PUNCH, OR THE LONDON CHARIVARI.—NOVEMBER 24, 1888.

EXTREMES MEET.

SIR EDMUND. "MY DEAR WARREN, YOU DID TOO MUCH!" SIR CHARLES. "AND YOU, MY DEAR HENDERSON, DID TOO LITTLE!!"
MR. PUNCH (sotto voce). "H'M!—SORRY FOR THE *NEW MAN!!*"

was the finest man we had in Whitehall, but probably the worst appointment, because he must be independent, and the Commissioner of Police is held in very tight bonds by the Home Office.' It was 100 years before he would be given such fair treatment in books on the police or the Ripper case.

WATTS, ALBERT, KPM Married name of Det Sgt Alberta Law.

WENSLEY, CHIEF CONSTABLE FREDERICK PORTER (1865–1949) The fourth officer to rise from PC to Chief Constable (cf. Adolphus Williamson, Sir James Olive), and arguably the most influential Metropolitan detective officer of the 20th century.

Born in Taunton of a family whose yeoman ancestry could be traced back to the 12th century. From boyhood he cherished the ambition of becoming a detective, and in 1887 came to London, joining the Metropolitan Police in January 1888 (Warrant No. 73224). Posted to L Division (Lambeth) as a beat constable, where he encountered a good deal of casual violence from drunks whom he arrested. Drafted to H Division, Whitechapel among the extra patrols mounted at the time of the Jack the Ripper murders, though he acknowledged that he played no part in the investigation of the case. In 1891, transferred from L Division to E Division to replace officers dismissed following the abortive Police Strike, 1890. From there transferred to Whitechapel, much against his wishes, as H Division was far more violent than L or E Division. He concentrated on trying to enter the CID, but after passing the requisite exams was dependent on a recommendation from the local Inspector, Tom Divall. Although PC Wensley built up a remarkable record for working overtime to secure valuable arrests of thieves, Divall disliked the young man and refused to recommend him. It was not until 1895 that H Division Superintendent Dodd, stepped in and insist-

ed that Wensley be placed as a probationer detective. Wensley never looked back, making his name by his action in the Turner Street murders of 1896, when he followed a ruffian who had just murdered an old receiver and his housekeeper on to the roof, causing him to jump off and break his thigh.

Wensley's dishevelled appearance on the rooftop led to his being mistaken by the crowd

THE ORIGINAL 'BIG FOUR' OF SCOTLAND YARD, (LEFT TO RIGHT) ARTHUR HAWKINS, FREDERICK WENSLEY, FRANCIS CARLIN AND ARTHUR NEIL.

for an accomplice, and this in turn led to his meeting Chief Constable (later Assistant Commissioner) Melville Macnaghten, who visited H Division HQ at Leman Street to ask about the supposed escaped confederate. Macnaghten charmed Wensley by informally calling him 'Fred', and Wensley amused and impressed Macnaghten when he argued the Chief Constable's way into Turner Street past a very determined local civilian who had been instructed by an Inspector to admit no one, 'Not even the Commissioner!' Thereafter Macnaghten took a positive and beneficial interest in Wensley's career.

For three years Wensley cultivated informants and familiarized himself with the criminal ways of the Division, learning all he could from such locally distinguished colleagues as Detective Inspector Stephen White and Detective Sergeants William Thick and Eli Caunter. At this time he abandoned teetotalism, as no informant would

trust a policeman who refused a drink with him. When he applied for promotion to Sergeant, he was refused on the ground that this would mean his transfer to another Division, and he was now too useful in Whitechapel. Wensley thereupon appealed to Scotland Yard, and Macnaghten authorized his promotion and retention in Whitechapel as a supernumerary on the strength.

In 1901 he played an important part in breaking up a gang of German burglars led by a woman named Bertha Weiner. In 1904, he and his friend Sergeant Ben Leeson were a part of Inspector Tom Divall's team investigating the murder of an elderly Commercial Road tobacconist, Miss Emily Farmer, by two young tearaway half-brothers called Conrad Donovan (or Rotten) and Charles Wade. Wensley was impressed by the sudden appearance of Macnaghten in evening dress at Leman Street. The Assistant Commissioner had left a formal function on hearing that the case had been imperilled by a man making a false confession.

Wensley's East End cases naturally included more investigations of theft, fraud and counterfeiting than the sensational murders which attracted later attention. One of his most painful memories was his role in a raid on an illegal gambling club catering to soldiers. Wensley and a colleague penetrated the club in disguise, with riding crops and the skin-tight breeches of Hussars officers. At a given signal, Wensley threw himself face down over the gaming table with his arms outstretched to conserve the chips and money which constituted evidence to be seized by a large body of his uniformed colleagues who were to rush in from a pantechnicon where they were hiding outside. Unfortunately, with excessive caution, the uniformed men had locked themselves in their Trojan horse, and could not make an instant entry. A delighted club member seized Wensley's riding crop and administered a severe thrashing to the skin-tight breeches, while Wensley gritted his teeth and hung on to the evidence.

Later he succeeded Divall as H Division Local Inspector. By now he was the most prominent policeman in the East End, nicknamed 'the Weasel' by the underworld. When the King's Police Medal was instituted in 1909, he was the first detective awarded the honour for outstanding service.

He placed great importance on rapid response to information about serious crimes. He noted that in 1909 the pimps Morris and Marks Reubens who assaulted two seamen named McEarchen and Sproull in a sinister backstreet room near Leman Street nearly got away with the murder of Sproull. Only the alertness of a PC Mackintosh led the police immediately from McEarchen's drunken ramblings to the alley where a trail of blood ran between the trick pad in 3 Rupert Street and Sproull's body, dumped on the other side of the road. Only prompt entry ensured the Reubenses' arrest before they could conceal evidence, and only an instant search of the room gave Wensley the chance to find Marks Reubens' bloodstained clasp-knife hidden behind the gas-stove. That clue was decisive in overturning the brothers' plea of self-defence and unpremeditated manslaughter, for the time it took Marks to draw and unclasp his knife was accepted as a murderer's 'malice aforethought'. It was enough to hang them both (to Wensley's personal satisfaction and the discomfiture of other East End pimps contemplating the 'badger game'). And the knife would certainly have been destroyed by the girls who hid it had not the police occupied their room within an hour of the murder.

Two major cases in 1910 convinced Wensley that it was absolutely vital that Divisional CIDs (and separate forces, when necessary) should cooperate closely across their boundaries. Had not his old friend Alfred Ward, the Divisional Detective Inspector of W Division (Clapham), accepted Melville Macnaghten's advice that he seek Wensley's help in investigating the murder of Leon Beron, Stinie Morrison would never have been brought to justice. The murder took place in Clapham, but the events leading up to it all took place in Whitechapel and Stepney.

At the same time, H Division was inevitably called in to help look for George Gardstein's gang of jewel thieves, who went to earth in Stepney after murdering three of the City of London policemen who interrupted their burglary of a shop in Houndsditch. Wensley willingly threw time and men into the hunt for these killers. He liaised with the City Police, and when Fritz Svaars and 'Joseph' were located, he played a prominent part in the shoot-out with them at the Siege of Sidney Street. He personally declined to carry a gun on this occasion, but he went forward under fire to rescue Ben Leeson, who had been shot and seriously injured in the first attempt to flush out the assassins.

In the same year, the City Police cooperated with him to seal off the roads around Old Street Magistrates' Court and arrest the East End villain Arthur Harding and his 'Vendetta gang', who had turned up in the City intending to murder their rival, 'Darky the Coon' Bogard. Another operation which impressed Wensley greatly was an inter-Divisional investigation that exposed the far-flung activities of a gang of coiners. He regretted that the *ad hoc* detective squad was broken up as soon as convictions were achieved.

In 1912 Wensley was promoted to Chief Inspector, an advance which normally entailed transfer to the Commissioner's Office at Scotland Yard. Until the outbreak of the Great War, however, an exception was made in his case, and he remained in the East End with freedom to extend his operations beyond the boundaries of H Division. In the early years of the war he was much concerned with the problems of possible espionage and sabotage which engrossed Assistant Commissioner Basil Thomson. In 1916, on the death of his friend Alfred Ward, he was finally transferred to Scotland Yard as the senior Chief Inspector in the CID, and spent the rest of his career as effective operational head of the Met's detectives.

He approached Thomson with two important suggestions based on his experience in the Divisions. To ensure that Divisional Superintendents and Local Inspectors did not jealously guard their territory from colleagues who needed to work across territorial boundaries, he proposed that the Metropolitan Police District should be divided into three or four large Areas, each controlled by a Detective Superintendent in Scotland Yard who would have the power to enforce Divisional cooperation. And to combat criminals' increasing mobility in motor cars across the metropolis, he recommended that a small body of detectives should be given their own means of fast transport and empowered to operate anywhere in London, without reference to senior officers in the Divisions. Thomson favoured the suggestions, but was too busy with war-related work to put them into practice, and they were shelved for the time being.

In 1917 Wensley pioneered a new method of detection when he asked a French butcher called Louis Voisin to write the words 'Bloody Belgium', which had been scrawled on the paper wrapping up the mutilated torso of his mistress before it was dumped in Regent's Square. Voisin obliged, and repeatedly reproduced the spelling error 'Blodie' which had appeared on the paper. After his conviction, he appealed, claiming that asking him to give specimens of his handwriting and spelling constituted entrapment. Mr Justice Lawrence dismissed the appeal contemptuously, noting that the same argument might be used to disallow any responses prisoners gave to investigating officers before they had been charged.

The press was becoming aware of Wensley's real distinction as a detective, and started to nickname him 'Ace'. His juniors at Scotland Yard, however, with their normal irreverence, nicknamed him 'Elephant' in honour of his long nose.

The deaths of his elder son in action and his younger son in the flu epidemic of 1918 were a deep personal distress. His quiet family life at Palmer's Green had always been important to him. He tried to feel patriotic pride in having given his sons for England, but colleagues noted that his eyes would always mist over when he spoke of them.

In 1919, Wensley was given the chance to put one of his proposals into effect. He summoned 12 outstanding detectives to Scotland Yard and gave them a roving brief under the command of DI Walter Hambrook to travel around London in a tarpaulin-covered wagon, following up crimes and hunting down criminals wherever they might hear of them. This was the genesis of the Flying Squad, which was consistently protected and supported from the top by Wensley whenever its budgets or activities were challenged.

The same year Wensley's second great reform was carried out. The Metropolitan Police District was divided into four Areas, and he and DCI Albert Hawkins were promoted to Superintendents. With Acting Superintendents Arthur Neil and Francis Carlin they constituted the Big Four (John Ashley later made this the Big Five), each taking overall charge of a quarter of Metropolitan detection. Wensley, whose area was all London east of the City, together with Bow Street (E Division) and the River Police, was very much *primus inter pares*, as was recognized in 1925 when the post of Chief Constable (CID) was reinstated specifically for him, and he became the only detective since Williamson to rise through the ranks to this status. His prestige throughout the force was enormous. His former Sergeant Ben Leeson in his memoirs misremembered him as having been promoted to Assistant Commissioner (a rank he fully deserved). Detective Inspector George Cornish, interviewing bootboy Henry Jacoby for the murder of Lady White in 1922, echoed the Wensley of 1896. To his surprise, one of the top brass turned up in white tie and tails to see how the case was proceeding – but this time it was Wensley who had broken his journey to a formal function in the interest of good detection. Deputy Commander Reg Spooner, who headed the Flying Squad after 1954 and died in harness in 1963, was justifiably proud of having been welcomed into the CID by Wensley. But as a straightforward cockney copper, Spooner took it for granted that Wensley had reached his exalted rank via the normal old school tie network of those days, and all his life wrongly recollected him as 'Colonel' Wensley. Detective Chief Superintendent Ted Greeno was equally proud of having been inducted into the CID by the man he regarded as the greatest policeman of all time.

With the Flying Squad and Area Detective Superintendents in place, Wensley concentrated his future reforming efforts on the encouragement of forensic scientific investigation, which was yielding obviously good results. He also continued the battle against professional gangs, though he was optimistic in thinking (as did Arthur Harding) that 'Darky the Coon's' power had been broken by the events of 1910, or that

he had been ultimately successful in breaking Darby Sabini's Clerkenwell-based mob of protection racketeers. In comparing his generally successful results with the manifest failure of the American police to contain organized crime, he undoubtedly underrated the difficulties the Americans had put themselves under by the ridiculous social experiment of prohibiting alcohol. Wensley seems never to have noted the difficulty of stamping out victim-free vice by legal prohibition, with its concomitant danger of bringing law enforcement into conflict with a non-larcenous public.

Given the opportunity, he was no chairbound warrior against crime. In 1922, hearing that the wife of murdered Percy Thompson was rumoured to have a lover, he had himself driven to Ilford police station to supervise her interrogation. When the lover was identified as Frederick Bywaters, he galvanized his recently formed Flying Squad to race to Bywaters' mother's home and search his room, thus uncovering the love letters which led to Mrs Thompson's conviction. And he pointed out that his passion for speed was justified once again, for Bywaters would have been well away to sea with every opportunity to destroy incriminating evidence had the

CHIEF CONSTABLE FREDERICK PORTER WENSLEY KPM.

Flying Squad failed to trace and arrest him within 24 hours of first hearing of him. The execution of Edith Thompson was and is highly controversial. Wensley, who met her, was convinced that it was justified, as her encouragement provoked Bywaters to murder Percy. He did not believe that she was a romancer who never expected to be taken seriously.

When Wensley retired in 1929 he was a national figure. He had probably received more commendations and awards than any other policeman ever, and his tremendous prestige gave his beloved CID a position of power in the Yard that would not be challenged until the 1970s. (Cf. Sir Robert Mark.) The serialization of his memoirs (*Detective Days*, 1931) was treated by the press as though he were royalty. He was invited to go to New York as a consultant to District Attorney Tom Dewey's successful investigation and prosecution of some leading figures in organized crime, but he refused to be involved in such a major piece of gang-busting unless he could be given complete control of the case. Given the scale of the American problem, it was probably just as well for his reputation that he never tried to make good his belief that he had coped with an equally dangerous gangland.

For the next 20 years he lived quietly at Palmer's Green, assembling a notable collection of Goss china, which he took immense pleasure in showing off to his guests. He was a genial host. Like many policemen, he treasured the memory of villains who liked and respected him as a copper who was always straight, but it is probably as great a tribute that Arthur Harding detested him and tried to blacken his memory when he dictated his 'memoirs' in the 1970s. Wensley always differentiated between wilful villains and people who were driven to crime by want, or could not 'go straight' because no one would employ them. Likewise he disapproved of capital punishment for people who killed in a moment of unrepeatable passion, or under immense provocation.

His professional ability, not always equalled in practical terms by his seniors, played no small part in giving us a professional police force, without ex-army officers, lawyers, colonial administrators, civil servants and other figures from the old boy

THE BLUE LAMP OF WEST END CENTRAL POLICE STATION.

network commandeering its highest ranks. His encouragement of Inspector Lilian Wyles, the first woman in the CID, may look paternalistic and patronizing by 21st-century standards, but it was a vital stage in overcoming the force's resistance to women police. And Miss Wyles perhaps wrote his finest epitaph: 'He was a diamond of the roughest kind, yet when I got to know him, it was to discover a heart of pure gold.'

See also Royal Commission, 1908.

WEST END CENTRAL Famous Divisional police station.

Purpose-built in Savile Row to replace Great Marlborough Street and Vine Street stations as the principal police centre controlling public disorder and street prostitution in the West End (C Division), West End Central station was opened on 14 July 1940. Two months later, on 24 September, it was gutted and all its movable fittings destroyed by a parachute mine that fell on the front doorstep. Three officers were killed and another 30 injured. For four days 'normal' duties continued in the shell of the building, but then Great Marlborough Street was reopened and the Divisional Headquarters Staff moved to Trenchard House until December, when West End Central was reopened. The following April King George VI and Queen Elizabeth visited the station to congratulate the staff on their devotion to duty.

Bow Street Magistrates' Court now shared with Great Marlborough Street the usual responsibility for fining street prostitutes, and they were still frequently charged at West End Central, where one postwar night young Edna May Collins, the despair of the Probation Service and Juvenile Courts, announced proudly that she had now turned 16, and could go to Bow Street 'with the big girls'.

By 1958 the volume of West End business was too great for a single Divisional structure, and the command at West End Central was divided into CD1 and CD2. By 1971 they had jointly outgrown the accommodation, and Vine Street had to be opened for the next 25 years. In 1995 the station closed until November 1997 for major refurbishment.

WHICHER, INSPECTOR JONATHAN (1814–1881) First widely known Scotland Yard detective.

Born in Camberwell. Worked as a labourer before joining the Met in 1837. (Warrant No. 13072). PC on E Division (Holborn), 1837–41. Detective Sergeant, A Division (Scotland Yard), 1842–56. Detective Inspector, 1856–64. Resigned 1864, due to 'congestion of the brain'. Retired to Holywell Street, Millbank.

Jonathan Whicher was one of the original members of the Detective Branch, and might be said to have been called to the specialization before the Branch existed. He attracted notice in the year he joined the force by spotting a prostitute in a Gray's Inn Road brothel wearing a stolen feather boa whose description had appeared in a route paper two days previously. He arrested Sophy Weller, and she was transported for the theft. Two years later, he was one of the constables dressed in plain clothes and sent by Inspector Nicholas Pearce to hunt for Daniel Good. PC Whicher accompanied Sgt Stephen Thornton in surveilling Good's wife Molly in Spitalfields. When the permanent Detective Branch was founded in the wake of the case, Whicher was promoted to Sergeant and drafted.

Known to friends and colleagues as Jack, he was also regarded as 'the Prince of Detectives'; a man who never made a blunder. He inspired Wilkie Collins's fictional Sergeant Cuff in *The Moonstone*, and his deliberate contemplative manner seems to have impressed most acquaintances as a mark of shrewdness and caution – which makes it unfortunate that he is best remembered today for his association with unsuccessful cases.

Charles Dickens' 1850 account of the detectives visiting *Household Words* describes Whicher as a short man – he was in fact 173cm (5ft 8 inches) tall – with a pock-marked complexion (his official records refer to smallpox marks). Inspector Field apparently introduced Whicher as the Branch's great expert on the 'Swell mob' – London pickpockets who infested race meetings all over the country. Whicher himself told of his pursuit and arrest of a well-known criminal who had gone to earth under a false name in Devon. His account reveals four things about his methods. He preferred to base his investigations on the known practices and associations of habitual criminals. Even when carrying out surveillance, he eschewed disguise (something he was known to despise). He could persuade the Post Office to let him read letters in the mail. And he diligently interviewed neighbours and asked questions wherever his perpetrator seemed to have been – a sort of precursor of the house-to-house inquiry.

In 1858 he was sent to Dagenham to investigate the reopened murder case on PC George Clarke. Whicher's prompt arrest of George Blewett, the newly accused suspect, has been described as somewhat precipitate and apparently at odds with his reputation for caution. But despite Blewett's acquittal, the most thorough recent examination of the case by Lee Sheldon indicates that there was strong evidence supporting the local certainty that the charge was well-founded.

In 1860 Whicher suffered his best-known setback. With his protégé Adolphus Williamson, he was sent to Wiltshire to unravel the Road House mystery. Four-year-old Francis Savile Kent was taken from his cot during the night, and his body was found in an outside privy the following morning. His throat had been cut and he had been stabbed to the heart. An open library window which the servants swore had been locked the previous night suggested the murderer's means of access and escape. Savile's father, Samuel Kent, was locally unpopular because of his sexual misconduct with servants. His second wife, Savile's mother, had formerly been the first Mrs Kent's nursemaid, and Samuel's liaison with her had started during the first Mrs Kent's lifetime. The Wiltshire constabulary felt that Mr Kent had deliberately impeded their investigation, misdirecting them toward some gypsies. The first constables in the house had been locked in the kitchen by some mischance, giving the household every opportunity to conceal any clues. The local suspicion was that Mr Kent had been engaged in dalliance with the current nursemaid, Elizabeth Gough, when Savile woke up and observed the guilty couple. They had promptly, and perhaps accidentally suffocated him, taking the body to the privy and stabbing it to cast blame on outsiders.

Whicher disagreed. He believed that 16-year-old Constance, daughter of Mr Kent's first marriage, had committed the murder, probably with the assistance of her brother William. He could find no direct evidence to support his suspicion of William, but Constance's influence over him had been demonstrated when the two ran away from home, Constance having first cut off her hair and dressed as a boy. Her manner elicited suspicion, and one of her nightdresses had suspiciously disappeared from the laundry. Whicher believed Constance had burned the bloodstained garment. He had her arrested and charged, but the case was thrown out for insufficient evidence. It seemed impossible, for example, that the girl could have held her little brother's corpse and opened the library window to get outside silently. Whicher protested that he was handicapped by having no legal support to overcome the magistrates' prior conclusions. But in the eyes of the public he had failed resoundingly, and he never again enjoyed the reputation of the Great Detective.

Five years later he was vindicated in the eyes of his colleagues. Under the influence of an Anglo-Catholic clergyman, Constance confessed and was convicted of the murder. Subsequent historians have objected that her confession is flawed: she claimed, for example, to have injured

Savile with her father's razor, yet this could not have stabbed his chest. Whicher's reputation has never been fully restored.

Nonetheless, an examination of his reports in 1860 show that he had a very strong case. He regarded the library window as a red herring. He was sure the body had been taken through a side door that led directly to the privy. He noted that Constance had used the same privy as the hiding place for the hair she cut off when she ran away, and remarked that whoever put the body there was too naive to see that it would be caught by the splashboard and would not disappear into the cesspit below. He pinpointed an exact time when Constance had the laundry to herself and could have extracted the nightdress. He found evidence from Constance's schoolmates that she was unusually strong and aggressive, and had often expressed her hatred of her father's second family. And, most important, he was sure (though he could not prove) that William was implicated. This (we may say with hindsight) could explain the inadequacy of Constance's confession, just as it is possible that Mr Kent's horrified suspicion of his older children might explain his apparent attempts to frustrate the investigation.

But a second setback immediately after the Road House case set the seal on Whicher's downfall. He was sent to Kingswood Rectory in Surrey, where burglars had tied up a Mrs Halliday, who was sleeping there as caretaker in the rector's absence, and had accidentally suffocated her with a gag. They fled, leaving behind a pocketbook dropped by one of them belonging to a German named Johann Franz, and containing the last page of a letter from a famous opera singer. Enquiries revealed that in Reigate the previous day, two Germans had bought string of the kind used to tie up Mrs Halliday. The search was on for Franz, and when he was found in London, he tried to escape by giving a false name. When he finally admitted his identity, he told an improbable story of having come to England with two fellow countrymen, one named Adolphe Krohn, who had stolen his pocketbook while he was asleep. He had given the false name because he had heard he was wanted for murder.

He was charged and put on trial, but the case collapsed when the opera singer turned up,

AN OFFICER SOUNDING THE ALARM ON HIS WHISTLE DURING WORLD WAR II.

denied knowing Franz, and said her letter had been written to Adolphe Krohn. Jonathan Whicher's reputation and spirits did not recover from this failure. He became increasingly depressed, until his resignation with what would seem to be a mental breakdown.

But he recovered, and in retirement played a part in exposing Arthur Orton, the obese Wapping butcher who was convicted of fraudulently impersonating the long-lost baronet Sir Roger Tichborne in 1872, having tied up the Tichborne estates in litigation for the previous eight years. Whicher knew he might be unpopular for this contribution to justice. Orton enjoyed considerable popular support, many people illogically seeing him as a working man (and therefore a fraud) being done out of his 'rights' by the wealthy aristocracy.

Whicher's judgment of Orton was absolutely right, and in this last case he showed, as he so often had done, the invariable value of painstaking investigation, repeatedly interviewing possible witnesses and carefully noting all possible evidence. If his manner was slow and deliberative, this reflects his true ability as the first great Metropolitan detective whose genius was, indeed, more perspiration than inspiration.

'WHISPERING SQUAD' Sub-section of the Drugs Squad, dissolved in 1972 when six of its members were charged with perjury and conspiracy to pervert the course of justice. Three of the perjury charges resulted in convictions, and the officers were imprisoned despite the jury's observation that the offences were not really significant.

In 1968, at a time of heightened press publicity about drugs, Detective Chief Inspector Victor Kelaher, at that time the youngest DCI in the history of the Met, was transferred from the Flying Squad to head the Drugs Squad. Kelaher, a brilliant detective and both a policeman's son and an old boy of the Orphanage, encouraged Detective Sergeant Norman 'Nobby' Pilcher to use methods which included allowing informants to set up crimes with which they would not be charged. Pilcher's little group of officers were so secretive and successful that they became known to colleagues as 'the Whispering Squad'. (Cf. the Ghost Squad.)

Eventually a misremembered date in evidence given against a family charged with attempted drug smuggling led to examination of Pilcher's and his junior officers' notebooks, where deliberate misstatements were found to have been made and a few pages replaced in one notebook. The result was the trial of Kelaher and five others for conspiracy, and all but Kelaher for perjury. Three were convicted and jailed for perjury. Kelaher was acquitted, but retired early, suffering from severe nervous stress. One of the remaining two officers resigned, and the sixth, a woman Detective Constable, was reprimanded and temporarily returned to uniformed duty.

The squad's over-zealous corner-cutting methods helped ensure the appointment of Sir Robert Mark as Commissioner and encouraged his reforms of the CID, along with the accelerated retirement of several old-style detectives who were not willing to see their former supremacy and methods superseded.

WHISTLES Since 1885 carried among appointments as means for patrolling officers to summon assistance. Still carried, although now supplementary to personal radios.

The River Police always used whistles to hail watermen. Wooden whistles were carried on the galleys, and the dockyard police carried naval bo'sun's whistles. Suggestions that patrolling uniformed police might carry whistles instead of rattles were put forward as early as 1845, but encountered initial resistance from the men who found the rattle a useful supplementary weapon. However, tests showed that whistles were audible over a greater distance, and the Manchester police force found them very satisfactory. In February 1885 the Met ordered 7175 whistles of the pattern used in Manchester, and issued them to all officers. For another couple of years rattles were held in stations for issue to night patrols, but in April 1887 they were called in and the whistle reigned supreme.

Hardly ever used after the introduction of the personal radio, the whistle is still sometimes carried. In the late 1990s, motorcycle police found that the referee's type of whistle with a reverberating pea in the small drum emitted an extremely useful blast which could attract attention over the noise of traffic and they began to be used informally, especially by the Special Escort Group.

WHITEHALL PLACE Original address of Metropolitan Police Headquarters. A street running east off the upper (northern) end of Whitehall, parallel with Great Scotland Yard. When No. 4 Whitehall Place, a government office, fell vacant in 1829, Sir Robert Peel acquired it as the office of the Metropolitan Police Commissioners Sir Charles Rowan and Richard Mayne. It was given up when the purpose-built New Scotland Yard on the Embankment was occupied in 1890, the name Scotland Yard having by then passed into general currency from the greater frequency with which visitors entered the HQ through its Back Hall.

WHITEHALL 1212 Famous telephone number of the Scotland Yard PBX (Private Branch

WHITEHALL PLACE. NO.4 IS THE SECOND DOOR FROM THE LEFT.

Exchange, or internal switchboard).

Introduced in April 1932, when WHItehall Automatic telephone exchange was installed to transmit dialled calls by machinery instead of headphoned GPO operators making manual connections from spoken numbers. (Previously New Scotland Yard had been on the Victoria exchange.)

Ms Dorothy Annie Nye (d.1985) was seconded by the Post Office to operate the PBX for Scotland Yard, and became known as 'Miss Whitehall 1212' to those who heard her answer incoming calls, after the manner of the day, by repeating the number the caller had dialled.

Until it was overtaken by 999 (see Nine Nine Nine) in 1937, WHItehall 1212 was the 'Urgent Police Call' number, and as such the best-known telephone number in the UK. It remained a part of everyone's mental furniture throughout the 1940s and 1950s while radio continued to dominate nascent television, and at the same time the GPO telephone service respected subscribers' preference for telephone numbers comprising an easily memorable combination of letters and digits rather than an endless string of digits.

When the telephone numbers are available, the digits 1212 and 1113 (a common later number for police stations) are still used by some Scotland Yard branches and some modern station numbers.

WHITE SLAVERY BRANCH Small short-lived Branch under Assistant Commissioner Frederick Bullock, formerly known as White Slave Traffic Branch and dissolved on the outbreak of WWI after planting the seeds of Interpol.

International efforts to secure a protocol prohibiting the transportation of women for immoral purposes followed claims in the 1880s that women and children were held against their will in Belgian brothels. Continual campaigning (by the National Vigilance Association in England) led to the signing of the protocol and the passing of severe laws against procuring and living off immoral earnings. Chief Constable Frederick Bullock, like senior police representatives from other countries attending international conferences on the subject, repeatedly reported that the police found no actual kidnapping or orga-

nized compulsion of women to lead immoral lives, though (with the support of Miss Eilidh Mac-Dougall and other charitable ladies) they could perform valuable work rescuing juveniles who put themselves in moral danger.

The NVA, whose long term hope was the complete elimination of prostitution, nevertheless pressed on with claims that false 'employment agencies', spurious 'theatrical contracts', and even drugging by chloroform and hypodermic syringe were all used to entrap women into continental, South African and South American brothels. These myths were reported in the press until the 1930s, putting steady pressure on the Met to put down an arguably non-existent crime. The short-lived Scotland Yard White Slavery Branch, however, did useful work against 'ponces' who maltreated and extorted money from women under their control, and the network of international (often Latvian) pimps which sprang up in response to prostitutes' need for assistance in circumventing the protocol and travelling to capital cities (including London) where they wished to work. Three cases of living on immoral earnings were reported by B Division in 1913, when only 9 Divisions had cases to report, but the totals are uncertain.

In 1914 Prince Albert of Monaco called an International Judicial Police Conference to regularize extradition procedures, frontier controls and anti-White Slavery measures. Its work was terminated by the outbreak of WWI, but its usefulness was recognized, and the second IJPC, called in Austria in 1923, led to the establishment of Interpol.

HENRY WHITING (1819–1894) The 'Police Philanthropist'.

Impressed by the courage of DI John Jacob Thomson in arresting Richard Burke in 1868, (see Clerkenwell Bombing) Mr Whiting of Lavender Hill was given permission to present Thomson with 'a small sum' to purchase some little token as a souvenir, and at the same time made his first donation of £1000 to endow the Bow Street Police Fund.

In 1870 he became the first name on the subscription list for the projected Police Orphanage, with a donation of £100. In 1885, when the two

little boys of a Cumberland policeman were orphaned by his murder, Mr Whiting persuaded the Orphanage to waive its exclusive London admissions policy and accept the lads. He supported his argument with a cheque for £500, and his first act on his birthday every year was to write a cheque for £100 for the Orphanage.

He gave £3000 toward the acquisition of the 'Seaside Home' (Police Convalescent Home) at Hove, and for the last 24 years of his life, sent £5 to Bow Street and £10 to his local Division in Battersea and Wandsworth every Christmas for distribution among the most needy and deserving police officers. He reacted speedily to reports of police suffering, as in the case of a constable who had his teeth knocked out and his jaw smashed by a ruffian with an iron bar. Mr Whiting placed the man in the Royal Dental Hospital and promised him a full set of false teeth as soon as his mouth could bear them. He made other generous contributions to the provincial and Royal Irish constabularies, and

HENRY WHITING.

PC HARRY COLES, 'THE ANIMALS' FRIEND', WHO BETWEEN 1890 AND 1915 SECURED 1500 CONVICTIONS FOR CRUELTY TO ANIMALS, A CRIME WHICH HE ABHORRED.

at the time of his death was arranging a new trust deed to extend the Police Relief Fund to the City of London Police.

Mr Whiting's income, derived from rents, was estimated at £6000 per annum, and of that he gave away £2000 every year to philanthropic causes. He asked for a funeral without pomp and ceremony, which prevented the police from mounting the massive demonstration of respect and affection they intended.

In 1895 his widow (who was an equally generous philanthropist in her own right) presented a clock and a plaque in his memory to the Orphanage.

WILDLIFE CRIME UNIT The Wildlife Crime Unit is based at New Scotland Yard and coordinates the work of the Met's Area Wildlife Officers, who deal with illegal persecution of badgers and wild birds (particularly birds of prey),

illegal hare coursing, poaching and, especially, the illegal wildlife trade in London.

Operation Charm, the Met's initiative against the illegal trade in endangered species, is run by the Wildlife Crime Unit and has led to the seizure of large quantities of wildlife products, from traditional Chinese medicines derived from tigers, rhinos and bears to elephant ivory and shahtoosh, the wool of the critically endangered chiru, or Tibetan antelope. Interpol estimate the illegal trade in wildlife to be worth $US 5 billion every year, and Operation Charm is an ongoing initiative.

WILLIAMSON, CHIEF CONSTABLE FREDERICK ADOLPHUS (1830–1889) First senior officer in the CID. First Chief Constable promoted from the ranks.

Son of the original Superintendent of T Division (Hammersmith). Educ. Hammersmith Grammar School. 1847–9, temporary clerk in the Royal Ordnance. 1849–50, assistant clerk in the Metropolitan Police. 1850, joined Met. 1852, transferred to Detective Branch and promoted to

Sergeant. 1863, Inspector. 1867, Chief Inspector, and senior officer in the CID when Howard Vincent formed it. 1870, Superintendent. 1888, Chief Constable 1889, retired and died soon after.

Possibly because he was a 'pup of the truncheon' or perhaps because his clerical experience had given him some familiarity with the bureaucratic ropes, 'Dolly' Williamson's promotion to Sergeant in the Detective Branch was exceptionally fast. He showed himself serious in his ambition for promotion by studying French in the evenings. Yet despite being apparently a swot and a seniors' favourite, he was very popular with his contemporaries. He was noted for his high spirits and willingness to participate in high jinks, as well as being skilled at avoiding letting them get him into trouble. He sang popular songs at parties and dinners. He kept fit by sculling on the Thames. Until at least 1877 he never missed the Oxford and Cambridge Boat Race. In due course he married his sweetheart, Miss Emma Macpherson.

He was trained as a detective by Jonathan Whicher and accompanied him to Wiltshire on the Constance Kent case. He retained a great respect for Whicher, whose adverse opinion of disguise he shared and retained throughout his career. When Whicher finally lost public credit in 1862, it was observed that Williamson's youthful high spirits died away. A friendly man but an efficient detective with notable ability at extracting the vital essence from complicated paperwork, he was thenceforward an essentially serious man. This was, perhaps, reflected in his detestation of any form of slang. He was never to become known to the public for any remarkable solution of sensational cases; essentially he trained and oversaw others.

Within a year Williamson was the senior Inspector in the Detective Branch. His attention through the mid-1860s was focused on the Fenians' activities, and so he was slow to observe the shortcomings of his colleagues which led to the Trial of the Detectives. He emerged with his integrity unquestioned, but his Branch's reputation severely damaged. After that, his kindness to younger colleagues was always remembered with deep affection, but it was noted that he had no close friends. Friendship, it seemed, had let him down.

But he was promoted to Superintendent as he took charge of Howard Vincent's new creation, the CID. Notes by Williamson preserved in the MEPO files suggest that he originated many of the ideas Vincent incorporated. He bought No. 4 Smith Square, SW1 as his home, and became noted for the roses he cultivated in its tiny garden. Working closely with Assistant Commissioner James Monro and the Home Office spymaster Dr Robert Anderson, he scored several successes against the renewed campaign of Fenian bombing, notably travelling to France to prevent the planned disruption of Queen Victoria's Jubilee celebrations by a bomb in Westminster Abbey.

By the late 1880s he was becoming somewhat disillusioned with his job. Robert Anderson, who left the only inside account of the events surrounding Williamson's promotion to Chief Constable, remarked that Williamson

CHIEF CONSTABLE ADOLPHUS WILLIAMSON.

threatened to resign because he believed that the incomprehensible secrecy enforced on Anderson and Sir Charles Warren as they prepared for Anderson to take up the post Monro had just resigned showed that there was some plot against Warren. It is not clear why this should have entered Williamson's mind, though it is known that at the time of Warren's resignation at the end of the year, the Superintendents as a rank (of whom Williamson had recently been one) unanimously deplored his going.

But a more obvious reason for Williamson's disgruntlement would seem to be Monro's (and Warren's) wish to pass him over in appointing Melville Macnaghten to the newly created position of Chief Constable, CID. It was well known that the proposal of the new rank in Sir Edmund Henderson's day had been accompanied by the hope that it should be used for promoting outstanding Superintendents into the 'gentlemanly' grade. It can hardly have gone down well with

Superintendent Williamson that Commissioner Warren explicitly disagreed, and thought that Chief Constables should be ex-army officers or old boys of public schools. At any rate, around the time Williamson apparently threatened resignation, Warren withdrew his support from the inexperienced young Macnaghten, and Williamson became the first Chief Constable drawn from the ranks and the last for the next 30 years.

It was too late to restore his sunny outlook. His health was breaking down. When Macnaghten was brought into the force as his deputy in 1889, he told the young man that it was a funny place to work: he'd be blamed if he did his job and blamed if he didn't. Soon after that he retired, and before the year was out he had died.

Although the press was damning about his antiquity and presumed incompetence at the time of the Jack the Ripper murders, every detective who worked under him and left memoirs recorded great respect for his ability and encouragement to his juniors. While the glamorous and innovative Vincent was rightly respected as the creator of the CID, Dolly Williamson was seen by working policemen as the man who got it off the ground.

WILLINK COMMISSION Royal Commission on the Police chaired by Sir Henry Urmston Willink MC.

Interim Report, 1960, Cmnd 1222. Final Report, 1962, Cmnd 1728. Set up by Home Secretary 'Rab' Butler to examine pay and conditions, questions of relations with the public, and the organization of provincial forces where two Chief Constables (at Brighton and Worcester) had been charged with fraud, one being convicted and imprisoned.

The interim report produced a prompt and needed revision of pay scales, raising basic pay from £510 to £695 over nine annual increments to £600 to £910 over the same period.

Concern about investigations of assault and other criminal offences allegedly committed by police officers were resolved by a recommendation that all cases should be referred to the Director of Public Prosecutions for a decision on prosecution or the need for further enquiries.

The tripartite responsibilities of Police Authorities, Chief Constables and the Home Secretary were clarified on a national basis, regardless of whether they were city or county forces, and the recommendations were put into force by the Police Act, 1964, which formed the basis of police organization for many years. Two exercises of amalgamation of forces followed the Act, and resulted in a reduction in their numbers from 129 to the current 43 in England and Wales.

In interesting minority reports, Sir George Turner and H. A. Hetherington revived the call for a separately recruited and more highly educated CID, and Professor A. L. Goodhart revived the call for a single national police force.

The Taverne Report on police manpower, equipment and efficiency followed, and was influential in the introduction of the Unit Beat (Panda) cars, Home Beat Officers and personal radios.

POLICEWOMEN TRAINING IN SELF DEFENCE IN THE 1940s.

WINSTON (1940–1957) Chestnut gelding acquired as a three- or four-year-old for the Mounted Police.

Ridden by HM King George VI at Trooping of the Colour ceremonies from 1947, and by HM Queen Elizabeth from her accession until 1956. Winston became widely known and immensely popular with the public when film of the Queen riding him accompanied the National Anthem as it was played at the end of cinema programmes for the first 10 years or so of her reign.

In February 1957 Winston had to be put down after falling and breaking his back at exercise. A huge volume of mail was received at Scotland Yard after newspaper reports suggested that he would be disposed of as cat food. In fact, he was given a seemly burial at Imber Court.

WOMEN POLICE Introduction of women police officers into the Met was preceded by the activities of two separate organizations, the uniformed Women's Police Service founded in 1914, and the non-uniformed Women Police Special Patrols.

1918–22, Metropolitan Women Police Patrols approved under Superintendent Mrs Sofia Stanley. Twenty-five women recruited early in 1919 and a further 50 later in the year. 1922, as an economy measure, reduced to 20 women sent out to the Divisions under the authority of Divisional Superintendents. 1923–30, Inspector Bertha Clayden, senior woman police officer, directed to liaise with Divisional Superintendents and, under their direction, supervise women police, who were now fully attested and given limited powers of arrest. 1930–69, A4 Branch (Women Police) established under a female Superintendent. 1969, Women's Branch dissolved in anticipation of Equal Pay Act, but Women Police still treated as an essentially separate section of the service and listed as a separate strength. 1973, Women Police integrated directly into the main force.

Scotland Yard was relatively slow to employ women police: Grantham, Birkenhead, Lancashire, Salisbury and Reading Constabularies were all earlier in the field. Commissioner Sir Nevil Macready's claim to have 'invented women police', has to be offset against his stated objection to the term, so that the 112 women he ultimately recruited had to be called 'Metropolitan Women Police Patrols' rather than constables. He completely bypassed the organizers of the Women Police Service, and appointed Mrs Sofia Stanley of the National Council of Women's Women Special Police Patrols as Superintendent of his new policewomen, with Mrs Elinor Robertson, a former senior officer in the Women's Forage Corps of the RASC, as her assistant. Neither of them, nor any of the patrols, were sworn in and given powers of arrest. The women recruited had to be spinsters or widows between the ages of 25 and 35. They were given uniform and sent out to the Divisions, who made little use of them at first, except for patrolling streets where prostitutes loitered, leaving it to the male constabulary to arrest any seen soliciting and make the case against them in court. Gradually they increased their duties to include escorting women and children to the courts, and watching clubs where illegal drinking and gambling was suspected. Sir Nevil wanted them to take over vice policing, because he felt 'it is difficult to eradicate the sex instinct [in men] unless they are religious fanatics, the worst type to deal with that form of vice'. The women police themselves quickly realized that some of their male colleagues were extremely selective in visiting the law upon brothels and prostitutes, and they strongly suspected that some sort of bribes or favours were being passed.

These early policewomen were sceptically received by some policemen. Macready's response was to urge his men to accept that women were useful for the duty of moving on fornicating couples in the parks, a job which, he suggested, belittled the standing of men who undertook it. At first Mrs Stanley shifted her women very frequently from Division to Division, but more, it transpired, from a fear that they might become too close to the men they worked with than to break up hostilities. In 1927 General Orders laid down that a WPC must resign if she married, though married women already serving were not affected.

In 1920 Major Sir John Baird, Parliamentary Under Secretary at the Home Office, set up and chaired a Committee on the Employment of Women on Police Duties. The Baird Committee heard misleading testimony from Macready, Superintendent Stanley and Sergeant Lilian Wyles, all of whom claimed that relations between the men on the beat and the women patrols were excellent. In terms which would be amazing by today's standards, where women's duties are equal, Macready insisted that he must have some policewomen who were 'in an unprovocative sense, ladies', for him to put in evening dress with 'some diamonds or whatever they wear', and some from 'the other end of the scale' – domestic servants and bus conductresses, perhaps, though he admitted to hardly knowing what the class of bus conductresses was. He was most concerned that his women should be 'the right type' and not 'vinegary spinsters'. The Committee's report recommended that women police should be sworn in and given limited powers of arrest with better pay, but with covert Home Office encouragement, the Met, like most other constabularies, ignored it. Commissioner Sir William Horwood, who took over from Macready in 1921, was hostile to women police and welcomed the recommendation in 1922 that they be disbanded immediately

under the 'Geddes Axe' (Sir Eric Geddes' notorious attempt to make public savings by reducing the pay and numbers of public sector employees). Superintendent Stanley, Chief Inspector Robertson, Inspectors Wyles and Dixon and Sergeant Butcher fought for delay and compromise with the strong support of Lady Astor and Mrs Wintringham, the two women members of Parliament. They managed to extract an assurance from Home Secretary Edward Shortt that a nucleus of 20 women would be retained, but in the process Chief Inspector Robertson had tendered her resignation and Inspector Wyles had accepted the offer made to her that she should accept attachment to the CID as a civilian sex statement taker (cf. Miss Eilidh MacDougall), subsequently regretting it and complaining that she had been put under improper pressure by Mrs Stanley. A disciplinary enquiry concluded that Chief Inspector Robertson had tried to shoulder the blame for Mrs Stanley's machinations under the threat of the Geddes axe, and all four women had to a greater or lesser extent lied to the Commissioner's Office about their mutual discussions and relations with Lady Astor. All but Lilian Wyles were threatened with dismissal, though only Mrs Stanley was ultimately discharged. The 20 uniformed patrols were distributed around the Divisions under the control of the Divisional Superintendents. They were, however, sworn in and given powers of arrest. Married women and widows with small children were prohibited from joining. In 1923 Inspector Bertha Clayden was given authority over them, though under their respective superintendents. In this limited form, the women police slowly built up their numbers again until, by 1930, they had regained the strength of about 100 originally intended, and three more of their number had been transferred to the CID.

At this point they were regrouped as A4 Branch with ranks equivalent to male police, and Miss Dorothy Peto was appointed Staff Officer over Miss Clayden's head to command it. After two years she was promoted to Superintendent. It became accepted procedure that a woman police officer should be present whenever women or children were interviewed (cf. Irene Savidge); that women police should provide the escort ser-

vices to and from court for women and juveniles, and that women should become primarily responsible for overseeing children taken before the Juvenile Courts as being in need of Care and Protection. Under Miss Peto the A4 Index was started, recording and classifying all information on missing and wayward juveniles.

The maximum number of posts was raised to 200 in 1934, and the posts were filled just as the war broke out. As had happened in WWI, the efficient war work carried out by women convinced larger numbers of men that sex discrimination was unnecessary. A new Commissioner, Sir Harold Scott, and a new Superintendent of A4, former Group Officer Elizabeth Bather of the WAAF, seized the opportunity to increase the strength to 300 in 1946, and drop the prohibition on matrimony. (The approved total establishment of the Metropolitan Police was 19,500, though shortfalls in the postwar period reduced the actual strength to 14,000.) Their pay rates were roughly 90% of those of their male colleagues.

Women Police were now given the same training as male recruits and sat the same examinations to qualify for promotion. Under Chief Superintendent Bather's leadership their duties were much enlarged. By the time the strength had been brought up to 450, 10% of them were in the CID undertaking all types of duties, including service with Special Branch.

From 1951 women were added to the House of Commons police detail. At the Coronation in 1953, women police managed the 30,000 schoolchildren placed to watch the procession on the Embankment. And in 1972 when 'School Kids' primed by their own 'Little Red Book' mounted their own demonstration in imitation of their Maoist and radical elders, women policed it, thereby defusing any suggestions of 'police brutality', and diminishing the status of the demonstration.

As beat patrols now involved WPCs in more or less the full range of peacekeeping, and they were still not supplied with truncheons, many were trained in self-defence, ju-jitsu being especially popular. They were also used increasingly for the dangerous work of decoying violent offenders. Sergeant Alberta Law received her KPM

WOMEN POLICE SERVICE OFFICERS CIRCA 1916.

following injury in this work, and Sergeant Ethel Bush and WPC Kathleen Parrott received their George Medals under similar circumstances. Perhaps the most unpleasant decoy work was that undertaken by WPCs who passed themselves off as street prostitutes soliciting motorists during the mid-1960s hunt for 'Jack the Stripper'. WPC Margaret Cleland was awarded the George Medal for a rooftop rescue in 1964 and WPC Bertha Cleghorn of C Division, killed in a bombing raid in 1944, is believed to be the first woman officer killed on duty. The killings of Jane Arbuthnot, Yvonne Fletcher and Nina MacKay (see Appendix 4) underline the risks that female officers face equally with their male colleagues.

In 1969 it became clear that it would be difficult to justify the separate and lower payment of women police once the promised Equal Pay Act had been introduced, and thereupon, instead

of being a separate Branch, the Women Police were completely integrated with the men, became qualified for every type of police work, and competed on equal terms for promotion. Sir Robert Mark finally dissolved the Women Police as a separately recorded strength in 1973. Henceforth, women were simply police officers. They were given truncheons and handcuffs. They frequently accompanied men on patrols instead of operating exclusively as women, which had tended to limit public perception of their duties. By 1980 their uniform allowed trousers as an alternative to skirts at the officer's discretion, except on ceremonial occasions. Women were accepted into the River Police and the Mounted Police.

There were some objections that women were no longer specially trained for child care, victim support and similar 'caring' roles. These were met by the introduction of Child Protection Teams, Domestic Violence Units and the Juvenile Bureaux. But in the eyes of most people, the 4032 women now serving in a Service of 26,563 have played and continue to play a major part in mak-

ing the Metropolitan Police fully integrated in a community which is no longer the patriarchal society in which it was founded. It is noteworthy that of the thousand or more complaints about the police made each year, almost none are against women police.

See also Lee Commission, Commander Shirley Becke.

WOMEN POLICE SERVICE Originally Women Police Volunteers, subsequently Women's Auxiliary Service. First organization of uniformed policewomen on the London streets, subsequently a somewhat confusing rival to the Metropolitan Women Police.

Founded in September 1914 by wealthy philanthropist and anti-White Slavery campaigner Margaret Damer Dawson and militant suffragette journalist and speaker Nina Boyle. Miss Damer Dawson wanted a uniformed organization of women to deter pimps and discourage young women from entering prostitution. Miss Boyle wished to take advantage of the war situation to put women temporarily in men's places, with the expectation that their usefulness would prove itself, leading to their permanent continuation after the war. Commissioner Sir Edward Henry gave the volunteers permission to patrol the streets, effectively undertaking rescue work among prostitutes, and issued them with identity cards, asking the police to render them any necessary assistance. He did not enlist their services to support the Metropolitan Police in any way, but the women renamed themselves the Women Police Service and adopted the Metropolitan Police ranks of Sergeant and Inspector.

Provincial forces, starting with Grantham, asked the WPS to supply them with occasional policewomen, who were recognized as especially useful in dealing with women and juveniles. Most policewomen remained WPS members, wearing its uniform, while effectively on loan as auxiliary civilian support in the provinces. But in 1915 Grantham swore in and attested Mrs Edith Smith, making her the first proper policewoman in Britain with full powers of arrest.

Miss Boyle resigned in the same year when she learnt that Mary Allen, the original WPS member sent to Grantham, had been used to impose a curfew on women, intended to protect the morals of servicemen stationed nearby. Miss Damer Dawson, now calling herself Commandant of the WPS, was content to collaborate with men in attacking prostitution by harassing women without acting against their clients. The WPS also supplied large numbers of uniformed women officers to police women munitions workers at the request of first Lloyd George and then Winston Churchill, successive Ministers of Munitions.

Miss Damer Dawson pioneered some useful innovations. She trained women for police work, including attendance at court and giving evidence, and introduced motorcycles with sidecars for the transport of senior officers (at a time when Metropolitan Superintendents were travelling by pony and trap). But the WPS attracted unfavourable notice by its obtrusive policing of prostitutes and young women whose appearance or manners offended their sense of respectability in the West End, and when Sir Nevil Macready replaced Sir Edward Henry he flatly refused to adopt them as Metropolitan Police aides, preferring the National Council of Women's Special Police Patrols who were untainted by past association with militant suffragettes and became the nucleus of the future Women Police. Mrs Stanley, head of the Patrols, was intensely hostile to the WPS, whose uniforms and use of the Metropolitan ranks misled the public in her opinion. Under her instigation, Sir William Horwood forced the WPS to change its name to the Women's Auxiliary Service in 1921 and to add red flashes to the uniform, distinguishing its members from the Metropolitan Women Police Patrols.

Soon after the Baird Committee on Women Police (1920) had failed to recommend that the WAS play any part in policing London, Miss Damer Dawson died. Although a WAS contingent made extremely valuable contributions to the Royal Irish Constabulary during the Troubles, the writing was now on the wall for the service. The new Commandant, Mary Allen, was awarded the OBE, but after 1930 she became increasingly eccentric, rarely appearing except in her uniform with breeches, adopting a monocle, and finally declaring herself to be a Fascist and an admirer of the 'much misunderstood' Hitler

and Goering (who shared her passion for uniforms). She toured the world lecturing on the need for uniformed women police, But she was more of an oddity than an influence. In 1940 a questioner in the House of Commons asked why she had not been interned, and the WAS suspended its activities for the duration of the war. They were never revived.

See also Lee Commission.

WOMEN SPECIAL POLICE PATROLS
Forerunners of the Metropolitan Women Police.

A variety of Christian and philanthropic societies, of which the most important was the National Union of Women Workers (subsequently the National Council of Women) set up a Women's Patrol Committee in July 1914, under the presidency of Mrs Creighton, wife of the Bishop of London. The intention was to restrain the mushrooming growth of prostitution in wartime by sending women volunteers to police the areas around service camps. They were to try to persuade young girls not to be lured into sexual relations with soldiers, and to inhibit acts of public indecency by their discreet presence. The Committee approached Commissioner Sir Edward Henry and Home Secretary Reginald McKenna, both of whom approved, especially as the patrols might combat the spread of venereal disease among the troops. The volunteers in London were issued with identity cards signed by the Commissioner, directing the police to assist them when necessary, and McKenna directed provincial Chief Constables to issue similar cards, though not all did so.

The patrols wore no uniforms, only an armband. Most, however, rapidly preferred the formality of plain dark blue skirts and jackets, with white blouses or shirts and large pudding-basin hats similar to those designed for the Women Police Service. They also added positive welfare work to their duties, referring young women in moral danger to professional rescue workers, opening clubs to provide respectable evening entertainment for young women (and some mixed groups), and increasingly taking responsibility for the welfare of distressed children. The NUWW collaborated with the Women Police Service in setting up a training school in Bristol

under Miss Dorothy Peto, though this led to friction later when Miss Damer Dawson of the WPS felt that her ideas were plagiarized without acknowledgement.

The Police Act, 1916 included an enabling clause permitting women to be employed on police duties. Sir Edward Henry promptly set half a dozen Special Patrols to work, mainly in Hyde Park where acts of public indecency were a continual nuisance. (See Sir Basil Thomson, Irene Savidge.) The women remained officially employees of the NCW, but the Home Office made them a grant of £400 a year. They were to work in pairs, accompanied at a little distance by a policeman with the power to make arrests if necessary.

Although a couple of women blenched at hearing the lewd acts they had witnessed described in court, the system proved extremely successful. Early in 1917, Mrs Annie Morgan-Scott and Mrs Bagster fought with and arrested two men who had overpowered their escort, PC Albert E. Silverson of A Division (Warrant No. 96487). In March that year, Mrs Sofia Stanley was appointed paid Supervisor of Special Patrols with a subsidy from the Home Office, her title (unlike that of the WPS officers) explicitly avoiding any confusion with official police ranks. She commanded 37 patrols in central London and 29 in the suburbs. Their duties now included policing the underground stations which the public used as shelters during Zeppelin raids, and taking drunks off the street to sober them up

In October Mrs Stanley succeeded in getting Sir Edward to furnish the patrols with serge greatcoats from Harrods for the winter, and 6d a week boot money. The Home Secretary and the Commissioner were preparing to investigate the possibility of creating a more official women's police force when the Police Strike of 1918 led to Sir Edward's sudden resignation and replacement by Sir Nevil Macready, the Commissioner who would subsequently describe himself as 'the inventor of women police'.

What he actually did in November 1918 was to appoint Mrs Stanley Superintendent of Metropolitan Women Police Patrols, and put her on an appointments board chaired by Mrs Carden, secretary of the Women's Patrol Committee. The board immediately appointed 25 women, all members or former members of the existing Special Patrols. Although these women were neither sworn in nor given special powers of arrest, they were directly employed by and directly under the orders of Scotland Yard, and their duties were policing. They were, therefore, *de facto* the first Metropolitan Women Police.

WOOTTON LAMP A 2-volt electric lantern powered by an accumulator and capable of

POLICE OFFICERS TRAINING WITH GAS MASKS IN 1937 AT HARROW ROAD.

throwing a wide or a narrow beam. Invented by George Wootton (subsequently Chief Engineer from 1930 to 1935), and standard issue to night patrols from 1924 to 1949. See Lanterns.

WORLD WAR II The period 1939–1945 was one of the most testing in the history of the force. Not only was it at full stretch with its normal role, it also had to encompass such duties as assisting with the evacuation, enforcing the blackout and restoring communications and order following the Blitz and other bombing from the V1 and V2 rockets. Many officers

and Civil Staff fought in the Armed Services, but the Met was able to call on re-engaged police pensioners, Special Constables and War Reserve officers. *See* Appendix 3 and Sir Philip Game.

WOVENDEN, INSPECTOR SQUIRE (FL.1834) Wrongfully dismissed following political pressure from Whigs antipathetic to the police force in what has been described as Rowan and Mayne's darkest hour.

Served in Peninsular War. Probably joined the Met as a Sergeant when the force was started in 1829. Warrant No. 679. D Division. Promoted to Inspector, January 1830.

Accused by prostitute Ruth Morris of having raped her in the cells on 19 June 1834 when she was detained for being drunk and disorderly. Superintendent Lazenby, after hearing her complaint, refused to take action as it was transparently untrue. But when he reported the matter to the Commissioners, Sir Richard Mayne insisted that such a serious accusation must be heard before an independent magistrate. Ruth Morris, however, refused to proceed with the charge.

A sergeant reported the incident to Chief Magistrate Frederick Roe of Bow Street, who was actively campaigning against the new police force, and Roe took the matter to the newly appointed Whig Home Secretary Lord Duncannon. On Duncannon's orders and over the heads of Commissioners Rowan and Mayne, Roe issued a warrant for Wovenden's arrest, and after his own private investigation sent him on for trial. The grand jury dismissed the case out of hand on hearing the evidence. Rowan and Mayne conducted their own investigation and reported in September that Wovenden and Lazenby had committed no impropriety and the whole incident had been exaggerated because of Roe's personal hatred of the police. Nonetheless, on 31 October Duncannon instructed them to dismiss Wovenden and Lazenby.

It was apparent that Roe hoped the Commissioners would resign and be replaced with malleable partisans who would allow the stipendiary magistrates to retain their own constables, and possibly even supervise the disinte-

gration of the Metropolitan Police. Despite their wish to support Wovenden and Lazenby, Rowan and Mayne decided that they could not put the entire force at risk. The Superintendent and Inspector were dismissed (and never reinstated, despite protests from many quarters), and Rowan contented himself with a dignified letter of protest to the Home Secretary.

WYLES, DET-INSP LILIAN MARY ELIZABETH, BEM (1885–1975) First woman member of the Metropolitan CID.

Educ. Thanet Hall, Margate and finishing school in Paris. Joined Metropolitan Women Police Patrols as Sergeant i/c Central London and the East End, 1919. Woman Patrol Divisional No. 4. Promoted to Inspector, 1921. CID, 1922. Attested with Woman's Warrant No. 23 in 1923. Sex statement taker for London north of the Thames throughout 1920s. Retd, British Empire Medal, 1949. Lived in West Cornwall in retirement, and published her memoirs in 1952.

The daughter of a wealthy Lincolnshire brewer who wanted her to read for the Bar, Lilian Wyles chose instead to nurse as war work in 1914, until a serious illness necessitated her going to South Africa in 1917. On her return, joined the National Council of Women's Women Special Police Patrols in June 1918. The following November she was one of the first batch of 25 women inducted into the Metropolitan Women Police Patrols, and was appointed Sergeant commanding patrols in central London and the East End. By 1922 she had been promoted to Inspector when she and Mrs Sofia Stanley, Inspector Grace Dixon and Sergeant Violet Butcher were among the last tranche of Metropolitan women police awaiting disbandment under the 'Geddes axe' of harsh economy measures. As a compromise, the Home Office offered Misses Wyles, Dixon and Butcher continued employment as civilian sex statement takers, to relieve the load on Miss Eilidh MacDougall. Lilian Wyles alone accepted, but then apparently regretted the imminent reduction to civilian status this would mean, and complained that Mrs Stanley had urged her and the other women to delay accepting in the hope that Lady Astor's parliamentary questions might force the Home

Office to retain them all as policewomen. An unseemly wrangle followed, and the upshot was that Mrs Stanley was dismissed and Miss Wyles

LILIAN WYLES.

was retained and sent to serve as a sworn-in police sex statement taker attached to the CID. For many years she remained responsible for the statements taken north of the river while Miss MacDougall continued to take all statements in south London. In 1923 Chief Constable Wensley had her rushed to Ilford, where Mrs Edith Thompson was being interviewed about the murder of her husband Percy. Miss Wyles was required to sit with Mrs Thompson and, without actually questioning her, take note of anything she said. Miss Wyles was not present when Edith Thompson made the giveaway remark, 'Why did he do it?' which led Wensley to investigate and charge her later.

In 1928 Miss Wyles was involved in the Irene Savidge affair and was summoned by Wensley to meet the Home Secretary and listen to the parliamentary debate as to whether Miss Savidge had been improperly questioned by Miss Wyles, Chief Inspector Collins and Detective Sergeant Clarke. Wensley also entrusted her with preventing Chief Inspector Collins from fortifying himself with brandy (which made him belligerent) before he faced the parliamentary inquiry into the case. This concluded that Miss Wyles had not behaved improperly, and she took pride in having shielded Chief Inspector Collins, who practised the sort of patronizing male chauvinism she resented in some senior colleagues.

In 1930, when Miss Dorothy Peto was appointed Superintendent of A4 Branch and three more women were posted to the CID, Lilian Wyles took on more serious functions as a detective officer with particular responsibilities for cases involving women and children. When she retired and went to live near Land's End, she was awarded the British Empire Medal. She had acquired great standing as the longest-serving woman in the CID and she was popular with her senior men colleagues. Her extremely interesting but somewhat self-serving memoirs silently pass over the unhappy imbroglio of 1922 (see Women Police) and an interview she gave to *Woman* magazine three years before her death embroiders and at times heightens by outright contradiction her role in notable events as she had earlier recorded them.

YARDLEY, CHARLES (FL.1829–1864) Head of the Metropolitan Police secretariat (Civil Staff).

Served in the Commissariat during the Napoleonic Wars. Trained in law, and applied for the post of Chief Clerk to the Commissioners when the police were being formed in 1829. Came provisionally for one month's trial in October, after Maurice Dowling had been dismissed in October 1829 for leaking information to the press. Retired 1864.

Yardley had two clerks working under him in 1829, and a third was added in 1840. Their duties were writing and copying correspondence, checking the lists of supplies and property, extrapolating data for annual statistical tables, and recording and circulating the Commissioners' Orders and Morning Reports from the Divisions. There was too much work for four clerks, and Yardley was compelled to use police clerks from A Division (Whitehall) to supplement his staff. He disliked this: Victorian clerks were acutely aware of their status as educated gentlemen, compared with policemen, who were artisans. Moreover, once trained, police clerks were liable to be posted to new and more responsible positions on the Divisions.

Yardley was also touchily insistent that his office's work was far more demanding than the mere accountancy of the Receiver's Office. But Yardley's diligence and loyalty made a significant contribution to the successful establishment of the Metropolitan Police. This was especially true after the retirement of Commissioner Charles Rowan and the Receiver John Wray, when Yardley was the sole fellow-survivor of the founding Department heads to give support to the ageing and increasingly difficult Richard Mayne. Both men were workaholics, and tended to stay at their desks from 10.00 a.m. until late at night. This was especially hard on the junior clerk ordered to be available at all times for Sir Richard Mayne.

Appropriately for the founder of a Secretariat, Yardley was more of a consolidator than an innovator. His one important technical upgrading was the replacement of quill pens with steel nibbed pens in 1860. (This entailed the pur-

chase of over 2000 steel pens for the Divisions.) His one attempt at something akin to restructuring was an abortive attempt to have his own title changed to Secretary, a titular upgrade not achieved until 1919.

When he finally retired in 1864, to be succeeded by the son of Superintendent John May of A Division, he was sorely missed. Within a month he had been recalled temporarily to advise on office restructuring. And though Supt John May's constant presence in Scotland Yard during its first decade and his effective responsibility for what was not yet called the Executive Branch ought to have prepared his son well for the duties of Chief Clerk, Edmund

May and his Department rapidly found themselves at odds with the uniformed officers in ways that had never occurred previously. The last tired four years of Richard Mayne's life were undoubtedly made worse by the lack of the fine Chief Clerk who established the embryo Civil Staff.

YERBA (D.1984) Police dog shot in attempting to apprehend a bank robber.

The dog's curious name is a result of the Met's habit of working systematically through the alphabet, naming all puppies in each successive single litter with names beginning with the same letter.

On 15 August 1984, Yerba's handler, PC Martin Coxon, was walking the dog in Petts Wood, Kent, when they fortuitously came across men in the process of robbing a bank in Station Square. PC Coxon immediately released Yerba, who gave chase, whereupon one of the robbers, 44-year-old Toni Baldessare, shot her with a .38 revolver. Yerba continued to pursue

POLICE DOG YERBA'S GRAVE.

THE Z-WAGON IN ACTION.

him, whereupon he aimed carefully again and shot the dog in the head. When Yerba fell to the pavement, Baldessare put another carefully aimed bullet in her back before running off. Yerba died in PC Coxon's arms, and was buried at Keston. A plaque was erected at the scene to commemorate the incident.

Police later tracked Baldessare to a flat in Streatham, where they surrounded the house for siege containment, before telephoning him and telling him to come out. Baldessare refused, barricading himself in and indicating that he wanted to be remembered for dying in a shoot-out with the police. In the event, the only shot fired was the one with which Baldessare committed suicide, after burning thousands of pounds of banknotes in the kitchen sink, and telling the negotiator he was 'burning the evidence'.

YOUTH AND COMMUNITY SECTIONS

Support the work of Community Liaison Officers replacing the former Juvenile Bureaux, providing educational and socially beneficial contacts with schools and youth groups, and monitoring children at risk of offending as well as those who come before the courts. YACS officers liaise with social workers and other agencies at meetings and case conferences to determine the childrens' best interests, receive recommendations from local authorities' Juvenile Panels, and communicate with parents and guardians about their children's conduct.

School Involvement Officers attend special training courses and deliver relevant lessons in schools on personal safety, the history of the police, crime and its consequences, drugs, and issues relevant to the Personal and Social Education elements of the National Curriculum.

Z-WAGON The huge flatbed truck with lifting equipment used for removing clamped or otherwise immobilized and untowable cars from illegal and obstructive parking on the roadway.

APPENDIX ONE: UNIFORMS

In 1829 when the Metropolitan Police was formed, Sir Robert Peel believed it was essential to establish in the public's mind that the London police was a civilian body and not a military force. The colour decided on was blue, to distinguish officers from the military who wore red. Top hats, which were in common use on London's streets, were chosen as headgear, and the uniform even included white trousers for summer! As the years progressed, styles changed. Around 1863 a high-necked tunic was adopted, with a coxcomb helmet similar to that worn by City of London police today. The more familiar modern shape was first introduced in 1870, and progressed through various design changes. High-buttoned tunics were to last until 1948 when the tunic began to resemble the present style.

Women police adopted an almost colonial form of skirt and helmet in 1919, but reverted to a traditional service pattern after World War II. The late 1960s saw the eye-catching but short-lived Norman Hartnell design. Female officers started to wear trousers in the 1980s, followed by woollen pullovers. By the late 1990s the traditional jacket was reserved for formal occasions, and the traditional helmet may also be reviewed.

A woman police officer gives directions to a member of the public in Trafalgar Square. She is wearing the first Women Police uniform, in use from 1919 to 1926. Note that the Divisional letter on her collar is followed by the letters MP, standing for Metropolitan Police.

A woman police officer sporting a 1937–1946 tunic, white gloves and helmet stops a vehicle turning from Rochester Row into Vincent Square, SW1.

The National Gallery in Trafalgar Square forms the backdrop for this picture taken around 1955. WPC Sylvia Croake wears the 1946–1968 uniform, known as the Bather uniform after its originator, Elizabeth Bather. It was modelled on Women's Auxiliary Air Force uniform during World War II.

The women police in this picture are wearing the uniform designed by fashion designer Norman Hartnell, worn from 1968–1973. Hartnell was only responsible for the uniform, not the hat. Two officers also sport the Hartnell-designed cape, designed to be worn over the uniform.

The officer in the middle is Sislin Fay Allen, the first black woman police officer in the Metropolitan Police, who served from 1968 to 1972.

This officer is pictured in the traditional Peeler's uniform jacket worn from 1829 to 1864. The Divisional letter and numbers are on the collar, and on the chair is the service top hat.

From left to right: Inspector David Baldry, Superintendent Robert Walker (mounted), Inspector Donald Warren and Chief Inspector Eleazar Denning, shown here at Epsom races wearing the tunic introduced in 1864, the first to dispense with 'tails'.

This photograph was taken at a shooting competition on Wimbledon Common around 1870. The A Division officers are wearing the coxcomb helmet, introduced in 1863 and phased out in 1870. The officers are wearing eight-button tunics with snake-clasp belts, also introduced in 1864, along with the new-style tunic. Note that two officers appear to be carrying truncheons in spring-loaded carrying cases.

Taken in Ickenham village in 1936, this photograph features officers wearing the unique five-button tunic, manufactured from a rather coarse cloth. It was introduced as part of a long-awaited improvement to the uniform in 1897, and lasted until 1934. This version was only used for daytime duty – at night officers wore an eight-button tunic.

Officers training in Peel House, Regency Street, SW1 in 1948. The male officers are dressed in the seven-button tunic used for daytime duty between 1934 and 1948, while the women officers are wearing the Bather uniform.

This A Division officer directs traffic in Parliament Square wearing white gauntlets, introduced in the 1930s. He wears the first open-neck tunic, used by the Met from 1951–9.

APPENDIX TWO: COMMISSIONERS

1829–50	Col. Sir Charles Rowan, KCB and Sir Richard Mayne, KCB
1850–55	Sir Richard Mayne, KCB and Captain William Hay
1855–68	Sir Richard Mayne, KCB
1868–69	Lt–Col. Douglas Labalmondière, CB (Acting Commissioner)
1869–86	Col. Sir Edmund Henderson, KCB
1886–88	Col. Sir Charles Warren, GCMG, KCB
1888–90	James Monro, CB
1890–1903	Col. Sir Edward Bradford, Bt, GCB, GCVO, KCSI
1903–18	Sir Edward Henry, Bt, GCVO, KCB, CSI
1918–20	Gen. Rt Hon Sir Nevil Macready, Bt, GCMG, KCB
1920–28	Brig-Gen. Sir William Horwood, KBE, KCB, DSO
1928–31	Gen. Rt Hon Viscount Byng of Vimy, GCB, GCMG, MVO
1931–35	Marshal of RAF, Lord Trenchard GCB, OM, GCVO, DSO
1935–45	Air Vice-Marshal Sir Philip Game GCB, GCVO, GBE, KCMG, DSO
1945–53	Sir Harold Scott, GCVO, KCB, KBE
1953–58	Sir John Nott-Bower, KCVO
1958–68	Sir Joseph Simpson, KBE
1968–72	Sir John Waldron, KCVO
1972–77	Sir Robert Mark, GBE, QPM
1977–82	Sir David McNee, QPM
1982–87	Sir Kenneth Newman, GBE, QPM
1987–93	Sir Peter Imbert, QPM
1993–	Sir Paul Condon, QPM

APPENDIX THREE: FOR GALLANTRY

The King's Police Medal was instituted on 7th July 1909 to reward 'courage and devotion to duty' after the **Tottenham Outrage**. The list in this Appendix covers officers who were awarded these medals for courage, together with the later King's Police and Fire Service Medal, the British Empire Medal awarded for bravery, the George Cross, the George Medal, the Queen's Police Medal awarded posthumously for bravery, and the Queen's Gallantry Medal. Two cases of awards of the rare Albert Medal are also included.

The brief descriptions of the incidents leading to the medal reflect the numerous occasions when police officers have been thrust without notice into situations where they have shown extraordinary bravery and have acted with great courage. The highest traditions of the Service have been formed by them.

Details have been drawn from the book 'Police Gallantry' by J Peter Farmery, from records, and from the Metropolitan Police Gallantry Awards book which dates from 1947. We believe that this list is the most comprehensive catalogue of Metropolitan Police bravery to date. It is not complete, however. Between 1947 and 1999, for instance, no fewer than 320 officers were awarded the King's, and later the Queen's, Commendation for Brave Conduct. The Royal Humane Society and the Society for the Preservation of Life from Fire make highly appreciated awards to the successors of some officers whose exploits are recorded below. The dates shown relate to the time of the award, rather than of the incident.

ALBERT MEDAL

1885 PC WILLIAM COLE Awarded the Albert medal in gold (the only police officer to have been so honoured) when he removed a Sinn Fein bomb from Westminster Hall which badly injured him when it exploded.

1918 INSPECTOR FREDERICK WRIGHT Awarded the Albert medal in bronze for saving 13 lives during a Zeppelin raid in Camberwell in October 1917.

KING'S POLICE MEDAL (1909–1941)

1910 PC JOHN WILLIAM CATER, PC CHARLES DIXON , PC CHARLES EAGLES Pursued anarchists Lepidus & Hefeld throughout the **Tottenham Outrage** and broke into Lepidus' room, knowing him to be armed and to have murdered PC Tyler and Ralph Joscelyne, and injured others.

1910 DC ALFRED YOUNG Arrested two armed thieves in Swiss Cottage who tried to fire at him.

1911 PC ARTHUR CAMBERS Attempted rescue of sewerman from poison gas down a Southall manhole.

1911 PC GEORGE HAYTREAD With help of Mrs Francis White, arrested armed man who had fired at him five times.

1912 PC SIDNEY RYALL Recaptured violent prisoner in Croydon who had stunned him and drawn copious blood from his head with a 15in iron case-opener in attempting escape.

1913 PC WILLIAM SILVER Arrested armed robber, who himself admitted to being amazed by the constable's courage.

1914 PC ALBERT ENGLISH Arrested Albert Bowes who had just shot and wounded Commissioner **Sir Edward Henry**.

1914 PC GEORGE JAMESON Injured by armed man shooting a revolver whom he arrested when dispersing a disorderly crowd.

1915 PC JOHN WALKER Felled by lead mallet wielded by one of two men he was questioning; nonetheless contributed to the man's arrest.

1915 PC THOMAS WRIGHT Injured by thief wielding shoemaker's knife as he arrested him in Springfield Rd, Stoke Newington.

1916 DS ALBERT HANDLEY Shot at in 1899 by a gang member, but the medal was also awarded for 26 years service in Bethnal Green during which he received 148 commendations.

1917 PC HERBERT ARCHER Rescued boy from a caisson chamber at 5.20 a.m. on a March morning while on secondment to Rosyth dockyard.

1917 DS ARTHUR ASKEW Arrested armed assailant in dark passage who had just shot and killed the constable accompanying Sgt Askew.

1917 PC WILLIAM LONGHURST Rescued miner overcome by poison gases in sewer at the Royal Arsenal.

1917 **PC EDWARD GEORGE BROWN GREENOFF** (Posthumous) Died staying outside the burning Silvertown Chemical Works to warn passers-by of likely TNT explosion.

1918 PC JAMES HARDY Severely injured by armed poacher in Ruffetts Wood, West Wickham, whom he nevertheless succeeded in arresting. PC Hardy died in a road accident before his investiture with KPM.

1918 PC JESSE CHRISTMAS, PC ROBERT MELTON Accompanied Inspector Frederick Wright into a bombed house to rescue 13 people trapped in a basement

---

The following officers were awarded the medal as the result of actions to save people from drowning in the River Thames, in other rivers, in docks or in canals.

1910 PC WILLIAM LAMBERT	1927 PC LESLIE LYDDON
1910 PC JOSEPH GEORGE TAYLOR	1927 PC ALEXANDER CUNNINGHAM
1911 PC WILLIAM DENIHAM	1928 PC GEORGE HAINSBY
1911 PC ALFRED PUFFETT	1928 PC FREDERICK MARK STONE
1911 PC WALTER BALDWIN	1930 PC ALBERT HIGHGATE
1913 PC JOSEPH ROOT	1930 PC RONALD KING LOVEJOY
1914 PC GEORGE PORTER	1931 PC JAMES DUNSMORE ADAMSON
1915 PC HENRY BROWN	1931 PC ERNEST JACOBI
1915 PC FREDERICK WEST	1931 PC THOMAS JACK KENWOOD
1916 PS CECIL SMITHERS	1934 PC LAURIE ANDREW MCLAREN
1916 PC CHARLES KEMP	1935 PC WALTER MORRIS
1917 PC GEORGE BURTON	1935 PC ARTHUR GEORGE RUSSELL
1918 PC ALFRED BENCE	1935 PC HARRY TIMMINS
1919 PC ARTHUR RICHARD BELLAMY	1936 PC CHARLES EDMOND FOX
1919 PC CHARLES KIDD	1939 PC WILLIAM DALE PAXTON
1921 PC GEORGE DAY	
1921 PC HARRY HAYES	
1921 PC WILLIAM BURTON	

The following officers showed great courage in dealing with runaway horses, sometimes towing vans, and invariably suffered serious injury as a result.

1911	PC GEORGE GATLAND	1925	PC GEORGE FISHER
1911	PC WILLIAM JESSIMAN	1925	PC ROBERT HARDING
1912	PS WILLIAM CLAPP	1925	**PC PERCIVAL NORMAN**
1913	PC THOMAS RAVENING	1925	PC HAROLD PECKOVER
1913	PC BERTIE SPENCER	1926	PC WILLIAM HOPKINS
1914	PC WILLIAM LOCKWOOD	1926	PC THOMAS MEAD
1914	ACT. PS ARTHUR STIFF	1927	PC CHRISTOPHER JONES
1915	PC GEORGE ROBERTS	1929	PC THOMAS FARRANCE
1916	PC WALTER CARPENTER	1929	PC HENRY GEORGE SPARKS
1916	PC JOHN DEW	1933	PC HERBERT COCKBURN
1916	PC FRED DRABBLE	1934	PC THOMAS JOHN HAYNES
1916	PC ALBERT HUGHES	1934	PC JAMES LEMMON
1917	PC THOMAS SLIPPER	1935	PC BERTRAM WELLESLEY
1918	PC ROBERT GEORGE		RUDDOCK
	WILSON	1935	PS EDWARD ONAN SHELAH
1918	PC CHARLES PENN	1936	PC ALLAN DENSHAM
1920	PC WALTER HEARN	1936	PC EDWARD MORRIS
1921	PC PERCY GREEN	1937	PC LAWRENCE AUSTIN
1923	PC EDWARD GEER		PERIGO
1923	PC HARRY HUTCHINGS	1938	PC JOHN HEARN MM
1924	PC JOSEPH ALLEN	1940	PC FREDERICK CHARLES
1924	PC JOHN COOPER		WALTON
1924	PC HENRY LOVEGROVE		

with a gas escape which had ignited and set fire to the very dangerous and tottering debris above. Inspector Wright, who had chopped the hole in the flooring through which the officers entered, received the Albert Medal.

1919 PC FRANK BRYANT Recovered a deranged man from the River Roding after the man had attacked him with a cutthroat razor, and died from his injuries.

1919 PC DAVID DAVIES Rescued two workmen overcome by gas in a Mitcham sewer.

1919 PC FRANCIS STUBBS Arrested an army deserter despite being kicked and injured by a knife.

1920 SGT ROYAL BIRD, PC GEORGE RICHARDSON, PC FREDERICK RICHES, PC WILLIAM WILLIAMS All four officers went to Waterloo Station to arrest a suspect wanted by Surrey Police. The man produced an automatic pistol with which he incapacitated PC Richardson and injured PC Williams, before Sgt Bird and PC Riches arrived to chase him through backstreets and corner him, still armed with the loaded pistol, in a wash-house.

These officers risked their lives by entering burning buildings in order to rescue occupants threatened by engulfing flames and smoke.

1911	DS JOSEPH JOSLIN	1921	PC SAMUEL TAYLOR
1912	PC MICHAEL BARRY	1924	PC JOHN COZENS
1912	PC GEORGE SPRINGETT	1924	PC CHARLES SADGROVE
1913	SGT EDMUND WATERS	1928	PC ALBERT TURPIN
1913	PC THOMAS LITTLE	1929	PC CECIL NEWING
1913	PC ALBERT WINTON	1930	**PC JAMES COLE**
1914	PC NOAH JONES	1934	PC FREDERICK GILBERT
1914	PC CORNELIUS GOODWIN		BLUNDELL
1915	PC FREDERICK BROWN	1934	PC WILLIAM FREDERICK KING
1915	PS SIDNEY BURFIELD	1936	PC GORDON JACK GREEN
1917	PC GEORGE BOWLES	1936	PC KENNETH WALTER
1918	PC CHARLES DEDNUM		STEELE
1918	DC MATTHEW LANDY	1938	PC ROBERT MACINTYRE
1918	PC AUGUSTUS RALPH		STARKEY
1921	PC HARRY POWELL		

1920 PC PERCY CARR, PC WILLIAM MEWTON, PC WILLIAM MONNERY The three officers extinguished fires in two adjacent trucks of a 26 truck train of small arms ammunition, standing beside a magazine at Woolwich Arsenal. To reach the fires they had to approach through exploding bullets and fuses to unfasten the sides of the trucks and get at their contents.

1920 PC GILBERT DARKE, PC FRANCIS MOORE After a struggle and threats against them, arrested an armed bank robber who had escaped to the cover of a wood.

1920 PC FREDERICK OST, PC FREDERICK WRIGHT Arrested an armed burglar who had fired seven shots at them and put shots through their clothing as they attempted to arrest him with an accomplice.

1920 PC MAURICE SULLIVAN Arrested one of two armed burglars he had been chasing as they fired five shots at him, and later attacked him with a jemmy.

1920 PC ALBERT WEBBER Rescued a workman from poisonous fumes following a gas explosion in the lower compartments of the German battleship 'Baden', undergoing a refit at Invergordon, where PC Webber was seconded to the Royal Dockyards.

1920 PC HARRY WILLIAMS Disarmed and arrested a drunken US Marine who was shooting at him near Grosvenor Square.

1921 PC JOHN ABBOTT, PC WALLACE CHURCHYARD Disarmed and arrested a mentally disordered man who was threatening them with a loaded rifle.

1921 PC BERTRAM ALLISON Pursued an armed youth stealing equipment from a Camberwell dentist's house, despite threats and a shot fired at him.

1921 PC PERCY SWEET, PC ALEXANDER JAFFRAY PC Sweet quietened a domestic incident in Endell St, Covent Garden where a man used a poker, tongs and chair to attack both the woman he was living with and PC Sweet. Later, the man pushed PC Sweet out of the house, and attacked both constables with the poker when they returned to arrest him.

1921 PS THOMAS BUCHANAN Pinned an armed robber to the wall in a cinema office until help arrived.

1921 PC CHARLES HALL, PC JACK LEWIS Having been supplied with revolvers to apprehend four armed Sinn Fein fugitives, found themselves engaged in a short gunfight with one of them as the suspects decamped from a taxi in Bromley. All were subsequently arrested.

1921 PC GEORGE SMITH Rescued a hysterical housemaid from a dangerous rooftop in Battersea.

1921 PS JOHN THOMAS Rescued a would-be suicidal lady from a dangerous window sill, despite her attacking him with a curtain rod.

1923 PC WALTER BUSH, PC JAMES DUFF, PC WALTER MARCH, DC CECIL SAYER Arrested the Fenians Reginald Dunn and Joseph O'Sullivan, who had just murdered Field-Marshal Sir Henry Wilson on his Belgravia doorstep, and retreated down Ebury Street firing at bystanders. In attempting their escape they shot PC March in the stomach and DC Sayer in the leg, disabling both before PCs Bush and Duff completed the arrests.

1923 PC FREDERICK CARTER, PC JOHN HAYES Chased and arrested an armed man who had intimidated people in the Green Dragon public house, Croydon, and shot at the officers as they approached.

1923 DC CHARLES MARTIN, DC PERCY MCDOUALL Arrested an armed confidence trickster, even though in resisting arrest he pushed DC McDoull's head through the plate glass window of the Brownie Restaurant in Victoria Street.

1924 DS ALFRED BEESLEY, DS WALTER HOBBS Completed arrest of bicycle thief who tried to escape from their arrest on the way to the station by wrenching free, shooting Sgt Beesley in the leg, and firing five more shots as the two officers overpowered him.

1924 PC JOHN DUBBER Arrested armed burglar who shot at him twice.

1924 PC ALBERT FLINT Severely injured by knife-wounds inflicted by robber he arrested threatening a woman in Hyde Park.

1924 DC JOHN RUTHERFORD Arrested armed gang leader who shot at him when two armed gangs were threatening to fight each other in a Holborn pub.

1925 PC HAROLD VINCENT Calmly talked armed burglar into putting down his weapon and surrendering to arrest.

1926 PC RICHARD BONNER, PC ALBERT GRAVETT Overpowered and arrested drink-maddened knife-wielding seaman who was terrorising and wounding others in Limehouse Asiatic seamen's home.

1926 PS JAMES HEDGES Arrested warehouse thief after a difficult rooftop chase at the end of which both Sergeant and thief fell through a collapsing roof and the ceiling below it.

1926 DDI ALBERT WARD, DI JAMES BELLINGER, DS ROBERT ELLIS Overpowered and arrested a known dangerous armed prison escapee who threatened them with a revolver which misfired.

1927 PC ALFRED GREEN Rescued two men from coal gas in a sewer shaft at Potters Bar.

1927 PC WALLACE WOOD Rescued two workmen from poisonous bitulac gas in a narrow water main at Feltham.

1928 PS ALFRED CLAYDEN, PS HENRY PEGLER Overpowered and arrested a known dangerous armed criminal wanted on a bench warrant, who tried to shoot at them.

1928 PC DUNCAN DUNN, PC WILLIAM MARSHALL Made precarious climb along roof edge guttering to rescue woman from fourth floor window of a burning house in Newman Street.

1928 PC PERCIVAL ROBERTS Overpowered and arrested a man who was terrorising a public house with a pistol, and fired at the PC.

1930 PS CHARLES BACON Rescued a boy from the sea while on holiday at Yarmouth.

1930 PC HENRY BEACHAM Singlehandedly chased five shopbreakers in Old Kent Road, leaping on their car running board and stopping it by hitting the driver. Chased them again as they made escape on foot after attacking him, and arrested one.

1930 PC HARRY HALL Arrested deranged man threatening bailiffs with a pistol in Holloway.

1930 DC REGINALD GRANVILLE JONES MM Overpowered and disarmed a suspect who was in the act of shooting at him in Southwark.

1930 DI EDWARD MICHAEL OCKEY Leapt from **Flying Squad** car on to running board of suspects' 50mph getaway car. Beaten off with a jemmy hitting his hands and head, and almost killed by fall and police pursuit car.

1931 PC ROBERT HENRY BAKER, PC ALEXANDER MCLEOD IRVINE Overpowered and arrested three of four armed shopbreakers who threatened to shoot them and then put up strong resistance.

1931 SGT GEORGE CHARLES COLVIN Overpowered (with assistance from passers-by) and arrested a deranged man, who had kicked another officer in the head, and had fired a revolver at Sgt Colvin.

1931 PC ALFRED CHARLES JAMES With the help of two members of the public, overpowered and arrested suspected car thief who pushed a pistol against the constable's body when told he was to be arrested.

1931 PC ROBERT HENRY MINNIS Seriously injured, throwing himself in the path of a car to push clear a four-year-old girl who had dashed out into the traffic. The incident was seen by HRH the Duke of York, (later George VI), whose detective called the ambulance.

1931 PS FREDERICK GEORGE MUGGRIDGE, PC JOHN LAIDLAW BERTRAM Overpowered and arrested a burglar who had fired four shots at them, and produced a second weapon to try again.

1931 PC DENNIS HENRY MURPHY Permanently injured when hit by a car out of whose path he was pushing an 11-year-old boy who had started to run across the road.

1931 PC WALTER ERNEST RAYMOND Restrained a woman threatening suicide from a parapet 40ft above the road, and carried her to safety along the roof edge guttering.

1932 PC HARRY CLAUDE VIVIAN BARWICK While on sick-list with foot injury, rescued a boy from Teddington Weir, further injuring his foot in the process.

1933 DI WILLIAM CAIN Jumped from Flying squad car on to running board of three suspect thieves' blocked car; and jumped on again when he was knocked off as the thieves accelerated away. Successfully grappled with the driver to bring the car to a halt again, and all three were arrested.

1933 PC SIDNEY PATTENDEN Shot three times, once close to the heart, by thieves he and a colleague interrupted in a Thames Ditton tennis pavilion. Invalided out of the Force because of his injuries.

1933 PC ALFRED SCHEIDE Seriously injured in unsuccessful attempt to push a little girl out of the path of a car in Brentford.

1933 PC ROBERT SWAN Arrested one of a gang of safebreakers he interrupted in Walworth, despite being knocked to the ground with a jemmy and severely injured.

1933 PS ROBERT WALLEN Seriously injured and invalided out of the Force when he successfully pushed a young girl out of the path of a car in Clerkenwell Road.

1934 PC WILLIAM BUNCE, PC FREDERICK ERNEST HAWKES Overpowered and arrested one of two robbers leaving a jeweller's shop after being threatened with a sawn-off double-barrelled shotgun and attacked with a knife.

1934 PC WILLIAM ALBERT ROBINS Rescued from the River Lea a violent suspect he had been pursuing while in plain clothes, and sustained injury from the man's struggle.

1934 PC WALTER HENRY TODD Arrested armed thief escaping from a garage whose confederate had just fired at him.

1935 DI CLAUD DOUGLAS SMITH Overpowered and arrested an armed robber who tried to shoot him at point blank range, having already shot down one of the constables accompanying Inspector Smith and fired several times at police.

1936 PC JAMES AIRTON Extinguished fire in an underground cable box at Ashley Square, Westminster; then entered smoke and fume-filled box in unsuccessful attempt to find a trapped workman.

1936 PC CHARLES FREDERICK ROBINSON Laboured to rescue a man from a falling shopfront following an explosion in Southwark, while 22 tons of debris rained down.

1936 **PC JAMES WARRENDER THOMSON** (Posthumous) Sacrificed his life clearing pedestrians from the path of a heavy cement lorry out of control down Barnet Hill.

1937 PC JOSEPH HENRY HOOD Although a non-driver, leapt on to the running-board of an inadequately parked police car which started to roll down Gipsy Hill, and succeeded in steering it away from pedestrians until the car overturned. Invalided out of the Force as the result of his injuries.

1937 PC REGINALD ERNEST RALPH MOUNCE Rescued 7-year-old boy trapped under a barge in the Grand Surrey Canal at Peckham, and almost saved his life with artificial respiration.

1938 PC CECIL FRANK CAVALIER MM , PC ERNEST WALTER SWAYNE Made unarmed search of a church hall, including its darkened loft, looking for a dangerous gunman who had just shot the verger and killed the vicar. Leapt at threatening crouching figure, which proved to be the gunman who had killed himself.

1938 PC JOHN WILLIAM CHESTERMAN Remained on running board of Soho car thieves' getaway car, despite violent and ultimately successful attempts to dislodge him. Promptly telephoned Scotland Yard, and the thieves were caught.

1938 PC EDWARD ERNEST FREELAND, PC HOWARD JAMES PERRY Both overcome by hydrogen cyanide gas which was being used to fumigate an old house in Cumberland Terrace. But Constable Freeland first rescued the old lady who had been trapped in the house, and Constable Perry pulled the two of them to safety before he himself collapsed. All three recovered in hospital.

1938 PC HARRY JOSEPH TURNELL Rescued small child from electrified train line near Blackheath and brought the child to safety despite the danger from trains and receiving severe shock.

1939 DS RONALD TOM BAILEY Forced car of thieves to stop by leaping on to running board.

1939 PC MATTHEW BURSNALL Succeeded in arresting a drunk despite being seriously injured by gun shot wounds in Bayswater.

1939 PC ALEXANDER CARMICHAEL Shot in the leg while assisting a colleague to arrest two fugitives known to be armed running from Dollis Hill Station.

1939 PC FREDERICK HENRY CHAMPS Without a torch to identify the live rails, went on to the railway line at Sudbury at night to rescue man from an oncoming train.

1939 PC ALBERT EDWARD COSHAM Drove more than 40 miles at very high speeds in successful pursuit of Post Office robbers whose reckless driving included serious attempts to force him to crash.

1939 PS GEORGE EDWARD HEMLEY, PC FREDERICK WILLIAM GROUND, SPS CECIL RACKHAM, DC ELLIOTT PILLAR While off duty, Constable Pillar was forced to drive his car from Woolwich ferry to Barking by two armed deserters. The officers overcame and arrested the men despite repeated revolver fire after PC Pillar deliberately crashed his car outside the police station.

1939 PC ARTHUR JAMES MCKITTERICK Repeated entry into gas filled house to rescue occupants.

1940 **DI ROBERT HONEY FABIAN** Dismantled second IRA bomb at scene of an explosion at Piccadilly.

1940 PC ERNEST VICTOR EDGAR HAYWARD Dismantled an IRA bomb he found in a shop window in Tottenham Court Road in the middle of the night.

1940 PC GORDON DONALD MORRISON Arrested an escaping prisoner in Woolwich who had pulled a loaded pistol on him.

1940 DC THOMAS CHARLES SHEPHERD Jumped on the running board of a smash and grab gang's getaway car in Croydon, and forced it to crash, leading to their arrest.

1940 PC WILLIAM TARRY, PC MAURICE HENRY WRIGHT Jointly rushed a burglar in Chislehurst who was pointing a rifle at them.

KING'S POLICE AND FIRE SERVICES MEDAL, 1941–1953

Retitled in 1940 to recognize the bravery of firemen during the Blitz.

1941 PC WILLIAM ALBERT BRIDGE Mounted running board of jewel thieves' car until it was stopped and the men arrested.

1941 SPECIAL CONSTABLE GEORGE THOMAS MYERS Stopped runaway horses and van bolting in Stepney.

1941 PC ALFRED JOHN PATEMAN Arrested store thief in Bethnal Green, and held on to his prisoner despite serious assault by three accomplices who broke the constable's nose and a tooth.

1941 PC JAMES THOMAS BARTON , PC THOMAS JOSEPH PRITLOVE Disarmed man holding shotgun at PC Barton's stomach after a Post Office robbery.

1942 SPS JOHN KANE Chased, disarmed and arrested a suspected deserter who had tried to escape being taken in custody at Streatham Police Station by threatening officers with a loaded revolver.

1942 PC SIDNEY COLLYER, PC FREDERICK WALTER LEE Chased, caught and held an armed suspect after a violent struggle, despite both officers being shot and wounded.

1942 PC DOUGLAS MARTIN BARNES While investigating a robbery committed by soldiers in Piccadilly, pursued and arrested suspect after being shot at three times.

1942 PS JOHN BANNISTER Went twice into fiercely burning house in Farleigh Rd, Stoke Newington and rescued two of the three occupants before being overcome by smoke.

1942 DC JOHN MCVERNON Arrested a larceny suspect after a long chase through Pimlico streets in the course of which he was shot at.

1942 DC WILLIAM MONTEITH Disarmed and arrested a youth previously escaped from custody who was threatening him at point blank range with a pistol.

1942 PS WILLIAM OLIVER Disarmed and arrested one of two men he and a constable were taking to Croydon Police Station for questioning, although the suspect had twice stuck a pistol in his ribs.

1943 PS WILLIAM POTTER Disarmed and, with the help of two constables, arrested a Canadian soldier who had produced a revolver and taken him hostage by pressing it into his side on realizing Sgt Potter believed him to be the man wanted for the murder of another police Sergeant in Bognor Regis.

1943 PS FRANK GEORGE BEAVIS, PC ERNEST DREW Overpowered and arrested a man who had threatened them with a loaded rifle and fixed bayonet pointed at them as they rushed his locked door in Diss St, Shoreditch.

1943 WRC REGINALD CARPENTER, PC GEORGE SIDNEY GRANT, PC CHARLES LINDSELL, PC PERCY HENRY SALTER Set up a road block at Staines Bridge for Canadian soldier who had stolen a machine gun, revolver and lorry from his base and broken through two road blocks in Surrey. When he approached, PC Lindsell stationed his car in the lorry's path and switched on his headlights, blinding the soldier who swerved into the kerb. WRC Carpenter and PC Grant jumped in the cab and disarmed the Canadian.

1943 PC DENNIS STURGESS COURT Badly wounded by a US soldier whom he chased after the man had wounded a woman in Coventry Street. The constable was stabbed three times, once in the face, during the pursuit, but tackled the suspect and arrested him.

1943 WRC TOM ALEC PAGE Pursued an armed soldier he found breaking into a house in Lyndhurst Gardens, Finchley. Continued the chase until the soldier disabled him by shooting him in the leg and striking him in the face with his rifle butt.

1943 PC JOHN CHARLES SALMON Rescued a woman from a burning house in Somerford St, Bethnal Green. In attempting to re-enter upper storey to rescue a child, almost fell from roof before passing out.

1944 SD INSP JAMES ARTHUR COLE (bar to 1930 medal), INSP JAMES PRICE, SP.INSP. HOWARD TERRY In a 13-hour siege, the officers tried to extract an armed mentally disordered man who fired a shotgun at any movement, and held his sister as a hostage in his house at Barry Rd, East Dulwich. Insp Price tried to gain access and climb the stairs while the man was distracted, but was shot at.

Inspectors Cole and Terry rescued the sister under cover of tear-gas, and later rushed the man's room, at which point he shot himself.

1944 PC ALFRED CHARLES SALMON Suffered multiple fractures to left arm and leg when violently thrown from the running board of a suspect's car in Abbey St, SE1. Managed to secure car number which ensured the man's arrest.

1945 PS HERBERT GEORGE MAYGER Successfully disarmed and arrested an intruder who had threatened the manager of a block of flats with a pistol, and proceeded to threaten the Sergeant, and struggle violently after his gun had been knocked from his hand by Sgt Mayger's truncheon.

1947 PC CECIL SNELLING Chased and struggled with an armed housebreaker, even after a bullet in his thigh nearly severed the main blood vessels.

1947 PC BERTIE ROWSWELL BEM, PC NORMAN STRANGE Chased an armed man, wanted for murder, from Russell Square along Upper Woburn Place, despite his firing at them constantly, one bullet passing through PC Strange's plain-clothes jacket, and another hitting PC Rowswell's eye, which had to be removed.

1947 WDS ALBERTA WATTS (NÉE LAW) Suffered violent assault during chase and struggle with suspect while voluntarily acting as decoy in relation to series of attacks on women on Tooting Bec Common.

1947 PS WILLIAM HOSIE DEANS Suffered violent assault, and was bound, gagged, and dumped in the snow in a remote place, having voluntarily impersonated a Kentish Town bank manager on information that he was to be kidnapped and his keys stolen.

1947 PC JAMES BRYCE CUTT Hung on to the running board of an Islington gang of shop thieves' getaway car for three miles before it crashed into a lamp post and the driver was arrested.

1948 PC THOMAS BEALE Suffered shock and nervous disability after successfully stopping a runaway horse and cart in Noel St, Islington.

1948 PS RALPH DONALD SHEPPARD, PC HARRY PATTERSON KAY Investigating reports of a break-in at a factory Sgt Sheppard was threatened with a burning oxyacetylene lamp and a revolver, and PC Kay was shot in the stomach in the course of arresting two burglars.

1949 INSP WILLIAM ARTHUR MOODY, PC ROBERT HENRY HIDE, WRC GEORGE CHARLES SEARLE, PC DENNIS EDWARD WHEELER The three officers burst in on and arrested the armed killer of PC Nathanael Edgar, after WRC Searle had identified his whereabouts in Stockwell and kept observation.

1949 DS HAROLD BLAND, DC JOHN MALCOLM BAXTER DC Baxter tried to stop the car of a suspect making an escape from Eastern Auction Market, Stepney, but was thrown off. In the same incident, DS Bland was shot through the clothing by a second suspect who tried to escape from arrest in a police car.

From 1950, the KPFSM was only awarded for Gallantry posthumously.

1953 PC SIDNEY GEORGE MILES Shot on a warehouse rooftop in Croydon, going to assist colleagues in the arrest of Christopher Craig and Derek Bentley.

QUEEN'S POLICE MEDAL (Only awarded for Gallantry posthumously) Instituted 19 May 1954.

1956 TEMP PS LEONARD DEMMON Killed in a gunfight accompanied by Temp PS Maurice Eden GM at Nicosia General Hospital in Cyprus when terrorists opened fire in order to free a prisoner.

1961 INSP PHILLIP PAWSEY, PS FREDERICK GEORGE HUTCHINS Both shot by a suspect with an automatic pistol attempting to escape from questioning at West Ham Police Station.

1974 PC MICHAEL ANTHONY WHITING Thrown from a car whose suspicious movements had led police to question the driver, who then tried to escape at reckless speed, deliberately colliding with other vehicles to try and shake PC Whiting off. When this succeeded, the constable's skull was broken, and he died the same day.

1976 PC STEPHEN ANDREW TIBBLE While riding his motorcycle off-duty, saw a man with a gun being chased by three plain-clothes officers. PC Tibble overtook him, dismounted, and approached, whereupon the suspect, an IRA terrorist, shot him three times at close range.

THE GEORGE CROSS

Instituted in 1940, the George Cross is the highest non-military gallantry award, sometimes known as the civilians' Victoria Cross. It has been awarded to five Metropolitan Police officers.

1952 DC FREDERICK FAIRFAX, while only armed with his truncheon, arrested and held burglar Derek Bentley after having been shot in the shoulder by Bentley's accomplice Christopher Craig. When issued with a pistol, advanced on Craig, who had been shooting at officers, and had killed **PC Sidney Miles**.

1958 PC HENRY WILLIAM STEVENS, covering the back door of a house in Bromley where a break-in was reported, gave chase to an armed man who ran away through the garden. As PC Stevens gained on him and shouted that he was a police officer, the man pulled a gun and shot him in the face, breaking his jaw. Despite this, PC Stevens caught up with him, seized and disarmed him. The prisoner broke free, but the officer caught him again and, before collapsing, kept hold of the priosner's jacket which led to the assailant's arrest.

1967 PC ANTHONY GLEDHILL, driving a patrol car in Rotherhithe and Deptford, became involved in the 80mph chase of a car containing five armed criminals, who repeatedly fired at the police car with a sawn-off shotgun and a revolver. Both PC Gledhill and his partner, PC McFall GM, were injured and required subsequent hospital treatment, despite which PC Gledhill kept the car on track until the criminals collided with a lorry and the men abandoned it. PC Gledhill and his partner pursued them on foot and succeeded in overpowering one.

1974 INSPECTOR JAMES BEATON, Princess Anne's personal protection officer, was shot in the chest, shoulder and arm when protecting the Princess and Mark Phillips from the attempt to kidnap them in the Mall. Despite his injuries, and the simultaneous attempt to kill the chauffeur, the Inspector secured the safety of his principals, held his ground and returned one shot before his gun jammed. Following the same incident, probationer PC Michael Hills was awarded the GM for disarming the assailant, despite having been shot in the liver, and DC Peter Edmonds was awarded the QGM for tackling and arresting the man in St James's Park.

1976 (POSTHUMOUS) EXPLOSIVES OFFICER CAPTAIN ROGER GOAD BEM, who had just completed an assignment, was called to Kensington Church Street where a national newspaper was advised an explosive device had been left in a shop doorway. With the area cleared, Captain Goad started to defuse the bomb, which exploded, killing him instantly.

GEORGE MEDAL

Instituted in 1940 for acts of bravery which did not reach the outstanding level of the George Cross. By the end of 1983, over 2,000 awards had been made, over 1,400 of which were during the Second World War. The names of the 80 recipients of the medal during the War are followed by 56 other awards of the medal.

George Medals awarded in connection with war activities

PC WILLIAM ALLEN	PC WILLIAM GRAY
SP CONS CHARLES ALMOND	PC WILLIE GRIFFITHS
PS HENRY BASS	PS DAVID GRIGG
INSP HARRY BATES	PC REGINALD GROSE
SPS FREDERICK BLAKE	PC WILLIAM GUNN
WRC RALPH BLOCK	PS ALBERT HACK
PC HENRY BRANDON	PC WILLIAM HACK
PC WILLIAM BRIDLE	PS CHARLES HALES
PS FREDERICK BURGESS	PC LEONARD HALL
PC HENRY BURGOYNE	SP CONS VERNON HITE
PC CHARLES BURROWS	PC LESLIE HUGHES
INSP FREDERICK COKER	PC EDWARD JACKSON
DC SIDNEY COOMBER	SPS EVAN JAMES
PS WILLIAM COX	PC JOHN JAMES
PC JOHN CRUMP	PC STANLEY JOHNSON
PS JACKSON DAVISON	PC WILLIAM KEERY
SP SGT GRAHAM DEACON	PC EDWARD KERRISON DCM
PC GEORGE DEAN	PC BERNARD LEES
SPS WILLIAM DOUGLAS	PC JAMES LESLIE
PC WALTER EDWARDS	STN INSP CLARENCE MCDONOUGH
PC LESLIE FINBOW	PS NEIL MCFARLANE
WRC JAMES FLETT	PC JOHN MCKENNING
PS GEORGE FOSTER	STN INSP THOMAS MAHIR
WRC ALBERT GARRARD	PC CHARLES MANN
WRC ERNEST GILBERT	PS ALBERT MARTIN
WRC ALBERT GORDON	PS JASPER MARTIN
JUNIOR STN INSP JOHN GOTT	

PC JOHN MEAD	PC WILLIAM SCHERMULY
WRC THOMAS MORRISON	WRC ARCHIBALD SEXTON
PC WALTER CHARLES NICHOLSON	PS JAMES SHERLAW
JUNIOR STN INSP RONALD NOBLE	PC ROY SLOWLEY
PC REGINALD OAKES	PC EDWARD STONE
WRC ALBERT PARSONS	PC FREDERICK STONE BEM
PC BRINLEY PEDRICK	WRC THOMAS TANNER
PC EDWIN POPE	PC WALTER TAYLOR
WRC LAMBERT PORTER	PC LEONARD THORNE
INSP JOHN PULHAM	PC ERNEST TRICKER
PC MATTHEW RIDDELL	WRC GEORGE VOIZEY
PS JAMES ROBSON BEM	PC GEORGE WHITMORE
PC ERNEST ROSE	PS HARLEY WRIGHT
PS GEORGE ROSIE	SPS HAROLD YOUNG
	WRC WILLIAM YOUNG

1951 PC LESLIE ALAN SMITH For courage and determination in arresting an armed man in Hounslow.

1951 PC OWEN ASHWIN, PC JOHN KERR MCCALLUM, PC IVAN STANLEY KING For courage and tenacity in tackling two violent criminals, one of whom used a firearm to resist arrest in Biggin Hill, Kent, severely wounding PC Ashwin.

1952 PC FREDERICK MARK STONE BEM For great courage and devotion to duty in tackling a violent shop-breaker armed with an iron bar, whereby he was severely injured.

1952 PC KENNETH ALFRED BAILEY, PC SYDNEY DARBY, INSP ALFRED LEONARD SHIPTON For courage and tenacity in effecting the arrest of a dangerous criminal who made a determined resistance to arrest by using an automatic pistol in Sutherland Avenue, Maida Vale.

1952 PC JOHN SHERRARD EDWARDES For courage and determination in effecting the arrest of a dangerous motor car thief at Kensington High Street.

1952 PC JAMES MCKENZIE Dealing with an armed man in a Paddington public house.

1953 **PC NORMAN HARRISON, PC JAMES CHRISTIE MCDONALD** For courage and devotion to duty in relation to dealing with Christopher Craig and Derek Bentley on the roof of a warehouse in Croydon.

1953 DC EDWARD NORMAN SNITCH, PC GEORGE EDWARD DORSETT For courage and tenacity in effecting the arrest of dangerous criminals, one of whom used a firearm to resist arrest at a bomb site at Clapham Place, Hackney.

1954 PC LEONARD GEOFFREY BOCKING, PC GEORGE ALEXANDER SINCLAIR For outstanding courage and tenacity in attempting to arrest an armed murderer in Clifton Gardens, Maida Vale.

1954 PC JOHN RICHARD THOMAS BAILEY For courage and determination in effecting the arrest of a dangerous criminal in Mitcham who used a firearm to resist arrest.

1955 **WPS ETHEL VIOLET BUSH, WPC KATHLEEN PARROTT** For outstanding courage and devotion to duty acting as crime decoys in Croydon, whereby they sustained injury.

1956 PC KEITH TREVOR BURDETT Courage and tenacity in effecting the arrest of a dangerous criminal who used a firearm to resist arrest and injured the officer in Vauxhall.

1956 DS ALBERT ERIC JOHN CHAMBERS, PC DAVID EVANS WOOD, PC GEORGE WILLIAM KARN For courage and tenacity in effecting the arrests of a gang of dangerous criminals in Mayfair who used firearms to resist arrest whereby DS Chambers and PC Wood were injured.

1956 PS NORMAN GEORGE LOXLEY, PC THOMAS OLIVER For courage and promptitude in rescuing a man from a burning railway carriage after an accident at Barnes.

1956 TEMP PS MAURICE EDEN Involved with Temp PS Leonard Demmon QPM in exchange of gunfire with terrorists at Nicosia General Hospital, Cyprus. Died just before his GM was awarded.

1959 PC GEORGE EDWARD DORSETT Awarded bar to GM for tackling and disarming a youth armed with a loaded shotgun outside his home in Chingford.

1961 PC CHARLES EDWARD COX Tackled a man armed with a loaded automatic pistol resulting in a gunshot wound to PC Cox. (Inspector Pawsey and Sergeant

1964 WPC MARGARET SHAW CLELAND Spent over an hour on a rooftop, and eventually rescued a 20 month child from the arms of his deranged father at great personal risk.

1966 PC ALASDAIR CAMERON FERGUSON MACLEOD, PC TERENCE VICTOR BROWN, PC KENNETH JAMES BOWERMAN, PC DOUGLAS WHITHAM Dealing with an escaped prisoner in a roof top incident who used a pistol to escape, but was eventually arrested after the officers used a broom handle and other means to prevent him from driving off in a car despite being fired at on several occasions in Piggott Street, Stepney.

1966 DS PETER ALAN WOODMORE, PC MICHAEL JAMES WHEELHOUSE Involved in a prolonged chase between Kingston and Chelsea of a stolen car during which two police officers, including PC Wheelhouse, were shot and wounded, and a police dog killed, before DS Woodmore arrested him.

1966 PS MICHAEL JOHN ROSE Confronted a youth at a break-in who threatened him with a pistol. PS Rose advanced towards him, the youth fired, but missed.

1967 DS LAWRENCE SCOTT Threatened with a rifle when he attempted to arrest a prison escapee in a house at Highbury. The suspect tried to fire the gun at him but the bullet transpired to be of the wrong calibre, and did not work.

1967 PC TERENCE FREDERICK McFALL Following the car chase of five suspects from Creek Side, Deptford, during which shots were fired at the police car, the criminals stopped and attempted to commandeer the police car. PC Gledhill GC got hold of the police car, and was thrown off. The front tyres of the police car then burst. PC McFall opened the passenger door, the suspect pulled the trigger of his gun, but it did not fire, and he was then arrested.

1969 TDC PHILLIP JOHN DIXON WILLIAMS, DS JOHN STUART NORTHMORE WHARTON The officers intercepted an armed gang in the course of a bank raid in Streatham. PC Williams made several attempts with his motorcycle to run down an armed robber who repeatedly threatened him and fired a gun. DS Wharton pursued on foot a robber with a shotgun and eventually overpowered him.

1972 SPS ARTHUR GARNER Pursued and overpowered a wanted criminal despite his ramming a police car, driving a car at the officers on foot, and firing a shotgun at the officers involved in Shepperton.

1973 PC PETER SLIMON In possession of a firearm in connection with protection duties, the officer intervened in a bank robbery in Kensington, was wounded in an exchange of gunfire, and attempted to pursue the bank robbers as they escaped from the scene.

1974 PC MICHAEL HILLS Involved in an incident involving a kidnap attack on HRH The Princess Anne in The Mall, in which Inspector Beaton was awarded the George Cross. PC Hills disarmed the assailant, despite having been shot.

1976 MAJOR DONALD VICTOR HENDERSON Awarded as the result of displaying courage and calmness during his work as an Explosives Officer attending numerous IRA bombing incidents.

1976 PC DAVID MICHAEL CLEMENTS Called to a bank raid and confronted by armed robbers, the officer was shot at several times and wounded while chasing the suspects in St John's Wood.

1976 MAJOR GEOFFREY WILLIAM BIDDLE MBE Defused four terrorist bombs during his work as an Explosives Officer.

1977 PC RAYMOND PETER KIFF Involved in chasing, overcoming and disarming a terrorist after an IRA train explosion and shooting at West Ham.

1977 INSP JOHN FRANCIS PURNELL, PS MURTAGH PHILLIP MCVEIGH, DI HENRY DOWSWELL Involved in an operation which intercepted IRA terrorists and resulted in the **Balcombe Street siege**.

1979 DC BRIAN ERNEST PAWLEY Wrestled with an armed and dangerous man and received gunshot wound saving a colleague from death in Bethnal Green.

1981 **PC TREVOR JAMES LOCK** Held hostage during the Iranian Embassy siege, and intervened at crucial stages in attempts to ensure safety of other hostages.

1983 KENNETH HOWORTH Killed while dealing with an IRA bomb in Oxford Street during the course of his duties as an Explosives Officer.

1983 PETER EDWIN SPENCER GURNEY MBE GM Awarded bar to his George Medal for disarming an explosive device immediately after his colleague Kenneth Howorth had been killed by a similar bomb.

1988 PS DAVID PENGELLY Involved as Sergeant of a team of officers protecting firemen during the **Broadwater Farm** riot in 1985, in which PC Keith Blakelock was

killed. **PC Blakelock** and ten other officers were awarded the Queen's Gallantry Medal.

1992 DS ALAN KNAPP, DS STEPHEN THOMAS Involved in an operation to arrest men attempting to rob a Post Office. Both were shot and seriously wounded, but continued their endeavours to arrest the culprit despite being unarmed.

BRITISH EMPIRE MEDAL (BEM)

Instituted in December 1922 for meritorious service. It ceased to be awarded for gallantry in 1974.

1946 PC JOSEPH BARRETT Gallant Conduct.

1948 DS THEOBALD BUTLER, DC JACK BARLOW Tackling a violent criminal armed with a loaded pistol.

1951 PC EDMUND WHEELER Rescuing a man from drowning in the Thames.

1952 PS ANTHONY LOWNDES Effecting the arrest of an armed criminal.

1952 DS ALBERT FRANK WELLS, PC JOHN FOSTER, PC MAURICE FURNER Effecting the arrest of an armed criminal.

1952 PC JOHN SIMPSON BURKE Effecting the arrest of a mentally unstable criminal armed with a revolver.

1953 **PC ROBERT JAMES WILLIAM JAGGS** Involved in the operation to arrest Christopher Craig and Derek Bentley from the roof of a warehouse in Croydon.

1954 PC JOHN ALAN GULLIVER Effecting the arrest of a dangerous criminal.

1954 DS CYRIL CHARLES NICHOLLS Involved with DC John Bailey GM in the arrest of a criminal who used a firearm to resist arrest.

1956 DS GEORGE HENRY FRAMPTON, PC ROBERT NEVILLE GREEN, PC WYNDHAM DAVID MORGAN, PC JOHN ATKINSON LEWIS Involved with PC Keith Burdett GM in effecting the arrest of a criminal who used a firearm to resist arrest.

1956 PC DONALD CAMERON Involved with DS Albert Chambers GM, PC George Karn GM and PC David Wood GM in effecting the arrest of a gang of dangerous criminals.

1956 PC ANTHONY GAIUS WALL Effecting the arrest of two juveniles, one of whom used a firearm to resist arrest, whereby he sustained injury.

1957 PC BRENDAN THOMAS BULLARD, PC THOMAS CHARLES WILLIAM THOMPSON, PC JOHN KAY Outstanding courage in tackling four violent criminals armed with iron bars whereby all were injured.

1957 PC JOHN RICHARD HARRIS Outstanding courage and determination in arresting an armed youth.

1958 PC STEWART JOHN WINTER Courage and determination in arresting a man for taking and driving away a motor vehicle after he had sustained injury.

1960 PC THOMAS YOUNG Clung to a motor car which was being driven erratically and at speed before arresting the driver despite injury.

1961 PS DAVID JONES FINDLAY Outstanding courage and determination when dealing with a youth armed with a loaded shotgun.

1961 PC LESLIE CHARLES ENGLAND Involved with Inspector Philip Pawsey QPM, PS Frederick Hutchins QPM, and PC Charles Cox GM in tackling a man armed with a loaded automatic pistol.

1962 DCI HUBERT MELVILLE REES Outstanding courage and leadership in arresting a man armed with loaded shotgun.

1962 PC THOMAS FORBES WATT While off duty intervened in a fight outside a club, sustained slash injuries requiring 60 stitches to his face, and chased his assailant for a quarter of a mile before arresting him.

1963 PC NORMAN ERIC BARTHOLOMEW, PC RICHARD ELLIS THOMAS. Rescued a drunken man from a building under construction 18 storeys high. The man fell, but the officers dragged him to safety.

1963 SPECIAL CONSTABLE JOHN MICHAEL LAURENCE While off duty climbed a gasometer and held on to a boy until assistance arrived.

1963 DI ROBERT HUNTLEY, PC JOHN GEORGE RUSSELL Went to a club to arrest a man after a shooting incident and despite threats from a loaded revolver, tackled the man, disarmed and arrested him after a tremendous struggle.

1963 SPS LESLIE JOHN MACKEY, DC FRANK VICTOR KEYLOCK Subdued and restrained a violent mentally disordered man wielding an axe and throwing missiles from a roof top.

1964 PC ROY ALBERT HOBBS, PC ROY STAMPER Chased an armed man on foot from a night club and with assistance from the public arrested him despite being shot at.

1965 PC CYRIL CHARLES CROSSINGHAM Broke into house to arrest violent man brandishing a carving knife and was stabbed in the arm.

1965 STN PS JOHN KENNETH LANE, PC THOMAS EVERETT Following the chase of a stolen car in a private motorist's car, a chase ensued on foot after which the officers subdued and arrested the suspect despite threats from a loaded hand gun.

1966 DS ALLEN ROBSON, DS ROY GORDON EYLES, DS PATRICK GLANVILLE GIBBINS Involved with PC Alasdair MacLeod GM and others in a prolonged struggle to subdue an escaped prisoner who was involved in a roof top incident, a chase in the street and an attempt to escape in a car.

1966 PS ARTHUR WILLIAM PORTER, DC ROGER KEITH OLIVER, PC DEREK EDWIN BIRKHEAD Involved with DS Peter Woodmore GM and PC Michael Wheelhouse GM in car chase, siege and arrest of an armed man between Kingston and Chelsea.

1966 PC JOHN HENRY BARRETT Jumped on to the bonnet of car suspected of being stolen which was being driven at him, and clung on despite determined efforts to dislodge him.

1966 DS HENRY CLEMENT, TDC DENNIS BARTLETT Involved in arresting two suspects despite having ammonia squirted in their eyes, and being attacked with an axe.

1966 TDC BRIAN CARNEY Disarmed and arrested man with converted starting pistol.

1966 PC STUART JONES Clung to the bonnet of a car trying to dislodge him, tried to subdue driver through the broken windscreen, and was eventually thrown off the moving car by the criminals.

1966 PC JOHN ANTHONY DAWSON, PC DEREK HEATON Involved in chase of suspect who threatened police officers who eventually arrested him despite the man firing what transpired to be an air pistol.

1966 PC JOHN CHORLTON While off duty climbed the drain pipe of a burning house, rescued two people from the first floor, but was overcome by smoke during a further rescue attempt inside the building.

1966 DC WILLIAM CYRIL CONNELL, DC ERNEST ARTHUR PACKMAN Involved in the arrest of a man who fired shots and injured DC Connell during a violent struggle.

1967 TDC VICTOR JOHN LOCK, TDC CHARLES BROWNE VON After chasing an armed robber on foot, confronted the suspect who threatened and pulled the trigger of a gun which did not fire as it was set at the only empty chamber.

1967 PC BRIAN EDWIN WHEELER, PC WILLIAM ARTHUR NIELD Overpowered powerful and violent man who seriously injured both officers with a barber's razor.

1967 DS DOUGLAS FRANK DAVIES, DS ALEXANDER ANTONY EIST Involved with DS Laurence Scott GM in arresting an escaped prisoner armed with a rifle.

1967 INSPECTOR GORDON GEORGE MCDOWELL On a conservatory roof top incident, disarmed and overpowered a youth armed with a loaded shotgun who had already fired once.

1967 PC LESLIE MANNS Arrested a youth despite being threatened with and shot in head by air rifle.

1968 PC JOHN ANTHONY ROBB With other officers, grabbed a man and prevented him from throwing himself from a high roof.

1968 PC TERENCE MICHAEL COX Pursued a youth in Epping Forest and detained him despite being fired at with an air rifle.

1968 SPS TERENCE JOHN PAGE, PC ANTHONY PAUL RICH, PC JOHN DAVID ROSS Involved in subduing a prisoner who threatened them with a Walther automatic pistol in the charge room and elsewhere in **West End Central** police station.

1968 PC FRANK PULLEY After being assaulted by suspect, was threatened by a revolver and then disarmed and arrested him.

1969 PS PETER LAIDLAW LAWSON, PC CLIVE LESTER ARNOLD Forced their way into house and arrested a man who had been threatening to shoot and stab his wife.

1969 DS LEONARD JOSEPH RYLAND Involved in the arrest of an armed suspect. He forced the gun away for a first shot. His hand became jammed in the gun's mechanism which prevented a second shot.

1969 TDC REGINALD ALFRED JENKINS, DI JAMES WILLIAM MARSHALL, DS PATRICK LAWRENCE O'BRIEN, DC RAYMOND CHARLES ADAMS Involved with TDC Phillip Williams GM and DS John Wharton GM in detaining a gang of armed bank robbers who fired at police.

1969 PC RICHARD HONEY, PC WILLIAM BUCHANAN LENNOX With assistance from a fireman, restrained violently struggling man trying to throw himself from a slippery ledge of Archway Road bridge.

1970 DS PATRICK GLANVILLE GIBBINS Bar to GM. Involved in arrest of men armed with ammonia and iron bar despite being seriously injured.

1970 PC JOHN MILLER Chased and detained youth who fired what transpired to be an air pistol to prevent his arrest.

1970 PC JOHN GRIFFITHS Disarmed man with loaded double-barrelled shotgun, and chased and arrested him despite threats from lock knife and iron bar.

1970 PC RONALD SHACKLOCK Disarmed suspect who threatened him with gun.

1970 PC RUSSELL JONES Jumped from Waterloo bridge into the River Thames to rescue woman who had jumped into the river.

1971 PC ANTHONY REYNOLDS, PC COLIN PETER BURCH Disarmed man after a car chase after he had fled from house where he had gone berserk with a gun.

1971 PC JOHN MOGFORD, PC GEORGE BLACK, PC RONALD TURNBULL Involved in violent struggle where the officers were shot at and threatened with a knife. PCs Mogford and Turnbull were both rendered unconscious.

1971 PC WESLEY WILLIAMS Arrested driver after being thrown on to bonnet of stolen car and after driver had driven at speed to dislodge him.

1971 PC JAMES DONNELLY, PC JOHN PHILIP WHITEHEAD Rescued child from blazing house.

1971 PC PETER EDMOND BUTCHER Disarmed man who threatened him with a pistol after a police car chase following a robbery.

1971 PC MALCOLM JOHN KNIGHT Pursued suspect despite being threatened with gun.

1971 INSP PETER MARSH Broke into house and arrested man armed with gun.

1971 PC RODNEY PHILLIPS Chased a man who repeatedly threatened him with gun and struck him several times before being arrested.

1971 PC JOHN DILWYN PRICE Attempted to disarm man threatening him with a shotgun, and detained him despite being struck over head.

1971 PC ROBERT GRAHAM DENCH, PC PETER JOHN BOWCOCK Pursued man who abandoned his car after a chase and then rescued him from fume-filled sewer.

1971 PC ANTHONY JOHN SEPRINI Detained man who had threatened him with a gun.

1972 PC BRIAN PARSONS, PC KEITH GILES Involved with Stn PS Arthur Garner GM in detaining wanted criminal who fired shotgun at police.

1973 DC RONALD JAMES ARNOLD Tackled man, who had barricaded himself in a house with two large knives, despite the effects of CS.

1973 PC DAVID ROBERT RUMBLE Pursued and detained one suspect from wages van robbery in Bethnal Green despite being repeatedly threatened with a shotgun.

1974 PC KIM CLABBY Persisted in attempting to pursue and arrest suspect despite effects of spray to eyes, a number of shots from a pistol and being driven at by a motor car.

1974 PC STANLEY CONLEY, PC GEORGE BURROWS, DC JAMES SMITH PC Conley and PC Burrows intervened in a hostage incident at the Indian High Commission and shot two suspects dead after being threatened with (replica) firearms. DC Smith disarmed a suspect while armed only with a truncheon.

1974 PC DAVID ANDREW WOLFENDEN Rescued a mentally unstable man standing on a 100 foot high ledge at Swan and Edgars department store.

1974 DS WILLIAM IAN GRIFFITHS Persisted in detaining a struggling and violent man despite being stabbed, and bleeding profusely.

QUEEN'S GALLANTRY MEDAL

Instituted 20th June 1974 for exemplary acts of bravery.

1974 DS ALAN WORDSWORTH Entered a hotel room while armed, confronted suspect who had committed a jewel robbery and made suspect drop his gun.

1974 DC PETER EDMONDS Involved with Insp James Beaton GC and PC Hills GM. Arrested armed man who attacked HRH The Princess Anne in the Mall.

1974 PC BARRY NEIL GAGE, PC ALAN TENYON POINTER, PC GODFREY HENRY CHAFFEY Involved in chasing a car and made arrests despite a number of shots being fired at police.

1974 DC JOHN RAYMOND YOUNG Pursued suspects by car to Swanley, and was fired at twice from shotgun and wounded in the course of attempting an arrest.

1974 PC GORDON USHER, PC FRANK HUMM Arrested man who attacked them with carving knife.

1975 SPS MICHAEL THOMAS PEFFER, PC DAVID BRADY, PC RYAN KENNETH DAVID During a prolonged car chase following a post office robbery, shots were fired at a police car, and the suspects eventually arrested after one officer grabbed a shotgun from a suspect and their getaway car was rammed by a police car.

1976 SUPT WILLIAM JOHN BRESLIN Arrested an armed man wanted for the murder of a Surrey police officer.

1976 PC RYAN KENNETH DAVID Bar to QGM awarded for rescuing a person attempting suicide from Archway bridge.

1977 DC JOHN ALLPORT Involved in a car chase of armed suspects.

1977 PC WILLIAM KINNIBURGH Chased a man armed with a gun in Camberwell.

1977 DS PHILIP WILLIAM MANSFIELD, PC BARRY CHARLES COURT, PC STEPHEN WILLIAM KNIGHT, PC ANDREW STEPHEN CLAIDEN, PC ROBERT FENTON Involved with Inspector John Purnell GM, DI Henry Dowswell GM and PS Murtagh McVeigh GM in intercepting **IRA** terrorists which resulted in the **Balcombe Street siege**.

1977 PC NORMAN WRIGHT Arrested an armed man at the Chilean embassy.

1979 PC BRYAN ERROL GROVE Involved in pursuit of armed robbers at Ley Street, Ilford in 1974.

1979 PC GORDON HEYES Chased an armed man who had robbed a petrol station, continuing on to an arrest despite being shot in leg.

1979 INSP DAVID BERT MARTIN Arrested and retained prisoner despite being surrounded by a group of dangerous and excited youths, one of whom fired a revolver at him.

1982 **PC PHILIP OLDS** Shot while intervening when two armed men robbed an off licence in Hayes, Middlesex.

1983 PC FRANCIS JOSEPH O'NEILL Stabbed and killed by offender while stopping and then pursuing a suspect who had been trying to obtain drugs by deception in Kennington.

1983 PC MALCOLM HENLEY While off duty, disarmed a gunman after he had robbed a security guard.

1988 PC MARTIN PROCTOR Entered an Underground train tunnel and pulled a woman intending suicide back to the platform despite the presence of an oncoming train.

1988 **PC KEITH BLAKELOCK,** PC RICKY PANDYA, PC MAXWELL ROBERTS, PC ALAN TAPPY, PC RICHARD COOMBES, PC MICHAEL SHEPHERD, PC STEPHEN MARTIN, PC KENNETH MILNE, PC ROBIN CLARK, PC MILES BARTON, PC MARTIN HOWELLS Involved in serious public disorder at **Broadwater Farm** on 6th October 1985. Under the leadership of Sgt David Pengelly GM, the officers went to protect firemen engaged in attempting to extinguish a fire caused by rioters. PC Blakelock was killed during the incident.

1989 DEREK CHARLES PICKFORD, EXPLOSIVES OFFICER, PC MICHAEL CHIPPERFIELD Both involved in prolonged search of a hotel room and found a concealed terrorist device which Mr Pickford made safe.

1989 PS IAN THOMAS Threatened with a pistol and wounded by a gunshot during the chase and subsequent arrest of two suspects in West India Dock Road, E14.

1991 PS DAVID HADAWAY, PC PHILIP RAINSFORD, PC JOHN ANDREW HEALY Involved in pursuing a violent armed robber who fired a gun at police whereby all three officers were injured.

1994 PS PETER WILTSHIRE Involved in tackling and arresting robbers while off duty.

1994 DC JAMES MORRISON While off duty, pursued a violent thief on foot, who stabbed him to death.

1995 PC EDWARD KEMP, PC PATRICK KIELTY Confronted by three armed robbers but chased and arrested a suspect despite being threatened and fired upon during the chase.

1996 PC DAVID BOYCE, PC MARK O'BRIEN Involved in incident where police officers were shot at several times during a high speed chase and hostage incident following a robbery.

1996 PS DEREK ROBERTSON Called to an armed robbery at New Addington and tackled a robbery suspect who stabbed him to death.

1997 PS PATRICK KIELTY Awarded bar to QGM for dealing with and disarming a violent man who took a child, and later a woman as hostages.

1997 PC ANTHONY FITZPATRICK Chased suspect who produced a gun and fired five shots, one of which wounded the officer, and one narrowly missed his head while the officer persisted in his pursuit.

320 OFFICERS HAVE BEEN AWARDED THE SOVEREIGN'S COMMENDATION FOR BRAVE CONDUCT BETWEEN 1946 AND 1999.

APPENDIX **FOUR:** ROLL OF HONOUR

The Roll of Honour was introduced after discussions in 1935 between Lord Trenchard and the Police Federation as a means of giving special recognition to the heroic death of **PC James Thomson KPM** who met his death in that year. The Roll of Honour was introduced in the form of a book with inscribed pages briefly describing how the officers met their death, and it was backdated to 1920 when Police Orders first began to record such entries. Over the years, the entries have come to be restricted to cases where death has ensued as the result of an act of special gallantry or in connection with duties involving special risks. As a tribute to the many members of the Metropolitan Police Service who have given their lives in the course of policing London, the names contained in the Roll of Honour are set out later in this Appendix.

On 27 July 1950, the Metropolitan Police War Memorial book was dedicated in Westminster Abbey in the presence of the King and Queen. This memorial also took the form of a Roll of Honour and contains details of 1,076 names, embossed on vellum, in memory of all the members of the Metropolitan Police Service who lost their lives during the 1914–1918 and the 1939–1945 Wars either while serving in His Majesty's Forces or as the result of enemy action at home. Between the formation of the Metropolitan Police in 1829 and the First World War, there were also many members of the Service who lost their lives in the Boer War and other conflicts.

In a tribute to officers who died before the Roll of Honour started in 1920, and in recognition of other officers who have died in the course of their duties, but whose names have not been formally recorded, a List of Remembrance precedes the Roll of Honour. This has been drawn from the honourable and conscientious research project conducted by Sergeant Anthony Rae, a former Metropolitan Police officer, now of Lancashire Constabulary, Hutton, Preston, PR4 5SB, who has been engaged in drawing up a Book of Remembrance for the National Police Memorial at the National Memorial Arboretum relating to all officers in the United Kingdom who have lost their lives in the line of duty. This list uses wider criteria, and may be incomplete, but research is continuing and Sergeant Rae is willing to deal with any queries.

LIST OF REMEMBRANCE

Pre-Metropolitan Police

1798 REGISTERED STEVEDORE GABRIEL FRANKS, shot dead in **Marine Police Office** Riot on 16th October

1813 WATERMAN CONSTABLE ABRAHAM BROWN, killed at Wapping on 20th August

1820 WATERMAN CONSTABLE MARK ARNOLD, drowned on duty on 4th January

Metropolitan Police

1830 **PC JOSEPH GRANTHAM**, kicked in the head attempting to arrest a drunken man at a disturbance in Somers Town.

1830 PC JOHN LONG, stabbed to death when he challenged three suspects near Gray's Inn Road

1831 PC MICHAEL PRATT, collapsed and died from a ruptured heart chasing four suspected thieves in Old Kent Road

1833 **PC ROBERT CULLEY**, stabbed to death during a riot at a political meeting in **Coldbath Fields**, Clerkenwell

1839 PC WILLIAM ALDRIDGE, died from a fractured skull after he was stoned by a mob during an arrest at Deptford

1841 PC JAMES CARROLL, attacked by a mob and struck with his own truncheon while making an arrest in Shoreditch

1842 PC TIMOTHY DALY, shot dead attempting to arrest a man for highway robbery at Highbury

1842 PC CHARLES REYNOLDS, drowned in the London Docks while on night beat duty

1844 PC JOHN BIRKMYRE and PC JOHN WRIGHT, both killed at a fire in Guildford Street when the floors of a burning house collapsed on them

1846 PC JAMES HASTIE, died from injuries after being assaulted by several men in a street disturbance at Deptford

1846 **PC GEORGE CLARK**, brutally beaten and stabbed to death while on night duty at Dagenham

1848 PC DANIEL HARKER MONK, struck with his own truncheon by a man attempting to free a prisoner at St Giles'

1849 PC WILLIAM SIBLEY, collapsed and died from supposed over exertion at a fire

1849 PC JOHN WELCH, suffocated in a sewer trying to rescue three workmen after bringing out two of them

1850 PC ALEXANDER SCOTT, died during a hospital operation to an injury received in an affray at Deptford

1851 PC HENRY JAMES CHAPLIN, attacked and struck with bricks by a disorderly crowd at Vauxhall Walk

1852 PC MICHAEL MADIGAN, found drowned in the Thames adjoining his beat

1855 PC FRANCIS STOKER, killed while endeavouring to save the lives of six persons whose house had collapsed

1856 PC MALACHI SHANNON, thrown from his horse and died in consequence of the injuries sustained.

1858 PC HENRY MORGAN, died from injuries received in an affray.

1859 PC WILLIAM FULLER, killed while taking a police horse to the station when it suddenly reared and fell on him

1860 PC GEORGE BROWN, killed by falling down an area at Parsonage House, St Stephens' while in the execution of his duty

1862 INSP WILLIAM HARD, died from a fractured skull caused by a fall from his horse

1862 PC RICHARD LILLICRAP, collapsed from over exertion when in pursuit of a thief in Petticoat Lane

1863 PC WILLIAM JOHN DAVEY, shot through the head on his doorstep by a man whom he was investigating for a crime at Acton

1863 PC FREDERICK WILLIAM PATRICK, found dead in a barge under Hungerford Bridge, having fallen through a hole while on night duty

1864 PC CHARLES PEARCE, fell from a police boat and drowned at Devonport Docks

1864 PC DANIEL LANGFORD, died from injuries he received when assaulted on duty in 1862

1864 PC GEORGE EDWARD SAUNDERS, drowned at night in the London Dock while on duty.

1866 PC WILLIAM FITZGERALD, violently assaulted by a drunken prisoner in Drury Lane

1866 PC THOMAS LEY BAKER, violently assaulted when apprehending two burglars in 1863

1866 SGT HENRY COLLINS, apparently thrown from his horse while on duty at West Drayton

1867 PC DENNIS POTTER CLARKE, assaulted in the execution of his duty in 1864

1868 INSP DANIEL BRADSTOCK, stabbed by an insane prisoner at King Street Police Station

1868 PC JOSEPH EITE, died from injuries received by being kicked by a drunken man.

1870 PC CHARLES COX, accidentally drowned when he fell from the river bank near Kew Bridge while on night duty

1870 PC JAMES NICE, died from the effects of injuries received when he was kicked on duty in 1869

1870 SGT GEORGE ROBINS, killed by a kick from his horse while practising mounted drill

1870 PC GEORGE FREDERICK WARING, died from injuries received when badly kicked by a drunken prisoner in Shoreditch

1872 PC JAMES BOWLER, found drowned on duty, in suspicious circumstances, in the Limehouse Cut Canal

1872 PC MOSES PARROTT, dropped down dead while on duty in Parliament Street from the effects of previous injuries and assaults

1873 PC ALFRED BENNETT, died following injuries received when assaulted during an arrest

1875 PC SAMUEL BELL, died from injuries received on duty when he was struck on the head by a gate

1877 PC THOMAS GROOMES, found drowned on duty

1878 PC RICHARD COOK, died from multiple injuries received from his horse falling on him.

1879 PC WILLIAM STEVENS NAZER, drowned while on duty at Chatham Dockyard

1879 PC JAMES COLLIS, died from multiple injuries when he was run over by a train while on duty at New Barnet Station

1879 PC WILLIAM TWINN, died from injuries received when knocked down by a runaway horse

1881 **PC FREDERICK ATKINS**, shot three times and fatally wounded when he disturbed an unknown burglar at Kingston Hill

1881 SGT WILLIAM BACON, accidentally drowned while in the execution of his duty

1882 PC WILLIAM GODDARD, accidentally drowned when he fell into a dock during stormy weather while on duty at Lambeth

1882 PC HENRY FITNUM, drowned while on duty

1882 INSP JOSEPH HUGHES, thrown from his horse and broke his neck while returning from Sunbury Petty Sessions

1882 **PC GEORGE COLE**, shot in the head attempting to arrest a burglar at Dalston

1883 PC WILLIAM SILVEY, died through falling from a wagon while in the performance of police duty

1884 INSP WILLIAM ROBSON, accidentally drowned when his police boat was hit by a steam tug while visiting river patrols near Charlton

1885 PC ALBERT THOMPSON, run over when he attempted to stop a horse and cart for furious driving while on point duty in Piccadilly

1885 DC RICHARD BARBER, fell through a glass skylight while chasing a burglar across a goods depot roof in Whitechapel

1886 PC HAROLD RICHARDSON, accidentally drowned on duty when he fell in the canal near Enfield Lock in stormy weather

1887 PC ROBERT MCGAW, died from a fractured skull after being kicked by his police horse in Fulham stables

1887 PS DAVID GROOMBRIDGE, died from injuries received when beaten and kicked by two men during an arrest at King's Cross in 1886

1888 PC MICHAEL LEWIS, died of a ruptured heart after a violent struggle arresting a suspected thief at Chelsea

1888 PC ALFRED ELLIS, accidentally drowned on duty when he fell in the river off steps near Barnes Bridge

1888 PC THOMAS DEAN, drowned in the Surrey Canal while patrolling his beat on a foggy night

1890 PC WILLIAM PASKER, drowned attempting to rescue a man in heavy seas at Margate off duty.

1891 PC GEORGE COLE, died when he was run over and fatally injured trying to stop a pair of runaway horses and van on Brixton Hill

1892 PC ARTHUR MAY, died from effects of injuries received when he fell into a canal while on duty

1892 PC HENRY GRAHAM, died as a result of injuries sustained in an accident while on mounted duty at the Lord Mayor's Show

1892 PC JOSEPH DANIELS, choked to death when he swallowed his false teeth while assisting in the arrest of a prisoner at Bow Street

1892 DS JOSEPH JOYCE, shot twice and fatally wounded when arresting a burglar at Charing Cross Road

1892 SGT DAVID GARNER, collapsed and died from heart disease and over exertion in securing a prisoner

1893 INSP GEORGE DIXON, found drowned on duty in suspicious circumstances at Hampton Court

1893 PC ROBERT WRIGHT, killed while searching for persons believed trapped in a burning house at Croydon

1895 PC CHARLES WALPOLE, crushed while on patrol by the accidental fall of a stack of timber in a wood yard at Dulwich

1896 PC EDWIN STONE, collapsed and died from heart disease while assisting in a violent arrest

1897 DC WILLIAM JAMES KEMP, died from internal injury aggravated through having strained himself while chasing a prisoner

1898 PC JAMES BALDWIN, fatally stabbed when attempting to arrest a man for causing a disturbance in the street at Hoxton

1900 PC GEORGE STEPHEN FUNNELL, died from injuries received rescuing three women from a fire in a public house at Hackney

1900 PC WILLIAM GOULDER, drowned when he fell in the Thames at Barnes while on patrol during a foggy night

1900 PC ERNEST THOMPSON, stabbed in the neck by a man whom he had moved on after a street disturbance in Whitechapel

1900 PC FREDERICK KIDD, drowned in Shadwell Dock while on night duty.

1901 PC JAMES NEWBOLD, drowned when he fell overboard from a patrolling police steam launch

1901 PS NEIL MACDOUGALL, accidentally shot in the neck at annual police revolver practice at Eltham

1902 PC ARTHUR HEALEY, fell through a glass roof while checking insecure premises at Kensington

1904 PC LEONARD RUSSELL, collapsed and died while in the act of arresting a man for drunkenness at Tottenham

1904 PC JAMES MACEY, collapsed and died following the arrest of a drunken woman at Kennington

1905 PS THOMAS WILLIAM PERRY, collapsed and died at the station after arresting two men for drunkenness at Walworth

1905 PC WILLIAM CROFT, died in consequence of injuries received when he fell into a pit while chasing burglars at Chiswick

1908 PC JOSEPH WILLIAMSON, died from injuries received when kicked in the head arresting a violent drunk in 1907

1909 PC WILLIAM FREDERICK TYLER KPM, shot in the head by armed robber Paul Hefeld whom he was pursuing in the **Tottenham Outrage**

1911 PC FREDERICK WILLIAM FREE, drowned while operating a security boom at the Royal Gunpowder Factory, Waltham Abbey

1912 INSP ALFRED DEEKS, collapsed and died after dispersing youths causing a nuisance outside a church while off duty at West Ealing

1912 PS WALTER JAMES HEATH, died after being accidentally shot while unloading a revolver used on night duty at Greenwich

1913 PS GEORGE ERNEST SPOONER, drowned when his police motor patrol boat was hit by a barge at Southwark Bridge

1914 SC JAMES JOHN CHRISTOPHER POPPS, collapsed and died after assisting officers in the arrest of a violent prisoner while off duty

1914 SC JOHN QUINNELL, drowned when on duty at Winchmore Hill pumping station

1915 PC WILLIAM WILLIAMSON, knocked down by motor bus while on duty observing searchlights.

1915 DC ALFRED YOUNG KPM, shot dead when attempting to execute an arrest warrant for fraud at Hampstead

1915 SC ALEXANDER ADDISON MARNIE, slipped between a wharf and a vessel fracturing his skull at Southwark

1916 PC FRANK RICKETTS, drowned when going to the assistance of a drowning boy at Teignmouth while off duty

1916 SC WILLIAM ALFRED ELLIS, drowned when he fell from a footbridge into the Regents Canal lock while on patrol on a stormy night

1916 INSP DANIEL HUBBARD, killed in a road accident when he was run over by an omnibus at Putney

1917 **PC EDWARD GEORGE BROWN GREENOFF KPM**, killed in an explosion while evacuating a burning munitions factory at Silvertown

1917 PS LAWRENCE QUIBELL, killed during fire engine practice at Rosyth dockyard

1917 PC MICHAEL DONOVAN, drowned while on patrol during a stormy night at Chatham Dockyard

1918 PC GEORGE HENRY RICHARD JUDGE, fatally injured while on night duty at Cricklewood by a motor car which failed to stop

1918 PC JAMES HARDY KPM, killed in cycling accident on eve of investiture for his KPM for bravery.

1918 PC HERBERT BERRY, died from injuries sustained while making an arrest in Euston Road

1919 PC FREDERICK WILLIAM LAMBERT, killed when he was run over attempting to stop a runaway horse and cart at Stamford Hill

1919 SPS THOMAS GREEN, struck on the head and killed by a mob attempting to free prisoners in the **Epsom police station siege**

1919 PC FRANK BRYANT KPM, died from injuries received on duty after rescuing a dangerous lunatic from drowning in 1918

1919 CI FREDERICK JAMES RIVETT, killed when he fell from his horse and fractured his skull while on duty at Westminster

1919 PC THOMAS ELDRED BRIGGS ROWLAND, died from a fractured skull after being assaulted while attempting an arrest at Walworth

1920 PS ALFRED JAMES TYLER, knocked down by a motor van while on patrol in Hampstead

1920 PC JAMES KELLY, shot three times and killed while pursuing a burglar he had disturbed at Acton.

1921 PC WILLIAM GEORGE HALLETT, killed on patrol in Drury Lane by a car driven by a drunken driver

1924 PC EDWARD LOCK, knocked down by a motor car after stopping a cyclist at Kingston Hill

1929 INSP ARTHUR VISTOR TULLETT, killed when a motorcycle driven by a colleague collided with a lorry

1934 PS HAROLD GLASBY, drowned while saving the lives of his wife and sons after their boat capsized

1936 PC JOSEPH ALFRED ALLAWAY, knocked down and killed by a car while on duty at Harlington

1939 PC GEORGE RODNEY SOUTHWORTH, fell attempting to put out a light in the blackout in Harley Street.

1939 WRC JACK MORGAN, knocked down crossing tramlines to deal with an accident on Victoria Embankment

1940 WRC ERNEST TAYLOR, fell from a wall while extinguishing a light during the blackout at Chelsea

1940 PC HENRY THOMAS BROOKS, accidentally shot with a police revolver at Chelsea Police Station

1941 SC ARTHUR CECIL GUEST, killed accidentally by an instructor during a firearms training class

1942 SGT EDWIN TOWERS, died after being concerned in an accident while travelling on the prison van

1944 PC WALTER CHARLES TRALAU, fatally injured in an accident while on duty on J Division

1944 PC HENRY CHARLES ERNEST HOWELL, struck by army truck while riding a pedal cycle on duty

1947 SDI OSCAR THOMPSON, killed in a car accident with Allied Control Commission for Germany

1948 PC ARTHUR EDWARD QUEMBY, killed when his police motorcycle skidded on an icy road

1948 PC PATRICK GEORGE FITZGERALD, died as the result of an accident while on motorcycle patrol

1949 PC HARRY HARDING, died from injuries received in road accident while on traffic patrol

1950 PC GEORGE RONALD COOPER, killed in collision with a lorry while on motorcycle traffic patrol

1950 PC ROBERT GILCHRIST MARTIN, skidded on a wet road while on motorcycle patrol at Hampton

1950 PC SAMUEL LOCK, accidentally shot while cleaning a police pistol at Wood Green Police Station

1954 PC DAVID BARRETT, collided with a lorry at Hunton Bridge while on an advanced motorcycle course

1956 PS GEORGE GOGGINS, collided with a lorry while undergoing car driver training near Dunstable

1956 PC MAURICE EDEN GM, died from a gunshot wound while serving with the British Police Unit in Cyprus just before the award of his George Medal was announced.

1958 PC EDGAR GERALD ALLEN, crashed on police motorcycle while pursuing a speeding car in Chiswick

1960 PC RONALD ALAN ADDISON, died from a heart attack suffered chasing two youths in Pentonville Road

1960 PC TERENCE DANIEL FURNELL, observer in patrol car which crashed while on its way to an emergency

1962 PC RODERICK MACKAY MUNRO, observer in patrol car which crashed into a tree in Catford

1964 DC JOHN BELL MAUGHAN, killed when a car collided with a police car in which he was the observer in Thornton Heath

1964 PC DAVID ALYN JONES, killed in an accident while under instruction on a lightweight motorcycle course

1964 PC GEORGE ERNEST WHITE, patrol car observer killed in a crash escorting heart technicians urgently to hospital

1965 PC DENNIS EDWARD COWELL, drowned after a police launch capsized towing a disabled Customs vessel

1966 PC SIDNEY SEAGER, a traffic patrol motorcyclist killed when an articulated lorry overturned and fell on him

1967 PC JAMES BRIAN MAY, killed when he was run down by a lorry while directing traffic at a road junction

1967 PS DAVID EDWARD WESTNEY, instructor killed when two training machines collided at Hendon driving school

1967 PC PAUL ROBERT CHERRY, radio operator in patrol car which crashed answering an emergency call in Bromley

1969 PC MICHAEL JOHN DAVIES, stabbed off duty after identifying himself to warn a man who had accosted him

1969 PC RONALD REGINALD PELL, killed in a road accident while on duty as an observer in a police car

1971 PC MICHAEL EATON DE LISLE INCE, killed in a collision between two police cars answering an emergency call

1971 TDC ALAN CHOULES, drowned off duty after saving the life of a boy after a boat capsized in the Thames at Staines

1971 PC ROBERT BEAZER, killed when his panda car crashed on an emergency call to a 4 year old savaged by a dog

1972 PC GEORGE WILLIAM HIGGS, and PC WILLIAM RANDALL killed in a traffic car crash on an urgent hospital escort.

1972 PC DOUGLAS JOHN PRICE, killed by motor cycle landing on him during training for a police motorcycle display

1973 PS STEWART WILL, drowned on holiday in Scotland. attempting to rescue a girl in difficulties in rough seas.

1974 TDC VERNON RUPERT WEATHERSTON, died when he was involved in a collision while driving a CID car

1977 PC DEREK JAMES BOTTOMLEY, passenger in a police car on an advanced driving course in collision with a lorry

1977 PC ALAN MICHAEL BAXTER, killed when his police car crashed while chasing a suspect car at Croydon

1977 PC RICHARD KENRICK HAMILTON, crashed in his panda car while answering an emergency call in Balham

1978 PC PATRICK ALAN CROAKE, traffic motorcyclist killed after colliding with an elderly pedestrian in the Mall

1979 PC KEVIN KELLIHER, crew member in a police van which crashed while in pursuit of a stolen car in Stepney

1981 PC DAVID IAN LUKE, collapsed at swimming pool while on duty training on fourth day of service

1981 PC DANIEL CLARKE, traffic motorcyclist killed at Holloway while en route to escort an abnormal load

1982 PC ROBERT MERCER, radio operator in police car which crashed while pursuing a stolen car at Northolt

1983 PC STEPHEN WALKER, killed by a car while chasing two suspected car thieves across a road at Ashford

1983 PC MARK SIMPKINS, area car observer killed in a crash while answering a call to a bank alarm in Chingford

1983 PC GORDON CORNISH, killed on advanced motorcycle training after collision with a lorry in Cambridgeshire

1983 PC FRANK BELLENIE, patrolling Home Beat officer killed by a car which mounted the pavement in Hillingdon

1984 PC GRANT CLIFFORD SUNNUCKS, area car driver killed in a crash pursuing a stolen car in North London

1986 PC MARTIN BELL, killed when his unmarked car was hit by a drunk driver pursued by police in West Putney

1989 PC MARK PEERS, drowned while searching for a submerged car during Underwater Search Unit training

1993 PC MICHAEL PERRY, whose panda car crashed answering an emergency call to a man suspected of murder

1993 PC NOEL CHARLES FRICK, killed when his surveillance duty police motorcycle crashed at Shepherds Bush

1993 DC THOMAS NEED, killed when his surveillance duty motorcycle was in collision with a car in Surrey

1994 PC MICHAEL TRING, killed in accident driving an area car on an emergency call for assistance to colleagues

1994 PC MATTHEW JAMES PARSONSON, passenger in police vehicle which crashed on a call for urgent assistance

1994 WPC GAIL DOREEN PIRNIE, collapsed and died from a heart attack while baton training at the Peel Centre

1996 PC STEPHEN ROBERT WILLIAMS, DPG motorcyclist killed in a crash on security patrol in North London

1998 DC IAN HERBERT, killed in a road accident while engaged on a training exercise in Kent

ROLL OF HONOUR

1924 PC ARTHUR HOLDAWAY, knocked down by a tram while on traffic duty at Camberwell, and died after retiring from the Service because of his injuries.

1927 SGT LEONARD CARTER, fell into uncovered pit when searching a basement near Pall Mall.

1927 PC PERCY EDWIN COOK, overcome by fumes while attempting to rescue workmen from a long disused inspecting chamber in Notting Hill.

1928 PC RAYMOND MITCHELL, struck by motorcycle combination when on traffic duty at Wallington.

1929 PC DAVID FORD, fell through glass roof pursuing suspects in Westminster Bridge Road.

1929 PC JOHN ARTHUR SELF, violently struck to the ground by man he was questioning in Golders Green.

1930 PC ARTHUR LAWES, deliberately struck by hit and run driver in unlighted stolen car in Tooting.

1931 PC WILLIAM GEORGE WARE, drowned when a tug struck a police motor boat at Chiswick.

1931 PC HARRY CAUTHERLEY, PC GEORGE WILLIAM ALLEN killed in accident in Beckenham while pursuing a car on motorcycle combination.

1933 PC FREDERICK PERCY, crushed by a van during a collision when he was on traffic duty in Chelsea.

1934 PC JAMES ROBERT CARTER, knocked down by a car when on traffic duty in Hampstead.

1935 **PC JAMES WARRENDER THOMSON KPM**, killed by cement lorry from whose uncontrolled path down Barnet Hill he was clearing pedestrians.

1935 PC HENRY ARTHUR GROVES, thrown by his horse as he was forcing it to avoid bolting into Trafalgar Square.

1937 PC BERNARD TUTT, crushed as he attempted to push children clear of the path of a motor vehicle which had been involved in a collision in Marylebone.

1937 SPS FREDERICK PARNCUTT, PC ALBERT TAYLOR drowned on duty near West India Dock when a tug was in collision with a police patrol boat.

1938 PC GEORGE SHEPHERD, thrown from running board of a car whose driver he was seeking to stop when the suspect collided with a bus in Hampstead.

1940 WRC JACK WILLIAM AVERY, stabbed by a man sketching gun emplacements in Hyde Park.

1943 PC HARRY PICKETT, run down by a lorry while standing in the roadway questioning another lorry driver in Banstead.

1947 PC LESLIE EDWIN THOMPSON, PC GILBERT EDWARD PERKINS, killed when their patrol car collided with a tree while responding to an urgent call to a housebreaking in Woodford.

1948 **PC NATHANAEL EDGAR**, shot while on plain clothes patrol when questioning suspect burglar in Southgate.

1952 **PC SIDNEY GEORGE MILES KPFSM**, shot while attempting the arrest of two suspects on a warehouse roof in Croydon.

1954 PC PERCY JAMES CLAXTON, killed by a gas explosion when called to investigate a suspected suicide in Hampstead.

1956 PC REGINALD WILLIAM TIPPLE, shot by an unknown assailant while serving with the British Police Unit in Cyprus.

1956 PC LEONARD ALFRED DEMMON QPM, A Division, shot by terrorists while serving with the British Police Unit in Cyprus.

1957 SUPT CORNELIUS CARSON, overcome by fumes rescuing a child from married quarters during a fire at Hackney Police Station.

1958 PC RAYMOND HENRY SUMMERS, stabbed while breaking up a gang fight in Seven Sisters Road, Holloway.

1959 **DETECTIVE SGT RAYMOND WILLIAM PURDY** shot by a prisoner escaping arrest in South Kensington.

1960 PC EDWARD ROY DORNEY, struck by a train when his dog picked up the scent of a burglar along a railway line in Peckham.

1960 PC LESLIE EDWIN VINCENT MEEHAN, struck by motor car after he was thrown off a car which had driven off after he had been questioning the driver about stolen property in Woolwich.

1961 SPS FREDERICK GEORGE HUTCHINS QPM, INSPECTOR PHILIP PAWSEY QPM, shot by a man escaping from questioning in West Ham Police Station

1966 DS CHRISTOPHER TIPPETT HEAD, PC GEOFFREY FOX, DC STANLEY BERTRAM WOMBWELL members of crew of F11 Q car in **Shepherd's Bush Murders**

1967 PC DESMOND MORGAN ACREMAN, struck by a passing car while trying to arrest two suspects.

1971 PC DOUGLAS FREDERICK BECKERSON, fell through glass roof at Baker Street Station, pursuing drunken youth who was running amok and smashing glass with an iron bar.

1973 PC MICHAEL ANTHONY WHITING QPM, killed after clinging to car which had driven off after he had stopped and questioned the driver in Charing Cross Road.

1975 PC STEPHEN ANDREW TIBBLE QPM, shot while off duty pursuing a suspected terrorist

1975 CAPTAIN ROGER PHILIP GOAD GC BEM, Explosives Officer, killed dealing with IRA bomb in Kensington

1980 PC FRANCIS JOSEPH O'NEILL QGM, stabbed by suspect attempting to obtain drugs from a chemist's shop in Lambeth.

1981 KENNETH ROBERT HOWORTH GM, Explosives Officer, killed while dealing with an IRA bomb in Oxford Street.

1983 INSPECTOR STEPHEN JOHN DODD, PS NOEL JOSEPH LANE, WPC JANE PHILIPPA ARBUTHNOT, killed by IRA bomb explosion at Hans Crescent, Kensington.

1984 PC STEPHEN JONES, run down attempting to stop drunken drivers racing on Seven Sisters Road, Holloway.

1984 **WPC YVONNE JOYCE FLETCHER**, murdered by gunfire from the Libyan People's Bureau, St James's Square.

1985 **PC KEITH HENRY BLAKELOCK** QGM, murdered during serious public disorder at **Broadwater Farm**.

1985 **DC JOHN WILLIAM FORDHAM**, stabbed while keeping surveillance on a suspected bullion receiver at West Kingsdown, Kent.

1987 PC RONAN KONRAD AIDAN MCCLOSKEY, killed while clinging to a car which drove off after he attempted to administer a breath test to the driver in Kilburn.

1989 PC PAUL MAURICE BREEN died in accident while on duty in a military ambulance on an emergency call.

1990 PC ASHLEY DAY, died in accident while on duty as radio operator in an Area Patrol car responding to an emergency call on Ealing Division.

1990 PC LAURENCE PETER BROWN, killed by suspect with sawn-off shotgun in Hackney.

1991 PC ROBERT CHENERY GLADWELL, killed by blow to the head while making an arrest on Harrow Road Division.

1991 SGT ALAN DEREK KING, stabbed by a suspect he stopped in Chingford.

1991 DC JAMES MORRISON QGM stabbed to death after chasing a suspect on Charing Cross Division while off duty.

1993 **PC PATRICK DUNNE**, shot when responding to a report of gunfire in Clapham.

1994 SGT DEREK ROBERTSON QGM, stabbed when intercepting three armed robbers leaving a Post Office at New Addington.

1995 PC PHILLIP WALTERS, shot when dealing with three men for causing a disturbance in Ilford.

1997 CONSTABLE NINA MCKAY, stabbed during the course of attempting to detain a man known to be violent towards police at a house in Forest Gate.

APPENDIX **FIVE**: ACRONYMS AND ABBREVIATIONS

(**Bold type** definitions indicate an entry in the main text)

ABACUS	Activity Based Accounting for Cost Units Servicewide
AC	Assistant Commissioner
ACIS	Article Classification Identification System
ACPO	Association of Chief Police Officers
ACSO	Assistant Commissioner, Special Operations
ACTO	Assistant Commissioner, Territorial Operations
AFO	Authorised Firearms Officer
AMIP	Area Major Investigations Pool
ARO	Aliens Registration Office
ARV	Armed Response Vehicle
CAD	Computer Aided Despatch
CIB	Complaints Investigation Bureau
CID	Criminal Investigation Department
CI	Chief Inspector
CJPU	Criminal Justice Protection Unit
CLO	Community Liaison Officer
CO	Commissioner's Office
CPT	Child Protection Team
CRIS	Crime Report Information System
CRO	Criminal Records Office
DAC	Deputy Assistant Commissioner
DACSO	Deputy Assistant Commissioner, Specialist Operations
DACTO	Deputy Assistant Commissioner, Territorial Operations
DC	Detective Constable

DCI	Detective Chief Inspector
DDI	Divisional Detective Inspector
DI	Detective Inspector
DPA	Directorate of Public Affairs and Internal Communications
DPG	Diplomatic Protection Group
DPP	Director of Public Prosecutions
DS	Detective Sergeant
DVU	Domestic Violence Unit
HBO	Home Beat Officer
HCR	Habitual Criminals Register
HOLMES	Home Office Large Major Enquiry System
IPA	International Police Association
IRV	Immediate Response Vehicle
JADPU	Joint Automatic Data Processing Unit
KPM	King's Police Medal
KPFSM	King's Police and Fire Services Medal
MACC	Mutual Aid Coordinating Centre
MEPO	Metropolitan Police Files held in PRO
METOPS	Computer control system in Special Operations Room
MP	Metropolitan Police
MPD	Metropolitan Police District
MPS	Metropolitan Police Service
NRC	National Reporting Centre
NUPPO	National Union of Police and Prison Officers
NSY	New Scotland Yard

OCG	Organised Crime Group		SOCO	Scenes of Crime Officer
OCU	Operational Command Unit		SPG	Special Patrol Group
OHA	Occupational Health Assistant		SPS	Station Police Sergeant
OSPRE	Objective Structured Performance Related Examinations		SRO	Station Reception Officer
OTIS	Operational Technology Information Service		TDC	Temporary Detective Constable
OVRO	Overseas Visitors Registration Office		TFU	Tactical Firearms Unit
PACE	Police and Criminal Evidence Act		TSG	Territorial Support Group
PBO	Permanent Beat Officer		VPU	Vulnerable Persons Unit
PCO	Public Carriage Office		WAS	Women Auxiliary Service
PNC	Police National Computer		WPC	Woman Police Constable
PRO	Public Record Office		WPO	Woman Police Officer
PS	Police Sergeant		WPS	Women Police Service or Woman Police Sergeant
PSU	Police Support Unit		WPV	Women Police Volunteers
PTI	Physical Training Instructor		WRC	War Reserve Constable
QPM	Queen's Police Medal		YACS	Youth and Community Section
SC	Special Constable			

APPENDIX SIX: A SELECTION OF SLANG

'AUXILIARY' Or 'Police auxiliary'. Late Victorian police jargon alternative to 'copper's nark' for informant.

'BANDIT TERRITORY' Jocular Met slang for home counties areas on the fringes of MPD, policed by county police forces.

'BARROW' Police slang for a hand ambulance.

'BATPHONES' Police slang for personal radio, by analogy with the telephone via which cartoon-book Gotham City's Police summon Batman and Robin to descend the Batpole, enter the Batmobile, and rush away to fight crime.

'BERTIE, DOING A' Police and underworld slang for turning supergrass. After Bertie Smalls, the bank robber who was the first to shop all his associates in past crimes in return for an amnesty from conviction for them (a degree of immunity not granted to his imitators) and security with a new identity for himself and his family after convictions had been achieved.

'BLACK RAT' Nickname for traffic patrol officer.

'BLUES AND TWOS' In-service jargon for operating the flashing blue lights and two-tone horn or siren on a patrol car.

'BOBETTES' Nickname for Metropolitan Women Police Officers adopted by US and Canadian press in 1962 during the X Division International Police Association official tour of the USA and Canada.

'BREATHING ACT' Identified by Lilian Wyles as Section 54 of the Metropolitan Police Act, 1839, empowering officers to arrest people for 'Using threatening, abusive or insulting words or behaviour with intent to provoke a breach of the peace or whereby a breach of the peace is likely to be occasioned.'

The vagueness of this offence allowed officers to act decisively when trouble threatened, but an argument or dispute had not yet risen to the point of actual violence. The fact of being arrested for a chargeable offence when only engaged in a shouting match tended to take the wind out of the sails of the potential offender and rapidly defused the situation. Thus it gave policemen valuable 'space to breathe', and was nicknamed 'the Breathing Act'. Between the 1920s and the 1960s, the term also came to be applied to the 'Sus Laws', on the jocular ground that people could be 'arrested for breathing'. The jocularity in itself hints at the possibility of abuse which led to the anxieties causing those laws against 'suspicious loitering' to be repealed.

'DABS' Self-explanatory police and underworld slang for fingerprints.

'DARBIES' OR 'DERBIES' Police and underworld slang for handcuffs. Probably obsolete today, though slang has a deceptive habit of lurking out of sight and suddenly coming back into current usage. A very old term for fetters and manacles, in the 17th century strongly associated with 'Derby bands' by which creditors secured debtors. It has been speculated that the term derived from the name of some noted usurer.

'DOING ONE'S LEGS' Police slang for inflicting a severe blow to a colleague's career prospects.

'DRINK' Police and underworld slang for a bribe offered to a police officer. Evidently related to the habit of many 19th-century publicans, reported in various memoirs, of having a pint of beer standing ready for the constable on beat duty, despite regulations strictly prohibiting patrolling policemen from drinking on duty. Some publicans followed this practice for the law-abiding reason that the presence of a uniformed officer ensured trouble-free closure of the premises for the night.

'FINGER A COLLAR' Police slang for 'make an arrest'. From the extremely firm grip inside the back of a shirt collar which provides the safest initial grip on a retreating offender.

'GENTSTABLE' 1930s Metropolitan Police slang for PC recruited from public school to attend Hendon Police College.

'GESTAPO' Drugs Squad slang, c.1970, for traffic police. Also, general, 'drummed out of the Gestapo for cruelty', as description of a senior officer perceived as unduly authoritarian.

'GN51' A 'tear-up', or rambling letter without any apparent cohesive purpose (categorized GN51 in the General Registry).

'GRASS' Underworld slang for an informant, sometimes used by police, and adopted in the compound 'supergrass'. Transitive verbal form is 'to grass up'.

Two derivations are claimed: from rhyming slang 'grasshopper; copper', and from the Country and Western song 'Whispering Grass'. The former is probably correct, the latter being wrongly presumed when prisoners in the dock took to humming or singing the tune at supergrasses giving evidence against them. There is the remote possibility of a connection with the 19th century Salopian slang 'Grasshoppers' for Shropshire's first constabulary, whose uniforms were rifle green.

'GUNSHIPS' Metropolitan Police slang for Flying Squad cars when firearms are carried, or Armed Response Vehicles.

'HEAVY MOB, THE' Police and underworld nickname for the Flying Squad, in which the squad took some pride.

'HOOKS' Obsolete slang (c.1870–1935) for pickpockets.

'HORTY' Vocalization of Home Office Road Traffic form no. HO/RT. See 'Producer'.

'JOB, THE' Standard police term for the police force as an institution and employer, and the occupation and duties incurred by being a policeman. Usage in an episode of American television series NYPD Blue suggests that the term has now crossed the Atlantic.

'JOCKEYS' Slang term for police, c.1930–50. Recalled by Detective Superintendent John Gosling (retired 1956). The authors have been able to discover no other source for this term and can offer no explanation of its origin beyond the speculation that it was an extremely hostile derivation from Victorian underworld slang 'jocker' or 'jockey': a thief.

'JUMP-UPS' Police slang for theft from parked lorries, wherein one or more thieves would 'jump up' on the tailboard and throw down goods to confederates. Unhappily largely superseded by armed or violent hijacking today.

'KOJAKS' Blue magnetic lamps which can be placed temporarily on the roofs of unmarked cars. So named because they first came to British notice in the American television series.

'MANOR' Police slang for an officer's territorial area of responsibility: most frequently section or Division.

'MORNING PRAYERS' Police slang for a management team's daily briefing on the work to be done.

'NARK' Or 'copper's nark'; old-fashioned thieves' cant for a police informant, sometimes used by police. Today would more usually be 'snout' in police idiom, and 'grass' in the underworld. See also 'auxiliary', supergrass.

'NEW TOY' A newly introduced piece of equipment, but allegedly extended to refer to a new recruit .

'NICK' (1) Noun. Police slang for police station. (2) Verb. Police and underworld slang for arrest.

'NONDY' Police vernacular abbreviation for 'nondescript vehicle': a van or covered truck apparently parked for business purposes from which surveillance may be maintained.

'NOSE' Criminal slang for an informant, current 1900 to 1930s. Deriving from Victorian thieves' cant, 'nose': (noun) a spy; and (verb) to keep watch on or spy out. Not used by police. Superseded by **'snout'**.

'OBBO VANS' Police slang for unmarked vans from which **observation** or **surveillance** can be mounted. They may be equipped with binoculars. Although the sides may be windowless to conceal the occupants, care has to be taken that visibility from the van suffices to allow the observing officers to get a clear and convincing view of what they are looking at.

'OGPU SQUAD' Nickname for a small group of Central CID officers in the 1930s commanded by Inspector F. D. 'Nutty' Sharpe, which was employed for secret enquiries on such offences as forgery, illegal immigration, receiving, coining and race-track protection racketeering. Named after the notorious Soviet Secret Police of the time.

'OLD BILL' Slang term for the police which seems relatively devoid of hostile or patronizing overtones, or thieves' cant obfuscation. Often shortened to 'Bill'. No fewer than 13 derivations have been proposed. 1. 'Old Bill' was King William IV, whose constables the early police were. (This is often put in the erroneous form that he was on the throne when the police were founded. Actually he did not succeed George IV until 1830.) 2.. *The Custom of the Country*, a play of 1619 by John Fletcher has constables of the watch refer to themselves as 'us peacemakers and all our bill of authority'. 3. Constables of the watch were sometimes nicknamed for the bills, or billhooks they carried as weapons. 4. Kaiser Wilhelm I of Prussia visited England around the time in 1864 when the police uniform changed from top hat and swallowtail coat to helmet and tunic. Such 'Prussian militarism' may have led to their being nicknamed after the first (and today less remembered) 'Kaiser Bill'. 5. The 'old bill' was, in Victorian times, a bill presumed to be presented by the police for a bribe to persuade them to turn a blind eye to some nefarious activity. 6. New laws for the police to enforce all come from Bills passed through Parliament. 7. 'Old Bill' might refer to Bill Bailey of the music-hall song ('Won't you come home . . . ?') with a pun on the Central Criminal Court at Old Bailey. 8. In the 1860s there was a Sgt Bill Smith in Limehouse. He was a popular character, and people used to ask after 'Old Bill'. 9. Many police officers wore authoritarian-looking 'Old Bill' moustaches like that adorning Bruce Bairnsfather's famous WWI cartoon character, the wily old soldier in the trenches. 10. The original vehicles used by the **Flying Squad** were all registered BYL, so the Squad became known as 'Old Bill'. 11. The London County Council at one time registered all police, fire and ambulance vehicles BYL, leading villains to spot unmarked police cars and say, "There's old Bill". 12. According to old Etonian illegal gaming club organizer and *roman policier* author the late Robin Cook ('Derek Raymond'), 'old bill' is a racing term for an outsider or unknown quantity; hence a dodgy figure and, from the illegal gambler's point of view, a policeman. 13. In 1917 the government adopted Bairnsfather's cartoon character in posters and advertisements putting over important wartime messages under the heading 'Old Bill says...' For this campaign, the character was dressed in **special constable**'s uniform, thus leading to his being popularly perceived as the representative figure of a policeman. Despite all these suggestions, the earliest documented usage traced by the **Historical Museum** is 1970, and Partridge's *Dictionary of Slang*, without giving citations, dates it from the 1950s or 'perhaps earlier'. So the term may well be post-WWII, and have been given wide currency by television.

'PATCH' Police slang for an officer's territorial or specialized professional area of responsibility.

'PEEL'S RAW LOBSTERS' Derogatory reference to police by reference to military red uniforms, known as 'lobsters', whereas blue police uniforms suggested uncooked lobsters.

'PERCHER' CID slang for an easy arrest where suspect and evidence are immediately forthcoming (e.g. a shop-lifter taken red-handed).

'PIPED OFF' Victorian police and criminal slang for 'under surveillance'. Used by Inspector Druscovich (see under **Trial of the Detectives**) to warn criminal confederates he was suspected at Scotland Yard. From 'pipe': thieves' cant for a spy or watcher.

'PLOD' Nickname for police deriving from the very deliberate pace laid down by **Rowan** and **Mayne** for **beat patrols**, and the somewhat stately **demeanour** found valuable in avoiding provocation and preventing violent incidents on the streets.

'PLONK' Male police slang for Woman Police Officer. Despite some late 20th-century fear that the word might derive from the derogatory 'plonker' (a stupid person) or 'plonk' (cheap wine), the actual derivation was from the heavily mannered step of women wearing the long hobble skirts fashionable around the time when women patrols were introduced. Thus WPOs 'plonked' heel and toe down together, while PCs plodded along the beat. Surprisingly, given the overt hostility of many beat constables to their new female colleagues in 1917, there appears to have been no derogatory overtone whatsoever in the term.

'PRINCIPAL' Special Branch jargon for a VIP being given personal protection.

'PRODUCER' In-service slang for form HO/RT/1 forms (also 'Horty') requiring motorists to produce their driving documents at police stations within five days. The system requires much administrative effort and some inconvenience to motorists, few of whom carry their driving licences with them.

'PUP OF THE TRUNCHEON' Victorian police slang for a policeman's son who joined the police.

'PUPPY-WALKING' A term used for handlers training a young dog.

'RAMBLING LETTERS' Correspondence addressed to Scotland Yard which does not appear to make any particular point or request capable of being followed up. (See also **'Tear-ups'**.)

'SCROTE' Police slang for an undesirable young criminal, a worthless and nasty piece of work. Derives from 'scrotum'. According to author Andrew Brown, it was originally adopted as an ironic, lightly self-mocking 'tough guy' term by officers who learnt it from Joseph Wambaugh's American police novels.

'SHAKY JOB BLUES' Anxiety about potentially unconvincing evidence at court or for disciplinary enquiry.

'SKIPPER' Police slang for Sergeant.

'SMUDGES' Obsolete Obscene Publications Branch slang for crude old black-and-white pornographic photographs.

'SNATCHER' According to Sgt Harry Daley, slang term used between c.1920 and 1930 for officers who preferred to make arrests and bring charges for all minor infractions of the law before the use of cautions was made official policy by **Commissioners Byng** and **Trenchard**.

'SNIPS' Criminal slang for **CID** officers, recalled by Supt Walter Hambrook as used in the interwar period.

'SNOUT' Police slang for an **informant**. Probably jocular variant of **'nose'**.

'SOUP REPORT' In-Service slang for shorter legal aid reports submitted to the **Solicitor's Department** prior to the creation of the Crown Prosecution Service. Prosecuting officers were then afforded legal representation at higher courts if defendants were sent on to them for sentence after conviction by magistrates.

'STOOGE' A petty criminal who confesses falsely to a crime committed by a more powerful villain and takes the rap for him. One of the commonest forms of stooge was a man employed to be arrested in place of a street bookmaker.

'SWEDES' Term for potentially naive provincial police officers investigating complaints in London.

'SWEENEY, THE' Rhyming slang for the **Flying Squad** ('Sweeney Todd'). Made familiar to the public by Thames Television series of that name (1975–8).

'SWIFTING' Making an arrest quickly when it may not be clear that all elements of the offence could be proved.

'TEAPOT ONE' Nickname for the **Catering Department**'s emergency response vehicle. Now used in official signals, designating Teapot One, Two or Three as these welcome refreshment vans are deployed to officers on emergency or crowd control duties.

'TEAR-UPS' Long but valueless letters addressed to Scotland Yard, including crank mail and delusions. Several letters over the same signature will be received and acknowledged before it is decided that the correspondence is worthless.

'TOM' Police slang for a prostitute. Alleged by former DAC Ian Forbes (Met, 1938–72) to derive from continental 'cat-houses' or brothels. It has also been understood by some officers to imply that prostitutes prowl the streets at night like tom-cats.

'TOPSY' In-Service slang, 1985–95 for **Territorial Operations** Computer system.

'VERBALS, THE' Self-incriminating statement falsely alleged by an arresting or interrogating officer to have been made by the arrestee.

'WALLY' CID slang for uniformed officer, current c.1970.

'WENDY HOUSE' Nickname for the Duty Chief Inspector's office in the **Information Room** at New Scotland Yard.

'WHEELS COMING OFF' Police jargon for a **public order** situation getting out of hand. The most notable and tragic recent London occasion when 'the wheels came off' was the **Broadwater Farm Riot**.

'WOODENTOP' Early 1980s **CID** slang for a uniformed officer, adopted by scriptwriter Geoff McQueen for the television play from which the series *The Bill* was developed.

AUTHORS' ACKNOWLEDGEMENTS

When this work was mooted, the Policy Board appointed former Chief Superintendent Alan Moss to liaise with us and the publishers. His help has been invaluable. He read every single entry as it was written, correcting us when we had facts wrong, directing us to people and printed sources for further information. He has drafted suggested rewrites and entire entries where we were not understanding administrative structures and changes. He compiled more than half of the 'For Gallantry' Appendix. He liaised with Branches and Departments and was our defender and envoy when we inadvertently wrote things that offended people.

In the period running up to the submission of our manuscript, Robin Gillis, former Curator of the Metropolitan Police Historical Museum was temporarily seconded to work with us. He proved a powerhouse of instant information, or immediate connection to sources of information, as well as a fund of knowledge about the Service's history and photographs. He saved us from making many foolish errors and joined us in liaison with the publishers. As we found ourselves with less and less time to reach our deadlines, Robin more or less disregarded his official working hours and gave us the benefit of long stretches of unpaid overtime work. He and Alan Moss also worked twelve-hour days with us to complete proofing the text. If two more names could be added to the title page, they would be Alan's and Robin's.

Mr Bob Cox of the Directorate of Public Affairs was appointed to oversee and help our work. He has conferred with us regularly to discuss progress, given us encouragement, and kept us in touch with policies, plans and opinions we could otherwise only have guessed at. He, Alan and Robin have been our constant friendly way in to the distant parts of the Met.

Ken Stone, formerly Deputy Curator of the Historical museum, has provided excellent guidance on photographs and many general and specific points of Met history. Ken's overall contribution has been deeply appreciated by all of us working on this book. Paul Rason, Geoff Taylor and Charles Hasler have all offered a stream of corrections, advice and information which were invaluable as our research progressed.

Norman Fairfax, formerly of the Civil Staff and the author of more Met history deposited at the Historical Museum than anyone else, has read every piece hot off the press, and returned us full and valuable comments, often garnished with wonderful personal memories. The authors are profoundly grateful for Norman's time and input.

At the Historical Museum, Paul Dew and Ray Seal generously allowed us to plunder their quite magnificent collection of documents and photographs, while John Ross entrusted into our care a couple of valuable items from the Crime ('Black') Museum. Alan Oakley, Andrew Brown, Maggie Bird, Richard ('Nutty') Sharp, and Christine Thomas of Archives have all given us information whenever requested, and allowed us to use documents in their keeping, a massive quantity of which Julia Todd has painstakingly photocopied for us. Ellie Haynes, Kumari Dharmeratnam and the staff of the Metropolitan Police Library have gone far beyond the call of duty in letting us have a huge number of books out for an inordinate length of time, not to mention letting us into dusty cupboards to scrabble through musty Reports. Paul Savory of Marathon Music not only supplied the Apple Mac without which the work could not have been started, but replaced it when its main board failed during the summer of 1998.

Some books provide such a comprehensive study of the particular aspect of Scotland Yard they describe that some of our entries are largely updated and enhanced digests of individual authors' work. Notable are John Bunker's *From Rattle to Radio*, Geoffrey Budworth's *River Beat*, J. Peter Farmery's *Police Gallantry*, Robert Gould and Michael Waldren's *London's Armed Police*, Gerald Lambourne's *The Fingerprint Story*, Philip Paul's *Murder Under the Microscope*, Norman Fairfax's several unpublished manuscripts and former Detective Sergeant Dick Kirby's unpublished history of the Flying Squad. Sergeant Anthony Rae (Lancashire Constabulary) let us use unpublished material representing years of his work in listing all officers who died on duty nationwide: a project which is Grant Aided by, amongst others, the Police History Society, and for which sponsors are always welcome.

Stewart Evans, formerly an officer in the Suffolk County Constabulary, has lent illustrations from his large personal collection of police and crime memorabilia, and at his own expense has photographed pictures, objects and documentary material at our request.

And we also gratefully acknowledge the help of: Andy Aliffe, Melanie Anderson, Helen Barnard, John Beck, Shirley Becke, Paul Begg, Emma Bott, Terry Bown, Bernie Brown, Beverley Brown, Galla Cassettari, Ken Castle, Michelle Cefai, Andrew Cole, Melanie Constance, Jean Cooper, Undine Concannon, John Davison, Cynthia Dill, Charles Dodsworth, Tim Dolphin, Dave Douglas, Steve Earl, Eileen Eggington, Bryn Elliott, Pam Evans, Allen Evershed, Ian Fairley, Dick Fedorcio, Michael Fountain, Michael Ferguson, Chris Forester, Susan Gangoo, Maurice Garvie, Ian Gillis, Keith Gotch, Anne E. Graham, Roger Gregory, Tim Harvey, Neil Haynes, Chris Heron, Baroness Hilton, Denise Himsworth, Tony Hodges, Spike Hughes, Lord Imbert, Brian Jenkins, Peter Kennison, Dick Kirby, Joan Lock, Bernard Luckhurst, Ron McAdam, Karen McCall, Keith MacKenzie, Michael Mackey, Sir David McNee, Sir Robert Mark, Sir Peter Matthews, Brian Morris, Barry Moss, Sir Kenneth Newman, Debbie Packman and the staff of *The Job*, Sue and Andy Parlour, Margaret Pereira, James Perry, Barry Phillips, Tom Pine, Peter Prentice, Anthony C. Purbrick, Tim Richardson, Norwell Roberts, Hilary Roper, Donald Rumbelow, Dominique Sargent, Lee Shelden, Roger Smith, Harry Spain, Leslie Stowe, David Tilley, Mei Trow, Mike Waldren, Teresa Want, Nick Warren, Ian Watt, Mark Watts, Stephen Wicks, Mrs Mavis Widocks, Chris Williams, Deborah Woollon-Kemp, Canon Barry Wright.

BIBLIOGRAPHY

Adam, H.L., C.I.D.: *Behind the Scenes at Scotland Yard*, Sampson Low, London, 1931

Adamson, Iain, *The Great Detective: A Life of Deputy Commander Reginald Spooner*, Frederick Muller, London, 1966

Allason, Rupert, *The Branch: A History of the Metropolitan Police Special Branch 1883-1983*, Secker & Warburg, London, 1983

Anderson, Sir Robert, *On Criminals and Crime*, Nisbet, London, 1907

- *The Lighter Side of my Official Life*, Hodder & Stoughton, London, 1910

Arrow, Charles, *Rogues and Others*, Duckworth, London, 1926

Ascoli, David, *The Queen's Peace: The Origins and Development of the Metropolitan Police 1829-1979*, Hamish Hamilton, London, 1979.

Babington, Anthony, *A House in Bow Street: Crime and the Magistracy 1740-1881*, Macdonald, London, 1969

Barker, Malcolm J. with T.C. Sobey, *Living with the Queen: Behind the Scenes at Buckingham Palace*, Barricade Books, Fort Lee, 1991

Begg, Paul and Keith Skinner, *The Scotland Yard Files*, Headline, London, 1992

- Martin Fido and Keith Skinner, *The Jack the Ripper A to Z*, Headline, London, 1996

Best, William C.F., QPM, *'C' or St. James's: A History of Policing in the West End of London 1829-1984*, Privately published, Kingston-upon-Thames, 1985

Boyle, Andrew, *Trenchard*, Collins, London, 1962

Brett, Dennis T., *The Police of England and Wales: A Bibliography*, Police Staff College Publications, Bramshill, 1979

Bristow, Carol, *Central 822*, Bantam, London, 1998

Britton, Paul, *The Jigsaw Man*, Bantam, London, 1997

Brown, Andrew, *Watching the Detectives*, Hodder & Stoughton, London, 1988

Browne, Douglas G., *The Rise of Scotland Yard*, Harrap, London, 1956

- and E.V.Tullett, *Bernard Spilsbury: His Life and Cases*, Companion Book Club, London, 1952

Budworth, Geoffrey, *The River Beat*, Historical Publications Ltd, London, 1997

Bunker, John, *From Rattle to Radio*, K.A.F.Brewin Books, Studley, 1988

Burke, Marc E., *Coming Out of the Blue*, Cassell, London, 1990

Burt, Leonard, *Commander Burt of Scotland Yard, by Himself*, Pan, London, 1962

Campbell, Duncan, *The Underworld*, BBC Books, London, 1994

Cavanagh, Ex-Chief Inspector, *Scotland Yard Past and Present: Experiences of Thirty-seven years*, Chatton & Windus, 1893

Challenor, Harold and Alfred Draper, *Tanky Challenor: SAS and the Met*, Leo Cooper, London, 1990

Cherrill, Fred, *Cherrill of the Yard*, Transworld Publishers, London, 1956

Chesshyre, Robert, *The Force: Inside the Police*, Sidgwick & Jackson, 1989

Childs, Maj-Gen Sir Wyndham, *Episodes and Reflections*, Cassell, London, 1930

Cobb, Belton, *Critical Years at the Yard: The Career of Frederick Williamson of the Detective Department and the C.I.D.*, Faber & Faber, London, 1956

- *The First Detectives*, Faber, London, 1957

- *Murdered on Duty: A Chronicle of the Killing of Policemen*, W.H.Allen, London, 1961

Cole, Harry, *Policeman's Story*, Chivers Press, Bath, first published 1985

Cornish, G.W., *Cornish of the 'Yard': His Reminiscences and Cases*, John Lane, London, 1935

Cowell, David, Trevor Jones and Jock Young (editors), *Policing the Riots*, Junction Books, 1982

Cox, Barry, John Shirley and Martin Short, *The Fall of Scotland Yard*, Penguin, Harmondsworth, 1977

Critchley, T.A., *A History of Police in England and Wales*, Constable, London, 1978

Daley, Harry, *This Small Cloud: A Personal Memoir*, Weidenfeld and Nicolson, London, 1986

Darbyshire, Neil and Brian Hilliard, *The Flying Squad*, Headline, London, 1993

Delano, Anthony, *Slip-Up: Fleet Street, Scotland Yard and the Great Train Robbery*, Quadrangle/NY Times Book Co, New York, 1975

Dew, Ex-Chief Inspector Walter, *I Caught Crippen*, Blackie & Son, London.., 1938

Dictionary of National Biography, OUP, London

Dilnot, George, *The Trial of the Detectives*, Geoffrey Bles, London, 1928

- *Scotland Yard: Its History and Organisation 1829-1929*, Geoffrey Bles, London, 1929

- *The Real Detective*, Geoffrey Bles, London, 1933

Fabian, Robert, *Fabian of the Yard*, Naldrett Press, Kingswood, 1950

Facts About the Metropolitan Police Service, Metropolitan Police DPA, London, n.d.

Fairfax, Norman, *Police Dog Story: A history of the use of dogs for law enforcement purposes*, Unpublished ms., Metropolitan Police Museum, 1969

- *From Quills to Computers: The History of the Metropolitan Police Civil Staff 1829-1979*, Unpublished ms., Metropolitan Police Museum, 1979

with J. Lakin and V. Wilkinson, *History of Metropolitan Police Uniforms*, Unpublished ms., Metropolitan Police Museum, n.d.

Fallon, Tom, *The River Police*, Frederick Muller, London, 1956

Farmery, J. Peter, *Police Gallantry*, Periter & Associates, N.Manly, NSW, 1995

Fido, Martin, *Murder Guide to London*, Academy Chicago, Chicago, 1990

- *The Chronicle of Crime*, London, Carlton Books, 1993

Fielding, Nigel C., *Community Policing*, Clarendon Press, Oxford, 1995

Fitch, Herbert T., *Traitors Within*, London, Hurst & Blackett, 1933

- *Memoirs of a Royal Detective*, Hurst & Blackett, London, 1935

Fleming, Robert with Hugh Miller, *Scotland Yard*, Penguin, Harmondsworth, 1995

Forbes, Ian, *Squad Man*, W.H.Allen, London, 1973

Fraser, Frankie, with James Morton, *Mad Frank: Memoirs of a Life of Crime*, Warner Books, London, 1995

Frost, George 'Jack', *Flying Squad*, Youth Book Club, London, 1950

Gifford, Lord et al, *The Broadwater Farm Inquiry: Report of the Independent Inquiry into the Disturbances of October 1985 at the Broadwater Estate, Tottenham*, Broadwater Farm Inquiry, London, 1986

- *Broadwater Farm Revisited: Second Report of the Independent Inquiry into the Disturbances of October 1985 at the Broadwater Farm Estate, Tottenham*, Karia Press, London, 1989

Gosling, John, *The Ghost Squad*, W.H.Allen, London, 1959

- with Dennis Craig, *The Great Train Robbery*, Signet, New York, 1965

Gough, W.C., *From Kew Observatory to Scotland Yard*, Hurst & Blackett, London, n.d.

Gould, Robert W. and Michael J.Waldren, *London's Armed Police: 1829 to the Present*, Arms & Armour Press, London, 1986

Greeno, Edward, *War on the Underworld*, John Long, London, 1960

Grigg, Mary, *The Challenor Case*, Penguin, Harmondsworth, 1965

Hambrook, Ex-Det Supt Walter, *Hambrook of the Yard*, Robert Hale, London, 1937

Hatherill, George, *A Detective's Story*, Andre Deutsch, London, 1971

Henderson, Major (ret'd) Donald, GM, *Dragons can be Defeated - A complete record of the George Medal's Progress 1940 - 1983*, Spink & Son Ltd 1984.

H.M.S.O. *Cmd 2193 REPORT of the Commission appointed to enquire into the case of ex-Inspector John Syme*, 1924

Hobbs, Dick, *Doing the Business: Entrepreneurship, the Working Class, and Detectives in the East End of London*, Clarendon Press, Oxford, 1988

Holman, Arthur, *My Dog Rex: The Story of Police Dog Rex III*, Harrap, London, 1957

Honeycombe, Gordon, *Adam's Tale*, Arrow, London, 1975

Howe, Sir Ronald, *The Pursuit of Crime*, Arthur Barker, London, 1961

H.M.Howgrave-Graham, *Light and Shade at Scotland Yard*, John Murray, London, 1947

- *The Metropolitan Police at War*, H.M.S.O. 1947

Huntley, Ex-Commander Bob, *Bomb Squad: My War Against the Terrorists*, W.H.Allen, London, 1977

Huxley, Ann, *Four Against the Bank of England*, Playboy, New York, 1980

Jackett, Sam, *Heroes of Scotland Yard*, Robert Hale, 1965

Jackman, Elspeth, *Never Off Duty, Never Alone*, Pearl Books, Worthing, 1983

Jackson, Sir Richard, *Occupied with Crime*, Harrap, London, 1967

Jennings, Andrew, Paul Lashmar, and Vyv Simson, *Scotland Yard's Cocaine Connection*, Arrow, London, 1990

Judge, Tony, *The Force of Persuasion*, The Police Federation, 1994.

Kee, Robert, *Trial and Error: The Maguires, the Guildford Pub Bombings and British Justice*, Penguin, Harmondsworth, 1989

Kelland, Gilbert, *Crime in London*, Grafton, London, 1987

Kennedy, Ludovic, *10 Rillington Place*, Grafton, London, 1971

Kirby, Ex-Det Sgt Dick, *The Squad: A History of the Men and Vehicles of the Flying Squad at New Scotland Yard 1919-1983*, unpublished ms, Metropolitan Police History Museum, London, 1993

Kray, Reg, *Born Fighter*, Arrow, London, 1990

- and Ron, with Fred Dineage, *Our Story*, Pan, London, 1989

Lambourne, Gerald, *The Fingerprint Story*, Harrap, London, 1984

Lambrianou, Tony, *Inside the Firm: The Untold story of the Krays' Reign of Terror*, Pan, London, 1992

Lansdowne, Andrew, *A Life's Reminiscences of Scotland Yard*, Leadenhall Press, London, 1890

Leeson, B., *Lost London: The Memoirs of an East End Detective*, Stanley Paul, London, 1934

Lane, Brian, *The Encyclopedia of Forensic Science*, Headline, London, 1992

Laurie, Peter, *Scotland Yard: A Personal Inquiry*, Bodley Head, London, 1970

Lefebure, Molly, *Evidence for the Crown: Experiences of a Pathologist's Secretary*, Harborough Publishing, London, 1957

Littlechild, John George, *The Reminiscences of Chief-Inspector Littlechild*, Leadenhall Press, London, 1894

Lock, Joan, *Lady Policeman*, Michael Joseph, London, 1968

- *The British Policewoman: Her Story*, Robert Hale, London, 1979

- *Tales from Bow Street*, Robert Hale, London, 1982

- *Blue Murder? Policemen Under Suspicion*, Robert Hale, London, 1986

- *Dreadful Deeds and Awful Murders: Scotland Yard's First Detectives, 1829-1878*, Barn Owl Books, Taunton, 1990

- *Scotland Yard Casebook: The Making of the CID 1865-1935*, Robert Hale, London, 1993

Lucas, Norman, *WPC 'Courage'*, Weidenfeld & Nicolson, London, 1986

Lynch, Tony, *The Bill: The Inside Story of British Television's Most Successful Police Series*, Boxtree, London, 1991

Mackenzie, Colin, *Biggs: The World's Most Wanted Man*, William Morrow & Co, New York, 1975

McNee, Sir David, *McNee's Law*, Collins, London, 1983

Mahir, Tom, *Police Dogs at Work*, J.M. Dent & Sons, London, 1970

Mark, Sir Robert, *In the Office of Constable*, Collins, London, 1978

Marriner, Brian, *Forensic Clues to Murder*, Arrow, London, 1991

Mitton, Mervyn A, *The Policeman's Lot - Antique British Police Equipment*, Quiller Press 1985

Metropolitan Police, *General Instructions*, 1829

Metropolitan Police, A8 Branch *The Anguilla Report* n.d.

Monk, John (ed), *The Memoirs of Chief Inspector John Monk (Metropolitan Police) 1859-1946*,

Unpublished ms., Met Police Library, Scotland Yard, 1969

Moser, Maurice, with Charles F. Rideal, *Stories from Scotland Yard*, John Barker, London, 1890

Morton, James, *Gangland: London's Underworld*, Warner Books, London, 1993

- *Bent Coppers: A Survey of Police Corruption*, Warner Books, London, 1994

Molloy, Pat, *The Cannock Chase Murders*, Hodder & Stoughton, Sevenoaks, 1990

Moylan, Sir John, *Scotland Yard and the Metropolitan Police*, Putnam, London, 1929

Murphy, Robert, *Smash and Grab: Gangsters in the London Underworld*, Faber & Faber, London, 1993

Nash, Jay Robert, *World Encyclopedia of Twentieth Century Murder*, Headline, London, 1992

Nock, O.S, *Historic Railway Disasters*, Arrow Books 1966

Oliver, Ted and Ramsey Smith, *Lambs to the Slaughter*, Warner Books, London, 1993

Paul, Philip, *Murder Under Microscope: The Story of Scotland Yard's Forensic Science Laboratory*, Futura, London, 1990

Perkins, Vanessa with Maureen Owen, *Sorry, Vessa*, Chapmans, London, 1991

Peto, Dorothy, *The Memoirs of Miss Dorothy Georgiana Olivia Peto OBE*, Organising Committee for the European Conference on Equal Opportunities in the Police 1992, London, 1993

Petrow, Stefan, *Policing Morals: The Metropolitan Police and the Home Office 1870- 1914*, Clarendon, Oxford, 1994

Police and Constabulary Almanac (passim), R.Hazell & Co., Henley-on-Thames, published annually from 1861.

Price, John, *The Metropolitan Police... Why It Was Established and How It Developed*, Unpublished research paper, Metropolitan Police Museum, 1983

- *The Metropolitan Police and the Public... The First Five Years*, Unpublished ms, Metropolitan Police Museum, 1991

Prothero, Margaret, *The History of the Criminal Investigation Department at Scotland Yard from the Earliest Times until Today*, Herbert Jenkins, London, 1931

Pulling, Christopher, *Mr Punch and the Police*, Butterworths, London, 1964

Read, Leonard with James Morton, *Nipper: The Story of Leonard 'Nipper' Read*, Warner Books, London, 1991

Reay, Colonel W.T, *The Specials - How They Served London*, Heinemann, 1920

Reynolds, Bruce, *The Autobiography of a Thief*, Bantam, London, 1995

Reynolds, Gerald W. and Anthony Judge, *The Night the Police Went on Strike*, Weidenfeld & Nicolson, London, 1968

Rivers, Chief inspector K., *History of the Traffic Department of the Metropolitan Police*, Privately published, Newtownabbey, Co.Antrim, 1969

Rose, Andrew, *Stinie: Murder on the Common*, Bodley Head, London, 1985

Rose, David, *A Climate of Fear: The Murder of PC Blakelock and the Case of the Tottenham Three*, Bloomsbury, London, 1992

Rumbelow, Donald, *I Spy Blue: The Police and Crime in the City of London from Elizabeth I to Victoria*, Cedric Chivers, London, 1971

- *The Houndsditch Murders & The Siege of Sidney Street*, revised edn., W.H.Allen, London, 1988

Samuel, Raphael, *East End Underworld: Chapters in the Life of Arthur Harding*, Routledge & Kegan Paul, London, 1981

Savage, Percy, *Savage of Scotland Yard*, Hutchinson, London, 1934

Scott, Sir Harold, *Scotland Yard*, Penguin, Harmondsworth, 1954

- *Your Obedient Servant*, Andre Deutsch, London, 1959

Sellwood, A.V., *Police Strike - 1919*, W.H.Allen, London, 1978

Sharpe, F.D. *'Nutty'*, *Sharpe of the Flying Squad*, John Long, London, 1938

Simpson, Professor Keith, *Forty Years of Murder: An Autobiography*, Grafton, London, 1980

Slipper, Jack, *Slipper of the Yard*, Sidgwick & Jackson, London, 1981

Stern, Chester, *Dr Iain West's Casebook*, Warner Books, London, 1997

Stowe, Leslie *London Medley - The Story of the Metropolitan Police Male Voice Choir*, Privately published, 1999.

Thomson, Basil, *My Experiences at Scotland Yard*, A.L.Burt, New York, 1922

Thorp, Arthur, with A. Noyes Thomas, *Calling Scotland Yard*, Allan Wingate, London, 1954

Thorwald, Jürgen, *The Marks of Cain*, Pan, London, 1968

Thurston, Gavin, *The Clerkenwell Riot: The Killing of Constable Culley*, Allen & Unwin, London, 1967

Tullett, Tom, *No Answer from Foxtrot Eleven*, Michael Joseph, London, 1967

- *Murder Squad: Famous Cases of Scotland Yard's Murder Squad*, Triad/Granada, London, 1981 (originally *Strictly Murder*, Bodley Head, London, 1979)

- *Clues to Murder: Famous Forensic Murder Cases of Professor J.M.Cameron*, Grafton, London, 1987

Van den Bergh, Tony, *Who Killed FreddieMills?* Constable, London, 1991

Villiers, Peter, *Without Fear or Favour: Policing in a Changing Democracy*, Unison Education, London, 1995

Wensley, Frederick Porter, *Detective Days: The Record of Forty-two Years' Service in the Criminal Investigation Department*, Cassell, London, 1931

Williams, Jeffery, *Byng of Vimy: General and Governor General*, Leo Cooper, in association with Secker & Warburg, London, 1983

Wilson, Colin, *Written in Blood: A History of Forensic Detection*, HarperCollins, London, 1995

Woodhall, Edwin T., *Guardians of the Great*, Blandford, London, 1934

- *Secrets of Scotland Yard*, John Lane Bodley Head, London, 1936

Wyles, Lilian, *A Woman at Scotland Yard*, Faber, London, 1952

Young, Filson (ed), *The Trial of Hawley Harvey Crippen*, William Hodge, Edinburgh, 1920

In addition, documents from the Scotland Yard Archives and the Metropolitan Police and Home Office files in the Public Record Office have been consulted throughout.

INDEX

The authors and publishers deeply regret that it has been impossible to include in this alphabetical index the names of all those officers who gave their lives on duty or were decorated for their gallantry in serving the public. Chronological lists can be found in Appendices Three and Four between pages 299 and 310.

Page numbers in italics refer to illustrations, and those in bold refer to main entries.